Sitting with Job

Selected Studies on the Book of Job

Edited by

Roy B. Zuck

Wipf and Stock Publishers
EUGENE, OREGON

Wipf and Stock Publishers
199 West 8th Avenue, Suite 3
Eugene, Oregon 97401

Sitting with Job
Selected Studies on the Book of Job
By Zuck, Roy B.

ISBN: 1-59244-384-2
Publication date 10/7/2003
Previously published by Baker Book House, 1992

Contents

ABBREVIATIONS

AAR	American Academy of Religion
AB	Anchor Bible
AfO	*Archiv für Orientforschung*
ALUOS	*Annual of Leeds University Oriental Society*
ANEP	J. B. Pritchard, ed., *Ancient Near East in Pictures*
ANET	J. B. Pritchard, ed., *Ancient Near Eastern Texts*
AOAT	*Alter Orient und Alter Testament*
ArOr	*Archiv orientální*
ATD	Alte Testament Deutsch
AV	Authorized Version
BA	*Biblical Archaeologist*
BARev	*Biblical Archaeology Review*
BASOR	*Bulletin of the American Schools of Oriental Research*
BDB	F. Brown, S. R. Driver, and C. A. Briggs, *A Hebrew and English Lexicon of the Old Testament*
BHT	*Beiträge zur Geschichte der biblischen Hermeneutik*
Bib	*Biblica*
BibOr	*Biblica et orientalia*
BJRL	*Bulletin of the John Rylands Library of Manchester*
BWL	W. G. Lambert, *Babylonian Wisdom Literature*
CBC	Cambridge Bible Commentary
CBQ	*Catholic Biblical Quarterly*
CT	T. G. Pinches, *Cuneiform Texts from the Babylonian Tablets in the British Museum*
CTM	*Concordia Theological Monthly*
CurTM	*Currents in Theology and Mission*
DG	S. R. Driver and G. B. Gray, *A Cultural and Exegetical Commentary on the Book of Job*

DJD	*Discoveries in the Judean Desert*
E, Eng.	English
ET	English translation
ETS	Evangelical Theological Society
FOTL	The Forms of the Old Testament Literature
HKAT	Handkommentar zum Alten Testament
HUCA	*Hebrew Union College Annual*
ICC	International Critical Commentary
IDB	G. A. Buttrick, ed., *Interpreter's Dictionary of the Bible*
IEJ	*Israel Exploration Journal*
Int	*Interpretation*
IOT	Robert H. Pfeiffer, *Introduction to the Old Testament*
JAOS	*Journal of the American Oriental Society*
JBL	*Journal of Biblical Literature*
JEOL	*Jaarbericht . . . ex oriente lux*
JETS	*Journal of the Evangelical Theological Society*
JJS	*Journal of Jewish Studies*
JNES	*Journal of Near Eastern Studies*
JQR	*Jewish Quarterly Review*
JSOT	*Journal for the Study of the Old Testament*
JSOTSup	Journal for the Study of the Old Testament Supplement Series
JSS	*Journal of Semitic Studies*
KAR	*Keilschriftexte aus Assur religiösen Inhalts*
KAT	Kommentar zum Alten Testament
KAV	*Keilschriftexte aus Assur verschiedenen Inhalts*
KJV	King James Version
KMW	Robert Gordis, *Koheleth—the Man and His World*
LMBH	Robert Gordis, "Lisegullot HaMeliṣah Bekhitheb hei Hagodeš"
LXX	Septuagint
MHHH	Robert Gordis, "Al Mibneh Haširah Haivrit Haqnedumah"
MT	Masoretic text
MVAG	Mitteilungen der Vorder-asiatische-Ägyptischen Gesellschaft
NAB	New American Bible
NASB	New American Standard Bible
NCB	New Century Bible
NCE	M. R. P. McGuire et al., eds., *New Catholic Encyclopedia*
NEB	New English Bible
NIV	New International Version
NJPS	The Tanakh (Jewish Publication Society)
NT	New Testament

OT	Old Testament
PBS	H. F. Lutz, *Selected Sumerian and Babylonian Texts*
PEQ	*Palestine Exploration Quarterly*
Phillips	*The New Testament in Modern English*, J. B. Phillips
QTg	Qumran Targum of Job
RA	*Revue d'assyriologie et d'archéologie orientale*
RB	*Revue biblique*
Restoration Q	*Restoration Quarterly*
RQ	*Romische Quartelschrift für christliche Altertumskunde und Kirchengeschichte*
RSV	Revised Standard Version
RV	Revised Version
SBL Proceedings	Society of Biblical Literature Proceedings
SBT	*Studies in Biblical Theology*
Soundings	*Soundings: An Interdisciplinary Journal*
SVT	Supplements to Vetus Testamentum
Syria	*Syria: Revue d'art oriental et d'archéologie*
TDNT	G. Kittel and G. Friedrich, eds., *Theological Dictionary of the New Testament*
TDOT	G. J. Botterweck and H. Ringgren, eds., *Theological Dictionary of the Old Testament*
Tg	Targum
ThR	*Theological Review*
ThZ	*Theologische Zeitschrift*
TOTC	Tyndale Old Testament Commentary
TRu	*Theologische Rundschau*
UT	Cyrus H. Gordon, *Ugaritic Texts*
VT	*Vetus Testamentum*
VTSup	Vetus Testamentum Supplements
WMANT	Wissenschaftliche Monographien zum Alten und Neuen Testament
WTJ	*Westminster Theological Journal*
WVDOG	Wissenschaftliche Veröffentlichgungen der deutschen
WZKM	*Wiener Zeitschrift für die Kunde des Morgenlands*
ZAW	*Zeitschrift für die alttestamentliche Wissenschaft*
ZDMG	*Zeitschrift der deutschen morgenlandischen Gesellschaft*

Contributors

Francis I. Andersen
Professor of Old Testament, New College of Advanced Christian Studies, Berkeley, California.

Albert Barnes
Pastor, First Presbyterian Church, Philadelphia, Pennsylvania. Deceased.

D. A. Carson
Professor of New Testament, Trinity Evangelical Divinity School, Deerfield, Illinois.

David J. A. Clines
Professor of Biblical Studies, University of Sheffield, England.

Édouard Dhorme
Professor of Hebrew, Assyrian, and Old Testament Exegesis, College de France, Paris. Deceased.

Michael Brennan Dick
Professor of Biblical Studies, Siena College, Loudonville, New York.

Edwin M. Good
Professor of Religious Studies, Stanford University, Stanford, California.

Robert Gordis
Rapaport Professor of the Philosophies of Religion and Professor of Bible, Jewish Theological Seminary of America, New York City, New York.

Norman C. Habel
Professor of Religion Studies, University of South Australia, Underdale, South Australia, Australia.

R. Laird Harris
Professor Emeritus of Old Testament, Covenant Theological Seminary, St. Louis, Missouri.

John E. Hartley
Chair, Department of Biblical Studies, C. P. Haggard School of Theology, Azusa Pacific University, Azusa, California.

Mark R. Littleton
Freelance writer, Columbia, Maryland.

David McKenna
President, Asbury Theological Seminary, Wilmore, Kentucky.

R. Lynne Newell
Senior Lecturer in Old Testament Studies, South East Asia Bible Seminary, Malang, Indonesia.

G. Frederick Owen
Professor of Archaeology, Pasadena College, Pasadena, California. Deceased.

Gregory W. Parsons
Professor of Biblical Studies, Baptist Missionary Association Theological Seminary, Jacksonville, Texas.

Sylvia Huberman Scholnick
Former lecturer in religion, College of William and Mary, Williamsburg, Virginia.

Elmer B. Smick
Professor of Old Testament, Gordon-Conwell Theological Seminary, South Hamilton, Massachusetts.

Matitiahu Tsevat
Professor Emeritus of Bible, Hebrew Union College, Cincinnati, Ohio.

Claus Westermann
Professor of Old Testament, University of Heidelberg, Heidelberg, Germany.

James G. Williams
Professor of Religion, Syracuse University, Syracuse, New York.

Philip Yancey
Freelance writer, Chicago, Illinois.

Roy B. Zuck
Vice president for Academic Affairs, Academic Dean, and Professor of Bible Exposition, Dallas Theological Seminary, Dallas, Texas.

Introduction

The problem of pain continues to puzzle and confound many people. Evil stands as an enigma; suffering presents a dilemma; misery is a mystery. This problem intensifies when we see individuals suffer who obviously do not deserve it. This issue is especially apparent in the Book of Job. Why should a righteous, upright man who feared God endure immeasurable loss and intense pain? Why should he be allowed to suffer such physical, emotional, financial, and spiritual agony, while also enduring the verbal abuse of friends and the seeming silence and indifference of God? This dilemma, along with the way it is presented, gives the Book of Job a universal and perennial appeal. Many writers have lauded it as a uniquely remarkable book.

Several years ago when I was writing a commentary on the Book of Job,[1] I was surprised to find a book on Job written in 1898 by William Johnston Zuck. I did some genealogical hunting and discovered that he was a great-great-great-uncle. As a professor of English literature at Otterbein University, he certainly understood works of literary quality. He wrote, "The book of Job is the masterpiece of the world's literature. For depth of thought, sublimity of conception, and beauty of expression, it is unsurpassed. The keenest criticism and the most profound scholarship the world has ever known have endeavored in vain to exhaust the matchless wealth of this material; it yet remains the brightest and, perhaps, most distant star in the literary firmament."[2] In his view "the poem surpasses every other single work in the whole world of poetic literature."[3]

1. Roy B. Zuck, *Job,* Everyman's Bible Commentary (Chicago: Moody, 1978).

2. William Johnston Zuck, ***The Book of Job, with an Introduction and Notes*** (Dayton, Ohio: United Brethren Publishing House, 1898), ix.

3. Ibid., xiv.

Because of its universal appeal and its unequaled literary quality, the Book of Job has drawn *lay persons and scholars alike* over the centuries. For lay believers, this book shows that suffering is common, that friends may misunderstand one's pain, that God, though silent, is not absent and does manifest his providential care for his own and calls on them to recognize his sovereignty, love, and wisdom. Scholars are challenged by the Book of Job because of its difficult Hebrew, its outstanding literary architecture, and its numerous problem texts. Its theology, its literary luster, its probing of the world's greatest mystery, its poetic style and beauty—these and other elements give it a fascination beyond description. In Thomas Carlyle's judgment, it is "one of the grandest things ever written."[4]

Studying and teaching the Book of Job over the years has introduced me to the voluminous literature: books and journal articles on Job flow like a river. *Taken from that flow, this anthology of articles and portions of books on Job brings together some of the best thinking on the Book of Job.* The chapters deal with many facets of the Book of Job: its purpose, literary structure, genre, language, and argument; specific problems such as the location of the land of Uz, mythology in the book, and the interpretation of selected passages; Elihu's role in the book; and the Lord's speeches.

Readers will readily note a conservative bias in my selections. Also evident is the diversity of background of the writers (many names are familiar to Joban scholars). Another easily recognizable feature is the *intentional variation in the kinds of articles included. Some are popular, others are more technical.* No doubt some readers familiar with the literature on Job will wonder why I did not include other selections. Subjectivity and one's theological perspective naturally influence an editor's choice of what to include in his anthology. Another factor is the limitation of space.

I do not agree with everything presented in these essays; probably no reader will either. For example, I believe the Book of Job was written much earlier than the postexilic period, though a few of the scholars whose works are included here do hold the late date.

No attempt has been made to conform the essays to one editorial style; each chapter has been left virtually as it was originally published. As an example, some writers transliterate the Hebrew ריב as *rīb* and others as *rîb*.

I hope these writings on the Book of Job *will challenge readers to a new appreciation of this book of the Bible, and will deepen their sense of God's sovereign wisdom and love in the midst of pain and suffering.*

I am grateful to the publishers for kindly permitting me to reprint from their works, and to the authors for their outstanding contributions to the study of what Alfred Lord Tennyson said is "the greatest poem, whether of ancient or modern literature."

4. Thomas Carlyle, "The Hero as a Prophet," in *On Heroes, Hero Worship, and the Heroic in History*, ed. Archibald MacMechan (Boston: Ginn, 1901), 55.

Part 1

Overviews of the Book of Job

1

The Structure and Purpose of the Book of Job

Gregory W. Parsons

It is common knowledge that the Book of Job is universally admired as a literary masterpiece in world literature. Although most of the superlatives have been exhausted to describe its literary excellence, it seems to defy more than a superficial analysis.[1] There has been little agreement with regard to the purpose and message of the book. This article will seek to delineate the literary structure of the Book of Job in order to determine the major purpose of the book. The goal is to demonstrate how the author of Job utilized certain key themes in developing the purpose and message of the book.

1. See Henry L. Rowold, "The Theology of Creation in the Yahweh Speeches as a Solution to the Problem Posed by the Book of Job" (Th.D. diss., Concordia Seminary in Exile, 1977), p. 1.

From Gregory W. Parsons, "The Structure and Purpose of the Book of Job," *Bibliotheca Sacra* 138 (April–June 1981): 139–57. Used by permission of Dallas Seminary Press.

Literary Structure

The unity of the Book of Job will be assumed in the analysis of its literary structure. It is believed that each component of the book has a necessary place in the overall design and argument of Job.[2]

Job is a complex literary work in which there has been a skillful wedding of poetry and prose and a masterful mixture of several literary genres.[3] The basic structure of Job consists of a prose framework (the prologue in chapters 1 and 2, and the epilogue in 42:7–17) which encloses an intricate poetic body.[4]

The prologue very concisely narrates how God's servant Job lost his family and his wealth in a rapid-fire succession of catastrophic events. Then it relates that when Job's health was removed his wife urged him to curse God and die. Job's three friends, Eliphaz, Bildad, and Zophar, arrived to comfort Job who remained firm in his devotion to God in the midst of his intense suffering. The reader is taken behind the scenes and informed that the reason for these events is that God was permitting Satan to afflict Job in order to test the motivation for Job's piety. This is done by rapidly alternating between the earthly setting and the heavenly court.

2. In order to do accurate exegesis of the Old Testament, it is necessary that one examine the extant text in its final canonical form with emphasis on synchronic analysis as opposed to diachronic analysis. The latter dissects the text in an attempt to hypothesize about the original form of the text and its transmission but never seems to put things back together again (Allen Paul Ross, "The Table of Nations in Genesis" [Th.D. diss., Dallas Theological Seminary, 1977], pp. 14–17). One definite contribution of "structural analysis" has been its stress on dealing with the text as it is rather than preoccupation with a "dehusking" process to eliminate "what does not fit" (Robert Polzin, "The Framework of the Book of Job," *Interpretation* 28 [1974]: 182–83). Cf. Robert Polzin, *Biblical Structuralism: Method and Subjectivity in the Study of Ancient Texts*, Semeia Supplements (Philadelphia: Fortress Press, 1977), for the nature of structuralism.

This "dehusking" procedure has been often employed (in varying degrees) on the Book of Job. The outer "folktale" is separated from the inner speeches because it contains "a patient Job" whereas the dialogue displays an "impatient Job." The speeches of Elihu are discarded as a later insertion because they seem to contribute nothing to the argument and appear to anticipate much in the Yahweh speeches. The hymn of wisdom (chap. 28) is isolated as a foreign insertion into Job's speeches (chaps. 27–31). The literary scalpel then slices off, at least, the Behemoth and Leviathan pericopes (40:15–41:26) from the Yahweh speeches because they seem unnecessary and are "obviously" inferior to the rest of the speeches. Others have even eliminated the Yahweh speeches altogether as irrelevant. It is ironic that with regard to the Book of Job (itself a study in irony), which teaches the mysterious nature of God's ways, man attempts to judge this divine book by subjective human standards. To fall into this trap is to miss one of the main teachings of the book.

3. As Andersen has noted, the Book of Job is an amazing mixture of almost every kind of literature which is found in the Old Testament (Francis I. Andersen, *Job: An Introduction and Commentary* [Downers Grove, Ill.: InterVarsity Press, 1976], p. 33). Besides the main genres—the lawsuit, the lament, and the controversy dialogue or dispute (see this author's article in the July-September 1981 issue of *Bibliotheca Sacra*)—many riddles, hymns, curses, and proverbs can be isolated within the various speeches of the book.

4. For two Egyptian parallels to this arrangement, see Berlin papyrus 3024 and "The Protests of the Eloquent Peasant" in James B. Pritchard, ed., Ancient Near *Eastern Texts Relating to the Old Testament* (Princeton: Princeton University Press, 1967), pp. 405–10.

The poetic body (3:1–42:6) begins with a personal lament by Job (chap. 3) in which he curses the day of his birth. This introductory soliloquy corresponds to the final soliloquy by Job (chaps. 29–31), and particularly to chapter 31 (his oath of innocence) which includes a self-curse. These two soliloquies enclose three cycles of disputations (*Streitgespräche*) between Job and his three friends. A cycle consists of speeches by the three friends (Eliphaz, Bildad, and Zophar, in that order) which are interspersed by a reply of Job to each speech.

This pattern is followed for the first two cycles of speeches (chaps. 4–14 and 15–21) but breaks down in the third cycle when Zophar fails to speak following Job's response to Bildad (chap. 26).[5] Rather than subjectively attempting to restore the allegedly jumbled text, one should recognize that this alteration of structure contributes to the development of the argument of the book. There are two basic lines of interaction which run through Job—Job's crying out to God and Job's disputations with his three friends. The absence of the third speech of Zophar is consistent with the fact that each of the speeches of the three friends is progressively shorter in each cycle and that Job's responses to each of the friends (which also are progressively shorter) are longer than the corresponding speech of the friends. This seems to signify Job's verbal victory over Zophar and the other two friends.[6] It is also indicative of the bankruptcy and futility of dialogue when both Job and the three friends assume the retribution dogma[7] (which for the friends implies Job's guilt and for Job implies God's injustice). Consequently, this structural design marks a very gradual swing toward a focus on Job's relationship and interaction with God in contrast to the earlier primary interaction between Job and his friends.[8]

5. Many different speculative attempts have been made to juggle the speeches of the final cycle or to attribute portions of chapter 27 (Job's reply in the extant canonical book) to Zophar. This has been attempted because portions of chapter 27 (esp. vv. 13–23) seem to be more consistent with Zophar's arguments than Job's. For a concise defense of retaining all of chapter 27 as Job's speech, see Roy B. Zuck, *Job*, Everyman's Bible Commentary (Chicago: Moody Press, 1978), pp. 119, 121.

6. The only exceptions to the rule that both the friends' and Job's speeches are progressively shorter are the second speech of Zophar (chap. 20) and the third response of Job to Eliphaz (chaps. 23 and 24). See the similar conclusion of Zuck (*Job*, pp. 30, 121). Cf. also *Encyclopaedia Britannica*, s.v. "Job," by Andrew Bruce Davidson and Crawford Howell Toy (reprinted in *The Voice of the Whirlwind: The Book of Job*, ed. Ralph E. Hone [San Francisco: Chandler Publishing, 1960], p. 93). Note also the remarks by Elihu concerning the failure of the argumentation of the three friends (Job 32:3).

7. This dogma will be discussed later in this article.

8. This is not to say that Job's focus of attention was always on his friends. He was constantly either crying out to God for response (cf. 10:2–22) or making accusations against Him (16:7–17; 19:7–12; 24:1–12) but was constantly being sidetracked by the dogmatic and virtually unsympathetic speeches of the friends. From the first cycle of the dialogue onward, Job often directly addressed God (see 7:12–21; 16:7–8; 17:3–4; and 30:20–23). Good argues that this indicates the hopelessness of appealing to God (Edwin M. Good, *Irony in the Old Testament* [Philadelphia: Westminster Press, 1965], pp. 231–32). This appears at first glance to contradict

This swing toward an emphasis on Job's dispute with God continues in chapters 27–31. Following a possible pause in which Job waited in vain for Zophar's third response,[9] Job concluded his words to the friends in chapter 27 by collectively addressing them[10] and declaring that they had failed to convince him that he was a sinner who deserved his calamity.[11] Chapter 28, a wisdom hymn, may be a kind of interlude which marks the transition between the two major parts of the poetic body—the previous dialogue between Job and his friends, and the forthcoming long discourses by Job (chaps. 29–31), Elihu (chaps. 32–37), and God (chaps. 38–41) which are almost monologues.[12] Chapters 29–31 are comprised of Job's soliloquies[13] in which he longs for his past blessed state of prosperity (chap. 29) and laments his present state of misery because of God's afflictions (chap. 30, which includes an aside to God in direct speech—vv. 21–23). The concluding chapter (31) consists of Job's oath of innocence (common in ancient Near Eastern juridical cases) in the form of a negative confession complete with self-imprecations.[14] Job concludes the chapter with a legal indictment against God to present his charges in writing (31:35–37). The result is a pregnant expectation of God's response.

However, the Elihu speeches (chaps. 32–37), which seemingly interrupt the

---

the author's own sensing of a change to a focus on Job's relationship to God. However, Job often talks about God in the third person as an enemy, etc., in these sections, which indicates the impersonal nature of God to him. After chapter 27, Job ignored the friends completely (except indirectly in 29:25) and looked to God (though indirectly) in his soliloquy.

9. Zuck, *Job*, p. 119.

10. The plural personal pronoun "you" is employed in verses 5, 11, and 12 and the plural verb in verse 12 (Zuck, *Job*, p. 119).

11. Möller argues that in 27:2–12 Job summarized his own basic arguments of the three cycles of speeches which he juxtaposed with the utterly nonsensical argument of the friends which he satirized in 27:13–23 (Hans Möller, *Sinn und Aufbau des Buches Hiob* [Berlin: Evangelische Verlagsanstalt, 1955], pp. 61–63).

12. Andersen suggests that this interlude was written by the anonymous author of the Book of Job (*Job*, pp. 222–29). However, it is possible to understand this wisdom poem as Job's words which summed up the typical wisdom teaching he had heard all his life (to fear God and depart from evil—see 28:28, i.e., to trust and obey Yahweh because He alone has the wisdom by which the world was created and is to be governed: cf. 42:5) (Robert Laurin, "The Theological Structure of Job," *Zeitschrift für die alttestamentliche Wissenschaft* 84 [1972]: 86–89). This would sum up Job's stance before God (cf. 1:1, 8; 2:3) in contrast to the friends' assertion that he must repent of his sins and fear God (cf. 4:6–11; 11:13–20; 15:4–5; 22:4–30). The last verse of chapter 28 (v. 28) may also serve as a fitting link to Job 29–31 wherein Job gave evidence that he had feared God (namely, his past virtues—chap. 29) and had departed from evil (his oath of innocence—chap. 31) (Zuck, *Job*, pp. 126–27).

13. These correspond to the initial soliloquy by Job (chap. 3).

14. Although this oath was common in ancient Near Eastern court cases, the emphatic nature of Job's oath is indicated by its length and its rare self-imprecation (Michael Brennan Dick, "The Legal Metaphor in Job 31," *Catholic Biblical Quarterly* 41 [1979]: 42, 47). This is strikingly similar to the Egyptian "Protestation of Innocence" in chapter 125 of the Book of the Dead (Pritchard, *Ancient Near Eastern Texts*, pp. 34–36). Because Job denied some of the charges made by Eliphaz against him (cf. 31:16–22 with 22:6–11), it is evident that he was saying to God that he was innocent of the charges brought against him by his friends.

argument of the book,[15] actually set the stage for the Yahweh speeches. Elihu appears as a type of mediator (an impartial witness) who speaks on behalf of God (36:2)[16] by rebuking the three friends (cf. 32:3, 6–14; 34:2–15; cf. 35:4) and by suggesting that Job needed to repent of his pride, which developed because of his suffering (cf. 33:17; 35:12–16). He recommended that Job should exalt God's works which are evident in nature (36:24–37:18) and fear Him who comes in golden splendor out of the north (37:22–24).[17] These basic ideas of Elihu are either assumed or developed by the Lord in His speeches.

The climax to the Book of Job appears in the symmetrical Yahweh speeches (38:1–42:6)—the two divine speeches with Job's two responses—which are the culmination of the skillfully designed poetic body of the book.[18] This pericope comprises two divine speeches (each of which is also divided into two principal parts) and two human responses. The precise symmetrical arrangement is illustrated in a comparison of the two "rounds" of divine-human interaction (see the following chart).

Thus except for the summary challenge in 40:2 for Job to respond (introduced by a transitional editorial remark), these two rounds are perfectly symmetrical in basic structure. That no summary challenge was needed at the end of the Lord's second speech is indicative that Job's second response (42:1–6) was a willing one in contrast to his initial reluctant reply (40:3–5).

15. These speeches have almost universally been rejected as a later insertion into the book because the flow of the book is smoother without them, because Elihu is not mentioned in the prologue or epilogue, and because of the alleged differences in literary style and vocabulary. See William Ewart Staples, *The Speeches of Elihu: A Study of Job* XXXII–XXXVII (Toronto: Oxford University Press, 1924), pp. 12–24. However, the present author holds that the Elihu speeches are a necessary complement to the Yahweh speeches. The speeches of Elihu, who served as a self-styled mediator in God's behalf, are assumed by Yahweh in His speeches; thus Elihu was not condemned since his arguments were essentially correct. For an excellent summary of the objections to the authenticity of the Elihu speeches followed by a rebuttal, see John Peter Lange, ed., *A Commentary on the Holy Scriptures*, 25 vols., vol. 8: *The Book of Job*, by Tayler Lewis and Otto Zöckler, trans. L. J. Evans (New York: Scribner, Armstrong & Co., 1874), pp. 268–73; and H. D. Beeby, "Elihu—Job's Mediator?" *Southeast Asia Journal of Theology* 7 (October 1965): 47–50. Also it seems providentially significant that three of the four manuscript fragments of Job which are extant from Qumran are portions of the Elihu speeches—namely, two manuscripts from chapter 36 (4Q Job[a] and 4Q Job[b]) yet unpublished (see Christoph Burchard, *Bibliographie zu den Handschriften von Toten Meer*, 2 vols. [Berlin: Alfred Topelmann, 1965], 2:327) and a tiny portion of 33:18–20 from Cave 2 (published by M. Baillet, J. T. Milik, and Roland de Vaux, *Les "Petites Grottes" de Qumran*, 2 vols., *DJD* [Oxford: Clarendon Press, 1962], 2:13 [#15], cf. 1:71).

16. This theme, which is prevalent in Job, provides a connecting link to the previous dialogue and at the same time is proleptic of Yahweh's theophany.

17. Zuck, *Job*, pp. 141–42.

18. Because the double exchange between God and Job is similar to the double exchange between God and Satan in the prologue, Andersen has suggested an unorthodox division of the Book of Job: introduction (1:1–5), speeches (1:6–42:6) and conclusion (42:7–17) (*Job*, pp. 20, 49). The speeches would be divided as follows: the interviews of Yahweh with Satan (1:6–2:13), the dialogue of Job with his friends (3:1–37:24), and the two interviews of Yahweh with Job (38:1–42:6).

	First Round (38:1–40:5)	*Second Round* (40:6–42:6)
Divine Speech	38:1–40:2	40:6–41:34
Introductory editorial note	38:1	40:6
Thematic challenge	38:2–3	40:7–14
Main body (in two principal parts)	38:4–38 (Inanimate creation)	40:15–24 (Behemoth)
	38:39–39:30 (Animate creation)	41:1–34 (Leviathan)
(Transitional editorial note)	40:1	—
Summary challenge	40:2	—
Human Response	40:3–5	42:1–6
Introductory editorial note	40:3	42:1
Reply per se	40:4–5	42:2–6

The epilogue (42:7–17) in prose is basically a counterbalance to the prologue. In the prologue Job offered intercessory sacrifices for his family; in the epilogue he offered an intercessory prayer for his three friends. In the former God commended Job as being of blameless character; in the latter God gave a qualified commendation of Job's words in contrast to the three friends. The prologue narrates the removal of Job's family, prosperity, and health, whereas the epilogue relates the restoration of Job's family and health and a doubling of his former wealth.

However, both Satan and Job's wife (who are prominent in the prologue as agents of evil who try to get Job to curse God)[19] are intentionally omitted in the epilogue. This deliberate omission emphasizes a major teaching of the book, namely, that man's relationship to God is not a "give-and-get" bargain nor a business contract of mutual benefit.[20]

Purpose of the Book

Statement of the Purpose

It is this writer's belief that the purpose of the Book of Job is *to show that the proper relationship between God and man is based solely on the sovereign grace of God and man's response of faith and submissive trust.*

19. See 1:9–12; 2:4–6, 9–10. Cf. Wilhelm Vischer, "God's Truth and Man's Lie," *Interpretation* 15 (1961): 132.

20. Zuck, *Job*, pp. 15, 19, 189–90. This biblical concept, which is in direct contrast to the ancient Near Eastern concept of man's relationship to God, will be developed further in the next section of this article.

This involves (in a negative fashion) the refutation of "retribution theology" (a dogmatic employment of the concept of divine retribution so that there was an automatic connection between deed and state of being) and its corollary that man's relationship to God is a business contract of mutual claims that is binding in court. This statement of purpose involves the assumption that the relationship between God and man is the basic problem of the book.[21] Although there are several subthemes which have been cited by scholars as the main theme,[22] it is the belief of this writer that only *the basis of the proper relationship between God and man* sufficiently encompasses these subthemes and qualifies, therefore, as the central focus of the book.

This problem is articulated in the prologue where Satan challenges the basis for Job's piety by claiming that he served God only for profit (i.e., because he prospers—see 1:9–11; 2:4–5).[23] Satan's challenge is reinforced by the fact that Job's wife urged Job to curse God and die (2:9). That Job refused to curse God (2:10) was graphic testimony that his worship was genuine and that Satan's allegation was false.[24]

Thus Job's suffering as an innocent party was not the main focus but was introduced only as a means of isolating and intensifying the question of the proper basis of man's relationship to God.[25]

Key Themes

Certain key themes are employed by the author to serve the purpose of the book and to assist in developing its argument. Perhaps the most important theme is the doctrine of divine retribution which pervades the Book of

21. Others who have recognized this as the main problem of the Book of Job include Rowold ("Theology of Creation," pp. 11, 19): John W. Wevers (*The Way of the Righteous: Psalms and the Books of Wisdom* [Philadelphia: Westminster Press, 1961], p. 75). "The basic problem of Job . . . is the *relation of finite man to an infinite God*" [italics his]): and Robert William Edward Forrest who says that the main issue is "what, if any, is the nature of the divine-human relationship and how may a man live in this universe" ("The Creation Motif in the Book of Job" [Ph.D. diss., McMaster University, 1975], p. 20). Cf. also Good, *Irony in the Old Testament*, pp. 197–98; Zuck, who writes that "one of the grand purposes in the book" is "to deal with motive behind worship, to demonstrate that it is possible to view life as other than a give-and-get bargain with God" (*Job*, p. 189); and Alfred von Rohr Sauer, "Salvation by Grace: The Heart of Job's Theology," *Concordia Theological Monthly* 37 (May 1966): 259–70.

22. These suggestions include the significance of the suffering of the innocent, the right behavior in suffering, the refutation of the principle of divine retribution, and the meaning of faith. Rowold gives a sampling of scholars who have held to these options as the main theme of Job ("Theology of Creation," p. 18). He notes that these subthemes have hindered the recognition of the real central problem.

23. Ibid., p. 20.

24. Zuck, *Job*, p. 189.

25. That this is true is demonstrated by the fact that the main problem of the book was posed before suffering entered the scene and was resolved (see 38:1–42:6) before Job's suffering was removed (Rowold, "Theology of Creation," pp. 20, 29 n. 22).

Job. Other main motifs . . . include the concept of a "mediator" and the persistent employment of creation and of legal metaphors. These major motifs relate to the purpose of the Book of Job.[26] (The concept of a "mediator" will be mentioned in conjunction with legal metaphors since it seems to be employed in such a context.)

The dogma of divine retribution. The principle of divine retribution, which is operative in some portions of the Old Testament,[27] and which lay at the core of ancient Near Eastern religions,[28] became a dogma for Job's friends. Because the validity of this principle (namely, that Yahweh the righteous Judge rewards the righteous with prosperity and punishes the wicked with calamity) had become an unquestioned dogma with no exception, it was automatically assumed that all suffering was caused by sin.

Eliphaz and Bildad asserted that since God, who is an impartial judge, did not punish the upright man nor preserve the evildoer, Job's suffering was a sign of hidden sin (see 4:7–11; 5:8–16; 8:3, 11–22; cf. 18:5–21). Thus it seemed evident to the three friends that Job was a sinner who needed to repent of his sins and to become piously obedient so that God would bless him again (see 22:4–11, 21–30, for Eliphaz's words and 11:13–20 for Zophar's similar sentiment). Bildad also stated that Job's children were killed as punishment for their sins (8:4). Both Eliphaz (15:17–35) and Zophar (20:4–29) argued from experience and the traditional wisdom of old[29] that Job's initial prosperity was explained by the accepted idea that the wicked enjoy only temporary prosperity and bliss before God metes out retributive judgment.

Because of the friends' unquestioned acceptance of the dogma of divine retribution, they were championing the view that the basis of the relationship between God and man was "God's impartial, retributive justice and man's pious fear of God."[30] As man related to God in obedient piety, so God would bless him. As in Satan's challenge of Job's motive for serving God, the demarcation between piety and prosperity became blurred.[31]

Job patiently denied the accusation of the three friends that he was guilty of sin for which he was being recompensed; he openly questioned the validity of the dogma of divine retribution because of the prosperity of the wicked (21:31).[32] Yet it is ironic that because Job accused God of injustice in order to maintain his own righteousness (see 40:8)—operating on the assumption that God was punishing him for sin, though unjustly—he was unconsciously

26. Though these are not the only motifs used, they seem to be the most significant ones.

27. This principle occurs particularly in Deuteronomy and many of the prophets.

28. See the present writer's work, "A Biblical Theology of Job 38:1–42:6" (Th.D. diss., Dallas Theological Seminary, 1980), chapter 1.

29. Cf. Job 8:8–10, where Bildad also appealed to tradition to support his argument.

30. Rowold, "Theology of Creation," p. 22.

31. Ibid.

32. In 21:19 Job objects to the friends' argument that God stores up punishment for a wicked man's sons by questioning why God does not recompense the wicked themselves.

retaining the dogma of divine retribution.[33] Because of this, Job could not harmonize his suffering with God's being an impartial judge. Rather, Job conceived of God as being an arbitrary and capricious Sovereign who abused his power (9:15–24; 12:13–25) and who maliciously treated innocent Job as a personal enemy (13:24–27; 16:7–17; 19:7–12). As a consequence of his suffering, Job viewed man's relationship to God as being based on God's sovereign caprice; therefore man could hope for happiness only by adhering to an ethical rightness superior to God's whereby man could demand vindication (Job 31; cf. 35:2b).[34]

Although Elihu was closer to the truth than the three friends because he seems to have sensed that Job was guilty of pride (33:17; cf. 35:12 and 36:9)[35] and emphasized suffering as mainly remedial in purpose (cf. 33:16–30; 36:8–12),[36] he also was wrong to defend God's justice by assuming that Job was guilty of sin before his suffering (34:37).[37] The explanation for this reasoning was Elihu's failure to divorce himself from the dogma of divine retribution (see 34:11, 25–27; cf. 34:33; 36:17; 37:13). However, Elihu was right in pointing out the fallacious nature of Job's position, which implied that God owed man something for his righteousness (35:3–8).[38]

Although a major thrust of the Lord's speeches (38:1–40:2; 40:6–41:34) was to polemicize against all potential rivals to his lordship over the cosmos,[39] there is also a subtle refutation of the dogma of divine retribution. Although granting that the control of chaotic forces of evil (which in some instances is inherent in the design of the universe—38:12–15) is somewhat consistent with the principle of divine retribution,[40] God demonstrates that the universe

33. In Job 31:2–3 he assumes God punishes the wicked; in 19:11 and 16:9 Job's assumption that God was angry with him implies that Job subconsciously felt that God was punishing him for some unknown sin of which Job was unaware. He wished that God would reveal this to him (10:2). This is consistent with Elihu's interpretation of Job's position as believing that God owed him something (or was obligated to him) because of his righteousness (35:3; cf. Elihu's quotation in 34:9). He refuted Job's position by appealing to God's transcendence (35:4–8; cf. Eliphaz's similar understanding in 22:2–3, 12).

34. Rowold, "Theology of Creation," pp. 23, 27. Two possible translations of this verse are given in the NIV and its margin. Job's hope of vindication because of his valid legal claim of righteousness assumes that he considered his relationship to God as a judiciary one in which God was obligated to repay him.

35. Zuck, *Job*, p. 149. The divine analysis was that Job was guilty of hubris (after his suffering began) in his challenge of God's justice. He unconsciously became a rival to God's position as ruler of the cosmos.

36. However, this angle of disciplinary suffering was also approached once by Eliphaz (see 5:17–27). That Elihu's argument had much truth seems to be implied by Yahweh's absence of rebuke of Elihu in contrast to the three friends.

37. Zuck, *Job*, pp. 148–49, 152.

38. See note 33.

39. This is the purpose stated in a negative fashion. See the author's "A Biblical Theology of Job 38:1–42:6," chapter 3.

40. However, this may be an ironic statement which shows that the wicked are indeed not broken but only controlled. Tsevat argues that this passage teaches that no provision for retribu-

is not always geared to this principle. Rain, which not infrequently appears in the Bible as a vehicle of reward and punishment (cf. Job 37:13 [NIV] and 5:10), is inherently designed to fall on the desert where it has no relevance for man (38:26).[41] In Job 41:11 (3)[42] the Lord may be refuting Job's apparent contention that God's relationship to man was a juridical relationship in which God was obligated to repay him.[43]

The epilogue, which records the restoration of Job and a twofold recompense of his prosperity (42:10, 12–17), seems, at first glance, to confirm the doctrine of divine retribution. However, in actuality this restoration was not a reward or payment but a free gift based solely on God's sovereign grace.[44] This is clear from the import of the Lord's speeches and from the fact that Job's original prosperity was not directly related to his piety.[45]

The Book of Job shows that only by dispensing with the traditional dogma of divine retribution was it possible to reconcile Job's innocence with God's permitting him to suffer.[46] The refutation of this dogma aids in the demolition of its corollary (which undergirds ancient near Eastern religions) that man's relationship to God is based on a juridical claim. Consequently, it complements the purpose of Job, which is to demonstrate the only proper basis for the relationship between God and man.

Creation motif. During Job's lament in which he cursed the day of his birth and deplored its creation (i.e., wishing that he had never been born [3:1–10] or that he had died at birth [3:11–19]), he summons the agents of chaos to annihilate that created day in order that he might live in peace (3:8–10). Job seems to have employed an anti-creation motif in which he wishes for the reversal of creation.[47] This motif was apparently utilized to

tion nor its manifestation is found in the order of the world. He says that although "the dawn of every day provides an occasion to punish the wicked, . . . this possibility is not in practice realized and is therefore not in the plan of the world" (Matitiahu Tsevat, "The Meaning of the Book of Job," *Hebrew Union College Annual* 37 [1966]: 99).

41. Ibid., p. 100. However, perhaps the main function is found in its implication that man is not the center of the universe. This is part of the polemic against man (who is not even mentioned with respect to his creation).

42. The enumeration of verses in parts of Job 40 and all of chapter 41 of the Hebrew Bible differs from that in English Bibles. In this article the English verse numbers will be cited with the Hebrew counterpart in parentheses (when noted).

43. See Job 35:3 and supra, note 33. The NIV translates 41:11 as follows: "Who has a claim against me that I must pay? Everything under heaven belongs to me."

44. Rowold, "Theology of Creation," p. 29 n. 22.

45. See note 25.

46. According to Tsevat, Job demonstrates the impossibility of the coexistence of the three ideas of an accessible God who turns His face to man (G), Job as an innocent man (J), and the philosophy of retributive justice (R). The friends eliminated J, and Job practically gives up G in order to maintain J. Only by giving up R can the other two be reconciled ("The Meaning of the Book of Job," pp. 372–73).

47. Job seems to castigate light (3:20), the first act of creation (Gen. 1:3–4), and wished that it would become darkness (3:4–5, 9). Also he disparaged the goodness of life (3:20), which was

emphasize the depths of his despair and the intensity of his anguish as a result of his abrupt transition from a life of bliss to a mere agonizing existence. Because life and creation had become hopeless and inexplicable to him, he preferred to abandon the created order to the confines of Sheol (nonexistence) (cf. 7:15–16, 21).[48]

Forrest has cogently argued that the reason Job desired nonexistence was his lack of perception of his own relationship to God or to the universe (i.e., Job's belonging within the universe). Thus Forrest has suggested that since creation must "somehow be explicable to him to be worthy of credence (i.e., illustrative of the divine-human relationship in a comprehensible manner so that Job would want to live in the universe)," creation provides the scenario for Job's basic inquiries into the nature of God's relationship to man.[49] The evidence from the text seems to support this hypothesis.

Job said that the wondrous acts of God in nature are inexplicable to him. He could not perceive God's nature[50] in these sovereign works (see 9:10–12; cf. 26:14 and perhaps chap. 28). Rather, God's sovereign control of nature (creation) appeared to indicate an arbitrary abuse of power and wisdom (9:12, 14–24; 12:13–25; cf. 30:18–23).[51] At the same time, Job appeals to nature to be a witness for him of the obvious injustices of God against him (12:7–10; 16:18–19) and of his own ethical purity (see 31:8, 12, 38–40).[52]

This latter tactic of Job was diametrically opposed to the friends' appeal to creation to support their theory of retributive justice as the basis of God's relationship to man (Eliphaz in 4:9–11; Zophar in 20:27–29; and Bildad in

---

extolled in Gen. 1:27–31; 2:7, wishing that he had perished at birth (3:11–19) so that he would have tranquility in the grave (Forrest, "The Creation Motif in the Book of Job," pp. 71–73). Fishbane's argument that Job 3:3–13 is a systematic *bouleversement*, or reversal, of the cosmic acts of creation in Genesis 1:1–2:4a by the use of magic spells and incantations in intriguing but lacks much evidence to support it (Michael Fishbane, "Jeremiah IV 23–26 and Job III 3–13: A Recovered Use of the Creation Pattern," *Vetus Testamentum* 21 [1971]: 153–54). It is probable that if Job had gone this far, he would have taken his wife's advice and perished or committed suicide (Forrest, "The Creation Motif in the Book of Job," pp. 68–69). However, in contrast to the "Dialogue of Pessimism" (Pritchard, *Ancient Near Eastern Texts*, pp. 437–38, 600–601) and to the Egyptian Papyrus 3024, it is doubtful that Job ever considered suicide.

48. Forrest, "The Creation Motif in the Book of Job," pp. 67, 74–75, 188–89. This is apparently the reason Job also identified himself with the forces of chaos (see 7:12).

49. Ibid., pp. 56, 67, 185; cf. p. 188. This is also a major reason the creation motif is employed in the Yahweh speeches. Job failed to see the significance of this doctrine for actual life situations.

50. Job admitted his inability to understand God's power and knowledge especially as manifested in creation. Apparently he could not truly appreciate God's role in creation because of the overtones of arbitrariness (ibid., p. 82).

51. Because of God's sovereign comprehensive power which includes even Sheol, Job had to abandon his wish for safety in Sheol as mere fancy (cf. 26:5–14).

52. This may be explainable in light of the ancient Near Eastern concept of the unity of the natural cosmos with the moral cosmos and the cosmos as a whole. See the author's "A Biblical Theology of Job 38:1–42:6," chapter 1.

22:15–18 [cf. vv. 19–20]; cf. also 5:8–16). Eliphaz advised that if Job would submit under God's corrective punishment, even the wild animals (as chaotic forces opposed to man) would be at peace with him (5:23).

Elihu's speeches include a lengthy section on God's sovereign and benevolent dealings in nature (36:26–37:24).[53] Elihu cited these acts of God as proof that God's sovereign power and justice are beyond man's comprehension. (Thus he apparently empathized with Job's failure to perceive God's nature in creation.) Although Elihu acknowledged that God used nature for His retributive purposes (37:13 NIV) and that nature is sometimes in chaotic opposition to man (37:6–7), he argued that the proper response of man to the sovereign (though inexplicably just) God is reverential trust (37:23–24). In this advice to Job from creation, Elihu prepared the way for the Lord's speeches.

The Lord's speeches (which are saturated with the creation motif) demonstrate that God's sovereign cosmic power was not the retributive justice (as the friends had argued) nor the "uncontrolled caprice" (as Job had perceived it) of an impersonal cosmos, but rather the majestic omnipotence and mysterious creative genius of a personal and gracious God.[54] The absence of a reference to the creation of man is part of a polemic against Job (and man in general) which has as one purpose to show that God was not obligated to fulfill Job's defiant demand for vindication because of his ethical righteousness (cf. 41:11 [3]).[55] God could not be manipulated or coerced like the impotent and immanent gods of the ancient Near East.

Because of Job's perception of this and of God's active participation in creation, Job responded in repentance and trust (42:2–3, 5–6).[56] Thus it is clear that the Book of Job teaches that the basis of the relationship between God and man is not one of mutual benefit or of a juridical obligation which binds God; rather, it is to be based on the Lord's sovereign "creative, life-affirming, joyous grace and of man's open, joyous trust"[57] in Him.

Legal metaphors. The Book of Job extensively employs legal terms and metaphors in the process of its dialogue concerning the disputed innocence of Job before God. That the dialogue is saturated with judicial terminology is quite consistent with the prominent role Job had previously played in the legal affairs of his town (29:7–17).[58] The use of legal metaphor also plays a part in illustrating the proper basis for man's relationship to God.

Scholnick's valuable study of the legal terminology in the Book of Job has

53. Zuck, *Job*, pp. 158–62.

54. Rowold, "Theology of Creation," pp. 168, 171.

55. Ibid., p. 168.

56. Job was shown the inconsistency of his theoretical knowledge of God's sovereignty and his haughty actions against God. The root cause was Job's faulty perception of Yahweh's sovereignty (cf. notes 33 and 45).

57. Rowold, "Theology of Creation," p. 183.

58. Sylvia Huberman Scholnick, "Lawsuit Drama in the Book of Job" (Ph.D. diss., Brandeis University, 1975), pp. vi, 103–4.

demonstrated that the terms זָכָה, זָכַךְ, טָהֵר, and נָקָה (which can be employed in the Old Testament in the sphere of worship—"pure, clean"—or in the sphere of the court—"innocent, free of legal claim") are employed in Job almost exclusively in a forensic context to explore the question of Job's legal status, both before God and in his community.[59] Other legal terms employed include יָשָׁר (1:1, 8; 2:3; 8:6; 23:7), צדק (which is used by each speaker, e.g., 6:29; 8:6; 9:15, 20; 11:2; 22:3; 35:2, 7–8; 40:8) and תָּמִים (1:1, 8; 2:3; 27:5; 31:6).[60]

Perhaps the most significant single legal term used is the root ריב which is used eleven times in Job (seven times as a verb—9:3; 10:2; 13:8, 19; 23:6; 33:13; 40:2; and four times as a noun—13:6; 29:16; 31:13, 35). As a verb in the Old Testament, it means "to make a complaint or accusation (by engaging in hostile unilateral speech activity) against an aggrieving party." As a noun, it denotes "a complaint or accusation by an aggrieved party against one held responsible for a grievance."[61] Although the word רִיב in the Old Testament sometimes describes a dispute outside court, it is used in Job solely in a legal sense as a metaphor to portray a "lawsuit" between Job and God.[62]

This idea of a man going to court with God is unprecedented in the Old Testament.[63] Thus at first Job was somewhat dubious that he could raise litigation with God (9:3; cf. 9:16) since he views God as a sovereign and unjust judge who has abused His authority (9:19–24, 28; 23:7). But Job insists that God make His charges as a legal opponent rather than . . . as an unjust judge (10:2).[64] Job's legal plight before God, who is simultaneously his legal adversary[65] and his judge, accentuates the urgency (and yet the hopelessness) of Job's cry for a neutral party to hear his case.[66]

59. These four terms are employed in the speeches of all characters except God. Few exceptions occur to this forensic usage: זָכַךְ in the context of sanitation in 9:30 and in an "astrological" context in 15:15 and 25:5, and טָהֵר in a metallurgical context (28:19) and in an "astrological" sense in 37:21 (ibid., pp. 3–4). In some cases it is man in general whose lack of legal innocence before God is mentioned (e.g., 25:4), but this is ultimately done to explore Job's innocence or guilt.

60. Ibid., p. 3.

61. See ibid., pp. 109–10, and cf. James Limburg, "The Root ריב and the Prophetic Lawsuit Speeches," *Journal of Biblical Literature* 88 (1969): 291–304, esp. 293–96, 301.

62. In all but two instances Job is the speaker. Also in two instances Job describes his previous judicial activity in the city gate (29:16 and 31:13). Scholnick's suggestion that Job is a "lawsuit drama" is not comprehensive enough to explain the multifaceted genres employed in Job. Scholnick overlooks the possibility that the Yahweh speeches may discontinue the legal metaphor. See the author's article in the July–September 1981 issue of *Bibliotheca Sacra*.

63. However, a servant could litigate against his master (Job 31:13) or a subject against his king (1 Sam. 24:8–22). See Scholnick, "Lawsuit Drama," p. 132. This unprecedented act perfectly illustrates Job's audacity and hubris for which he must repent.

64. See Scholnick, "Lawsuit Drama," pp. 133, 136, and Dick, "The Legal Metaphor," p. 50.

65. In Job 31:35 God is called Job's איש ריב (literally, "man of complaint"), a technical term for a legal adversary (see Judg. 12:2; Isa. 41:11; Jer. 15:10) (Limburg, "The Root ריב," p. 298); cf. Scholnick, "Lawsuit Drama," p. 149.

66. See Dick, "The Legal Metaphor," p. 50.

The concept of a mediator (or neutral party) is introduced in Job 9:33 where Job wished for an impartial מוֹכִיחַ to arbitrate a settlement between God and himself.[67] This arbitrator was probably the ancient Near Eastern judge whose "verdict" was probably no more than a "settlement proposal" which could be accepted or rejected by the parties involved.[68] Job's appeal for an impartial trial is continued in 13:7–12 where he accused the three friends of being partial witnesses on God's behalf who argue His case for Him.[69] The theme of a mediator (or arbitrator) is continued in 16:18–21. Job expressed confidence that surely someone in heaven was his witness or advocate (v. 19, which uses עֵד followed by its Aramaic equivalent שָׂהֵד).[70] The context (especially v. 21) supports the NIV translation of מְלִיצַי (v. 20) as "intercessor": "My intercessor is my friend as my eyes pour out tears to God; on behalf of a man he pleads with God as a man pleads for his friend."[71]

Similar to Job's plea for an impartial "go-between" (9:33) and his confidence of a heavenly witness or intercessor (16:18–21) is his confident assertion that his גֹּאֵל was alive (19:25). Because of the acknowledged complex difficulties and the diverse interpretations of Job 19:25–27,[72] it is impossible to speak dogmatically about verse 25. However, because of the widespread usage of the legal metaphor in Job, it seems likely that Job spoke metaphorically of the גֹּאֵל as one who was "a helper in a lawsuit to see that justice was done to his

67. The NIV has suggested this nuance of the word.

68. Dick, "The Legal Metaphor," p. 46. Veenker gives a summary of scholars who favor this as the function of the ancient Near Eastern judge and of those who question it (Ronald A. Veenker, "An Old Babylonian Legal Procedure for Appeal," *Hebrew Union College Annual* 45 [1974]: 4 n. 14).

The concept of an intermediary figure to advocate his case before God is reminiscent of one role of the personal god in the ancient Near East. For thorough documentation of this intermediary role of the personal god in Mesopotamia, Asia Minor, and Syria-Palestine, see Hermann Vorländer, *Mein Gott: Die Vorstellungen vom persönlichen Gott im Alten Orient und im Alten Testament*, Alter Orient und Altes Testament (Neukirchen-Vluyn: Neukirchener Verlag, 1975), pp. 87–90, 132–34, 162–63. Although it is impossible to prove, it may be that this concept could have surfaced in Job's mind for an instant. However, Job's monotheistic conviction (cf. 31:26–28) would have prevented him from seriously considering such a possibility (Marvin H. Pope, *Job: Introduction, Translation and Notes*, 3d ed., The Anchor Bible [Garden City, N.Y.: Doubleday & Co., 1973], p. 76).

69. Scholnick argues that Job summoned the friends to act as judges and witnesses, a role which apparently was not clearly differentiated ("Lawsuit Drama," p. 138). In Job 31:21 Job himself spoke of his having previous legal help in his city court.

70. Cf. the NIV, and see Francis Brown, S. R. Driver, and C. A. Briggs, *Hebrew and English Lexicon of the Old Testament* (Oxford: Clarendon Press, 1972), p. 962.

71. Job 16:20–21 NIV. Less likely (but possible) is the understanding of מְלִיצַי as "scoffer" or "one who mocks" Job. Cf. NASB and the NIV margin. For the nuance "mediator" or "intercessor," see Job 33:23.

72. For an introduction to some of the difficulties, see the recent helpful work of William Modawell Kruidenier, "The Interpretation and Theological Contribution of Job 19:25–27" (Th.M. thesis, Dallas Theological Seminary, 1978), esp. pp. 2–10.

protégé"[73] (cf. Ps. 119:154; Prov. 23:11; Jer. 50:34; Lam. 3:58). Job's thinking seems to have progressed somewhat from the thought of a mere impartial arbitrator (9:33) to a legal advocate who could present his case and vindicate him as innocent before God (cf. 16:18–21). Consequently it appears unlikely that Job conceived of his "kinsman redeemer" (or legal advocate) as being God Himself. Rather, by using the legal metaphor Job expressed his conviction that he would be vindicated as innocent (which in an earthly lawsuit might require a vindicator or legal advocate).

> The point in Job 19:25 is that just as there is a vindicator in an earthly lawsuit, so in Job's dispute with God there must also be one who intercedes for him, but it does not make clear who this vindicator might be. Accordingly, what we have here is an inexact statement: Job wishes to express the conviction that he must be acquitted in the end, and he clothes this thought in the figurative language of the lawsuit: someone must vindicate him to prove his innocence.[74]

However, in light of Job's legal plight in which God is both judge and legal opponent, Job realized that his hope for an impartial judge was futile. Thus Job could only wish for someone to hear him (31:35). (Possibly the concept of an impartial judge [or arbiter] is continued here.)[75]

Elihu, who stated that he would be an impartial witness (32:21–22),[76] suggested that if there were an angel, a מֵלִיץ (a mediator or intercessor), avail-

73. *Theological Dictionary of the Old Testament*, s.v. "גָּאַל" by Helmer Ringgren, 2:352.

74. Ibid., p. 355. It might be argued that verses 26–27, which mention Job's seeing God, indicate that the גֹּאֵל Job expected was God. But since the legal advocate or vindicator (גֹּאֵל) as previously sought for (9:33 and 16:18–21) was to be an impartial middle party between Job and God, the גֹּאֵל need not be (indeed probably is not) synonymous with God. Although it is unlikely that Job conceived of God per se as his גֹּאֵל, this is not to say, in the final analysis, that God was not his גֹּאֵל (in Job 42:7 Job was vindicated to some extent). Also, in light of the New Testament (1 Tim. 2:5; Heb. 7:25; 8:6; 9:15; 12:24), Zuck is undoubtedly correct in stating that Job's "longed-for Arbiter (9:33), Witness-Advocate (16:19)" and "living Redeemer-Vindicator" (19:25) was the person "whom we know as Jesus Christ, the Son of God" (*Job*, p. 92). However, one must be careful lest he should be guilty of imposing the New Testament back onto the Old Testament by saying dogmatically that Job knew who his גֹּאֵל was.

75. In light of Job's oath of innocence in chapter 31 (a common juridicial procedure in the ancient Near East), Dick has suggested that the participle is the equivalent of מוֹכִיחַ (9:33), the arbitration-judge. Second Samuel 15:3–4 may indicate that this person "was an official appointed by the king to mediate legal disputes" (Dick, "The Legal Metaphor," pp. 47–48). The forensic usage of the cognates of שָׁמַע to designate the activity of a judge (as documented by Scholnick, "Lawsuit Drama," pp. 188–89) seems to confirm this.

76. Because Elihu was apparently a mere bystander from the beginning (or a silent observer who came on the scene a little later than the friends), he qualified to be more neutral and objective in the dispute than either Job or his friends. Thus Elihu appears to serve as a type of arbiter who recommends a settlement. The fact that he was not actually a part of the dispute may explain why he was not rebuked (nor mentioned) by God in the epilogue nor mentioned earlier in the book. Beeby suggests that Elihu was Job's "covenant mediator" necessary for Job, a non-Israelite, to know God face-to-face ("Elihu–Job's Mediator," pp. 42, 48).

able to Job to plead for God's clemency, actually this "mediator would be on God's side, interpreting God's will and leading Job to repentance rather than defending his integrity (33:23–30)."[77]

The legal metaphor often employed heretofore in the Book of Job rarely appears in the Lord's speeches (38:1–42:6). This rare usage of legal metaphor (cf. 40:2, 8 and perhaps 38:3, which is identical to 40:7, and the absence of legal metaphor in Job's responses) which may be used ironically (in contrast to the frequent usage earlier in the book) is significant.

Although impossible to prove, it seems likely that the Lord employed the verb אָזַר "gird up [the loins]" in a forensic sense in 38:3 (and 40:7) in order to heighten the irony of his twofold interrogation of Job.[78] A main function of the Lord's speeches is to show the absurdity of Job's attempt to manipulate God by a "lawsuit," which assumed that his relationship to God is a juridical one. Consequently the Lord virtually ignored Job's allegations of His injustice (except for 40:8).[79]

In 40:2 the Lord summarized His interrogation of Job concerning the universe by ironically asking Job, "Can he who contends with the Almighty correct (or instruct) him? Let him who accuses God answer all this!" (author's translation). Yahweh ironically challenged Job to teach (or correct) Him in the matters of the universe to prove that he was equal to God and thus capable of arguing with God in court.[80]

In 40:8–14 God demonstrated the fallacy of Job's impugning His justice in order to vindicate himself. The Lord's usage of מִשְׁפָּט (in the context of divine kingship over the universe, 40:8–10; cf. Elihu's usage in 34:17 and 37:23) serves as a corrective to the misunderstanding of justice (מִשְׁפָּט) by Job and his friends. The friends viewed מִשְׁפָּט as God's retributive judgment on guilty Job (8:3–4; cf. Elihu's usage in 34:11–12, 23–30); Job considered מִשְׁפָּט as litigation in court to prove his innocence (9:19, 32; 14:3; 19:7) or the processing of a case (13:18; 23:4; 31:13).[81] Both understandings were faulty because of an improper perception of the relationship between God and man.

77. Norman Habel, "Only the Jackal Is My Friend," *Interpretation* 31 (1977): 235. It is ironic that Job himself played the role of an intercessor in 42:8–9 when he prayed for his three friends at the Lord's beckoning.

78. It is possible that belt-wrestling as an ordeal in court (as found in a Nuzi tablet in which it was proscribed by the judges) lay behind the usage of אָזַר as a legal metaphor (Cyrus H. Gordon, "Belt-Wrestling in the Bible World," *Hebrew Union College Annual* 23 [1950–51]: 131–36, esp. 134–36). Contrast Zuck, *Job*, p. 165 n. 6. The present author considers forensic overtones probable for אָזַר because of the ironic usage of the legal metaphor in 40:2 and because of the function of the Yahweh speeches in showing that man's relationship to God is not a juridical one.

79. Zuck, *Job*, p. 163.

80. מוֹכִיחַ ("the one who accuses or argues") is probably a "pun" on Job 9:33 which prepares the way for the Lord's suggestion that Job had tried to be his own "mediator" or "redeemer" (esp. 40:14).

81. Scholnick, "Lawsuit Drama," p. 265.

This improper perception is refuted in the Book of Job. By the incongruity of the legal metaphor in which the Lord functions both as Job's judge and legal adversary and by the Lord's ignoring Job's plea for vindication (or even a trial),[82] the Book of Job "reveals the bankruptcy of conceiving the man-God relationship along the lines of legal justice."[83] Thus it is the legal metaphor "which most forcefully communicates the thesis of the Book of Job that religious piety is not amenable to the *quid pro quo* principle of divine retribution."[84]

Conclusion

The basic literary structure of the Book of Job (a prose framework—prologue and epilogue—which encloses the intricate poetic body) is a part of the almost architectonic symmetry of the book which is also evident in the poetic body. Three cycles of disputations between Job and his three friends are enclosed by two soliloquies of Job (chaps. 3 and 29–31). However, the fact that the symmetry is lacking at the end of the third cycle of speeches (where Zophar did not speak) focuses the reader's attention on the futility of dialogue between Job and his friends and aids in focusing on the interaction between Job and God. It also accentuates the need to resolve the main problem of the book (which was articulated in the prologue, 1:9–11; 2:4–5), namely, the basis of the proper relationship between God and man.

Thus the main purpose of Job is to show that the proper relationship between God and man is based solely on the sovereign grace of God and man's response of faith and submissive trust. This involves (in a negative fashion) the refutation of the retribution dogma and its corollary that man's relationship to God is a business contract binding in court. Three key themes (the dogma of divine retribution, the creation motif, and legal metaphors) were expertly employed in the development of this purpose.

82. This is heightened by the infrequent (and ironic) usage of legal terminology in the Yahweh speeches (see nn. 79 and 80, and cf. nn. 59 and 62).

83. Dick, "The Legal Metaphor," p. 50.

84. Ibid. See also Job 41:11 (NIV).

2

Literary Features of the Book of Job

Gregory W. Parsons

Literary Genre

The consensus that Job is a literary work of the highest magnitude does not make the task of classifying it with regard to its literary type any easier. Many literary critics have attempted to place the Book of Job into one overarching literary genre or category. However, this writer views all attempts to fit the book into one category as failing to do justice to the complex nature of its literary fabric.[1]

Suggestions as to the basic (or comprehensive) literary genre of Job normally have fallen into three major categories: the lawsuit (ריב), which is a legal or judicial genre; the lament genre, which is frequent in the Psalms; or the

1. Even scholars who attempt to fit Job into one literary genre normally acknowledge the presence of other elements. However, they modify what they view as the overall genre in an attempt to include these other literary elements.

From Gregory W. Parsons, "Literary Features of the Book of Job," *Bibliotheca Sacra* 138 (July–September 1981): 213–29. Used by permission of Dallas Seminary Press.

controversy dialogue or dispute, which is similar to the wisdom genre of contest literature in the ancient Near East.

Basic Views

Lawsuit. Because of the occurrence of legal terminology in Job, many scholars have argued that the juridical sphere is the backdrop of the book.[2] Richter understands the Book of Job as a secular lawsuit by Job against God whereby the friends serve as witnesses (who apparently place a counter-suit against Job). Chapters 4–14 are viewed as a preliminary attempt at reconciliation out of court, and chapters 15–31 are seen as formal court proceedings between Job and the friends. The resumption of the case against Job by Elihu and the judgment of God (38:1–42:6) in the form of a secular counter-lawsuit between God and Job result in the withdrawal of the accusation by Job.[3]

Scholnick has presented a scholarly argument for viewing Job as a "lawsuit drama," whereby the man (Job) takes his opponent (God) to court. The issue of the legal guilt or innocence of the two parties involved is resolved through a lawsuit in which the friends are judges and witnesses.[4]

Lament. Although Westermann recognized the existence of a controversy dialogue in Job 4–27, he argued that the most important element in the book is the lament (the personal lament well known in the Psalms). The lament by Job, which begins (chap. 3) and ends (chaps. 29–31) the dialogue proper, completely encloses the controversy speeches.[5]

Gesé suggested that the original "folk book" of Job, now allegedly extant only in the prose sections—the prologue, the epilogue, and in 3:1 and 38:1—was a "paradigm of the answered lament" patterned after three Mesopotamian texts in which an answer of God came to the sufferer.[6] How-

2. However, as noted by Michael Brennan Dick, "'legal language' itself does not constitute a distinct literary form, for the juridicial sphere encompasses a broad area of human life and does not correspond to a specific situation (*Sitz im Leben*)" ("The Legal Metaphor in Job 31," *Catholic Biblical Quarterly* 41 [1979]: 37).

3. Heinz Richter, *Studien zu Hiob: Der Aufbau des Hiobbuches, dargestellt an den Gattungen des Rechtsleben* (Berlin: Evangelisches Verlagsanstalt, [1958]). Cf. James L. Crenshaw, "Wisdom," in *Old Testament Form Criticism,* ed. John H. Hayes (San Antonio: Trinity University Press, 1974), p. 254.

4. Sylvia Huberman Scholnick, "Lawsuit Drama in the Book of Job" (Ph.D. diss., Brandeis University, 1975). Scholnick's view is the most persuasive of any writer who tries to fit Job into one *Gattung;* however, she fails to recognize that the Lord's speeches actually serve to discontinue this metaphor. See this writer's article ("The Structure and Purpose of the Book of Job," *Bibliotheca Sacra* 138 [April–June 1981]: 139–57). Scholnick provides a convenient summary of some other scholars who have noted the idea that Job represents the proceedings of a lawsuit ("Lawsuit Drama," pp. x–xi; cf. also Crenshaw, "Wisdom," pp. 253–54).

5. Claus Westermann, *Der Aufbau des Buches Hiob* (Tübingen: J. C. B. Mohr, 1965), pp. 4–5; and his *Handbook to the Old Testament,* trans. and ed. Robert H. Boyd (Minneapolis: Augsburg Publishing House, 1967), pp. 226–33.

6. See James B. Pritchard, ed. *Ancient Near Eastern Texts Relating to the Old Testament,* 3d ed. (Princeton, N. J.: Princeton University Press, 1969), pp. 589–91; 596–601. Note the actual

ever, Gesé argued that the author of Job changed the original intent of the "paradigm of the answered lament," whose form he ironically employs, by substituting in the poetic sections a demand for a trial with God instead of the allegedly original plea for mercy.[7]

Controversy dialogue. Some scholars have proposed that Job is a variant of the philosophical dialogue, namely a controversy dialogue similar to the disputation or contest literature in the ancient Near East.[8] Although Crenshaw acknowledges that Job cannot be squeezed into one narrow genre, he considers the controversy dialogue, which is influenced by its function within prophetic literature as self-vindication, as the major literary type in the book.[9]

Conclusion

Three views which have been proposed to describe the comprehensive literary genre of the Book of Job have been cited. However, the realization that each of the three positions has at least some validity underlies the fact that none of them succeeds in adequately accounting for the diversified nature of this complex literary work.[10] As a matter of fact, the author of the Book of Job skillfully interwove at least three major literary genres into the fabric of his composition. Using the terminology of Lévêque, the author skillfully played from three different "keyboards"[11] in his polyphonic work—wisdom types, a genre from Psalms, and a genre from the legal sphere. Consequently it can be concluded that the Book of Job is a "mixed genre" in which its author expertly blended a variety of literary types in order to serve the function of the book.[12]

---

contrasts between Job and these three texts as pointed out by the present writer ("A Biblical Theology of Job 38:1–42:6" [Th.D. diss., Dallas Theological Seminary, 1980], pp. 21–22, 24).

7. See Hartmut Gesé, *Lehre und Wirklichkeit in der alten Weisheit: Studien zu Sprüchen Salomos und dem Buche Hiob* (Tübingen: J. C. B. Mohr, 1958), pp. 63–64, 73. For a helpful summary of Gesé's argument, see John Charles Holbert, "The Function and Significance of the *Klage* in the Book of Job with Special Reference to the Incidence of Formal and Verbal Irony" (Ph.D. diss., Southern Methodist University, 1975), pp. 41–43. Note, however, that Horst Dietrich Preuss states that Gesé no longer holds to this theory ("Jahwes Antwort an Hiob und die sogenannte Hiobliteratur des alten Vorderen Orients," in *Beiträge zur alttestamentlichen Theologie: Festschrift für Walther Zimmerli zum 70. Geburtstag* [Göttingen: Vandenhoeck & Ruprecht, 1977], pp. 333 n. 47).

8. Crenshaw, "Wisdom," pp. 228, 254. See W. G. Lambert, *Babylonian Wisdom Literature* (Oxford: Clarendon Press, 1960), pp. 150–212, for contest literature in Mesopotamia.

9. Crenshaw, "Wisdom," pp. 253–54.

10. For instance, none of these adequately accounts for the prose framework of the book. Note the interesting suggestion of Francis I. Andersen that Job stands closest to the epic history of Israel in which a major point of interest is the speeches, often in poetic form (cf. Genesis and Samuel) (*Job: An Introduction and Commentary* [Downers Grove, Ill.: InterVarsity Press, 1976], pp. 36–37).

11. Jean Lévêque, *Job et son Dieu: Essai d'Exégése et de Théologie Biblique*, 2 vols. (Paris: J. Gabalda, 1970), 1:235. On the combination of these three genres see Georg Fohrer, *Das Buch Hiob* (Gütersloh: Gütersloher Verlagshaus Gerd Mohn, 1963), pp. 50–51; and his *Studien Zum Buche hiob* (Gütersloh: Gütersloher Verlagshaus Gerd Mohn, 1963), p. 70.

12. The Berlin Papyrus 3024 from Egypt, which bears a resemblance in form to Job with its prose framework surrounding its poetic body, also employs several different literary genres. The

Literary Devices

Two key literary devices which are employed by the writer of Job are the usage of irony and of mythopoeic language. The present author will analyze the significant manner in which these two major literary devices are utilized to assist the development of the argument and purpose of the book. Also less important literary devices will be briefly noted.

Irony[13]

The Book of Job is truly a study in irony. Irony is a significant literary feature which saturates nearly every portion of the book.[14]

It is interesting that dramatic irony (similar to that used in Greek tragedy)[15] plays an important role in the basic format of Job. The readers and the heavenly court share the knowledge presented in the prologue, of which Job and his friends are not aware—namely, that Job is innocent of wrongdoing and is being tested as part of the cosmic purpose of God.

It is precisely because of the reader's knowledge of Satan's statement that God had put a protective hedge (שַׂכְתָּ) about Job (1:10), that the irony of

---

theme of the dispute between the man and his *Ba* is developed by using three or four different literary forms including a legal dispute, a direct dispute, and two prose allegories. See Hans Goedicke, *The Report about the Dispute of a Man with His Ba: Papyrus Berlin 3024* (Baltimore: Johns Hopkins Press, 1970), pp. 14–17. Thus it should be recognized that literary types are not frozen forms but are utilized in various situations which may deviate from the supposed original *Sitz im Leben*.

13. A concise definition of irony is practically impossible because it involves several nuances of meaning. There are at least three major types of irony: (1) Socratic irony (or irony of character) which is closest to the meaning of the Greek word εἰρωνεια—"dissimulation" (i.e., ignorance feigned to provoke or confound an opponent); (2) verbal irony, which is a figure of speech in which the intended meaning is the opposite (or a modification) of the literal sense of the words used; and (3) irony of events (in drama being called dramatic or Sophoclean irony and in real life called cosmic irony or irony of Fate), which involves an audience (or onlooker) who "perceives that a character is acting in complete ignorance of his true condition." The last type of irony was prominent in Greek drama in which the audience knew in advance the outcome of the legend being enacted in contrast to the actor's own limited understanding of his own actions. See William Joseph Ambrose Power, "A Study of Irony in the Book of Job" (Ph.D. diss., University of Toronto, 1961), pp. 19–26. Holbert, a student of Power, has suggested another classification of irony in Job, namely, "formal irony" to designate those instances in which it is assumed that Job borrowed Old Testament literary formulas and then altered them in such a way as to heighten the ironic intent of the verbal ironies (see Holbert, "Function and Significance of the *Klage* in the Book of Job," p. 4 n. 6). However, Holbert's suggestion is too subjective and involves too many assumptions which cannot be proved. His assumption that elements in Job are parodies on the biblical Psalms depends on a date of Job after the Psalms and ignores similar forms in the ancient Near East from a much earlier date. Thus only verbal irony and irony of events are clearly present in the Book of Job.

14. Since an exhaustive study of irony is impossible here, only selected examples will be noted. For other possible examples (some of which are questionable) see the excellent studies by Power ("A Study of Irony in the Book of Job") and Holbert ("Function and Significance of the *Klage* in the Book of Job"). See also Edwin M. Good, *Irony in the Old Testament* (Philadelphia: Westminster Press, 1965), pp. 196–240.

15. See supra, n. 13.

Job's words in 3:23 becomes evident. Job bemoans that God had placed a hedge around him (וַיָּסֶךְ)[16] so that he could not die. The very protective hedge which (although removed to a greater distance by God) prevents Job's death (cf. 2:6) and which was intended for good is conceived of as a restrictive hedge intended for evil.[17] Job consciously speaks ironically about this "hedge" or security guard (מִשְׁמָר) in 7:12. His question drips with irony as he asks God if he himself was so dangerous as the sea monster that he must be put under twenty-four-hour surveillance (vv. 17–20). In 13:27 Job again alludes to God's guard being restrictive. It is ironic that Job (in 29:2) longed for the bygone days when Yahweh's guard was a blessing rather than a restrictive hindrance.[18] It is this background which enables the reader to understand the full impact of the irony of the Lord's words in 38:8 when He asks Job who hedged in the sea with doors (cf. 7:12). The Lord here uses the same verb—וַיָּסֶךְ—Job employed in 3:23.

The "comforting" friends make use of irony in a subtle attempt to prove that Job is wicked. Their words are aimed at the wicked man with whom they implicitly identify Job by means of verbal irony, whereby they twist Job's words in an attempt to incriminate him.[19] For example, Eliphaz's statements in 4:7–11 are an attempt to equate Job with the wicked man whose lot is trouble (עָמָל—cf. Job's usage of the same word in 3:10, 20 to describe his own condition).[20] In 4:10–11 Eliphaz obliquely refers to Job's "roar" (or "moaning," cf. 3:24) as actually the roar and groan of a lion (as a symbol of the wicked)[21] whose cubs had been scattered and killed because of God's anger.[22] However, a deeper irony (of which the reader is aware) overshadows this pas-

16. The root סוך used in 3:23 is related to the root שׂוך used in 1:10. Between three and ten Hebrew manuscripts have סַכֹּתָ (from the root סוך) in 1:10. For a concise summary of the relationship between שׂוך and סוך as well as שָׂכַךְ and סָכַךְ, see E. Dhorme, *A Commentary on the Book of job*, trans. Harold Knight (London: Thomas Nelson & Sons, 1967), p. 7.

17. This is technically called Sophoclean irony since the use of the root סוך in this verse is a device which brings the reader's attention to his superior understanding of Job's situation in contrast to Job's complete ignorance of it (see Power, "A Study of Irony in the Book of Job," pp. 39, 25). The irony is accentuated by the fact that, when the hedge is moved outward, Job interprets it as becoming unbearably restrictive (cf. 13:27).

18. Power notes that the Sophoclean irony is "the hedge and guard that once were forsaken and despised but now are desired and esteemed have throughout the long and tortuous struggle at all times been present" (ibid., p. 138). It is not necessary to emend בְּסוֹד to בְּסוֹךְ in verse 4 (as Power, p. 136, and others do) to gather this from verse 2 and the overall context.

19. See Good, *Irony in the Old Testament*, pp. 201–12.

20. Whereas Job seems to blame God for his trouble (3:20), Eliphaz plainly implies that the fault is Job's alone because of his wickedness (Holbert, "Function and Significance of *Klage* in the Book of Job," pp. 120–21; cf. Power, "A Study of Irony in the Book of Job," pp. 42–43).

21. See Pritchard for the comparable usage of the lion as a symbol of the impious in the "Babylonian Theodicy" (*Ancient Near Eastern Texts*, p. 602, lines 48–55, 59–64).

22. Job's children had been killed as described in the prologue (1:18–19). See Power, "A Study of Irony in the Book of Job," pp. 42–43, and Holbert, "Function and Significance of *Klage* in the Book of Job," p. 121.

sage. Eliphaz's question, "Were the upright ever destroyed?" (4:7b), which implies, according to the retribution dogma, that no upright person was ever destroyed, is disproved by the very fact that Job sits before him on the ash heap (cf. 1:1, 8; 2:3 where Job is designated יָשָׁר)."[23] Rather than proving Job to be a sinner, Eliphaz displays his own naïve acceptance of an invalid dogma. This not only reinforces Job's innocence in the eyes of the reader[24] but also emphasizes the absurdity of the retribution dogma. In similar fashion, Bildad's possible ironic twisting of Job's words (7:21) in 8:5[25] rebounds against him by the deeper irony of Bildad's own statements of 8:6 and 8:20.[26]

Job counters the ironic jibes of the friends with his own ironic remarks. In 12:2 Job retorts sarcastically (or perhaps satirically)[27] that his friends had such a monopoly on wisdom that wisdom would cease when they died. On the other hand he ironically states that what they say is common knowledge to all men (12:3c). Job says that he himself was not inferior to them in knowledge (12:3b and 13:2b). Beneath the irony of this retort and his statement "what you know, I also know" in 13:2a lies the deeper irony that the equality of their knowledge (especially with regard to the assumption of the retribution dogma) consisted of virtual ignorance of the Lord's ways.[28] Once again Sophoclean irony reinforces the absurdity of the dogma of divine retribution. Here it also illustrates the futility of a "dialogue" between Job and the three friends and adumbrates the necessity for the divine perspective which comes in the Lord's speeches.[29]

23. Holbert calls this verbal irony ("Function and Significance of *Klage* in the Book of Job," p. 122). However, this is more accurately dramatic or Sophoclean irony since Eliphaz is unaware of the events of the prologue.

24. Ibid., p. 123.

25. It is possible that Bildad intentionally reverses the way שָׁחַר is employed by implying that Job should be more concerned with *seeking* God than with God's hypothetically *seeking* him (ibid., p. 157, and Power, "A Study of Irony in the Book of Job," pp. 57–58).

26. Holbert, "Function and Significance of *Klage* in the Book of Job," p. 157.

27. Sarcasm, which is often used interchangeably with irony, often can only be differentiated from it by the tone of voice used. Its tone is ordinarily very heavy and seldom hides its feelings in contrast to irony which uses a lighter tone and has a far more ambiguous effect (Good, *Irony in the Old Testament,* p. 26). The distinction between irony and satire seems to be that the latter, which involves subtle ridicule, is "militant irony." It has a bit of fantasy which the reader recognizes as grotesque or absurd (i.e., inconsistent with reality). See Northrup Frye, *Anatomy of Criticism: Four Essays* (Princeton, N.J.: Princeton University Press, 1957), pp. 223–24, and *The Oxford English Dictionary,* s.v. "Satire." Sarcasm, a biting and cutting criticism, is similar to satire in that its intention is to wound and even destroy, which is not usually the case with irony (Good, *Irony in the Old Testament,* pp. 26–29, 214; and *The Oxford English Dictionary,* s.v. "Sarcasm").

28. Cf. Henry L. Rowold, "The Theology of Creation in the Yahweh Speeches of the Book of Job as a Solution to the Problem Posed by the Book of Job" (Th.D. diss., Concordia Seminary in Exile, 1977), pp. 69–70, esp. n. 9.

29. Also it neutralizes Job's ironic exposition of God's wisdom and power (12:13–25). It seems clear from the context of verses 14–25 and from Job's earlier attacks on God that verse 13 was spoken "tongue in cheek" by Job.

The usage of irony in the dialogue of Job, although especially frequent in the first cycle, occurs almost throughout the three cycles. For example, from the second cycle, Bildad in 18:4 reverses the meaning of Job's words of 14:18 that the "rock is moved from its place."[30] Then Bildad seemingly presents the simple orthodox view of the wicked and his fate (18:5–21). However, it is more likely "a masterpiece of irony" in which Bildad fits the words Job had already spoken about his own condition into the description of the wicked man's fate.[31] Job, who apparently sensed the irony of Bildad's words, responded in 19:2 by mocking Bildad's introductory words of his last two speeches (עַד־אָנָה—"how long?").[32]

In the third cycle, for example, Eliphaz in 22:15–18 turns around Job's quotation of the wicked man (21:14–16) to support his contention that Job has ironically fallen into the same path as wicked men of old (cf. Job's statement in 7:19).[33] Consequently, Eliphaz counsels Job to put away his wickedness in order that his prosperity would be restored (22:22–30). He concludes by stating (in 22:30) that *if* Job would repent, his prayers would once again become efficacious, not only for those who are innocent, but even for the guilty (those not innocent).[34] This would later find ironic fulfillment (in a way not envisioned by Eliphaz) when Job's prayer for his three friends (including Eliphaz himself—42:8–10) was heard so that they, who were not innocent, were forgiven.[35] Again the reader is enabled to see the incongruity of the retribution dogma Eliphaz champions.

Job's words in 27:5–6, where he insists that he would cling to integrity and maintain his righteousness till death despite the allegations of his friends bears ironic resemblance to the Lord's analysis of Job in 2:3. The irony that results from the use of the word "integrity" (תֻּמָּה) causes the reader to wonder if the Lord would still describe Job in the same way after Job's long and blas-

30. See Good, *Irony in the Old Testament,* p. 206, for the precise meaning of this reversal.

31. For an elaboration of how this was done, see Power, "A Study of Irony in the Book of Job," pp. 100–102.

32. See 8:2 (עַצד־אָן) and 18:2 (עַד־אָנָה). Job is tired of hearing Bildad's "how long?" (ibid., pp. 102–3).

33. Ibid., pp. 118–19; cf. Roy B. Zuck, *Job,* Everyman's Bible Commentary (Chicago: Moody Press, 1978), p. 105.

34. Cf. Job 1 where Job offered sacrifices on behalf of his children. The retention of the Masoretic text (both in its text and vocalization), as found in the NIV, is preferred for two reasons: (1) it is theologically more difficult, that is, it appears to contradict the argument of the friends that the innocent—***not*** the guilty—are saved; and (2) the versions (namely, the Theodotionic addition to the Septuagint, the Vulgate, and the Syuriac) had to change the person of verse 30b to fit their translation of "innocent one." Cf. Lester L. Grabbe, ***Comparative Philology and the Text of Job*** (Missoula, Mont.: Scholars Press, 1977), p. 85. As Gordis has proved, this understanding of verse 30 is in perfect harmony with the Jewish doctrine of corporate responsibility (as in Abraham's appeal to God to save Sodom) (Robert Gordis, "Corporate Personality in Job: A Note on 22:29–30," ***Journal of Near Eastern Studies*** 4 [1945]: 54–55).

35. Ibid.; cf. Grabbe, *Comparative Philology and the Text of Job,* p. 85.

phemous attacks on God.[36] The usage of this literary device causes the reader to desire (and anticipate) the voice of God from the "whirlwind."

There is a noticeable lessening of irony in chapters 29–31. Apart from the mild "self-irony" of 29:2[37] and 29:18–20, which contrasts Job's former state with his present state (chap. 30), there is almost no irony either about God (cf. perhaps 31:3–4) or toward the friends. There may be an "implied ironic slap" toward the friends in 29:25c ("like one who comforts mourners").[38] This technique of "deironization" (which allegedly verifies the spurious nature of 29–31)[39] is fitting for Job's soliloquy in which he ignores the friends and turns his hopes toward God (though indirectly) in an almost hopeless "last-ditch" appeal for vindication. The brunt of the irony, which is directed toward Job, consists of a dual contrast—between his former expectations (chap. 29) and his present state, and between his earlier flagrant attacks on God and his present somber appeal for vindication. These contrasts are indicative of Job's desperate situation and prepare the way for the Lord's speeches.

The speeches of Elihu are particularly ironic (or even sarcastic) toward the friends for their failure to deal properly with Job (32:7, 9–11, 15–16). They also contain a few gently ironic utterances directed toward Job (cf. 34:33 and 37:17–20).[40] This may illustrate the somewhat neutral (or perhaps mediatorial) role of Elihu.

The Lord's speeches (particularly the first) are permeated with obviously ironic remarks which border on sarcasm (38:4–5, 18, 21). However, they also contain more subtly ironic remarks. For example, the Lord's usage of מוֹכִיחַ in 40:2 seems to be an implicit reference to Job's hypothetical מוֹכִיחַ (9:33).[41]

Mythopoeic Language

The observant reader of the Book of Job is struck by the prevalence of mythopoeic language (the poetic usage of mythological allusions), which is perhaps more prominent in Job than in any other biblical book.[42] Smick has

36. Power, "A Study of Irony in the Book of Job," pp. 127–28.

37. Cf. supra, p. 215 [pp. 38–40 in this volume].

38. See Good, *Irony in the Old Testament,* pp. 224–25, 234.

39. See Holbert's allegation, "Function and Significance of *Klage* in the Book of Job," pp. 258ff.

40. Good, *Irony in the Old Testament,* pp. 208–12.

41. Ibid., pp. 234–36. See the present writer's "A Biblical Theology of Job 38:1–42:6," pp. 110–12, for the significance of these and other ironic remarks. See also Elihu's use of מוֹכִיחַ in 32:12 where he says that there is no מוֹכִיחַ for Job. See Power, "A Study of Irony in the Book of Job," pp. 139–40.

42. Matitiahu Tsevat, "The Meaning of the Book of Job," *Hebrew Union College Annual* 37 (1966): 86. Although obviously genuine mythological allusions are numerous, one must be careful not to be victimized by the mythological approach of Walter L. Michel, "The Ugaritic Texts and the Mythological Expressions in the Book of Job" (Ph.D. diss., University of Wisconsin, 1970), which attempts to read mythology (esp. Ugaritic) into almost every verse by textual emendation and by speculation. Pope is also often guilty of a mythological approach to Job (Marvin H.

divided the mythological terminology into four categories: (1) the forces of nature (the fire, the sea, etc.); (2) "creatures cosmic or otherwise"; (3) cosmography; and (4) pagan cultic practices.[43] How do these various mythological allusions fit with an evangelical view of the origin and purpose of the Book of Job?[44]

The only reference to Smick's last category occurs in Job 3:8 where Job calls for enchanters to curse the day (of his birth) by arousing Leviathan (presumably to swallow the sun).[45] (Thus the context supports the retention of יוֹם in the Masoretic text instead of its emendation to יָם [sea or the god Yamm]—a chaos force in Ugaritic as the counterpart of Leviathan, the sea monster.) However, there may indeed be a subtle play on the similar sound of יוֹם ("day") and יָם ("sea") and the parallel between Leviathan and Yamm in Ugaritic mythology.[46] Job apparently employed "the most vivid and forceful proverbial language" available to him to emphasize the depths of his despair and the intensity of his anguish.[47] Because of Job's clear statement of his monotheism (in 31:26–28), this mythological allusion (as well as others in the book)[48] should not be considered as indicative of Job's belief in the validity of pagan cultic practices or of the existence of other deities.[49]

As a matter of fact, at least two passages where Job speaks contain possible polemical overtones. The first passage (9:5–13), which includes a host of

---

Pope, *Job,* 3d ed. [Garden City, N.Y.: Doubleday and Co., 1973]). However, neither ought one to go to the extreme to deny that any mythological expressions occur in Job "in a strained attempt to remove the writers of Scripture from such contamination" (Elmer B. Smick, "Mythology and the Book of Job," *Journal of the Evangelical Theological Society* 13 [1970]:101–21).

43. Smick, "Mythology," p. 101.

44. Ibid. The amazing thing is that the mythological allusions abound most in Job's speeches and in the Lord's speeches (where one would least expect them). In contrast, the friends employ little mythopoeic language.

45. It was a common belief among ancient peoples all over the world that a solar eclipse was caused by a dragon or monster which swallowed the sun. For a collection of several of these traditions see Theodor H. Gaster, *Myth, Legend, and Custom in the Old Testament,* 1st ed. (New York: Harper & Row, 1969), pp. 878–88, and also his book, *Thespis: Ritual, Myth and Drama in the Ancient Near East,* rev. ed. (New York: Harper & Row, 1961; reprint ed., New York: Harper Torch Books, 1966), pp. 228–29. The daily opposition of the sun god Re by the serpentine monster Apophis in Egyptian mythology probably also included the concept that a total solar eclipse indicated the temporary triumph of Apophis who had swallowed the sun (cf. Pritchard, *Ancient Near Eastern Texts,* pp. 6–7, 12; and Luis I. J. Stadelmann, *The Hebrew Conception of the World: A Philological and Literary Study* [Rome: Pontifical Biblical Institute, 1970], pp. 21–22). Gaster has suggested that the promise of the protection and friendship of the sun goddess by Koshar-wa-Khasas (in the Ugaritic text—UT 62:35–52) belies a similar concept *(Thespis,* pp. 228–30).

46. Elmer B. Smick, "Another Look at the Mythological Elements in the Book of Job," *Westminster Theological Journal* 40 (1978): 215.

47. Ibid.

48. See, for instance, the use of עַפְעַפֵּי־שָׁחַר in 3:9, "the eyelids of Dawn," a personification of dawn which is equivalent to the Ugaritic goddess *šḥr* ("Dawn"). See also Job 38:12 and 41:18(10).

49. However, Job's error in chapter 3 was questioning the sovereign purpose of God by condemning the day of his birth (Smick, "Another Look," p. 215).

mythological allusions,[50] emphasizes the sovereignty of the Lord over the sea[51] and the uniqueness of the Lord as the God who alone (לְבַדּוֹ) made the heavens, which are worshiped by pagans (9:8).[52] Also 9:7 makes it clear that it is the Lord, *not* a monster, who is the cause of the eclipse of the sun.[53] The sun (here denoted by חֶרֶס) is never referred to as שֶׁמֶשׁ[54] by the man Job, which seems to be a conscious but subtle polemic against sun worship.[55]

The second passage, 26:5–14, also contains several mythological allusions.[56] However, the emphasis is clearly on the sovereignty of God over all the forces of nature. Verse 7 seems to contain a merism whereby the Lord's creation of the north (probably the "heavens" or "skies")[57] and His establishment of the earth upon nothing[58] indicate His total control of the universe

50. Job 9:6 describes mountains as "the pillars" (of the earth) (cf. 26:11). In verse 8 בָּמֳתֵי יָם, literally, "the high places of Yamm" (no article), has been translated as the "back of Yamm (or Sea)" by many scholars because of the Ugaritic cognate *bmt* ("back"). For example, see Pope, *Job,* pp. 68, 70, and Charles Lee Feinberg, "Ugaritic Literature and the Book of Job" (Ph.D. diss., Johns Hopkins University, 1945), p. 55. Verse 9 speaks of the constellation Orion which was conceived of as a giant hunter in ancient mythology (see 38:31). Verse 13 mentions עֹזְרֵי־רָהַב, the helpers of Rahab, רָהַב ("boisterous, arrogant") being the peculiarly Israelite name for Leviathan (see Ronald Barclay Allen, "The Leviathan-Rahab-Dragon Motif in the Old Testament" [Th.M. thesis, Dallas Theological Seminary, 1968], pp. 2–5, 66–67, 76). See also Francis Brown, S. R. Driver, and Charles A. Briggs, *A Hebrew and English Lexicon of the Old Testament* (Oxford: Clarendon Press, 1972), p. 923; and Mary K. Wakeman, *God's Battle with the Monster: A Study in Biblical Imagery* (Leiden: E. J. Brill, 1973), pp. 58 and 79.

51. Although the absence of the article permits יָם to be a proper noun, the article is not mandatory in poetry. The presence of the plural בָּמֳתֵי (lit., "backs") emphasizes that Yamm has many "backs" or waves because he is actually nothing more than a natural force (the waves of the sea) and not a deity at all.

52. Smick, "Another Look," pp. 218–19.

53. Ibid., p. 218.

54. שמש is cognate to Akkadian *šamaš* and Ugaritic *špš*, both of which are employed to designate the "sun" as well as the "sun deity."

55. חרס is a rare Hebrew word for "sun" used elsewhere only in Judges 14:18 (except for place names) (Brown, Driver, and Briggs, *A Hebrew Lexicon,* p. 357). In Job's disavowal of sun worship (31:26), he employs the word אוֹר "light" (cf. Elihu's usage in 37:21); in 30:28 he uses the word חַמָּה "heat" which is rarely used in the Old Testament to describe the sun (see Song of Sol. 6:10; Isa. 24:23; 30:26) (Brown, Driver, and Briggs, *A Hebrew Lexicon,* pp. 328–29). The only occurrence of שמש in the Book of Job is in 8:16 where Bildad speaks.

56. In 26:7 צָפוֹן ("the north") was the cosmic mountain in Ugaritic mythology; verses 10–11 may denote a primitive cosmography of the earth as a flat disk floating in the subterranean waters (cf. v. 7) and of the mountains as pillars supporting the heavens. However, this is more likely phenomenological language (language describing the way things appear—such as meteorologists use "sunrise" or "sunset"—without necessarily endorsing this scientifically). Verses 12–13 describe Rahab, the chaotic monster (see supra, n. 50) which the Lord smashed to pieces. (See the similar description in UT 67:I:1–3, 27–30, where Mot seems to question the possibility of Baal's defeating the chaos monster.) In 26:13 the monster is designated נָחָשׁ בָּרִחַ "the fleeing serpent" whom the Lord pierced (cf. Isa. 27:1 and also Anat's claim of destroying the serpent in *'nt* III: 38–39).

57. See Smick, "Another Look," pp. 222–23, and the NIV translation.

58. This assertion of faith supports the probability that 26:10–11 (and other verses where Job speaks) describe the cosmos in a phenomenological manner.

(see vv. 8–14). Therefore verse 12, which refers to הַיָּם (*the* sea—with definite article indicating *not* a proper name), seems to be at least an effort at "demythologizing,"[59] if not antimythical polemicizing.

In the speeches of the friends and of Elihu, besides the few references to cosmography,[60] very little mythopoeic language is used. Eliphaz (in 5:7) speaks of בְּנֵי־רֶשֶׁף "the sons of Resheph" to describe the "flames" or "sparks" which fly upward. Resheph is well-attested as the Northwest Semitic god of plague and pestilence.[61] Similarly Bildad in 18:13 refers to Death's firstborn (בְּכוֹר מָוֶת).[62] The mention of "holy ones" (by Eliphaz in 5:1 and 15:15) is reminiscent of the "divine council" motif (cf. 15:7–8) of the ancient Near East in which the lesser divine beings participated in an assembly of the gods who made the decisions (cf. "the sons of God" in the prologue—1:6; 2:1).[63]

Now that the basic data concerning mythopoeic language in Job have been cited,[64] how does one explain the usage of such mythological language? The fact that the mythopoeic language is much more frequent in the speeches of Job (where polemical overtones appear to be present) than in the friends' speeches strongly suggests that these allusions are merely borrowed imagery from the ancient Near Eastern cultural milieu.[65] Corroboration of this may be indicated by noting the presence of mythopoeic language in the Lord's speeches.[66] Mythopoeic allusions are clearly present in the descriptions

59. The present writer uses this term to describe a neutralization of the mythical concepts of the ancient Near East. This usage in 26:12 is in contrast to 7:12 where Job asked if he were Yamm (יָם without the article) or the sea-monster (תַּנִּין) that God placed a guard over him (cf. *'nt* II:37 where Anat claims to have muzzled the dragon, *tnn*). See Smick, "Another Look," p. 223. תַּנִּין, unlike Leviathan and Rahab which are personal names for the monster, is more properly a generic term for the sea-monster (Wakeman, *God's Battle with the Monster,* p. 79).

60. See 22:14 and 37:18 where the sky seemed to be a solid dome (רָקִיעַ) over the earth. This is also probably phenomenological language.

61. Thus the term "sons of Resheph" describes the various types of pestilence (here "flames") (see Smick, "Mythology," p. 105, and "Another Look," pp. 219–20; also Pope, *Job,* pp. 42–43). For references to Resheph, see Gaster, *Myth, Legend, and Custom,* pp. 670–71, 789.

62. Mot was the Ugaritic god of drought, death, and the underworld. See Smick, "Mythology," p. 105, and "Another Look," p. 220.

63. See Smick, "Another Look," pp. 216–17.

64. The evidence from the Lord's speeches has been deliberately omitted so far. Also some evidence was not included from the rest of the book such as several instances of personification of the forces of nature (cf. אֲבַדּוֹן—[28:22; 31:12] and תְּהוֹם [28:14]).

65. This is consistent with the strict monotheism of Job (31:26–28) and his friends as well as all the Old Testament writers. Allen's excellent analysis of the Leviathan motif concludes that the mythopoeic language of the Old Testament was merely literary allusion, not "borrowed mythology" ("The Leviathan-Rahab-Dragon Motif in the Old Testament," pp. 60, 63; cf. Bruce K. Waltke, *Creation and Chaos* [Portland, Ore.: Western Conservative Baptist Seminary, 1974], pp. 13–14).

66. If one assumes that these speeches are really the words of the Lord and not merely words placed in His mouth by the poet (the typical neoorthodox view), the presence of mythological language is a cogent indication that mere imagery is being employed.

of the restraining of the sea with bars and doors (38:8–10),[67] of Leviathan breathing fire and smoke (41:19–21 [11–13]),[68] and probably of the underworld as having gates (38:17). It is also probable that mythopoeic language occurs in the personification of the stars (38:7—parallelism with בְּנֵי אֱלֹהִים),[69] of Dawn (שַׁחַר) in 38:12,[70] and of the constellation Orion (כְּסִיל) in 38:31.[71]

Why did God use mythopoeic language in His speeches to Job? The present writer has argued elsewhere[72] that polemical overtones exist in the usage of this language. These polemical nuances stress the contrast between the uniquely sovereign Lord who operates by grace and the ancient Near Eastern gods who were bound by the dogma of retribution.

A twofold purpose may be seen in this subtle polemic against the gods: (1) to endorse Job's monotheistic stance[73] in the process of exposing the inconsistency of Job's action (unconscious self-deification) with his theological position; and (b) to emphasize that the Lord cannot be manipulated

67. In the so-called Akkadian creation epic *Enuma Elish,* the goddess *Ti'āmat* (Old Akkadian word for "sea"), who apparently represented the powers in the primeval salt water ocean, was slain and bound by Marduk in his storm chariot. After her corpse was cut in half to make the sky out of one half, Marduk provided for bars and posted guards so that her waters could not escape. (See tablet IV, lines 93ff., and esp. 139–40 in Pritchard, *Ancient Near Eastern Texts,* p. 67.) Also see Alexander Heidel, *The Babylonian Genesis: The Story of Creation,* 2d ed. (Chicago: University of Chicago Press, 1951; reprint ed., Phoenix Books, 1963), pp. 40–42. Heidel interprets the guard to refer only to the waters contained in the sky (see p. 42 n. 94).

68. See Job's allusion in 3:8 to the mythical Leviathan as a force of chaos.

69. The stars were worshiped as mighty gods in pagan cults of the ancient Near East (cf. Deut. 4:19). For instance, the Ugaritic poem sometimes called "The Birth of the Gracious Gods" (UT 52) celebrates the birth of the astral deities Dawn (*šḥr*) and Dusk (*šlm*)—lines 52 and 53—probably the brilliant star Venus regarded by many as both the morning and evening star (cf. Pope, *Job,* p. 292). For a transliteration and translation of UT 52 (= SS), see G. R. Driver, *Canaanite Myths and Legends* (Edinburgh: T. & T. Clark, 1956), pp. 120–25. The mention of "the sons of God" (cf. Job 1:6 and 2:1) bears a resemblance to the assembly of lesser gods in the ancient Near East.

70. See the reference to the Ugaritic god *Šaḥar* in n. 69. See also the reference to the "eyelids of Dawn"(עַפְעַפֵּי־שָׁחַר) in Job 41:18 (10) and 3:9. The star Venus, likely called *Šaḥar* in Ugaritic, was also venerated and associated with Inanna in Sumerian myths, with Ishtar in Akkadian, and with Attar (Astarte) in Ugaritic myths. See Helmer Ringgren, *Religions of the Ancient Near East,* trans. John Sturdy (Philadelphia: Westminster Press, 1973), pp. 9, 59–60, 141–42.

71. In ancient mythology Orion was a giant hunter. According to Dhorme (*Commentary on the Book of Job,* p. 132) and Theodor H. Gaster (*Thespis,* p. 322). Orion was the Babylonian god of the chase and was called Ninib (equivalent to Sumerian Ninurta, the stalwart warrior god with his hunting gear of bows and nets). In Egyptian literature the god Osiris (forebear and prototype of all dead kings) was alive in Orion. The dead king could go to the "Field of Rushes" (the Hereafter) with Orion; even the common (nonroyal) men rose and set with Orion as night stars. See Henri Frankfort, *Ancient Egyptian Religion: An Interpretation* (New York: Columbia University Press, 1948), pp. 102–3, 105–6, 109–11.

72. See the writer's "Biblical Theology of Job 38:1–42:6."

73. This included not only a belief in the sovereignty of God (see the writer's article, "The Structure and Purpose of the Book of Job") but even polemical statements against other gods (Job 9:5–13; 26:5–14).

according to the dogma of retribution which bound the gods of the ancient Near East.[74]

The scope of this article permits only one example of polemic from the Lord's speeches, namely, the subtle reaffirmation of Job's implicit polemic against sun worship.[75] The Lord's control over the sun is shown by His daily command for sunrise and sunset, although the word "sun" (שֶׁמֶשׁ) is never directly mentioned in His speeches.[76] This polemic against the sun, however, does much more than endorse Job's monotheistic stance. Since the sun god was almost universally considered to be the guardian of justice in the ancient Near East,[77] the Lord's control of the sun (and its limiting of the activities of the wicked—38:13–15)[78] demonstrated that the Lord (and the Lord alone) was the guarantor of justice.[79] Explicit in this was the fact that the Lord, not Job, was responsible for meting out justice (see 38:12–15 and 40:8–14).[80]

Furthermore the portrayal of the Lord's sovereignty over Leviathan, not only a symbol of chaos and of the wicked and proud (see 40:12), but also of Satan himself,[81] may involve a subtle double entendre for the reader which implies God's victory over Satan who has been proved wrong.[82]

Other Literary Devices

The author of Job also employed several other literary devices in the composition of his masterpiece. Only some of these can be noted, and then very

74. Job's failure to part with this dogma (see 40:8) was not only inconsistent with his theology, but also caused him to adopt a distorted view of God's sovereignty, namely, that it was cruel caprice.

75. See supra, p. 219 [p. 44 in this volume].

76. Indirect mentions occur in the use of בֹּקֶר ("morning") and שַׁחַר ("dawn") in 38:12–15 and of אוֹר ("light") in 38:19–20.

77. See chapter 1 of the writer's "A Biblical Theology of Job 38:1–42:6."

78. In the ancient Near East, it was believed that the sun god drove the demons and other chaotic forces (often embodied in animals) back into their hiding places each morning. See the representation of the god of light (probably Shamash) in opposition to demons in Othmar Keel, *The Symbolism of the Biblical World: Ancient Near Eastern Iconography and the Book of Psalms,* trans. Timothy J. Hallett (New York: Seabury Press, 1978), p. 54, fig. 53. See also Shamash seated in judgment of a lion-headed demon (ibid., p. 208, fig. 286). In Egypt the concept was that of Re in his sun boat emerging victoriously over the underworld serpent of darkness, Apophis (see Frankfort, *Ancient Egyptian Religion,* p. 18 and fig. 8).

79. Job 38:12–15 is an answer to Job's objections of 24:13–17 that wickedness was rampant at night.

80. Job assumed that the Lord was bound to the dogma of retribution like the sun god and in doing so unconsciously placed himself as judge.

81. See Revelation 12:3–17 (esp. v. 9) and 20:2 where Satan is called a serpent and a dragon. See also Allen, who argues that the Leviathan motif is consistently an emblem of Satan in the Old Testament ("The Leviathan-Rahab-Dragon Motif in the Old Testament").

82. See Smick, "Another Look at the Mythological Elements in the Book of Job," p. 227. (While the present writer arrived at virtually the same conclusion independently of Smick, it was a real encouragement to find another evangelical who recognized the significance of the mytho-

briefly, because they do not contribute in an obvious way to the overall purpose of the book.

Several somewhat related literary devices employed in Job may be conveniently lumped together under the general term "paronomasia."[83] Selected examples of various types of paronomasia which occur in Job will be briefly noted. Some indication of the existence of alliteration is found in 5:8 where every word begins with the letter א except the last word.[84] Another common literary device is assonance. This is used, for example, in 12:2 where six of the seven Hebrew words contain the humming sound ("m") which accentuates Job's mocking sarcasm.[85] Rhyme occurs occasionally as in 10:8–18[86] and in 19:3–4, 17–21.

The use of assonance in Job 3:8 borders that of a play on words (or "sense"-paronomasia) where the use of וֹם (which is suggestive of יָם)[87] is heightened by the pun between אֹרְרֵי ("those who curse") and עֹרֵר ("those who arouse"), two virtual homonyms. Eliphaz's play on the words "ground" (אֲדָמָה) and "man" (אָדָם) in conjunction with the repetition of the word עָמָל "trouble" (5:6–7) serves as an effective device to aid his clever argument that trouble does not spring from the ground but from man.[88]

Job 13:24 may contain a pun by Job on his own name (אִיּוֹב with the use אוֹיֵב "enemy") to describe his relationship to God.[89] This pun is similar to the

logical overtones of Leviathan for understanding the Book of Job. Except for Allen ["The Leviathen-Rahab-Dragon Motif in the Old Testament," pp. 82–84], other evangelicals have minimized the mythological aspect of Leviathan for the Lord's speeches and have ignored the possible significance of it as a Satanic emblem.) It is only through the permission of the Lord that Satan was allowed to use his forces of chaos and evil against Job. Although Job is quite ignorant of Satan's role as described in the prologue, it may be through the familiar anti-creation symbol of chaos (Leviathan) that the Lord communicated the fact that chaos forces (within the sovereign restraint set by the Creator) were responsible for the calamities which befell Job and the apparent injustices which Job had observed and lamented.

83. Immanuel M. Casanowicz (*Paronomasia in the Old Testament* [Boston: Norwood Press, 1894]) divides this term into "sound-paronomasia" and "sense-paronomasia." The former includes alliteration ("the recurrence of the same initial letter or its phonetic equivalent in two or more words in close or immediate succession"), rhyme (the agreement of sound at the end of words), and assonance (the coincidence of sound in the middle of words). The latter, sense-paronomasia, is a "play on words" or pun in which the combination of words of similar sounds produces a witticism or jest (see pp. 3–4, 8, 12). Casanowicz lists some fifty-two examples of paronomasia in Job (pp. 91–93), but his list is far from exhaustive.

84. Robert Gordis, *The Book of God and Man: A Study of Job* (Chicago: University of Chicago Press, 1965), p. 166.

85. Ibid., pp. 166–67.

86. Charles Lee Feinberg, "The Poetic Structure of the Book of Job and the ugaritic Literature," *Bibliotheca Sacra* 103 (1946): 290.

87. See supra, p. 218 [p. 43 in this volume].

88. Good, *Irony in the Old Testament*, p. 203.

89. This was suggested as long ago as the Talmud (Baba Bathra, 15a). See Holbert, "Function and Significance of the *Klage* in the Book of Job," p. 182, and Good, *Irony in the Old Testament*, p. 230. The *plene* spelling of "enemy" אוֹיֵב (rather than אֹיֵב) seems to confirm this.

subtle device of double entendre (or what Gordis designates *talḥin,* after the Arabic rhetoricians) which sometimes occurs. The author wished to bring both meanings of a word (especially when homonyms existed) to the consciousness of the reader simultaneously. For example, in 7:6 the use of תִּקְוָה ("hope") also brings to mind its homonym which means "thread" because of the figure of the weaver employed in the verse.[90]

Conclusion

It has been argued that the Book of Job does not fit into a single literary genre; rather, its author skillfully interwove literary forms from a least three major genres (the lawsuit, the lament, and the controversy dialogue) into the fabric of the book in order to serve its function.

In a previous article the present writer suggested that the purpose of Job (stated in a negative fashion) was the refutation of the retribution dogma and its corollary that man's relationship to God is a business contract binding in court.[91] In the present article this contention is supported by demonstrating how two major literary devices (irony and mythopoeic language) were expertly employed in the development of this purpose. Furthermore several other literary features (such as assonance, alliteration, and double entendre, which may be collectively called paronomasia) were noted. These less obvious strokes from the poetic brush, which often do not contribute significantly to the overall purpose, may be called the "finishing touches" to the literary masterpiece known as the Book of Job.

90. Gordis, *The Book of God and Man,* pp. 167–68. He suggests that this device also occurs in 3:6–7, 22; 5:24; 9:17; 12:6; 21:13; and 22:25 (see p. 347 n. 51).

91. Parsons, "The Structure and Purpose of the Book of Job," pp. 139–57.

3

The Literary Genre of the Book of Job

Claus Westermann

Is the Book of Job to be classified as wisdom literature? Until now this question has been answered predominantly in the affirmative, yet recently several voices have been raised in opposition.[1] Essentially they contend that so far as literary form is concerned the Book of Job is utterly

1. In my opinion the soundest and most important objection has been raised by Paul Volz (*Das Buch Hiob*, Schriften des Alten Testaments 3/2 [Göttingen, 1911], pp. 25–26 ["Hiobs Klage kein Lehrgedicht"]). Subsequent defenders of the same view include Artur Weiser, *Das Buch Hiob*, Das Alte Testament Deutsch 13 (Göttingen: Vandenhoeck & Ruprecht, 1951); Johannes Fichtner, "Hiob in der Berkündigung unserer Zeit," *Wort und Dienst*, N.F. 2 (1950): 71–89; Aage Bentzen, *Introduction to the Old Testament*, vol. 2 (Copenhagen: G. E. C. Gad, ²1952); Priedrich Baumgärtel, *Der Hiobdialog: Aufriss und Deutung*, Beiträge zur Wissenschaft vom Alten und Neuen Testament 61 (Stuttgart, 1933); and Moses Buttenweiser, *The Book of Job*

From Claus Westermann, *The Structure of the Book of Job: A Form-Critical Analysis*, trans. Charles A. Muenchow (Philadelphia: Fortress, 1981), 1–15. Used by permission of Augsburg Fortress.

unique.[2] The whole question of literary form would become significant only if the judgment concerning literary classification were to have a decisive effect upon the exegesis of the book. Historically this seems not to have happened; at least interpreters of Job have not argued much about this matter of literary classification.[3] In fact, however, the categorizing of Job as wisdom literature has clearly exerted a pervasive, perhaps even controlling, influence upon nineteenth- and twentieth-century exegesis. This becomes apparent at one particular point: most modern interpretations proceed on the assumption that the Book of Job deals with a "problem." For example, Theodore H. Robinson writes: "The subject of this poem is the most serious problem that has ever troubled the human mind."[4] In the words of Johannes Lindblom, the poet "discusses, upon the occasion of the misfortune of Job, the problem of divine retribution and of the justice of God."[5] Sellin and Rost say that Job treats the problem "How is the suffering of a just man to be reconciled with the existence of a just God?"[6] This basic proposition—that the Book of Job deals with a problem—reflects a prior decision regarding the "meaning" of the Book of Job, a decision which cannot help but exert a controlling influence upon the exegesis of the book.[7] However, one cannot avoid noticing that those interpreters who agree on the basic proposition that the Book of Job deals with a problem obviously disagree on just what that problem is. Furthermore, the history of interpretation shows no progress on this crucial question as to the

(New York, 1922). All these see the lament as the chief component of the Book of Job, and they question the classification of Job as wisdom literature on the basis of that observation. The reason this recent view of the Book of Job has not been generally accepted may well lie in the fact that the true character of the lament in the Old Testament has not been sufficiently investigated. In any case, the contemporary situation with regard to this question is ambiguous: some simply continue to classify the Book of Job as wisdom, while others cautiously question this classification. The following statement by Kuhl is characteristic of the latter tendency: "One ordinarily reckons Job as part of the wisdom literature. . . . However, the poem does not readily fit into the framework of the usual corpus of wisdom literature. The poem's affinities with the poetry of the psalms, above all, its similarities to the genres of the lament and the hymn, are every bit as pronounced as its relationship to wisdom" (Curt Kuhl, "Neuere Literarkritik des Buches Hiob," *Theologische Rundschau*, N. F. 21 [1953]: 311).

2. E.g., Weiser, *Das Buch Hiob*, pp. 8–9. Cf. the remark by Kuhl: "One would therefore be well advised to see in Job an 'utterly unique poem' (Beel, p. 268), an 'independent type' (Kraeling, p. 226), which fits into none of the usual categories (Spalding, p. 290)" ("Literakritik," pp. 311–12).

3. Kuhl's essay is the first really comprehensive presentation of the history of research on the Book of Job. Thanks are due to the author for this exceptionally painstaking survey, which has drawn together an extraordinarily immense number of individual studies.

4. Theodore H. Robinson, *The Poetry of the Old Testament* (London: Duckworth, 1947), p. 68.

5. Johannes Lindblom, *La composition du livre de Job* (Lund: C. W. K. Gleerup, 1945), p. 35.

6. Ernst Sellin and Leonhard Rost, *Einleitung in das Alte Testament* (Heidelberg: Quelle & Meyer, ³1950), p. 160; cf. Ernst Sellin and Georg Fohrer, *Introduction to the Old Testament*, trans. David E. Green (Nashville: Abingdon, 1968), p. 334.

7. Volz, who explicitly denies that the Book of Job deals with a problem, points this out with particular clarity in his commentary (*Das Buch Hiob*, p. 25).

nature of the problem. Regarding this decisive question Kuhl confirms, "The history of Job research simply does not reveal clearly recognizable and distinctive stages."[8] Might not this lack of progress indicate that the widely shared assumption that the Book of Job deals with a problem needs now to be reconsidered? Does the Book of Job really address a problem—perhaps even several problems—that can be expressed in the form of a question such as that formulated by Sellin and Rost? But if the Book of Job does in fact deal with a question, then surely it is not a theoretical question but an existential question.[9] This is clear from the conclusion of the book, which, as more recent interpreters generally agree, does not offer a conceptual or theoretical answer.[10]

To inquire about something is to make of it an object. Whatever the thing may be, inquiry concerning it involves the attempt to grasp it conceptually. If the thing in question is suffering, or, more precisely, the suffering of a just man, then in a certain sense that just man becomes an object—the object of thought.

Existential questions are put differently. For example, the existential question "Why must I suffer?" does not arise because a person thinks about his own suffering and makes it an object of thought. It arises out of the suffering as such, as a kind of direct reaction to it; it is a *reactio* arising in response to a previous *actio*. There are various kinds of reaction to pain and suffering, such as screaming or remedial action. When the reaction is verbal we call it a lament. The question "Why must I suffer?" is a lament, insofar as it is an existential question. To be sure, it can go on to become a theoretical question, but by then it is only a derivative question.

The lament is widely attested in the Book of Job; in fact, it dominates the book. Fundamentally the book treats an existential question. Therefore interpretation of the Book of Job must take as its starting point the existential question, in other words, the lament. It cannot take as its point of departure some problem, such as "the problem of suffering." A lament is something fundamentally different from a treatment of the problem of suffering. A lament does not arise out of mournful reflection on suffering—what some interpreters call elegaic thought. On the contrary, a lament is an existential process which has its own structure. This has far-reaching consequences for exegesis. Where it is supposed that, in the lament sections, the poet of the Book of Job is dealing with the problem of suffering, Job's being a case in point, the interpreter will be inquiring into the thoughts of any given section (e.g., chaps. 3 or 30) and their interconnections. However, where it is seen that the poet is not merely using the style of the lament in order to express his thoughts after the manner of songs of lamentation, but that these are real

8. Kuhl, "Literarkritik," p. 167.

9. Cf. Weiser, *Das Buch Hiob*, p. 9.

10. Esp. Fridolin Stier (*Das Buch Ijjob, hebräisch und deutsch* [Münich: Kosel, 1954]); cf. Weiser: "It is inappropriate . . .to try to limit the problem of Job to a theological question" (*Das Buch Hiob*, p. 9).

laments, the interpreter will have to examine to what extent and how in these sections the lament develops along the lines of its own forms and in consonance with its own rules. In the Book of Job the poet does not string together mournful reflections whose interconnections we can figure out by our logic. On the contrary, in his laments he stands in a tradition of fixed forms whose richness and impressive design can be appreciated only against the background of the whole history of the lament in the Old Testament, from whence these forms derive.[11]

What has been said so far applies to only one component of the Book of Job, not to the book as a whole. Hence one might argue that, while it may well have significance for the lament sections of the book, it is inconsequential for interpretation of the book as a whole; the whole—or in any case the chief part—is dialogue, a dialogue which has the character of a discussion, and the Book of Job as a whole therefore is still a discussion of a problem. Here one must ask, though, whether it really is a discussion; it is certainly *not* a discussion in the sense in which we customarily understand the word. Rather, it is a disputation, and that is something quite different. Köhler has clearly delineated the distinguishing characteristics of the disputation and its affinity to courtroom speech.[12] Lindblom has emphasized that the manner of speech in a disputation is essentially different from that in an "objective" discussion.[13] A disputation is a forensic process; the parties involved do not discuss a problem, but rather argue a matter before a court of law.

This clarification does not close the matter, however, for it does not yet adequately explain the dialogue form in the Book of Job.[14] Indeed, the friends come to Job neither to have a discussion with him nor to carry on a disputation; they come to console him. Here I agree with Bentzen that the dialogue form in the Book of Job is simply the dialogue of consolation, even though from the very beginning consolation is transformed into disputation.[15] The intended consolation misfires and is replaced by disputes, as we shall see later. This dialogue section (chaps. 4–27) is framed by the laments of Job (chaps. 3 and 29–31) which stand outside the disputation and are strictly laments, lacking any sort of address to the friends. This means that the dialogue stands *within* the lament. The lament is there both before and after the

11. Cf. Volz: "The poet has not written a treatise but a lament" (*Das Buch Hiob,* p. 26). Baumgärtel has apparently also noticed this distinction. However, he has drawn from it the conclusion to which one is forced if one rigidly adheres to the presupposition that the Book of Job deals with a problem: he has stricken out all those passages which he recognizes as being laments in the proper sense.

12. Ludwig Köhler, "Justice in the Gate," postscript to *Hebrew Man,* trans. Peter R. Ackroyd (London: SCM, 1956), pp. 158–63 (= "Die hebräische Rechtsgemeinde," postscript to *Der hebräische Mensch* [Tübingen: J. C. B. Mohr (Paul Siebeck), 1953], pp. 153–58).

13. Lindbolm, *La composition,* pp. 40–41.

14. Cf. Kuhl, "Literarkritik," pp. 294–306.

15. Bentzen, *Introduction,* 2:174–79.

dialogue with the friends; it has both the first and the last word. Out of Job's lament, however, a new "dialogue" arises; disillusioned with his friends, Job turns directly to God and demands an answer. And the Book of Job reports that God did answer. God's answer to Job (chaps. 38–41) clearly has—at least in part—the character of a disputation. As figure 3.1 reveals, disputational speech connects the characters of the drama with the dialogue between Job and God following after that between the friends and Job, even though the foundations for it were laid already at the beginning. This sequence is necessitated by the fact that Job has to appeal to a higher court when his

Fig. 3.1
Disputational Speech in the Book of Job

friends refuse to hear his case. In the decisive places, especially at the end of chap. 31, Job's appeal to God employs the language of a legal proceeding. The whole process, whose contours are thus sketched out, in no way resembles the character of a discussion about some theme or problem. What is presented is rather a legal proceeding terminating in a decision.[16] The legal decision demanded by Job is preceded by a disputation. Because the chief element on Job's side of this disputation is the lament, God's decision is at the same time the answer to Job's lament. The most important element in the speeches of the friends is something quite different. They alone advance arguments in their speeches; in Job's speeches—except for one at the end, as we shall see—the lament stands in the place of the argument. This incongruity between the speeches of the friends and the speeches of Job is the most noticeable and also the most important structural clue in the book. Disputational speech is common to all three parties, as we have seen; that is to say, for all three something is being contested. However, the disputational speech in any given instance serves only as the introduction.The resemblance between the speeches of Job and those of the friends is purely superficial: each speech is introduced by a personal address, upon which follows a speech about something. The friends in every case present arguments, their chief argument being the doctrine about the fate of the transgressor. In place of the arguments, however, Job inserts a lament. (In only one place in the dia-

16. This interpretation of the Book of Job stands out especially clearly in the recent study by Stier; cf. my review of *Das Buch Ijjob, hebräisch und deutsch,* by Fridolin Stier, in *Eckart Jahrbuch* 25 (1955/56): 260–65.

logue section do thesis and antithesis stand in clear juxtaposition: in chap. 21, the last speech of the second cycle of discourse, Job sets his thesis over against that of the friends regarding the fate of the transgressor; only here does Job directly contest the doctrine of retribution.) It is this incongruity which gives the book its peculiar drama. Throughout the whole dialogue section there is this juxtaposition of doctrine and lament. The doctrine, which comes directly out of tradition but is now rigidified, stands over against the burning lament, which arises directly out of an existential anguish. The lament finds no hearing and elicits no consolation; the doctrine ricochets off the reality of pain. Thus the disputation must run its course without resolution; only the higher court can decide.

However, Job had already turned to this higher court—cryptically, to be sure—*before* the onset of the disputation. A straight line leads from this opening accusation against God in chap. 3 to Job's summoning of God at the end of chap. 31. The bracketing of the dialogue section (chaps. 4–27) by the element of lament, in which Job turns directly to God, corresponds substantively to the incongruity noted within the dialogue section. There is then only one way to see the whole of the Book of Job: the encompassing confrontation is that between Job and God, while within this confrontation stands the one between the friends and Job. What happens between the friends and Job begins with the first speech of Eliphaz (chap. 4) and ends with Job's answer to the third speech of Eliphaz (chap. 23; on chaps. 24–27 see below). What happens between Job and God begins with the lament in chap. 3 and ends with God's answer to Job's final, summarizing lament in chaps. 29–31, which climaxes in Job's summoning of God (31:35–37). This divine-human interaction is never totally interrupted in the middle section (chaps. 4–27) but rather is continued in Job's laments, which are components of his speech in the dialogue section. When finally Job turns irrevocably away from his friends, he once again confronts God alone. Chapters 4–27 are therefore in no way the whole; to be sure, they are the longest part, but they are a part of the whole. Figure 3.2 depicts the whole narrative framework. The whole, then, is neither a disputation nor a dialogue. What is depicted is an event involving three partners or parties: Job, the friends, and God. Thus the Book of Job is really a drama.[17] Of course, it is not a drama in the firmly fixed literary sense the word has for us now, but it is a drama in the original sense of the world. The poet presents an occurrence, an event. He presents it not, or at least not only, in the style of a narrative or a report. Instead he works an event into the framework of a narrative. This event commences with a lament, upon which an act of consolation is supposed to follow. The consolation, however, turns into disputation. This disputation breaks off without resolution, at which point the

17. Similarly Volz (*Das Buch Hiob*, p. 24), who refers to a remark by Luther which already points in the same direction; cf. also Buttenweiser, *Book of Job*.

Fig. 3.2
The Narrative Framework of the Book of Job

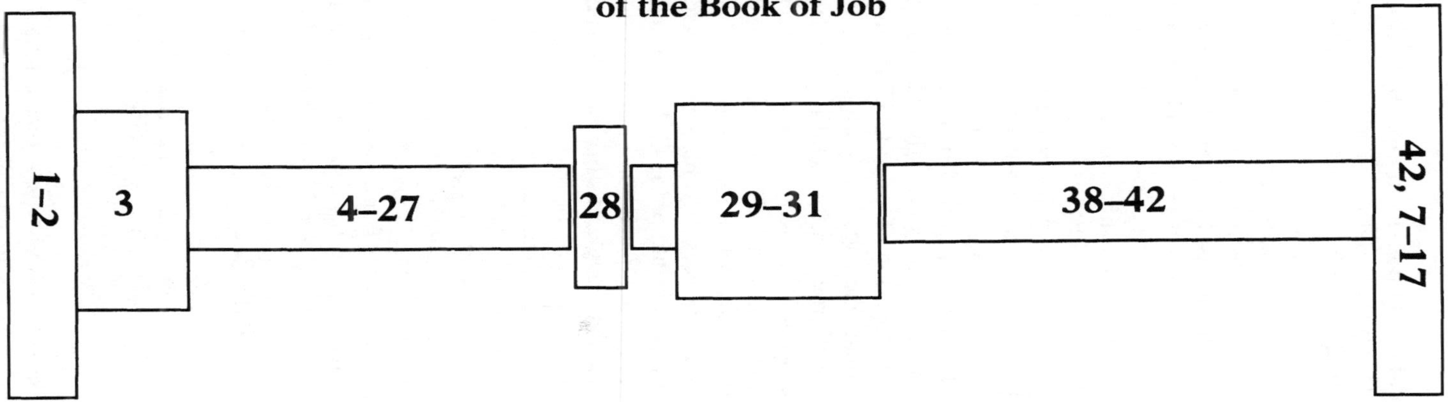

lament resumes and leads up to a summoning of God. God answers, and Job submits to God. This is the event depicted by the Book of Job.

The event is fitted into the framework of a narrative. What significance does this narrative have for the whole?[18] As we said above, the poet depicts an event, one which happens to a definite, real, living human being with a specific name and living in a particular place. In like manner, his three friends are not just any sort of characters, but men with names and personalities. The poet presents a true story about real people. Now this does not mean that Job and his friends are historical in our sense of the word, namely, that their existence can be established on the basis of documentary evidence. However, it does mean that Job is not just an instance in which something is to be demonstrated.[19] On the contrary, Job was a real person, a unique individual.

The narrative framework of the Book of Job is necessary in order to make all this clear at the outset. The narrative framework is in no way superfluous to the book as a whole; it simply *must* be there. This is further established, in my mind, by the fact that the poet of the "drama" chose to employ a story already current in the tradition of his people. He did not want to invent a figure; he speaks of a man who had already lived. That this traditional story does not agree in places with the event which the poet depicts in lament, disputation, and divine response is actually a sign of "authenticity"—in a sense other than the literary one. The poet lets us recognize, and *wants* us to recognize, that he is appropriating an earlier, long-since-fixed story.[20]

If one looks closely, one sees that this is the same process which frequently shows up in the historical books of the Old Testament, only in reverse: a participant in a story has a song placed on his lips, but in such a way that we can still clearly recognize that song and story each has a different point of origin, that each stands in its own line of tradition, and that both have here been deliberately fused together. Examples of this include the song of praise which a king sings at the high point of his reign (2 Sam. 22 = Ps. 18), the lament of an ill king (Isa. 38), the lament of a childless woman (1 Sam. 1), the song of the prophet Jonah, and the songs of the community in Chronicles, which are constructed out of psalms. The Song of Hannah (1 Sam. 2) is probably the example closest to Job. What is framework in the Book of Job is here the real focus of interest, namely, the narrative of the birth of a child. A song is inserted into this narrative, but it does not really fit. One would have expected a song of thanksgiving at this juncture in the story, but instead one finds a descriptive song of praise which is clearly recognizable as a secondary

18. Cf. Otto Eissfeldt, *The Old Testament: An Introduction*, trans. Peter R. Ackroyd (New York: Harper & Row, 1965), esp. pp. 462–66 (= *Einleitung in das Alte Testament* [Tübingen: J. C. B. Mohr (Paul Siebeck), [3]1964], pp. 624–30).

19. Unfortunately, Job is described all too often as a "case" even by the most recent interpreters of the Book of Job!

20. Hermann Gunkel rightly saw this; cf. his "Hiobbuch," in *Die Religion in Geschichte und Gegenwart* (Tübingen, [2]1929), vol. 2, cols. 1924–30.

insertion. Thus the song, which one well knows was frequently sung and familiar to many, is here placed in the mouth of a particular person on a specific occasion. Moreover, it matters neither to the author not to the hearers that the song does not quite fit in with the story. The reverse situation is found in the Book of Job: the story is affixed to the poem as its framework. This gives the poem its character as an event; the one lamenting in the poem is a real person. That two constructs of different origin are hereby joined is not concealed, nor is it meant to be concealed. One must therefore differentiate between the Job-poem proper and the narrative framework, but one must also constantly keep in mind that the Job-poem cannot be thought of apart from the framework.

However, the Job-poem proper must now be even more precisely defined. Can one be more explicit about the nature of the event presented? In my opinion, Bentzen has here suggested a whole new interpretation which can open the way to a shift in one's overall view of the Book of Job. Bentzen starts out from Lindblom's observation to the effect that the closest religio-historical parallel to the Book of Job is the Babylonian poem "I will serve the Lord of Wisdom." As Bentzen says,

> "I will serve the Lord of Wisdom" . . . is in reality a psalm, a combined psalm of lamentation and of thanksgiving, which has certainly been used in the temple-cult. . . . The parallel poems in dialogue form are only a further development of the situation of the psalm of lamentation and its forms. . . . *The dialogue is a "dramatization" of the psalm of lamentation*, more accurately, of the "prayers of the accused," placed in the frame of a narrative.[21]

Bentzen then inquires into the background of the origin of this process of dramatization in the Book of Job and finds a possible answer in the poem itself:

> According to the framework of the book, the narrative, the friends of Job arrive to *console* Job. Is it not probable that this feature has been borrowed from reality? . . . So the dialogue in a natural way grows under the hand of the poet, and in this situation he is able to use the many forms, especially of psalms of lamentation, which he displays in his lyrics.[22]

If one looks closely one sees here two different explanations. To start with the second, the dialogue is conditioned simply by the situation of consolation. Because the speeches of the friends are anything but consoling, this straightforward explanation of the dialogue form has heretofore never been seriously entertained. Now admittedly the speeches offer no consolation. However, the conclusion generally drawn from this fact is open to question.

21. Bentzen, *Introduction*, p. 182.
22. Ibid.

Simply because the speeches of the friends, who had come to console Job, were not actually consoling, it does not follow that the dialogue form has nothing to do with the process of consolation. On the contrary, the *situation* of consolation remains in effect: Job *remains* the lamenter, and nothing alters the fact that the proper role for the friends, to the very end, was that of offering consolation. This is no mere hypothesis; it is repeatedly and clearly stated by Job himself:

> As for you you whitewash with lies;
>   worthless physicians are you all. (13:4)
>
> Are the consolations of God too small for you,
>   or the word that deals gently with you? (Eliphaz, 15:11)
>
> I have heard many such things;
>   miserable comforters are you all. (16:2)
>
> I could strengthen you with my mouth,
>   and the solace of my lips would assuage your pain. (16:5)
>
> Listen carefully to my words,
>   and let this be your consolation. (21:2)
>
> How then will you comfort me with empty nothings?
>   There is nothing left of your answers but falsehood. (21:34)
>
> How you have helped him who has no power!
>   How you have saved the arm that has no strength!
> How you have counseled him who has no wisdom,
>   and plentifully declared sound knowledge!
> With whose help have you uttered words,
>   and whose spirit has come forth from you? (26:2–4)

As the citation from 15:11 clearly shows, not only Job but also the friends know well that the proper office of the latter is consolation. In my opinion the beginning of the first of the friends' speeches displays the same realization, for how else would one understand the fact that this speech follows directly upon Job's lament? In any case, Job does not open chap. 3 with a disputation speech; he laments, and furthermore, his lament contains no trace of an attack on the friends. What else besides a word of consolation should follow such a lament? No speech by a friend is so amicable, reserved, and sympathetic to Job as the beginning of the first speech of Eliphaz; the properly intended consolation still sounds forth here. Contrary to his own intention, Eliphaz's word of consolation leads to disputation.

There is yet another reason why it has never before been seen, or at least conceded, that the dialogue between the friends and Job has grown out of the situation of consolation. We are accustomed to regard consolation as a one-way process. In other words, we understand by "consolation" simply a consoling or comforting word. However, the real process of consolation is a dialogue. In such a process it is essential that the sufferer or mourner be led to speak amid his suffering; thus the consoling words assume the character of an answer to the lament. What it comes down to is that a repeated exchange of words belongs to the very essence of the process of consolation. In real situations of consolation—as experience demonstrates thousandfold—it almost never happens that the sufferer speaks only once and the consoler replies only once. It is furthermore essential to the process of consolation that the one doing the lamenting be allowed to express himself. Therefore an attitude of reservation is incumbent upon the consoler in such a conversation, whereas the one doing the lamenting has the right to be expansive in his lament. The particular structure of the dialogue in the Book of Job shows precisely this arrangement. The sufferer speaks first (chap. 3); Job's speeches are usually longer than those of the friends; above all, the friends allow Job to respond after each individual utterance on the part of one of them (i.e., AB, AC, AD, AB, AC, AD, etc.; not ABCD, ABCD). Job's speeches remain laments to the very end (23:2); instead of disputations, he expected consolation from his friends right up to the end—even though in vain (21:34).

In terms of its content, therefore, the whole dialogue section is actually consoling conversation. Our arguments advanced above confirm Bentzen's supposition. However, in one place in this consoling conversation, namely, where the friends were obligated to extend comforting words to Job, disputation has instead intruded—disputation corresponding to that found in the realm of jurisprudence and finally leading up to an indictment. Köhler has expounded upon this aspect of the dialogue section.[23] But now—as we have already indicated—the two sides of this disputation are not congruent. On the one hand, the speeches of Job contain laments rather than arguments, even though introduced as disputational speech. On the other hand, the disputation is encompassed by the lament (chaps. 3 and 29–31). From Job's perspective it appears as though the lamenter is assailed by his friends and left in the lurch when his friends were supposed to stand by him. So Job turns on his friends and accosts them. Bentzen's other explanation applied to this aspect of the dialogue section, namely, that we have here a dramatized lament. In support of this view, Bentzen refers to Psalm 41:9[10] and 51:11–13[13–15], in which the lamenter laments that his friends have become enemies to him. It is true that the same procedure is intimated here which is widely developed in the Book of Job. However, this does not yet explain the presence of the dialogue form. Fortunately, among the so-called individual lament psalms there is a small group in which the transition from

23. Köhler, "Justice," pp. 158–63.

lamentation to disputational speech is already carried out on the part of the lamenter—even if only in suggestive, stylized fashion. These are the psalms in which the lamenter addresses his opponents in such words as:

> O men, how long shall my honor suffer shame?
> How long will you love vain words, and seek after lies?
> But know that. . . . (Ps. 4:2[3])

> Depart from me, all you workers of evil;
> for the Lord has heard the sound of my weeping. (Ps. 6:8[9])[24]

In these places there really is a dramatizing of the lament! These cases in Psalms are not hard to explain. First of all, a very considerable expansion shows up at the place of the third component of the lament (viz., the indictment of the enemies) in the genre of the individual lament.[25] In this regard, sometimes the evildoers step so strongly to the fore that they dominate the whole psalm. Corresponding to the degree to which this happens, the proper confrontation—namely, that between the lamenter and God—is overshadowed by the confrontation between the lamenter and his friends. The result, on the one hand, is a very extensive discourse *about* the enemies, which actually breaks through the genre of the lament;[26] on the other hand, the discourse leaps over into an address directed *to* the enemies. Psalm 4:2[3] could stand unaltered in a speech of Job! The direct address of the friends in the speeches of Job has its parallels in the address of the enemies in the individual lament psalms already cited. In both places, this element of address arises out of the lament and remains encompassed by the lament. Of course, a considerable gulf separates those few verses from the individual lament psalms and the speeches of Job; however, a real correspondence exists with regard to the genre of speech and the situation.

The formal elements of the Book of Job have thus been determined. The dialogue is supposed to become a consoling conversation in which the speech of the one partner would have to be lament and that of the other consolation. Controversy crops up in the place of the consolation offered by the friends, and this leads to arguments. On Job's side, the lament remains the chief component. However, alongside the lament there must now appear opposition to the friends, with the result that the whole comes to be depicted as a disputation. Nevertheless, this disputation, which has come together out of different elements, remains encompassed by the lament (chaps. 3 and 29–31), which has the first and the last word. Direct address of the friends is

24. Cf. also Ps. 119:115; 52:1–4[3–6]; 58:1–5[2–6].

25. Cf. Claus Westermann, "Struktur und Geschichte der Klage im Alten Testament," *Zeitschrift für die alttestamentliche Wissenschaft* 66 (1954): 44–80.

26. The lament becomes a lamenting description (ibid., p. 64).

missing in this lament. However, the secret third partner in the conversation *is* addressed in the lament, namely, God. The whole ends with the summoning of God at the end of the last lament (31:35–37). The controversy is thereby taken to the higher court. Only Job and God are left to face one another. The dramatizing of the lament now demands that some sort of an answer be given in response to Job's summons, whereby the word which will resolve the controversy will be spoken. This whole happening is placed within the framework of a narrated story. With this dramatizing of the lament, the poet has not constructed an illustrative case but has reported an event which befell a real human being.

The three partners in this event, or drama, correspond to the three parts of the lament.[27] Thereby the explanation of the whole as a dramatizing of the lament receives still further confirmation. This determination of the formal elements of the Book of Job is of vital importance for the exegesis of the book. Each individual sentence of the book stands in a twofold context. First of all, it stands in the respective context of a speech by Job, by one of the friends, or by God. At the same time, however, it is also a part of the depicted event, which is itself composed of the formal elements pointed out above. The character of this event is not to be ascertained in the way attempted by most up to now, namely, by pursuing a line of thought which supposedly penetrates the whole Book of Job. On the contrary, it is to be determined only by way of placing each individual sentence in the context proper to it in the respective genres of speech. This means that a line from Job's lament must be seen in the context of the total lament throughout the whole book, that a line in praise of God must be seen against the background of all the sentences praising God, and that a single disputation must be viewed in the context of the whole of the disputation. Allied with this is the fact that each individual genre of speech must be investigated throughout the whole book. Thus it is important just *where* an avowal of trust stands, *where* one part of a lament dominates while another part is totally lacking, *where* and *how* wishes and petitions are inserted, and *how* the distribution is made between references to personal matters and remarks of a substantive sort. This sort of questioning opens up avenues and perspectives which simply could not come to light through an inquiry into the book's course of thought. Only in this way can one come to recognize the poem's structure, which has grown out of living genres of speech and not out of abstract thinking.[28]

27. See below.

28. Édouard Paul Dhorme, *A Commentary on the Book of Job*, trans. Harold Knight (London: Nelson, 1967), pp. lxi–lxii (= *Le livre de Job* [Paris, 1926], pp. xlix–l).

4

The Genres and Message of the Book of Job

John E. Hartley

Genres

Several form-critical studies have been made of the portions of the Book of Job.[1] Two major efforts have attempted to identify the genre of the book. Richter identifies it as a lawsuit.[2] The various sections of the book correspond to different stages of a lawsuit. The first section is the procedure to reach a settlement through a pre-trial hearing (chs. 4–14). Since

1. Cf. G. Fohrer, "Form und Funktion in der Hiobdictung," *ZDMG* 109 (1959) 31–49; repr. in *Studien zum Buche Hiob* (Gütersloh: Gerd Mohn, 1963), pp. 68–86. R. Murphy, *Wisdom Literature: Job, Proverbs, Ruth, Canticles, Ecclesiates, Esther*, FOTL 13 (Grand Rapids: Eerdmans, 1981), pp. 13–45.

2. H. Richter, *Studien Zu Hiob, Der Aufbau des Hiobbuches dargestellt an den Gattungen des Rechtslebens* (Berlin: Evangelische Verlagsanstalt, 1959).

From John E. Hartley, *The Book of Job*, New International Commentary on the Old Testament (Grand Rapids: Eerdmans, 1988), 37–50. Used by permission of Wm B. Eerdmans Publishing Company.

this attempt fails, a formal trial follows (chs. 15–31). The friends' silence after Job's oath of innocence means that they have conceded their case and Job has won. Deeply disturbed by this state of affairs, Elihu enters and appeals the decision (chs. 32–37). Finally, God appears as litigant (chs. 38–41). Under his questioning, the defendant Job withdraws his complaint so that reconciliation between God and himself is achieved (42:1–6).

C. Westermann has presented another major analysis of the structure of this book.[3] He argues that Job is a dramatized lament. Legal language is incorporated into the lament in order to develop Job's complaints and his accusations against God. The friends' speeches are designed as words of consolation, but disputation intrudes into their speeches as they feel compelled to persuade Job of the orthodox position. The Yahweh speeches are also a disputation. Whereas Richter's study is too one-sided, Westermann describes the genres in the Book of Job; but "dramatized lament" is a descriptive term, not a literary genre, and it fails to categorize the entire work.[4]

The author, a literary genius, created a masterpiece that is *sui generis*. The book both recounts the story of Job's trial and triumph and debates the issue of human suffering through the medium of speeches. That is, the book is both an epic and a wisdom disputation. In order to probe deeply into the issue of the suffering righteous and its attendant issue of theodicy, the author has drawn on numerous genres in the composition of the speeches. These genres are identified throughout the commentary. At this point an overview of the component parts of the speeches is given to show their interrelatedness and to show how they contribute to the nuance of the message.

The speeches of the friends are essentially disputations, for these men seek to persuade Job to adopt their particular theology. Their speeches consist of multiple genres. The following table lists the broadest categories of genres in their speeches (many of the units are a blend of several genres).

First Cycle

genre	*Eliphaz*	*Bildad*	*Zophar*
word of consolation	4:2–6		
accusation (in litigation)		8:2–4	11:2–6
wisdom instruction	4:7–11[5]	8:8–10	
fate of wicked	5:1–7	8:11–15	
fate of upright	5:17–28	8:16–19, 20–22	
praise of God	5:9–16		11:7–11
exhortations to seek God	5:8, 27	8:5–7	(11:12) 11:13–20

3. C. Westermann, *Structure of the Book of Job*.
4. See R. Murphy, op. cit., pp. 16–17.
5. The first Eliphaz speech also contains a vision report (4:12–21).

Second Cycle

accusation	15:2–6	18:2–4	20:2–3
wisdom instruction	15:7–16		
fate of wicked	15:17–35	18:5–21	20:4–29

Third Cycle

accusation	22:2–9	
threat	22:10–11	
praise of God	22:12	25:2–6
disputation	22:13–20	
fate of wicked		27:13–23
call to repentance	22:21–30	

In the first cycle the friends seek to console Job by recounting to him the just and wise ways of God. They juxtapose descriptions of the calamity that befalls the wicked with those of the blessings that attend the righteous. These descriptions function both as a warning of impending doom and as an exhortation for Job to repent. In defense of their instruction the friends quote hymnic lines in praise of God's power and wisdom. They also exhort Job to seek God, promising him prosperity, security, and joy.

In the second cycle the friends, suspecting that Job must have done something seriously wrong to be so afflicted, omit any words of consolation as they deliver harsh accusations against him. Each of them describes the terrible fate that awaits the evildoer as a powerful warning that he must forsake his evil course. Absent from this cycle are hymnic lines in praise of God and calls to repentance; the friends concentrate on trying to convince Job that he is numbered among the wicked.

In the third cycle Eliphaz directly accuses Job of specific sins, and adds a threat about his precarious circumstances. He quotes briefly from a hymn and then proceeds to dispute with Job about the fate of the wicked. He concludes with a vivid, energetic call to repentance. Next, Bildad merely quotes from a hymn in praise of God's majesty and describes the downfall of the wicked. Unfortunately, the end of the third cycle has been disturbed and some lines have been lost.

Job's responses may be divided according to the party addressed—either the friends or God.

Response	*1*	*2*	*3*
First Cycle	Friends (ch. 6)	Friends (ch. 9)	Friends (12:1–13:17)
	God (ch. 7)	God (ch. 10)	God (13:18–14:22)

Second Cycle	Friends (16:1–6)	Friends (ch. 19)	Friends (ch. 21)
	God (16:7–17:16)		
Third Cycle	Friends (chs. 23–24)	Friends (ch. 26; 27:1–12)	

In the first cycle Job's responses are fairly evenly divided: he alternates between the friends and God.[6] The next two cycles are not as balanced. Job's first response of the second cycle is directed primarily to God; in the rest of the dialogue he speaks solely to the friends.

The multiple genres in Job's responses may be listed as follows:

Lament:
- description of suffering: 6:2–4, 11–13; 7:3–6; 9:25–28; 10:1; 16:6–17; 17:1–2, 6–9; 19:13–20; 23:2
- apprehensive fear:
  - of death: 13:28; 14:18–22; 17:11–16
  - of God: 23:15–17
- sorrow at general human suffering: 7:1–2; 14:1–12
- justification of lamenting: 6:5–7
- complaint:
  - against friends: 6:14–27; 12:2–6; 13:1–3; 16:2–5; 17:10; 19:2–6; 21:34; 26:2–4
  - against God: 7:7–10, 11–21; 9:17–18, 21–24; 10:2–7, 13–17; 16:7–14; 19:7–12

Lawsuit:
- with the friends: 13:4–12
- with God: 9:2–4, 14–16, 19–20, (28b), 29–33; 13:13–17 (purposed), 18–27; 23:3–7 (wish)

Petition:
- to the friends: 6:28–29; 19:21–22
- to God:
  - wish to die: 6:8–10; 7:15
  - wish for some relief before death: 7:7–10, 16–21; 10:18–22; 14:(5–6), 13–17
  - request for the easing of his suffering so that he can dispute with God: 9:34–35; 13:20–21
  - plea for vindication: 16:18; 17:3–4; 19:23–24
  - plea for deliverance from enemies: 27:7–10

6. For a further discussion see D. Patrick, "Job's Address of God," *ZAW* 91 (1979) 268–82.

Hymnic lines in praise of God: 9:5–13; 10:8–12; 12:13–25; 23:8–9, 13–14; 26:5–14

Avowal of innocence: 6:28–30; 16:17; 23:10–12; 27:2–6

Affirmation of trust in God: 16:19–22; 19:25–27; 23:6–7

Wisdom instruction: 12:7–12

Warning to friends: 17:5; 19:28–29

Disputation on the success of wicked: 21:2–33; 24:1–17 (followed by a curse on the wicked, 24:18–24, and a challenge to be proven wrong, 24:25)

The skillful blending of genres in Job's speeches yields a splendid result. Through his lamenting Job reveals the depth of his agony. He not only laments his own suffering, but he groans over human suffering in general (7:1–3; 14:1–12). The generalizing tendencies in his laments allow all people to identify with Job. In the hymnic segments Job alludes to the primordial conflict between God and the forces of chaos (e.g., 9:13; 26:12–13). In this way he addresses the cosmic dimensions of his trial and reinforces his belief that God is master over all forces, terrestrial and cosmic. Sorely troubled that his affliction witnesses to some wrongdoing, Job ponders how he can demand that God vindicate him. Thus he draws on the language of a lawsuit to confront God. Thinking of litigation against God, he affirms his own innocence. Also, out of faith he states his trust in God as the one who will prove his innocence.

Two speeches of Job stand outside the dialogue, those in ch. 3 and in chs. 29–31. The first is a curse-lament, a mixture of a curse pronounced against the day of one's birth (3:3–13) and a lament (3:14–26). Job's last formal speech is an avowal of innocence. It is composed by expanding elements of a lament: remembrance of past glory (ch. 29), a detailed description of present suffering (ch. 30), and an oath of innocence (ch. 31). This avowal of innocence is an expression of Job's complete confidence in God's commitment to justice.

As for the Elihu speeches, they are disputations with the intention of teaching Job about God's disciplinary use of suffering and God's just and wise rule. His speeches are very orderly; the elements for the first three are:

	1	*2*	*3*
Introductory apology	32:6–22		
An apology or exhortation to listen	33:1–7	34:2–4	
The presentation of Job's position	33:8–11	34:5–9	35:2–4
A disputation or instruction	33:12–30	34:10–30	35:5–15
An invitation for Job to answer or a judgment	33:31–33	34:34–37	35:16

The fourth speech is composed of two elements—an instruction (36:2–21) and a hymnic description of a theophany (36:22–37:24). Elihu's role is that of Job's instructor and Yahweh's forerunner.

Yahweh's two speeches (38:2–40:2; 40:6–41:26 [Eng. 41:34]) follow the general pattern of a disputation. Yahweh opens by ordering Job to answer his interrogation (38:2–3). The core of the first speech is composed of a hymn praising the Creator and Sustainer of the world. By turning the lines into questions, the author changes the speech into a disputation.[7] The latter part of the speech is made up of animal portraits, an infrequent genre in the OT (38:39–39:30). In his second speech Yahweh comes closer to presenting a direct challenge to the defendant. He challenges Job to prove his superiority (40:6–14) and expands that challenge with the two long portraits of the primordial creatures Behemoth and Leviathan (40:15–41:26 [Eng. 41:34]).

Job's two responses are short. The first one (40:3–5) is simply a statement that he has nothing more to say. His second response (42:1–6) is an acknowledgment of Yahweh's lordship and a recantation.

The identification of the genres that make up the speeches is important to determine more precisely the meaning of the speeches. An understanding of the life setting of each genre clarifies the meaning of its words, phrases, and metaphors. Nevertheless, the author of Job has used these genres freely to his own purpose. Thus the setting in the book is far more important in determining the function of each genre than its setting in life.[8] For example, a description of the fate of the wicked, which usually serves to teach the moral order of the world, functions in 15:20–35 as a warning to Job. Thus for interpreting this work one must give careful attention to the interplay between a genre and its literary setting.

Message

The message of the Book of Job will be presented on two levels: first, on the basis of the book's dramatic framework, and second, in the light of its themes.

Dramatic Framework

A consideration of the dramatic framework of the Book of Job offers great insight into the book's message. The author penetrates deeply into the issue of human suffering by setting up many sharp contrasts.[9] The interplay of these contrasts gives dramatic movement to the story.

7. Cf. G. von Rad, "Job XXXVIII and Ancient Egyptian Wisdom," in *The Problem of the Hexateuch and Other Essays,* tr. E. W. Trueman Dicken (Edinburgh/London: Oliver and Boyd; New York: McGraw-Hill, 1966), pp. 281–91; repr. in *Studies in Ancient Israelite Wisdom,* ed. J. Crenshaw (New York: KTAV, 1976), pp. 267–77.

8. Cf. G. Fohrer, *ZDMG* 109 (1959) 32–33; idem, *Das Buch Hiob,* p. 52.

9. See R. Polzin, *Biblical Structuralism,* Semeia Supplements (Philadelphia: Fortress, 1977), pp. 54–121.

The basic tension is between one's belief in God and one's personal experience. In the prologue these two dimensions of human existence are in harmony for Job:

Job fears God.	God blesses Job.

Job serves God wholeheartedly, and God's blessing makes Job the noblest, richest chief in the East. God confidently praises Job before the Satan, who questions the integrity of Job's fear of God, claiming that Job does not fear God for nought, but for the great wealth God freely gives him. The Satan then challenges God to let Job's devotion be tested. God accepts the challenge and permits the Satan to afflict Job. Nevertheless, despite his losses and his debilitating illness, Job continues to fear God. Now, however, his daily experience is no longer in harmony with his belief:

Job fears God.	Job is sorely afflicted.

Initially Job mourns his plight in silence, but later he bursts forth in a bitter lament (ch. 3):

Job laments in silence.	Job laments loudly and bitterly.

Job's three friends, who have come to comfort him, are sorely troubled by the severity of Job's affliction. At first they try to console him, but in their dialogue with Job they become deeply offended by Job's posture of stubbornly holding onto his innocence and accusing God. Their understanding of retribution leads them to conclude that Job has sinned and has escaped worse punishment only through the mercy of God. Therefore, they earnestly exhort him to repent in order to enjoy God's favor again. Since they place their system of belief above their compassion for their troubled friend, their exhortations to repentance become a temptation by encouraging Job to seek God for reward, not for God himself. The conflict that arises between their purpose and their actions may be charted as follows:

The friends wish to comfort Job.	They accuse him of flagrant sins.
	Their exhortations tempt him to seek God for material gain.
Job rejects the friends' counsel.	

At the end of the dialogue the hymn to wisdom (ch. 28) teaches that people cannot find wisdom, whose dwelling place is known only to God, save in the fear of God; thus this hymn judges the counsel of the comforters as lacking in wisdom.

The friends are wise men, defenders of accepted beliefs.	The hymn to wisdom denies that humanity knows wisdom.

In the epilogue God will confirm this judgment by saying that the three friends have not spoken about him rightly (42:7–9):

The friends think they honor God in their exhorting and condemning Job.	God condemns them and requires sacrifices for them.

Job's experience of undeserved suffering makes him apprehensive that God may be a ruthless tyrant rather than a merciful Lord. His conviction that he is innocent leads him to call God's justice into question. Therefore, he decides that if he could enter into litigation with God, God would confirm his innocence. But he is apprehensive that God will overpower him. Nevertheless, his conviction that God is just prods him to pursue a lawsuit with God. Job also knows that in court he must have a witness to testify on his behalf, a witness more credible than the condemning testimony of his body. At this point Job's faith in God rises above his experience of suffering, leading him to declare that God is his Witness (16:19), even his Redeemer (19:25–27), whose testimony will vindicate him. Still, his pain terrorizes him and his dread is compounded by God's silence. Finally, his confidence in his own innocence and God's justice drives him to take a desperate course that will force God to act: he swears an avowal of innocence (chs. 29–31). Now God must answer him; for God to remain silent would be to concede Job's claim to innocence. These conflicting motifs may be charted as follows:

Job believes that he is innocent and God is just.	Job experiences suffering for no apparent reason.
Job pleads for mercy.	God is silent and allows Job's affliction to continue.
Job accuses God of condemning him unjustly.	Job affirms his faith in God as his witness and his redeemer.
	Job swears an avowal of innocence.

Job's belief in God as just and merciful impels him to look to God for a just resolution to his situation.

Job's complaints against God receive two responses, one from Elihu and one from God himself. Elihu teaches that God, who never perverts justice, uses suffering to discipline his servants and that God sends an intermediary to rescue from certain death those who turn to him. Furthermore, he argues that God governs the world in justice and also reveals himself to humanity.

Thus Elihu counters Job's complaint by modifying the traditional belief about suffering and by defending the belief that God governs the world justly:

Job suffers and complains that God is silent.	Elihu teaches that God disciplines by suffering and that God sends an angel-mediator to rescue those near death.
Job accuses God of injustice.	Elihu argues for God's justice and concludes that Job is wrong in condemning God.

Thus Elihu prepares Job to hear God's speech.

Finally God himself answers Job. God's words sharpen the contrast for Job. Whereas Job is confident of his innocence, God accuses him of darkening counsel. Whereas Job demands that God show cause for his affliction, God questions Job about his knowledge of the world . . .:

Job longs for God's presence.	God appears.
Job claims that he is innocent and that God has wronged him.	God accuses him of darkening counsel.
Job demands a resolution to his case.	God questions him about creation and the government of the world.

Instead of explaining to Job why he has afflicted him, God recounts the marvelous way he has created the world and the wise, judicious way he governs it. If he can both expand Job's understanding of his governance of the world and make [Job] perceive the limits of human understanding of the world order, he can persuade Job that it is possible to believe that he is just and merciful, caring for every creature. Job's initial response to God's questioning is startling—the loquacious Job has virtually nothing to say:

Job states that he is well prepared to argue his case before God.	Job declines to take advantage of the opportunity God gives him to speak.

Next, God challenges Job to don regal garments and rule the world justly, subduing the proud and the wicked. Then God questions him about his ability to master Behemoth and Leviathan. If Job cannot rule more justly than God, he will forfeit his case against God. Persuaded by God's argument, Job relinquishes his complaint and humbles himself before God. This act of contrition stands in stark contrast to his bold claim of innocence:

Job swears that he is innocent.	Job surrenders his complaint and his oath of innocence.

Realizing that to pursue his lawsuit against God, after God has reasoned with him, would be to stand in outright rebellion against God, Job acknowledges God's complete lordship over his life by humbly surrendering himself to God. Thus at the end of the speeches, there is a major resolution to the contrast in the dialogue:

Job asks God to speak to him.	God appears to Job and addresses him.

Job submits to God.

In the epilogue the remaining contrasts are resolved. God accepts Job's act of contrition:

Job submits to God.	God accepts him.

God's earlier accusation against Job gives way to affirmation:

God accuses Job of darkening counsel.	God affirms that Job has spoken rightly.

Whereas Job has darkened counsel in accusing God of ruling unjustly, he has spoken rightly in holding onto his innocence and in asserting that God is his Redeemer. At the same time God holds the friends accountable for their speaking wrongly of him and orders them to make atonement by offering up sacrifices and having Job pray for them. God's instructions both authenticate Job and provide a way for the reconciliation of Job and his friends:

God instructs the friends to offer up sacrifices.	The friends obey God and Job prays for them.

Afterward God manifests his presence in Job's life by blessing him abundantly:

God blesses Job.	Job's estate doubles and Job lives a long, full life.

The epilogue illustrates the basic truth that God is gracious and good, seeking the welfare of his servants. "This realistic this-worldly conclusion of the book shows powerfully that the real decision whether God is truly God falls in *this* life. Here and now faith must prove true."[10]

Themes

The author probes the multiple aspects of human suffering and presents many insights into this issue. Six prominent themes will be noted here: (1) a righteous person may suffer; (2) the dimensions of human suffering; (3) a righteous person's struggle to overcome suffering; (4) qualifications to the doctrine of double retribution; (5) the question of theodicy; (6) an encounter with God.

1. Through Job's experience the author sets forth the tenet that an upright person may suffer terribly, even though he has not sinned. Calamity is not necessarily a hostile witness against a righteous person's integrity.

2. Job, a man of great faith and flawless character, suffers deeply in every dimension of his existence—physical, social, spiritual, and emotional. These dimensions, to be sure, are intertwined in human experience and can be separated only for purposes of discussion. In the physical realm Job loses his vast wealth and all his children in a single day (1:13–14). In these events, Job suffers from both the suddenness and the totality of his losses. A little later he is struck down by a dreaded disease (2:8–10). In the social dimensions Job, the noblest elder of his community, is alienated from his family and friends as he sits in shame on an ash heap outside the city's walls (2:7–8; 19:13–19). There the crowds, even the lowest rabble, scorn him as they make him the subject of their taunt songs (16:10; 30:1–15). Since even those who have come to console him turn against him, he feels the treachery of disloyal friends (6:14–23). Spiritually God's silence terrifies Job (23:8, 9, 15). God's apparent hostility leads him to imagine that God is a capricious despot, who delights in afflicting his servant (cf. 6:4; 7:17–19; 19:25). Troubled on all sides, Job feels the range of disturbed emotions: troubled thoughts (7:4, 13–14), uncertainty (9:20), rejection and hostility (10:3; 12:4), fear (9:28), dismay (21:6), loneliness (19:13–19), distaste for life (9:2), i.e., the lack of any sense of inner tranquility (3:26). No wonder he often groans that his soul is bitter (7:11; 10:1; 27:2).

3. The center of Job's test is that the anguish caused by God's apparently unreasoned anger threatens to break his moral resolve. Desperately he gropes for some way out of this dark abyss. By vigorously lamenting his bitter feelings, he comes to grips with his anguish and channels his mind to seek some resolution to his predicament. As he probes for a resolution, his thinking is governed by three principles: God is all-powerful and just; he himself is innocent, undeserving of such affliction; and a premature death will be an unbearable disgrace, leaving him unvindicated. His unwavering conviction that he

10. W. Vischer, "God's Truth and Man's Lie" (tr. D. G. Miller), *Int* 15 (1961) 145.

has never departed from God's commandments (23:12) prevents him from becoming trapped in the selfish application of spiritual axioms and wise sayings, a trap set by his friends' counsel. Positively it leads him to swear that he will never speak falsely or act deceitfully by confessing some contrived wrongdoing solely to win God's favor (27:4). By focusing on God as his Witness and his Redeemer, Job makes bold statements of trust in God (16:19; 19:25–27). Finally, with an avowal of innocence he places his destiny in God's hands and demonstrates that a person's moral resolve can grow stronger even amid the worst adversity. Job thus stands as the prime example of how an upright person can maintain his own integrity even when overwhelmed, for no apparent reason, by the most painful suffering.

4. The author challenges directly a simplistic understanding of the doctrine of double retribution—that the righteous are always blessed and that the wicked experience untold hardship, leading to premature death. Job's three comforters articulate the traditional understanding of retribution in its various nuances. Because of their rigid understanding of this doctrine they can only explain Job's suffering as the result of some sin that he has committed. Then the only solution they can offer to him is the way of repentance. Because they encourage Job to repent primarily to escape his suffering and to receive God's blessing, they unsuspectingly tempt him to use God for personal gain, the essence of sin. Therefore, if Job followed their counsel, he would confirm the Satan's proposition that human beings are totally self-serving in their worship of God. Through the example of these three comforters the author strongly denounces the practice of using deceptive arguments to defend God (13:7–12).

5. Suffering opens Job's eyes to the discrepancy between the belief that God punishes the wicked and the reality that in numerous cases the wicked are never punished and the innocent are caught by sudden disaster. He wonders whether God is a capricious deity, doing good or ill according to his whims (9:22–24; 21:7–33; 24:1–17). Thus Job raises the issue of theodicy.

Both the Elihu speeches and the Yahweh speeches address the issue of God's being just. Elihu teaches that God uses dreams and suffering as rods of discipline to turn a person from error, even if the error is only potential (33:12–22, 29–30; 36:16–21). Pain is often an instrument of God's mercy. Thus Elihu wishes to direct attention to the purpose of suffering, rather than to try to discover its origin. Furthermore, he acknowledges the great gulf between humanity and God and teaches that God himself directs the deliverance of an afflicted person from death by graciously sending a mediating angel to proclaim that a ransom has been found (33:23–28). If that person will pray, accepting the deliverance God provides, God will deliver his life from death. Moreover, Elihu portrays God as mercifully just in all his dealings (ch. 34), arguing that he has nothing to gain by acting unjustly (ch. 35).[11]

11. N. Snaith, *The Book of Job*, SBT 2/11 (London: SCM; Naperville: Allenson, 1968), p. 90.

Elihu also extols this great God as one who reveals himself in an awesome display of power in order to inspire people to worship him (36:22–37:13).

Addressing Job, God affirms that he has structured the world exactly according to his blueprints (38:4–8). With this metaphor he claims that he has built justice into the structure of the universe. Moreover, God asserts that no corner of the world is outside his authority (38:16–24), thereby refuting any theory that injustice and suffering exist because God is in a struggle with a strong foe. Furthermore, God argues for his wise management of the world by pointing to his ordering of the heavenly elements and his care of the wild animals (38:25–39:30). His argument that he manages the heavenly elements so wisely and provides for the creatures of the desert so caringly implies that he certainly watches over people just as wisely and caringly. Furthermore, in questioning Job so intently about the created order and the creatures Behemoth and Leviathan, symbols of hostile cosmic forces, God brings Job to realize that no human being has a proper perspective to judge the course of matters in the universe, let alone to accuse God of acting unjustly. The foundation of God's argument in his speeches is that power and wisdom (justice) are one in the supreme ruler of the universe. That is, by demonstrating that he exercises his power in wisdom, God proves that he rules the world in justice. Thus the analogies of the created order that God puts before Job offer him the grounds for believing in "the essential rightness of things."[12]

6. Awed by God's majesty and overwhelmed that God in grace reasons with him, Job surrenders his complaint against God, realizing that a person must surrender even his rights to God because God is Lord. In yielding himself to God Job reveals beyond any doubt that he serves God out of love, not for material gain or prestige. Also, in abandoning his avowal of innocence he removes all barriers between himself and God.

In praise of God Job confesses, "I had heard you with my ears, but now my eyes have seen you" (42:5). Clearly the author finds the profoundest personal answer to undeserved suffering to reside in the divine-human encounter. That God both appears to Job and speaks with him means that Job's encounter is more than a mystical experience with a numinous force; it is a meeting with the personal God. God's presence authenticates Job, drawing him out of his self-love to focus his affection on God. Job gladly abandons the complaints against God, conscious of the fact that he can trust God in his grace to accomplish that which is worthwhile from his undeserved suffering. The value of an encounter with God goes beyond the experience itself, as demonstrated by the fact that God continues both to speak with Job after he recants and to work in his life.

God acknowledges Job's faithfulness by giving him the privilege of interceding for his friends as they offer up sacrifices to atone for their having spoken wrongly about God (42:7–9). This divine directive contains many

12. Robert Gordis, *The Book of God and Man*, p. 156.

insights. The friends, who have seriously erred by misleading Job in their defense of traditional beliefs, must now seek God's forgiveness. Job now possesses new authority with God by reason of his obedient endurance of undeserved affliction. God's directive also teaches Job that he must not harbor any ill feelings toward his friends for their failure to comfort him.

In conclusion, the Book of Job teaches that a person may serve God faithfully, whether his circumstances are bleak or filled with promise, for he has the assurance that God is for him, seeking his ultimate good. A person can triumph over suffering through faith in God.

5

THE LANGUAGE AND STYLE OF JOB

Robert Gordis

Every writer of consequence wishes to be more than a writer—he aspires to be a thinker, even a philosopher. For the author of Job this desire was abundantly gratified, if we interpret "philosopher" in its original sense as a lover and practitioner of wisdom. The rich content of the book, the range and the depth of its thought, bear witness to the extraordinary intellectual gifts of the author.

The profundity of Job is matched by its literary greatness. The author is generally included among the half-dozen transcendent literary geniuses of all time, along with Homer, the Greek dramatists, Dante, Shakespeare, and Goethe.

The artistry of Job is revealed in its superb structure. . . . The traditional prose tale of the pious suffering Job is utilized by the poet in masterly fashion as a framework for the dialogue. Both parts, the prologue and the epilogue,

From Robert Gordis, *The Book of God and Man: A Study of Job* (Chicago: University of Chicago Press, 1966), 157–68. Used by permission of the Univesity of Chicago Press.

are linked to the poetry by brief jointures written by the author. The prose tale itself has been retold with consummate artistry. In terse moving style the five scenes of the drama unfold, alternating between earth and heaven. The four disasters that befall Job come in a climactic series—the first two through human agencies, robbing him of his possessions; the last two of divine origin, destroying his family, and all but destroying him.

Then follow the three cycles of speeches by Job and his friends. The progression they reveal lies not in the logical development of ideas, such as we meet in a Platonic dialogue, but in the crescendo of emotion. The friends who have come to comfort Job by reminding him of the eternal verities grow more and more helpless and angry as the chasm between them widens. As the dialogue continues, Job is driven both to greater bitterness and to a new and deeper faith. As he sees himself thoroughly misunderstood by even the wisest and best of men, his conviction grows that he will be vindicated by God, the great arbiter—nay more—his eternal witness, indeed, his ultimate redeemer.

But before God appears there is another word to be spoken by man. The poet introduces Elihu, who opposes Job for attacking God's justice, and the friends, for defending it so poorly. He himself proceeds to set forth his own solution, which is the secondary answer to the problem of evil. Elihu's words serve as a foil and a prelude to the great speeches of the Lord, which contain the primary answer. Here the poet sets forth his basic insight: the universe, miracle as well as mystery, is the background against which the dark burden of suffering is to be borne even when it cannot be understood. Before this truth, which neither belittles or justifies Job's tragic experience, the sufferer submits and is reconciled.

The last word has now been spoken. It remains only to take up the strands of the familiar tale. In the highly significant jointure which links the poetry to the prose narrative it is made clear that Job has been vindicated. It is he who must intercede for the friends who, in spite of their role as God's defenders, have not spoken the truth about him. The story is now resumed in all its naïve simplicity. Job is restored to prosperity, the number of his sons is doubled, his newborn daughters are beautiful, and he lives twice the normal life span, dying an old man, "satisfied with life."

The beauty of Job is revealed not only in its over-all structure, but in many specific details as well. Again and again, the author reveals a keen observation of all the phenomena of nature, whether it be the streams in the desert, the river flowing into the sea, the wild beasts in search of prey, the sturdy plant cleaving its way through rocks, the transplanted tree coming back to life, the mountain goats crouching to give birth, or the eternal constellations of the heavens. He looks at life with the fresh and unclouded eyes of the poet who sees the world being created anew each day, with the morning stars singing together and all the sons of God shouting for joy. And like the God whom he worships, he exults equally in the swift grace of the horse and the sluggish might of the crocodile.

Thomas Carlyle's enthusiastic panegyric is in no way extravagant:

> There is the seeing eye, the mildly understanding heart. So true everyway; true eyesight and vision for all things; material things no less than spiritual: the Horse—"hast thou clothed his neck with thunder?"—he "laughs at the shaking of the spear!" Such living likenesses were never since drawn. Sublime sorrow, sublime reconciliation; oldest choral melody as of the heart of mankind;—so soft and great; as the summer midnight, as the world with its sea and stars! There is nothing written, I think, in the Bible or out of it, of equal literary merit.[1]

Equally acute is the poet's eye for the human parade. The limitless ills of human existence, the ravages of disease, the miracle of human birth, the clash of wills in the law court, the rise and fall of classes and nations, the attack of the warrior upon his adversary, the thief plotting his evil schemes, the poverty-stricken harvest worker shivering in the cold of night, the rich malefactor living in luxury and ease—all these are transfixed through a telling phrase, a striking image. Nowhere else has the existential tragedy of man, whether in the brief hour of his contentment and joy or in the moment of his death and nothingness, been caught more poignantly or unforgettably.

Each reading discloses new beauties in Job, even if the book is read in a language other than Hebrew. The wonder is that so much has been successfully captured in translation, particularly in the magnificent King James Version. The reasons for its success are several. The Committee of Translators of 1611 possessed native literary gifts of the highest order and an ear for the cadence and sound of words second to none. Moreover, it was their good fortune to live at the flood tide of the Elizabethan era, when English possessed a richness and plasticity never attained before or since. Finally, the translators made themselves willing captives of the Hebrew original, even when it meant creating new English idioms out of Semitic turns of phrases. These ultimately became integral to the English language because of the sway held by the Authorized Version over the English-speaking peoples.

It does not derogate from the achievement of the translators to point out that their work was facilitated by the character of biblical poetry. Unlike classical Greek and Latin poetry, biblical meter does not depend on a pattern of long and short syllables arranged in a given form. Nor does biblical poetry depend on rhyme and the fixed succession of stressed and unstressed syllables, as most modern verse does—features generally impossible to capture in translation. Rhyme is practically non-existent in biblical verse.

Biblical poetry is characterized by two features that are bound up with its content rather than its form. First, the patterns of biblical rhythm are generally based on the principle of one beat or accent for each word or thought-unit, irrespective of the number of syllables. The second feature is that of par-

1. "The Hero as Prophet," *On Heroes, Hero Worship and the Heroic in History* (New York, 1905), pp. 69–70.

allelism: the impact of an idea or emotion is heightened by having one poetic line or stich followed by another line which echoes, contrasts, or completes the content of the first.[2] Both these features, the non-syllabic meter based on thought-units and the ***parallelismus membrorum,*** pose a substantial challenge to any translator, but they are not totally beyond the scope of a gifted writer.

As is to be expected, the poetic qualities of the book are fully revealed only in the original. Our understanding of the rich texture of Job's style has been tremendously advanced by the last three hundred years of research in Semitic linguistics and prosody and by the discovery of significant remains of ancient Near Eastern literature.

Job has more words of unique occurrence and a richer vocabulary than any other biblical book.[3] For example, the author uses four nouns for "lion," six terms for "trap,"[4] and four synonyms for "darkness."[5] He knows the names of the constellations,[6] of metals, and of many precious stones.[7] He is familiar with the detailed anatomy of great beasts,[8] the technical language of the law courts,[9] and the occupations of mining[10] and hunting.[11]

The richness of his vocabulary stands the poet in excellent stead. Because of the variety of language at his disposal he is able to sustain the reader's interest through forty chapters of poetry written in parallelistic style. His skillful use of synonyms prevents the repetition of the same idea in adjoining stichs from becoming monotonous.

At the same time, he is master of the rules, not their captive. In spite of his extraordinary command of the resources of Hebrew, he does not hesitate to break with the pattern. At times he will use the root twice in the same verse. Thus in 13:7 the same verb (***dibber,*** "speak") occurs in both stichs:

> Is it for the sake of God that you speak falsehood,
> On His behalf that you utter lies?

2. On biblical poetry, cf. G. B. Gray, *The Forms of Hebrew Poetry* (London, 1915); R. Gordis, *Al Mibneh Hasirah Haivrit Haqedumah* ("On the Structure of Ancient Hebrew Poetry") in *Sefer Hasanah Liyehudei Amerikah* (New York, 5705 = 1944), pp. 136–59; T. H. Robinson, *The Poetry of the O. T.* (London, 1947). The attempts of E. Sievers and others to establish a quantitative meter for biblical poetry have not thus far succeeded. Cf. W. H. Cobb, *A Criticism of Systems of Hebrew Metre* (Oxford, 1905). The problem of biblical metrics is complicated by a consideration all too often overlooked: biblical poetry was not recited, but chanted, and the musical value that was given to any word or phrase which affected its stress and length is totally lost to us today.

3. Cf. the list of ***hapax legomena*** in F. Delitzsch, *Das Buch Iob* (Leipzig, 1864), p. 125.

4. Job 4:10–11; 18:8–9.

5. Ibid., 10:22, for example.

6. Ibid., 9:9; 38:31ff.

7. Ibid., 28:1–2; 28:15ff.

8. Ibid., 40:15ff.; 40:25ff.

9. Ibid., 9:2ff.; 14:15.

10. Ibid., 28:1–10.

11. Ibid., 16:12ff., for example.

This repetition is, moreover, too frequent in Job to be a scribal error.[12] We may be sure that the poet's command of the language was at least equal to that of his modern readers.[13] The usage is due either to the desire for emphasis or to some psychological reason that now eludes us.

In order to elucidate the rich vocabulary of Job, the modern scholar has recourse to other Semitic languages such as Akkadian, Ethiopic, and Ugaritic, but most especially to Arabic, Aramaic, and post-biblical Hebrew. The varied rationale for this technique is not always clearly understood even among students. When we turn to a cognate language for help in elucidating a Hebrew text, there is, to be sure, the possibility that the particular term was borrowed from a neighboring people together with the object which it represents.[14] This is, however, a comparatively rare phenomenon. The basic assumption in involving cognate roots is that Hebrew and its sister languages are all descended from a proto-Semitic tongue. Hence a word that has come down to us in the relatively limited vocabulary of the Hebrew Bible may be explained by its use in another Semitic language where it occurs more frequently and its meaning is more certain.

It has long been noted that Job has a large number of Arabisms, that is to say, words that are best explained by reference to the rich vocabulary of classical and dialectical Arabic.[15] It does not follow that the poet knew Arabic, although this assumption is not completely ruled out by any evidence at our disposal. There is, however, no basis whatever for assuming that our book is a translation of a non-existent Arabic original.[16] These so-called Arabisms are generally not borrowings but authentic Hebrew words fortunately attested by their provenance in the far richer Arabic lexicon.

12. The repetition of the same vocable occurs also in Job 8:3 (*'iwwēt*); 11:7 (*māṣā'*); 15:31 (*šāw'*); 17:15 (*tiqwāh*), as well as in Eccles. 3:16 (*rešaʿ*) and 4:1 (*mᵉnaḥem*).

13. The Septuagint, intended for non-Semitic readers to whom parallelism was alien and who might find the repetition monotonous, tends to substitute a Greek synonym for one or the other stich in these cases. On the basis of this practice, modern scholars have often, and uncritically, assumed an error in the Hebrew text and exhibited their ingenuity by proposing a Hebrew synonym to replace the repeated root.

14. There is no need to document this phenomenon. For an illustration, cf. Hebrew *pardes* and Greek *paradeisos* from the Persian *pairi-daeza*; Hebrew *'apiryon* (Song of Songs 3:9) from Sanskrit *paryanka*, on which see Gordis, *Songs of Songs*, ad loc. The list can be extended indefinitely. In modern languages, cf. French *redingote* (from English *riding-coat*) and *bifteck* (from English *beefsteak*), to say nothing of thousands of technological terms that are today international.

15. Cf. the standard commentaries passim, esp. Delitzsch, Dhorme, Tur-Sinai, and Yellin.

16. This idea was suggested by the medieval scholar Abraham ibn Ezra, who was struck by the Arabisms in the book (cf. his Commentary on 2:11). On the theory of an Arabic origin, see chapter xv. Carlyle, whose praise of the Book of Job we have quoted, is not alone in being able to combine reverence for the Bible with prejudice against the people that produced it. He says: "Biblical critics seem agreed that our own book of *Job* was written in that (i.e., Arab) region of the world. *One feels indeed as if it were not Hebrew;* such a noble universalism different from noble patriotism or sectarianism reigns in it" (my italics). Carlyle's approach, which can scarcely be regarded as objective, is, unfortunately, not lacking even in modern scholarship.

Even more frequent are the so-called Aramaisms in Job.[17] Here the situation is more complex because of the close relationship of the two languages and the extensive contacts of the Hebrews with Aramaic at several periods of history. This has often been overlooked or misunderstood. Not only are Hebrew and Aramaic both Semitic languages, but they also belong to the same sub-group of North-West Semitic, so that the resemblances are closer than between any other two languages in the Semitic family. The relationship between the Hebrews and the Aramaic-speaking peoples of Mesopotamia and Syria existed throughout the history of the Hebrew nation. According to the Bible, Jacob's father-in-law Laban, with whom he lived for twenty years, spoke Aramaic (Gen. 31:47). Throughout the First Temple period, the Aramean kingdoms and Israel shared a common border and stood in close contact, friendly or hostile, with one another.[18] During the Babylonian Exile and in the post-Exilic period, Aramaic became the *lingua franca*, universally used for government and business throughout the Middle East.

The decrees from the Persian government archives cited in the Book of Ezra are written in Aramaic. So are the letters sent to the Persian governor Bagoas in Jerusalem by the Jewish military colony at Elephantine on the upper Nile, as indeed are all the extant remains of that fascinating outpost of Jewish life. These documents and other inscriptions testify to the extensive use of Aramaic throughout the Middle East during the fifth century B.C.E., if not earlier.[19] Ultimately, Aramaic pre-empted the position of Hebrew in the Jewish community of the Second Temple, becoming the language of law, literary composition, and ordinary conversation.[20]

It is therefore methodologically unsound to lump all Aramaisms together, and on that basis to assign a later date to the literary documents in which they occur.[21] Actually, the Aramaisms in biblical Hebrew are to be subsumed under four distinct categories: (1) examples of the North-West Semitic vocabulary and usage indigenous to both Aramaic and Hebrew, at times frequent in Aramaic but remaining rare (or poetic) in Hebrew (such forms are gener-

17. Cf. DG, I, xlvi ff., for a careful tabulation and analysis of the Aramaisms, real and alleged.

18. See John Bright, *A History of Israel* (Philadelphia, 1959), pp. 210–58.

19. Cf. the standard collection of these texts by E. Sachau, *Aramäische Papyrus und Ostraken* (Leipzig, 1911), and the supplementary collection by E. G. Kraeling, *The Brooklyn Museum Aramaic Papyri* (New Haven, 1953), as well as the smaller collection by A. Ungnad, *Aramäische Papyrus aus Elephantine* (Leipzig, 1911).

20. Cf. the second-century Book of Daniel, which entered the biblical canon, and the later so-called *A Genesis Apocryphon*, or "Midrash on Genesis," found at Qumran, published by Y. Yadin (Jerusalem, 1956). Some early sections of the Mishnah are also given in Aramaic.

The complex question of when Hebrew ceased to be a spoken language in Palestine is unsolved today. For the view that Hebrew remained a living tongue throughout the mishnic period, and a conspectus of the evidence, see E. Ben Yehuda, *Thesaurus Linguae Hebraicae, Prolegomena* (Tel Aviv, 1948), pp. 80–254. It is certain that Hebrew continued to be spoken in certain "pockets" of population as late as the third century C.E.

21. See E. Kautzsch, *Die Aramäismen im A.T.* (Halle am Saale, 1902), which was significantly criticized by Th. Noeldeke in *ZDMG*, LVII (1907), 412–20.

ally early and cannot be invoked for a late date);[22] (2) earlier Hebrew borrowings from nearby Aramaic during the pre-Exilic period, especially in the heyday of the Syrian kingdom;[23] (3) later Hebrew borrowings during the Babylonian Exile and the post-Exilic period;[24] (4) idioms and morphological forms introduced into Hebrew and patterned after Aramaic usage, with which the Hebrew writer or speaker was familiar.[25]

It follows that the occurrence of a few Aramaisms in a Hebrew text is insufficient to determine its age or origin. Only when we encounter a heavy concentration of words, idioms, or grammatical forms patterned on Aramaic, is it a fair presumption that the author was accustomed to thinking in Aramaic and used it freely in his daily speech.[26] This last situation obtains in Job, where Aramaisms are plentiful both in vocabulary and in morphology.[27]

Another source for the understanding of biblical Hebrew in general, and the language of Job in particular, is to be found in the extensive works of post-biblical literature. In the past, the significance of rabbinic Hebrew was all too often ignored or minimized on the ground that it was a "degenerate" or "artificial" form of the language. Today it is generally recognized that the Hebrew of the Mishnah, the Talmud, and the mishrashim, and even of the medieval era, represents later stages in the evolution of the same language. By every canon of scientific method, parallels from later Hebrew should be recognized as being at least as significant as cognates from other languages and alien culture-spheres, with which the Hebrews may have had only slight and superficial contacts, or perhaps none. This is not intended to deny the value of the "horizontal" aspect, through space, of comparative Hebrew philology, but to underscore the importance of the "vertical" aspect, through time.[28]

In Job, as in other biblical books, there are usages best explained by rab-

22. As, e.g., *'athah,* "come" (Deut. 33:2; Mic. 4:8; Jer. 3:22; often in Deutero-Isaiah and Job); the *Lamed accusative,* as, e.g., after *'āhabh* (Lev. 19:18, 34; 2 Sam. 3:30) or *hārag* (2 Sam. 3:30; see BDB, p. 512a); *mālal,* "speak" (Gen. 21:7).

23. As, e.g., *rā'āh,* "chase, desire," parallel to *rādaph* (Hos. 12:2).

24. Cf. such use as *bar,* "son" (Prov. 31:2).

25. Cf. such idioms as *'im' al hammelekh tobh* (Esther 7:3; cf. Ezra 5:17), as against the classical Hebrew phrase *tōbh b^e 'einei* (1 Sam. 29:6), and the use of *in* as the masc. plur. ending, as in Prov. 31:3; Job 4:2; 24:22; 31:10; Dan. 12:13. Yet even this indubitably Aramaic ending occurs in such earlier texts as Judg. 5:10; Mic. 3:12; 1 Kings 11:33; 2 Kings 11:13; Ezek. 4:9; 26:18.

26. A striking illustration, and a rare one, is afforded by Ps. 139, where the opening verses contain at least four Aramaisms: *lere'iy* (vs. 2), *ribh'iy* (vs. 3), *millāh* (vs. 4), and *'essaq* (vs. 8).

27. Cf. the verb *ḥawah* (15:17; 32:6, 10, 17; 36:2) and the noun *'ahwāh* (13:19), a root occurring in only one other passage outside Job (Ps. 19:2); the *in* masc. plur. ending as, e.g., *hayyin* (24:23), *millin* (4:2, and elsewhere). In 36:2a, we have an entire stich which is Aramaic in vocabulary: *Kathar li z^e'er va' ahawwekkā.*

On the higher concentration of Aramaisms in the Elihu chapters (32–37), see chapter ix. On the bearing of the Aramaisms on the date of Job, see chapter xv.

28. On the need to recognize these two aspects of comparative philology, see Gordis, "Studies in the Relationship of Biblical and Rabbinic Hebrew," in *Louis Gensberg Jubilee Volumes* (New York, 1945), English Section, pp. 173 75 et seq. This paper presents a substantial number

binic Hebrew.[29] This, in spite of the fact that Job uses poetic diction, while most of the extant rabbinic sources are in prose, much of it being technical to boot. The frequency of Aramaisms in Job supports the conclusion, to which other criteria also point, that Job was written in a period when Aramaic was widely used for conversation and that the author was thoroughly familiar with the language.[30] To be sure, there are relatively fewer Aramaisms and late Hebrew locutions than in other biblical books that emanate from the same era. The reason inheres in the important distinctions in style between poetry and prose. In poetry, the author has a tendency to use exalted speech and therefore to archaize and to retain the vocabulary and forms of the classical language. Thus, even the latest of the Psalms are far freer of Aramaisms than the prose works of the post-Exilic period, like Ecclesiastes, Esther, and Chronicles. The Dead Sea Scrolls exhibit the same feature. The prose writings of these sectarians, like the *Manual of Discipline* (*Serekh Hayahad*), approximate proto-mishnaic Hebrew, while the poetic *Hymns of Thanksgiving* (*Hodayot*) betray late Hebrew influences much more rarely, being modeled after the biblical Psalms.[31] The dialogue of Job may therefore be described as the supreme example of late biblical poetry in both style and vocabulary.

The prose tale in the prologue and epilogue is written in exquisite biblical Hebrew, on a par with the classic narratives in Genesis and Samuel. This has suggested to some scholars a very early date for the prose tale, but as we have seen, there are irrefutable considerations of content that preclude a pre-Exilic date for the story in its present form. What we have here is a superb example of literary archaizing, a striking *tour de force* by the author, who wished to place his protagonists in the patriarchal past. Moreover, the readers knew the tale as one of hoary antiquity. Hence in retelling it, the author uses perfect classical Hebrew with practically no trace of a later style.[32] There are other examples of such skillful archaizing by gifted writers who give few telltale

of instances in which post-biblical Hebrew sheds welcome light on biblical usages. Additional examples are adduced in Gordis, "Lesōn Hamiqrā Le'ōr Lesōn Hakhamîm," in *Sefer Tur-Sinai* (Jerusalem, 5720 = 1960), pp. 149–68.

29. Cf., e.g., *hiqsāh* in Job 9:4, on which see the Comm.

30. Cf. chapter xv.

31. For some of the often overlooked implications of the stylistic differences between prose and poetry and their bearing on the evaluation of different literary genres, cf. Gordis, "Qoheleth and Qumran—A Study in Style," *Biblica*, XLI (1960), 395–410, esp. 402ff.

32. The one exception is the root *kibbel* (2:10) which occurs only in late biblical texts (Esther 4:4; 9:21, 23; Ezra 8:30; 1 Chron. 12:18; 21:11; 2 Chron. 29:16, 22; Prov. 19:20 cannot be dated with any assurance, but may be late), and frequently in the Mishnah. Though W. F. Albright believes he has discovered the root in a Canaanite gloss in the Tel-el-Amarna Letters of the fourteenth century B.C.E. (cf. *BASOR*, No. 89 [1943], 29ff.), the exclusively late usage of the verb makes it a late word in Hebrew.

The use of *bērēkh*, "bless," as a euphemism (1:5, 11; 2:5, 9) occurs elsewhere only in 1 Kings 21:10, 13, and Ps. 10:3. It is likely that these are both late sources. Kings was obviously completed in the Exilic period and the acrostic form of the psalm suggests a late date (cf. R. Gordis, "Psalm 9–10: A Textual and Exegetical Study," in *JQR*, XLVIII (1957), 104–22.

signs of their own age. The Book of Ruth, likewise post-Exilic, is written in a style reminiscent of the Book of Judges. In modern literature, Thackerary's *Henry Esmond* follows the style and structure of the eighteenth-century English novels, while Thomas Love Beddoes, a Victorian poet, wrote in Elizabethan and Jacobean style.

As has been noted earlier in this chapter, the poetic sections of Job are naturally marked by the two basic traits of biblical poetry, *parallelism* and *meter.* Scholars have disagreed on the question of the basic meter employed in the book. While most regard the 3:3 pattern as basic, Pfeiffer has argued strongly for 4:4 as the meter.[33] Many commentators have insisted that the book consists exclusively of distichs. Hence, whenever a verse in the present text contains a third stich, they have proceeded to eliminate it as spurious. Since the problem is gratuitous, the proposed solution is uncalled for. In a work as long as Job, any single rhythm pattern would have become unbearable. Indeed, other biblical poems which are far shorter than Job, like "The Song of the Sea" (Exod. chap. 15), "The Song of Deborah" (Judg. chap. 5), Isaiah's "Great Arraignment" (Isa. chap. 1) and Koheleth's "Allegory of Old Age" (Eccles. 11:7–12:8), all exhibit a variety of meters, since monotony is the cardinal sin of literature.[34] To be sure, redoubtable surgeons did not hesitate to subject these texts as well to amputation in order to make the meter conform to their preconceived theories. But the discovery of a variety of meters in the Ugaritic poems[35] has demonstrated what should have been clear all along—that while a poem is written in a basic meter, the author will often introduce variations in the pattern in order to express different emotions and to stimulate the reader's interest.

The facts are clear and beyond dispute. There is, however, room for differ-

33. Pfeiffer, *IOT,* p. 687.

34. Thus the "Song of the Sea" (Exod. chap. 15) is written basically in a 4:4 rhythm. However, it exhibits the following meter-patterns: 4:4 (vs. 1); 3:3 (vs. 2); 3:2 (vs. 3); 5:5 (vs. 4); 4:4 (vs. 5, giving *tehomōt* and *yᵉ khasyūmū* each two beats, and vss. 6–18). In the latter half of the song, monotony is avoided by varying the number of stichs per verse. Thus we have distichs (vss. 5, 6, 7, 10, 11, 13, 14, and 16, which contains a pair of distichs), tristichs (vss. 8, 9), as well as monostichs (vss. 12, 18).

The "Song of Deborah" (Judg. chap. 5) is basically in 3:3 meter but exhibits similar variations in meter and stichometry, as is the case with Isa. chap. 1. With regard to the "Allegory of Old Age" in Eccles., see *KMW,* p. 323, for a discussion of its varied meter.

On the use of variations in meter and stichometry, cf. "MHHH," pp. 142 ff. On variations in the accent of longer words or thought-units, cf. op. cit., pp. 140–41.

35. Cf. C. H. Gordon, *Ugaritic Manual* (Rome, 1955), pp. 108–9, especially p. 108, n. 1: "Structurally different verses and strophes occur constantly within the same poem in Ugaritic. It is therefore unsound to attribute similar variety in the Bible to the blending of different poems. . . . All that is asked of those who maintain metric hypotheses is to state their metric formulae and to demonstrate that the formulae fit the texts. Instead, they emend the texts to fit their hypotheses. A sure sign of error is the constant need to prop up a hypothesis with more hypotheses." Cf. also G. D. Young in *JNES,* IX (1950), 124–33; W. F. Albright in *HUCA,* XXIII (1950–51), 1–39.

ences in interpretation. Thus, Gordon believes that "the poetry of the ancient Near East, Akkadian, Ugaritic, Hebrew, Egyptian, did not know of exact meter."[36] In view of the variety, complexity and technical skill exhibited by biblical and oriental poets, this view does not commend itself. Their conception of meter differed from that of classical or Western poetry. Their meter patterns, however, are much too regular to be dismissed as non-existent. In view of our ignorance of the musical modes in which ancient oriental verse was intoned, we can only assume the general principle of one stress for each word or thought-unit, modified in rare cases by metric considerations. As for variations in meter, they are thoroughly explicable as part of the poet's craft.

In Job the basic pattern is a verse consisting of two stichs, each containing three beats. But this meter (which is, incidentally, the most frequently used in biblical poetry) undergoes every conceivable variation, in the number of stichs in the verse and the number of stresses per stich.[87] In addition to the balanced rhythm pattern, where each stich has the same number of beats, we also meet with the haunting meter called the *Kinah* rhythm, where the second stich is shorter than the first.[38] Special power inheres in the rarer use of a staccato rhythm.[39] As is true of other biblical poets, the author will at times follow the natural tendency to conclude a speech in a literary crescendo, bringing it to an end with an increase in either the number of stresses or stichs in the closing line.[40] The general principle is exhibited everywhere: while one meter predominates, variety is nearly always present.[41]

36. Gordon, op. cit., p. 108, n. 1.
37. See "MHHH," pp. 143–44, and see nn. 41 and 42 below.
38. See n. 41 below.
39. Cf., e.g., Job 17:1.
40. This is achieved in a variety of ways:
   (a) In a section containing distichs, the closing verse will end with a tristich, cf. Job, chaps. 10, 11, 19, 26. So also Ps. 13, 14, 16, 18, 19, 37, 47, 53, 55, 63, 73, 90, 94, 103, 104, 111, 119, 125, 129, 148.
   (b) The closing stich will be extended by the use of more words or by longer ones. Job, chaps. 5, 17, 18, 21. So also Ps. 17, 21, 26, 41, 45, 71, 81, 91, 116.
   (c) The composition or the section will change in the closing verse from a shorter to a longer meter, as in Ps. 19 (vs. 11), 24, 27, 34, 41–42, 51 (vs. 19), 82, 89.
   (d) The meter may be lengthened in the closing stich only. Thus Job 18, basically in 3:3 meter, ends in 4:4. Cf. Ps. 4, 8, 10, 13, 15, 20, 47, 50, 52, 59, 62, 63, 66, 67, 84, 86, 123, 145. The ritual term *Hallelūyā* apparently served also to extend the meter of the closing stich, as in Ps. 113, 117, 146, 147.
   (e) Two of these devices may be used simultaneously, as in Ps. 47. For a detailed examination of this important poetic usage, not hitherto adequately recognized, see "MHHH," pp. 144ff.

41. Thus Job's opening soliloquy (chap. 3) exhibits the following rhythm pattern: 4:4 (vs. 3), 4:4:3 (vs. 4), 3:3:3 (vs. 5), 4:3:3 or 4:4:4 (vs. 6), 4:4 (vs. 7), 3:3 (vs. 8), 3:3:3 (vs. 9), 3:3 (vss. 10–16), 4:4 (vs. 17), 3:3 (vss. 18, 19), 4:3 (vs. 20), 3:3 (vs. 21, where two beats are to be assigned to either of the two longer words in stich b, *Vayaḥpᵉrūhū mimmatmōnīm*, and vs. 22, giving two beats to *hassemēḥīm*), 4:3 (vs. 24 and vs. 25, giving two beats to *vayeʾetāyēnī*, 3:2 or 2:2:2:2 (vs. 26).

This chapter is more varied than is usually the case. Thus in chap. 4, the 3:3 meter predomi-

It should therefore be clear that it is a methodological error to delete words or stichs merely for metrical reasons. Metrics can play a legitimate role in textual criticism only when re-enforced by other textual and exegetical considerations.[42]

In biblical poetry it is usual for the stichs to be in *consecutive parallelism* to each other; that is to say, stich *a* is parallel to *b*, and stich *c* to *d*.[43] This pattern (*a*|*b*; *c*|*d*) occurs in the vast majority of poetic lines, as, e.g., in Job 4:4, 5:

a) Your words have upheld the stumbling,
b) and you have strengthened the weak-kneed.
c) But now that it has come to you, you cannot bear it;
d) it touches you, and you are dismayed.

Much rarer is the pattern of *alternate parallelism*, where the first stich is parallel to the third, and the second stich to the fourth ($a, b | a^1, b^1$).[44] A good example occurs in Hos. 5:3:

a) I have known Ephraim,
b) and Israel is not hidden from me.
a^1) For now you have committed harlotry, O Ephraim,
b^1) and Israel has defiled itself.

Of the greatest interest is the pattern of *chiastic parallelism*, where the first stich is parallel to the fourth and the second stich to the third ($a, b | b^1, a^1$).[45] This less obvious form often proves a valuable clue to the connection and meaning of difficult verses and of entire passages. An instance occurs at the end of Psalm 1, where it establishes the link between verses 5 and 6 and obviates the need for the emendations proposed by some scholars:

a) Therefore the wicked shall not stand in judgment,
b) nor sinners in the community of the righteous,
b^1) for the Lord loves the righteous,
a^1) but the way of the wicked must perish.

---

nates. The pattern is as follows: 4:4 (vs. 2), 3:3 (vss. 3, 4), 4:3 (vs. 5), 3:3 (vss. 6, 7, *zᵉkōr nāʾ* is an anacrusis outside the meter), 4:4 (vs. 8, giving *yīqṣᵉrūhū* two beats), 3:3 (vs. 9), 4:3 (vs. 10), 3:3 (vss. 11, 12, 13, 14, 15), 3:3:3 (vs. 16), 3:3 (vss. 17, 18), 3:3:3 (vs. 19), 3:3 (vss. 20, 21).

42. Cf. "MHHH," pp. 143ff., 148–49, where Deut. 33:11; Hos. 8:11; Ps. 4, 7–8; and Job 19:14, 15; 20:29, are adduced as instances of the proper use of metrics in textual criticism.

43. On the various patterns of parallelism, see "MHHH," pp. 151ff.

44. Loc. cit., for analysis of such examples of alternate parallelism as Hos. 5:3; Ps. 33:20, 21. This usage occurs also in prose, cf. Exod. 29:27; Deut. 22:25–27, as Ehrlich acutely noted. It is the key to the difficult passage in Eccles. 5:17–19. See *KMW*, ad loc.

45. Loc cit., for such instances of chiastic parallelism as Hos. 2:21–22; 8:14; Ps. 1:5, 6; Prov. 23:15, 16; Job 20:3; Lam. 2:13. For the structure and meaning of Job 29:25, see the translation and the Comm.

Another striking example of chiastic parallelism is found in Job 20:2, 3:

a) Indeed, my thoughts force me to answer
b) because of the feelings within me.
*b*¹) I hear words of censure which insult me,
*a*¹) And my spirit of understanding impels me to reply.

Chapter 8 is so difficult that commentators have been unable to decide whether the closing section (vss. 16–19) refers to the wicked or to the righteous! Chiasmus supplies the key. When this rhetorical form is recognized it becomes clear that verses 12–15 describe the destruction of the wicked (*a*), and verses 16–19, the survival of the righteous (*b*). Then comes the conclusion of the chiasmus in 8:20:

*b*¹) Indeed, God will not spurn the blameless man,
*a*¹) nor will He uphold the evildoers.

We have noted the author's freedom from slavish adherence to the usual canons of meter and parallelism. This applies also to his use of rhetorical figures. Alliteration is common, but he does not carry it to mechanical extremes. A case in point is afforded by 5:8:

As for me, I would seek after God [*El*]
And to God [*Elohim*] entrust my cause. . . .

In the Hebrew text, consonantal *Aleph* begins every word except the last (*dibhrāthî*). It is easy enough to substitute a synonym beginning with *Aleph,* such as *'imrāthî*, "my word," as some textual critics have proposed. The poet is less hidebound and departs from the alliteration at will.

Even more common than alliteration is his remarkable use of assonance. In 12:2, Job addresses a sarcastic utterance to his friends:

No doubt you are the people that count,
And with you all wisdom will die!

Here every one of the seven words in the Hebrew contains the humming sound, "m," which suggests Job's mocking sarcasm.

The book is characterized by various rhetorical figures which are expounded by the Greek and Latin grammarians as well as the Arab rhetoricians. Similes and metaphors are both common and self-explanatory.[46] We also encounter other rhetorical usages which help our understanding of the

46. For an analysis of their basic role in poetry in general and in Job in particular, see chap. xiv.

book, such as *zeugma, hendiadys,* and *hysteron proteron,* all familiar from classical literature.[47]

One of the most familiar figures of speech in the Bible is *paronomasia,* in which the author uses one word because of its similarity in sound to another.[48] For example, Isa. 5:7:

> He hoped for justice (*mišpāṭ*),
> but behold bloodshed (*mišpāḥ*).
> For righteousness (*ṣedāqāh*),
> but behold, a cry (*ṣᵉāqāh*).

Here the prophet selects these two pairs of nouns, rather than any of their synonyms, because he wishes to point up a contrast which is heightened by the similarity of sound. Plays on words are extremely common in all languages and literatures. In our day they tend to be looked down upon as a low form of humor, but they were far more highly regarded in the past, as the Bible, Homer, and Shakespeare abundantly attest.[49]

One more literary device of greater subtlety, which has not been sufficiently noticed heretofore, should be indicated. The Arab rhetoricians in their study of Arabic poetry called it *talḥin*.[50] No other biblical writer uses it as frequently or as effectively as the author of Job.[51] This usage is to be distinguished from paronomasia, the pun or the play on words. In *talḥin,* the effect derives not from the sound but from the meaning. The poet uses a word which has two distinct denotations, one primary to the context and the other secondary but also appropriate. His choice of the particular word, rather than a synonym, is dictated by the desire to bring both meanings simultaneously

47. For *zeugma,* cf. Job 4:10; 10:12. For *hendiadys,* cf. 5:15; 10:12; 25:2. (For other biblical examples, see "LMBH," pp. 263 ff.) For *hysteron proteron,* cf. Job 14:10; 16:9; 20:19, and other biblical examples in "LMBH," pp. 262 ff.

48. Cf. I. M. Casanowicz, *Paronomasia in the O. T.* (Boston, 1894); E. König, *Stilistik, Rhetorik, Poetik* (Leipzig, 1900); D. Yellin, *Kethabim Nibharim Letorat Hamelitzah Batanakh* (Jerusalem 5699 = 1939). See also "LMBH," pp. 253–67, esp. pp. 255ff., on paronomasia and *talhin.* It was noted by the medieval Hebrew grammarians Menahem ben Saruk, Jonah Abulwalid ibn Ganah, and Abraham ibn Ezra. Cf. Yellin, op. cit., p. 67, note.

49. Thus, the noted Shakespearean scholar and Elizabethan linguist, Helge Kökeritz, "discovered several additional and more complicated puns that amused Shakespeare's contemporaries. *Some of them were not merely double but triple and even quadruple in meaning.*" (The italics are mine.) (Naboth Hedin in *American Swedish Monthly,* cited in the *New York Times,* March 28, 1964.)

50. The Arabic term means, among other things, "mode of speech, dialect, error in pronunciation, leading to a change in meaning or construction." Arab rhetoricians distinguished between (a) *'istaḥda'm,* lit. "use, serving, ministering," where "only one meaning is intended, and another, less common, is suggested by phonetic similarity" (i.e., *paronomasia*), and (b) *tawrīya,* "concealment," where "both meanings are intended" (i.e. *talhin*). Cf. Yellin, op. cit., p. 87 and n. 7.

51. *Talhin* occurs in Job 3:6–7, 22; 5:24; 7:6; 9:17; 12:6; 21:13; 22:25. For other examples see "LMBH," pp. 255–62.

to the consciousness of the reader, who derives a delicate aesthetic pleasure from the instantaneous recognition of both meanings.

Thus in Lam. 2:13 we have an example which can fortunately be imitated in English: "For your break is great as the sea." Here the poet uses the Hebrew word *šebher*, "break," rather than any of its countless synonyms, because of his simile "like the sea." *Šebher* suggests the related word *mišbār*, "breaker, wave," and is thus doubly appropriate to the context.

A very moving instance occurs in Job 7:6, which cannot be duplicated in translation. The Hebrew text reads:

> My days are swifter than the weaver's shuttle;
> They end in the absence of hope.

The word for "hope" used here is the common *tiqwāh*. This noun, however, has a homonym, identical in form, which means "thread" (as in Josh. 2:18). The poet has spoken of man's days as fleeing swiftly and lacking in hope. The figure of the weaver suggests the secondary meaning of the shuttle of life running out of thread. Both senses of the word *tiqwāh* enter the reader's consciousness together and are experienced simultaneously.

These attributes of style suggest but do not exhaust the boundless artistry of the poet. In the magnificent architecture of the whole and in the perfection of each detail a master stands revealed.

6

The Language of the Book of Job

Édouard Dhorme

We should take as the basis of this study the oldest parts of the Book of Job: the prose narrative, the poetic dialogue, and the speeches of Yahweh. We have already noted that the style of Elihu was distinct from that of the rest of the work and had a more pronounced Aramaic colour.

The language of the Book of Job, thus reduced to its essential elements, reveals a strong literary personality. The author has his own vocabulary, grammar, and special technique of expression. He copies hardly at all and imitates only rarely.

A list of the words which are found only in Job has been drawn up by Fried. Delitzsch.[1] They can be classified into a number of categories which bear witness to the author's fondness for neologisms or uncommon words.

1. *Das Buch Hiob,* pp. 125ff. We have left out of account those words which are due to distortions of the text. Our list is moreover independent of that of Delitzsch.

From Édouard Dhorme, *A Commentary on the Book of Job,* trans. Harold Knight (1926; reprint, London: Thomas Nelson & Sons, 1967), clxxv–clxxix. Used by permission of Thomas Nelson Publishers.

For example, he has recourse to the feminine form which corresponds to the ***numen unitatis*** of the Arabs נהרה (3:4), עננה (3:5), חילה (6:10), דאבה (41:14). Sometimes the masculine will be substituted for the feminine which is usual elsewhere: נחוש (6:12). The form alone distinguishes שׂעפים (4:13; 20:2) from the same word in the Psalms (cf. Comm. on 4:13).

Most of the terms peculiar to the Book of Job are to be explained by reference to Hebraic or Semitic common roots: תהלה (4:18), סלד (6:10), חתת (6:21), נדדים (7:4), גוש or גיש (7:5), מחנק (7:15), מפגע (7:20), מסת (9:23), רקבון (13:28; 41:19), ניד (16:5), התלים (17:2), תפת (common noun 17:6), מלכדת (18:10), שׂיא (15:31; 20:6), צהר (24:11), בלימה (26:7), הליך (29:6), שחר (30:30), באשה (31:40), חתלה (38:9), אגל (38:28), משכות (38:31), ירוק (39:8), רננים (39:9[*sic*; 39:13]), רעמה (39:19), נחר (39:20), and נחיר (41:12), אבר (39:26), חברים (40:30), חדוד (41:22).

Sometimes a transformation of the root explains the new word: כלח (5:26), נתס (30:13), יזרבו (6:17), מעדנות (38:31).

The unusual term is sometimes borrowed from other branches of the Semitic family of languages. Thus Assyrian, Arabic, and Aramaic possess the equivalents of גֶּלֶד (16:15) and of מֹחַ (21:24). Assyrian and Arabic explain אֵבֶה (9:26), שֻׂכּוֹת (40:31), and the verb זקק of 28:1; 36:27. Aramaic and Arabic enable us to recognise the verbs גרד (2:8), נהק (6:5; 30:7), רפף (26:11), the nouns גְּבִינָה (10:10), זְכוֹכִית (28:17), עֲטִישָׁה (41:10). Through Assyrian we can analyse the terms מְזִיחַ (12:21), גָּבִישׁ (28:18), מִשְׁטָר (38:33), בוּל (40:20), תּוֹתָח (41:21). Aramaic, the influence of which we have already detected,[2] explains a certain number of words: נתע (4:10), סוש (9:26), אחוה (13:17), סד (13:27; 33:11), רזם (15:12), חב (31:33), ערוד (39:5), שׂריר (40:16), דוץ (41:14). The Arabic language also supplies keys to the understanding of terms peculiar to Job: כידור (15:24), הכר (19:3), בצר (22:24, 25), הדך (40:12), מטיל (40:18), צאלים (40:21), צלצל (40:31), כידוד (41:11), מסע (41:18), שׁריה (41:18). The terms שׂכוי and טחות of 38:36 are perhaps of Egyptian origin.

If the author of the Book of Job does not hesitate to introduce into his vocabulary words of foreign origin or of new formation, we shall not be surprised to find, apart from the ***hapax legomena***, a certain number of roots, verbs, nouns, whole expressions even, which betray the infiltration of other Semitic tongues. Here we shall simply give the references which will enable the reader to find in the Commentary the words in question and their etymology.[3]

Explanations by Assyrian, Aramaic, Arabic: 2:7; 8:16; 14:5.

By Assyrian and Arabic: 14:19; 20:2; 28:9; 31:3; 40:22; 41:12.

By Arabic and Aramaic: 8:12; 16:15.

By Assyrian or Babylonian[4]: 1:10, 15; 3:5, 8, 14; 6:4, 21; 12:21; 15:26, 32; 16:22; 17:11; 18:2, 17; 19:17, 23; 20:7, 23, 25, 28; 21:17, 21; 26:9, 15,

2. See above, p. lxxxv. On the Aramaisms of Elihu, see pp. civf.

3. This list completes the preceding one. It is here a question not of special terms but of words and expressions in general.

4. We normally use the term 'Akkadian', which denotes the Assyro-Babylonian language.

18; 28:15, 16; 30:3, 25: 31:26; 33:6, 9, 18, 19; 34:3, 13 17; 36:8, 16, 17, 32; 37:1; 38:5, 6, 23, 33; 39:8, 9, 10, 13, 23; 40:20, 23.

By Aramaic[5]: 3:25; 4:20; 5:22; 6:5, 6, 16; 8:2, 13; 11:7; 12:5; 14:6, 10; 15:17, 24; 16:2; 17:1; 18:5; 20:16; 21:7, 10, 12; 22:16; 24:24; 28:1, 8, 16; 30:3, 6; 31:9; 38:30.

By Arabic: 6:3, 10; 10:8, 17; 11:6; 14:20; 15:23; 16:6, 16; 17:8, 13; 18:8; 19:20; 20:18; 21:32; 26:13; 28:26; 29:4; 30:4, 6, 17, 22; 31:31; 33:21; 34:19; 36:10, 18; 37:2, 6, 9, 11, 20; 38:25; 39:1, 3, 4, 21.[6]

These phenomena are to be explained by the affinity between the various Semitic languages. A certain Hebrew word belongs to a root which has disappeared from the domain of Hebrew itself but still persists in all other domains. It is not then necessary to assume a direct borrowing. Furthermore, the scantiness of our documentation explains the disappearance of a certain number of words or expressions which were known in popular or literary speech but which have not been established in the Bible. Thus the *hapax legomena* are often due to the chances of the written tradition of the Bible. A word which is found only very rarely in Holy Scripture may have been perpetuated in current speech.

The truly significant facts are those whose only explanation lies in the definite influence of a foreign language. From this point of view, it has long been noted that the author of the Book of Job was often subject to Aramaic influences.

A study of the vocabulary reveals the fact that sometimes an Aramaic word has been chosen to supply, in the parallelism, the equivalent of the Hebrew word. We have already drawn attention to this fact in our discussion of the speeches of Yahweh. To the Hebrew עֵד 'witness' corresponds the Aramaic שָׂהֵד (16:19); to the Hebrew פֶּרֶא 'onager' the Aramaic עָרוֹד (39:5); to the Hebrew עֶצֶם 'bone' the Aramaic גֶּרֶם (40:18). The case is typical. The poet quite naturally uses Hebrew. When he seeks a synonym, it is Aramaic which supplies him with one. Note that Aramaic always comes second.

Another significant procedure of the author is to use Aramaic rather than the current Hebrew word, either to vary the style or because Aramaic has become so deeply rooted in his mother-tongue. Thus 'to come' is in Hebrew בוא but אתה in Aramaic. In the Book of Job we find that בוא sometimes takes the place of אתה, for example in order to avoid the repetition of the word בוא in 3:25, or for the sake of the rhythm in 16:22 (cf. 37:22, Elihu). The Aramaic מִלֵּל replaces the Hebrew דִּבֵּר 'to say' in 8:2 (cf. 33:3, Elihu). Its derivative מִלָּה 'word' is quite characteristic of the Book of Job, in which it appears 34 times.[7] Note that its plural[8] sometimes assumes the Hebraic form

5. As regards the Aramaisms in the speeches of Elihu, cf. above, pp. civf.

6. The many Arabic etymologies of 40–I are noted in the list of the *hapax legomena* above.

7. Cf. E. Kautzsch, *Die Aramaismen im A.T.*, I, p. 61.

8. Cf. Comm. on 4:2.

מלים (10 times), sometimes the Aramaic form מלין (13 times). Very symptomatic again is the substitution of כָּפָן (Aramaic) for רָעָב 'famine' in 5:22; 30:3; of חוָּה (Aramaic) for הִגִּיד 'to explain' in 15:17 (cf. 32:6, 10, 17; 36:2, Elihu); of כֵּפִים (Aramaic) for סְלָעִים 'rocks' (30:6).

Sometimes it is one of the consonants of the root which is to be explained by an Aramaic pronunciation: thus דעך 'to become extinguished' instead of זעך.[9]

Aramaic makes its influence felt even in regard to grammar. We have mentioned the plural מלין alongside מלים. Again, we find אֲחֵרִין in 31:10. The reflexive is expressed by נַפְשִׁי 'my soul' (an Aramaism) in 4:21. It is above all the use of הֵן 'if', instead of אם, which betrays the habit of using Aramaic (4:18; 9:11, 12; 12:14, 15; 13:15, etc.). It appears that in poetry either conjunction is used indifferently.

We have here confined ourselves to pointing out the most characteristic features. They suffice to situate the language of the Book of Job in that period when Aramaic was penetrating into Israel to a very considerable extent, that is, in the post-exilic period.[10] The exile in Chaldaea and the return to the mother-country had the effect of bringing the Jews into unceasing contact with populations for whom Aramaic formed a bond with other Semites. Under the hegemony of the Persians, as the papyrus records testify, Aramaic became the language of commerce and of international exchanges.[11] The Jewish colonies in Egypt used this idiom, and we have seen that the author of the Book of Job had probably visited his compatriots in the valley of the Nile. His language confirms the conclusions we have reached with regard to his date and personality.

9. Cf. Comm. on 17:1.

10. Cf. E. Kautzsch, op. cit., p. 6. We do not at all deny the inter-penetration of the Syrians of Damascus and the Hebrews, especially those of the Northern Kingdom, well before the exile. But Aramaic, even in the time of Hezekiah, was still understood only by a tiny minority, as may be seen from the dialogue in which the envoys of the King of Judah ask the Assyrian general to speak 'in Aramaic' and not 'in the Jews' language' so that his words should be understood only by the initiated and not by the people (2 Kg. 18:26).

11. See Cowley, *Aramaic Papyri*, pp. xvff.

7

Literary Features and the Message of the Book of Job

Norman C. Habel

Literary Features and Their Significance

We have already discussed the significance of the narrative plot and ancient heroic setting for an appreciation of the literary dimensions of the Book of Job as a totality. The literary techniques employed by the artistic designer of this book are diverse and complex. They extend to the adaptation of traditional literary forms, motif development, repetition, verbal irony, varying patterns of parallelism, and the creation of provocative literary designs. Our examination of these literary features will be neither exhaustive

From Norman C. Habel, *The Book of Job: A Commentary*, Old Testament Library (Philadelphia: Westminster, 1985), 42–69. Used by permission of Westminster/John Knox Press.

nor an end in itself. Our task will be to illustrate the major ways in which the author appropriates literary techniques to capture and heighten the theological conflicts developed within the book.

Form and Focus

It is a mark of creative genius that this author rarely appropriates literary forms or genres in their ideal traditional form. Rather, they are adapted, modified, and transformed to meet particular artistic and theological ends. Nowhere, for example, does the complete lament genre as exemplified in the Psalms appear in the speeches of Job (cf. Westermann, *The Structure of the Book of Job*). The one major feature of the lament genre which the poet employs and adapts is the complaint (*Klage*). The typical lament in the Psalms assumes a triangular relationship involving the sufferer, the enemy, and God. The sufferer complains to God about the enemy, whether that enemy be disease, death, physical danger, persecution, or personal foe. In Job the situation is radically different. There is no third party about which Job may complain to God. God is himself the problem, the enemy, and the object of Job's complaint. Even in ch. 7, where Job commences each unit with an axiom about the miserable condition of mortals on earth, his complaint is ultimately directed against God as the taskmaster. Instead of being hailed as a deity to whom pleas of help could be addressed, God is dubbed with ironic titles such as "Seeing Eye" (7:8) and "Watcher of Humans" (7:20). God is the enemy and the spy. Job's cries are defiant accusations, not humble cries for deliverance. The author even parodies famous hymnic lines from Ps. 8 acclaiming the exalted nature of human beings. He does this by transforming them into another axiom about the plight of mortals which he then cites as an additional ground for complaint (7:17–18). Thus the poet adapts a rich variety of materials, including complaints, hymns, axioms, taunts, and sarcastic pleas, to focus on the intense alienation between Job's understanding of himself as a mortal and the character of God as an oppressive celestial spy. The complaints of Job against his God are distinctive modes of expression which deserve to be analyzed in their own right (cf. Fohrer, *Studien zum Buche Hiob*, 70).

Hymnic materials in praise of God may lie behind passages such as 9:5–10 or 12:13–25, but in the hands of this poet they are reoriented to announce the violent ways of a Creator bent on disrupting his created order and producing chaos in society and nature. These materials no longer serve as a vehicle of praise but rather of blame. Even the hymnic passages cited by Eliphaz (5:9–16) or Elihu (36:26–33) are not employed as expressions of praise but as "proof texts" to substantiate arguments in the dispute with Job. An even more violent adaptation of hymnic materials is found in ch. 10. Here Job alleges that the tender techniques employed by the Creator in forming him as a precious human being (10:8–12) were not motivated by love but by an insidious hidden desire to spy on Job with the hope of finding flaws in his character (10:13–17).

At appropriate points, oaths (27:2), curses (3:2), proverbs (5:2), parables (8:12ff.), traditional sayings (2:4), disputations (ch. 21), and other genres are incorporated into the speeches of the protagonists. In each case these literary forms are pieces of a larger fabric and their distinctive character must be discerned in the light of the governing structure of the literary unit as a whole. Appeal to ancient tradition as a literary form also seems to have been adapted for use in several speeches (8:8ff; 20:4ff., Habel, *ZAW* 88, 1976, 253–272). An ironic adaptation of this appeal to authority is reflected in Job's appeal to the animals (12:7–12).

The adaptation of diverse genres to serve literary and theological ends, raises the vexing question of the genre of the Book of Job as a whole. Terrien recognizes that these diverse genres have been appropriated by the poet but concludes that the book is a festal tragedy, a paracultic drama for the celebration of the New Year festival. Terrien's interpretation recalls the influential work of Horace Kallen, whose reconstruction of Job (*The Book of Job as a Greek Tragedy,* 1918) consisted of four acts in direct imitation of Euripidean theater. Some scholars have argued that, given the theological orientation of the Old Testament, no true tragedy is to be found in its pages (G. Steiner, *The Death of Tragedy,* London: Faber & Faber, 1961, 4–6). B. Kurzweil argues that only when "the Biblical text has ceased to serve as a document of faith and only when the intrinsic truth of the Biblical narrative has ceased to exist for the poet, can he turn it into a subject of tragedy" (in I. Cohen and B. Y. Michali, eds., *Anthology of Hebrew Essays,* Tel Aviv: Massada Publishing Co., 1966, I, 97–116, esp. 111). According to Aristotle's classic interpretation, tragedy involves a plot within which the hero moves from success to disaster (cf. Halperin, *Semitics* 7, 1980, 28–39). This relentless downhill progression is linked with the hero's *hamartia* (sin, error, faulty judgment), a weakness of which he may be ignorant. This weakness leads to a horrible deed (*to deinon*) perpetrated by the hero and the consequent reversal of his fortunes (*peripeteia*). Finally the hero comes to a recognition (*anagnōrisis*) of his true character and experiences deep suffering (*pathos*). Elements of this structure could be identified in the narrative plot of Job. At the very heart of Job, however, the hero defies God to demonstrate that his character is without flaw and his life free from any terrible deed worthy of his deep suffering. If the poet of Job was familiar with tragedy as a paradigm, he has clearly transformed it to underscore the reality that the source of human pathos may lie totally outside the human being. Job's reversal of fortunes [is] due to a divine decree, not a character fault. The hero's retraction at the end of the story is not a confession of sin but an admission of ignorance. Finally, Job's fortunes are restored and he enjoys blessings greater than those he knew before his ordeal.

It is precisely this U-shaped plot which supports the proposal of Whedbee that the Book of Job is serious comedy rather than tragedy (*Semeia* 7, 1977, 1–39). According to Whedbee, the essentials of comedy are, first, "a perception of incongruity that moves in the realms of the ironic, the ludicrous and the ridiculous," and, second, "a basic plot line that leads ultimately to the happiness of the hero and his restoration to a serene and harmonious society." According to this paradigm, Job suffers unwarranted disasters, struggles to encounter God in a lawsuit, and finally comes to terms with God after he appears in person from a whirlwind. The hero's new relationship with God is "employed throughout the work in a deft manner that befits dark comedy rather than the comical. Yet, as Aharoni points out (*Tarbiz* 49, 1979, 1–13), irony, incongruity, and paradox are features which are not confined to comedy. They are also found in tragedy. Moreover, the comic hero has a different nature from that of his tragic counterpart. The former is able to adjust, maneuver, and overcome his plight by cunning, luck, or intrigue. The latter is a man of integrity whose inflexibility and destiny leads to his inevitable downfall.

Rather than compare the Book of Job with classical Greek genres, it seems preferable to ascertain ancient Near Eastern prototypes which clarify the genre of Job as a whole. As we demonstrated earlier, the narrative plot of Job is consistent with the ancient Near Eastern paradigm of the righteous sufferer who *(a)* experiences undeserved suffering; *(b)* complains bitterly to his deity; and *(c)* is heard by his deity and restored to life (Gesé, *Lehre und Wirklichkeit,* 64–65). Both the so-called Sumerian Job text (Kramer, *SVT* 3, 1960, 170–182) and the Babylonian Ludlul Bel Nemeqi (*BWL,* 33–62) have the same skeletal plot structure. The author of the Book of Job, however, has adapted and expanded each component of this plot to highlight the existential complexities and theological paradoxes involved in exploring this plot.

Embedded in the plot is a dispute about the plot and the characters of the plot. Job and the friends debate the cause and nature of Job's unwarranted suffering, the appropriate way to "complain" to God in such a crisis, and the means of gaining God's ear and achieving restoration. This dispute form can be classified as a *Streitgespräch* (controversy dialogue, or disputation). The original life setting for such disputes was probably the exploration of truth at gatherings of the wise. An obvious prototype for this kind of disputation is the dialogue between the sufferer and the friend in the Babylonian Theodicy (*BWL,* 71ff.). The speeches of the sufferer and the friend alternate as they argue about the source, purpose, and nature of the misery experienced by the sufferer.

In the progression of the narrative plot of Job, however, the hero moves from disputing the issue of his innocent suffering to planning a vehicle for vindicating his innocence. Job changes from a disputant to a litigant. His final pronouncements, the speeches of Elihu, and the challenge of Yahweh all assume a forensic context. Consequently the dispute scene between Job and the friends, which is but one of six major scenes in the plot, takes on the character of pretrial proceedings. The legal dimensions of the plot have led scholars such as B. Gemser (*SVT* 3, 1960, 134–135) and J. Stamm (*Jaarbericht . . . Ex Oriente Lux* 9, 1944, 104) to classify the Book of Job as a *rîb*, or court trial. The creative literary work of Job, however, does not conform to any single traditional genre structure. Traditional forms are incorporated, adapted, and transcended through the integration of curses, disputation, lament, trial speeches, wisdom poems, and hymnic materials into an underlying narrative plot. Plot and dialogue interact in a complex structure. Their interaction highlights counterpoint and controversy, ambiguity and audacity in the account of a mortal struggling to discover the meaning of life in the face of tradition, experience, and faith. Perhaps, as our earlier plot analysis suggests, the Book of Job has its closest affinities in genre with the epic history of early Israel (cf. Andersen, *Job*, 36). Yet even classic legend form has been transformed to heighten the underlying conflict of the plot through extended dialogue and major speeches.

Structure and Parallelism

The various genres, traditions, and formulae appropriated by the artist of Job are incorporated into distinctive literary structures and designs. . . . Whether the literary artist was always conscious of the structures created may be a matter of dispute. In some instances the design we have outlined might also be disputed, but in general the structures examined are abundantly clear and evidently constructed by the artist to bring particular themes or ideas into focus.

A common balanced arrangement of larger literary units is the palistrophe (cf. chs. 29; 31). A key line or passage is often located at the pivot point of the typical A-B-C-D-C-B-A palistrophe pattern (cf. 16:9–14). In 19:21–29, for example, the reference to the redeemer (19:25–26a) stands at the pivot point of a thematic palistrophe. In Job 14 the structural arrangement highlights the centrality of the hope motifs at the pivot points (14:3–4 and 13–17) of an otherwise pessimistic passage. In some literary designs the materials reflect a progression of ideas developed sequentially (cf. ch. 28). A striking example of this technique is found in chs. 9–10, where Job begins with an announcement that litigation is futile, considers the odds against pursuing litigation, explores several alternatives, rehearses an imaginary suit against God,but finally closes with another cry of futility.

A frequent structuring device of the author is the *inclusio* or envelope construction, in which a key term, form of speech, image, or motif given at the beginning of a unit is repeated or complemented as a signal of closure at the end of that unit. Within the total framework of the Book of Job, the correspondence between the opening verses (1:1–3) and the closing verses (42:12–17) has long been recognized. What has not been fully appreciated is that 28:28 clearly echoes 1:1 and seems to constitute an *inclusio* which signals a closure at the midpoint of the scenes in the book as a whole. The use of the term *bînā*, "discernment," which introduces the closing vignette (39:26–30) of Yahweh's speech from the whirlwind, recalls the same key term in the opening vignette (38:4–7) and thereby emphasizes its significance for interpreting the speech as a whole. The speech is clearly a challenge to Job's "discernment/wisdom," not to his guilt or integrity. . . .

Each major literary unit reflects a structure designed to integrate the governing themes and functions of the materials incorporated in that unit. The three balanced units of ch. 7 are each introduced by axioms about the human condition and concluded with taunts addressed to God. The very last expression of each taunt refers to emptiness and nonexistence (7:8b, 16b, 21d). . . .

Our discernment of structural patterns is not motivated by a desire to discover symmetry for its own sake. The materials of the text must dictate the structure. A close examination of ch. 3, for example, reveals that the traditional arrangement of the text into three balanced "strophes" (3–10, 11–19, and 20–26; cf. Freedman, *Bib* 49, 1968, 503–508) may be a misleading mechanical division of the text. A detailed examination of the formal and thematic features of the text reveals only two major literary units. The first is a curse (vs. 3–10) grounded in a closing *kî* clause (v. 10), and the second is a complaint characterized by a series of "why" passages and grounded in a double *kî* clause in the closing verses (vs. 24–26).

This example, among many others, illustrates the futility of dividing the poetic passages of Job into stanzas or strophes of relatively equal length based on a common theme or structure. One may point to the series of vignettes on discrete topics so brilliantly presented in Yahweh's first speech (38:4–39:30). Yahweh's second speech, however, breaks the preceding pattern quite deliberately; the treatments of Leviathan and Behemoth are much longer and more convoluted than the preceding vignettes. Accordingly, it seems preferable to avoid terms like "strophe" and "stanza" and employ the neutral term "literary unit," allowing the materials of the text to dictate the size of such units.

Since the programmative work of Bishop Robert Lowth entitled *De Sacra Poesi Hebraeorum* (1753), parallelism has been recognized as a fundamental structuring device of Hebrew poetry. A common parallel structure consists of two lines, the members of the first line corresponding in some sense to the members of the second line. Kugel (*The Idea of Hebrew Poetry*) has demonstrated that the threefold classification of parallelism into synonymous, antithetical, and synthetic is inadequate and restrictive. The numerous patterns of correspondence which can be discerned between verse lines in the poetry of Job are beyond the scope of this limited introduction. It is significant, however, that the antithetical pattern common in Proverbs (e.g., 12:21; 17:22) is relatively rare in the Book of Job. Ambiguous variation rather than direct antithesis of ideas seems to characterize the style of this poet.

By playing with the broad patterns of correspondence in Hebrew poetry, the author of Job creates vehicles of ambiguity, interaction, and equivocation. There is rarely an instance where one line repeats exactly the thought of the preceding line. The subtlety of the poet's art is also apparent even in those verses where both lines appear to correspond closely in thought and form. A good example is found in 1:21:

Naked I came from my mother's womb
And naked I shall return there.

The first pair of members here consists of a repetition of the word "naked," which carries both its literal sense and the implied connotation of "having no possessions." The second pair, "came" and "shall return," are antithetic euphemisms for "birth" and "death" respectively, while the final term, "there," is an ambiguous designation for the grave/earth. This disarmingly simple term "there" pulls the listener up short and forces a reinterpretation of the earlier expression "mother's womb." At first hearing, this expression is taken literally by the listener, but in conjunction with the second line referring to death it must also carry the connotation of Mother Earth. It is precisely this ingenious process of leading the listener/reader back to hear again what has preceded that demonstrates the brilliant way the poet adapts poetic structures to create ambiguity and double entendre. The same process happens, for example, in Job's complaint in ch. 7. It is only in the verses which follow 7:17 that the hidden negative connotation in Job's interpretation of Ps. 8 is disclosed.

A related technique of the poet is the creation of implicit wordplays. Thus 3:8 reads:

Let it be damned by those who curse day,
By those ready to rouse Leviathan.

The traditional parallel for Leviathan is *yām,* "Sea," rather than *yōm,* "day," a word which sounds very similar. The alert Israelite listener would have known this tradition and caught the hidden wordplay in the text. By implication, the cursing of "day" is of the same order as the cursing of "Sea." To emend the text and read "Sea" is to level out the original and lose the subtlety of the text.

Most of the standard formal features of Hebrew poetry are represented in Job. Examples can be cited of traditional word pairs (such as day/night in 3:3, or womb/belly in 3:11); chiasm (5:14; 6:25–26; 20:2–3); double-duty modifiers (as in 3:23, where the idiom "Why does he give light?" is to be supplied from 3:20); assonance (16:12); onomatopoeia (41:10[18E]), repetition (41:15–16 [23–24E]), wordplay (7:2, 6), and similar poetic devices. Another creative technique of the poet is to take a traditional poetic verse and play with the key terms of themes in the subsequent verses. The opening lines of Job's curse in ch. 3 refer to day and night as a standard word pair. In the verses which follow, "that day" and "that night" are signal words to introduce a series of imprecations which play on the polar images of light/darkness and ordered time/chaos. The *kî* clause which grounds the opening verse (v. 3) is only given at the conclusion of the unit (in v. 10). Verses 4–9 intervene as a lyrical elaboration of the opening traditional curse formula, based on the passing of day and night.

Numerous examples of poetic structures and patterns could be explored. Many are discussed at the relevant points in the commentary. The patterns we have discerned demonstrate a freedom and creativity of approach that enables the poet to employ traditional forms and structures to create distinctive designs which emphasize a paradoxical interpretation of reality.

Repetition, Allusion, and Irony

Purposeful repetition as a literary technique is typical of both biblical narrative and poetry. While this technique may have had its origins in oral storytelling and recitation, it has lost its oral roots and been appropriated as a literary vehicle for creating intentional associations and connections between units which may be immediately juxtaposed or separated by extended speeches.

The simplest form of repetition involves the use of the same word or word root in a single line, verse, or literary unit. In 38:27, for example, the same verbal root appears in juxtaposed words to emphasize the arid nature of "the wasted wasteland." The repetition of the term "way" (*derek*) in the opening and closing lines of 38:24–25 highlights the mysterious cosmic structures established to control the movement of lightning and thunderstorm. A word may also be repeated as a key word at several points in a speech. While the theme of the wisdom poem (ch. 28) may be the quest for wisdom, the key word, *māqōm*, "place," focuses on the primordially assigned "home" of all things in the cosmic order, including wisdom herself. The repetition of a term as such may not be as important as the variation in meaning which the same term assumes in another context. In the curse of Job, for example, the term "light" (*'ōr*) appears three times (3:9, 16, 20). In the context of the light/darkness polarity it may mean the light of day (v. 9). In the context of Job's existential struggle it means the "light" of life. Thus the sequence of "hoping for light" (v. 9), "seeing light" (v. 16), and "giving light" (v. 20) is tantamount to a portrayal of the process of "coming to life." In 24:13–17, "light" and "day" are symbols for more than "life." They stand for righteousness and the good; conversely, "darkness" means death and evil.

The repeated use of the verb "see" (*r'y*) in conjunction with a number of synonyms (e.g., *šmr,* "watch," *šwr,* "look at/gaze upon"), highlights the motif of God as the eye who spies on Job to detect his faults. In 7:8 "the Seeing Eye" is an ironic designation for God's eye. He is "the Watcher of Humans" (7:20; cf. 10:14; 13:27; 14:16). It is with biting sarcasm that Job asks God, the eternal eye, whether he has "eyes of flesh" like mortals (10:4). Job's agony is exacerbated by the realization that God, the eye, is forever watching Job, but that he cannot "see" his hidden and elusive foe to confront him with the truth (23:9). At several points Elihu rubs salt into the wounds by reiterating the truth that the "eyes" of God watch the ways of mortals (34:21; 36:7), and that if Job would simply "look at" the heavens and "see" the skies with eyes of faith, he would experience the transcendent presence of

God. Ironically, Job concludes with the victorious claim, "But now my eyes see you" (42:5; cf. 19:27). The creative interplay between the various terms associated with seeing illustrates how the author develops a governing theological motif from a diversity of contending perspectives.

In addition to the patterns of repetition illustrated above, mention should be made of recurring expressions which are sometimes designated formulae. These formulae are interpreted by Urbrock, among others, as evidence of oral antecedents in the Book of Job (*SBL Proceedings* 2, 1972, 459–487) and assume a prior stage of oral performance. Whatever the processes by which these formulae were appropriated by the author and incorporated into the text, they are now an integral part of that text as a literary work of art and they function as vehicles of repetition in that context. The repetition of idioms or scenes is often a signal to watch for subtle variations which focus the distinctive meaning of the passage. In 38:19a and 34a, for example, the verses commence with the common formula "Where is the way . . .?" Yet the same term "light" which is introduced by this formula in both lines has two discrete meanings in context. The first refers to the phenomenon of "light" as opposed to darkness and the second refers to "lightning."

In his opening speech Eliphaz cites the hymnic formula "who does great inscrutable deeds, wonders beyond reckoning" (5:9). Eliphaz, it seems, has extracted this expression from its cultic context and employed it as a proof text to justify his argument about the nature of God. When Job employs the same expression (in 9:10), his interpretation of the formula is sarcastic. God's wondrous deeds are in fact disruptive acts (9:5–9). His inscrutability makes him inaccessible to a suffering mortal like Job (9:11–13). Elihu picks up the same expression and transforms it again to suit his own purposes: the great and wondrous acts of God are revealed from the sky through meteorological marvels (37:5). Job makes a final allusion to these inscrutable "wonders" in his closing speech (42:3b), where he acknowledges a hidden design of the cosmos which is beyond his mortal comprehension. Thus the diverse use of the same expression reflects the dynamic interplay of the speakers and a continuity of language that enables their conflicting interests to surface clearly. . . .

Contrary to the opinion of some scholars, the Book of Job is not a disparate collection of narration and speech materials with relatively little internal cohesion or connection. We have argued above that the underlying narrative plot of Job provides an integrating framework for the book as a whole. To this argument can be added evidence from the author's technique of verbal allusion and motif repetition. The artist's way of integrating materials does not reflect a pedantic, point-for-point correspondence between argument and rebuttal, or between challenge and response. The approach is tangential; verbal associations are made by indirect allusion; and literary connections are often playful. Style corresponds to theology; ambiguity is both a mark not only of the literary design but also of the paradox apparent in the design of the cosmos. Wordplays, puns, double entendre, and verbal irony are part of the author's stock-in-trade. The verbal irony of the language corresponds to the dramatic irony of the plot.

In our preceding discussion of the foreshadowing technique of the author, we highlighted a number of terms, themes, and plot developments found in the prologue which reappear in the subsequent speeches. One of the most significant of these is the motif of the "face" of God, which is developed in chs. 13 and 23. Close literary connections between 1:21 and ch. 3 illustrate the purposeful integration of the prologue and ch. 3. Both the substantive issues and terminology of the prologue are incorporated in subsequent speeches to underscore both thematic continuity and ironic discontinuity between the speeches and their framing narrative.

The theophanic address of Yahweh from the whirlwind is also closely related to the speeches which precede. Yahweh does not fall into the trap of quoting Job's arguments and refuting them seriatim, in the style of a modern debate. Instead he employs the technique of posing a range of impossible challenges which together constitute a unified defense. Job's questions are not answered directly. Rather, Yahweh's defense embraces a series of subtle allusions, innuendos, and ironic references to previous claims and accusations of Job. In every vignette of Yahweh's speech, these tangential connections can be discerned. . . . In some cases the interplay between two passages may be quite extensive, as Elihu's appropriation of Job's terminology in 13:17–28 clearly illustrates. . . . In most cases, however, the allusion is subtle and indirect; a word or image suffices to conjure up the essentials of a preceding speech. . . .

The full force of the literary play and interplay of the various constituent units of the book can only be appreciated when we take into account its ironic dimensions. At least two modes of irony seem to operate in this work as a whole—the dramatic and the verbal. Irony reflects the author's consciousness of the disparity between pretense and reality, between the ideal and the actual, between the role of the *alazōn,* the fool or pretender, and the *eirōn,* the person of integrity who exposes the *alazōn.* Irony plays with incongruities, the gap between the knowledge of the audience and that of the performers, the incongruity between word and action, or the mismatch between what is fitting and what happens. We understand dramatic irony to be concerned with the events of the plot from the omniscient vantage point of the audience. Verbal irony deals with the way various speakers attempt to play the role of *eirōn,* and expose a preceding speaker by using terms, images, or expressions with nuances of meaning which trip that speaker on his or her own words. The exposé, however, may backfire and reveal the would-be *eirōn,* to be an *alazōn* instead (cf. Good, *Irony in the Old Testament;* Robertson, *Soundings* 56, 446–469).

One of the most striking examples, integrating both ironic modes, is the use of "hedge" in 3:23. The audience knows that the Satan has employed this term to describe the blessings with which God has surrounded Job (1:10).

Job, however, uses the word without knowing the connotation it carried in the wager which led to his afflictions at God's hand. For Job the hedge refers to those very disasters and evils which prevent him from discerning the purpose of life. Thus the same term is employed to refer to opposite perceptions of reality, both of which are attributed to God.

Job and the friends repeatedly use verbal irony and sarcasm as a technique for exposing the false perceptions of their opponents. An extended example of this technique is found in ch. 11, where Zophar incorporates a variety of terms from Job's earlier speeches and locates them in a totally different context than Job's original. . . . Job complains that he experiences extreme "misery" whenever he "lies down" (7:4), even though he is free from "deceit" (6:29, 30) and knows the "mind" of God (10:13). Zophar glibly replies that Job can be assured of a life without "misery" and can be free from anguish when he "lies down" if he but turns his "mind" to God and dismisses "deceit" from his tent. Zophar's response is not a rational rebuttal of Job's preceding arguments, but a conditional assurance embracing a variety of veiled allusions which attempt to expose Job's true situation with verbal irony and sarcasm. In other passages the ironic language is more cruel and cutting. From Job's complaint in ch. 7, for example, Eliphaz selects the emotive terms "emptiness" (v. 3), "no return" from Sheol (v. 10), "torment" (v. 11), and "terrify" (v. 14) and incorporates them in his portrayal of the anguish experienced by the wicked (15:22ff.). Elphaz' portrait thereby allows Job's own words to indict him and by allusion prove the point Eliphaz made earlier that "your own mouth condemns you" (15:6). . . .

The verbal irony of the book assumes an even richer dimension when located within the wider framework of the narrative plot and heroic setting discussed above. The decision of the celestial council to afflict Job takes place in camera. Job and his friends are ignorant of the "test" being administered. Yet the audience knows both what Job does not know and the fact that Job does not know. Job was framed. In the course of the speeches which follow Job's affliction, the incongruity of the announced reason for Job's trials and the several alleged reasons offered by Job and his friends for this trial continues to intensify. Allusions back to the death of Job's family (8:4), the fall of his house, and the ugliness of his diseases (7:5) keep alive this disparity between the ostensible narrative portrait of Job's situation and the experiential interpretations by Job and his friends.

The friends are also framed. They are depicted as protagonists of an orthodox stance which the audience knows, from the outset, to be patently false in this particular case. The fate of the friends belies their honest claims and exhortations. They sincerely call on Job to repent and remove "deceit" from his mouth. In the end it is they whose words are found false, for they did not speak the truth about God as Job did (42:7). And Job, the alleged wicked man, is the only intercessor Yahweh will accept to rescue them (42:8–10). This ironic ending comes as a shock, since Job, during his hours of bitter anguish, had portrayed God's dark and alien side. Now, it seems, this characterization is declared true by God himself. Job is revealed as the true *eirōn* by exposing the dark side of God as the beast, the hunter, and the spy.

If Job is the epitome of the *eirōn*, Elihu is the exemplar of the *alazōn*, the fool. He pursues the orthodoxy of the friends to the absurd and attempts to play the role of arbiter in God's place. He attempts to deflate Job but in the process exposes himself as a fool (see Habel, in *In the Shelter of Elyon*). The poet places language and terminology in Elihu's mouth which he ignorantly uses to describe himself but which had previously been employed by Eliphaz to characterize a bombastic fool full of hot air (see on 32:18–22). Elihu presumes to speak the final orthodox word that God is transcendent and does not dirty himself in dialogue with humans.

After Elihu's closure comes Yahweh's shock entrance. Elihu is deflated by the very act of Yahweh speaking to a mortal hero. Yet the pattern of incongruities continues. For the answer of God is a coherent self-defense which neither reveals the hidden facts of the prologue nor deals explicitly with Job's demand for vindication of his innocence. His responses are tangential. Job is left to draw his own [conclusions.]

In the end Job retracts his case, even though he has spoken "the truth" about God. He is right about God but submits to God. The incongruity of the plan of heaven and the interpretation of events on earth obtains to the end of the book. Job, the hero, may be the *eirōn* exposing the traditions and beliefs of the friends, but in the artistic hands of this author reality is also uncovered. The literary techniques of this artist thereby highlight the central theme that life is lived in the gap between heaven and earth, between the ideal and the real.

The Legal Metaphor

Integral to the structure and coherence of the Book of Job is the development of the legal metaphor. As our earlier analysis of the narrative plot suggests, this metaphor is a major literary device which integrates narrative progression and theological motif. The centrality of this metaphor has been highlighted by the recent work of H. Richter (*Studien zu Hiob*); Gemser (*SVT* 3, 1960, 120–137); Scholnick (*Lawsuit Drama*); Frye (*Legal Language*); Roberts (*RQ* 16, 1973, 159–165); and Dick (*CBQ* 41, 1979, 37–50). This research has identified a wide array of technical forensic terms employed by the author at strategic points. Though the use of this metaphor does not require that the genre of Job be classified as a "lawsuit drama," as Scholnick suggests, the metaphor does organize major components of the work in a creative and dramatic way. The major stages in the development of this metaphor in the book as a literary whole are reflected in figure 7.1.

The forensic language and motifs associated with the legal metaphor permeate the speeches of the book, but the preceding sequence reflects the skeletal design of the author in developing this metaphor in the plot and pro-

Fig. 7.1
The Development of the Legal Metaphor in the Book of Job

A. Ironic Anticipation (1:6–11; 2:1–6)
  B. Contemplating Litigation (chs. 9–10)
    C. Challenging the Accuser (ch. 13)
      D. Announcing an Arbiter (16:18–21; 19:21–29)
        E. Testimony of the Accused (chs. 29–30)
        E1. Oath and Challenge by the Accused (ch. 31)
      D1. Verdict of an Arbiter (chs. 32–37)
    C1. Challenging the Accused (38:1ff.; 40:6ff.)
  B1. Retracting Litigation (42:1–6)
A1. Ironic Exculpation (42:7–9)

gression of the book. Literary technique and theological direction move toward a common goal: the question of innocent suffering as exemplified in the case of Job, and the vehicle by which such a case can be judged.

The hero is presented as a champion familiar with the legal procedures of the city gate. He upholds the rights of the underprivileged (29:7–16); handles the legal suits (*rîb*) of strangers (29:16); and guarantees litigation (*mišpāṭ*), even when a member of his own household has a legal complaint (*rîb*) against him (31:13). Ironically, when the case of Job's integrity is presented before the council of heaven (1:6–11), Job is accused *in absentia* by the Satan, the professional accuser of the celestial court (cf. Zech. 3). Yet in the dialogue which follows, the original accuser fades from the scene and God is identified by Job as the accuser and legal adversary.

Job's consideration of litigation as the means of handling his dispute with God seems to have been triggered by a comment of Eliphaz that no mortal can be "righteous/in the right" (*ṣdq*) before God (4:17). Job begins with the same starting point: a mortal cannot possibly win a legal suit against El (9:2). Yet Job explores this apparent impossibility further (see on chs. 9–10). The problems involved in bringing God to trial (*rîb*, 9:30) are legion. He would never answer the charges of mortals (9:3) and would probably not even listen to them (9:16). Mortals are expected to plead for mercy, not bring charges or demand legal proceedings (9:14–15). Then, of course, the overwhelming presence of God in court would intimidate mortals on the stand (9:17, 34). Because God is so powerful, ordinary mortals cannot arraign him or force him to appear in court and submit to a fair legal process (9:19, 32–34). Job nevertheless rehearses the legal complaint (*śîaḥ*, 10:1) which he would present before God in court if he had the chance (ch. 10), commencing with a demand that God identify the "legal case" (*rîb*) he has against Job (10:2), even though he must know that Job is not guilty (*ršʿ*, 10:7).

After first contemplating the difficulties involved in litigation (chs. 9–10), Job announces his plan to argue his case (hiphil of *ykḥ*) with El anyway and handle the various pretrial preliminaries (13:3). He warns his friends that they will be found false witnesses when they are cross-examined by God in court (13:6–12). Job takes his courage into his own hands and announces that he will argue his case (hiphil of *ykḥ*, 13:15) directly to God's "face" (13:13–16). Job claims to have "prepared" (*ʿrk)* his "lawsuit" (*mišpāṭ*) and is ready to face the court (13:18). He then issues a formal challenge to his adversary at law: "Who will contend this suit (*rîb*) with me?" (13:19). In issuing this challenge Job calls for a fair trial in which his divine adversary restrains the intimidating terror of his powerful presence (13:20–21) and presents a bill of particulars specifying the charges against the accused (13:23). To this point Job's guilt has been assumed by the friends; a formal trial would make the charges against Job a matter of public record. Job's shriveled appearance testifies against him (16:8), though no charges have been made. With Job's formal challenge a new catalyst has been introduced into the plot of the narrative.

Job anticipates the appearance of an arbiter (*mōkîaḥ*) to handle his case, even though he at first announces that no such person exists (9:33). He calls on the earth to let his blood cry out against the injustice of his lot until his heavenly witness comes to "arbitrate" (hiphil of *ykḥ*) his case (16:18–22). One day his mediator will rise in court and Job will be vindicated (19:25–27). Job is also frustrated by the fact that he cannot locate God's abode. Job is willing to present his case before God in person if he can but find his elusive adversary (23:2–7). Job closes his dialogue with the friends by taking an oath that he has not perjured himself in any of his speeches and that he has held fast to his integrity to the end. Job is not willing to concede that God is "in the right" (*ṣdq*) and he, Job, is in the wrong (27:2–6).

The turning point in the development of the legal process in Job is the public testimony Job addresses to those assembled (chs. 29–31). For Job that assembly constitutes his court, even though no arbiter has yet arisen and the accuser has so far remained silent. Job testifies to a life of righteousness, an obsession for justice, and a concern for public approbation. His formal oath of innocence is designed to clear job of any guilt relating to the sins enumerated (ch. 31). The climax to Job's testimony is his final challenge with its twofold summons for an arbiter (*šōmēaʿ*) to hear his case and for his adversary at law (*ʾîs rîb*) to appear with a written document making his position public (31:35–37). If neither an arbiter nor Job's adversary appears, Job's oath of innocence stands. He is cleared of all charges and his integrity vindicated.

In response to Job's call for an arbiter, a brash youth called Elihu steps forward and presents his credentials, such as they are (ch. 32). He summons Job to take his stand (hithpael of *yṣb*) and to present his case (*ʿrk*, 33:5). Elihu examines Job's arguments, formally addresses the assembled court in flattering terms (34:2, 10, 34), and presents a verdict in favor of God (chs. 34–37). Central to Elihu's presentation is his claim that it is not for mortals to set a time to come before El in litigation (*mišpāṭ*, 34:23). God is the norm of justice. The very act of a mortal challenging God's justice is evidence of guilt (cf. 34:17; 35:2).

When the divine adversary speaks from the whirlwind he apparently assumes the legal context created by Job and acknowledges Job as "the one with a suit (*rîb*) against Shaddai" and "the one arraigning (hiphil of *ykḥ*) Eloah" (40:2). Thus Yahweh answers Job's legal challenge, even if not in the way Job may have hoped. For Yahweh's defense is a challenge of his own (chs. 38–41). Yahweh ignores the question of whether Job is guilty of specific sins that may have provoked his afflictions and focuses on Job's attempt to undermine God's "justice / just rule" (*mišpāṭ*) in order to prove his own case. Job makes God appear guilty (*rš'*), when the question before the court is Job's innocence (*ṣdq*, 40:8). It is Job, not God, who is on trial. Only if Job could demonstrate his capacity to control the evils of the earth could he presume to challenge God's justice and put him on trial (40:9–14).

In the end the author has Job retract his case (42:1–6). Why? On one level it is presumably because Job's oath of clearance stands undisputed, no sin has been charged against him, and no divine sanction has been directed against him. Job is innocent, even if no formal verdict has yet been passed. On another more profound level, Job's retraction reflects his new understanding of how God operates. He is not bound in his administration of the cosmos by a moral law according to which the wicked are necessarily afflicted and the righteous inevitably blessed. A lawsuit based on the assumption that God operates by this moral law is therefore shown to be futile. God is above any such law and the design of the cosmos reveals this higher order of God's ways. To demand that God conduct a trial based on a law of reward and retribution to which he is not bound is pointless. God's ways reflect a different order of things, which leaves Job without a legal basis for pursuing his case.

Ironically Job receives confirmation that his integrity has been vindicated in God's address to Eliphaz. Job spoke the "truth" about God (42:7–9). Thus Job is cleared and the friends, who tried to defend God, are found to be false witnesses. The legal process is thereby brought to completion. Yet the artist's use of this legal metaphor has an additional implication for interpreting the problem of Job. For while the metaphor provides the vehicle for the hero to challenge and confront God as the apparent administrator of justice in the earth, the answer of God throws into question that same metaphor as a serious vehicle for relating to God. The human tendency to find necessary laws by which to comprehend God's ways or control his favor is revealed to be foolish. Yahweh is bigger than the law or any legal metaphor.

Imagery and Analogy

Imagery and analogy are developed by the author of Job within the broad parameters of a wisdom cosmology. In creating the world, God established an order whose governing principle was wisdom (cf. 28:20–28; Prov. 8). In the primordial design of that cosmic order each component has its fixed locus (*māqōm*) and "way," or mode of operation (*derek*).Through this design all components were organized into an interdependent whole. The order of the natural world could also be expected in the social world. Analogies could be drawn from nature to confirm principles and axioms in the social or moral order of things. To live in harmony with this eternal principle of order was to uphold righteousness in the earth (cf. Schmidt, *Gerechtigkeit als Weltordnung*). Analogies were drawn from nature to confirm principles and axioms in the social and moral order of things, since a consistent ordering principle was assumed in all domains of the cosmos. The use of imagery from nature is therefore more than a poetic device to add color and poignancy to a particular argument (cf. 35:10–11). The social, moral, and natural spheres were believed to interlock and be governed by a common set of principles which have their source in a common Creator.

The principle of moral retribution is substantiated by Eliphaz with the axiom that "those who plough iniquity and sow trouble—they reap it" (4:8). He supports his position by appealing to the fate of lions who perish for lack of prey, apparently because of their evil and ravenous impulses (4:10–11). The Babylonian Theodicy echoes this same principle: "For the crime which the lion committed, the pit awaits him" (*BWL*, 75). Thus the lion becomes a symbol for what is dangerous and evil in the world. A significant feature of the poet of Job, however, is the use of facts and analogies from nature to challenge this very same principle. Job declares that he is the innocent victim and that God pursues him like a lion so that he can demonstrate his prowess as a hunter (10:16). Job is perfectly willing to have the birds, beasts, fish, and earth testify to the truth of God's ways (12:7–8). Living creatures will verify that there is no consistent operation of a moral principle of just retribution in the natural realm, though Job still assumes there ought to be one. The approach of wisdom demands a critical examination of the evidence, for analogy is always ambiguous.The ear tests arguments as the palate tastes food, insists Job (12:11). Ambiguity is evident also in Yahweh's response about the needs of the lion. The lion may be ferocious, but God provides food for the lion according to his providential plan. Yet the food God provides is another innocent victim like Job.

Botanical imagery employed by the artist also demonstrates that one reality can be interpreted from diverse perspectives. "Grass" may be employed as an analogy for flourishing offspring (5:25) or for the miracle of life that God gives to the desert when it rains (38:27). Bildad cites the traditional parable of two plants as evidence that there are two similar categories of humans, those who die quickly as plants die for lack of liquid sustenance, and those who take deep root (8:8ff.). The former are the wicked and the latter are the righteous who find their sustenance in God. According to Job, however, trees are not like mortals. The tree, like the plant with deep roots, may be cut down, but its trunk will sprout again when its roots scent water (14:7–9). The tree may die, but it has an innate hope which enables it to come back to life. Mortals do not have the same hope. They die and never return to life. Later Job himself modifies the analogy of the tree with hope. God, he declares, has uprooted him like a tree and prevented the possibility of hope or life (19:10).

The cloud may represent the ephemeral nature of mortals (7:9) or symbolize the mysteries of the heavens (37:15–16). The endlessly changing clouds are signals of God's master mind at work (37:15–16), the spectacular pavilion of his presence (36:29), his messengers traveling on high (38:34–35), and the principle of wisdom governing the mysterious nature of the sky (38:36–38). Clouds, though they may appear flimsy, have a remarkable capacity for enveloping and containing weighty celestial waters (26:8), and God has his own special cloud as a mask for the glory of his holy throne and his terrifying face (see on 26:9). The same phenomenon of nature, be it plant, cloud, light, thunder, or lion, is subject to diverse interpretations and used as an analogy for differing views of reality. This poetic technique of using nature analogies and symbols to support more than one interpretation or side of an argument seems to be deliberately employed to corroborate the substantive argument that the cosmic order is multivalent and ambiguous. To deduce eternal moral principles on the basis of the natural order, therefore, is foolhardy.

The imagery of Job is also drawn from the mythological domain. Leviathan is summoned as a destructive force from primordial times to negate Job's birth (3:8). Later Leviathan appears as a fire-breathing chaos dragon whom Job is challenged to subdue as God himself once did in bringing order out of chaos (40:25ff. [41:1ff.E]). In a brilliant appropriation of a related chaos symbol, the author has Job ask whether he poses a formidable threat like Sea (*yām*) or Dragon (*tannîn*). According to Job, God was forcibly trying to muzzle his expression of the truth about God's unjust treatment of a mortal (7:12). The poet, who was no doubt familiar with the sea as a symbol of destruction for the enemies of God and Israel, has transformed this image into a personal symbol applied to one emaciated mortal sitting among his potsherds. Symbols and images, whatever their origin, are subject to appropriation, interpretation, and transformation.

Yahweh's majestic answer from the whirlwind draws together images, symbols, and analogies from the preceding speakers into a colorful panorama of natural phenomena. His dominant approach is to explore this diverse array of phenomena by posing challenge questions. The God who comes with the answer poses questions about the order from which the previous disputants drew their conclusions. The edifice called earth, with its deep pillars and cosmic cornerstone, may shake as Job contended, but its construction was a celebrated primordial act (38:4–7). The Sea with which Job saw himself identified as God's enemy was once reduced from a threatening chaos monster to a controllable force like a baby in its playpen (38:8–10). Death, into whose arms Job sought to escape, and Darkness, whom he summoned to reverse his birth, were both assigned their destined places in the cosmic order

(38:16–21). These great acts of God in establishing the earth are the work of God alone. He knows the complexity of its operation. All the symbols of life and death, chaos and order, are subsumed under his cosmic design. He precedes and oversees that design but is not bound by any laws which operate within it, least of all any presumed law of reward and retribution.

The animals portrayed in Yahweh's speech are also figures with symbolic associations deliberately juxtaposed to depict a panorama of opposites and a collage of paradoxes. The terrifying lion is contrasted with the timid ibex (38:39–39:4). The self-sufficient wild ass and the unmanageable wild ox (39:5–12) are beyond human control. Yet the horse, with thunder in its mane and fire in its soul, relishes joining in human wars (39:19–25).The hawk and the eagle are the epitome of innate wisdom (39:26–30), while the ostrich is a perfect example of the opposite (39:13–18). Thus the author combines contrasting symbols to reflect a paradoxical world where the wild and the wonderful, the wise and the foolish, the controlled and the chaotic unite in one cosmic design.

To argue from that paradoxical world to necessary moral laws of operation in human life is foolish. The natural world has its controls and constraints, but any argument from analogy from one case can be countered by analogy from another. God's cosmic design is ambiguous, and God is free to govern it as he wishes. For mortals to prove how God should or would act by observing the ways of nature is to limit God in his eternal goodness and sovereignty. That message of the book is supported by the poet's adaptation of ancient symbols in his portrayal of the primordial design of the cosmos, a portrayal which is itself an artist's interpretation.

An argument from analogy seems to govern the poet's formulation of Yahweh's speeches. If the observable world is characterized by diversity, ambiguity, and possibility, the cosmic design in its grand totality must be even more complex. Potential rather than necessity is the hallmark of cosmic order. To glimpse that reality is to look beyond laws to life, beyond any mechanical codes of operation which might be deduced from patterns in the cosmic order to Wisdom as the primordial principle behind the order. The personification of Wisdom (ch. 28) points to an eternal agent or will rather than a set of uncompromising laws that govern the universe. The metaphor of God discovering and acquiring wisdom emphasizes even further the personal and relational in the *modus operandi* of the world. Through a rich use of imagery and analogy the poet highlights this interpretation of the cosmic design as one characterized by imagination and potential, complexity and constraint. The author of Job is indeed one of the wise and a critic of those who would change wisdom into law.

Message and Meaning

The Book of Job is a brilliant tapestry of literary art and theological dispute. Ambiguous images of the world are interwoven with conflicting perspectives about the world. The quest of the wise to interpret reality, suffering, and the order of things is integrated with a struggle to understand the quest itself and the God who launched them on that quest. The artist combines literary techniques and traditional motifs to sustain theological suspense within a narrative boundary. The question of what will happen is continually bound up with what is right and true. Subtle ironies, blatant sarcasm, ambiguities of language, and complexities of plot all unite to portend a theology of paradox.

Central to the Book of Job is the conflict between God and Job, between the integrity of the Creator and the integrity of a particular mortal. Heaven and earth are at odds again. The conflict is signaled in the opening scenes of the narrative, where the goodness of Job is portrayed in terms so idealistic that they hardly seem believable (1:1–5). Yet such is the character of ancient heroes. Job's integrity is fair game in the arena of living history. The way in which God agrees to test Job's integrity, however, raises serious doubts about God's own integrity. He is apparently vulnerable to incitement by the Satan in his heavenly council. He succumbs to a wager—twice (1:6–12; 2:1–6). He afflicts Job without cause or provocation by Job, and his capacity to rule justly is thrown into question. That question, which is anticipated in the prologue, is probed relentlessly by Job in the subsequent dialogue with his friends. It is a question which assumes a moral order in the world where retributive justice is the norm. The doubts injected by the Satan challenge this principle of retributive justice from another angle (1:9–10). Mortals, he proposes, only worship God out of self-interest; they are righteous because they expect to be rewarded. Their integrity is therefore suspect. God will have to afflict an innocent mortal to prove otherwise.

Job and the friends explore numerous realities of their world, including the ground of knowledge, the nature of the wicked, the human condition, the role of friends, the analogy of nature, the rule of God, and the moral order. Throughout their dialogue, Job is intent on vindicating his own integrity at the expense of his divine antagonist. Job exposes the dark side of God. Job's personal experience as an innocent sufferer gives him a new vision of heaven. God is an enemy, a spy rather than a protector, a hunter rather than a healer, a destroyer rather than a sustainer of the cosmic order (6:4; 9:5–13; 12:13–25; 16:9–14). Job views God as devious, fashioning mortals with an ulterior motive to discover their weaknesses and harass them until they die (10:8–17). To live as a human being on earth is to be oppressed by a ruthless heavenly taskmaster (7:1–8). In the context of the traditional law of retributive justice, God's integrity is clearly in question. He is supposed to bless the righteous, not afflict them. What has been said about his ways in the past and what he does in real life are in conflict. In the cold reality of history, mortals are dehumanized by their celestial overlord. They are prevented from attaining their potential (ch. 7). But the hero of this legend refuses to allow heaven to be exonerated. He assumes the sufferer's right to be angry and "tell it like it is," no matter what the consequences.

The friends and Elihu, in turn, support the integrity of God as an axiomatic truth and challenge the integrity of Job. God, by his very nature and position as cosmic ruler, acts righteously in all things and upholds the principle of distributive justice within the social and natural orders. The eternal law of reward and retribution is guaranteed by his righteous character. In accord with widespread ancient Near Eastern belief, they contend that the just are rewarded and the wicked are punished. But they also endorse the converse of that principle: those who are suffering affliction must be sinners who deserve the suffering. Job's arguments and outbursts about the alien character of God are evidence that Job is deceitful and lacking integrity. His guilt may be hidden but his speech betrays him (15:4–6). Causality in the moral order is guaranteed by God. There is a necessary nexus between sin and affliction. Job's affliction, therefore, must be interpreted as divine punishment and living proof of that axiom. Those who plow iniquity and sow trouble inevitably reap it (4:8).

The problem of how suffering is to be interpreted is reflected in the polarity between the way Job, as an insider, understands his plight and the way outsiders like the friends view the same plight. The insider and the outsider have different views of the world. Their perspectives highlight the conflict between belief and experience, between the consolation offered by tradition and the living despair of a crushed hope. The conflict is intensified throughout the dialogue, not only as a substantive issue, but also by the poet's technique of having each side in the dispute employ innuendo, ironic allusion, and sarcastic comment to undermine its opponent. Each party deliberately reinterprets the text of the opponent and, in the process, tends to misinterpret. The author's quest to interpret suffering becomes a quest to understand interpretation. At various points in the book, suffering is interpreted as punishment for sin (e.g., 4:7–9), the inevitable lot of frail mortals who have an inherent propensity for evil (e.g., 15:14–16), a calculated disciplinary work of God (e.g., 33:15–28; 36:8–15), part of a mysterious divine plan (11:5–11), or a test imposed on a righteous mortal to satisfy a heavenly dispute (1:6–12). These diverse answers leave the wisdom teacher with the even deeper question of the criteria or ground for interpreting suffering and whether, in the end, the book offers a genuine solution to the problem of innocent suffering.

The efforts of the friends to solve Job's problem move from friendly persuasion to vehement indictment. The ground of their claims is a tradition which reaches back to primordial times (8:8; 15:17–19) and is confirmed by personal visions (4:12–16) or careful investigation (5:27). In the light of this tradition, Job's only hope of salvation is to repent of his sins, even if they be secret sins, and turn in humble submission to God. The Creator will then reverse Job's fortunes. A striking feature of the presentation of the friends is the extended portraits of the wicked man who is paraded before Job like a mirror, in which he is supposed to see himself, his mental anguish, and his inevitable fate (e.g., 15:20–35; 18:5–21). The possibility that Job is innocent is never seriously entertained by the friends. His pathetic condition is proof positive of his guilt. The friends demonstrate, in the underlying scheme of the author, the folly of arguing from a limited theological perspective on reality and pursuing that argument to its logical absurdity. The friends take one aspect of reality and make it prescriptive for all reality.

The presence of unwarranted suffering, hardship, and evil in life poses the further question of the purpose of life. Is it not better to follow the advice of Job's wife to "curse God and die" (2:9)? Death seems an inviting world where one is free from the ordeal of living (3:11–19). Why, exclaims Job, should human beings see the light of day if God prevents them from discerning their "way," that is, their direction and purpose in life (3:23)? Though Job does not plan suicide, he prefers death to an endless life of oppression at the hands of an arbitrary God (7:11–16). The crisis of Job is not only the problem of unjustified suffering but also the question of meaning in life when there is no future, no justice, no relief, and no purpose he can discern. He is completely separated and alienated from God and his community. The hero stands alone in his misery (19:6–20). Every avenue of hope he explores proves illusory. Trees have a greater hope than mortals. Trees may be felled and die, but they have an inner resource which enables them to come back to life again (14:7–10). Mortals, in spite of their fantasies (14:13–17), descend to Sheol and their hope dies with them (14:18–19; 17:11–16). Yet death, with all its terrors, is ultimately more appealing than suffering through life with no goal or hope. Job, however, refuses to commit suicide. His very alienation from God provokes him to act. The vindication of his integrity gives him the reason to keep struggling with God, no matter what the consequences. He does not turn to God in penitence or submission, but in righteous indignation.

Job, however, is not content with indulging his anger, berating his friends in typical disputational style, protesting his innocence, bewailing his miserable mortal condition, or exposing the wanton cruelty of his celestial foe. Nor will he tolerate the course of action demanded by the friends. Instead, he explores a bold alternative for resolving the conflict between himself and God. He contemplates and plans litigation, a court hearing in which both parties can be heard without fear of intimidation or false witness (see discussion under "The Legal Metaphor," above). Job begins rather tentatively with his planned lawsuit but progressively takes his life in his hands and eventually challenges his adversary at law to appear in court with an appropriate writ (31:35–37). Repeatedly Job turns from disputing with the friends to confront God with the truth and the option of litigation.

Job explores the possibility of various legal arbiters or celestial mediators who could handle his case and assure him of a fair trial (9:31–35; 16:18–21; 19:23–27). He is convinced that, were his case brought before an impartial court, be it before or after his death, he would be totally vindicated. He maintains his integrity to the bitter end. Under oath he vows he is free of perjury or deceit (27:2–6). This oath foreshadows Job's climactic oath of clearance in his concluding speech (ch. 31). After closing the dialogue with the friends, Job addresses an assembled community as if it were a court in session (chs. 29–31). In that setting Job challenges God by taking an oath of clearance. By that terrible act he takes his life in his hands. If he is guilty, God ought to strike him with sudden disasters, many of which Job describes in horrible detail. In the belief system of that ancient world, a righteous God would be bound by the oath to respond. If God did not react with the appropriate calamities, the surviving mortal would be cleared of guilt. In the design of the author, provoking God into action is presented as a right and an option for the audience to contemplate.

The conflict thereby assumes new proportions. In the very act of calling the bluff of his divine antagonist, Job appears to overstep the bounds of humble faith and assume a posture of Promethean arrogance. His obsession with his righteousness borders on hubris and self-righteousness. Yet for Job the vindication of his integrity is the one thing left in life; he is ready to defy God rather than deny his integrity! In this he is a true hero. He not only takes an oath of clearance but summons God to appear in court and state his case unequivocally (ch. 31). Job wants the unthinkable—to see God face to face. The "face" of God and the "seeing" of God are two motifs which highlight the exalted level of Job's anticipated confrontation with God (13:15–16, 20, 24; 23:4; 19:26–27; 42:5). Job challenges the ancient tradition that the invisible God is too holy for the eyes of wise and righteous mortals to behold. Job summons God to emerge from his celestial corner and show himself for what he really is.

Elihu's intervention delays the final showdown between Job and his opponent but heightens the improbability that such a showdown could ever take place. Elihu presumes to play the part of the impartial arbiter whom Job had earlier sought to handle his case. According to Elihu, God is truly transcendent and above the petty demands of a mortal obsessed with gaining a glimpse of his face (chs. 34–35; cf. 35:14). Job's demand for God to present his legal case in person is ludicrous. God does not appear in court at an hour set by self-serving earthly litigants (34:23). He is a distant ruler of the heavens who leaves evidence of his character and will among the intrusive phenomena of one's personal life and the meteorological activities of the sky (chs. 33 and 36–37). God has left all the clues necessary to understand his nature; it is simply a matter of interpreting them correctly. A young man with an insightful spirit, claims Elihu, is as likely to have the answer as old men steeped in traditional wisdom. Once again the author throws open the question of the criteria by which the cosmic order and its Creator are to be interpreted.

Contrary to Elihu's reasonable expectations, Yahweh makes a shock appearance in a whirlwind. The transcendent adversary steps out from behind the veil of his invisible holiness and manifests himself to Job. The hero has provoked his God to appear in person. Perhaps no prophet had arisen in Israel like Moses, "whom the Lord knew face to face" (Deut. 34:10), but the author is signaling that the experience of Moses was anticipated by a great non-Israelite hero. Job's faith in himself is vindicated. He sees God and survives! Yahweh's personal appearance is the first stage in the resolution of the conflict between Job and his God. Job's innocence is affirmed. None of the sanctions given in Job's oath of clearance are imposed. Yahweh's appearance, however, is accompanied by a lengthy divine speech which is apparently designed to resolve the issues raised in the conflict but which, at first reading, appears to complicate the question even further.

The one who challenged God is himself challenged. The opening divine challenge, however, is not directed specifically toward Job's integrity or the problem of innocent suffering, but toward Job's level of discernment about the design of the cosmos (38:2). Job's innocence is not in question but his understanding of God's ways is deficient. It is God's integrity as the designer of the cosmos which is at stake. The challenge questions addressed to Job about the various components of the cosmic design point to the Creator as the only one who could comprehend its primordial complexity and rich ambiguity. Its intricate design incorporates structural, functional, and celebrative aspects. The structural aspect highlights internal laws governing the cosmos, the functional points to God's containment of evil and his providential care, and the celebrative emphasizes the paradoxical, incongruous, and festive features of this design. They lead Job back to the primordial fundamentals involved in the construction and control of the cosmos.

How does Yahweh's speech answer Job's problem about the justice of his case or the suffering of the innocent? It depicts a world ruled by the freedom of God within the constraints of his cosmic design. That design has the sun rising on the evil and on the good, and the rain falling on desert as well as arable land. Natural laws govern the cosmic order. But these natural laws are not governed by a higher law of reward and retribution which is applied mechanically each dawn. The natural order is amoral (cf. Tsevat, *HUCA* 37, 1966, 72–106). The wicked may be restrained, because the dawn arrives and deprives them of the darkness where they hide, but the darkness is not eliminated and the wicked are not struck down by the sun each morning (38:12–15). The food for the lion and the kill for the raven are innocent creatures who no more deserve to die than any others. God cares for and controls the cosmos within the laws he has established in creation. One cannot deduce from these laws that the wicked will inevitably be punished or the innocent be immune from suffering. There is no eternal principle of natural justice inherent in the natural order. The operations of the cosmos are controlled within certain broad parameters and constraints. The mechanical operation of a moral causality is not a necessary feature of that order, even though mortals like Job's friends may seek to substantiate a universal principle of retributive justice by appealing to the natural order.

Yahweh's second challenge to the hero is focused precisely on this question. Does a righteous ruler intervene in the routine operation of things to abase all the proud and crush all the wicked on earth? Should divine retribution be automatic, immediate, and obvious? If Job has the capacity to achieve this kind of direct retribution equitably, Yahweh will concede Job's superiority in the debate (40:7–14). There is, however, another basic question which Job must first consider: "Would you prove me wrong so that you may be in the right?" (40:8). Does Job need to negate God's integrity to uphold his own? Only if Job assumes that God is bound to run the world on the basis of the principle of justice articulated in the law of moral causality and epitomized by the traditional doctrine of reward and retribution. If in his governance of the cosmos God is not bound by that principle but by an integrity of his own, then the ground for a court case, where the operation of this principle is assumed, has been removed.

God admits there is evil and chaos in the world. He does not annihilate it but contains it within certain boundaries, just as he contained Leviathan and Behemoth (chs. 40–41), the great primordial chaos monsters. The forces of chaos are harnessed and the threatening sea confined like a baby to its playpen (38:8–11). The universe is a paradoxical world where the regular and the unexpected, the good and the bad, the successful and the sufferer coexist. The eagle may soar freely by innate wisdom, while the foolish ostrich needs continuous attention (39:13–18, 26–27). Death and life are intricately united in a cycle of growth and decay, pleasure and pain. The innocent do suffer unjustly in a cosmic order where natural laws and structures operate without repeated divine interruption. Those who do good and act righteously are not necessarily rewarded in this world either by direct divine compensation or by the necessary operation of inherent natural laws. That answer brings the audience back to the opening prologue where Job is afflicted in spite of his goodness. Thus the principle of retributive justice as a mechanical law of the cosmos is repudiated in three contexts—by the message of the prologue, by the experience of Job, and by the answer of God.

Job's personal experience of God through whirlwind and word leads him to retract his legal suit. Since the design of the cosmos is not bound by the law of retributive justice, there is no point in proceeding. Job affirms God's integrity by acknowledging that he did not understand the structure of God's cosmic design or the powerful freedom operating within that design (42:2–6). Job learns the truth about God's paradoxical ways without ever learning about the wager which forced him to undergo his ordeal. God is indeed the "source" of the evil that Job suffered (2:10), just as he is the Creator who controls chaos. Job's integrity is also intact. He did not succumb to the pressure of friends, accede to their interpretation of God's way, and repent. Job's presentation of the dark side of God is acknowledged as a more honest expression of the truth than the traditional formulations of justice promoted by the friends (42:7). Accordingly, Yahweh announces that the lives of the friends are in jeopardy, because they have not spoken the "truth" as Job has done. In a backhanded way, Yahweh's words to Eliphaz vindicate Job's integrity publicly and concede that Job had exposed the "truth" about God's treatment of humans like Job. The ironic circle is complete: Job was afflicted without cause and subsequently acclaimed for demonstrating that God may act in just that way.

Finally the hero who defied God to defend his own integrity is honored as the one intercessor who can confront God on behalf of his disgraced friends. Job had repeatedly explored the need for mediation between an afflicted human and God. It is the allotted role of a friend, according to Job, to show loyalty (*ḥesed*) to a despairing person who has forsaken the fear of Shaddai (6:14). A friend comforts and sustains another even if it means taking sides against God (cf. Habel, *Int* 31, 1977, 227–236). Job denounces his three friends because they have betrayed him by defending God in the interests of their orthodox teaching and at the expense of Job's spiritual need. They added "trouble/misery" (*ʿāmāl*) to Job's life rather than alleviating it (see on 16:2). Job also looked for a celestial advocate, a friend before Eloah, who would arbitrate a lawsuit on Job's behalf (16:18–21). When God and a mortal are locked in combat, the mortal needs a mediator (cf. 9:32–35), though the services of the holy ones above are generally not available (5:1). Job even reaches a point where he envisages the appearance of a figure who is more than an arbiter. He foresees a redeemer who will rise in court to vindicate Job before God, even if Job is already dead. The redeemer will act as kin, friend, and defender against God (19:23–27). Elihu claims he can act as the arbiter for Job's case, but instead of defending Job he defends God. He suggests that an angel might perhaps act as an intermediary for Job, if Job were bent on repentance (chs. 32–33). In the end it is Job, the man in search of a mediator, who becomes a mediator and friend. His heroic encounter with God made him the only person fit to intercede for the lives of the three friends (42:7–9). Job is declared the one intercessor who can move God to intervene, just as he did when he provoked God to appear in the whirlwind. Since God is not bound by the law of retributive justice, he may set aside judgment on the friends if Job acts on their behalf. God is not a remote ruler of the heavens, but a personal deity accessible to the bold human mediator.

Just as the deliverance of the friends was an act of grace mediated by Job, so the restoration of Job's family and goods was a gesture of divine goodness, not a reward for Job's integrity or heroic persistence. God freely chooses to bless Job with good, just as he chose to afflict him with evil. Job experienced the freedom of God by being afflicted even though innocent and by being blessed even after defying God and accusing him of being demonic. The integrity of Job and God is confirmed, but integrity has taken on a new meaning that transcends conformity to a mechanistic moral or natural law of reward and retribution.

The traditional hero returns from his exploits with a boon for others to share. In the context of a wisdom writing, we might expect that Job's boon is the gift of wisdom. But is wisdom the gain and goal of Job's experience? It is significant that the author of the Book of Job never has any of the human participants actually designate himself "wise," though each in turn lays claim to an authoritative source of knowledge and accuses his opponent of claiming to have wisdom (cf. 15:2–20; 26:3). The quest for wisdom as distinct from knowledge is the central theme of the author's poem on wisdom (ch. 28). Wisdom is not portrayed as an attribute of God, but personified as a figure whom God discovered and acquired in the process of creating the cosmos. Wisdom is that primordial principle or design which governs the ordering of the cosmos. Primordial Wisdom is inaccesible to mortals (28:12–15; cf. 11:7–9; 26:14). By speaking without full knowledge of the cosmic order, Job was obfuscating the primordial principle and design of the cosmos (38:2). Job lacked "discernment" (*bînâ*, 38:4) of the primordial "way" of God. The cosmos has an apportioned "place" (*māqōm*) and "way" (*derek*) for all things. Rules and structures govern the cosmic order. Beyond these rules and structures, however, lies the principle of Wisdom. Wisdom is apparently God's own "way" (Prov. 8:22; Job 26:14). Wisdom, however, is depicted not as an eternal law established by God but as a figure with whom he has a personal relationship. The force and freedom of God's personal relationship with wisdom lies behind the cosmic design. What Job discovers is not primordial wisdom, but the reality of God in a direct personal relationship and an honest confrontation. God is known through the passionate questioning of Job rather than through the complacent submission of the friends; through the ambiguity of life rather than through his adherence to a moral law. God may establish a personal relationship with mortals on earth as he once did with Wisdom in the primordial (cf. Habel, *CTM* 10, 1983, 142–154).

The message of Job, then, is bound up with the interplay of tradition and experience, the search for moral laws and the discovery of a cosmic design with laws which are not in themselves the guarantors of moral order; the right of the sufferer to be angry with God and the need of outsiders to interpret that suffering; the dilemma of a hidden transcendent deity and the living experience of his holiness; the unexpected dark side of God and his elusive sovereign goodness; the paradox of an ambiguous reality called life and the search for meaning in the face of death; the inaccesibility of primordial wisdom and the eternal quest for understanding the mysteries of the cosmos; the laughing Leviathan silenced by God's might; and the comical ostrich in need of God's personal care. Job finally understood that "the Lord gives and the Lord takes away" (1:21), but not in the manner many mortals may wish, expect, or understand. For Job experienced God and his paradoxical ways as an insider. The design of God frees Job from a mechanical, blind submission to a moral law of retributive justice. God creates the space in his order for the freedom of humans and the freedom of God, for the integrity of mortals and the integrity of God, for the angry complaints of those in agony and the challenge of God in whirlwind or whisper. Job discovers his God and in so doing finds his own "place" (*māqōm*) and "way" (*derek*), a "way" once hidden from him by God himself (3:23). Job, like God, comes to transcend the moral order by his innocent suffering.

8

The Shape and Argument of the Book of Job

David J. A. Clines

Shape

We cannot begin to comprehend the Book of Job piecemeal, beginning at the first verse or opening of the book at random. What we need to do, with this book more than many others, is to start by identifying and becoming familiar with its shape.

The shape of a book, as of anything, is not an intrinsic property of the object itself, but a design in the mind of the observer. Without any arbitrariness, different readers of the book may discern different shapes in it, esteeming and highlighting this part or that part in varying degrees. Even the one

From David J. A. Clines, *Job 1–20,* Word Biblical Commentary (Waco: Word, 1989), xxxiv–xlvii. Used by permission of Word Books.

reader may see more than one way of grasping the overall shape of the work. Here are three ways of seeing shape in the Book of Job.

Framework and Core

We may distinguish between the *framework* of the book and its *core* or *center*, using the image of a painting surrounded by a frame. The book itself suggests this view of its shape through its use of *prose* and *poetry*. The *framework* of the book is *prose*, the *core* is *poetry*; and since the framework is naive (or so it seems) and the core is sophisticated, the distinction between the relatively cheap and unimportant frame of a painting and the painting itself sounds a convincing analogy. We can also distinguish framework from core by noticing that the *framework* of Job is *narrative* and the *core* is *didactic poetry*. The book as a whole is thus both a *narrative* and an *argument*, or, perhaps more precise, an *argument* set within the context of a *narrative*. We may represent it diagrammatically as follows:

1:1–2:13	Framework:	prose	narrative
3:1–42:6	Core:	poetry	argument
42:7–17	Framework:	prose	narrative

Exposition, Complication, Resolution

A somewhat different shape emerges if we pay more close attention to the narrative thread that runs throughout the book. The analysis of shape given above, though valid in general, ignored the fact that there is a certain amount of prose narrative within the poetry, and it paid little attention to the *content* of the narrative. If we now emphasize the narrative elements, noting especially the marks of closure embedded in the narrative, we may discern an alternative structure.

The narrative of the Book of Job begins with God afflicting Job in order to discover whether Job's piety depends only upon his prosperity; will Job still loyally worship God if God deprives Job of all his possessions? By 2:10 we find that Job is unshakable in his piety. "In all this, Job did not sin with his lips," says the narrator. So, to all appearances, the story is over; no further development of the plot is required by the story, and we have reached a point of closure.

The narrative continues, nevertheless. We soon learn that Job *feels* more than he has *said*, and we soon find him "curs[ing] the day of his birth" (3:1). This more aggressive behavior of Job will continue for many chapters,with Job demanding that God cease his unreasonable treatment of him. Thereafter Job challenges God to a lawsuit, that is, to justify his actions legally. When he has finally delivered his challenge, and his oath that he is innocent of any cause for which God could be punishing him, we reach a second point of closure, the narrator's sentence. "The words of Job are ended" (31:40).

In the third segment of the book, a fourth friend, Elihu, lectures Job in speeches to which Job has no opportunity to reply before a dramatic turn is taken in the narrative: God himself responds to Job—not by answering Job's challenge, but by issuing a challenge of his own to Job. What right has Job to dictate how the universe should be run? Job admits in the end that he has no right to question God's actions, and he withdraws his case against God (42:3). God shows he is free either to afflict or to bless by showering Job with wealth and extending his life. The final point of closure comes with Job's death, "an old man, and full of days" (42:17).

These three segments of the book, which we have identified from the story line and from the marks of closure, may now be analyzed as the three basic elements that are to be found in every story: exposition, complication, resolution. In the *exposition* the scene is set, the characters are introduced, and all the necessary conditions for the plot are established. In the *complication*, the characters encounter difficulties or dangers, and tensions emerge that excite the reader's curiosity as to how they can possibly be resolved. The *resolution* portrays how the narrative problem posed by the story is solved.

The three segments are further distinguished from one another by another device of the narrative: new characters are introduced at the beginnings of each of the segments. In the first it is Job (1:1–3); in the second it is the three friends who come to commiserate with Job (2:11–13); in the third it is the fourth friend Elihu, who is angered by the speeches of the other friends (32:1–5), and more especially God himself, who enters the scene in 38:1.

The shape of the book from these perspectives can now be displayed diagrammatically:

1:1–2:10	God afflicts Job	exposition	new character: Job
2:11–31:40	Job challenges God	complication	new characters: 3 friends
32:1–42:17	God challenges Job	resolution	new characters: Elihu, God

Prologue, Dialogue, Epilogue

Yet another way of viewing the shape of the book follows the indications given by the book itself about the speakers. The whole book may be seen as a series of *speeches,* the *narrator* speaking in prologue and epilogue, and the *characters* in the dialogue. Thus:

I. Prologue (1:1–2:13)
  Narrator
II. Dialogue (3:1–42:6)
  1. Job and the three friends, First Cycle
    Job (3:1–26)
      Eliphaz (4:1–5:27)

Job (6:1–7:21)
    Bildad (8:1–22)
Job (9:1–10:22)
    Zophar (11:1–20)

2. Job and the three friends, Second Cycle
   Job (12:1–14:22)
       Eliphaz (15:1–35)
   Job (16:1–17:16)
       Bildad (18:1–21)
   Job (19:1–29)
       Zophar (20:1–29)
3. Job and the three friends, Third Cycle
   Job (21:1–34)
       Eliphaz (22:1–30)
   Job (23:1–24:25)
       Bildad (25:1–6)
   Job (26:1–14)
   Job (27:1–28:28)
   Job (29:1–31:40)
4. Elihu
   Elihu (32:1–33:33)
   Elihu (34:1–37)
   Elihu (35:1–16)
   Elihu (36:1–37:24)
5. Yahweh and Job
   Yahweh (38:1–40:2)
       Job (40:3–5)
   Yahweh (40:6–41:34)
       Job (42:1–6)

III. Epilogue (42:7–17)
     Narrator

This analysis alerts us to different realities in the book. First, the narrator's words enclose those of all the characters, at first predisposing the reader to certain views of how all of the speakers in the dialogue are to be heard, and at the end leaving the narrator's perspective uppermost in the reader's mind. Second, it is Job who for the most part initiates conversation; he speaks and the friends reply to him. Indeed, after Bildad's third speech the friends do not speak again, but Job speaks three times without any intervention by them, as if they have faltered and he has gained new energy. Elihu speaks four times, without receiving any reply from Job, as if Job is no longer listening; is he waiting for someone else to speak? When Yahweh speaks, it is he and not Job who takes the initiative; though Job has summoned Yahweh to speak,

Yahweh's speeches are less a reply than a new approach. Third, all the speaking moves toward silence: Job, who has done most of the talking, in the end lays his hand on his mouth (40:4–5); the friends run out of steam and do not even finish the third cycle of speeches. The question has to be raised: what has all this talk achieved? Is the real resolution to the problem of the book a verbal one at all, or is it perhaps only a resolution when Yahweh too stops speaking and actually does something about Job's suffering by "restor[ing] Job's condition" (42:10)?

Argument

We have distinguished between the narrative of the framework of Job and the argument of the poetry that forms the core of the book. But this distinction is not wholly valid. For we have been able to speak of the narrative of the book as a whole, that is, of a narrative that does not only *frame* the book, but which runs *through* it. And we can now speak of the argument not just of the *speeches* in which the characters are obviously arguing with one another, but of *the book as a whole,* narrative and speeches included.

What is "the argument" of the book? It is the view the book takes of the principal issue it is addressing. We may either suppose, with most readers of the Book of Job, that the major question in it is the problem of suffering. Or we may suggest that the chief issue is the problem of the moral order of the world, of the principles on which it is governed. Each of these issues will provide us with a different perspective from which to consider the book.

The Problem of Suffering

To understand the book well, it is first of all important to know what exactly *is* the problem of suffering according to the book.

Many think that the essential question about suffering is, *Why* suffering? That is to say, What is its origin and cause, or, more personally, Why has this suffering happened to me? These are serious questions, but the Book of Job gives no satisfactory answer to them. It is true that this question about the origin or cause of suffering is ventilated in the book, and partial answers to it are given by the friends. They say that suffering comes about sometimes as punishment for sins, sometimes as a warning against committing sin in the future, and sometimes, as in Job's case, for no earthly reason at all, but for some inscrutable divine reason. In the end, however, readers cannot discover from the book any one clear view about what the reason for their own particular suffering may be, nor any statement about the reason for human suffering in general; for the book is entirely about the suffering of one particular and unique individual.

A second problem about suffering is whether there is such a thing as *innocent* suffering. The intellectual background of the book is obviously one in which cut-and-dried theologies of guilt and punishment have prevailed; for all the friends of Job, in their different ways, insist that if Job is suffering he must in some way be deserving of his suffering. It is still today a natural human tendency to ask, when one is suffering, What have I done to deserve this? The Book of Job, while of course it does not deny the possibility that sometimes suffering is richly deserved by the sufferer, speaks out clearly against the idea that such is always the case. Job is an innocent sufferer, whose innocence is not only asserted by himself (6:30; 9:15), but is attested to by the narrator (1:1), and above all by God (1:8; 2:3; 42:7–8). Nevertheless, even this question about the possibility of innocent suffering and the answer to it given by the book are not the primary issue in the book's concern with suffering.

The third, and essential, problem of suffering in the Book of Job may be said to be a more existential one, namely: In what way am I supposed to suffer? Or, What am I to do when I am suffering? To such questions the book gives two different but complementary answers. The first is expressed in the opening two chapters. Here Job's reaction to the disasters that come upon him is a calm acceptance of the will of God; he can bless God not only for what he has given but also for what he has taken away (1:21; 2:10). Sufferers who can identify with Job's acceptance of his suffering, neither ignoring the reality of suffering by escaping into the past, nor so preoccupied with present grief as to ignore past blessing, are fortunate indeed. The patient Job of the prologue is a model for sufferers. But Job does not remain in that attitude of acceptance. Once we move into his poetic speeches, from chap. 3 onward, we encounter a mind in turmoil, a sense of bitterness and anger, of isolation from God and even persecution by God. Job makes no attempt to suppress his hostility toward God for what has happened to him; he insists that he will "speak in the anguish of [his] spirit" and "complain in the bitterness of [his] soul" (7:11). What makes this protesting Job a model for other sufferers is that he directs himself constantly toward God, whom he regards as the one who is responsible, both immediately and ultimately, for his suffering. It is only because Job insists on response from God that God enters into dialogue with Job. Even though Job's intellectual questions about the justice of his suffering are never adequately answered, he himself in the end is satisfied, as a sufferer, by his encounter with God.

Viewed as an answer to the problem of suffering, then, the argument of the Book of Job is: By all means let Job the patient be your model so long as that is possible for you; but when equanimity fails, let the grief and anger of Job the impatient direct itself and yourself toward God, for only in encounter with him will the tension of suffering be resolved.

The Moral Order of the World

Another way of stating the argument of the book is to see it as addressing the question whether there is any moral order in the world; that is to say, whether there is any rule whereby goodness is rewarded and wickedness is punished. The belief that there is an exact correspondence between one's behavior and one's destiny is known as the doctrine of retribution. In one form or another it is shared by most human beings, not just religious people, since it is the foundation of most people's childhood upbringing: certain behavior will earn you rewards, while certain other behavior will bring pain or disaster. There is indeed a mismatch between this principle, which we seem to require in some form or other for the world to have coherence, and the realities that contradict the principle; and to this mismatch both the narrator and the characters of the Book of Job turn their attention. Each of them has a distinctive standpoint on this question of retribution or the moral order.

Narrator. The narrator in fact founds the whole story upon the doctrine of retribution. Job, the wealthiest of all orientals, is equally the most pious; there is no coincidence here, the narrator means to say. "That man was blameless and upright, fearing God and turning away from evil" (1:1)—that is deed. And here is consequence: "And there were born to him seven sons and three daughters [the perfect family], and he had 7,000 sheep, 3,000 camels," and so on (1:2). Here in the first two sentences of the book we find spelled out the doctrine of retribution, wearing its more acceptable face: piety brings prosperity. Into that prosperity there then breaks on one day the most terrible of calamities: Job loses all he has—which is not only his children and his wealth, but worse than that, his social significance, and, worse still, his reputation as a righteous man. For the other, and more unlovely, side of this principle of world order is that suffering is caused by sin.

Up to this moment Job himself has believed in retribution, but now, unshakably convinced that he has done nothing to deserve his misery, he is launched on a quest for another moral order. The doctrine has failed the test of reality—reality, that is, as he experiences it. Job's three friends, too, find their dogma challenged by Job's experience, for they have always taken Job at face value, as a pious man. After all, he is a conspicuous testimony to the validity of the dogma: his exceptional piety has brought about his exceptional wealth, has it not? It does not take them long, however, to decide against Job and in favor of the dogma, though they each restate it differently.

What the friends have in common is their unquestioning belief that suffering is the result of sin. Their doctrine of retribution, that sin produces punishment, is also reversible: see a man suffering and you can be sure he has deserved it. There is no doubt in their minds of the order: Job's misery is by the book. But there is room for difference of opinion over what precisely Job's sufferings signify.

Eliphaz. Eliphaz, the first friend, starts from the assumption that the innocent never suffer permanently: "What innocent man ever perished, where were the upright ever annihilated?" (4:7). For him Job is essentially one of the innocent, so whatever Job has done must be comparatively trivial, and so too his suffering is bound to be soon over:

> Is not your piety your source of confidence?
> Does not your blameless life give you hope? (4:6)

he asks. Job is blameless on the whole, pious in general. Eliphaz's search for order leads him to nuance in this way the concept of innocence; that is how he can explain the mismatch between theory and experience. Even the most innocent of humans, like Job, must expect to suffer deservedly on occasion.

Bildad. The second friend, Bildad, is if anything even more convinced of the doctrine of retribution, for he has just now seen a compelling exemplification of it. Job's children have died, cut off in their prime; it is the classical picture of the fate of the wicked:

> Your sons sinned against him,
> so he has abandoned them to the power of their guilt. (8:4)

The very fact that Job still lives is proof that he is no gross sinner, like his children. However serious his suffering, it is not as bad as it might be; therefore his sin is not as serious as he may fear.

Zophar. Now whereas Eliphaz has set Job's suffering in the context of his whole life (his suffering is just a temporary pinprick), and Bildad has set it in the context of the fate of his family (the children are dead, Job is not), Zophar, the third friend, perceives no such context for Job's pain. The fact is, he would say, that Job is suffering, and suffering is inevitably the product of sin. To contextualize Job's suffering and try to set it in proportion is ultimately to trivialize it. Zophar is for principle rather than proportion; the bottom line is that Job is a sinner suffering hard at this moment for his sin.

Since Job refuses to acknowledge his sin, claiming,

> My doctrine is pure,
> I am clean in your sight, [O God]. (11:4)

it follows that he is a secret sinner. In fact, if only the truth were known, it would no doubt transpire that Job is a worse sinner than anyone suspects:

> If only God would speak,
> if only he would open his lips to you,
> if only he would tell you the secrets of his wisdom . . .
> you would know that God exacts of you
> less than your guilt deserves. (11:5–6)

For all his talk about divine secrets, "higher than heaven—what can you do? deeper than Sheol—what can you know?" (11:8), Zophar holds a theology of the essential knowability of God. God's wisdom is not of a different kind from human wisdom; it only means that he knows more about humankind than anyone realizes, and that means more about their sins. Where there is suffering but no visible reason, we can be sure, says Zophar, that God's wisdom holds the reason. What is more, it will not be some mysterious, ineffable, transcendental reason, but a reason that could easily be comprehended by a human being "if only God would open his lips." So while we cannot always be sure why God is punishing people, we can be sure that when they are suffering he is punishing them for some reason or another, never without cause or gratuitously.

Zophar has in addition a more distinctive contribution to make: it concerns the role of God's mercy in the outworking of the principle of retribution. Job might be tempted to think that even though there is doubtless no escape from the working of the law of retribution, perhaps he could appeal for mercy to soften its blows. But what you must know, says Zophar, is that "God has already overlooked part of your sin" (11:6). Any mercy that God is going to allow to temper justice has already been taken into account when the law of retribution comes into play. Discounts for mercy's sake are included in the price you pay.

Elihu. Another participant in the dialogue enters only after the first three friends have completed all they have to say. Elihu, the young man, at first "timid and afraid to declare [his] opinion" (32:6), in the end intervenes, realizing that "it is not the old that are wise" but rather "it is the spirit in a man, the breath of the Almighty, that makes him understand" (32:8–9). His point about retribution is that it is not some balancing mechanism in the universe that operates ruthlessly and inescapably, but rather is a channel by which God speaks to humans. Suffering is not so much a mystery; it is more a revelation.

Sometimes, for example, God speaks in visions of the night, in terrifying nightmares, to warn people against committing sins they are contemplating. At other times, a person may be

> chastened with pain upon his bed
> and with continual strife in his bones. (33:19)

like Job. The purpose of such suffering is not retribution, but to lead to confession by the sinner, one's restoration by God, and one's public praise of God (33:27). The other friends, and Job, have been narrow-minded in their view of retribution as a tit-for-tat process. Look to its design, says Elihu, and you will find that it is an instrument of divine communication.

For these four theologians, the retribution principle stands unshaken by Job's experience. Eliphaz has allowed a redefinition of "innocent" to mean "well, hardly ever wicked," Bildad has stressed that the law of retribution has a certain sensitivity (if you are not extremely wicked, you don't actually die), while Zophar has declared that the principle of retribution is not at all a rigorous quid pro quo, for a percentage of the punishment that should light upon you has already been deducted for mercy's sake. Even Elihu, while recognizing that there are more important theological truths than strict retribution, still affirms its validity.

Job. By contrast with the friends' singleminded and static positions, Job's mind is confused, flexible, and experimental. In every one of his eleven speeches he adopts a different posture, psychologically and theologically. In the end he admits that he has nothing to rely upon, not even God—nothing except his conviction of his own innocence.

His first religious instinct is to accept what has happened to him as God's doing, and to bless God even for calamity: "Yahweh has given, and Yahweh has taken away; blessed by Yahweh's name" (1:21; cf. 2:10). But his second thoughts are more reflective and theological, because he realizes that order has collapsed about him. When in chap. 3 he wishes he had never been born, it is not mainly because he is suffering from his physical illness and from the grief of bereavement; he is expressing a psychic reaction to disorder. Since it is too late now to strike his birthdate out of the calendar—which is the first thought that occurs to him (3:6)—in his second speech he cries out for God to kill him and so put an end to his disorientation:

> O that it would please God to crush me,
> that he would let loose his hand and cut me off! (6:8)

When nothing makes sense any longer, and especially when the most fundamental moral order of all—the principle of retribution—is subverted, and disproportion reigns, there is nothing to live for:

> Am I the sea, or a sea-monster? . . .
> I loathe my life, I would live no longer. (7:12, 16)

Even so, to have nothing to live for, and to live without order, does not mean for Job that he can have no desire. In his third speech he openly desires what he lacks: a declaration that he is innocent. It is a desire impossible of fulfillment, but it is his desire all the same.

> How can a man be declared innocent by God?
> If one took him to court [to prove one's innocence]
> one could not answer one in a thousand of his questions. (9:2–3)

The problem with God is not just that he is superwise and superpowerful (9:19); it is rather that he is by settled design hostile to his creation. As Job puts it, sardonically: "Being God, he never withdraws his anger" (9:13). The ancient myths were right, thinks Job, when they recounted that the first thing God ever did was to create the world by slaying the chaos monster, in a primeval act of aggression (9:13). Not only toward creation at large but toward Job in particular God's attitude has been, since Job's conception, one of perpetual hostility and cruelty, masked indeed by an apparent tender concern:

> Your hands fashioned and made me;
> and now you turn about to destroy me. (9:8)

It is hopeless to seek vindication, he says; so he will not do it. But in the very act of saying to God, "It is hopeless to ask you for what I deserve," Job is in reality demanding what he believes he is entitled to.

Something has happened to Job in expressing his hopelessness. For in his next speech (chaps. 12–14) he has moved to a decision: nevertheless, I will present my case to God.

> No doubt he will slay me; I have no hope;
> yet I will defend my ways to his face. (13:15)

His decision is more startling than that, however. He cannot *defend* himself against the pain which God is inflicting on him; he can only defend himself *verbally*. But since God is not *saying* anything, Job can only defend himself verbally by creating a scenario where both he and God are obliged to speak, each in his own defense. In short, Job summons God to a lawsuit! He challenges God to give an account of himself—to explain what Job has done wrong to deserve such suffering. But of course since Job believes he has done nothing wrong, implicitly he challenges God to confess that he and not Job is the criminal.

This is a case that must be heard promptly, for Job does not believe he can have much longer to live, considering how God is buffeting him. If Job's name is not cleared now it never will be, and certainly not in any afterlife.

> For a tree there is hope,
> that if it is cut down it will sprout again,
> that its fresh shoots will not fail.
> Though its root grows old in the ground
> and its stump begins to die in the dust,
> yet at the scent of water it may bud
> and put forth shoots like a plant new[ly] set.
>
> But a man, when he dies, loses every power;
> he breathes his last, and where is he then?
> Like the water that has gone from a vanished lake,
> like a stream that has shrunk and dried up,
> Man lies down and will not rise again,
> till the heavens are no more he will not awake,
> nor be roused out of his sleep. (14:7–12)

What is now certain, in all the uncertainty that surrounds him, is that his word of challenge to God has been uttered—and cannot be unsaid. It is written into the heavenly record, and stands as his witness to himself in heaven. It is his own assertion of his innocence that he is referring to when he says in his fifth speech (chap. 16–17):

> Even now, my witness is in heaven,
> my advocate is on high.

> It is my cry that is my spokesman;
> sleeplessly I wait for God's reply. (16:19–20)

And it is the same affirmation of innocence that in his sixth speech (chap. 19) he speaks of as his "advocate":

> I know that my advocate lives. (19:25)

He has in mind here no heavenly figure who will defend his cause before God, since there is none—and least of all God himself, who has proved to be nothing but his enemy. He is compelled to undertake his own defense, and leave his own affidavit to speak in his behalf.

The climax to Job's defense of his own innocence and his demand upon God that he explain for what reason he has been tormenting Job comes in the last of Job's speeches (chaps. 29–31). Here Job reviews his past life in a final attempt to discover whether there can be any cause in himself for the suffering he has been enduring. Whatever area of his life he considers, he can judge himself blameless. He brings his speeches to a conclusion with a mighty oath affirming his righteousness. Still working within the metaphorical scenario of the lawsuit, he imagines himself signing a declaration:

> Here is my signature [to my oath of exculpation];
> let the Almighty answer me!
> Oh, that I had the bill of indictment written by my adversary! (31:35)

So brief would any bill of charges against Job be, and so trivial would be the faults that could be leveled against him, that Job would be proud for all the world to see how little he had offended against God and how greatly he had fulfilled the ideal of human piety:

> Surely I would carry [the indictment] on my shoulder;
> I would bind it on me as a crown.
> I would give him an account of all my steps.
> Like a prince I would approach him! (31:36–37)

Job's impressive and convincing protestation of innocence poses a desperate problem for the moral order of the universe, however. For if Job is innocent, the doctrine of retribution is false. And there is no other principle available to replace it.

God. Only God can address the problem. He is compelled, by Job's metaphor of the lawsuit and by the logic of the author's narrative, to enter the conversation. But what divine word can both defend Job's innocence—to which God committed himself in chap. 1—and at the same time affirm the working of a moral law in the world?

In reality, God's speeches (chaps. 38–41) are remarkable as much for what they omit as for what they contain. There is, in the first place, not a word of the retributive principle here. This must mean that it is not so fundamental to understanding the world as all the previous characters of the book have thought. But it must also mean that it is not entirely wrong, either. If God were passionately in favor of it or violently against it, would he not have had to mention it?

In the second place, the divine speeches are notorious for their insistence on asking questions rather than giving answers, quite apart from the seeming irrelevance of the questions themselves to the fundamental issues of the book.

> Where were you when I laid the foundation of the earth? . . .
> Have you entered into the springs of the sea? . . .
> Do you know when the mountain goats bring forth? . . .
> Is it by your wisdom that the hawk soars? (38:4, 16; 39:1, 26)

Those—and suchlike excursions into cosmology and natural history—are, amazingly enough, the substance of the divine speeches. The purpose of God's parade of unknown and unknowable features of the natural world can hardly be to browbeat Job with dazzling displays of his power and intelligence—for Job has not for a minute doubted that God is wise and strong, too wise and strong indeed for human comfort and for his own good. Rather, God invites Job to reconsider the mystery and complexity—and the often sheer unfathomableness—of the world that God has created.

God's questions to Job are arranged in three distinct sequences. First there is the series that focus on Job's nonparticipation in creation, such as: "Who shut the sea with doors?" (38:8). These mean that Job is not qualified to hold views on the nature of the universe. Second, there is the series on the management of the world, among which we find:

> Have you ever in your life ordered the morning forth? . . .
> Can you bind the chains of the Pleiades
> or loose the cords of Orion? (38:12, 31)

Job has never organized the appearance of a new day; how can he speak then about the governance of the universe? Third, there is the sequence of questions about the animals, lion and raven, goat and hind, wild ass, ostrich, warhorse, hawk and eagle. Through these questions Job's gaze is deliberately fastened upon animals that serve no purpose in the human economy but are, instead, useless to humans, their habits mysterious to us. In these chapters there is no mention of those domesticated animals, sheep, ass and camel, that Job possessed in abundance and knew the ways of. The subject here is wild animals, the purpose of whose existence is unintelligible to humans. By the end of the second divine speech (40:7–41:34) the focus has come to rest upon two animals, Behemoth and Leviathan, hippopotamus and crocodile, symbols of primeval chaos, who of all the animal creation are supremely wild and terrible.

The point must be that hippopotamus and crocodile, however alarming, are part of God's creation. God expects Job to realize, and Job is not slow at grasping the point, that the natural order—the principles on which the world was created—is analogous to the moral order—the principles according to which it is governed. In both these orders, there is much that is incomprehensible to humans, even threatening their existence, but all of it is the work of a wise God who has made the world the way it is for his own inscrutable purposes. Innocent suffering is a hippopotamus. The only sense it makes, it makes to God, for it is not amenable to human rationality.

Job has no right to an explanation for his suffering, any more than he has a right to have the purpose of crocodiles explained to him. He is not even entitled to be told whether he is being punished for some fault he has committed, or whether he is indeed the innocent sufferer he believes himself to be. The order of creation sets the standard for the moral order of the universe; and that is, that God must be allowed to know what he is doing, and lies under no obligation to give any account of himself.

What does this viewpoint expressed by the character God do to the doctrine of retribution? It neither affirms nor denies it; but it marginalizes it. In Job's case, at least, the doctrine of retribution is beside the point. We, the readers, have known from the beginning of the book that Job is innocent, for the narrator and God have both affirmed it (1:1, 8; 2:3); Job himself, though suffering as if he were a wicked man, is unshakably convinced of his innocence. We and Job, therefore, know that the doctrine of retribution is not wholly true. But God never tells Job that he accepts Job's innocence; so Job never learns what God's view of the doctrine is. All that Job learns from God is that retribution is not the issue, but whether God can be trusted to run his world.

Job capitulates. His religious instinct for reverence which prompted his initial acceptance of his misfortune (1:21; 2:10) had become overwhelmed by his more intellectual and theological search for meaning. But now his religion and his theology are suddenly able to cohere. He replies to God:

> "Who is this that darkens the [divine] design by words
>   without knowledge?" [so you have rightly said, Yahweh].
> You are right: I misspoke myself, I was beyond my limits. . . .
> I had heard of you by the hearing of the ear
>   but now my eye sees you. . . . (42:3, 5)

Which means to say: I knew you, but did not know you; what I knew of your workings (through the principle of retribution) was real knowledge, but it was not the whole truth about you. The whole truth is that you are ultimately unknowable, and your reasons are in the last analysis incomprehensible.

> Therefore I melt in reverence before you,
> and I have received my comfort,
>   even while sitting in dust and ashes. (42:6)

Religiously, Job finds this position acceptable, even actually comforting: to bow in awe before a mysterious God he cannot grasp, perceiving only the "outskirts of his ways" (26:14). This is the Job of the prologue, but with a difference: the religious instinct is now supported by a theological realignment. Now he not only feels, but also has come to believe, that it makes sense that God should not be wholly amenable to human reason. It was the theology of wild animals that convinced him, the inexplicability of whole tracts of the natural order, the apparent meaninglessness of creatures useless to humankind but unquestionably created by God nevertheless. Now he knows that was a paradigm for all knowledge of God.

Narrator. The book does not conclude at this point, however. The narrator has yet to tell us of the reversal of Job's fortunes. There is more to this happy ending of the book than at first appears, for the issues of the moral governance of the world and the doctrine of retribution are still on the agenda. What this concluding episode does for these issues is, surprisingly, to reinstate the dogma of retribution as the principle according to which the world operates. For the story shows at its end that the righteous man Job is also the most prosperous, just as he was at the beginning. Job is here described as the "servant" of the Lord, who has spoken of God "what is right," unlike the friends (42:7–8), and when he has prayed for forgiveness of the friends' "folly" he is rewarded with twice the possessions he had at first (42:10).

It must be admitted that the ending of the book undercuts to some extent the divine speeches of chaps. 38–41. For although the Lord has implied that questions of justice and retribution are not the central ones, the narrator's concluding word is that after all the principle of retribution stands almost unscathed by the experience of Job. By rights, according to the principle, the innocent Job should never have suffered at all; so the principle was partially defective. Yet in the end the principle becomes enshrined in the history of Job, and he functions as a prime witness to its general validity. Even if in every instance it does not explain human fates, in the main it is affirmed by the Book of Job as the truth about the moral universe.

9

A Fresh Reading of the Book of Job

Philip Yancey

A Misreading

If you had asked me when I began my study what the Book of Job was about, I would have been quick to respond. *Job? Everybody knows what Job is about. It's the Bible's most complete treatment of the problem of suffering. It's about terrible grief and bewildering pain.* Without doubt the bulk of the book does center on the theme of suffering. Chapters 3–37 contain no action to speak of, just the opinionated dialogues of five prickly men—Job, his three friends, and the enigmatic Elihu—concerning the problem of pain. They are all trying to account for the slings and arrows of outrageous fortune that have fallen upon poor Job, who sits forlorn in the ashes of what used to be his mansion.

I now believe I misread the book—or, more accurately, didn't take into

From Philip Yancey, *Disappointment with God: Questions Nobody Asks Aloud* (Grand Rapids: Zondervan, 1988), 162–74. Used by permission of Zondervan Publishing House.

account the entire book. Despite the fact that all but a few pages of Job deal with the problem of pain, I am coming to the conclusion that Job is not really about the problem of pain. Suffering contributes the ingredients of the story, not its central theme. Just as a cake is not about eggs, flour, milk, and shortening, but uses those ingredients in the process of creating a cake, Job is not "about" suffering; it merely uses such ingredients in its larger story, which concerns even more important questions, cosmic questions. Seen as a whole, Job is primarily about *faith* in its starkest form.

I am drawn to this conclusion mainly because of the introductory "plot" in chapters 1 and 2, which reveals that Job's personal drama on earth had its origin in a cosmic drama in heaven. I once regarded Job as a profound expression of human disappointment—something on the order of Meg Woodson's letter [in which she wrote about her daughter's death from cystic fibrosis at age twenty-three], only longer and more detailed, and with direct biblical sanction. As I studied the book further, however, I discovered that it does not really present the human viewpoint. God is the central character in the Bible, and nowhere does this come through more clearly than in the book of Job. I realized that I had always read it from the perspective of chapter 3 on—in other words, from Job's perspective.

Let me explain.

It helps to think of the Book of Job as a mystery play, a "whodunit" detective story. Before the play itself begins, we in the audience get a sneak preview, as if we have showed up early for a press conference in which the director explains his work (chapters 1–2). He relates the plot and describes the main characters, then tells us in advance who did what in the play, and why. In fact, he solves every mystery in the play except one: how will the main character respond? Will Job trust God or deny him?

Later, when the curtain rises, we see only the actors on stage. Confined within the play, they have no knowledge of what the director has told us in the sneak preview. We know the answer to the "whodunit" questions, but the star detective, Job, does not. He spends all his time on stage trying to discover what we already know. He scratches himself with shards of pottery and asks, "Why me? What did I do wrong? What is God trying to tell me?"

To the audience, Job's questions should be mere intellectual exercises, for we learned the answers in the prologue, the first two chapters. What did Job do wrong? Nothing. He represents the very best of the species. Didn't God himself call Job "blameless and upright, a man who fears God and shuns evil"? Why, then, is Job suffering? Not for punishment. Far from it—he has been selected as the principal player in a great contest of the heavens.

The Wager

In retrospect, I sometimes wonder how I could have misread the Book of Job so badly. Part of the reason, I think, lies in the eloquence of chapters

3–37, which express the human dilemma with such power that we can get trapped in their force field, forgetting that the questions they raise have already been answered in chapters 1 and 2. But there is yet another reason: no one knows quite what to make of the first two chapters. Even biblical scholars tend to view the prologue with embarrassment, or discount it as the addition of a later editor. The prologue shows God and Satan involved in—and you can almost see blush marks on the commentary pages—something resembling a wager. All Job's trauma traces back to, well, a kind of bet, placed by the two cosmic powers.

The trouble starts with Satan's claim that Job is a spoiled favorite, loyal only because God has "put a hedge around him." Satan scoffs that God, unworthy of love in himself, only attracts people like Job because they're "bribed" to follow him. If times ever get tough, Satan charges, such people will quickly abandon God. When God accepts the challenge to test Satan's theory, thus consenting to let Job's response settle the issue, the calamities begin to rain down on poor, unsuspecting Job.

I would certainly not deny the strangeness of this heavenly contest. On the other hand, I cannot sidestep the account of The Wager in Job, for it offers a rare peek through the keyhole of eternity. When people experience pain, questions spill out—the very questions that tormented Job. Why me? What's going on? Does God care? Is there a God? This one time, in the raw recounting of Job's travail, we the onlookers—not Job—are granted a view behind the curtain. What we long for, the prologue to Job provides: a glimpse into how the world is run. As nowhere else in the Bible, the Book of Job shows us God's point of view, including the supernatural activity normally hidden from us.

Job has put God on trial, accusing him of unfair acts against an innocent party. Angry, satirical, betrayed, Job wanders as close to blasphemy as he can get—just to the edge. His words have a startlingly familiar ring because they are so modern. He gives voice to our most deeply felt complaints against God. But chapters 1 and 2 prove that, regardless of what Job thinks, God is not on trial in this book. Job is on trial. The point of the book is not suffering: Where is God when it hurts? The prologue dealt with that issue. The point is faith: Where is Job when it hurts? How is he responding? To understand the Book of Job, I must begin there.

> *To believe in the supernatural is not simply to believe that after living a successful, material, and fairly virtuous life here one will continue to exist in the best-possible substitute for this world, or that after living a starved and stunted life here one will be compensated with all the good things one has gone without: it is to believe that the supernatural is the greatest reality here and now.*
>
> —*T. S. Eliot*

A Role in the Cosmos

> *Some say that to the gods we are like flies that boys idly swat on a summer day. Others say that not a feather from a sparrow falls to the ground without the will of the Heavenly Father.*
>
> —*Thornton Wilder, The Bridge of San Luis Rey*

To my friend Richard, who wrote a book about Job, that ancient man seemed a larger-than-life hero who had dared arm wrestle with God Almighty. Once, after listening to Richard expound on the valor of Job, I brought up the account of The Wager. Anger rose in his face. "All I can say," he snapped, "is that Job paid one [terrible] price just to make God feel good!"

I, too, found it hard to avoid such sentiments at first. There is no easy way around the difficulty, for the heavenly contest played itself out in Job's life in the form of marauders, firestorms, windstorms, and boils. How can God's winning a contest, *any* contest, be worth such a price? As C. G. Jung asked in his caustic book on Job, "Is it worth the lion's while to terrify the mouse?"

As I studied Job further, however, I saw that I had been harboring the wrong image of what took place. Yes, there was an arm wrestling match, but not between Job and God. Rather, *Satan* and God were the chief combatants, although—most significantly—God had designated the man Job as his stand-in. The first and last chapters make clear that Job was unknowingly performing in a cosmic showdown before spectators in the unseen world.

Disturbing the Universe

The strange scene of The Wager reminded me of a few other places where the Bible affords a brief glimpse behind the curtain. Consider, for example, Revelation 12, which depicts an even more bizarre contest: a pregnant woman, wearing the sun for a dress and twelve stars for a crown, opposes a red dragon so enormous he can dislodge a third of the stars from the sky with one sweep of his tail. The dragon lies in wait, seeking to devour the pregnant woman's child at birth. And there's more: a flight into the desert, a serpent who tries to drown the woman, and a fierce war in heaven.

Biblical commentators propose as many interpretations of the details in Revelation 12 as there are commentaries, but almost all agree that the weird images point to the great disruption in the universe caused by Jesus' birth in Bethlehem. In a sense, Revelation 12 presents another side of Christmas, adding a new set of holographic images to the familiar scenes of manger and shepherds and the slaughter of the innocents. Which is the "true" story of Christmas: Luke's pastoral version or Revelation's account of the cosmos at war? They are the same story, of course; only the level of viewing differs. Luke gives the view from earth and Revelation shades in details from the unseen world.

The two worlds come together vividly in three of Jesus' most famous stories, the parables of the lost sheep, the lost coin, and the lost son. All three make the same point: great joy breaks out in heaven when a sinner repents. Today, anyone can watch a sinner repenting, for televised Billy Graham crusades portray the scene live and in color. The camera follows a young woman as she makes her way through the stands to an area set aside for repentance and conversion. But Jesus' stories imply that far more may be going on out there: beyond that stadium scene, in a place concealed from all camera lenses, a great party has erupted, a gigantic celebration in the unseen world.

Belief in an unseen world forms a crucial dividing line of faith today. Many people get up, eat, drive their cars, work, make phone calls, tend to their children, and go to bed without giving a single thought to the existence of an unseen world. But according to the Bible, human history is far more than the rising and falling of people and nations; it is a staging ground for the battle of the universe. Hence what seems like an "ordinary" action in the seen world may have an extraordinary effect on the unseen world: a short-term mission assignment causes Satan to fall like lightning from heaven (Luke 10); a sinner's repentance sets off celestial celebration (Luke 15); a baby's birth disturbs the entire universe (Revelation 12). Much of that effect, however, remains hidden from our view—except for the occasional glimpses granted us in places like Revelation, and in Job.

An ordinary person in the seen world, Job was called upon to endure a trial with cosmic consequences. He had no glimmer of light to guide him, no hint that the unseen world cared about him, or even existed. Yet like a laboratory test animal, he was handpicked to settle one of the most urgent issues of humanity and to determine a small piece of the history of the universe.

Is it absurd to believe that one human being, a tiny dot on a tiny planet, can make a difference in the history of the universe? It certainly seemed so to Job's friends. Listen to Elihu, the last of Job's comforters:

> If you sin, how does that affect him [God]?
> If your sins are many, what does that do to him?
> If you are righteous, what do you give to him,
> or what does he receive from your hand?
> Your wickedness affects only a man like yourself,
> and your righteousness only the sons of men. [35:6–8 *Phillips*]

Elihu, however, was flat wrong. The opening and closing chapters of Job prove that God was greatly affected by the response of one man and that cosmic issues were at stake. (Later in a message to the prophet Ezekiel, God would point with pride to Job—along with Daniel and Noah—as one of his three favorites.)

Job's example, drawn in sharp relief, shows how life on earth affects the universe. When I began my study, I tended to avoid the "embarrassing" scene in chapter 1, but I have since come to believe that, whether drama or history, The Wager offers a message of great hope to all of us—perhaps the most powerful and enduring lesson from Job. In the end, The Wager resolved decisively that the faith of a single human being counts for very much indeed. Job affirms that our response to testing *matters*. The history of mankind—and, in fact, my own individual history of faith—is enclosed within the great drama of the history of the universe.

God has granted us "the dignity of causation," said Pascal. We may doubt, with Elihu, whether one person can make any appreciable difference. But the Bible rustles with hints that something like The Wager is played out in other believers as well. We are God's Exhibit A, his demonstration piece to the powers in the unseen world. The apostle Paul, borrowing an image from the processional of gladiators into the Colosseum, pictured himself on public display: "We have been made a spectacle to the whole universe, to angels as well as to men" (1 Cor. 4:9 *Phillips*). And in the same letter he commented, in an astonishing aside, "Do you not know that we will judge angels?" (1 Cor. 6:3 *Phillips*).

We humans inhabit a mere speck of a planet in the outer suburbs of a spiral galaxy that is only one of about a million million such galaxies in the observable universe, but the New Testament insists that what happens among us here will, in fact, help determine the future of that universe. Paul is emphatic: "The whole creation is on tiptoe to see that the wonderful sight of the sons of God coming into their own" (Rom. 8:19 *Phillips*). Natural creation, "groaning" in travail and decay, can only be set free by the transformation of human beings.

The Great Reversal

In the Christian view, all of human history takes place somewhere between the first part of Genesis and the last part of Revelation, which paint the same scene, with the same brush strokes: Paradise, a river, the luminous glory of God, and the Tree of Life. History begins and ends at the same place, and everything in between comprises the struggle to regain what was lost.[1]

After [humanity's] fall from Paradise, history entered a new phase. Creation God had done by himself, starting with nothing and ending up with the universe in all its splendor. The new work is Re-creation, and for this God employs the very human beings who had originally spoiled his work. Creation progressed through stages: first stars, then the sky and sea, and on through plants and animals, and finally man and woman. Re-creation reverses the

1. John MacQuarrie discusses our ultimate destiny in this passage from *The Humility of God:* "If the doctrine of original sin is not to have the last word, it must be confronted with a doctrine of original righteousness. After all, in the Old Testament story righteousness is more original than sin."

sequence, starting with man and woman and culminating in the restoration of all the rest.

In many ways the act of Re-creation is "harder" than creation, for it relies on flawed human beings. Surely, it has cost God more: the death of his Son. Still, God insists on healing the world from the bottom up, rather than from the top down.

As I studied Job, it struck me that The Wager was, at its heart, a stark reenactment of God's original question in creation: Will the humans choose for or against me? From God's point of view that has been the central question of history, beginning with Adam and continuing on through Job and every man and woman who has ever lived. The Wager in the Book of Job called into question the whole human experiment.

Satan denied that human beings are truly free. We have freedom to descend, of course—Adam and all his descendants proved that. But freedom to ascend, to believe God for no other reason than, well . . . for no reason at all? Can a person believe even when God appears to him as an enemy? Or is faith one more product of environment and circumstance? The opening chapters of Job expose Satan as the first great behaviorist: Job was *conditioned* to love God, he implied. Take away the rewards, and watch his faith crumble. The Wager put Satan's theory to the test.

I have come to see Job's trials as a crucial test of human freedom, an important issue in modern items as well. In our century, it takes faith to believe that a human being amounts to more than a combination of DNA programming, instincts of the gene pool, cultural conditioning, and the impersonal forces of history. Yet even in this behaviorist century, we want to believe differently. We want to believe that the thousand hard and easy choices we make each day somehow count. And the Book of Job insists that they do; one person's faith can make a difference. There is a role for human beings, after all, and by fulfilling that role Job set a pattern for anyone who ever faces doubt or hardship.

Very often, disappointment with God begins in Job-like circumstances. The death of a child, a tragic accident, or a loss of job may bring on the same questions Job asked. Why me? What does God have against me? Why does he seem so distant? As reader's of Job's story, we can see behind the curtain to a contest being waged in the invisible world. But in our own trials, we will not have such insight. When tragedy strikes, we will live in shadow, unaware of what is transpiring in the unseen world. The drama that Job lived through will then replicate itself in our individual lives. Once again, God will let his reputation ride on the response of unpredictable human beings.

For Job, the battleground of faith involved lost possessions, lost family members, lost health. We may face a different struggle: a career failure, a floundering marriage, sexual orientation, a body shape that turns people off, not on. At such times the outer circumstances—the illness, the bank account, the run of bad luck—will seem the real struggle. We may beg God to change those circumstances. *If only I were beautiful or handsome, then everything would work out. If only I had more money—or at least a job—then I could easily believe God.*

But the more important battle, as shown in Job, takes place inside us. Will we trust God? Job teaches that at the moment when faith is hardest and *least* likely, then faith is most needed. His struggle presents a glimpse of what the Bible elsewhere spells out in detail: the remarkable truth that our choices matter, not just to us and our own destiny but, amazingly, to God himself and the universe he rules.

In short, God has granted to ordinary men and women the dignity of participating in the Great Reversal which will restore the cosmos to its pristine state. All the reasons for disappointment with God . . . as well as all cancers, all deaths, all broken relationships, all the collected groanings of our savage planet—all these imperfections will be wiped away. We may at times question God's wisdom and lose patience with his timetable. (The disciples, after all, felt bitter disappointment when Jesus rejected their dream of a physical kingdom in favor of an invisible, spiritual kingdom.) But all the prophets' lavish promises will someday come true, and we, you and I, are the ones selected to help bring that about.

No one has expressed the pain and unfairness of this world more poignantly than Job; no one has voiced disappointment with God more passionately. We must still attend to Job's complaints and to God's fierce response. But the Book of Job begins not with the complaints—the human viewpoint—but with God's point of view. In the prologue, the scene of The Wager establishes a darkly shining truth: Job—and you and I—can join the struggle to reverse all that is wrong with the universe. We can make a difference.

The Book of Job gives no satisfying answers to the question "Why?" Instead, it substitutes another question, "To what end?" By remaining faithful to God through his trials Job, crotchety, sardonic old Job, helped abolish the very pain and unfairness of this world that he had protested so vigorously. And Meg Woodson, who stubbornly clings to God's love in the shadows, even after watching two children die . . . she too is helping to reverse those wrongs.

Why the delay? Why does God let evil and pain so flagrantly exist, even thrive, on this planet? Why does he let us do slowly and blunderingly what he could do in an eyeblink?

He holds back for our sakes. Re-creation involves us; we are, in fact, at the center of his plan. The Wager, the motive behind all human history, is to develop us, not God. Our very existence announces to the powers in the universe that restoration is under way. Every act of faith by every one of the people of God is like the tolling of a bell, and a faith like Job's reverberates throughout the universe.

Our present life feels *like a real fight—as if there were something really wild in the universe which we, with all our idealities and faithfulnesses, are needed to redeem.*

—William James, The Will to Believe

I had far rather walk, as I do, in daily terror of eternity, than feel that this was only a children's game in which all the contestants would get equally worthless prizes in the end.

—T. S. Eliot

10

The Doctrine of God in the Book of Job

R. Laird Harris

A few years ago, there was a man of the East—the eastern United States, that is—named Archibald MacLeish. And he wrote a rather famous play called *J.B.*, taking his theme from that ancient man for a distant eastern country, Job. The play was in no sense a commentary on Job, and it gave a radically different treatment of the problems of the relation of God, man and evil. But at least we may say that MacLeish's choice of his title underlines the perennial fascination of the Book of Job, even to those who may not agree with its teaching and conclusions. It is in every respect a great book. It deals with some of the deepest problems of man and directs us to the existence of a sovereign God for their solution. It treats these problems not in a doctrinaire fashion, but wrestles with them and gives us answers to proclaim to a

From R. Laird Harris, "The Book of Job and Its Doctrine of God," *Grace Journal* 13 (Fall 1972): 3–33. Used by permission of Grace Theological Seminary.

troubled age, to a generation that recognizes the antinomies of life, but cannot find a meaningful solution for them. We hope in these studies to see how the ancient godly philosopher and prophet explores deeply the basic questions of life and offers to the man of faith answers far wiser than much which passes for wisdom today. But first to turn to some technical questions.

The Date of Job

Probably the most common view of the date of Job in conservative circles has been that the book is very old. For example, the Scofield Reference Bible points to the patriarchal period. The Jewish tradition enshrined in the Talmud (Baba Bathra 14b) says Moses was its author. This Jewish tradition is quite late. The Talmud was not codified until the 5th century A.D., and our manuscripts of it come from a still later period. The tradition may have some value however. It may not be that the data on authorship was correctly remembered by the Jews, but that they came to the conclusion of early authorship from various factors that we too can observe.

That there was an ancient worthy by the name of Job is sure from Ezekiel 14:14, 20, which mentions him along with Noah and Daniel. The reference is similar to that in Jeremiah 15:1, which uses Moses and Samuel as ancient types of righteousness. It used to be remarked that the verses in Ezekiel mean little because Daniel is one of the trio, and the Book of Daniel is now regularly placed in the second century B.C. We are, of course, not willing to concede the late date of Daniel. A newly discovered Targum, a Targum of Job, interestingly, argues that the Aramaic of Daniel does not reflect the language of the second century B.C. in Palestine as has been so widely believed. It is claimed that this Targum of Job was translated about 100 B.C. and shows a later stage of Aramaic than Ezra or Daniel. In any case, this passage in Ezekiel is no longer held to be against the early date of Job, for the reference to Daniel is now differently understood. It is now said that the Daniel of Ezekiel refers not to the canonical Daniel, but to the Daniel mentioned in the Ugaritic texts as an ancient wise man, the father of the hero, Aqhat. Here again, we may enter a disclaimer. The Daniel of Ugarit is quite different from the righteous man of Ezekiel 14. Actually Ezekiel does not appeal to these men because they were ancient, but because they were righteous. But in any case, the verses do assure us that Ezekiel, about 600 B.C., did know the story of Job.

The only other external evidence for the antiquity of the book would come from cross references and allusions in other Biblical books. Proverbs 3:11 is one such passage, with the wording quite similar to Job 5:17. Job says, "Despise not the chastening of the Almighty." Proverbs says, "My son, despise not the chastening of the Lord." The wording of the two passages is identical in Hebrew, except that Job has the divine name, Shaddai, which it very frequently uses, and Proverbs uses the more common name, the Tetragram. It also adds a characteristic proverbial touch, "my son." The force of such a parallel is debatable, because it is hard to know which book quoted the other, granted that there was some verbal dependence. [Job 28] is an encomium of wisdom in terms of a search for wisdom in places which only God knows. The conclusion is that "the fear of the Lord that is wisdom; and to depart from evil is understanding." This conclusion is quite like Proverbs 1:7; 9:10; 15:33 and Psalm 111:10. Again the question is, did Job build a beautiful poem on the subject of wisdom as defined in Proverbs and use it in his context? Or did Proverbs and the Psalms take a theme already developed in Job and allude to it in various verses? We cannot be sure, but it does seem a little more probable that Proverbs and Psalms did the borrowing. The matter is somewhat complicated by the problem of the position of Job 28 itself. Critical commentators feel that the whole chapter is intrusive. It is indeed distinctive, but there is no need to object to such a poem being included in Job's asseveration of his righteousness. Actually the chapter is an important part of Job's argument. It builds up to a great climax in which Job establishes his ethical and moral standard.

Another parallel is between Job 71:17 and Psalm 8:5. Job says, "What is man that you magnify him?" The Psalm says, "What is man that you remember him?" The word "man" in each case is the less used word for man, *ᵓnōsh* making literary interdependence more likely. Another parallel is Job 2:13 and Proverbs 10:28. Job says, "The hope of the profane man shall perish." Proverbs puts it, "The hope of a wicked man shall perish." The two statements differ only in the words for a wicked man. The word "profane" is found several times in Job. It would be more natural for the somewhat unusual word to be found in the original passage. Another parallel is Isaiah 19:5 with Job 14:11. The last half of each verse "the waters shall fail from the sea" is identical. The verses are in different contexts, however, and it would be hard to prove which is copied from the other. Another passage showing a literary parallel is the section in which Job curses his day (Job 3:1–11). Jeremiah does likewise (Jer. 20:14–18). Driver, referring to this passage, quotes Dillmann as arguing that Job is earlier because [it is] more powerful and vivid. Driver questions this conclusion because, he says, Job was written by a greater poet in any case (*Introduction to the Literature of the O.T.*, New York: Doubleday, ed. of 1896, p. 408). One could now support Dillman's argument by reference to allusions in this passage to Ugaritic motifs (vs. 8 refers to Leviathan) of which we shall speak again later. Also, there is a parallel between Job 18:5, 6 and Proverbs 13:9. Driver believes that Bildad borrowed from Proverbs. But Bildad has a four-line poem against the "lamp of the wicked." Proverbs uses only this one phrase as a contrast to the bright shining of the lamp of the righteous. It is just as likely, perhaps more so, that Proverbs did the borrowing.

There are also interesting verbal parallels of Job 27:1 and 29:1 with Numbers 23:7, 18; 24:3, 15. Four times the Book of Numbers says Balaam "took up his parable and said." It is probable that the verbal parallel is only due to a common linguistic usage. But it is interesting . . . that the parallel is with Balaam, another man of the eastern area, and one living in Moses' day. To sum up, there are a few interesting verbal parallels with Psalms, Proverbs, Isaiah, and the Balaam oracles. These are not conclusive, but incline somewhat toward a pre-monarchy date for the writing.

There is also considerable internal evidence for a pre-monarchy date, or even for Mosaic times. This evidence is of two kinds—comparison of the book with Biblical data and comparison with the general archaeological picture of early times. On the first point, it has been widely noticed that the picture of Job's sacrificial ritual is like that of the patriarchs and bears no relation to the tabernacle ritual of Moses' day and later. Job served as a priest in his own house, as Abraham did, and as Melchizedek seems to have done. Of course, this may have been due to Job's locale as a righteous man off in the East believing in Israel's God, but not allied with Israel. But it is easier to say that the scene is patriarchal. At the same time, the book mentions names of the patriarchal circle. The land of Uz was presumably named after Abraham's nephew (Gen. 22:21) and Elihu the Buzite belonged to the clan headed by the brother of Uz. Bildad the Shuhite was a descendant of Abraham himself, by Keturah (Gen. 25:2). Presumably, the reason this record got into the circle of Israel's Scriptures is that Job and his people were distant cousins of the Israelites. We may even get a glimpse here of those other godly men of Abraham's day who, like Melchizedek, worshipped the true God though they were not in Abraham's immediate family. When God called Abraham to found the theocracy, there were others around who shared Abraham's faith.

There is another ancient touch, hard to evaluate. It is the use of the divine name Shaddai. This and Eloâh are the characteristic names for God in Job and are used sparingly elsewhere. Shaddai occurs some thirty times in Job, six times in the Pentateuch and seldom elsewhere. The matter is complicated first because we are not sure of its origin, and secondly, critics have argued that the P document teaches in Exodus 6:3 that all instances of "Jehovah" before Moses are anachronistic and are therefore useful for separating out Pentateuchal documents.

Personally I am of the opinion that the word is borrowed from the Akkadian or Amorite and was indeed used early in Israel's history. I feel the derivation from the word for "breast" is fanciful and does not explain what seems to be an archaic Lemedh-He ending. The hard "d" need not be a doubling, but a preservation of the old Akkadian pronunciation which had no soft "d." And the Akkadian *shalû* means mountain, which would be a very suitable expression of the eternality of God. The Psalmist often applies the Hebrew word, mountain, *ẓûr* to God. If this be the etymology of the word, its use would be an archaic touch.

We need not agree with critical source division of Genesis to believe that "Jehovah" was more widely used in late Hebrew than in early times. It may have been a Hebrew word and if so, would have been less used by the patriarchs who learned Canaanite as their second language. It is notable that none of the patriarchal families use the element Jehovah in their names. Shaddai-names also are rare, though the two we know are Pentateuchal, Zurishaddai and Shedeur.

There is little else internally to date the book. The mention of domesticated camels in 1:3 would indicate to the Albright school that the book was later than the 13th century. But the date of domestication of camels is in dispute. It may be that in the settled areas camels were not common, but that nomads of the desert used them earlier. At least Abraham also had his camels. The mention of iron (19:24; 20:24; 28:2; 40:18; 41:27) also might indicate a date after 1200 B.C. when the iron age began. But the occasional mention of iron at an earlier day is not surprising for iron was used in small amounts long before the discovery of better methods of iron working which made its use common in about 1200 B.C. Two talents of iron—about 150 pounds—are mentioned in a Ugaritic tablet from Moses' day. Marvin Pope, in his Anchor Bible Commentary on Job, points out that the unit of money (or item of jewelry) mentioned in Job 4:11, *qᵉśîṭā*, is mentioned elsewhere only in Gen. 33:19 and its parallel, Josh. 24:32. Job's longevity also—140 years after his trial—is of the patriarchal vintage.

Secondly, as to the historical background of Job, it seems to fit well with ideas and literature of the second millennium B.C. Pope remarks that "the ideas championed by Job's friends were normative in Mesopotamian theology from the early second millennium B.C." (p. xxxv) and he compares several works on suffering: From Egypt, the *Dispute over Suicide* and the *Tale of the Eloquent Peasant*, and from Mesopotamia, a lament called by S. N. Kramer *The First Job*. The Akkadian work *I Will Praise the Lord of Wisdom*, also called *The Babylonian Job*, describes a sufferer who recovers, and the *Dialogue about Human Misery*, sometimes called the *Babylonian Ecclesiastes*, is on a similar topic. Pope offers extracts from these works. They can be read conveniently in ANET. It should be noted that these works consider the problem of suffering, as does the Book of Job, but their answer is quite different. Pope is accurate in stating that they agree by and large with the viewpoint of the three comforters. That is, they teach that wickedness brings suffering and righteousness blessing. But the real answer of Job was distinctive and far above his comforters and different from these early treatments. However, it is of importance to notice that the subject received extensive treatment in early times and thus Job fits well against the background of that day.

Many, however, including Pope, have given a later date. Pfeiffer (*Introduction to the O. T.*) gives a date of about 600 B.C. Driver dated the book "most probably to the period of the Babylonian captivity" (*Introduction to the Literature of the O.T.*, New York: Scribner's ed. of 1892, p. 405). A. Bentzen is uncertain. He places the date of the book after the discussion of retribution in Ezekiel 18 and before the references to "the prophet Job who maintained all the ways of righteousness" in Ecclesiasticus 49:9 (*Introduction to the O.T.*, 4th ed. Copenhagen: G. E. C. Gad, 1958, vol. II, p. 179). Eissfeldt is not positive, but says "we should probably think of the post-exilic period, and perhaps most probably of the later period rather than the earlier, i.e., about the fourth century. The language of the book fits in with this, for it often reveals an Aramaic coloring" (*The O.T., an Introduction*, tr. by Peter R. Ackroyd, New York: Harper 1965, p. 470). Both Eissfeldt's date and his arguments seem now to be invalidated by the Dead Sea Scrolls and better knowledge of the Aramaic language. Fragments of Job are found among the Dead Sea Scrolls actually dating from about 200 B.C. They are written in the paleo-Hebrew Script implying that there was a considerable history of copying behind them. And now to the further surprise of many, the Targum referred to above, an Aramaic translation of Job, has been found among the Dead Sea Scrolls. The copy is from about A.D. 50, but the translation itself is dated by the editors at about 100 B.C. Evidently Job was already a loved and famous book in the second century B.C.

More scholars have now veered toward a pre-exilic date. Albright dates it in "the sixth or fifth century B.C." (*Supplement to Vetus Testamentum* 3, 1960, p. 14). Pope hesitatingly suggests the seventh century B.C. before the movements that brought the destruction of Israel (p. xxxvii) as the date of the dialogue but does not commit himself on the unity of the book. As we hope to show later, there are cross references from the main body of the book to every other part. There is therefore no need to question its unity and to say that it existed for centuries in partial form. Some have declared that the references to Satan betray Persian influence. Strange then that there are no Persian words in the book! Satan is a name of Hebrew derivation, not Persian. Actually, the theology of the book should not be used as a datum for dating because opinions will differ as to whether advanced theology indicates late borrowing or early revelation.

It would be nice if the language of Job could be used to indicate the date, but we do not have contemporary Hebrew—or eastern—dialects to use as a standard. The language of Job is difficult and must be discussed shortly, but it has been variously evaluated and can give us little help on the problem of dating.

In the absence of definite evidences for late dating and in view of numerous indications of a patriarchal milieu, it seems possible to hold to a Mosaic or slightly pre-Mosaic date in accord with much old Jewish and Christian sentiment. However, the New Testament does not speak on either Job's authorship or date, and the date is not of theological concern. We may therefore hold our conclusion provisionally expecting further light, especially from linguistic studies.

Job and the Canon

In our Hebrew Bibles, Job is the second or the third book in the third division called the writings. Practically all the works on O.T. introduction, both conservative and critical, trace this three-fold division back as far as the prologue to Ecclesiasticus about 130 B.C. Critical scholars suppose that the third division in the canon was placed last in the collection because it was latest in time. The canon is said to have developed in three stages with the law being canonized first at about 400 B.C., the prophets second at 200 B.C., and the writings last at about A.D. 90. This final canonization was the work of the council of Jamnia. The idea is that the books of the third division were not generally enough accepted to be included in the second division at 200 B.C. On this view, Job was finished at least at a relatively late date and attained canonical status only after 200 B.C. Some more recent scholars who would place Job in pre-exilic times do not face the question as to why it was not included in the earlier canonical divisions.

Conservative scholars like E. J. Young and R. K. Harrison suggests that the tri-partite division was due to different types of authorship, rather than to different stages of canonization. (E. J. Young, *An Introduction to the O.T.*, Grand Rapids: Eerdmans, 1949, p. 41; R. K. Harrison, *Introduction to the O. T.*, Grand Rapids: Eerdmans, 1969, p. 284.) The claim is that the second division was written by prophets and the third division by men who had the prophetic gift, but not the prophetic office. This characterization would apparently apply to the author of Job. I have elsewhere argued against this view (R. L. Harris, *Inspiration and Canonicity of the Bible*, Grand Rapids: Zondervan, 1957, pp. 129ff, 170ff). There is no biblical support for the distinction made between a prophet by office and a prophet by gift. Of course, in the case of Job, the matter is the more uncertain because, if Job were not the author, we have no valid information as to who was. Ecclesiasticus speaks of "the prophet Job" but his witness is too late to help, except that it reveals the attitude of Judaism of the second century B.C.

Harrison relieves the problem somewhat by emphasizing the self-authenticating character of the Biblical books. These books and no others won their way first into Hebrew hearts, and therefore into the Jewish canon. Job is surely a book that would have commanded wide acceptance by the people of God.

A further point, however, is important and is usually neglected by O.T. students. It is by no means certain that the division of books found in our Hebrew Bibles is the division common among the ancient Jews. Indeed, there is positive evidence that it was not. The present three-fold division with five books in the law, eight in the prophets, and eleven in the writings, cannot be traced back of the Talmud which was codified in the fifth century. There is a three-fold division mentioned in Ecclesiasticus, as stated above, but there is no proof that it was our three-fold division. On the contrary, Josephus, earlier than the Talmud, evidences a differing three-fold division with five books in the law, thirteen in the prophets, and only four in the writings. From his terminology, it is clear that Josephus regarded such a book as Job—also Chronicles, Daniel and others—as among the prophets. This evidence fits much better the reference in Ecclesiasticus to Job as a prophet and in Matthew 24:15 to Daniel as a prophet. Far too long, the Talmud has been used as the point of reference in canonical studies. Earlier witness leads to quite different results.

Actually the three-fold division of the canon was not the only one. The N.T., the LXX and the Qumran evidence combine to show that there was also an ancient two-fold division of the canon into the Law and the prophets. This too I have argued elsewhere and need not pursue. But according to this division, Job would have been from early times accorded the place of a prophetic book. As a consequence, we cannot use the position of Job in the Hebrew Bible to argue either for a late or early date of its composition. Job was accepted, as far as our scanty evidence goes, from the time of its writing. If its prophetic authorship wee acknowledged then, as it was believed later, this would doubtless have settled the matter of the acceptance of the book. In any case, the majesty of the style of Job and its other marks of divine inspiration would have commended itself to the ancient Hebrews. We need not doubt that it was accepted as canonical from the time of its writing, although the details are lost in the mists of antiquity.

The Language of Job

It is agreed on all sides that Job is a great book, as well as a beautiful one. It is also agreed by students beginning work in Hebrew poetry that Job is a difficult book to translate. Those who specialize in statistics say that there are more *hapax legomena* used in Job than in any other O.T. book. And the problems of translation are not entirely lexical either. There are unusual forms and some strange usages which, unless recognized, will lead the translator astray. An extreme example of the difficulty of translation is exhibited in the strange verse of the AV in 36:33. "The noise of it showeth concerning it; the cattle also concerning the vapor"—a verse which as it stands is quite meaningless! The language is so unusual that some (F. H. Foster referred to in M. Pope, *Job,* The Anchor Bible, Garden City: Doubleday, 1965, p. xliv, hereafter called: Pope, *Job*) have supposed that the book was written in Arabic and what we have is a translation into Hebrew. If this be true, I would suggest that the translator did a poor job of rendering the work into Hebrew! On the face of it, such a view is unnatural. The first written Arabic we have is from the 5th century A.D., and the first literature of any extent comes after the Hejira. It would be odd if our only monument of ancient written Arabic were in Hebrew!

It is true, however, that there are some words in Job that are neatly explained by reference to Arabic. For instance in 23:9, the words "work" and "hide" in the AV may be derived from words meaning "turn" in the Arabic. Also the word "drops" in the AV of 38:28, "the drops of dew" is found elsewhere only in Arabic. Again in 30:7, 17, the word for "flee" or "rest" in the

AV and found only here has an Arabic cognate "gnaw." (Though the sense hardly fits—to gnaw the wilderness! Commentators must supply something!) Actually, the Syriac has the same word, so an Arabic origin is not proved. Indeed, this example shows the difficulty of proving an Arabic original for a word. A root may be known at present only in Arabic and in Job, but our known vocabulary of ancient Aramaic is woefully small and the word in question may have been used in Aramaic also. Only occasionally can the phonetic differences between Aramaic, Arabic and other languages be used to identify the original language of the word concerned.

An example may be given from Job 35:10. The word "songs" of AV is translated by Pope as "protection" deriving it from the Arabic root *dmr* "who gives protection in the night." But the root also is now recognized in this sense in Ugaritic as a name of Baal (though not so recognized in Cyrus Gordon's *Ugaritic Textbook, Glossary*) (Pope, *Job* in loc.).

A word on the place of Aramaic. There have been others who thought Job was written in Aramaic and translated into Hebrew. On the face of it, this view would be more natural, for Aramaic was used to the east and north of Palestine in pre-exilic times. According to Genesis 31:47, Laban spoke Aramaic and it would be quite possible to hold that Job did too. There are several Aramaic touches in the book. In 16:19, the same pair of words for witness is found, as is used by Jacob and by Laban in Genesis 31:47, Galeed and Jegar-Sahadutha, and the word *śāhēd* is used nowhere else in the Bible. Students of beginning Hebrew will be relieved to find that the verb *qatal* does occur in Biblical Hebrew—twice in Job and once in Psalm 139, which has several Aramaic touches. By contrast, it occurs seven times in the short Aramaic section of Daniel and Ezra. Again, *millā* meaning "word" occurs several times in Job. This in itself is not surprising. It also occurs a number of times in other Hebrew poetry as a synonym of *dābār*. But in Job, the plural of *millā* thirteen times has the typical ending of the Aramaic noun—*iyn*. Job also uses the Hebrew masc[uline] pl[ural] form *in–iym* ten times. The force of this example is slightly blunted by the fact that Phoenician and Moabite also use this ending. It was not peculiar to Aramaic.

Other words cited as rare in Hebrew, in Aramaic are *ḥap̱* "clean" (33:9); *nākā* "smite" (30:8) and *zaʿak̠* "extinguish" (Job 17:1). The last example is curious for it presents an argument in reverse. This word is the same as another word *daʿak* "extinguish" which is used five times in Job, three in Proverbs, and once in Isaiah and in Psalms. The two words are cognate roots. But according to ordinary Semitic phonetic law, the root with "d" should be Aramaic and the one with "z" should be Hebrew. So it is Job that shows a variety of usage and the other books which use only the Aramaic form.

There is another Aramaic form of some interest for it shows mixture. In 37:4, the AV "stay them" (*yᵉʿaqqᵉḇēm*) comes from an Aramaic root *ʿqb* meaning to "hold back." But it now seems that the final "m" is not the pronoun "them" but the enclitic "m" common in Ugaritic. It would therefore seem that the form is not an Aramaism but an archaic form sharing some features of Ugaritic and some of later Aramaic. It should be pointed out that several grammatical features formerly thought to be Aramaic are now seen to be native to old Canaanite, as evidenced in Ugaritic—so much so that Albrecht Goetze even classified Ugaritic as Aramaic. Most now hold that these features were simply early Canaanite, some of which survived in or were borrowed into Aramaic. In short, many features formerly called Aramaisms (and words called "late and poetic" in Brown, Driver and Briggs *Hebrew Lexicon*) are now seen to be archaic.

It should be recognized that Job's peculiarities are not limited to Arabic and Aramaic evidences. The word for "vapor" in Job 36:27 (AV) is used elsewhere only in Genesis 2:6. The old translation "mist" or "vapor" was a guess. The word can now be identified as borrowed through the Akkadian from the Sumerian. It means "river" and refers to the river of Eden (see R. L. Harris, "Mist and the River of Eden," *Journal of the Evangelical Theological Society,* vol. 11 [1968] p. 177). Another Sumerian word may be concealed in the word for the constellation *Mazzaroth* (39:32 and "north" in 37:9 AV). It is possible that the "r" reflects the "l" of the Sumerian word for stars which still appears in the Jewish greeting "Mazal tov"—good luck!

There are also Akkadian influences in Job. In 33:6, man is said to be a creature "nipped from clay" i.e., created from, or of, the earth. The same expression occurs in the Gilgamesh Epic. Interestingly, it also occurs in the hymns of the Dead Sea Community, doubtless in dependence on Job (Pope, *Job* in loc. and T. H. Gaster, *The Dead Sea Scriptures,* rev. ed. Garden City, N.Y.: Doubleday, 1964, p. 133).

In 29:4, the word "secret" in AV is difficult but is cognate to the Akkadian *sadādu* meaning "to protect." "The protection of God was over my home."

In other cases, however, words in Job which are cognate to Akkadian are also found in Ugaritic. An example given by Pope (*Job* in loc.) is the root *ʿmq* which usually means "valley" and is so translated by AV in 39:21. But a better sense is gotten from the meaning "strength" attested in Akkadian and Ugaritic both.

One could well wonder if the peculiarities of Job were due more to similarities to the old Ugaritic material than to either Arabic, Aramaic or Akkadian. The borrowed Akkadian words concerned are few, although we have an extensive Akkadian vocabulary for comparison. Our vocabulary of old North Arabic is nil, and of Aramaic is limited. Even our Ugaritic comprises only a fraction of that dialect. So it is well to be cautious. But Ugaritic influences are of various kinds, both in vocabulary, grammar, and concept. It would seem more likely that Job was more indebted to the northern and western Ugaritic neighbors.

Only a few of the Ugaritic parallels need be given—more are pointed out by Pope who has made an important contribution to the study of Ugaritic in his book *El in the Ugaritic Texts.* The word "acquaint" of AV in 22:21 is better taken with the sense "yield" as in the shaphel conjugation in Ugaritic. The word "one" of AV in 23:13 could perhaps be the Ugaritic *'ḫd* cognate to Hebrew *'ḥz* and the phrase would mean "He, when he takes hold of a person. . . ." Pope prefers a slight emendation looking in a different direction. In 36:28, the word "abundantly" of AV is better taken as the Ugaritic *rb* "showers." In 39:14, the word "leaveth" of AV is better taken as the Ugaritic *ʿdb* cognate to Hebrew *ʿzb* meaning "set," "part" (Gordon, *Ugaritic Studies in Glossary*) and refers according to Pope (*Job*, in loc.) following M. Dahood to the ostrich laying her eggs in the sand. In 39:25, the word "among" of the AV is read *bd* by Pope and NEB with the Ugaritic significance "song" or trumpet "blast"—"at the blast of the trumpet he saith Aha!"

A more significant borrowing from the Ugaritic is found in 36:30, 33 where the preposition "upon" or "concerning" of AV is taken to be a shorter form of Elyon, the Most High as is witnessed to in Ugaritic. This rendition of the preposition *ʿal* is used repeatedly by Dahood in his studies on the Psalms, also in the Anchor Bible Series. The difficult vs. 33 would read: "The Most High speaks in thunder; his anger burns against evil."

There are other similarities of Job to the Ugaritic literature. The use of an enclitic "m" on the end of verbs occurs in Ugaritic as it does in Akkadian. The occasional use of this feature in Biblical poetry is now widely recognized and several instances where "m" formerly was thought to be a [third person masculine plural] objective pronoun are now classed as the enclitic "m." One instance has been noted above, Job 37:4. Other probable cases are 4:19; 17:1, and 24:1. Also, Gordon remarks (C. H. Gordon, *Ugaritic Studies—Grammar,* Rome: Pontifical Biblical Institute 1965, p. 138) that "waw" always stands first in a coordinating situation, but may be delayed if it is in a subordinate clause. The masoretes punctuated 36:7 so that the second "waw" began a new clause. Pope gets better sense by translating "with kings on the throne he seats them." Also the later "waw" in this verse may be so treated: "and they are exalted forever."

There are some cases of Ugaritic phrases used in Job. In the difficult poem on wisdom, 28:11 the AV says "He binds the floods from overflowing." The context apparently speaks of mining operations where precious stones are found but not wisdom. The phrase in 28:11 *mibbᵉkiy nᵉharot* has been taken as the preposition *min,* plus the root "to weep." But there is another root *nēbek* meaning "spring" used only in Job 38:16. This root was suggested already in Brown, Driver, Briggs for 28:11 and now the phrase is found in Ugaritic as the word for the "sources of the two rivers" where the dwelling of the Ugaritic deity El stood. The idea is that the miners reach the deep springs of water in their search for treasures.

Another such instance is 36:13, where the phrase "hypocrites in heart" AV is the same phrase "impious-minded" (Pope, *Job* in loc.), applied to the evil actions of the goddess Anath.

From this brief survey of lexical and grammatical features, we come to the astonishing conclusion that the Book of Job is difficult Hebrew! But it may be said with some confidence that it is not difficult because it is late and Aramaic, or late and Arabic in flavor. It shares some of these peculiarities regardless of their date or origin. But it also evidences touches of Mesopotamian language and clearly shows similarities to the old Canaanite dialect of Ugarit. It need not be supposed that the author lived in Ugarit. It may be remembered that Hinter Syria was a crossroads of caravans from Ugarit, from Canaan, from Arabia and from Mesopotamia. If Job wrote the book and was a rich and learned gentleman of the sons of the East, he would have had an international outlook and connections such as the Book of Job shows. We do not know enough about ancient dialects to date Job by its language. But there are indications that it would fit an early date, better than the later.

The Literature of Job

The structure of the book is well known. There is a prose introduction and conclusion. In between, there is an extensive poetic dialogue. Job in great affliction raises the problem of innocent suffering. There are two rounds of speeches of Job and his three friends, Eliphaz, Bildad and Zophar. On the third circuit, Eliphaz speaks, then Job, then Bildad speaks very briefly. Job gives a long speech ending with an oath of innocency.

The place of a third speech by Zophar is taken by a young upstart, Elihu, who is amazed that older heads have not put Job in his place. When Elihu is finished, or perhaps interrupting Elihu, Jehovah speaks to Job out of the storm. He speaks twice with Job and Job briefly responds each time in faith and humility. This leads to the final prose section chronicling Job's restoration to God's favor, to health, and to prosperity.

There is no Biblical parallel to the structure of Job, and no close parallel in ancient literature to the format, although, as mentioned earlier, there are other treatments of the problems raised. The problems of the suffering of the innocent and the prosperity of the wicked have perplexed many and are treated by the Psalmists. Asaph asked "Will the Lord cast off forever?" but confessed "this is my infirmity, but I will remember the years of the right hand of the Most High" (Ps. 77:7–10). He trusted that his affliction would be removed in God's time. Psalm 88 is full of complaint, but does not see through the problem to an answer. Psalm 37:35 complains that the wicked prosper "like a green bay tree." But the answer is that the wicked man is soon gone. Psalm 73 comes closest to the thought of Job. The double problem of the suffering of the righteous and the prosperity of the wicked is solved in the sanctuary of God and, like Job, the Psalmist's thought is directed to God alone in heaven. But Job draws out the argument in extenso and reaches a grander expression of his conclusion.

Efforts, of course, have been made to fragment the Book of Job, as has been done with almost every other O.T. book. The prose parts at the beginning and end have been cut off. The speeches of Elihu and of Jehovah at the end have been called additions. Chapter 28 on wisdom has been questioned as an intrusion.

Some conclusions are not only unnecessary, they go against the positive indications in the book of a unity. And there are other ancient compositions (e.g., the *Protests of the Eloquent Peasant, ANET*, pp. 405ff) which have a poetic body sandwiched between a prose introduction and conclusion.

It is true that the Tetragram YHWH is used in the introduction and conclusion, but not in the poetry. But 38:1 uses it to introduce Jehovah's highly poetic reply to Job from the storm. Also it seems that Bildad in Job 8:4 refers to the catastrophe that killed Job's sons as related in the introduction. There are many places where one speaker in the dialogue refers to what another has said. The reference to man born of woman being born to trouble is given by Eliphaz in 5:7, by Job in 14:1 and by Eliphaz again in 15:14 and by Bildad in 25:4. Job's long speech in 38:34 quotes a line of Eliphaz, 22:11. Also Job in 27:20 repeats a previous phrase of 21:19. The Elihu speech of 34:3 repeats Job's remark of 12:11. The same is true of 33:11 with 13:27. Even the wisdom chapter (28:26) is paralleled in the speech by Jehovah in 38:25.

It is of some interest that the newly discovered Aramaic translation of Job (J. P. M. Van der Ploeg and A. S. Van der Woude, *Le Targum de Job,* Leiden: Brill, 1971) follows the Hebrew text very closely. It is of course fragmentary. There are only two or three such instances of dislocation covered by the preserved text of the Targum (e.g., Pope's insertion of 26:1–4 between 27:1 and 2 and the dislocation of 31:38–40 in NEB). But to the several dislocations alleged by the New English Bible, by Pope and other commentators, the Targum gives no support. On the other hand, the Targum has one verse dislocated in Job's second response to the Lord (40:5 replaces 42:3). The witness of the Targum, of course, cannot be pressed. It only goes back to about 100 B.C., but such as it is, it is in the direction of the integrity of the text of Job.

The LXX text of Job presents problems of its own. Origen and Jerome say that it was considerably shorter than the Hebrew, but our major manuscripts do not show these lacunae. They presumably have been filled out from Theodotion or some other source. The Old Latin witnesses to the shorter text, but this witness is fragmentary and it is hard to evaluate Origen's witness without more information. The witness of the new Targum is the more welcome, as it reaches back almost to the days of the original LXX translation.

As to the poetry and style of the Book of Job, it may be helpful to apply to it remarks I have made elsewhere on the Psalms ("The Psalms" in *The Biblical Expositor*, ed. C. F. H. Henry, Phila: Holman, 1960, vol. II). It is well known that Hebrew poetry is characterized by parallelism and the use of synonymous expressions to gain repetition. But the secret of great Hebrew poetry is not its rhyme and meter. Mere rhyme and meter may be found in English doggerel like the Mother Goose rhymes for children. Humpty Dumpty had a great fall. But we can hardly say that he fell in great verse! So it is with Hebrew poetry. The poetry of Job is great because it deals in magnificent ways with great subjects. The thought and conception is great. For this reason, it is great poetry, even in a fairly literal translation, such as that of the AV. I once had a friend, in the family, not a Bible student or scholar, who characterized the lines in Job 38:7 as the most beautiful in the English language . . . "Who laid its cornerstone, when the morning stars sang together and all the sons of God shouted for joy?" The intensity of Job's trial is shown in the introduction with the successive reports of calamity punctuating his peace like pistol shots in the night. The depth of his trial is revealed in his facing in its stark reality the awfulness of the problem of a good God who grants no justice. Note that Job spends very little time on his physical ailments. Not once does he tell us where it hurts! Because Job's hurt is the hurt of the heart of lost humanity. And by the same token, the book rises out of the depths of despair to confident heights of faith and revelation of God. Some commentators profess to find contradictions in Job's speeches and even assign part of his last speech to Zophar. They fail to realize that Job is grappling with what some today call the antinomies of existence. He sees the problem deeply. But he never lets go completely of his faith that these problems of earth have an answer in God. And he rises almost to the beatific vision in his assurance that he himself with his own eyes will behold God and then all will be well. But as in the case of Martha, whose hope was for her brother's future resurrection, God graciously gave a larger promise. Jesus said to Martha, "I am the resurrection and the life." And to Job, God said I am the Almighty God. In my protection you are secure. Pope is correct that the "book presents profundities surpassing those that may be found in any of its parts . . . the values men cherish, the little gods they worship—family, home, nation, race, sex, wealth, fame—all fade away . . . confidence in this One is the only value not subject to time." (Pope, *Job,* p. lxxvii). Job is great literature. And it has answers from God.

Mythology or Revelation?

In addition to all the problems raised by the unusual dialect of the Book of Job and the problems of the theology yet to be considered, there are problems that we turn to now concerning the alleged mythical background of the book.

A prominent feature of the Book of Job is the reference to Behemoth and Leviathan in chapters 40 and 41. What are these creatures? They are famous enough that an ocean liner was named after one and the other has become a synonym for something of jumbo size. It is possible that these are ancient names for actual animals and the hippopotamus and crocodile have most often been nominated. However, advancing study of ancient times and, especially the discovery of the mythology of Ugarit, has inclined many to find here and elsewhere in Job a reference to the mythology of the cultures surrounding Israel. The question before us is, must we recognize in Job such mythology and if so, does it present theological problems?

The problem concerns not only Job, but Psalms, Isaiah and passages in a few other books as well. Leviathan is mentioned by name in Psalm 74:14; 104:26 and Isaiah 27:1, as well as in Job 3:8 and 41:1. The reference in Isaiah calls Leviathan the fleeing serpent, the crooked serpent. The former expression is found also in Job 26:13 in a context that also may be mythological. Pope (*Job* in loc.) says that the reference in Job 26:13 is to the dragon that causes eclipses! The line in Isaiah is very much like a Ugaritic text: "Because thou didst smite Lotan, the writhing serpent/didst destroy the crooked serpent/the accursed one of seven heads" (C. H. Gordon, *Ugaritic Literature, a Comprehensive Translation,* Rome: Pontifical Biblical Institute 1949; cf. also *ANET* p. 138). The words "writhing" and "crooked" are those used in the Isaiah passage. Furthermore Leviathan in Psalm 74:14 is pictured as multiheaded. It looks very much as if Leviathan sometimes in the Bible is a name for a mythological monster. This seven-headed monster is pictured on a seal and on a piece of shell as a somewhat dinosaur-like creature with seven heads placed one below another on the long neck. A hero with a spear is seen on the seal having pierced the lower four heads of the dragon. Apparently the seal depicts the conquest of Leviathan, or Lotan as the Ugaritic pronunciation has it. It is pictured in *ANEP.*

The question is, how does such a description of Leviathan fit in with Biblical revelation? The answer is not too difficult. The Bible uses the mythology of antiquity without approving of it. The symbolism of Daniel is instructive. In Daniel 7, the first kingdom, the Babylonian, is symbolized by a lion with eagle's wings. This symbol is well-known from Mesopotamian architecture. In Daniel's vision, God used this symbol to identify Babylon, but there is no approval or disapproval of the symbol. Actually the dreadful fourth beast of Daniel 7 with ten horns is pictured again in Revelation 13 as a dragon with seven heads and ten horns. The devil in Revelation 12 is also pictured as a dragon with seven heads. Presumably these instances tell us that the old mythological symbol of an evil dragon is used as a symbol of the devil and his minions. We may conclude that mythological symbols are used in the Bible for purposes of illustration and communication of truth without in the least adopting the mythology or approving of its ideas.

Albright argues that this process was widespread in ancient Israel and calls it "demythologizing," though rejecting the Bultmannian overtones of that word. (Albright, *Yahweh and the Gods of Canaan,* Garden City, N.Y.: Doubleday, 1968, pp. 183–207). He gives examples of pagan deities or practices which were part of Israel's background, but were robbed of their pagan meaning before they were made a part of Israel's religion. His example is the word "cereal" which we use daily without in the slightest taking part in the worship of the goddess Ceres or believing that she spent half of her time in the underworld.

Albright makes the flat statement, "It may confidently be stated that there is no true mythology anywhere in the Hebrew Bible. What we have consists of vestiges—what may be called the 'debris' of a past religious culture" (op. cit. p. 185). Actually Albright goes farther than is necessary in finding examples in the Bible. He assumes that the word *tehôm* in Gen. 1:2 comes from the ancient myths of Marduk's fight with Tiamat when he created the world from her carcass. Albright believes the old story was demythologized. Actually, we should remember that many of the ancient deities were named after natural objects and forces. Deus means sky, Chronos means time, Tiamat and *tehôm* mean fresh water, Yamm means sea. All of these items were deified probably because of animistic ideas. It is not clear that *tehôm* first meant the deity of the water, then became demythologized into water. Rather it was the reverse. There was a god Yamm in Ugaritic who was god of the sea, but the meaning "sea" in all probability came first, not vice versa. And usually when the word *yamm* is used in the Hebrew Bible, it is used without any reference to a deity of the sea at all.

Nevertheless, it is true that in Job there are several instances where mythological items are referred to and we should recognize these without concluding that the book had pagan overtones in its make-up. These are studied in a perceptive article by Elmer B. Smick, "Mythology and the Book of Job," *Journal of the Evangelical Theological Society,* vol. XIII part 2, 1970, pp. 101–8.

Job cursed his day at the beginning of his dialogue. In the process, he calls for a curse from "those who curse the day (*yōm*)" or "those who curse *yamm* (God of the Sea), those skilled to rouse Leviathan." This mythological reference is only an allusion and means no more than our use of Norse deities for the names of the days of the week. But it is probable that there is here an allusion to evil deities.

Other references to the sea as a deity may be found in 7:12. "Am I the Sea God (*Yamm*) or the Sea Serpent (*Tannīn*) that you set a guard over me?" asks Job, and in 9:8, Job acknowledges God as creator of the stars "who treads on the high places of the sea." The idea of "high places of the sea" is peculiar. The corresponding word in Ugaritic means the "back" of an animal or man or god (C. H. Gordon, *Ugaritic Studies—Glossary*). Therefore, the suggestion is that God the creator is pictured as trampling on the back of the god, Yamm, in confining the sea to its borders. A word of caution may be expressed. These may be references to mythology, but again, the words *yamm* and *tannīn* have literal meanings which are not impossible in these two contexts. We may find here the mythological motifs, but also we may have some reservations.

In 9:13, close to the *yamm* context, there is the mention of the "helpers of Rahab" who bow under him. Rahab is mentioned again in 26:12: "by his strength he put the sea [or the Sea God Yamm] to rest; by his wisdom he smote Rahab." The following verses speak of his conquering the fleeing serpent as already mentioned. It is true that Rahab can mean "proud ones," and to quell the sea is a natural figure, but it is perhaps more likely in these contexts that Job celebrates the power of God in conquering the evil and proud mythological deities of the heathen.

Another pair of deities is found by some in Job 38:36. "Who hath put wisdom in the inward parts (*tuhōt*) or who hath given understanding to the heart (*śekwîy*)?" Here Pope (*Job,* in loc.) and others find mention of the Egyptian god of wisdom Thoth and Mercury (Coptic: Souchi). Albright accepts the translation Thoth, but declares the alleged Coptic name of Mercury arose by a modern mistake (op. cit. p. 245ff). The traditional translation of the words seems quite enough in this passage.

Another alleged reference to a pagan god is in 5:7, "Man is born to trouble as sparks [sons of Resheph] fly upward." Resheph was indeed the god of burning and pestilence, but *resheph* also referred to literal fire and pestilence. The sons of Resheph are not understandable in this context if it refers to a deity. The traditional rendering is satisfactory.

There are a few other alleged mythological renderings, but they are probably not necessarily so. The references to Behemoth and Leviathan in 40 and 41 remain to be considered.

The word Behemoth is merely the plural of the word "cattle." The plural of majesty or excellence could thus designate a big cow-like beast and the hippopotamus has been suggested. Pope (*Job,* in loc.) adopts the mythological interpretation and speaks of the human-headed bull of heaven pictured like the water buffalo of the swamps above Galilee. What was said above is applicable here. There was a bull of heaven in mythology and the Behemoth could have been that. This reference in Job could be, on the other hand, a literal water buffalo. Or it could have been a hippopotamus with which Palestinians were familiar, even though these animals did not live in the Jordan area. Verse 23 does not demand that they did. Mention of the strong tail, however, fits neither the buffalo nor hippopotamus. I would suggest that most fearsome of beasts, the elephant. The elephant even more that the hippopotamus drinks up the river at a gulp and the African elephant is not tamed. It is true that the elephant's tail also is minimal, but the astonishing feature of an elephant is the appendage at the other end. Is it not possible that the Hebrew *znb* could refer to trunk equally as well as tail?

Leviathan is here pictured not as an evil deity, but as an animal. Again, we remember that the deity was usually invented by investing a normal object or animal with divine powers. There was probably at some time a literal animal called Leviathan. If this reference in Job is the deity Leviathan, it is odd that his main feature, his seven heads, is not mentioned. Rather his natural parts and physical strength and ferocity are dwelt upon. The sparks and smoke from his nostrils surely are but hyperbole. Whether it refers to the crocodile or to a whale, we perhaps cannot be sure. Obviously, it is a creature of the sea which was so greatly feared that in mythology it became worshiped.

This is, I believe the extent of the mythology of Job. We turn now to its theology.

The Theology of Job: The Character of God

We come in this last section to the climax of the Book of Job which is, as all realize, the revelation of God who speaks to Job out of the whirlwind. Job in his agony had sought for God and asked to set out his case before God. He had pleaded his innocence before God. Now at last God speaks and Job, though the confrontation is not what he had asked for, nonetheless has the answer to his deepest desire and he is satisfied.

There is somewhat of a problem in studying the subject of the character of God in the Book of Job, for much of the book is fallacious in its revelation. We can say this reverently, of course. All of the book is inspired and actually all the characters except Satan express some elements of truth, but at least the speeches of the three comforters are not normative for theology. Job himself, as we have seen, grew in his faith and understanding. Surely Job's idea of life after death progressed greatly during the course of his trial. Some things Job said about God are true. Some things are not. So, much of the dialogue is not divine teaching and for fully authoritative teaching about God, we are restricted to the speeches of Jehovah at the end and to the prose framework at the start and finish of the book. We may remark that the case is somewhat like that in Ecclesiastes. There also, there is much in the book that is preliminary to the conclusion. The author there tries various philosophies of life and finds them false. He is shut up to the final conclusion that the chief end of man is to fear God and keep His commandments. So also in Job, it is the final answer that we want. It was the ultimate vision of God that satisfied the patriarch's heart.

God reveals himself first to Job as creator. It is of interest to compare God's first revelation in Genesis. The sacred scriptures begin with the creative activity of God. Here God is superlatively shown to be God without competitor or equal. The corollary is that God is the only eternal one and all else sprang into existence at God's command. The first chapter of Genesis outlines a procedure in God's creation. Job gives none of these details. The teaching is contained in highly figurative rhetorical questions that remind us how puny man is in comparison to the power of God, the Creator of all. One need not explore the use of time as a fourth dimension to realize that time for us is very short. We are creatures of a day. The Psalmist says that we are like grass which grows up in the morning and is cast down in the evening (Ps. 90:6). But God is eternal. A thousand years to him is but a watch in the night. Where wast thou when I laid the foundations of the earth (Job 38:4)? How we would wish to know at least some of the secrets of God's creation! How old is the universe? Is the big bang theory of the origin of matter correct? And if so, did the original fireball spring into being when God first enunciated the laws that govern time, space, energy and matter? What is matter and what is energy after all, now that we have found to our horror that they are interconvertible? We have begun to see in recent years something of the ferocity of elemental force, as well as something of the immensity of the reaches of space. We might remember that we are not the first ones to know a little something of these things. Lightning probably awed the ancients as much as it frightens us. And among the Greeks at least, there was at least an idea of the distances of space. Two hundred fifty years before Christ, Eratosthenes in Egypt had measured the circumference of the earth to within ten percent of the correct figure (see the article "Eratosthenes" in the *Encyclopedia Britannica*). And Ptolemy, the astronomer, shortly after Christ, assures us that the distance to the stars is so great that the earth in comparison is a point without magnitude. His estimate was around a billion miles. We know now that his estimate was far too small. But man is about as puny beside a billion miles as beside ten-billion light years.

It is hardly necessary to add that God does not tell Job that the world is set on foundations with supporting pillars and a cornerstone. The morning stars do not really sing and the bounds of the sea are set not by doors and bars. Its bounds are set by gravitation—if only we knew what gravitation is! Elsewhere (26:7) Job had confessed that God hangs the earth on nothing. But how God hangs the earth and how he formed the earth and the world are still mysteries which we attempt to probe, but how little we understand of the power of God the creator.

I am convinced that one great problem of modern thought is the result of a determined denial of God's creatorship. Evolution is now in the popular mind today an explanation of how God created (a false explanation, I believe.) But it has become an alternative idea to God's creation. Evolution, however, cannot explain the beginning of things. It is accompanied by purely philosophical concepts of origin by chance, the eternality of matter, and a flat denial of God. One result is that human personality is unexplainably alone in a sea of chaos. Thought has no basis for validity. Art has no reason or coherence. Life has no meaning and death no hope. Against this torrent of despair comes the clear revelation of God. "Before the mountains were brought forth or ever thou hadst formed the earth and the world even from everlasting to everlasting, thou art God" (Ps. 90:2). It is significant that when John hears the angels in heaven praising the Father, their song is "thou art worthy . . . for thou hast created all things and for thy pleasure they are and were created." If God be really the Creator, we are assured that he is the ultimate reality. There is none behind or over him. Job no longer seeks an umpire. There is none beside Him.

But God is not only transcendent Being. He reveals himself to Job in his providence. The Westminster Shorter Catechism defines God's works of providence as his "most holy, wise and powerful, preserving and governing all His creatures and all their actions." God is immanent in the sense that He is active in His creation. He is not a part of the world process. But He directs the world process in wisdom that we are only beginning to appreciate. Because there are second causes, some men now stop with second causes and leave God out. The result is a material universe that can never explain itself or satisfy man who, if he has any significance at all, has a non-material aspect we call the soul. Does Job know the weather? Can he direct the thunder? I understand that the force of a hurricane is equal to several atomic explosions each minute. The mere force required to make the wind blow at sixty to a hundred miles per hour over a diameter of some hundreds of miles is staggering. It is no contradiction in the Bible when Isaiah 5:6 says that clouds bring rain and Job 38:28 asks "Hath the rain a father? Or who hath begotten the drops of dew?" Again the poetry of Job is striking in its figures of speech. And the thrust of it is that puny man can observe the stars, but it is the Almighty God who guides the stars in their courses. There is matter of great comfort here. We are not alone in the fell clutch of circumstance and we do not suffer under the bludgeonings of chance. We live under the protecting shadow of a Sovereign God.

The providence of God extends to the remarkable and peculiar phenomena of the animal world. Do you understand the gestation of the wild goats? Obviously, as an ancient cattleman, Job knew something of the mating and birth of his animals. We know much more. We know that sperm and ova are produced and that they unite in the miracle of life. The chromosomes and genes intermingle, then the cells multiply. Some become liver tissue, some nerve cells, some bones and some blood. And how is it and why is it that it all happens just this way? What man would have dreamed up the ostrich, that peculiar bird? The only bird, I understand, with eyelashes! Why, I have no idea. The only bird, I understand, equipped with a bladder! Again, why? There surely is a reason, but how strange are some of God's creatures! Some have questioned if the ostrich is as dumb as the verses seem to say. I suppose that depends on what you compare it with! Most would not think of turkeys as dumb, but I have seen young turkeys hang themselves getting out of the tree where they roosted! The ostrich is dumb on some counts. Yet as the passage says, when she lifts herself up, or as Pope . . . explains it, when she spreads her tail feathers and runs, she can outdistance any horse with ease. The wild ass, the ox, the ostrich, the horse, the hawk, the vulture—these are but samples of the varied, specialized and peculiar creation which God controls. And if God controls these creatures of the wild, he can care for me. Bryant said of the waterfowl,

> He who from zone to zone guides through the distant air thy certain flight
> In the long path that I must tread alone can guide my steps aright.

The example of Behemoth and Leviathan have been dealt with already. The teaching is that he who made Behemoth the chief of the ways of God can make his sword to approach unto him (40:19). Is it not a powerful thought that God is in control? And remember that this control depends not just on power, but on infinite wisdom as well.

The essential affirmation of the Book of Job, however, is not the mere power and wisdom of God, marvelous as these are, but the affirmation of the righteousness, the rectitude of God. This was Job's problem. He was ready to acknowledge the power of God. Indeed, that God's power was far beyond Job's was part of his problem. But is God good? Abraham confessed that the judge of all the earth will do the right (Gen. 18:25). Job had questioned. It is not right for God to destroy the perfect and the wicked (9:22). But God cannot let pass that charge. Job humbles himself in his first answer. But God demands a further answer. "Wilt thou annul my judgment? Wilt thou condemn me that thou mayest be justified?" (40:8). Job could see but the tiny fringe of God's purposes. God reveals himself as one who above all is holy, righteous and just. Job's sin was not final. His faith burned low at times but was never out. He trusted God even when he doubted God's ways and God led him through the sea, even if not on dry land.

But there comes a day when others must meet God. I quote . . . from Henley's poem, "I thank whatever gods may be / for my unconquerable soul." I am told that later, Henley lost his ten-year-old daughter and was broken up by the tragedy. Our souls are not unconquerable. Some day all will stand before the judgment seat of God in an experience not like Job's, and not like the alleged person to person encounter of existentialism, but in the dark. And in that dread day, all men will lay their hand upon their mouth for the judgments of God are true and righteous altogether and they are final. No man then will annul God's judgment and Satan will then be put away, and death and hell consigned to the lake of fire, and God's power, wisdom, glory, and righteousness will be fully revealed.

There is one more point. The conclusion of Job, like the prologue, is part of the book and has a lesson. God is merciful. You have heard of the patience (or endurance) of Job and have seen the end of the Lord that the Lord is very pitiful and of tender mercy. Job was restored even in this life. He had come to trust in a future life. But even this life is blessed for the child of God. So Satan was overcome as he will be vanquished at last in God's good time. He will overcome him by the blood of the Lamb of God, for the accuser of our brethren shall be cast down who accused them before the throne of God day and night. Therefore rejoice ye heavens (Rev. 12:10–12).

The Theology of Job: Rewards

Pope is correct, "The issues raised are crucial for men and the answers attempted are as good as have ever been offered" (*Job*, p. lxxvii). Pope himself misses, I believe, one grand answer in Job—the doctrine of the future life. The name "theodicy" was applied, I believe, by Leibnitz to the question of the justification of the ways of God with regard to evil in the universe. It is a problem for theism. Baudelaire, seeing the injustice in the world and hearing that God was in control, remarked that "your God is my devil." He was not so far wrong! The Bible says that in a sense the devil is in control of much that goes on in this world. The indispensable prologue to Job makes it clear that Satan has much power here and now—with the necessary caveat, under God. This is not the best of all possible worlds. That was the deists' perversion, not the Christian teaching. "In the world, ye shall have tribulation" is a further statement of Job's complaint: "Man is born to trouble as the sparks fly upward." We ask in our groaning, why does not God do something in Vietnam, in Bangladesh, or with the Berlin wall? We ask, worse yet, why did God do what he did years ago in the Lisbon earthquake, or today in the Calcutta tidal wave? Is God cruel? Is Krishna the destroyer actually a part of the deity? These were the awful thoughts that crowded in on Job when he was called upon existentially to face the question posed in Ecclesiastes 4:1, "the oppressions that are done under the sun."

Job did not know and the comforters did not know that Job was suffering for the honor of God himself and to the shame of Satan, the author of sin. A groaning world today has not read the prologue of Job. It does not believe in Satan as really evil, or in God as really good. As a result, a European [author] like Hermann Hesse turns to Eastern philosophy denying, as he does in his *Siddharta,* all distinctions of right and wrong, of pain and pleasure, of man and God and eternity. All becomes merged in a river of indistinction. There is no meaning. As Matthew Arnold has said in *Dover Beach,*

> We are here as on a darkling plain
> Swept by confused alarms of struggle and of flight,
> Where ignorant armies clash by night.

Job cursed his day. Pope remarks (*Job,* p. xiii) that James 5:11 gives an unbalanced view in referring to the patience of Job. That, however, was when the book began. Job gave absolute submission to the will of God. Because God was God, Job was at first content. And it should be noted from 1:22 and 2:10 that this is the truly acceptable attitude before God. But theory is one thing and life is another. God would give the world an example *in extremis.* He does that sometimes. Paul called himself an example of God's deepest grace. Ananias and Sapphira were made an example to the early church. D. L. Moody heard a preacher say, the world has yet to see what God can do with a fully yielded Christian. Moody said, I will be that man. And God made him a great example to bless the hearts of multitudes. God made Job an example and a comfort to thousands since his time. God may have even laughed as he used Satan to direct Job's longing, and ours also, to higher things than children, and sheep, and camels and oxen. God had a plan for Job's life—and for yours.

But Job now descended into the valley of the shadow. And in his misery, he longed for death as the final answer. In lines of great beauty he sought the grave "where the wicked cease from troubling and the weary are at rest." Hamlet pondered suicide. There are only two cases of suicide in the Bible—Ahithophel and Judas. Suicide is not the way out for one who believes that there is a God and that our life is sacred because we are made in God's image. And these great verities Job could not forget. But Job's first three speeches each end with the longing for the oblivion of the grave.

Eliphaz confronts Job with a different view. He even claims a revelation (4:13) though he was clearly a false prophet. He declares that foolish men, i.e., sinners, are the ones who suffer and that therefore God must be chastening Job. If Job repents, God will wonderfully restore. Eliphaz here, as far as I can see, speaks for the other friends including Elihu. I can see little progress in the argument of the "miserable comforters" as Job called them. They declare that Job must have sinned and therefore he suffers. If he will rectify his conduct, God will restore him. Actually this is the view expressed in those several related treatises on suffering from Egypt and Babylonia. . . . This is really the view of the world today. If there be a just God, he must punish sin now and reward righteousness now. If this is not done, we cannot believe that God is real. This attitude was dramatized by the skeptic, Robert Ingersoll. On the platform, he would dare God to strike him dead in one minute. The audience waited in silence and at the end of a minute, he pocketed his watch declaring that he had proved that there was no God. On one occasion, a newspaper editorial the following day asked if the little man had thought that he could exhaust the patience of the Almighty in sixty seconds! But twentieth-century man is not noted for his patience. We expect judgment now or else not at all. Really the view of the three comforters amounts to the idea that you get all your hell and all your heaven in this life! There has been some question about Job's doctrine of resurrection. But note that not one verse in the speeches of the three friends of Elihu direct Job's eyes to the hereafter for bliss or blame. Theirs is the little *quid pro quo* of the disciples, "Master, who did sin this man or his parents that he was born blind?" Christ's answer applied also to Job, "Neither . . . but that the works of God should be made manifest in him." And God's works in Job at the last were manifest to devils, angels, and men.

In Job's first round of speeches, he doesn't get much further than an anguished cry to God for relief and a plea for death. He declares that he is not wicked (10:7) and complains that God destroys the perfect and wicked alike (9:22). Job has no chance, for there is no possible umpire between him and God (9:33); he therefore asks God to take away his hand before he goes to the land of no return (10:21).

The picture of the grave that Job draws thus far is close to oblivion. Indeed this is his only hope (3:13–22). It is a place of quiet, of sleep; death (*māweth*) and the tomb (*qeḇer*) are in parallelism. In his second speech, Job pictures the grave as the end and therefore he will give rein to his complaint (7:11). He expects to "go down to Sheol" and not come up (7:9). He will "sleep in the dust" and he will not be. The same thoughts recur in his third speech. He wished he had been "carried from the womb to the grave (*qeḇer*)" (10:19). He longs for the land of darkness, disorder and gloom. It may be noted that Job's concept of that land differs notably from that of the Babylonian underworld (cf. the description in *ANET,* p. 109). Here are no monsters, gods or goddesses. It is not a peopled place of consciousness. It is as near soul sleep as we can get. But from another angle, it does not describe soul sleep. It does not describe the soul at all. It describes rather the tomb to which the body goes. This was, just then, the extent of his concern. Death, the tomb (*qeḇer*), Sheol, and the land of darkness are the terms used. The Palestinian tomb was cut in the rock. It was, of course, dark; it was down. It held the bones and dust of many generations. One decayed body was pushed back in the crypt when another was laid in. The body of course slept. The soul was not then in Job's view. Neither was any Babylonian place of departed spirits.

In Job's second round of speeches, he continues his bitter complaint, but something new has been added. Job now does not long for death. He holds on to his innocence and is sure of justification (13:18). He is confident that God will be his salvation (13:16). But there is a problem in the key verse, "though he slay me, yet will I trust in him" (13:15). RV translated "He will kill me, I have no hope." NEB says, "If he would slay me I should not hesitate." The problem concerns the word *lōʾ* (not) which may also be read *lō* (for it). The Hebrew consonantal text gives the first reading, the vocalic text the second. Most of the versions read it the second way. Unfortunately, the new Targum does not cover this section. In view of the uncertainty, it is not wise to be dogmatic, yet it may be pointed out that the verb "hope" or "wait for" usually is used with a prepositional complement "l" (for). If this be the case, the AV reading "though he slay me yet will I trust in him" is the true reading. It would fit the context very well.

In this same speech, Job rises to further heights which are often not noticed because translations do not always bring out the structure of the passage (14:7–15). Job is still in great distress. But now, like Hamlet, he looks beyond the moment of death and asks what dreams may come when we have shuffled off this mortal coil. Here for the first time in the book, someone raises the question of a future life. That alone is highly significant. Here is a new phase of the argument. "If a man die shall he live again?" The question of God's justice and acceptance of a man is here raised off the mundane plane into the sphere of the future. Job trembles on the threshold of a new hope. Is it perhaps that although this is not the best of all possible worlds, that there is another one to come? Job sees, as it were, a light in the keyhole of the door in heaven which John the apostle saw opened full wide.

Job's argument begins where it should begin. Job is God's child. He considers a tree, an insensate thing, yet it has persistent life. If it is cut down, though it seems to die, it will by water at the roots put forth a second growth. The verb is ***ḥālap***. It will bud and grow. This is for a mere tree. But man! Of greater worth, a child of God, the word of God's hands. Man dies and never rises till the heavens grow old. He does not awake (*qyṣ*) nor rise (*ʿwr*). Then Job wishes to be hidden in Sheol, until God's wrath passes over and God might remember him. Surely Sheol here means the grave. But will God remember him? Job answers his great question by a declaration that he would "wait" (same word as "trust" in 13:15 treated above) until his second growth (*ḥᵉlipah*) would come. Job seizes the thought that man is of far greater worth to God than a mere tree. "Thou shalt call and I will answer thee; thou wilt have a desire to the work of thine hands." Here Job in a pinnacle of faith looks beyond the tomb to the resurrection call of God. It is a pinnacle. Job does not maintain this hope undimmed. But he has cried out in faith and he has begun to see that the answers to the great questions after all lie in God who made us for himself, and we may reverently reverse Augustine's famous remark. God made us to fellowship with himself and he is not satisfied until he brings us to rest in him.

Tur-Sinai (*The Book of Job,* in loc.) is very unsatisfactory here. Tur-Sinai does not associate the two words for second growth. He rearranges some lines and emends others. On verse 13, he makes the surprising comment, "Job interrupts the presentation of facts (i.e., of man's eternal death) with rhetorical unrealistic wishes; would that the fate of man, and my own fate, were like that of a tree by the water, so that, after a period of waiting in Sheol, I might return to life." This quotation is simply an admission that some modern commentators find Job's affirmation of resurrection hopelessly unrealistic. But then perhaps the commentators have not had to think as deeply as Job did.

The next speech of Job, the fifth, does not advance. He castigates his miserable comforters and complains that God has turned him over to wicked men. But he declares that he is innocent and calls heaven to witness as he cries unto God for relief. Then he returns to the thought of death. This time he does not seem to long for death as he did earlier, but regards it as the end of his hope (17:15). The word "wait" (AV) of 17:13 is the same root as "hope" in 17:15. The persons of the verbs in the last verse of the chapter can be read differently in agreement with Pope (*Job,* in loc.) and NEB. But Pope's question marks need not be adopted. I offer this translation:

> If I have hope, sheol (the grave) is my house.
> I will spread my couch in the darkness.
> I have called corruption my father and the worm my mother and sister,
> Where then is my hope? and who will see my hope?
> When my hope goes down to sheol (the grave) and we descend together to the dust.

Job here plays with the word "hope," which he had used in 14:7. There is hope for a tree that it will have a second growth. Is Job's only hope extinction in the grave? No longer does Job seek for death and extinction. Now he reaches for every glimmer of hope beyond the darkness of the tomb.

Job's sixth speech is shorter than usual, but this one is a climax. Again he chides his "friends" with being his worst enemies. They should pity him when the hand of God is heavy upon him (19:21). And so he looks beyond the present. His friends have turned against him, but he would have his words engraved upon enduring rock. For his vindicator will arise at last.

These verses, 19:25–27, are both very important and very difficult. They are taken in Handel's *Messiah* as a great prediction of Christ. In the NEB translation, they say nothing of resurrection. Pope (*Job*, in loc.) and many modern commentators find no hope of resurrection here, feeling that to do so would contradict 14:12. But as shown above, 14:12 is in a context where Job poses the question of resurrection and answers it with the affirmation of faith.

Verse 25 begins, "For I know that my vindicator lives." The word is *gō'ēl* and refers to the next of kin who avenges a murder or relieves the oppression of the destitute. Job obviously is not referring to a mere man. God was Israel's *gō'ēl* who redeemed from Egypt (Exod. 6:6) from exile (Isa. 43:1) and from death (Hos. 13:14 quoted in 1 Cor. 15:55). In view of the fact that the vision of God is Job's desire (19:26), it seems proper to take the redeemer to be God himself—but probably not the messianic redeemer. Pope on the other hand declares that the redeemer whom Job hopes for is the umpire of 9:33 who will force God to come to terms. He compares Mesopotamian subdeities who thus interceded for men. But of all this, the verse says nothing. That Job actually hoped for help outside of God is against the whole tenor of this passage, regardless of his earlier outburst.

"And that he will stand at last upon the dust." "Upon the dust" may mean the earth, or it may mean the dust of Job's tomb (cf. 17:16). "Stand" or "rise" may be a legal term. The vindicator will appear on Job's behalf. But it is not to save Job from death—the "at last" argues otherwise. The vindicator will redeem Job in some future day of his expectation.

"And though after my skin worms destroy this body," note the italicized words of the AV. It is a difficult line. The preposition "after" refers to time or place, and neither in Hebrew or English is the word "after" appropriate for the noun "skin"! The context wants the infinitive construct of a verb. Pope takes the preposition with the verb "destroy" and translates it "after my skin is flayed." But then with the final pronoun "this" would be out of place and the verb following the pronoun should agree with it, but it does not. The NEB ad libs here with a footnote that the Hebrew is unintelligible. It is possible, however, to read the word "my skin" (root *ᶜwr*) as a verb in the infinitive construct. The same verb was used to mean "awake" in a resurrection context in 14:12 (see above). The reading would then be "after my awaking." The verb "destroy" is difficult. It is used only three times, though it is used in a second meaning "to encircle." It may be translated, "After my awakening when this (sickness or body) is destroyed."

"Yet in my flesh I shall see God." Pope, and others, translate "without my flesh, I shall see God." This translation is interesting, for it would make the passage refer not to resurrection, but to spiritual life in heaven—an equally happy thought for Job. The preposition *min* can indeed mean "apart from" as well as "from the standpoint of," and many examples of the latter use are given in the lexicon. [For example,] the Lord roars *min* Zion (Amos 1:2). In view of the next line, it seems hard to adopt Pope's idea. The whole thrust is that Job will see God in his resurrected body. Tur-Sinai (*The Book of Job*, in loc.) takes it to mean from the standpoint of his body—but before death.

> Whom I shall see for myself
> and my eyes shall see and not a stranger.
> (NEB, "I myself and no other.")

This verse put the capstone on Job's declaration of faith. Job at long last, after his body is consumed, will see God in a resurrection day. The following words are probably correctly placed with the later verses as the NEB and with them we are not now concerned.

How does this doctrine of the resurrection bear on the date of Job? Does this imply a late date because it would involve a borrowing of Persian ideas? Here much depends on one's background and viewpoint. If one is convinced that the doctrine of resurrection is late, then Job will be given a post-exilic date, along with Psalm 49, 73, 16, Isaiah 26, Hosea 13:14 and other passages. It would seem better to face the claims of revelation given in the Bible, rather than thus to restructure the O.T. on subjective grounds. Surely the argument in Job does not look like an item borrowed from an alien creed. The teaching of the resurrection in Job is hammered out by facing in a unique way the problems of life against the background of the revealed character of both God and man. Job seems rather to have the marks of an early and original treatment of this wonderful doctrine. It is easier to think that the Psalmists and prophets stood on the shoulders of Job in their resurrection doctrine.

And after all, what do we know of the Persian religion in the early days? We have some monuments of Persian grandeur and some reports of their kingdom and wars. But we have no early copies of the religious books of the Persians. We know not when or by whom these books were written. They were copied and recopied in lands where Christian influence was very strong in the first centuries of our era. What interpolations may have occurred and what influences may have been absorbed, who knows? Eventually these books were taken to India and brought to the modern world. But it is quite uncertain that Job could have been actually influenced in this, its basic doctrine, by such alleged teaching.

There is, further, a dark side to Job's insights on the future life. For Job had two problems to face. First, why do the righteous suffer, but secondly, why do the wicked prosper. For the wicked do prosper. Honesty is not always the policy that succeeds, and sometimes crime does pay. Job now attacks his comforters with the declaration that they are wrong also on the second count. "The wicked live, become old, yea are mighty in power" (21:7–16). The translation of the rest of the passage is in debate. The AV seems to make Job say that although the wicked seem to die happy, yet later (vss. 17–22) they shall drink of God's wrath. Then again (vss. 23–34) he says wicked and righteous die alike. The NEB and the NASB by the use of judicious quotation marks and question marks make Job consistently say that the wicked do not get the judgment the three comforters assign to them. The question is one of detail, but I rather favor the AV at this point. It is true that the wicked go to Sheol in peace (21:13). All lie down alike in the dust and worms cover them (21:26). But what then? Verse 30 is the key verse. It has two "l" prepositions, which can mean "to" or as we now know from Ugaritic "from." The AV takes the meaning "to" and says the wicked is spared from disaster. This is also the meaning of the NASB, though the "l" is translated "to." But the conclusion of the chapter in the AV seems to say that despite appearances, God will judge the wicked—and this thought is later developed.

Then Eliphaz viciously attacks Job again and accuses him of many sins. Job responds to this that God knows he is innocent and when God has tested him, "I shall come forth as gold" (23:10). Very different, however, is the case with the wicked. He outlines the extreme wickedness of some men and now he veers to the thought that indeed they will receive their judgment. (Sheol and the worm will consume them [24:19–20].) Their exaltation is short (25:24). Tur-Sinai (*The Book of Job,* in loc.) escapes this conclusion by saying Job is quoting from the three friends. Pope (*Job,* in loc.) also cannot follow the argument here. He believes that Job has contradicted his previous statement and that this speech should be attributed to Zophar. Pope is correct in recognizing a shift in the argument, but it seems quite possible to hold that Job himself is looking further. Especially so because after Bildad's short and final speech, Job returns to this argument in 27:13–23. Here he is a bit more explicit. The wicked man will not merely die, perhaps easily. He will be given a reward from the Almighty. His children shall suffer, his widows shall not mourn him, he suffers the terrors of God. Tur-Sinai (*op cit.*) escapes this conclusion by saying Job "used to say" this. Pope, of course, ascribes this also to Zophar, but it seems that Job himself may here be expressing in incipient form the even harder doctrine that the wicked, who seem to get by, will actually receive in the end the judgment of God. It cannot be said that Job expresses with any clarity the doctrine of future punishment for the wicked. But it is involved in his view and some of his statements look in that direction.

As for Job himself, he brings his argument to a grand conclusion. He summarizes his moral principles in words already referred to as taken up by Solomon. Wisdom may be found, but not by worldly search. Surely Job wanted wisdom. His friends claimed understanding. But Job declares that real wisdom is to worship God in reverence and holiness of life. The claim is distinct that Job did this, and in his final speech Job lifts his hand in a solemn oath of abjuration that before God he has lived in innocence of the great sins of which he has been so bitterly and unjustly accused. If he be guilty, he says at last, let thistles grow instead of wheat and weeds instead of barley! The words of Job are ended.

Elihu returns to the argument, but in a sense he seems to parrot the argument of the rest and thus to be a anti-climax. Job has nothing more to say. But Job has stood his trial. He has trusted God. He has continued in his principles of righteousness and he has seen beyond the grave to the final justice of God. It remains for God himself to answer Elihu and the three friends and to both humble and bless his servant with a vision of God in His greatness.

11

The Problems of Suffering in the Book of Job

Francis I. Andersen

In the story of Job the problem of evil in the world is not dealt with abstractly, but in terms of one man's agony. The three friends and Elihu do their best to apply general principles to Job's case; but they do not help him, and what they say is finally declared invalid by God Himself. This is a surprise, for their arguments have the familiar ring of sound doctrine.

Strictly speaking, human misery, or the larger sum of evil in all its forms, is a problem only for the person who believes in one God who is all-powerful and all-loving. Outside such faith there are many explanations of evil which involve a denial, or a limitation, of either God's sovereignty or of His goodness. The argument has been expressed with philosophical clarity as follows: If God were perfectly good, He could not tolerate the existence of violence,

From Francis I. Andersen, *Job: An Introduction and Commentary,* Tyndale Old Testament Commentaries (Downers Grove, Ill.: InterVarsity, 1976), 64–73. Used by permission of InterVarsity Press.

disease, etc.; therefore there must be some limit to His ability to control such events, that is, He is not almighty. Alternatively, if God does have complete power over everything that happens, His failure to curb the wrongs that occur must be due to the fact that He does not see anything wrong in them, that is, He is not good.

Many thoughtful people, horrified by the helplessness of humanity in the face of natural disasters or outraged by the ruthless exploitation of 'the down-trodden and the injured' by the unscrupulous masters of political or economic power, have lost faith in the goodness of God. 'If I had the power of God,' they protest, 'I could do more about these things than He seems to be doing!'

A reasoned theodicy—the justification of the ways of God to men—is a legitimate task for Christian apologetics. The Book of Job is not such a treatise, but the story of one man, his loss, his search and his discovery. This search takes place entirely within the household of faith. All the characters, the three friends and Elihu as much as Job himself, are fully committed to belief in one supreme God who is unquestionably just in all His acts. Solutions which lie outside such biblical revelation are not even considered in the Book of Job. Polytheism, in which each god has his own limited domain, survives in a simpler form in various kinds of dualism, in which evil (perhaps in the person of the Devil) exists over against good. Naturalistic belief in a closed universe where God does nothing has found expression in 'God is dead' theology. It is another kind of dualism; even if the world is said to be God's creation, His effective removal from the scene is a rag of deism, pitiful beside the robust biblical belief that God owns the world and is always at work in it. The Book of Job similarly accepts no suggestion of limitation in either the power or the goodness of God.

Like the rest of the Bible, the Book of Job also takes the world seriously. It is God's making, and God's property, and it is good. While God is delighted with all His creatures, human beings are His special friends, for only men share with God the wisdom which is His image in them. A man is able to talk to God, and God answers him. Human existence in this created world, as God's creature, is the place where the goodness of God is supremely displayed and experienced. Hence Job's insistence on a meaningful life, here and now, even though a man's life must be comprehended in the completeness that embraces birth and time and death.

But this joyful acceptance of creaturehood, this insistence on seeing the goodness of the Lord in the land of the living, accounts for the reluctance of Job to postpone satisfaction until after death, even though he confidently expects to go on living with God after that event. The moral question central to Job arises from the biblical teaching that a man reaps what he sows—in this life. Rewards for virtue and punishments for vice cannot all be postponed to heaven and hell. But troubles and benefits are not distributed to mankind by an even-handed justice, it would seem. The wicked prosper, the righteous suffer. Evil is not always—not often!—punished in proportion to guilt; good is not always—not often!—rewarded in proportion to merit. The case of Job precipitates the test of faith in its severest form—the supremely righteous man who sustains the most extreme calamities. How can he, or anyone, continue to believe that God is right and fair in what He sometimes does to people? There can be no doubt that it is God, only God, who is responsible for all that happens to Job. It cannot be blamed on 'Nature' or the Devil, for these are but His creatures.

It is worth observing that a solution that eastern religions have found attractive, viz. the reversal of the inequalities of one existence by compensation in some future reincarnation, never finds an entrance to biblical thought, with its vivid awareness of the once-for-all-ness of each man's individual existence in history.

We should notice also that the Book of Job does not resort to a line of thought that has been paramount in Western Christianity since the triumph of Augustine over Pelagius. The dogma of the original and inherited depravity and guilt of all mankind, if permitted to deny any possibility of goodness in human conduct, must contradict the premise of the Book of Job that its hero was a 'blameless and upright' man (1:1). Job's friends are the ones who infer, as they must infer in order to safeguard the doctrine that each person reaps what he sows, that Job is paying for his sins. On this basis there is no such thing as a righteous man, no-one ever receives as much punishment as he deserves, and most receive far less. Job's insistence on his integrity can, then, be only hypocrisy, adding to his sin. So speak Job's friends, with the sound of orthodoxy. It is no wonder that commentators whose exposition is controlled by the traditional doctrines of the fall and corruption of every member of the human race, have joined the friends in condemning Job, and seen the purpose of God as a discipline to bring Job to repentance. But such interpretations crumble at the word of God Himself that Job is 'blameless and upright' and that he, and not the friends, was correct in what he said in the discussion. That is, Job was right, but not self-righteous, to insist on his own integrity, to complain that his suffering was undeserved, and to demand from God Himself an explanation of how His justice was to be found in such unprovoked torture. The Book of Job loses its point if the righteousness of Job is not taken as genuine.

God's final endorsement of Job's speeches is also surprising for another reason. It silences the cant of those who remind us of the inscrutability of God, and smugly say, 'It is not for us to question the ways of the Almighty!' For that is precisely what Job does, and God says that he was fully justified in doing so. The Lord welcomes this exercise of moral judgment from man's side, even when it is directed in judgment on God Himself!

The apparent injustice of God is seen in the disproportionate share of ills that come to many good people. Experience contradicts the teaching that each person reaps what he sows. Within the accepted framework of common belief that God is sovereign and God is just, Job and the other speakers gather together most of the solutions to this problem which are presented in the Bible. When the wicked prosper and the righteous suffer, something more than a simple doctrine of rewards and punishments is needed.

The Bible, including Job, has several distinct ways of reconciling human suffering with the justice of God. Most of them are heard on the lips of Job's friends, and Job finds them unsatisfactory. But if they are not completely satisfying, and if, in particular, they do not apply in Job's case, this does not mean that they are wrong. What makes this collision of minds so dramatic is the soundness of their views and the cogency of their arguments. The author has not set up men of straw against Job. To that extent the argument ends in a stalemate, as Elihu recognizes.

The covenant of Yahweh with Israel set two ways before the people—life, through obedience, or death, through disloyalty. A simple correlation of these causes and their effects is expressed in the cursings and blessings recited with the covenant (Lv. 26; Dt. 27–30). Put simply, you reap what you sow (Gal. 6:7; Ps. 34:11–22; 1 Pet. 3:10). This is the starting-point of much biblical teaching. These are not just threats and bribes; God's moral administration of the world requires that the rightness of right should lead to well-being, and the wrongness of wrong should lead to disaster. But the connection is not often obvious, and life is much more complex than this simple formula. Human suffering is more than a system of rewards and punishments.

Holy men, brooding on this mystery, and anxious to protect the character of God from slander, saw that outward appearances might not give a true picture of what was happening between a man and God. The material prosperity of the wicked is not an index of his happiness, and its permission is not an oversight on the part of God. The rich are really miserable, because wealth is insecure and transient. If it is ill-gotten, their conscience is always in dread of a day of reckoning. By contrast, the inward joy of the righteous cannot be destroyed by outward misfortune, for his communion with God is safe from any change due to circumstances (Ps. 73).

By such a test, Job is condemned, and his agitation is inexcusable. But God did not suspend each individual in isolation, to find fulfilment solely in communion with Himself. God put each man with family and friends and things, with property and work. Only a false piety, a disdain for things as evil (the Manichean heresy), a contempt for emotions as weak (the Stoic error), would expect in Job an unflinching fortitude in the midst of such loss and pain. Job rightly grieves his bereavement; he is authentically depressed by his illness. He is human. The untrammelled serenity which some prescribe as the goal of 'victorious living' is a negation of whole areas of our experience as God has made us. Job lives fully. The calm attained by the psalmist (Ps. 73:23–28), and by Job also at the end, was reached only through, and as the fruit of, terrible suffering.

Men seek an explanation of suffering in cause and effect. They look backwards for a connection between prior sin and present suffering. The Bible looks forwards in hope and seeks explanations, not so much in origins as in goals. The purpose of suffering is seen, not in its cause, but in its result. The man was born blind so that the works of God could be displayed in him (Jn. 9:3). But sometimes good never seems to come out of evil. Men wait in vain. They find God's slowness irksome. They lose heart, and often lose faith. The Bible commends God's self-restraint. The outworkings of His justice through the long processes of history, which sometimes require spans of many centuries, are part of our existence in time. It is easier to see the hand of God in spectacular and immediate acts, and the sinner who is not instantly corrected is likely to despise God's delay in executing justice as a sign that He is indifferent or even absent. We have to be as patient as God Himself to see the end result, or to go on living in faith without seeing it. In due season we shall reap, if we do not faint.

So there are passages in the Bible which postpone the resolution of the incongruities in God's moral administration to the last eschatological moment, or even to an occasion beyond history itself. The Book of Job is moving in this direction, but its attention is mainly on this life. Given time, the wicked will receive his just deserts and the righteous will find deliverance and compensation. This teaching, expressed by Zophar in Job 20, puts a strain on Job's faith. He cannot wait indefinitely to see justice done. He contradicts Zophar vigorously (chapter 21). And, even if everything is set right later on, can this ever neutralize the wrong treatment that people have received before that later settlement? The biblical answer is that God (but only God!) can actually transform evil into good, so that in retrospect (but only in retrospect!) it is seen to have actually been good, without diminishing in the least the awful actuality of the evil it was at the time.

If the Book of Job cannot take on this full eschatological dimension, it is largely because it does not yet have the achievement of Jesus Christ to include in the picture. For in Him the greatest evils, the betrayal and crucifixion of the Son of God, become, and now are, the greatest good for all mankind. Job does see part of the answer by teaching that, when the experience is over, the sufferer will appreciate it in a new way because of what he has learnt. Suffering is not always punitive or even corrective. It can be instructive. It is a discipline and a warning. This is a common Wisdom theme (Pr. 3:11; Heb. 12:12f.). This is affirmed by Eliphaz (Jb. 5:17) and especially by Elihu. Suffering is morally therapeutic and prophylactic.[1]

Such answers to any man's question, 'Why am I suffering?' are confined to the individual. They are valuable and valid, because they take the human person seriously in his moral connections with God. But no individual exists in isolation. The Bible views man as both a singular and a social being.

1. For detailed discussion see J. A. Sanders, 'Suffering as Divine Discipline in the Old Testament and Post-Biblical Judaism' (*Colgate Rochester Divinity School Bulletin,* XXVIII, 1955).

Individual responsibility was emphasized by Jeremiah and Ezekiel, not as the only truth, not even as the highest truth, but to correct the error of those who quoted a proverb about social solidarity ('The fathers have eaten sour grapes, and the children's teeth are set on edge') in order to evade blame.

Neither side gives the whole picture. Each man stands directly before God; but no man stands alone. One man sins, and the consequences reverberate through the entire race. Others are more likely to profit from a man's goodness than himself. Each is linked to others, ultimately to all in one vast web of inter-personal humanity. No-one's suffering is ever completely private in either its causes or its results. The Bible recognizes as a fact that consequences of evil are inherited from our ancestors, shared with our contemporaries, bequeathed to posterity. This emphasis escapes from one problem only to fall into another. If a disaster is punishment for sin, why should Job suffer for anyone's faults but his own? Job knows that his troubles are caused by criminals, by the forces of nature, by disease—things that could happen to anyone. We know that behind these events lay the malice of the Satan. But behind all that it is harder to see the fairness of God, let alone His good intentions.

Yet, in spite of these disturbing thoughts, it is part of the answer that a person can willingly accept suffering as the tribute he pays to other people's freedom. He may be sobered by the remembrance of occasions when he has caused hurt to others, deliberately or carelessly. And, when tempted to complain, 'Why didn't God stop them from doing that to me?' he might ask himself what his life would be life if God paralysed his arm each time he lifted it to strike an angry blow, or to steal.

It is part of the answer that it is possible for one person to share the burdens of others. The price paid for this can be suffering. But, when done in love, such suffering becomes a person's noblest task. This aspect of the matter is barely glimpsed in Job. That suffering can be voluntary and vicarious is one of the most amazing and liberating of all the truths revealed in Scripture. The patient endurance of wrong can conquer evil by love. The sufferer can fortify others by his example. The ills of life can sweeten a man or turn him sour. The metal has no strength that has not been tempered in the fire.

In the extreme of self-giving, suffering can be redemptive. It must be admitted that this part of the Old Testament revelation, which finds its clearest expression in Isaiah 52:11–53:12, scarcely enters into the discussion between Job and his friends.

The Bible tries to affirm two contrary truths which collide in the Book of Job. Suffering is the common burden of all men and the lonely burden of each man. It explains it as punitive, corrective, exemplary, vicarious. From one angle, suffering is inflicted by God in justice; from another angle, it can be accepted by persons in love.

These truths have to be stated with great pastoral sensitivity to become true for any sufferer. It is amazing how trite, stale or sanctimonious they can become on the lips of Job's friends. Their ineptitude does not invalidate what they say. The truths in their speeches cannot be given up without leaving the universe a moral chaos. They are quite right, as far as they go. The teaching of the Bible is clear: 'God is no respecter of persons' 'He pays back every man according to his deeds.' This is where justice begins; but it is not where love ends. These truths do not cover all the facts. They certainly do not apply to Job, as he knows, and God knows, and as we, the readers, also know. But Job's friends cannot perceive the innocence of his heart as God does; they cannot detect the good-will of God—nor can Job. They must do the best with what theology they have, as we all must.

Job's friends were well-meaning, but presumptuous. Job's case was 'special' and escapes the generalized doctrines. Nothing but the Voice from the tempest can meet his case, and when that happens, Job keeps his secret. Beyond the frontier reached by the best human understanding of God's revelation—for we must remember that the theology of Job's friends is excellent—lies the abyss of undeserved suffering into which Job is plunged. The case of Job opens up a whole new dimension. There is a vast area of human misery which is neither penal, nor remedial, nor redemptive. It is just meaningless. The answer to the question, 'Who sinned, this man or his parents, that he was born blind?' is 'Nobody sinned' (Jn. 9:2f.). *Job did not sin* (Jb. 1:22).

To condemn the miserable wretch as one already rejected by God is the final human cruelty. Job's friends, trying to apply their best insights to help him to spiritual recovery, unintentionally add to his pain. What he needs is compassion, not advice. The helplessness of Job is pathetic. If he had sinned, he could repent. But he cannot dishonestly invent imaginary sins to repent of. There is nothing he can do, except to cry out to God from the depths (Ps. 130:1). In this gulf of anger he is alone, until he discovers that God has not deserted him permanently. But, like Jesus, he does not at first—not for a long time!—receive any answer to his desolate cry, 'My God, my God, why hast thou forsaken me?' Yet the *via dolorosa* becomes the road to God. Mary paid a price for bearing the Son of God; a sword was thrust through her own heart (Lk. 2:35). She could not escape her agony, which was also her holy privilege and her joy. Of all human beings, the innocent sufferer stands nearest to God. One might ask if there is any pathway into the light, except through dereliction. Job's final contentment is inexplicable unless he found in the valley of the shadow of death a place of spiritual growth.

The Bible, especially the New Testament, sees two sides to this opportunity. From the agony of abandonment by God comes a ministry of compassion that extends to all companions on this dreadful journey (2 Cor. 1:3–7). What is an unendurable indignity at the time becomes a holy honour in memory. Moses in Midian, David in his hide-out, Jeremiah and Joseph in the pit, Daniel in the lions' den, Paul in more than one prison. Like Job on the city dump, their life would seem to have reached its end. The long wait, sometimes for years. The silence of God. But deliverance came, and with it a gratitude never felt by those who never knew despair.

The heroes of faith in Hebrews 11 were all sufferers, and many died without deliverance. Now no suffering seems pleasant at the time, but *afterwards* 'it yields the peaceful fruit of righteousness to those who have been trained by it' (Heb. 12:11). This is not a thing for anyone to arrange for himself in order to gain spiritual benefits. God alone may send it. No-one who has felt His rod would wish to go that way again; but no-one who has come with Job to 'what the Lord is aiming at' (see Jas. 5:11) would ever wish not to have trodden his path. The body of Jesus for ever bears the scars of crucifixion, and they are its chief glory. If the passion of Job was an early sketch of the greatest Sufferer, it remains for His later followers to enter into 'the fellowship of his sufferings' (Phil. 3:10 AV) and joyfully to supply what is still needed to complete the sufferings of Christ (Col. 1:24). For He is the chief Pilgrim and Pioneer of this way, 'a man of sorrows, and acquainted with grief' (Is. 53:3). His Gethsemane was a human experience, but it exceeds all others in its intensity and in its healing power. The full burden of our anxieties crushed Him. What Job longed for blindly has actually happened. God Himself has joined us in our hell of loneliness, and acquired a new completeness through what He endured (Heb. 5:7–9). All the 'meanings' of suffering converge on Christ. He entered a domain of suffering reserved for Him alone. No man can bear the sin of another, but Jesus carried the sins of all. As the Substitute for all sinners, His sufferings were penal, a bearing of the death penalty for sin. They were also a full and authentic sharing of our human condition with a love that gave itself completely into the furnace of affliction. That the Lord Himself has embraced and absorbed the undeserved consequences of all evil is the final answer to Job and to all the Jobs of humanity. As an innocent sufferer, Job is the companion of God.

12

THE MEANING OF THE BOOK OF JOB

Matitiahu Tsevat

The opening of the Book of Job is a case of the rule that a great author can be recognized by the way he fashions the opening of his work.[1] As the prologue (chaps. 1f.) tells the events on earth and in heaven, it provides the reader with the factual background of what is to come and intro-

1. Special abbreviations used in this paper are: Kuhl 1953 and Kuhl 1954 = C. Kuhl, *ThR*, N. F. 21 (1953), pp. 163–205, 257–317; and *ThR*, N. F. 22 (1954), 261–316, respectively. Rowley = H. H. Rowley, *From Moses to Qumran* (1963), pp. 141–83. "Com." following the name of an author refers to his commentary; when it follows Tur Sinai, his 1954 Hebrew commentary is intended.

Views widely held and readily available in the scholarly literature are not identified or specifically referred to, nor are the arguments adduced for them. A balanced view, supported by detailed exegesis and a discussion of differing opinions is found in G. Fohrer, *Das Buch Hiob* (1963), 565

From Matitiahu Tsevat, "The Meaning of the Book of Job," *Hebrew Union College Annual* 37 (1966): 73–106. Used by permission of the Hebrew Union College.

duces him with equal clarity to the problem of the book.[2] The poetic part (3:1–42:6) may appear to modern readers overly long and, in places, wordy and confused (responsibility for which may be assigned, on the one hand, to an abundance of additions by later hands, textual confusion, and an exceptionally difficult language and, on the other, perhaps to the intention of the author to show by the growing repetitiveness of the *dramatis personae* that they have exhausted their arguments); the 35 verses of the narrative introduction are concise and pithy and yet contain everything the reader has to know.

There is Job, the pious man, on whom God's blessing rests. But this idyl of piety and prosperity is introduced only to be immediately menaced by the accuser, Satan, as he presents himself at the heavenly council and demands: "Is it for nought that Job is pious?" (1:9). He questions not Job's deeds but his motivation. Nor is this an act of viciousness on his part; God Himself has provoked him to probe and shake the foundations of the beautiful edifice of righteousness, serenity, and happiness and finally wreck it completely. For God has asked him: "Have you considered my servant Job, that there is no one on earth as blameless and upright as he?" (1:8). Job is the pious man, if there is one. The problem is: is there one? Which is secondary to the main problem: is there piety? Which is, as the accuser insists: is there disinterested piety? He claims that Job behaves according to standards of religion only as long as he finds it useful, whereas piety begins where usefulness ends. God accepts the challenge as proposed by the accuser and on his terms, and this acceptance determines the meaning of piety for the rest of the book. From now on, he who performs an action in expectation of material reward is not to be credited with religious or moral behavior. Different and less pure concepts of piety which find their way into the speeches of the friends later on (8:5–7, 20–22; 11:13–19; 22:21–28) are thus invalid and implicitly rejected *a limine*.

pages. The reader who prefers an English book is referred to S. R. Driver and G. B. Gray, *The Book of Job* (1921, and reprints), LXXVIII+376+360 pages. (The commentary of M. Pope did not reach me in time to make use of in this paper.) A detailed and excellent survey on Job research between ca. 1921 and 1953 is given by Kuhl 1953 and Kuhl 1954. It is supplemented by the more recent article of Rowley, first published in *BJRL* 41 (1958f.), pp. 167–207; re-edited and brought up-to-date in his *From Moses to Qumran*. Reference to these articles is primarily to the literature which Kuhl and Rowley survey and only infrequently to their own opinions.

2. There are three critical views as regards the relation of the prose frame, comprising the prologue (chaps. 1f.) and the epilogue (42:7–17), to the poetic colloquy it encloses. (1) The author of the poetic part (i.e., the author of the book, since there are almost forty chapters of poetry to two-and-a-half of prose; the reduction of the number of forty to about thirty for critical reasons, such as the excision of the Elihu section [chaps. 32–37; cf. n. 17], does not affect the point I wish to make) used and possibly adapted an older prose story, enclosing in it his own larger work. (2) The author wrote the prose as well as the poetry. (3) A later editor provided the narrative frame for the poet. Cf. Kuhl 1953, pp. 185–205; Rowley, pp. 151–56, 159. I hold with the great majority of students in favoring the first or the second view. A choice between them is of little consequence for the issue at hand, the question of the author's having composed the frame or appropriated an existing one being one of literary prehistory; in either case the resulting book is his creation, and the object of our concern is this book.

We now know what piety is; this is a question *quid iuris* in Kant's terminology. What we do not know is the answer to the first question: is there piety? This is a question *quid facti*. While we do not learn the answer at this early stage of the book, we have a preliminary indication that it is likely to be in the affirmative, that there is piety in the world, for it is God Who is the proponent of this view (2:3).

Amplifying what was touched upon before, the narrative content of the prologue and its thought content are not dissociated, but rather the two, plot and ideas, are intimately wedded, and this union now constitutes more than merely the sum of its two components. The prologue informs the reader of the cause of Job's suffering, information which Job himself cannot and must not have. We know more than the hero. But the hero, precisely because of his ignorance, will experience problems and gain insights before which our superior knowledge pales. It is not the spectator's knowledge of the drama but rather Job's problem that matters. The prologue *qua* prologue is a work of genius.

At the beginning of the poetic part we find ourselves in a different world, not only as regards the plot—if we may so refer to the regular change of speakers and their ever-increasing animosity—but also as regards the ideas. The latter, while not unrelated to the ideas of the prologue, assume very different forms, and it is only towards the end of the book that we recognize them in their earlier formulation. In our treatment the three friends and their philosophies will not be differentiated from one another but be seen as one group with one position, over against which will stand Job's philosophy.

One of the friends speaks up in response to Job's initial lament (of chap. 3). His purport, in which the others join him later: Job should behave himself, live up to the very convictions which he formerly preached to others, and rely on God because afflictions are God's chastisements (chaps. 4f.). As Job finds this counsel cold comfort, the friends become ever more adamant and finally quite aggressive as they develop their theology. Their view, they claim, is based on both tradition and observed reality. A web of causality is spun over the world. Man's fate is in his hand; what he gets depends on what he does. The just man is rewarded, the sinner punished. This cause-and-effect relation, widely accepted in the ancient Near East, they reverse: distress and tribulation are punishment meted out for sin. The inescapable conclusion is that Job, distressed and afflicted, is a sinner. His sins may be unknown to him, but they are no less real. Causality in the realm of morality is guaranteed by God; this is the meaning of the sentence "God is just." As for Job, let him search out his sins and repent, and the happiness of his former status will be restored to him.

The friends came to comfort (2:11), but their philosophy will afford a grievously harrowed man no consolation. Yet the literary device that spurs the action and aggravates the situation is the ever-increasing vehemence of the friends, their self-righteousness and unqualified condemnation of their disputant, all of which not only fails to console or at least convince Job but increasingly makes a true conversation impossible. There is no meeting of minds. Repeatedly Job says: "If you only would listen to my words" (13:5f.; 21:2f.). But they launch a massive assault, attacking him from all sides with such force and viciousness that one might expect his backbone to be broken and his personality, the pivot of the drama, extinguished. We must remind ourselves how hard it was for an ancient Israelite, grounded himself in tradition, to withstand the logic of the friends.

Job's backbone is not broken. Up to the last verses of the book he not only stands upright but actually grows in strength, and as the disputation continues we see the development and integration of his personality. He undertakes to demolish some of the friends' arguments and to reject others. Reality, he contends, does not accord with their theory. The world is not governed by the principle of measure for measure. Almost everywhere the wicked prosper. Against these incontrovertible facts, tradition and authority, to which the friends appeal, are without validity; wisdom is not necessarily found with the elders (12:12)[3]—a shocking pronouncement in those days. So clear is the discrepancy between theory and reality that the theory can only be saved by distortion of observation and misrepresentation of reality, in short by a lie. "You whitewash with lies [the dark side of life]," is the accusation Job hurls at the friends (13:4). A few verses later he demands: "Will you speak falsely for God, speak deceitfully for Him?" (13:7–11). This is probably the first time in history that pious fraud is clearly recognized and denounced for what it is: a contradiction in terms. Fraud is never pious, it is always impious.

But Job does not stop with presenting his own, very different view of the world. Decisive is his rejection of the principle which underlies the argument of the friends: the inference from observed reality to the causation of that reality, and this rejection is independent of the accuracy or inaccuracy of the observation. His misery is no evidence for sin on his part because he did not sin. Neither logic nor clever dispositions of commonly held opinions nor glib talk can produce what does not exist: his iniquity. To be precise, Job does not deny absolutely that he has sinned. He grants the possibility of minor transgressions (7:21; 13:26). But what he denies categorically is sins of such weight as to warrant their being related to his lot as cause to effect. The friends' argument rests on a doctrine; his argument is grounded in his life, his experience, his person. And since he knows himself, and since the course of his life lies open before everyone, he is compelled to affirm that the cause of the terrible atrocities that God has unleashed against him lies not in him but in God. God wants to torment him, torment him without reason, because God is cruel. From the lack of rational reason in a persons' behavior we take a clue to his character. God's outstanding characteristic appears therefore to be a

3. The verse presents a rhetorical question the answer to which is no. Cf. Tur Sinai, com.

demoniac ruthlessness. In ever-repeated and diverse ways Job accuses God of wanton cruelty. God's eyes are on man (and on Job as the representative of mankind) not, as the Bible frequently asserts and as the friends faithfully echo, to guard and protect him but to watch and destroy him. Would that He leave man alone to finish out his days in quiet; but no, He searches him out for horror and doom. The friends speak of God's might and wisdom. Surely, says Job, He is mighty and wise, but might is brute force, and wisdom is craftiness seeing that they serve God's caprice and outrage justice. No wonder that omnipotence and omniscience, ordinarily epithets of praise of God, turn in Job's mouth to expressions of blame.

But Job does not limit himself to such statements of facts, as he sees the divine facts. He describes them so keenly because they concern his own person. He is the target. Thus description becomes accusation. Job, the accuser, wants to bring God, the defendant, to court. Nor is this all. Job craving judgment, objective, rational judgment, knows that there is no judge but God. It is in the rational milieu of the tribunal that God will shed his demoniac features, and Job's troubles will be over. Again and again he wants the encounter, longs to see God. For it is his innermost and strongest hope, implicit for the most part but sometimes pronounced, that God also longs for him, His creature, the work of His hands. This hope upholds Job in the hours of his greatest despair. Beside this all else pales. Progressively his dispute with the friends loses in importance as his address to God—accusation, challenge, prayer, and prediction—gains in importance. In his final long speech (chs. 26f.; 29–31) the presence of the friends gradually becomes dim; in its last three chapters they are not mentioned at all. The only protagonists on the stage at the end are Job and the Deity, the best man and his God.

The concluding chapter of Job's speech (ch. 31), has a particular function in the economy of the book. Job is not satisfied with accusing, begging, and hoping; he takes more efficacious action compelling God to leave His uncommitted, whimsical transcendence and to take a stand, to relate Himself to his problems. Ancient man, as he conceptualized his world, had a means of challenging God: the oath. Man swears to a fact or a promise; if he perjures himself, God, Who is evoked in the oath, is bound to punish him; if it is a terrible oath, punishment will be terrible. (It is hardly necessary to remark that ordinarily an oath was not sworn in order to challenge God but to affirm a statement or a promise.) It is otherwise with Job. Ch. 31, 40 verses long, is his oath.[4] It is the most terrible oath in the Bible, for this reason: A full oath has the following form: "If I did or shall do this, or if I did not or shall not do this, then may God punish me." Ordinarily, however, the apodosis ("then may God punish me") is omitted. The very likely reason for this ellipsis is that

4. Vss. 35–37, probably to be placed after vs. 40, are not part of the oath but draw the sum total of Job's pleadings from ch. 3 through ch. 31. For the form of this oath, cf. S. H. Blank, *JJS* 2 (1951), pp. 105–107.

one shied away from conjuring up punishment in the unlikely event of an unintentional factual inaccuracy of the material content of the oath. Although uttered in good faith, such an inaccuracy may set in motion the mechanism of punishment for perjury that the oath envisages. Caution truncated the oath in biblical and post-biblical Israel and among her neighbors.[5] Job throws caution to the winds. Over and over he explicitly calls upon himself every conceivable punishment if what he says is not true.

He talks long but says in effect only one thing: that he has led an essentially good life, that he has not sinned. For all that he is not verbose. It is worth the reader's notice that the sins which he abjures are not, for the most part, monstrous crimes but minute deviations from the loftiest standards of ethics and piety. Here are a few examples: "If I have disdained the cause of my manservant or maidservant when they brought a complaint against me . . ." (vs. 13). "If I have withheld anything that the poor desired or have caused the eyes of the widow to fail . . ." (vs. 16). "If I have 'rejoiced'[6] at the ruin of my foe or exulted when evil overtook him . . ." (vs. 29). "If I have concealed my transgression as people (are wont to do) by hiding my iniquity in my bosom because I stood in great fear of the multitude . . . and kept silence . . ." (vss. 33f.). "If my land has cried out against me . . . if I have eaten its yield without payment and brought low the spirit of its owners"[7] (vss. 38f.).

The challenge to God is overt and clear. God is bound to act. If Job has perjured himself, God is to punish him even more than he is already punished, if that is yet possible. If not, he is pure; the oath proves it. Then he should be restored ***in integrum,*** for so judicial procedure requires. If neither of these immediate and plain alternatives result, God is challenged personally to respond to the oath. (Indeed, what Job desires above all else is the personal encounter with God, divine revelation.) Would that He produced counteraccusation; Job will make a crown and an ornament out of it—so certain is he of his case. He will stand up before God like a prince, he will not blink an eye (vss. 35–37). Job has grown to Promethean stature. The miracle is that it

5. The custom in Jewish Palestine of the first few centuries A.D. is described by S. Lieberman, *Greek in Jewish Palestine* (1942), ch. 5, especially pp. 121–24. It is as interesting as it is not surprising that the simple people were even more cautious than the rabbis in the formulation of the oath.

6. Read "וְהִתְרֹעַעְתִּי" with the Targum (ויבבית), commentaries; MT וְהִתְעֹרַרְתִּי.

7. The meaning of "my land" in conjunction with "its owners" is that Job had distrained real estate of defaulting debtors and, himself consuming its yield, had brought the impoverished original owners to the verge of despair. Had Job behaved in such a manner, he would have been fully within his legal rights, yet by virtue of his own highly developed conscience guilty of a cruel and antisocial act. M. Dahood, taking his cue from Ugaritic, has repeatedly insisted (most recently in *Biblica* 46 [1965], pp. 320f.) that בְּעָלֶיהָ is dialectical for פעליה (= פְּעָלֶהָ). This is possible but gratuitous. In general, we would observe that resort to dialectical features, non-standard sound shifts, or the like should not be had except with caution and primarily for the purpose of avoiding forced exegesis or unsupported emendations.

is not growth at the expense of piety. This is the most striking case in the Bible of a man so strongly asserting himself against God while yet remaining so loyal to Him.

From this vantage point, looking back over the disputation of Job and the friends and forward to the answer of God, we have no difficulty identifying the problem of the book in a preliminary way. It is the suffering of the innocent. There is broad agreement about this,[8] although the issue is sometimes blurred by the omission of the qualifier "of the innocent." The omission reduces the problem to suffering alone, but this is surely unintentional because the suffering of the non-innocent is deserved suffering, i.e., punishment. The friends indeed attempt repeatedly to construe Job's suffering as punishment. But no one has yet seen in this argument more than a straw man.

The problem of the suffering of the innocent is everywhere in the book. Where is the answer? It is a priori probable that it is found at the end. An answer comes after a question and not in the middle while the questioning is going on. This is a truism, to be sure, but its evocation is forced upon us by proposals that the answer lies in the middle of the book, e.g., in chaps. 19[9] or 28[10] or even in the speeches of Elihu.[11] As to the end, the prose epilogue presents no serious candidature. It contains little more than the story of Job's restoration to his former state of happiness and the pronouncement of his vindication. Thus by elimination we are directed to the final chapters of the poetry (hereinafter "final chapters"), 38:1–42:6, God's long speech and Job's short response. We assume that the answer is found in either or both of their components, and it will be our task to demonstrate that this assumption is correct, that here indeed lies the answer of the book. As the business of the demonstration begins immediately and extends to the end of the article, this assumption is henceforth our working hypothesis, one we hope will be vindicated in the course of this discussion.

Some critics, however, say that the final chapters are not part of the original book. Their argument runs as follows: The logic of literary structure as well as other considerations require that these chapters contain the answer of the book; this is their *raison d'être*. But they do not contain it (by which the critics mean: we have not detected in them an acceptable answer). Ergo, the chapters have no justification for existence; they were added later. Ergo, the

8. For a different opinion, cf. infra, p. 23.

9. For some of the champions of this proposal, notably those who hold that 19:25–27 refer to Job's resurrection or redemption, cf. Fohrer, com., pp. 318f. Further recent attempts to detect the solution in ch. 19 are mentioned by Kuhl 1953, p. 304. Add K. Fullerton, *ZAW* 42 (1924), pp. 116–36.

10. The opinions are cited and discussed by Kuhl 1953, p. 282; Rowley, pp. 166f. Add Tur Sinai, com., pp. 238, 388. It should be remarked, however, that a number of scholars who accept this view place the chapter at the end of the divine address.

11. K. Budde, com. (1913), pp. xlv–xlviii; others are listed by Kuhl 1953, pp. 261f.; Kuhl 1954, pp. 312f.

book has no answer to its problem.[12] This is lazy man's logic. The sentence "I have not detected the meaning" should signify to the philologist "I have not yet detected it," and this should spur him to further search in place of recourse to the easy alternative of denying the authenticity of the passage.

Yet since most of those who deny that the answer of the book is contained in its final chapters say that the book has no answer at all,[13] we have first to address ourselves to the question: does the book have an answer? This question we answer in the affirmative for the following reasons.[14]

First, were the book to contain no answer, we should be faced with a literary work posing a problem of the greatest moment without offering or even attempting a solution. The reader would be cut loose from his moorings of tradition and faith and left adrift. The Book of Job without an answer to its problem would constitute a literary torso, an anthology of verbalized doubts; it would betray an utter lack of appreciation of the controlling conceptions which are everywhere in evidence in the work. . . .

A second reason for postulating an answer to the problem of the suffering of the innocent in Job is the plain and obvious design of the book. It converges forcefully on the final chapters. Job's long concluding speech (chs. 29–31) containing his oath sums up his position but is not an absolute end. This speech is a transition, an expression of expectation; it culminates in his challenge to God as he subjects himself to the penalties enumerated in the oath; it is the strongest expression of his longing for confrontation. The final chapters bring the fulfillment; the desire to meet God, for a revelation, for an answer is granted there. To declare these chapters unauthentic is to reject the expected when it occurs.

A further support for the thesis that the problem of the book is answered is to be found in the beginning of the epilogue. It reads: "After having spoken these words to Job, the Lord said to Eliphaz, the Temanite: 'My wrath is kindled against you and your two friends; for you have not spoken of Me what is right as has My servant Job'" (42:7). As several scholars have observed, this verse refers to a revelation which God has just granted to Job. Job's wish has been fulfilled, his incessant questions have received a reply. Which means that explicit reference to an actual revelation is made in a different part of the book. God's answer to suffering Job is or contains His answer to the suffering of Job, i.e., it constitutes the solution to the problem of the book.[15] The answer of the book is anchored in its ground plan.

12. The latter conclusion is, of course, not shared by the comparatively small group of interpreters who are referred to in nn. 9–11.

13. Cf. n. 12.

14. Cf. also R. A. F. MacKenzie, *Biblica* 40 (1959), pp. 437–41.

15. Neither this nor the preceding arguments prove the genuineness of the present answer, 38:1–40:14 (for its extent, cf. n. 26); they admit of the highly improbable hypothesis that the original answer of the poem was replaced by the present one. (Whether an originally independent

Some scholars, however, for whom we may take C. Kuhl as a spokesman, share the extreme skepticism of the critics mentioned before. Overwhelmed by the difficulty of understanding God's reply, by the seeming unrelatedness of its content to Job's words, they say that God's answer is His theophany, the mere fact that He appeared to the man who deemed himself cast out from the presence of God. The theophany itself is genuine, but its verbal content, the long divine address, is a later addition.[16] At first glance, this opinion has much to recommend itself. The theophany rehabilitates Job. Job has suffered, but his suffering is no sign of his rejection. True, he as well as the friends have so interpreted it, but their interpretation is now corrected. Moreover, theophany, personal contact with God has been his greatest desire; now it is realized. Furthermore, revelation is the supreme good in biblical religion. Of Moses, Deuteronomy says (34:10): "There has not risen a prophet in Israel like Moses, whom the Lord knew face to face." Yet Job has come close to this. In general it may be said that all doubts, anguishes, and antagonisms to which a man may be prey, disappear in the presence of a vision. Job himself says as much in his last response: "I had heard of You from hearsay, but now my eye sees You. Therefore . . ." (42:5f.). The vision has transferred him into a new state. It is the fullest answer.

The importance of the revelation in the Book of Job is immense. It can be overemphasized in only one way: if it is made exclusive, if it is interpreted to be the whole answer. This, however, is a misinterpretation and must be rejected for the following reasons:

(1) The event of a revelation, distinct from its specific, articulate content, is personal, untransmissible, and unrepeatable. A report of a revelatory event as such is pure autobiography. Had the author of the book restricted himself to autobiography at this critical juncture, he would have proclaimed that his own problems were solved, but to his readers he would say implicitly: "If you are grievously afflicted, wait for a personal revelation; there is no salvation outside of revelation." Such an answer would be altogether incongruous.

(2) The design and the construction of the book do not lend themselves to Kuhl's interpretation. The book in its first thirty-one chapters[17] is the result of a supreme conceptual, literary, and poetical effort. Is it conceivable that the author invested this stupendous intellectual energy in the question only to seek, receive, and transmit the whole solution on a nonintellectual level?

---

prose story had a different disputation followed by a different speech of God [Fohrer, com., pp. 37, 538] need not detain us.)

16. Kuhl 1953, pp. 270f.

17. I accept the prevailing critical opinion that the Elihú pericope (chaps. 32–37) is secondary and therefore do not consider these chapters.

The reasoning and the conclusions of the preceding paragraphs are essentially formal, as this summary shows: the Book of Job presents a problem (it is the problem of the suffering of the innocent); the problem has an answer; the answer is contained in the final chapters; and the final chapters are authentic. The conclusions being formal, they must now be put to the test of substantiation through the interpretation of the final chapters that, according to our postulation, contain the answer.

"The Lord answered Job out of the storm" (38:1). Job is granted his request; God answers him. The answer comes from the storm, and since, in the Bible, a storm often precedes or accompanies a theophany, we are prepared for a theophany to occur with the answer. The occurrence is affirmed in Job's response: "Now my eye sees You" (42:5).

The divine speech has two introductory verses.

> Just who darkens the plan by words without knowledge? Gird up your loins like a man; I will question you, and you shall declare to me [38:2f.].

We shall learn soon which plan (עֵצָה) Job darkens. But irrespective of which and whose, his approach, possibly his very position, is rejected at the outset; he speaks "without knowledge." In vs. 3b, God formally accepts the challenge. Earlier Job offered God two alternatives: "Call, and I will answer; or let me speak, and You reply to me" (13:22). Now God chooses the first alternative. In contrast with the continuation of the verse, its beginning, "Gird up your loins," is figurative, possibly referring to an ancient custom, which C. H. Gordon calls "belt-wrestling."[18]

Now comes the substance of the speech. We know from vs. 3 that it will be presented in the form of a question, a question which breaks down into a series of detailed questions. The first group, vss. 4–11, concerns creation; within it, the first subgroup, vss. 4–7, contains questions about the creation of the earth, which means in the cosmology and language of the time, the dry land;

> Where were you when I laid the foundation of the earth? Tell me if you have understanding. Who determined its measurements—if you know that, or who stretched the line on it? In what were its bases sunk, or who laid its cornerstone, when the morning stars sang in unison and all the divine beings shouted for joy? (38:4–7)

"You, Job, were not present at the creation of the earth and, consequently, you know nothing about its nature." Take the problem of measurement. How can the infinitely large earth be measured? With which measuring line? After the measuring, the laying of foundations. This is even less comprehensible. On

18. Cf. *HUCA* XXIII:1 (1950f.), pp. 131–36.

what basis is this immense earth set? On the watery sea, as the Psalmist says (24:2)? Or maybe even on no basis at all, as the Book of Job itself has it ("He hangs the earth upon nothing," 26:7)? All this is a complete mystery. What makes it even more mysterious to man is that other beings, divine or celestial, are presumably able to answer these questions for they were present and involved when these things happened, they celebrated the great event—only human beings were not there and hence do not share the knowledge.

> 'Who'[19] shut in the sea with doors when it burst forth from the womb, when I made clouds its garment and dense fog its swaddling band, making breakers[20] 'its'[21] limit,[22] fixing bars and doors, and said: "Thus far shall you come and no farther; here shall your 'proud'[23] waves 'be stayed.'"[23] (38:8–11)

The author of Job was a well-educated man, familiar with the Jewish and non-Jewish literature of his time. His book abounds in allusions to the myths of the ancient Orient. One of the most prominent of them is the story of the fight of the supreme God, the leader of the present pantheon, with the sea which appears in the image of a gigantic dragon; the god is victorious and, according to one version, fashions the sky (and the earth) out of the body of the dead monster.[24] This myth is alluded to in other parts of the book (3:8; 7:12; 9:13; 26:12f.).[25] Yet nothing of it is present in this passage. The sea is not God's adversary; it is a giant baby, just born, that had to be confined at the moment of birth (vs. 8), when a baby must be wrapped in swaddling clothes. The stripes of fog on the surface of the sea are its swaddle (vs. 9). All this is subsumed under the question of vs. 4: "Where were you then?"

The text now turns from the creation of the world to its survey and management (38:12–39:30).[26] The form of the questions is maintained throughout. We are first shown the inanimate world (38:12–38). At the beginning there is the daily rise of the morning.

> Have you ever in your life commanded the morning, have you directed[27] the dawn to its place to take hold of the skirts of the earth so that the wicked are

19. Read 'מִי סָךְ', commentaries; so also the Vulgate (*quis conclusit*); MT וַיָּסֶךְ.

20. וָאֶשְׁבֹּר, denominative from מִשְׁבָּרִים "breakers, surf at the reefs of the shore."

21. Read 'חֻקּוֹ', commentaries; MT חֻקִּי.

22. Cf. 14:5.

23. Read 'יִשָּׁבֵת גְּאוֹן', commentaries; MT יָשִׁית בִּגְאוֹן.

24. Cf. the Assyro-Babylonian epic Enuma Elish IV:93ff.

25. Cf., e.g., Fohrer, com., pp. 502f., who offers an inclusive treatment of this and other mythological imagery.

26. I incline to the critical opinion that 40:15–41:26 are not authentic; cf. the references in Rowley, p. 166, n. 1; also Fohrer, com., p. 39. But the point this article is trying to make is not affected by one's critical position regarding this section; cf. also Rowley's view, p. 166. Other insertions in the final chapters will be critically recognized in their proper places.

27. Cf. the same meaning of a probably related form of this verb in 1 Sam. 21:3.

> shaken out of it—it changes like clay under the seal and 'it is dyed'[28] like a garment—so that light is withheld from the wicked, and their uplifted arm is broken? (38:12–15)

Has Job ever performed such a routine thing as bringing on a new day? Following up the broad question by special attention to one corner of the tableau, which is nothing but a manifestation of His interest in the world as it is, God describes the dawn by what it does to the earth. The latter looks like a broad piece of cloth, of indistinct color first, but the color changes soon and keeps changing with the brightening of the day. As the sun rises, the contours of the earth are beginning to stand out clearly like the impression of a seal on soft clay.

Next comes a paragraph which may be called "The dimensions of the universe."

> Have you reached the springs of the sea[29] or walked in the recesses of the deep? Have the gates of death been laid bare to your sight, and have you seen the gates to murk? Have you examined well (the universe) as far as the farthest (ends) of the netherworld? Speak, if you know any of this! Where is the way to the abode of the light, and where is the place of darkness, that you may lead either one[30] back to its realm or discern the paths to its home? You surely know all this[31] for you were already born then, and the number of your days is great indeed. (38:16–21)

"The first questions, all left unanswered, showed clearly enough," God continues, "that you were not present at the creation of the world. Have you at least seen its full expanse?" The question, like all the others, is rhetorical and

28. Read 'וְתִצְטַבַּע' or 'וְתִצָּבַע', commentaries; MT וְיִתְיַצְּבוּ.

29. The nouns in vss. 16–18 may refer to names of gods or demons in various ancient Oriental mythologies and accordingly be rendered as "Sea," "Deep" (or "Primeval Flood"), "Death," "Murk," and "Netherworld"; or "Yamm," *"Tiham," "Mot," "Ṣalmut," and *"Ars." (*Tiham, and *Ars may be hypothesized by their appearance [in feminine forms] in the cognate literature. Tiamtu, etc., is well known from the Assyro-Babylonian civilization. Remarkably, ארציח [= Erișitu] appears in Jewish folklore [M. Gaster, ספר מעשיות, here after S. Krauss, *HUCA* IV (1927), p. 352; Krauss, however, misinterprets the word].) I cannot decide whether the author, oscillating between the semantic foreground ("sea") and background ("Sea," "Yamm"), intends either of these pairs of meanings ("sea" or "Sea" [or "Yamm," respectively] and in like manner all the others) or both of them. The language of classical Hebrew poetry admits of both, and it is often beyond our means to settle on a single meaning ("sea" or "Sea/Yamm") or the double meaning ("sea-Sea/Yamm"). (A comparable problem is presented in Sumero-Akkadian cuneiform, where, for example, ***ᵈŠamaš***, for all the presence of the divine determinative, in many contexts conveys to the modern reader nothing more than "sun.") The program of the significance of Near Eastern mythology in Job will be discussed further on. . . .

30. "Either one" is an attempt to render the distributive function of the Hebrew personal suffixes; this function is present, e.g., in חַרְבּוֹ and קַשְׁתּוֹ. (Isa. 41:2).

31. The force of כֻלָּהּ after יָדַעְתָּ of vs. 18 extends to יָדַעְתָּ of this verse. The word is not repeated, perhaps in order to avoid crowding the stich.

has an ironical ring; the expected answer is no. Job knows only a small section of the world. The sarcasm of vs. 21, however, momentarily disregards the conclusion of vss. 4ff.: "You know all this because at the time of their creation you must have been alive—or so you behave."

The theme of the dimensions of the universe is continued in the next paragraph, dealing with precipitations and winds.

> Have your reached the storehouses of the snow and have you see the storehouses of the hail, which I have reserved for times of trouble, for the day of battle and war? By what route does the west wind[32] escape[33] or the east wind fan out over the earth? Who has cleft a channel for the rain flood and a way for the thunder cloud to cause rain on land where no man is, on a desert where no people live to satiate waste and desolate terrain and to sprout fresh grass?[34] Has the rain a father, and (is there one) who sired the drops[35] of the dew? From whose womb does the ice come forth, and who gives birth to the rime of heaven, when the water 'becomes solid'[36] like stone, and the surface of the waters is 'hidden'?[36] (38:22–30)

Vss. 28–30 raise a new point. God asks Job: "How do rain, ice, and frost come into being? Give a realistic answer. Do not give Me myths for facts." Mythological fragments or just allusions to myths are one of the secondary features of Job, probably more prominent in it than in any other biblical book.[37] But what was only an inkling in the passage about the sea (vss. 8–11), here becomes explicit. Myths in Job, as in general in the other (poetic) books of the Bible, are literary devices, a stylistic feature betraying the broad education of the author, but hardly constitutive elements of his belief. "Has the rain a father?" The myth says yes: explicitly or implicitly, rain is the semen of the

32. Vocalize 'אוּר' (?) <Aram. אוריה <Akkad. ***amurrū*** (Tur Sinai, com.).

33. Akkad. *ḫalāqu* means both "to flee, escape, slip away" and "to perish." M. Dahood considers the second meaning for some biblical passages (***Biblica*** 45 [1964], p. 408). The first, however, provides the basis for interpreting Jer. 37:12 (already Redaq, Rosenmüller, and Gesenius [***Thesaurus***] from the context, as well as Geller and Tur Sinai based on the Akkadian); Lam. 4:16 (following verbs of motion and naming the ultimate agent of it: "the face of the Lord chased them away" [cf. Num. 10:35]); 1 Sam. 23:28 (an etiological connection of the story with the "Rock of Escape"). There is no basis for judging the masoretic vocalization of the verb here and in the Jeremiah passage.

34. טֶעֶא, literally "plants" or "growth." Cf. Gen. 1:12.

35. The meaning of אֶגְלֵי is conjectural. (A. Guillaume's etymology, *Abr-Nahrain* 1 [1959f.], p. 6, had justly been questioned by [Driver and] Gray, com., four decades before it was proposed.)

36. Very uncertain. The translation of this verse follows a number of commentaries in (1) emending the text by exchanging the order of the verbs and (2) assuming for יִתְלַכָּדוּ the meaning "hold together" (41:9 || יְדֻבָּקוּ hence "pack, solidify," metaphorical for "freeze." Moreover, "waters" as the rendition of תְהוֹם has no better support than Ezek. 31:4 and Ps. 42:6. (It cannot mean here "primeval flood," or "sea," "rivers," since neither the one nor the others—in and around Palestine—ever freeze.)

37. Cf. supra, p. 12.

weather god. The Book of Job says no. This no, which is clad in the by now familiar form of a rhetorical question, destroys a world of fancy and coherence which everybody understands and in which he can orient himself,[38] without explicitly substituting another one of comparable serviceability.[39]

Vss. 31–38, not reproduced here, contain final questions about the inanimate world, in particular about various celestial phenomena. Beginning with vs. 39 to the end of the descriptive interrogation (39:30)[40] we find ourselves on the road through the kingdom of animals. Several of its members, from the lion down, pass before our eyes. Each member or group of members represents one side of animal life, and God questions Job about it. First providing food for wild animals; this is demonstrated at the lion.

> Can you hunt the prey for the lion or satisfy the appetite of the lions[41] when they crouch in their dens or lie in wait in the thicket? Who provides his prey 'in the evening'[42] when his whelps roving without food cry to God? (38:39–41)

Man is not wont to give much thought to the food supply of wild animals, but it is a problem all the same. Would Job assume the responsibility of providing food for one of their kind who normally has no difficulty in getting what he needs?

Next comes procreation; the texts speak about mountain goats and deer.

> Do you know when the mountain goats give birth, or do you observe the calving of the hinds? Can you number the months that they fulfil and know the time when they give birth, when they crouch to bring forth their offspring and cast their young? Their kids become strong, grow up in the open, and go forth never to return. (39:1–4)

Here it is not the question of responsibility and care but something less. It is only knowledge, obtained through observation of some phases of animal life. But alas, the animals are too swift for observation, or the phases are too long.

The next paragraph, speaking about the zebra(?),[43] the onager, and the wild ox, concerns the freedom and taming of wild beasts.

> Who has let the zebra go free and who has loosened the onager's bonds to whom I have given the steppe for his home and the salt land for his habitat?

38. Cf. infra, p. 30.
39. But note that vss. 34 and 37 suggest (different) explanations of the origin of rain.
40. Cf. n. 26 about 40:15–41:26.
41. (כפיר(ים, another of the several Hebrew words for lion.
42. The vocalization 'לְעֶרֶב '(cf. 4:10f.; Ps. 104:20f.) is preferable to masoretic לְעֹרֵב, commentaries; the raven is quite out of place before 39:26 or rather 39:30. Also, יְחַנּוּ is more appropriate as applied to young lions than young ravens, so much so, that many who retain לְעֹרֵב find it necessary to emend the end of the verse.
43. The identification is not certain.

> He scorns the tumult of the city; he does not hear the driver's shouts. He 'ranges'[44] the mountains as his pasture and searches after every bit of green. is the wild ox willing to serve you? Will he spend the night at your manger? Does a rope[45] bind the wild ox to the furrow? Will he at your heels plow up the valleys?[46] Can you depend on him for the greatness of his strength and shunt your work upon him? Can you rely on him to return,[47] 'to'[48] your threshing floor[48] bring home your grain? (39:5–12)

"Zebra and onager owe you nothing," says God, "not even their freedom. They are far beyond your ken and completely beyond your reach." Speaking of the wild ox, God continues the line of this argument but gives it a practical turn: "The wild ox could be quite a useful beast with his strength, but you are unable to domesticate him. You know little about the world and can do less about it. You are unable to effect so small a change in the order of the created world as would be the transferral of a wild beast to the category of the tame. It is your will against the will of the beast, yet it is his which prevails."

The rest of the road through the animal kingdom (39:13–30), passing in succession the ostrich (vss. 13–18), the horse (vss. 19–25), and the hawk and the vulture[49] (vss. 26–30), need not be traversed here. The form of a string of (rhetorical) questions is preserved throughout. At the end of the journey God looks back as He draws the sum of His questioning. The beginning of the concluding section of His speech (40:2, 8–14)[50] is transitional in form in

44. Vocalize 'יָתוּר', commentaries; MT יְתוּר.

45. Literally "his rope," i.e., the rope which would bind him. But the text of the stich is suspect. רֵים, not in the LXX, is perhaps a vertical dittography from vs. 9. If so, the translation is: "Can you bind 'I' his rope (as he plows, or: in order that he plow) in the furrow?" Cf. Tur Sinai, com.

46. The passage would be consistent with the use of a two-handle plow which requires two plowmen, one handling the plow, the other leading the ox; or, since it is highly unlikely that such plows were used in biblical Palestine (cf. J. Feliks, החקלאות בארץ ישראל בתקופת המשנה והתלמוד [1963], p. 29), it might have reference to the custom of drawing border furrows which require two plowmen irrespective of the type of plow (cf. Fohrer, com., after Guthe); or to a special plowing, before or after the main plowing, similarly requiring two men, which may be the intention of יְשַׂדֵּד (cf. Isa. 28:24; and see the comment of Feliks, supported by rabbinic passages, ibid., pp. 37f.; "to harrow" is wrong).

47. The *ketiv* ישוב is adopted; the *qere* is יָשִׁיב.

48. Read 'יְזָרְעֲךָ גָרְנֶךָ' commentaries ('and' is not expressed in the translation); MT זַרְעֲךָ וְגָרְנְךָ. The word זֶרַע assumes the extended meaning "(seed grain>) grain = harvest."

49. The identification of נֶשֶׁר, "vulture" or/and "eagle," is not settled; cf. G. R. Driver, *PEQ* 86f. (1955), pp. 9f.; 90 (1958), pp. 56f.; M. Dor, לשוננו 27f. (1963f.), pp. 290–92; Z. Ben Hayim, ibid., pp. 293f.; (תשכ״ג-תשכ״ד) זיכרונות האקדמיה ללשון העברית, 1965, pp. 222–30.

50. The critical omission of a number of verses and the rearrangement of the remaining ones, which also affects Job's answer, represent the opinion of the scholars named by Kuhl 1953, p. 269; it is convincingly argued by Fohrer, com., pp. 37–39. But again (cf. n. 26), the meaning of this part of Job and thereby of the whole book does not depend on the critical surgery performed on the text here. The transmitted text as well as a number of different critical rearrangements are all compatible with the interpretation offered here.

that it continues, in vss. 2, 8f., the rhetorical questions of chaps. 38f.; but they are not longer questions about the world.

> Will the reprover enter suit against Shaddai? Let him who admonishes God give answer. Will you really nullify My judgment, put Me in the wrong so that you may be vindicated? Or is it that you have an arm like God and like Him can thunderously roar? Deck yourself with majesty and dignity, clothe yourself in state and glory. Give free scope to your raging anger. Seeing anyone haughty, bring him low; seeing anyone haughty, abase him and tread down the wicked in their tracks. Conceal them alike in the earth, wrap their faces in concealment. Then I, too, will acknowledge that your right hand is all-prevailing. (40:2, 8–14)

"Will the reprover enter suit?" The reprover, of course is Job, and reproof is exactly what he administered to the Deity throughout the disputation. These words of reproof were the overflow of an embittered soul; but is he really prepared to enter into litigation with Him? "Let him who admonishes God give answer. Yes or no? Do you now, having failed to answer even one of My questions about the world, yet desire to contend with Me? (40:2). Would you nullify My judgment so that you may be vindicated? Is this an issue which concerns your person alone? Are you so wrapped up in yourself as to be closed to all else? Or would you now perhaps admit the possible existence and validity of standards of which you had not dreamed or the possible nonexistence or invalidity of standards in which you have believed or which you have taken for granted? (40:8). Have you any of the divine attributes required to govern the world? (40:9). At this juncture it is might, not knowledge, which Job would have to possess for the task but does not.) If you have, don the robes of office, take up the scepter (40:10). Then, having dressed for the part, begin your rule: put the wicked in their place! (40:13). Do that, and I will recognize your potency" (40:14). The issue is now clearly drawn. Does Job have the power? Will he pick up the gauntlet?

It is precisely at this point, no earlier, no later, that Job must respond. This structural requirement is one of the reasons for the critical rearrangement of the text. Job's answer, however, is more than an indispensable element of the literary structure. It is the outgrowth of the peculiar form that the problem of the suffering of the innocent takes on in the book: the narration of the experience of a particular person.[51] The reader of this narration who has seen Job as more than a spokesman for a philosophical viewpoint, who has involved

51. There is a view recorded in the Talmud (not, however, unopposed) that Job was not a historical personage (Baba Bathra 14b and parallels). My own opinion is that the understanding of the book as fiction should not be accepted except in the narrow sense that events did not happen exactly as told. The book is too close to human experience to be taken as a total invention. In any case, the intensity of direct involvement shines through the haze rising out of the questions of historical literalness.

himself in the person of Job throughout the long, heart-rending disputation, must ask at its end: "Has the revelation of God in and of itself had any effect on Job? And if so, what? How does Job see himself and his problem now that God Himself has spoken? In other biblical revelations nothing is the same after the event; God calls and man responds. Is Job a biblical book in this dialogical sense of God's call and man's response? Is Job after the revelation a wiser, better man?" The answer to these questions lies in Job's last words, in the fact that he spoke at all, and in what it was he said.

> Then Job answered the Lord:[52] I am indeed of small account; what shall I answer You? I lay my hand on my mouth. I have spoken once but will not 'do so again,'[53] twice indeed, but will say no more. I know that You can do everything, that nothing You purpose is impossible for You. Verily,[54] I made pronouncements but understood not, about things too wondrous for me, beyond my ken. From hearsay I had heard of You, but now my eye sees You. Therefore I retract[55] and repent in dust and ashes. (40:3–5; 42:2, 3b, 5, 6)

The talk is coming to its end. Toward the conclusion of His address (40:2) God has called upon Job to answer. But this Job declines to do: "I cannot. I can no longer carry on. I am too light" (קַלֹּתִי RSV: "I am of small account," which is a paraphrase). The root קלל is antonymous to כבר which yields the noun כָּבוֹד "weight, value, substance, essence of personality."[56] Biblical man's כָּבוֹד was most precious to him; take away his כָּבוֹד and you deprive him of his better part. Job concerned himself with כָּבוֹד on two separate occasions in the earlier parts of the book (19:9; 29:20). But when God now asks him about the world and invites him to perform certain acts, Job who has no answer and is unable to meet the challenge disclaims all כָּבוֹד and says קַלֹּתִי. His position has crumbled, he cannot stand up and gird his loins like a man, he brings the disputation to a halt, he "will say no more" (40:4f.). But if he does not know the answers to God's specific questions about the world, he has gained knowledge about God and thus indirectly about the world in general. God began His speech with the rhetorical question intending Job: "Just who darkens the plan by words without knowledge?" (38:2). God made and is upholding the world according to His plan, but Job misinterpreted it in his words, i.e., according to the light of his own conceptions. Now Job has become wiser. He

52. On the arrangement of the text, cf. n. 50.

53. Read 'אֶשְׁנֶה', commentaries, literal translation "'do it twice'"; MT אֶעֱנֶה.

54. לָכֵן as in Gen. 4:15; 30:15; 1 Sam. 28:2. F. J. Goldbaum, *JNES* 23 (1964), pp. 132–34, sweepingly generalizes a special application of the word, viz., the introduction of a vow.

55. Cf. L. J. Kuyper, *VT* 9 (1959), pp. 91–94.

56. כָּבוֹד as a social concept is "honor." "Die Ehre ist, objektiv, die Meinung Anderer von unserm Wert, und subjektive, unsere Furcht vor sieser Meinung" (A. Schopenhauer, *Parerga und Paralipomena,* "Aphorismen zur Lebensweishiet," ch. 4. [*Sämtliche Werke,* vol. 4, Leipzig, Inselverlag, Grossherzog Wilhelm Ernst Ausgabe, no date, p. 426]).

sees that nothing God purposes is impossible—either of conception or of execution (42:2). Repudiation of his former position is now for Job both a necessary logical and existential consequence (42:3b).

Job's misinterpretation of God and the world was due to his conceptions which were by and large those of Israelite tradition. His argument with the friends rested on this ground common to all of them, and their disagreement was about secondary features and particularly had regard to the application of the philosophy of tradition to his fate. Tradition, the text calls it שֵׁמַע אֹזֶן,[57] was immensely important in ancient Israel. When it was tradition of religious doctrines, and when these doctrines were combined into a comparatively consistent whole, we speak of traditional theology. There is no part in the Old Testament which represents the most common variety of traditional theology better than the talk of Job and the friends. But let us remember that insofar as Israelite tradition was biblical it was given to eruptions, notably at the appearance of God. Job's experience of divine revelation has raised him above the hearsay of tradition; he has "seen" God. This "seeing" is not, to be sure, mere sensory perception by the eye but a personal meeting. And this meeting means for man that he has achieved the closest contact with the Deity and is now among His most faithful and intimate ones. Job had desired confrontation with God; he has received much more: communion. Be it clear, however, that this communion is not mystical oneness of man and God; "Gott bleibt Gott, Mensch bleibt Mensch."[58] It is the closest possible meeting of two personalities which remain distinct.

The communion of Job with God resembles the communion of the prophets with the Divine. As such it has important consequences for the understanding of the book, consequences in regard to which I find myself in disagreement with Fohrer despite the fact that he, too, recognizes the similarity of the experience of Job and that of the prophets.[59] The prophets are taken into God's counsel. "God does nothing without revealing His counsel to His servants the prophets," says Amos (3:7). God deliberates with Amos (7:1–9; 8:3), with Isaiah (6:8–13), and others as He deliberated aforetime with Abraham (Gen. 18:17–21, 23–33) and Moses (Exod. 32–34). Not only is the intellectual element characteristically present in their communion with God, the communion involves: usually the understanding of, often the approval of, sometimes an active sharing in His plan. Job's communion with God is not bought with an intellectual sacrifice, at the cost of renouncing his wish to understand the constitution of the world. True, of its creation, its expanse, its details—of animal life and of all the other things—he has no

57. Words for hearing, asking, telling, remembering, and the like express the concept of tradition in biblical Hebrew; e.g., 2 Sam. 7:22; Ps. 44:2; 78:3f.; Deut. 4:32; 32:7; Job 8:8, 10; Exod. 13:8, 14; Judg. 6:13; Ps. 77:6f.

58. Fohrer, com., p. 535, n. 6.

59. Fohrer, com., p. 53.

more knowledge now than he had before. But he now has gained an insight into its constitution, even as the prophets were granted new understanding in the communion with God (42:5).

"Therefore I retract and repent in dust and ashes." These are Job's final words. Outwardly nothing has changed for him. He is still sitting in the dirt: "He took a potsherd with which to scrape himself and sat in the ashes" (2:8). The ashes are the same, but it is a changed man who is sitting in them.

What has changed him? The revelation—by which we mean two things: the fact of the revelation itself and its content; and it is this content that is the answer to the problem of the work, the meaning of the Book of Job. The question is, however, just what is the answer, what is God's reply?

A review of a few interpretations is in order before I offer my own interpretation. The criteria governing the selection are durability, newness, or the importance of the interpretations.

The interpretation that probably enjoys the greatest popularity is the one that might be labelled "education through overwhelming." Job is shown the immensity, complexity, and mystery of the universe; these greatly exceed his comprehension. For all this he can and does relate himself to this stupendous world by recognizing in it its creator, ruler, and sustainer. God is not only infinitely mightier but also wiser than he. God's is that inscrutable business, the government of the world. While man thinks only of his own needs and problems, God sustains a whole world, providing for all His creatures. As Job is made aware of the world's material and spiritual dimensions—dimensions forever beyond his grasp—he is reduced to submission. The long catalog of the complexities and wonders of the universe, culminating in the evidence of the providential care for the animals, seems to bear out this interpretation; but its faults are so fatal—and glaring at that—that the fact of its wide acceptance must in itself be regarded as a problem in the history of the interpretation of the book. Job has never doubted God's power or wisdom. He has, in fact, repeatedly spoken of them, albeit mostly with bitterness because of God's capricious misuse of His superior might and wisdom to thwart justice (see, for instance, chaps. 9 and 12). Although the complexities of the governance of the world have not been Job's concern, we are given no reason to doubt his readiness to recognize them. They are not, however, the issue, nor is God's ability to keep things going. The issue is: Why do I suffer? Why do the righteous suffer?[60]

Distantly related to this interpretation is the one given by M. Buber,[61] with which can loosely be associated that of G. von Rad.[62] Buber does not fail to

60. It would be altogether consistent with the interpretation under scrutiny to make God answer this question with the counterquestion: "Are things not complicated enough the way they are now? Why do you want to make them more difficult with your question?"

61. *The Prophetic Faith* (1949), pp. 194f.; in the German original, *Werke,* vol. 2 (1964), pp. 441f.

62. *Theologie des A. T.*, vol. 1 (1957), pp. 414f.

see that the problem is not the dimensions and mysteries of the universe and that parading its complexities will not provide the answer. He sees that the problem is justice. But when it comes to the answer, Buber would have us believe that the answer is as follows: God teaches Job that divine justice, to be exact, the justice of God which is manifest in creation, is greater than human justice; that it is not retributory and egalitarian but allotting, spending, freely flowing; that God gives each creature that which is appropriate, ***suum cuique***. But this is no answer at all. For Job's question remains: Is it "appropriate" for the innocent to suffer and for the wicked to prosper? God's allotment of fates is not the issue; this Job has never doubted. What the issue does concern is the fate of the individual, its why and wherefore. What is the reason for God's not shaping this fate in accordance with the standards that He himself has set? In other words, not the ***cuique*** is the question but the ***suum***. But what is particularly disturbing in Buber's interpretation is the very application of the term justice to God's generosity (a generosity which would here consist of a liberal allotment of suffering to the righteous). Nothing is gained by such assignment of private meanings to terms which in ordinary and universal usage—the Book of Job not excepted—denote the opposite.

Robert Gordis has another interpretation, whose essence may be stated in his own words. "Nature is . . . a cosmos, a thing of beauty . . . Just as there is order and harmony in the natural world . . . so there is order and meaning in the moral sphere . . . When man steeps himself in the beauty of the world his troubles . . . dissolve within the larger plan . . . The beauty of the world becomes an anodyne to man's suffering—and the key to truth . . . and it is before this truth that he [Job] yields."[63] The operative words in the above argument are ". . . beauty becomes an anodyne to man's suffering—and the key to truth." If the question is justice, would anyone propose that the demands of justice are met by the administering of an anesthesia to the victim of an unjust sentence? And if the question is pain and torture, the beauty surrounding the tortured may in its contrast intensify the pain. It was just Bialik's sensitivity to the beauty in nature that indeed led him to write in בעיר ההרגה, a poem about the pogrom of Kishinev in 1903: [64]

כִּי קָרָא אֲדֹנָי לָאָבִיב וְלַטֶּבַח גַּם־יָחַד:
הַשֶּׁמֶשׁ ז רְחָה, הַשִּׁטָּה פָּרְחָה וְהַשּׁוֹחֵט שָׁחַט.

Moreover, one cannot fail to observe that Gordis does not distinguish between the reality and an artistic description of it. Thus the reader of chs.

63. In *Great Moral Dilemmas in Literature* . . ., R. M. MacIver ed. (1956), pp. 177f.; *Judaism* 13 (1964), pp. 48–63. The quotation is from *Judaism*, pp. 62f.

64. "The Lord called forth spring and killing at once:
The sun shone, the locust bloomed, and the butcher
butchered" (lines 21f.)

38f., admires the beauty of the description of the world, not the beauty of the world itself. The sea pictured as a baby just breaking forth from the womb and instantly wrapped in swaddling clothes, the fogs which lie on the surface of the waters, as in the words of 38:8–11, is art. The imagery is unquestionably beautiful, but is the sea beautiful? One may be impressed by the creation of the poet, yet not by the sea, which one may never even have seen. If the distinction is made between reality and literature, Gordis's interpretation becomes untenable.

The last interpretation to be examined, that of G. Fohrer, actually attacks the question of the problem itself.[65] The problem of the book, says Fohrer, is not: Why does the righteous man suffer? but: What is the proper conduct of man in suffering? It does not concern theodicy but man's life and his conduct. The question of theodicy is not even raised, for it is one which cannot be answered. From this it follows that the answer of the Book of Job cannot be found in the address of God but only in the final reply of Job. "In der vorbehaltlosen Hingable an Gott and in der persönlichen Gemeinschaft mit ihm trägt und erträgt Hiob sein Geschick . . . Hiob wird in das gross Leben und Leiden der Welt eingegliedert, zugleich aber durch die Gemeinschaft mit dem göttlichen Urgrund der Welt herausgehoben. Das ist das rechte Verstehen des Leides und das rechte Verhalten des Menschen in ihm: demütiges und hingebungsvolles Schweigen aus dem Ruhen in Gott . . ."[66]

My earlier remarks indicate how far I am able to go along with Fohrer.[67] Job's reply and the way he replies are essential to the book. The book is more than the exposition of a concept; it is the life story of a man,[68] written with his life blood. The end of the story, his reply to the divine questioning, is indispensable for without it the beginning and the middle are without justification. It completes the confrontation and complements the revelation. The fault of Fohrer's interpretation, as I see it, lies in its exclusiveness, i.e., in refusing to see in the Book of Job a theoretical treatise. It is my view that while it is not only a theoretical treatise, it is certainly that, and basically that. My criticism of those scholars who, disregarding the content of God's speech,

65. *ThZ* 18 (1962), pp. 1–24; com., pp. 532, 536, 557–59; cf. the opinions referred to on pp. 557f., n. 21.

66. Fohrer, com., p. 558. S. Terrien denies with Fohrer that the main theme of the book is the suffering of the innocent, the problem of theodicy; cf. his contribution to *The Interpreter's Bible,* vol. 3 (1954), pp. 877–1198, particularly pp. 897, 902; and his *Job (Commentaire de l'A.T.* 13; 1963), particularly pp. 35f., 45–49. Terrien differs from Fohrer in that he refuses to deconceptualize the essence of the book as radically and systematically as does Fohrer. But this difference seems, at times, to be only one of degree. In a context which only slightly mitigates the boldness of his statement he says: Man "transgresse les limites de son humanité chaque fois qu'il prononce un jugement sur le caractére de la divinité" (*Job,* p. 45). Cf. also Rowley, pp. 176, 183.

67. Cf. supra, pp. 18f.

68. Cf. supra, p. 18.

restrict the answer of the book to the fact of the revelation,[69] also applies, in some measure, to Fohrer. Indeed, man's conduct in suffering may not exist even as a secondary theme.[70] But be that as it may, the primary theme is the suffering of the innocent. For the overwhelming majority of readers and commentators this is, and always has been, the problem of the book.[71]

In a text of such demonstrated difficulty as is the speech of God (witness the numerous contradictory interpretations) the meaning often eludes a verse-to-verse approach. We shall, therefore, have recourse to another approach: first, we shall derive the answer to the problem of the book from its total conceptual content; second, seek the verification of the answer in the text of the divine address; third, apply two controls to the answer, one external to the address, the other to the book.

69. Cf. supra, pp. 9f.

70. It would be wrong to posit that in presenting Job's communion with God and his retraction the book sees a normative model for man's conduct in suffering.

71. At this juncture it may be remarked that the epilogue, which could be expected to be relevant to the answer of the book, fails notably to offer confirmation of any of the foregoing interpretations or any other interpretation known to me. The epilogue vindicates Job in general but also explicitly in relation to the friends: "After having spoken these words to Job, the Lord said to Eliphaz, the Temanite: 'My wrath is kindled against you and your two friends, for you have not spoken of Me what is right as has My servant Job'" (vs. 7). It is in this verse and in some of the following that the author takes the occasion, the only time in the entire work, to state explicitly his opinion of the friends and their philosophy and to sum up his evaluation of Job and his philosophy and conduct. But he does not even begin to explain why that which Job has spoken of God—as compared with that which the friends have—is right. (דִּבֶּר אֶל with the rare meaning "to speak of, concerning" [cf. 1 Sam. 3:12] is a case of the otherwise frequent interchange of אֶל and עַל; the standard phrase with this meaning is דִּבֶּר עַל) Of even greater moment is the fact that he does not in any way relate the epilogue's vindication of Job to what must be regarded as absolutely true, namely, the divine answer. This may be accounted for in terms of the literary prehistory of the book (if the hypothesis is accepted that the author used an existing prose frame and adapted it imperfectly) or of the genre and purpose of the existing prose frame and adapted it imperfectly) or of the genre and purpose of the prose epilogue (i.e., the narrative hurries to the eventful end and seeks to avoid retarding complications). Whatever the reason, the reader may regret that the author is not more helpful in his last verses.

A characteristically modern approach deplores the very existence of the epilogue coming, as it does, after the heights of the poetry achieved in the final chapters. Admitting the literary requirement of a complete narrative frame, beginning and end, and even the desirability of the idyllic tones of the final, a number of readers yet regard this finale as anticlimatic (cf. Kuhl 1953, pp. 204f.; Rowley, pp. 159f.). This approach elicits two comments. One, it cannot be assumed as a matter of course that the ancient Israelite would have been disturbed by this anticlimax in the same manner as the contemporary Westerner reared on the canons of Greek literary style and theory. The Israelite may indeed have welcomed it with relief. Secondly, the epilogue provides the needed resolution of the plot. Job was afflicted with physical ailments and social ostracism and suffered spiritual torments. He was freed of the last of these afflictions in the final chapters of the poetry; the physical and social penalties remain. The problem of the book, which is spiritual, is solved, and Job is vindicated—as will be shown—before the epilogue. But he remains in his physical pain and in social disgrace. His pain was a necessary device in the drama of ideas. This drama now over and pain having played out its role, that pain should be removed. The epilogue does just this.

Job and his friends, worlds apart in many respects, share one belief; the acrimoniousness of their disputation and its minute details are due to this shared premise: the world is founded on justice, i.e., *quid pro quo,* reward and punishment, which will hereinafter be referred to as the principle of retribution. This principle pervades the world. Job and the friends hold fast to this belief because they have been raised in it; because everybody has it; because man has an intense need to abide by it. The need is so great that he goes to the remotest extremes to uphold it. When reality does not agree with the principle of retribution, whose function is to structure and interpret reality, so much the worse for reality. Man distorts his experience of reality, disregards facts, imagines figments, fashions *ad hoc* theories, and erects superstructures, all so as not to give up or substantially change the principle. A parade example of this phenomenon is the discussion of Job and the friends. What accounts for this phenomenon? The fact that this principle of retribution is the touchstone of man's life and his conduct within his society. Whether in the rearing of children or the administration of justice, it is this principle which guides him. From it flow some of his noblest deeds. And so it is natural that God is conceived as guaranteeing it in the governance of the world.

But give up the principle, reject causality in the physical-ethical world, and the problem of Job, the man and the book, disappears. Where justice is possible, injustice is, too. Where it is not, where the principle of retribution has no validity, there can be no injustice. In the absence of this principle, for Job to expect a lot corresponding morally with his deed is absurd. Where there is no ground for expecting anything, it is pointless for him to complain of his disappointment: that though he has been pious and upright his lot is bitter. Nor is there any point to the inference drawn by the friends from Job's lot to his conduct. To repeat: only the awareness that the world of ideas, unlike the world of matter, is not governed by the category of cause and effect, i.e., only the elimination of the principle of retribution, can solve the problem of the book.

This is the inescapable conclusion from the conceptual content of the book and an analysis of its problem. Its verification must be sought in God's address. God says to Job: "You were not present when the universe was created. You do not know its blueprint or the stuff that went into its making." No less than three times God refers to the "foundation," "the basis," and "the cornerstone" of the inhabited world, the earth (38:4, 6). "What, then, makes you assume that it is justice which is its foundation?" "Moreover," God continues, "you do not know the mundane phenomena of the natural world." And He draws progressively tighter circles around Job, proceeding in order of diminishing expanse from the realm of heaven and the underworld to that of those wild beasts which Job, for all his desire, cannot domesticate. Arriving at what is most familiar to Job, He finally asks: "Perhaps, at least, you know your own homestead?" No answer. "If, then, you know nothing and can do nothing, why ever should you assume that retribution, justice (צֶדֶק), is a constituent element in the plan (עֵצָה [38:2]; מְזִמָּה [42:2]) of the world?" (38:2). Thus God leads Job through the macrocosm and microcosm, but nowhere does Job see justice. From the linguistic approach, it is striking that √צדק and other roots which express the idea of justice, viz. √ישר and √תמם , while moderately frequent in chs. 1–31,[72] are not found at all in the story of Job's journey through the world.[73] And, let us note, the centrality of the idea of justice in the book and the broadness of the canvas on which the universe is painted preclude the deprecation of this observation as an argument from silence.

But we are not left with negative argumentation alone. The divine address contains some passages that have not, it seems to me, received due attention in the commentaries. It is striking that the description of the inanimate world, comprising almost all of chapter 38, is interrupted by an evaluative and teleological proposition centering on man: "Have you ever in your life commanded the morning, have you directed the dawn to its place to take hold of the skirts of the earth so that the wicked are shaken out of it, so that light is withheld from the wicked, and their uplifted arm is broken?" (38:12f., 15). This can mean one thing only: there is no provision for retribution, nor any manifestation of it in the order of the world. The dawn of every day provides an occasion to punish the wicked, but this possibility is not in practice realized and is therefore not in the plan of the world. "Consider this fundamental fact," Job is told: "The sun rises over the righteous and the sinners alike. Can you change that?"

The end of God's speech is similar in meaning. Here is an excerpt: "Will the reprover enter suit against Shaddai? Will you put Me in the wrong so that you may be vindicated? Or is it that you have an arm like God? Seeing anyone haughty, abase him and tread down the wicked in their tracks. Then I, too, will acknowledge that your right hand is all-prevailing" (40:2, 8–14). Everything is rhetorical or hypothetical. God and Job know that he cannot possibly do these things; it is not in the plan, not in the plan for the wicked to be punished. If Job were able to perform these things, his criticism of God would be justified, not only by the demonstration of his own prowess but, more important, by the demonstration that retribution is at least potentially operative in the world and need only be actualized. Failing a demonstration of this ability, the assumption of punishment of the wicked and reward of the righteous is without ground, and Job has no right to blame God.

The third passage I shall cite is the least conspicuous but the most interesting: "Who has cleft a channel for the rain flood and a way for the thunder cloud to cause rain on land where no man is, on a desert where no people live to satiate waste and desolate terrain and to sprout fresh grass?" (38:25–27).

72. The Elihu chapters (32–37) are disregarded; cf. n. 17.

73. √צדק occurs 19 times, √ישר 7 times, √תמם 16 times. √צדק, with the legal meaning "to be vindicated," occurs in 40:8 after the journey through the world; the occurrence is therefore not counted. √תמם in 31:40 means "to finish," and this passage is also not counted.

As God describes the meteorological phenomena, he is implying: "Consider this, Job: precious rain, that would be so beneficial to human beings, is wasted on land uninhabited and uninhabitable. In the natural world, where the category of cause and effect is operative, man is not as central as you fancy." This is, in effect, God's polemic with Job. It is, by the same token, the author's polemic with the point of view found in the rest of the Bible, for Job represents the general biblical point of view. Rain, in the Bible, figures prominently as a vehicle of reward and punishment. It is given for good deeds and withheld for evil ones. Here, however, the phenomenon is shown not to be a vehicle of morality at all—the moral purpose ascribed to it just does not exist. (Be it noted that the text does not state that the rain falls partly on the desert and partly on the sown. The point is that it falls on the desert where it has no relevance for man.)

God says: "No retribution is provided for in the blueprint of the world, nor does it exist anywhere in it. None is planed for the nonhuman world and none for the human world. Divine justice is not an element of reality. It is a figment existing only in the misguided philosophy with which you have been inculcated. The world in which you and the friends are spun is a dream. Wake up, Job!" And wake up is what Job does at the end.

Let us now adduce controls for our thesis. One control, whose substance is acknowledged by all, yet whose significance in the total picture is commonly ignored, is the knowledge that we, the readers of the prologue, possess—we know that Job did not suffer in retribution for what he had done. We know that his presuppositions were wrong in part and those of the friends in toto; that their discussion, earnest though it was, was largely out of touch with reality. The Book of Job is, from the first chapter, the classical statement that a man's lot is not the consequence of his deeds. The prologue, for one thing, shows that in the one exemplary case with which it is concerned, divine justice, retribution, does not enter into the heavenly considerations. Against this reading of the whole book in the light of its prologue it may be argued that, our earlier remark notwithstanding,[74] allowance should be made for a narrative feature which exists purely for the sake of the plot and is probably not intended to have a bearing on the ideas of the book. The argument, however, while legitimate in principle, "makes allowance," i.e., it reckons with a literary flaw in a work so artistic as to make such allowance gratuitous. Be that as it may, the innocence of Job is a feature not confined to the narrative of the prologue but one providing the basis of the entire work; without it there is no problem of Job, indeed there is no Book of Job.

The other control is historical and circumstantial. It is stronger than the previous control for being external to the book and weaker because, resting on its date, it is prey to the uncertainties of literary history. Yet for all the difficulty of dating, the overwhelming majority of scholars, for a variety of rea-

74. Cf. supra, pp. 1–3.

sons date the Book of Job between the sixth and the fourth centuries B.C. Now that is the very period in which the earlier doctrine of collective retribution (represented, for instance, in the Pentateuch) had lost its sway without yet being replaced by the doctrine of individual retribution in the world-to-come. (From time to time there was attempted an application of the earlier doctrine of retributory justice to the individual rather than to the group. These attempts, notably in wisdom texts *sensu proprio,* remained ephemeral, the doctrine foundering on the rock of reality: the wicked flourish, and the righteous perish.) Now the earlier and the later doctrines have an effective answer to the problem of the suffering of the innocent. The former, the collective answer, operates with a social unit large in the number of its components, the individual Israelites, and extended in time, the people of Israel through the generations. When dealing with a group as large and long-lived as a nation it is possible to work out solutions in accordance with the principle of collective retribution. The latter, the belief of retribution in the other world, admits by definition no difficulties: retribution, deferred to a future life, cannot be contradicted by experience.[75]

Thus it would seem clear that the sixth through the third centuries represented that one period in the history of biblical religion which is not covered, or, at best, very scantily covered, by one or the other form of this idea of divine justice. It is in this period that the problem of the suffering of the innocent is most likely to have been answered in a way other than, hence opposed to, that of divine justice=retribution. And this is the very period to which the Book of Job is commonly dated. It is through the combination of our view, viz., that the solution which the book offers to the problem is the radical denial of the principle of retribution, and the accepted determination of the date of the book that the gap in the history of thought on this problem is neatly filled. At some time during the sixth through the third centuries a book was written which said to man: Neither hope for reward for good deeds nor fear punishment for evil deeds; moralists cannot shake the wicked from the surface of the earth and God will not. The laws of the natural order and those of the moral order are not of a piece. If you decide to do what is good, do it because it is good.

Let us now, laying aside our concern for checking conclusions, extend our consideration of the adventure of ideas beyond the biblical period. The Book of Job continues the intellectual and religious enterprise, begun in the earlier

75. In the later history of Judaism and in Christianity these religions continued to experiment with various combinations of the forms of retribution—individual, collective, and otherwordly. Enjoying the shelter of flexible retributory creeds, they have not been troubled by the problem central to the book in a measure at all commensurable with the concern of modern readers who find themselves unable to accept the theological shelter which ideological versatility makes possible for these religions. Hence it is that in modern times, when nontraditional religiosity has come to the fore, the Book of Job figures so much more prominently than was the case hitherto either in the thinking or the liturgy of Judaism and Christianity.

books of the Bible, of emptying the world of much that had been put into it during the preceding millennia by human fantasy operating to satisfy human concerns. These books demythologized the world.[76] The Book of Job, in this respect, does not lag behind any of them. It features, as has been observed before, an abundance of images from the then current myths but does not fail to provide its own understanding of them:[77] the world is not as the myths would have it. If, therefore, the myths do not describe reality, their appearance or allusions to them in the book is a matter of literary style and artistic convention somewhat in the manner of the tropes and mythological figures in the libretti of Metastasio.

But the Book of Job does more than demythologize the world; it also "demoralizes" it, which is to say, makes it amoral. It completes the process whose first phase is known to the reader of the Bible from the opening pages of Genesis: the removal from the conceptual world of an order of superhuman beings independent of the Deity. And it extends it by the denial of the realization of moral values—values deriving from the Deity, to be sure—other than realization effected by man. This new world is as harsh as it is simple, for in it man is deprived of the protection he enjoyed in a world saturated with myth and morality and populated with powers to which he might turn with a view to rendering them favorable to his well-being, foremost by his leading of a meritorious life.

The number of alternative explanations offered for the meaning of the Book of Job confronts each interpreter with the question: If what you say is right, why does the book not say so in so many words? An easy answer is that the dramatic and poetic nature of such a work, containing layer upon layer of depth and hinting at yet others, precludes a plain and direct proposition. The interpretation offered here suggests an additional answer, which might be adduced in support of the interpretation: the very radicalism of the book's answer, shattering a central biblical doctrine and a belief cherished in ancient Israel, would itself demand the protection of a veil. The book is, to be sure, uniquely daring in many other respects and according to any interpretation: the pronouncements of Job against God, agonized and agonizing, must have evoked a shudder in the biblical audience. Yet these outbursts do not constitute a new and radical doctrine; they can be passed off as cries of a man in pain. But the answer of God, presenting a doctrine as radical as it is new, a doctrine in diametrical opposition to the teaching of tradition, may never have been tolerated or preserved for us but for the protection of its form, its eschewal of the direct categorical pronouncement.

If we look once more at the structure of the work, the unity of frame and colloquy, whether primary or secondary,[78] now appears in a righter light.

76. "Myth" and its derivatives are used here in the narrow sense, referring to identifiable myths of the ancient Near East, their cognates, and their possible reflexes in Israel.

77. Cf. the remarks to 38:8–11, 28f., supra, pp. 12, 15.

78. Cf. n. 2.

Two questions were posed in the prologue; one, What is piety? the other, Is there piety?[79] We had some reason to answer the second question in the affirmative. The final chapters strengthen the affirmation: it is to Job, the man who, above all other men, exemplifies piety (1:8), that God reveals Himself. In this context, revelation connotes more than relativity and rank ("there is none as pious as he") denote; it constitutes, in effect, the affirmation by God that Job is pious. Our main interest, however, is in the first question, the essential feature of whose answer was put forward in the prologue without equivocation: piety, whatever its other attributes, must be disinterested. Egoistically motivated connection between the religio-moral and the natural worlds, common since the beginning of the history of the human kind and evident in many parts of the Bible, is forever precluded by this unequivocal answer of the prologue; for to make this connection is to deprive attitude, behavior, or action of the dignity of piety. God's answer, however, goes a step further. It severs any causal connection, hitherto assumed in the world at large and prominent everywhere in the Bible, between these two worlds; a person's fate is dissociated from, and unrelated to, his religio-moral attitude or actions. The prologue says that one ought not to, the divine address says that one cannot, expect anything for one's behavior.[80] Job behaved piously throughout, but his behavior had, in the narrated time[81] of 1:13–31:40, no consequences compatible with the accepted idea of reward and punishment; yet he most ardently hoped for these consequences and was utterly shaken when his hopes were not realized. God tells him in chaps. 38–40 that these consequences nowhere and never follow, and that it is, therefore, futile to hope for them. In his final reply (40:3–5; 42:2f., 5f.) Job acknowledges this fact and thus, free of misconception, is now prepared for a pious and moral life uncluttered by false hopes and unfounded claims. To resort to a simile: the unity of the book may be likened to a switchback traversing rugged territory yet ever maintaining the general direction toward the goal; on a lower bend, the answer of the prologue—on an upper bend, the divine answer.

The Book of Job, a supreme expression of religious faith, presents the purest moral theory in the Bible. Now it would be a grave error to interpret its denial of divine retribution as constituting a legitimate excuse for man

79. Cf. supra, p. 2.

80. This generalization has two aspects. (1) The prologue, to be sure, deals only with reward, the expected result of pious behavior, and not with punishment; only the discourse extends the doctrine to include punishment (4:7–11; and elsewhere). (2) Strictly speaking, the prologue does not say that man ought to expect nothing for his behavior; it says only that his behavior ought to be independent of the fulfillment or nonfulfillment of his expectations. The generalization is nonetheless, in my opinion, unobjectionable. The prologue is a narrative which singles out parts which characterize the whole and does not constitute a discursive, comprehensive treatment of the whole.

81. Cf. M. Weiss, *Biblica* 46 (1965), p. 182.

from his obligations to establish justice on earth. Justice is not woven into the stuff of the universe nor is God occupied with its administration but it is an ideal to be realized by society and in it. As to God Himself, while the book does not say so explicitly, it does not exclude the possibility of God's obligating Himself to abide by human standards in regard to specific occasions and contexts. Thus God, while often the author of the standards for human conduct, is Himself bound by them only in exceptional cases.

Fig. 12.1
The Central Ideas in the Book of Job

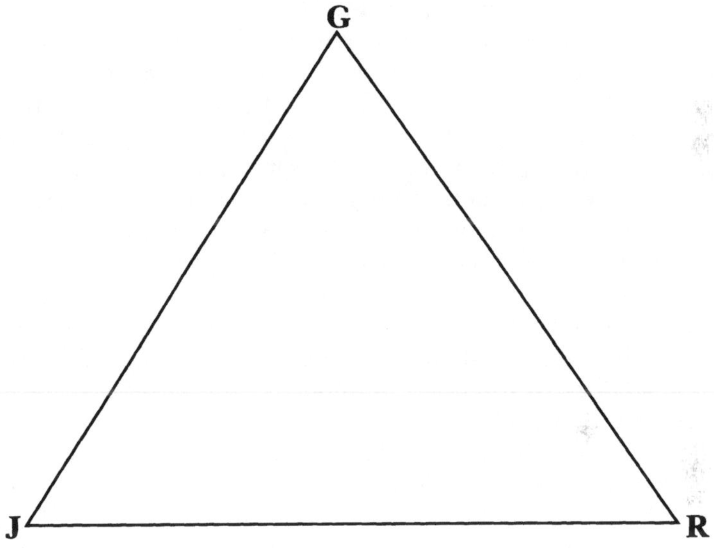

Let us imagine an equilateral triangle (figure 12.1), at the three vertexes of which we have *G* standing for God Who turns His face to man and is accessible to him, *J* for Job, the upright man, and *R* for the philosophy of retribution or justice in the world. The Book of Job, then, tells of an attempt to maintain these ideas simultaneously—an attempt which ends in failure. It is the purpose of the book to demonstrate the impossibility of the coexistence of these three ideas and the consequent logical necessity to give up one of them. The friends cancel *J*, maintaining *G* and *R*. God eliminates *R*, maintaining *G* and *J*. Job all but gives up *G*, as he maintains *J* and *R*. Now it is the limiting phrase "all but" that makes a religious book of what would otherwise have been merely a theological treatise. It epitomizes Job's struggle with himself and with God. He knew in his bones that he was just. At the same time he shared the concept of his age that it is the business of God to maintain the category of cause and effect in the moral as well as in the natural world.

Unable to compromise the fact of his innocence or to divest himself of the concept of his age, he distorted perforce the image of God. But this distortion accomplished nothing; he yet felt that he was wrong, he hoped and, for moments, even held the conviction that God had His face turned toward him, if not with favor then at least with interest, that God would one day "long for" him (14:15). He wanted therefore to "come" to God (23:3), to "see" Him, i.e., His true image (19:26f.). In his unflagging but futile attempt to interpret the vicious triangle he became ever more enmeshed in contradictions. He maintained *J* and *R* and despaired of, yet did not surrender, *G*. At times observation of reality led him nonetheless to the conclusion that *R* was wrong, i.e., that the world in not governed by justice. At these moments he came close to one aspect of God's position. Yet only close: he could only conceive of the dichotomy justice/injustice, until God showed him that this dichotomy is not adequate for the structuring of reality, for it lacks the third required element: nonjustice. These three elements should indeed by grouped in a dichotomy, but in the form: justice-injustice/nonjustice. The left side of the dichotomy, justice-injustice, is societal, the right one, nonjustice, is extrasocietal. The error of Job and the friends lay in this: that they permitted the societal aspect of the dichotomy to encroach on the extrasocietal one. This is the error or *R*. But once the error is recognized, *R* is eliminated, *G* and *J* remain—this is God's answer. Job accepts the answer. Unencumbered now by the old doctrine of justice and retribution, he receives confirmation of his former hope that God does turn His face to man, that He is accessible to him—confirmation provided by the theophany. To put it differently: He Who speaks to man in the Book of Job is neither a just nor an unjust god but God.

Of Job, enmeshed in his contradictions, who at the end recanted everything he had said, God says to the friends: "You have not spoken of Me what is right as has My servant Job" (42:7). The error that Job upheld and was compelled to renounce was yet closer to the truth than the arguments of the friends for all the support of many authorities that these arguments enjoyed. This is the judgment of the book. From the contradictions of Job there is a way to truth, from the consistencies of the friends, none.

Deeper and more beautiful yet are the words of the Midrash (*Pesiqta Rabbati*, ed. M. Friedmann, 190b): "Had he [Job] not clamored so—as it is now the practice to say in prayer 'God of Abraham, God of Isaac, and God of Jacob,' so one would say 'and God of Job'."

Part 2

Specific Themes and Passages in the Book of Job

13

Mythology and the Book of Job

Elmer B. Smick

Mythological elements in the Book of Job have long been recognized by critics who now use the newer literary materials from the Biblical world to confirm their opinion. Our purpose in this investigation is to examine certain key passages to determine where there are unmistakable mythological allusions and to explain how this fits with an evangelical view of the origin of the book and its interpretation.

There is a rather limited number of categories or subjects where mythological terminology is employed. The most frequent usage is when the speaker deals with the forces of nature, the storm, fire, the sea, etc. A second category has to do with creatures cosmic or otherwise. A third with cosmography and a fourth with heathen cultic practices. Only one passage has the latter, which may be dealt with summarily. Job 3:8:

From Elmer B. Smick, "Mythology and the Book of Job," *Journal of the Evangelical Theological Society* 13 (Spring 1970): 101–8. Used by permission of the Evangelical Theological Society.

Let those who curse a day curse it
or even those skilled to stir Leviathan.

Job calls for the enchanters to curse his day. [This curse] usually [is] taken [to refer to] the rousing of the sea monster who, according to primitive notions, was supposed to swallow the sun or moon and bring about an eclipse. This would fit the context, for Job has wished the day of his birth were indeed blotted out or made dark. Verse 5b seems to be a reference to the eclipse. This presents no special problem since Job's whole mood here is erroneous: he is using a common forceful expression as he yields to his anguish of soul even though he undoubtedly knew that use of enchanters was forbidden by the Lord. His real sin, for which he can scarcely be excused, was in damning the day of his birth, questioning the sovereign purpose of God.

A superficial acquaintance with the dialogues of the Book of Job will convince anyone that Job and his friends were theologically somewhat confused especially in the matter of theodicy. In some places, therefore, they could be mouthing contemporaneous notions. However, we would not expect this in the words of God as, for example, in the theophany of chapters 38–41, and may well ask, "Are there clear-cut mythological assumptions here?"

The tendency of the naturalistic critic to see mythology everywhere results in more misinterpretation than the well-meant but misdirected attempt to rule out all mythological expression. Reading primitive meaning into a piece of monotheistic literature where the idiom can be viewed as a result of simple observation or the use of quaint expressions is poor methodology. On the other hand, we must be cautioned against the rejection of all mythological usage in a strained attempt to remove the writers of Scripture from such contamination.

There are those references where the language of mythology appears as borrowed metaphors, use of names, etc. This is like the New Testament use of the heathen deity name Baalzebub for Satan. As the writer stated in an earlier paper, "this marks a time of religious vigor and verbal fluency . . . in artful poetic idiom without necessarily a thought given to polytheistic usage" ("Ugaritic and the Theology of the Psalms"). The Canaanite linguistic substratum was a readily available vehicle through which the prophets and poets could communicate the truth.

Job 26 is said to present a primitive cosmography. Verses 9 and 10 read:

He encloses the face of his throne
And spreads his cloud upon it.

He marked (described) a circle on the surface of the waters
As far as the fartherest (the very end of) limit of light and darkness.

How can it be affirmed that this represents a primitive cosmography when verse 7 says "he hanged the earth on nothing"? Verse 10 may mean that when one is on the water out of the sight of land everywhere one turns one sees only horizon. Verse 9 is said to picture God seated on a throne above a solid firmament conceived of as a dome sitting on the pillars of heaven (v. 11). The RSV saw correctly that *ksh* is not throne but *keseh* meaning "the full moon" as in Psalm 81:4 and Proverbs 7:20. So that 26:9 reads:

> He closes in the face of the full moon
> And spreads his cloud over it.

It may be quaint but is highly poetic to speak of the mountains as pillars (26:11) which support the low clouds.

No one has ever satisfactorily explained how verse 7 fits into any primitive cosmography.

> He stretches out the north over the void
> And hangs the earth on nothing.

Buttenweiser's famous comment on 26:7 is summarily dismissed in the Anchor Bible 15 which makes no attempt to explain mythologically or otherwise what it means. Buttenweiser translates:

> "He that suspended the earth over the vacuum"

and he comments:

> Our author, though naturally ignorant of the law of gravitation, had outgrown the naive view of his age about the universe, and conceived of the earth as a heavenly body floating in space, like the sun, moon, and stars. It is not surprising to meet with such a view in the Book of Job when one considers the advance astronomy in Babylonia, Egypt, and Greece. As early as 540–510 B.C. Pythagoros of Samos, on his travels in Egypt and the East, acquired the knowledge of the obliquity of the ecliptic and of the earth's being a sphere freely poised in space. . . . Job 38:6 bears out rather than contradicts the conclusion that the writer of Job had attained a more advanced view of the universe, since the question, "Whereon were its foundations set?" shows that he no longer shared the primitive notion that the earth was resting on pillars erected in the sea. (Buttenweiser, *The Book of Job,* in loc.)

The figure in chapter 38:4–6 is a description of the building of the earth as if it were a house. Buttenweiser's interpretation is weakened if we view the passage as God's questioning Job on whether the earth was built like this.

Buttenweiser also contends the north (26:7) is the celestial pole formed by the seven stars of Ursa Minor from which the movement of the universe was believed to proceed. But we cannot ignore what Ugaritic tells about Mount Zaphon as being the Canaanite Olympus (actually *Mons Casius, Jebel el 'Aqra*) where Baal built his marvelous dwelling. This explains why the

Hebrew word *ṣāphôn* means north. It is to be understood in Job as the celestial place where God dwells using the available Canaanite expression just as Isaiah does in Isaiah 14:13, 14:

> "You said in your heart,
> I will ascend to heaven;
>
> above the stars of God
> I will set my throne on high;
>
> I will sit on the mount of assembly
> in the far north
>
> I will ascend above the heights of
> the clouds
>
> I will make myself like the Most High."

Furthermore the verb *nth* is often used for the stretching out or bending or arching of the heavens (Psalm 104:2), and this concept parallels antithetically the other side of the bicolon "The earth he hangs on nothing" and "He stretches out the north (heaven) over the void."

Psalm 48:2 and 3 (Hebrew) reads:

> "Beautiful of height,
> Joy of all the earth,
>
> Is Mount Zion on the sides of the North, (or, Is Mount
> Zion in the heart of Zaphon)
>
> The City of (the) great king."

Biblical terminology here identifies *Ṣāphōn* with Mount Zion as the place where God dwells, which reminds us of Isaiah 2:2–4 where the Mount of the Lord's house is established at the head of the mountains with all the nations flowing to it. This Mount Zion is most assuredly eschatological Jerusalem where the Lord is enthroned and rules over a world of universal peace.

In Job 26:12–14 the terms used are again mythological, but the meaning is of God's powerful control over the raging force of the sea. We translate

> By his strength he stills the Sea, (Note article = improper noun)
>
> And by his understanding he smites Rahab
>
> By his wind he puts Sea in a bag, (Tur-Sinai, *The Book of Job,* in loc.)
>
> His hand pierced the fleeing serpent."

The two bicola are parallel. "The Sea is stilled" parallels "Sea is put in a bag." And "Rahab is smitten" parallels "the fleeing serpent is pierced." Job goes on to say that such dominion over the sea is only a bit of [God's] dominion, only a whisper, Who can understand the real thunder of his mighty acts?

Similarly in Job 9:13, the cohorts of Rahab are described as those who grovel beneath the Almighty who shakes the earth and removes mountains; who stretched out the heavens alone and made the constellations and who treads on the back of Yamm (the Sea). *Bmh* is never used for waves, but the Ugaritic cognate of *bhm* is always the back of a creature which yields a well-known Near Eastern symbol of overcoming one's foes (Isaiah 63:6). The metaphor pictures God's complete control of the sea. Likewise in 7:12 Job complains of imagined harassment by God when he says "Am I Sea (*Yam*) or *Tanin* (Sea Monster) that you set a guard over me?" In Hebrew monotheism God created and controls the *Taninim* in contrast to north-western Semitic mythology where the uncreated monsters of chaos are slain by hero gods who then proceed to create the land and sea from pieces of the slain monster.

We see none of this where we might expect to see it in Job 38 where the sea is personified and its birth is pictured (8–11). Shutting the sea within doors (8) is indeed like Marduk did after slaying Tiamat and creating the seas from her, but here it merely refers to the limitations of the sea's boundaries. There is similar use of swaddling bands in Job 38:9 and in the birth of the Ugaritic bovine monsters called Eaters and Devourers, but both are borrowed from events of human birth and the biblical account is tied closely to natural phenomena.

In Job 38:12b Morning and Dawn are personified just as Dawn and Dusk were a divine pair in Ugaritic, and in verse 13 Earth is personified with coming of day likened to the snatching off of her skirts and shaking the wicked out of it. But apart from personification no other mythological distinctive is employed in these verses.

Just as *Ṣāphōn* was a word originally meaning the abode of the gods, but in Hebrew was used for the habitation of the only true God, so the terms *Yam* and *Rahab* derived from the Canaanite Sea-God and his monstrous cohort, and it can be demonstrated that in a strong monotheistic context like the Book of Job these personifications were simply rich linguistic expressions of the powers of nature. Even when viewed as Canaanite gods, part of their function was to describe and explain natural phenomena. If Job and his friends did know the mythology, this in itself would not prove they believed the myth any more than my reference to Greek deities proves I believe them. This view is strengthened by Job 31:26, 27 where the patriarch by oath with sanctions denies ever being tempted to participate in heathen worship of the sun or moon.

We turn to Job 5:7 where the KJV and RSV read:

"But man is born to trouble as the sparks fly upward."

M. Pope in Anchor Bible 15 translates:

"And Resheph's sons wing high."

This is another clear case where the name of a northwest Semitic deity is used to refer to forces in nature with which the particular deity was identified in the mythology. In the Ugaritic pantheon Resheph is equated with Nergal, the Mesopotamian god of pestilence and the netherworld. In the Old Testament the word is used of pestilence in Deuteronomy 32:25 and Habakkuk 3:5, and the plural is used of lightning in Psalm 78:48. In Psalm 76:4, however, the reshephs (arrows) of the bow are in apposition to the shield, the sword and the battle. In Ugaritic Resheph is called "Lord of the arrow," probably referring to his skillful use of lightning. Just as Death had a first-born in Job 18:13 who devours wicked men's bodies, so here the sons of Resheph may be various forms of trouble or pestilence or flames which soar aloft. It is curious that in Song of Solomon 8:6 the Reshephs are associated with earthly love, but only in the sense that such love is like flashes of fire. It seems unnecessary to carry the thought to the ambivalent nature of Resheph sometimes mentioned in extra-Biblical texts.

". . . Love is as strong as death . . . and her reshephs are reshephs (flashes) of fire, a most vehement flame."

What of Behemoth and Leviathan in Job 40 and 41? There is something to be said for simply taking them as a great bovine creature (or hippopotamus) and crocodile respectively. Both are used in other Old Testament contexts without a hint of mythological or symbolic implication. (Pss. 8:8; 50:10ff.; 78:22; 104:26; Joel 1:20; 2:22; Habakkuk 2:17). The word *Behemoth* seems to be an intensive plural of *Behemah* (beast); hence the beast par excellence. *Behemoth* is called in 40:19a "the first of the ways of God." Pope translates this "a primordial production of God," but Dahood renders "He is the finest manifestation of God's power" (*drkt* = dominion in Ugaritic). In Ugaritic the goddess Anat conquered the seven-headed Leviathan along with a bovine creature called *'gl il 'tk* "the ferocious bullock."

Old Testament passages speak of great evil powers whether cosmic or political in terms of monstrous creatures. Such as Isaiah 27:1 where in the day the Lord punishes the inhabitants of the earth for their iniquity he also will slay Leviathan, the swift, crooked serpent. In Isaiah 51:9, 10 Rahab is Egypt and in Psalm 74:12, 13 the many-headed Leviathan is Egypt, and in Job 40 and 41 the description of Leviathan becomes highly symbolic. One must assume a considerable amount of hyperbole to make of this simply a crocodile. Could it be possible that after a description of the crocodile an unannounced transition occurs because God also intends to remind Job of those cosmic forces which Leviathan symbolizes and against which no human strength can prevail? For some reason the Hebrew text begins a new chapter in the middle of this description (41:9 = 41:1 Hebrew). We translate from this chapter verse 9–12 (1–4):

> "Behold any hope is false
> (For) the angels are hurled down at his appearance
> (And) he is fierce when one arouses him.
> (But) who can stand before me,
> Who can confront me and survive,
> For everything under the heavens is mine.
> Will not I silence his boastings
> His proud (high) talk and his fair array of words."

And verses 18–21:

> "His sneezings flash forth light,
> His eyes are like the glow (eyelids) of dawn.
> Out of his mouth go burning torches
> And sparks of fire leap forth.
> From his nostrils go smoke
> As out of a seething pot and burning brushwood.
> His breath kindles coals
> And a flame goes pours out of his mouth."

And verse 25:

> "At his terror the angels (mighty ones) are afraid
> By reason of despair they are cast down."

The swords, javelins, arrows, clubs, slingstones are no good against him 26–29). And according to verses 33 and 34:

> "Upon earth there is not his like
> One made without fear.
>
> He looks on all that is lofty
> He is king over all proud beings."

My studied conclusion is that this is not a mere crocodile but is to be understood in light of Isaiah 27:1 etc. (cf. the dragon symbol of Rev. 12).

The prologue of Job pictures the heavenly council before God. Eliphaz in 5:1 says,

> "Call now; is there any who will answer you,
> And to which of the Holy Ones will you turn?"

Eliphaz is taunting Job that it is hopeless for him to appeal to the *qedōšim* (holy ones). Critics take them to be the lesser divine beings, who, according to Mesopotamian concept, were available as personal intercessors in the divine assembly. It should be noted that whether here or in the prologue or in Psalm 89:5 "the assembly of the holy ones" is most assuredly made up of created beings. Even in Mesopotamian concepts the lesser divine beings were created; whether in the progress of revelation Eliphaz had made the clear-cut monotheistic distinction we cannot tell, but we can be certain that neither the Book of Job nor the Psalms attribute to these "holy ones" any of the pagan concepts of deity. In Job 15:8 Eliphaz condemning Job for self-exaltation questions his ability to sit in and eavesdrop on the divine council. In 33:23, 24 Elihu speaks of mediation by an angel. The Mesopotamian belief in a personal god who looked after the interest of his mortal client in the divine assembly may be a related concept, but it is not a proven stage in the development of Hebrew religion. These "holy ones," among whom a man might find a defender, should be tied to Job's appeal for an arbiter (*môkîaḥ*, 9:33) or witness (*ēd*, 16:19–21) or vindicator (*gō'ēl*, 19:25–27). In a most prophetic way Job is touching on the mystery of godliness in seeing that one who can stand between God and man must share in the nature of each, as Job says in 9:33 "that might lay his hand upon the two of us." This concept finds further expression in the Old Testament teaching regarding the suffering vicarious expiator.

Some scholars feel that Job 38:31a provides an example of how the KJV was influenced by the earlier Jewish interpretation taken over by Christian exegetes. Nachmanides and others understood the verse in an astrological sense, the "sweet influences" of Pleiades being the astrological forces which produce pleasure, flowers, and fruits in the spring. It is likely the key word should be rendered "fetters" parallel with "bands" of Orion following 1 Samuel 15:32 where Agag stands before Samuel, not delicately, but in fetters (ICC). Nor should verse 33 be taken astrologically "Knowest thou the ordinances of heaven? Canst thou set the dominion thereof in the earth?" Some take these words to be pre-Newtonian allusions to the forces of gravity. The words are *ḥuqqōt statutes* parallel with *mišṭār* (Akk. *mišṭāru* a writing). The stars in Akkadian are called *šiṭir šamē* "heavenly writing." I believe Tur-Sinai has come closest to understanding the verse by connecting it with Psalm 19 (*Archiv Orientalni* 17, II, 1949).

An example of a forced attempt to read mythology into the text is demonstrated by Dhorme followed by Pope who render 38:36:

> "Who put wisdom in Thoth *(ṭuḥot)*
> Who gave Sekwi understanding" *(šekwi)*

The RSV takes these difficult words as "clouds" and "mist" with some philological support. Since the verses before and after are dealing with the clouds, the rain and lightning, Thoth and Sekwi as gods are out of context.

Of this general subject Albright has said some cogent things in his *History, Archaeology and Christian Humanism*. Remarking how the Old Testament is a "masterpiece of empirical logic not expressed in formal categories," Albright claims the Old Testament has demythologized not the literature but the language of Canaan. "Old words are kept but with new meanings divested of all clear mythological connotations." Albright notes how the Puritan John Milton drew heavily on Greek mythology to enrich his poetic imagery even in his picture of creation.

For example, the use of plural *ʾelōhîm* and *ʾadōnāy* may have come from polytheistic usage but in Hebrew came to mean the totality of all the manifestations and attributes of deity which polytheism broke down into single elements. Even in some documents a single high god is referred to with the plural ending, the so-called plural of majesty (Amarna and Ugaritic). Nothing sounds more polytheistic to some ears than the words used by the Chronicler "for great is our God above all gods" (1 Chron. 2:5).

Albright observes "much of the onslaught on early Israelite monotheism comes from scholars who represent certain theological points of view with reference to monotheism, i.e., who deny that orthodox trinitarian Christianity . . . or orthodox Judaism or orthodox Islam are monotheistic. I do not need to stress the fact that neither of the last two religions can be called monotheistic by a theologian who insists that this term applies only to Unitarian Christianity or liberal Judaism. But no dictionary definition of monotheism was ever intended to exclude orthodox Christianity" (*History, Archaeology and Christian Humanism*, 155).

In conclusion let me say that the distinguishing mark of a mythology is not references to gods or the use of anthropomorphism and various descriptive metaphors which describe deity in concrete terminology but rather the narration of the actions of numerous gods who have the same limitations and sins common to man, including especially sexual relations. Neither the Book of Job nor any of the Old Testament has the slightest hint of belief in any such mythology.

14

Another Look at the Mythological Elements in the Book of Job

Elmer B. Smick

The Book of Job, like a microcosm of the Old Testament, bears witness to the will and purpose of the God who created and rules over nature and all creatures, especially his crowning creature man. In Genesis 3 as a result of the work of the tempter God must put in effect the death penalty of Genesis 2:17. But only the Tempter, the serpent, is cursed. Man gets a somewhat suspended sentence as far as the death penalty goes but with immediate punitive effects. The Book of Job brings us a step closer to the

From Elmer B. Smick, "Another Look at the Mythological Elements in the Book of Job," *Westminster Theological Journal* 40 (1978): 213–28. Used by permission of Westminster Theological Society.

mystery of godliness by adding a new dimension to the concept of punitive suffering. The ancient Near Eastern documents from Babylonia and Egypt agree with the punitive aspect of suffering but are shallow in the way they deal with the problem.[1] Man as a sinner must humble himself before the gods who are often perverse or not interested or they are incapacitated. But attention to both the continuities and discontinuities between the worship of Yahweh and the paganisms of the Old Testament world is an important feature of O.T. hermeneutics.

H. W. Wolff in his chapter entitled "The Hermeneutics of the Old Testament" (in the series of essays on that subject edited by Claus Westermann) says:

> The more distinctly the old Oriental religions are reconstructed before our eyes, the more clearly we see that the O.T. actively resists the attempt to understand it in analogy to the cults of its environment. This is all the more surprising since the connection of Israel with its environment in matters of a general world view, of profane and sacral usage, of Cultic institutions, yes even of prophetic phenomena, is constantly becoming clearer.[2]

To this may be added the observation that the mythological elements in Job conform remarkably well with the religious expressions from contemporary sources. But careful attention to certain features in context will show that any special problem these allusions may appear to pose for the monotheistic outlook of the author of this book is superficial. Our present purpose is to defend this last statement. Here we use the term myth in its traditional sense—not as another way of expressing the truth[3] but as the way a polytheistic people understood deity. In this sense, to see wide mythological commitment, as some have been prone to do,[4] results in as much misinterpretation as does the attempt to ignore mythological expression to protect the scriptures from such "contamination." Reading primitive meaning into a piece of monotheistic literature because the language is infused with the idiom of a primitive substratum is poor methodology. It is true that sometimes it is impossible to tell when the terms are mere figures and when they represent the view of the speaker.[5] We must be guided by the thrust of the context.

1. Marvin H. Pope in the Anchor Bible 15 (lvi–lxxiii) has a good summary of the parallel literature.

2. H. W. Wolff, "The Hermeneutics of the Old Testament," in Claus Westermann, ed., *Essays on Old Testament Hermeneutics* (Richmond, Va.: John Knox Press, 1963), 167.

3. John L. McKenzie in his article "Myth and the Old Testament" (*CBQ* XXI, 265–282) following Cassirer defines myth in this way but it assumes a unique set of presuppositions.

4. Pope seems to take this position. He takes issue with R. Gordis's statement that Job takes monotheism for granted (AB 15, xxxix).

5. See the quotation from T. H. Gaster below.

The language of mythology is inherent in every language from every age and is often used in religious contexts that are strongly monotheistic.[6] The Jews in Babylon borrowed pagan festival names for their religious calendar. Fanatically monotheistic Jews embellished their synagogues with zodiacal mosaics borrowed from Roman art depicting the sun god riding his chariot.[7] Matthew 12:24 uses the pagan deity name Baalzebub (2 Kings 1:3) for Satan simply as an idiom without a thought given to its origin. Isaiah and Ezekiel, both monotheists, were prone to using mythological allusion as a vehicle through which they communicated their messages.[8]

Nature is a theme which frequently evoked mythological language: the storm, fire, the sea, the heavens and the earth, and creatures in both spheres. Job 3:8 begins with a reference to an occult practice involving the celebrated Leviathan. Regarding the day of his birth Job says:

> May those who curse days curse that day,
> those who are ready to arouse Leviathan. (NIV)

Dhorme says "those who curse days" may refer to other sufferers like Job who also cursed the day of their birth. But in light of the parallelism the expression more likely refers to professional cursers like Balaam. Job appears to be making a play on the similar sound of the words *yām*, "sea," and *yōm*, "day," and the parallel between Leviathan the sea monster and the Yamm as a deity in Canaanite mythology.

Job, in a cursing mood, employs the most vivid and forceful proverbial language available to call for the obliteration of that day.[9] The figure then is of an awakened monster of chaos who could swallow that day. According to some mythological notions such swallowing of the sun and moon brought about an eclipse! There is no way of knowing how valid Job considered the work of such cursers, but in his negative confession Job presents himself as a monotheist who rejected current mythological conceptions of the sun (31:26–28). Job's error, for which he can scarcely be excused, was in damning the day of his birth, questioning the sovereign purpose of God. Job in his attempt to understand his theology in the light of his immediate experience, while constrained to speak only the truth before God, came perilously close to cursing God to his face as the Satan had predicted. His friends on the other hand uttered many perceptive truths. Paul could quote Eliphaz in 1 Corinthians 3:19.[10] What they said, however, did not necessarily apply to Job.

6. John Milton drew heavily on Greek mythology to enrich his poetic imagery even in his picture of creation.

7. *BASOR* 228, 61ff.

8. Isaiah 14 and 27, Ezekiel 28.

9. Although NEB renders 8b, "those whose magic binds even the monster . . . ," the same stem of the verb *'ûr* means "to awaken" the dead in Sheol in Isaiah 14:9.

10. Job 5:13.

It becomes increasingly clear that they had no concern for Job and as he said were only mouthing words to curry God's favor. Their original conciliatory attitudes quickly become harsh and vindictive. The words of the dialogue then are not normative and so we must consider the mythological allusions in that light.

Even so, it is difficult to tell when a speaker uses mythic terms metaphorically. Demythologizing was a process that was practiced in Israel.[11] But there are continuities as well as discontinuities between the normative theology of Israel and the surrounding nations. Our procedure will be to examine some passages in which mythological expression uniquely serves the purpose of the book. In some cases this reverses the effect of polytheism and shows Job's God is Sovereign Lord over all creation. Also mythopoeic language may provide a "sensus plenior" to the Divine speeches which implies Yahweh's victory over the Satan. This is more tenuous but if valid it helps us understand better the enigmatic words of Yahweh which are so important as a key to understanding the book.

Perhaps a distinction should be made between conscious demythologizing and simple metaphor. For example, Psalm 121 appears to be a conscious demythologizing, a polemic against the cosmic mountain motif and the notion of many patron deities. Since the pagan deities are no-gods (Ps. 5:4), where can one turn for help? The psalmist says:

> When I lift up my eyes to the mountains
>   where does my help come from?
> My help comes from Yahweh,
>   the Maker of heaven and earth.

The psalmist conceives of Yahweh as the patron deity:

> He will not let your foot slip . . .
> Yahweh watches over you . . .
> Yahweh will keep you from all harm . . .

We think immediately of Eliphaz's taunt of Job in 5:1:

> "Call now, is there any who will answer you, and to which of the Holy Ones will you turn?"

These "holy ones" are the *benê hā'elōhîm* of the prologue. The divine council motif may be considered an ideological continuity but the authors of Job and Psalms 82 and 89 have introduced a discontinuity in the way they handle the concept. The discontinuity can be appreciated in terms of the

11. See Albright's development of this idea in *Yahweh and the Gods of Canaan*.

Hebrew hierarchy of *'elōhîm*. There is only one creator—all the *q^ehal q^edōšîm* fear him and none can be compared with him (89:7–8). Men are *'elōhîm* to the animals, rulers and judges are *'elōhîm* to ordinary men, and the heavenly beings [are *'elōhîm*] to men. In the mythology there were lesser divine beings created by the cosmic gods to serve them. They are sometimes available as patron deities or personal intercessors and were general lackeys in the divine assembly. In Job 33 Eliphaz speaks of such an intercessor calling him a *mal'āk*[12] (messenger) and a *mēlîṣ* (interpreter). Both Job and his friends believe that among such "holy ones" a man might find a defender. Three times Job mentions such a one, feeling the need for an arbiter (9:33), a witness (16:19–21) and a vindicator (19:25–27). This is certainly evocative and part of the ideological preparation for the mediatorial work of the Christ who could stand between God and man, sharing the nature of each, as Job says in 9:33 "that he might lay his hand upon the two of us."

The Book of Job is replete with vivid imagery based on the mythic literature deeply engrained in the language and passed on through generations. There are too many examples to do more than sample a few themes. A widely used theme is the quelling of Chaos known in west Semitic literature as Yamm (Sea) and in Babylonia as Tiamat (the Deep). The sea monsters variously called Rahab (the boisterous), Tannin (the dragon) and Leviathan (the serpent) also play a part.

In 7:12 Job speaks out in anguish over his imagined harassment by God and says:

> Am I *Yamm* (Sea) or *Tannin*
> that you set a guard over me?

The tales of the conquest of Yamm, Tannin, and Lotan by Baal and Anat are well known. The Babylonian Tiamat is killed by hero gods who then proceed to create the land and sea from the pieces. The west Semitic literature provides no creation account but stresses the control of the sea by the weather god, Baal (Ugaritic texts 68, 129, 137). Job and his friends knew well the west Semitic myths. But were they committed to them as part of their view of deity? The only way we can know is from the total thrust of their words.

A look at the chaos terminology in the first part of chapter 9 will help us capture the thrust of Job's concept of deity. According to Job, El is indeed a God of profound wisdom and cosmic force and as such is too much for mere man. In verses 5–13 [El] moves mountains and shakes the earth off its foundations—the earthquake. He speaks and the sun doesn't rise—the eclipse. He seals up the stars from sight—movement of the stars and planets. He

12. The same term is used in Ugaritic for the lackey gods. Cf. A. Herdner, *Corpus des tablettes en cunéiformes alphabétiques,* 1.3, 17–21; 3.4.76–80, etc.

stretched out the heavens and trampled on the back of Yamm *(bomᵒtê yām)*—creation and overcoming of Chaos. He made the Bear, Orion, Pleiades, and the southern chambers and when angry even the cohorts of Rahab cower at his feet. Job here describes a deity who is unique when compared with what we know of any single contemporary god. The Ugaritic El is a character variously represented. Sometimes he is a forceful lone patriarch living in a tent, at other times a frightened deity who is forced to give up the young Baal to the messengers of Yamm. Baal can take things in his own hands and destroy Yamm with the weapons supplied by Kothar wa-Hasis.[13] But then Baal is killed by Mot. The issue is always sovereignty. El and the divine assembly are faced with the question of ascribing kingship to Yamm. Baal asserts kingship not only by eliminating Yamm but by demonstrating his power in the storm. This west Semitic story was imported to the east where Marduk, chosen as king by the gods, asserts kingship by slaying Tiamat.[14]

The point is that Job's God assumes all the functions of the gods whether Baal, El, or Yamm. Job's El is never subordinated to any of the *benê hā'elohîm.* In 9:8 he exercises his creative power all by himself *(lᵉbaddô).* The line is the same as in Isaiah 44:24. He is not only a deity who does not share his power and authority but he performs his numberless wonders while being invisible (verse 11).

> When he passes me I can't see him.
>   When he goes by I can't perceive him.

The psalmist expresses a similar discontinuity in Psalm 89:5–8.

> The heavens praise your wonders, O Yahweh,
>   your faithfulness also, in the assembly of the holy ones.
> For who in the skies above can compare with Yahweh?
>   Who is like Yahweh among the heavenly beings?
> In the council of the holy ones God is greatly feared;
>   he is more awesome than all who surround him.
> O Yahweh, God of hosts, who is like you?
>   You are mighty, O Yahweh, and your faithfulness surrounds you.

As in Job and Isaiah this theme is linked to God as Creator for it is precisely at this point the psalmist describes Yahweh as Creator of the heavens and earth and the One who rules over the surging sea, crushing Rahab and all his enemies. In his creating and saving power he is unique and incomparable. The psalmist's God also had that mysterious quality of invisibility. Was it

13. See H. L. Ginsberg's translation of the Baal-Yamm Cycle in *ANET,* p. 131.

14. Yahweh's lordship over Chaos is the theme of Psalm 29. There the *benê 'elim* are called to honor and worship the one who controls and sits enthroned forever over the flood (29:10).

not this quality that disturbed his idolatrous contemporaries when they chided "Where is your God?" (42:3, 10; 79:10). Psalm 115:2 reads:

Why do the nations say,
"Where is their God?"
Our God is in heaven;
he does whatever pleases him
But their idols are silver and gold,
made by the hands of men.

BDB notes that when *'ayyeh* is so used, the answer *nowhere* is expected. Even though ineffectiveness may be the point of Psalm terminology, invisibility is in mind in Job. Job is asserting that his God is both invisible and all-powerful.

Turning now to another theme in Job 5:7 where the KJV and RSV read:

But man is born to trouble
as the sparks fly upward,

it is better to translate:

Man is born to trouble
as sure as Resheph's sons soar aloft.

Who are "Resheph's sons"? Is this a metaphor for flames, sparks or lightning? Resheph is equated with Nergal, the Mesopotamian god of pestilence and the netherworld. In Deut. 32:24 the word is parallel with *qeṭeb* (destruction) and in Hab. 3:5 with *deber* (pestilence), and the plural is used of lightning in Ps. 78:48. In Ps. 76:4, however, "the reshephs" (arrows) of the bow are in apposition to the shield, the sword and the battle. In Ugaritic Resheph is called "Lord of the arrow," either referring to his skillful use of lightning or his attendance upon arrows in flight. Just as Death's firstborn (Job 18:13) devours the bodies of wicked men, so here the sons of Resheph are active trouble makers. On Resheph T. M. Gaster observes:

> When *Resheph* is said (Hab. 3:5) to attend upon Yahweh, or when the pangs of love are described as "fiery *reshephs*" (Song of Songs 8:6), do the writers really have in mind the figures of the Canaanite plague-god of that name, or is this simply a case of metonymy? This is a problem which I will not even attempt to resolve, but it must at least be mentioned.[15]

From my point of view Gaster is asking the wrong question. It makes little difference whether the figure of the plague god is in mind or not. Habakkuk

15. *Myth, Legend and Custom in the Old Testament,* p. xxxvi, as quoted in W. Michel's *Mythological Expressions in the Book of Job,* p. 8.

is using a highly anthropomorphic figure of Yahweh. The real question is, did Habakkuk believe Yahweh existed in the form of a warrior and did Job and Habakkuk believe Resheph or Resheph's sons really existed as gods? That must be answered in the light of other things these writers say.

Job 26 is replete with mythological allusions—the denizens of Sheol, Zaphon the cosmic mountain, Yamm and Rahab, all in a cosmography with some rather sophisticated observations.

Verses 5–14 may be rendered:

The spirits of the dead writhe,
  the Waters below and their denizens.
Sheol is naked in God's presence,
  Abaddon is uncovered.
He spreads out Zaphon over emptiness;
  he hangs the earth on nothing.
He wraps up the waters in his clouds;
  yet the clouds do not burst under the weight.
He covers the face of the full moon
  spreading his clouds over it.
He marks out the horizon on the face of the waters
  for a boundary between light and darkness.
The pillars of the heavens quake
  stunned at his rebuke
By his power he churns up the sea,
  by his skill he pierces Rahab.
By his breath the heavens become fair;
  his hand pierces the gliding serpent.
And these are only the outer fringes of his power;
  how faint the whisper we hear of him!
  Who then can understand the thunder of his might?

Buttenweiser in his famous comment on verse 7 said:

Our author, though naturally ignorant of the law of gravitation, had outgrown the naive view of his age about the universe, and conceived of the earth as a heavenly body floating in space, like the sun, moon, and stars. It is not surprising to meet with such a view in the Book of Job when one considers the advance astronomy in Babylonia, Egypt, and Greece. As early as 540–510 B.C. Pythagoras of Samos, in his travels in Egypt and the East, acquired the knowledge of the obliquity of the ecliptic and of the earth's being a sphere freely poised in space . . . Job 38:6 bears out rather than contradicts the conclusion that the writer of Job had attained a more advanced view of the universe, since the question, "Whereon were its foundations set?" shows that he no longer shared the primitive notion that the earth was resting on pillars erected in the sea.[16]

16. M. Buttenweiser, *The Book of Job*, 1922, in loc.

Both Buttenweiser and Dhorme contend "the north" *(ṣāphôn)* is the celestial pole formed by the seven stars of Ursa Minor from which the movement of the universe was believed to proceed. Two observations are needed. First, the cosmography is not in itself the purpose of the passage. Again God's power is in focus. Secondly, we cannot ignore what Ugaritic literature tells about Mount Zaphon as the Canaanite Olympus.[17]

The cosmic mountain concept is related to Sinai as the place from which God reveals himself and Zion as God's dwelling place.[18]

Psalm 48:1–2 says:

> Great is the LORD and most worthy of praise,
> in the city of our God, his holy mountain.
> It is beautiful in elevation,
> the joy of the whole earth.
> Like the utmost heights of Zaphon is Mount Zion,
> the city of the Great King.

Eschatological Zion in Isaiah 2:2–4 is the place where the LORD's house is established at the head of the mountains with all the nations flowing to it, where the LORD is enthroned and rules over a world of universal peace (cf. Isaiah 24:23).

The passage which most closely approximates Job 26:7 is Isaiah 14:13–14. Here the King of Babylon desires to place himself where the Most High dwells.

> You said in your heart,
> "I will ascend to heaven;
> above the stars of God
> I will set my throne on high;
> I will sit on the mount of assembly.
> On the slopes of Zaphon
> I will ascend above the heights of the clouds;
> I will make myself like the Most High."

There is a difference in the way the two passages use Zaphon. In the mouth of the pagan king it is used quite literally to mean the mount of assembly which, indeed, reaches into the heavens and is the divine abode. But in Job the choice of words points to metonymy. I came to this conclusion before I noticed that Clifford makes a similar observations in a footnote. . . .:

17. Actually *Mons Casius* due north of Israel where Baal-Hadad had his marvelous dwelling built. This explains why the Hebrew word *ṣāpon* means north. Compare Negev for south, Yam for west.

18. See *The Cosmic Mountain in Canaan and the Old Testament*, Richard Clifford.

> Zaphon's meaning seems to be practically "heavens." *Nōṭek* elsewhere is used of "heavens" in the Old Testament and it forms a reasonable merism with *'ereṣ* in the passage from Job. It is easy to imagine the development of the meaning of Zaphon, under Israelite impulse, from "mountain (dwelling of God)" to "heavens (dwelling of God)."[19]

It may also be that the heaven being like a dome-shaped canopy which may be stretched out was associated with the similarly shaped mountains as represented in the glyptic art.[20] So the mountain of all mountains is the mountain which God stretched out like a canopy which is his dwelling place —the heavens.

Even though mythopoeic language is used, there is a hint that the author is demythologizing. In contrast to 7:12 where he said "Am I Yamm, that you set a guard over me" here in 26:12 the definite article is used with *yām* which shows the writer did not consider it a proper name.

So I would not agree with Fohrer who over-literalizes the cosmic picture and suggests pillars must be supporting the heavens nor would I agree with Buttenweiser who moves in the opposite direction. Buttenweiser may not be wrong in 38:5, where Yahweh uses the figure of the earth as a building with foundations and a cornerstone and asks Job "On what were its footings set?"—an indication that this was considered a mystery. The purpose of the writer is not to tell us how much he knew of the cosmos but to tell how powerful God is. Job is saying El is the God of the heavens and the God of the earth—the God of all nature. Stretching out the heavens over emptiness and hanging up the earth on nothing are bold figures both derived from actions common to man. The marvel is that he can do these things with nothing for support. Other marvels of nature are also attributed to his vast power and dominion. He fills the clouds with water and they do not burst. He uses the clouds as a drape over the face of the full moon.[21] He marks out the circle of the horizon as with cosmic calipers. By a mere word he makes the mountains shake and by his power he controls the raging sea and its monstrous creatures. And all this is only a whisper of his power, only the fringe of his dominion.[22]

Understanding the mythological background sometimes accomplishes just the opposite of what is assumed. Rather than show ideological commitment to the pagan way of handling the mysteries of nature it throws the discontinuity into relief and helps us appreciate how monotheistic the writer was. For example: Sheol, the realm of Mot in Ugaritic where Baal enters and is powerless, is open before God so that its denizens tremble—a uniquely biblical concept that fits only monotheism.

19. Ibid., 162, fn. 85.

20. Ibid., 96, top.

21. In verse 9 *kissē'* (throne) should be read *kese'* (full moon) on the basis of Psalm 81:4 and Proverbs 7:20.

22. As early as 1957 Dahood suggested *derek* sometimes means "power" or "dominion" (*Biblica* 38, 306–320). In this he since has been generally supported (AB 15, 186).

Generally the mythology allots to the gods their separate domains. There are the gods of the heavens and the gods of the earth. With Baal dead Ashtar, the Rebel god, is permitted by El to attempt to sit on Baal's throne, but not having the stature he does not succeed and must be content to reign on the earth.[23] Each god is powerful in his own domain. As personifications of nature they are often in conflict with each other. The hero Baal faces a losing battle with Mot and has victory over Yamm. Unlike the Ugaritic El who sires deities but cannot control them, Job's "El" is the sovereign Lord over all natural forces—especially the domains of Mot, Yamm, and Baal.

This is what prompts Hans Wolff to write:

> Following the signposts of the OT itself, we must seek to understand it on the basis of the peculiar nature of Yahweh, the God of Israel. In his essence, Yahweh is not a figure of mythology in the sense that one could speak of him in the manner of the myths of the neighboring lands, which chatter so much of the "private life" of their gods and of their life together in the pantheon. Yahweh is the one beside whom no other is god, and before whom all others are shown to be no gods.[24]

Our final thesis is that mythopoeic language provides a *sensus plenior* in the Yahweh speeches which serves well the purpose of the book. But what is the purpose of the book? Is it not to show that the righteous may suffer for no other reason than to accomplish God's higher will? I summarize some of the thoughts of G. B. Gray[25] on the relationship of the Yahweh speeches to that purpose. He has noted that what the divine speeches do not contain is as important as what they do. The speeches do not reverse Yahweh's judgment in the Prologue about Job. The Satan was wrong in impugning Job's inner reasons for being righteous and the friends were wrong about Job's outward conduct as the reason for his suffering. God's rebuke of Job (38:2, 40:2) was for what he said after the calamity happened not for earlier sins which would have proved the penal theory of suffering was correct. The friends by their theory implied they knew completely God's way. One of the purposes of the Yahweh speeches is to show that neither they nor Job possessed such complete knowledge. Indeed, the speeches how how very limited man's knowledge is. On the surface it would appear that the speeches concentrate only on the natural world. But careful reading reveals something else. In the first speech (chapters 38 and 39) God's works in the natural creation are in view. God introduces this with the words (38:2):

23. A. Herdner, *Corpus des tablettes en cunéiformes alphabétiques*, 6.1.39–65. Clifford mentions another place where Ashtar does exercise kingship from Zaphon (*The Cosmic Mountain*, p. 168).

24. "Hermeneutics in the Old Testament," 168.

25. I.C.C. *Job*, Introduction.

Who is this that darkens my counsel
  by words without knowledge?

Then follow two chapters of proof that Job knew very little about God's world (something modern man has learned much more of only to discover how much more lies beyond him). Job is humbled. He agrees that his words were based on ignorance: "I put my hand to my mouth . . . I will say no more" (40:4–5).

The second speech begins on an entirely different note:

Would you discredit my justice?
  Would you condemn me to justify yourself?
Do you have an arm like God's,
  and can your voice thunder like his?
Then adorn yourself with glory and splendor,
  and clothe yourself in honor and majesty.
Unleash the fury of your wrath;
  look on every proud one and bring him low;
  look on every proud one and humble him;
crush the wicked wherever they stand.
Bury them all in the dust together;
  shroud their faces in the grave.

In keeping with this introduction the descriptions of Behemoth and Leviathan follow. The purpose this time is not only to humble Job by showing him that Yahweh is Creator and Sustainer of the natural world but to convince him that Yahweh is Lord of the moral order. And appropriately Job's response this time is repentance (42:1–6). The concentration on these two awesome creatures, placed as they are after this assertion of Yahweh's justice and moral order, lends weight to the contention that they are symbolic.[26] The figures may draw from the features of the hippopotamus and crocodile. Both terms are used in other O.T. contexts without symbolic significance (Pss. 8:8, 50:10, 78:22, 104:26; Joel 1:20, 2:22; Hab. 2:17). But they also symbolize evil political powers. The many-headed Leviathan of Psalm 74:12–13 is a poetic handling of Israel's crossing the Red Sea and Isaiah 27:1 describes Yahweh's destruction of the Evil One in the eschaton.

The word *b^{e}hēmōt* is an intensive plural of *b^{e}hēmāh* (beast); hence the beast par excellence. Behemoth in 40:19a is "the first of the ways of God." Pope translates this "a primordial production of God," but Dahood renders it "the finest manifestation of God's power" (AB 15, 272). In Ugaritic the goddess Anat conquered the seven-headed Leviathan along with a bovine creature

26. It is impossible to tell where the description of Behemoth ends and Leviathan begins. Some take 40:23 as the division. But it is possible they are left this way because both figures describe one being.

called "the ferocious bullock." Leviathan has power over which no human strength can prevail. For some reason the Hebrew text begins a new chapter in the middle of this description (41:9 = 41:1 Heb.). We translate beginning in 41:18:

> His sneezings flash forth lightning
>   His eyes are like the glow of dawn.
> Flames stream from his mouth;
>   sparks of fire leap forth.
> From his nostrils pours smoke,
>   as from a pot heated by burning brushwood.
> His breath sets coals ablaze:
>   a flame pours from his mouth.

And verse 25:

> When he rises the heavenly beings are afraid;
>   they are beside themselves because of the crashing.

Swords, javelins, arrows, clubs, slingstones are no good against him according to verses 26–29. And in 33 we read:

> Then even I will admit you
>   that your own right hand can save you. (40:8–14)
> Upon earth there is not his equal,
>   he was made without fear.
> He looks down on all that is lofty;
>   he is king over all proud beings.

Is this merely a crocodile or should it be understood in light of Isaiah 27:1, etc. (cf. the dragon symbol of Revelation 12)?

By telling of his dominion over Behemoth and Leviathan, perhaps by means of a subtle double entendre, Yahweh is celebrating his triumph in the moral sphere. The Satan, the Accuser, has been proved wrong though Job does not know it. The author and the reader see the entire picture which Job and his friends never knew. No totally rational theory of suffering is substituted for the faulty one the friends proffered. The only answer given is the same as in Genesis. God permits the Satan to touch Job as part of the cosmic contest.

On this general subject Albright has said some cogent things in his *History, Archaeology and Christian Humanism*. Remarking how the Old Testament is a "masterpiece of empirical logic not expressed in formal categories," Albright claims the Old Testament has demythologized the poems on which some Hebrew literature is based. "Old words are kept but with new meanings divested of mythological connotations."

There may be partial demythologizing in some cases. On 38:7 F. I. Andersen says:

> It is noteworthy that 11Qtg Job has completed the demythologizing, making the stars shine instead of sing, and calling the sons "angels."[27]

Is use of the plural in *ʾelōhîm* and *ʾădōnāy* demythologizing? In Hebrew this appears to mean the totality of all the manifestations and attributes of deity which polytheism broke down into single elements. In some Canaanite documents a single high god is referred to with the plural ending, the so-called plural of majesty (Amarna and Ugaritic). Nothing sounds more polytheistic to some ears than the words used by that monotheist the Chronicler: "for great is our God above all gods" (1 Chron. 2:5).

Albright observes,

> much of the onslaught on early Israelite monotheism comes from scholars who represent certain theological points of view with reference to monotheism, i.e. who deny that orthodox trinitarian Christianity . . . or orthodox Judaism or orthodox Islam are monotheistic. I do not need to stress the fact that neither of the last two religions can be called monotheistic by a theologian who insists that this term applies only to unitarian Christianity or liberal Judaism. But no dictionary definition of monotheism was ever intended to exclude orthodox Christianity.[28]

In conclusion let me say that the distinguishing mark of mythology is not references to gods or the use of anthropomorphism and various metaphors which describe deity in concrete terminology but rather the narration of the interactions of numerous gods including such characteristics as their pettiness, their wild acts of violence, and sexual exploits. The OT authors do not show such concrete mythological commitment.

27. Tyndale O. T. Commentaries, *Job*, p. 274.
28. W. F. Albright, *History, Archaeology and Christian Humanism*, 155.

15

THE LAND OF UZ

G. Frederick Owen

Uz (עוּץ; LXX Αὐσῖτις) was the name of three men mentioned in the Bible: (1) the son of Aram and grandson of Shem (Gen. 10:22–23); (2) the son of Nahor and Milcah and brother of Buz (22:21), where the KJV reads "Huz"; and (3) one of the sons of Dishan the Horite of the land of Edom (36:28). One of these settled in a district or a section of the country E of Pal[estine], and on the border of Arabia, which became known as "The land of Uz." In time it became famous as the home of Job.

The country is nowhere specifically located either in sacred or secular history or geography, yet biblical and traditional references provide several clues to its location:

1. It was a land of plentiful pastures (Job 1:3).
2. Portions of it were suitable for plowed crops (Job 1:14).
3. It was near the desert or "wilderness" (Job 1:19).

From G. Frederick Owen, "Uz," in *The Zondervan Pictorial Encyclopedia of the Bible,* ed. Merrill C. Tenney, 5 vols. (Grand Rapids: Zondervan, 1975), 5:852–53. Used by permission of Zondervan Publishing House.

4. It was sufficiently extensive to have a number of kings or "Sheikhs" over as many tribes or people (Jer. 25:20).
5. It was so situated as to be in more or less proximity to the tribes of the Temanites, the Shuhites, the Naamathites (Job 2:11), the Buzites (32:2), and to Dedan (Jer. 25:23).
6. There was a colony of Edom (called "daughter of Edom") in the Land of Uz (Lam. 4:21).
7. It was within raiding distance of the Sabeans and Chaldeans (Job 1:15, 17).
8. Ancient tradition, as found in the "Syriac book," affirmed that the Land of Uz lay "on the borders of Idumea (Edom) Arabia."
9. The LXX, in some vv. at the end of the Book of Job, says that contemporary tradition located the Land of Uz "on the border of Edom and Arabia." Job was "the greatest of all the men of the east" (Job 1:3, 13–19). And "the east," from the Biblical writer's point of view, almost always meant those countries on the rim of the Arabian desert, E and SE of the lower Jordan River and the Dead Sea, but a bit beyond Ammon, Moab, and Edom.

Wadi Sirhan, SE of Jebel ed Druz, is the one land area that fits the Biblical description of the "land of Uz," and falls into place and harmonizes with the setting in the Book of Job as no other area in the lands of the Bible. Wadi Sirhan is a great shallow plain-like depression some 210 miles long and averaging 20 miles wide. It begins at the present inland town of Azraq, a typical oasis with many palm groves, some fifty miles E of Amman, and continues in a southeasterly direction to within ten miles of Jauf, an important caravan junction of central Arabia. Many localities in the northwestern portion of Wadi Sirhan—(the general area where Job prob. lived)—are only 40 to 100 miles from the eastern borders of Edom.

Much of Wadi Sirhan is a vast, flat pasture land, fairly well suited to the raising of camels, donkeys, sheep, and goats. And to this day it sustains wild life such as gazelle, oryx, ostrich, and the wild ass, though in smaller numbers than in Job's day. The chief wealth of the plain lies in its abundant water supply. From the southern slopes of Jebel Druz, from the ranges of hills N and NE, and from the hundred miles long wadi-cut plateau stretching along its southwestern border, the water from winter and spring rains flow, either on the surface or subterraneously, into this depression. It becomes somewhat of a catchment basin for rain and run-off water, which means that such a reservoir of underground water is built up that in many places the water table is high enough to afford an abundance of water when a thin limestone sheet has been penetrated some eighteen to twenty-four inches below the ground surface. In other places there are wells and water holes where at times many thousands of camels and smaller cattle may be seen in the area at the same time. In some parts, however, they depend on rain water caught in cisterns and reservoirs.

In 1925, during the Druse rebellion against the Fr[ench] rule in Syria, many Druse chiefs with their people fled for refuge to Wadi Sirhan, where they pastured their vast herds and lived in their tents until the trouble was over. In ancient times the district lay near the caravan route from Sheba and Tema, and was exposed to the people of this area, and to the bands of Sabeans and Chaldeans as they came along the caravan route from the E. The residence of Job was in or near a city, at the gate of which he sat with the elders, to administer justice.

16

A Brief Explanation of Job 1–3

David J. A. Clines

Job 1–2

In these two chapters of seemingly artless prose, the problematic of the book has been exposed. It is that while the doctrine of retribution is initially taken for granted—as in the depiction of Job's piety and his consequent prosperity in 1:1–3—it has in the course of the narrative been first questioned and then overturned. It is questioned in 1:9 where it is asked whether Job serves God gratuitously, i.e., whether his piety may not be the result of his prosperity rather than the other way about—as has always been assumed; and it is overturned by the heavenly decision to decide that question by removing his prosperity. Once that is done, the retributive principle has been broken; for now the most pious man on earth is among the most wretched. It is irrelevant that 40 chapters later he will be restored to his

From David J. A. Clines, *Job 1–20,* Word Biblical Commentary (Waco: Word, 1989), 65–66, 104–5. Used by permission of Word Books.

wealth, for the bulk of the book revolves about what it signifies that a righteous person can be in such misery. What counts now is that in a world where it is believed and taught that actions have appropriate consequences (despite the many evidences to the contrary), heaven itself has now sabotaged that doctrine with a most shocking infringement.

This attack on the doctrine of retribution has both an intellectual and an existential dimension. The intellectual dimension has hardly been broached in the prologue, and innocent readers of the book may actually be deceived into thinking the prologue nothing but a simple folktale forming the machinery for the real intellectual issues of the dialogue. This is not so, of course, because here we have heard not some apparent and fictive exception to the doctrine that we may hope to find reconciled with it ultimately, but a categorical reversal of it which is certified by the narrator to be no misprision, and which no less a character than God authorizes explicitly. All the same, it will be much more the business of the dialogue than of the prologue to probe the intellectual conundrum of the innocent's suffering. What the prologue first turns its attention to is the existential dimension.

The existential problem is not the question, Do the innocent suffer?—that is, If they are suffering, can they indeed be innocent? Nor is it the question, Why do the innocent suffer?—that is, What reason can be given for such suffering?, which is to say, How can innocent suffering be comprehended or explained within some other set of concepts? These are all intellectual questions, and the book as a whole does indeed address them, even if it does not resolve them. But here what is posed is the existential question: What should innocents do when inexplicable suffering comes upon them? The portraiture of Job contains the answer the narrative seeks to convey: in mourning for his loss Job blesses the Lord who gave and who has taken away, never sinning in his speech or speaking irreverently of God (1:21–22; 2:10). This is not the only answer the book gives to the existential question, for the moment we turn the page (literally, as it happens, in my RSV) into chap. 3 we find the selfsame Job, who has abandoned neither his piety nor his integrity, first wishing he had never been born and then by stages moving to the most formal accusation of God a human can mount. In case we should be supposing that Job from chap. 3 onwards is making false moves, unworthy of imitation by readers, or losing his faith, or at least failing to maintain the moral and religious standards he exemplifies in the prologue, the end of the book has Job praised by God for speaking of him "what is right," and to such a degree in tune with the divine disposition that only through his prayer are the friends relieved of the consequences of their "folly" (42:8–9). There are not two Jobs, but there is more than one right way of coping with innocent suffering: when Job cannot bow in pious submission to the divine theft of his children, his property and his reputation he can still, with a piety equal but different, assert that it is with God and no other that he must treat and demand that from God and no other his innocence be vindicated, since not even his own complete assurance of his innocence can satisfy him. This attitude too, aggressive and febrile in contrast to the compliant and almost catatonic Job of chaps. 1–2, will in the dialogue be presented as an answer to the existential question, How can I endure suffering? But while we are still in the prosaic, formal, and antique world of the prologue, the more conventional piety prevails.

Job 3

This poem, one of the great masterpieces of the work, is striking above all for its restraint. Not for the restraint of Job's emotions, which are deep, raw, and terrifying, as he showers with maledictions every aspect of the world that gave him existence or continues to support it. That excessive and surreal rejection of life that imagines the night of his conception being swallowed up by the underworld (v. 6) or that depicts the world-weary as grave-robbers desperately digging their way into Sheol as into a treasure-house (vv. 21–22) is a quintessential instance of the vitality of the human spirit when freed from the bounds of custom, decorum and prosaic reality. The restraint that makes this a poem of world stature is the exclusive concentration on feeling, without the importation of ideological questions. For a book that is so dominated by intellectual issues of theodicy it is amazing to find here not one strictly theological sentence, not a single question about the meaning of his suffering, not a hint that it may be deserved, not the slightest nod to the doctrine of retribution. All that will come, in its time, but here we are invited to view the man Job in the violence of his grief. Unless we encounter this man with these feelings we have no right to listen in on the debates that follow; with this speech before us we cannot overintellectualize the book, but must always be reading it as the drama of a human soul.

What are Job's friends, who have sat silently with him seven days and seven nights (2:13), to make of this utterance with which Job breaks the silence? Trained themselves, as Job too must have been, in the doctrine of exact retribution, they must be astonished to hear from Job not the faintest concession to that fundamental explanation of human fortunes, nor the slightest admission of a guilt that had brought him to this point. This poem is not only powerful, it is improper. They have been wondering, no doubt, and their subsequent speeches confirm it, how to behave like friends at all when the evidence before their eyes marks Job out as a man who has deeply sinned, and whom it is not entirely safe to associate with. To hear Job speak, it sounds as if he knows of nothing to blame himself for, and so, whether gently or astringently, they will feel it their duty to point out to him in their speeches that the suffering that has brought him to this extreme of turmoil can have only one meaning: that he is nothing but a sinner being punished for his sin.

Another restraint, on the poet's part, that surprises us the more as we read further in the book is that God is not blamed, nor even especially held responsible, for the suffering Job is encountering. It is God indeed who continues to give life to those in "trouble" (v. 20), but that fact is mentioned only to wish that he wouldn't, not to blame him for doing so. And Job himself is a man "hedged in" by God (v. 23), overprotected, and not allowed to sink toward the grave; but that too is not said in order to charge God with cruelty, but to stress how inescapable a hold life has on Job. Even in the prologue, Job's responses to the double calamity had been to see God behind everything that had befallen him (1:21; 2:10), but here there is no word of that, simply the naked feelings. The accusations against God will begin in Job's next speech (6:4), and thereafter will fall thick and fast; but at this moment the poet shuts us up to a contemplation of Job's inner life that will only hereafter breed harsh words against God and the friends and will involve Job ultimately in a metaphorical lawsuit against God.

Yet another surprise in this poem has been referred to in v. 13. It is that the dominant note of the poem has been Job's restlessness or turmoil (vv. 10, 17, 20, 26) contrasted with the restfulness of Sheol (vv. 13–15, 17–19). This is not self-evidently the emotion people in Job's position would feel about their suffering: self-pity, anger, disgust, hopelessness, yes; but anxiety and turmoil, hardly. The reason can only be that it is the intellectual-existential implications of his suffering that "disturb" Job; though he will not ventilate them here, we are to understand that already he has been meditating on the religious significance of the disasters. His anxiety is not because of his foul skin disease, nor even because he fears he may soon be dead, but rather because he is experiencing a shaking of the foundations of cosmic moral order. He is disoriented by the anomie of his experience and longs for Sheol as a place where order reigns, the order, indeed, of inactivity and effacement of earthly relationships, to be sure, but an order where the conflicts of the absurd have been swallowed up by a pacific meaninglessness.

17

WHERE JOB'S "COMFORTERS" WENT WRONG

Mark R. Littleton

Job's "comforters" have gotten a bad reputation in our world. Anyone who is accused of being one of them suffers an unequivocal put-down. It's like saying, "You're worthless." Or, "What a miserable friend you are." Or, "Instead of helping matters, you've made them worse!"

The first time I realized I was in danger of becoming such a person was when my wife became pregnant with our first daughter. For several months, she suffered from a debilitating nausea that stayed with her all day. She couldn't keep food down, even after the morning. It was so bad that the doctor thought it could come to hospitalization and intravenous feeding.

Often, when I'd return from my day at the office, my first comment, after spying the load of dishes still sitting in the sink, was, "Instead of lying around all day, why don't you wash the dishes? That'll make you feel better."

From Mark R. Littleton, *When God Seems Far Away* (Wheaton, Ill.: Harold Shaw, 1987), 79–88. Used by permission of Harold Shaw Publishers.

Valerie replied, "But I can't bear the sight of food. The very smell of it makes me nauseous."

I angrily proceeded to wash them myself, then said, "It's all in your head."

There was a lot of disagreement in those days.

It really hit me when we sat down to dinner and my wife threw up right on her plate before she'd taken a bite. I was so callous I just went on eating. I coldly thought, "She's just trying to make it look worse than it is."

My wife stared at me through bleary eyes. "You're the most unsympathetic person I ever knew. I hope you get pregnant like this and have morning sickness too."

It was almost funny! *Almost.*

But before you lambaste me about this and tell me I'm virtual pond scum, please understand that I've reformed. However, it does take awhile.

Nonetheless, I know well what it is to be accused of being one of Job's "comforters."

Good Intentions

These three men who first visited Job actually started off rather well. When they heard about their friend's disaster, they immediately covenanted to come by, sympathize with him, and comfort him.

The Hebrew words used here are interesting. "Sympathize" actually translates a word that means to move about with anxiety and be disturbed, to shake one's head with agitation.

In effect, what they planned to do was hear Job's story and agree with him. How do most of us sympathize with others when they're in pain? We shake our heads, saying, "That sounds horrible." And, "Yes, I really understand. That's the most terrible thing I ever heard." We become agitated in our concern and shake our heads with horror.

The word for "comfort" means to "be sorry." One of the Semitic roots even translates a word meaning to breathe pantingly. When a person comforts someone he may sigh and weep. Their pain becomes his pain. He "feels sorry" for them and expresses compassion and grief over their agony.

That's what Eliphaz, Bildad, and Zophar planned to do.

When they finally saw Job as they walked toward him, they were astounded. No matter what they'd heard, this wasn't what they expected. They wept, tore their robes, and threw dust over their heads—Eastern expressions of mourning. These men weren't frauds. They were truly grieved.

One more indication of their own pain at the sight of Job is the fact that they were silent for seven days. This seems incredible, especially when we realize that the first thing most of us do when we see someone in pain is to say something ridiculous like, "I hope it's over soon," or, "I'm really and truly sorry, very sorry, so sorry. I really am," or, "I'm going to get the whole church to pray for you." Sometimes such expressions are euphemisms for,

"Good heavens! You look gross. I mean, I can barely stand the sight of you. If I don't get away soon, I'll be sick."

Regardless of our plans, few of us could stick to silence for seven days. The compassion of these three men was true. They were the real thing. No one can fault them for not caring.

Trying to Find an Explanation

After seven days, though, Job finally spoke. . . .

After Job expressed very normal feelings about his pain, Eliphaz jumped in. He was very polite about it. But he dropped the basic bombshell that forms the foundation of their whole argument: the only reason people suffer is because they've sinned.

The argument went on through three rounds of speeches for Job and each of the friends. Insults were slung. Harsh words of sarcasm were fired out from each person. It was obviously an uncomfortable and unnecessary situation. Why did it come to this? Simply because Job and his three friends became hardened in their respective theological positions. They said, "You've sinned, Job. And you've sinned horribly. You've committed so many sins, they're piled up before God like a heap. Just repent, and the whole thing will be over." Job said he was innocent.

The argument clearly moved from bad to worse. Job's counselors started out well, but they became entrenched in their position and ended up accusing Job of heinous crimes rather than helping him.

Job's three friends found themselves supporting an unsupportable argument. They *didn't* know why all this was happening to Job, but they felt compelled to come up with some explanation. They had no proof of his sin. But they were convinced that their so-called divine principle was correct. They were the classic, "Don't-give-me-the-facts, I've-already-made-up-my-mind" type of people. Even though Job repeatedly showed them they were wrong, they only became firmer in their convictions. As a result, they moved from subtle suggestion to outright accusation. Not only was it possible Job had sinned, they were sure he'd sinned on a level that one could only describe as total wickedness. What then did the comforters do wrong?

Mistakes of Human Wisdom

We all make mistakes. We're human and so were Job's friends. *Their first mistake was to say that Job must have sinned.* It's true that God does judge evil in this world (2 Peter 2:9–22). People do "suffer wrong as the wages of doing wrong" (2 Peter 2:13). But God does not settle all His accounts on the day of the crime. Some people's sins follow them after death to judgment (1 Timothy 5:24). They are never judged in this world.

Second, the three counselors proved their assumption on incomplete evidence. They observed that wicked men usually suffer. Job was suffering. Therefore, he must be a wicked man.

But wicked men don't always suffer. Even Job brought this out. Sometimes they escape. Sometimes they even prosper in the midst of their evildoing.

It's so easy to become an accuser on the basis of faulty evidence. In any case of suffering, before anyone makes a judgment call on why it's happening, he first needs to get the facts. No intelligent doctor would put a patient on the operating table simply because he complained of stomach pains. It might be the anchovies from the pizza the night before!

Third, when Job argued with them, the three counselors became indignant. Job proved them wrong over, under, sideways, and down. But they only became hardened in their conviction that he'd sinned. They went from subtle suggestion to outright indictment.

Again, this is typical of human nature. When we don't get our way, we not only get even, we determine that we'll prove ourselves right if it's the last thing we do.

I remember hearing a Christian leader speak of a situation he was in while driving toward Chicago. As he cruised along, he passed his exit and his wife said, "You missed the exit, honey."

Well, that just made him mad. He said, "I'm driving this car. I know where I'm going. I know if I missed an exit."

She said, "You'd better turn around."

He responded, "There's no need for that."

Silence.

He continued on and the signs ceased to say Chicago. They began telling about Detroit and other cities not so close to Chicago.

She remarked, "Honey, all the signs for Chicago have stopped. You're going the wrong way."

He gritted his teeth and opted for one more exit.

When they reached the exit there was still no sign for Chicago.

His wife piped up again, "Honey, stop being ridiculous and turn around."

At that point, he decided to prove her wrong whatever it took. He began trying to think of a way to get to Chicago without turning around.

There was no way.

Suddenly, he realized he was sinning. He confessed his sin, gave up and turned around.

She said, "See how easy it was."

He smiled. "Now why didn't I do that twenty miles ago?"

"Because you're too proud."

That's rough, but true. When we get entrenched in a losing position, even though we know it's lost, we tend to continue in that position anyway. We're just too proud.

Fourth, in the heat of their argument, Job's friends forgot their original purpose. They ceased to be comforters and became accusers.

That's the problem with human wisdom. We become more concerned about proving our opinions than meeting the needs of others. This was the real failure on Job's counselors' part.

A friend of mine says his wife's chief complaint is that he's always concerned to win an argument. She says, "All I want you to do is listen. But you're determined to prove I'm wrong."

One day she shared with him a certain frustration with their children. His immediate response was to show her why she shouldn't be frustrated! "If you'd discipline them like I do, you wouldn't have the problem."

They argued awhile and finally she blurted, "Why are you always trying to win? Why can't I just air my feelings without you having to prove me wrong? My feelings are my feelings. Can't you simply listen without passing judgment?"

She was frustrated, but my friend told me, "You know it's the hardest thing in the world for me just to listen. I always want to solve the problem. But sometimes what is needed is listening. Especially with wives."

I laughed. But it's true. When a person hurts, their hurt is valid, regardless of the reasons the hurt has happened. *Our job is not to show them why they hurt, but to offer them comfort the best we can—with love, kindness, understanding, and affection.*

Haddon Robinson used to tell his students, "When we go to God and ask Him why bad things are happening, He doesn't give us an explanation; He gives us Himself."

Why Is This Argument So Sinister?

Despite the problems the counselors had in dealing with a losing argument, there's another even more important question here. It's this: Why was their argument wrong? So wrong, in fact, that God told them to ask Job to pray on their behalf, that they might not be judged (Job 42:7–9)?

There are a number of reasons why this argument is straight from the pit. It's a lie of Satan that many people promote—a lie that does not have a single grain of truth in it.

It Becomes a Reason to Reject Hurting People

The first problem with this argument is that it divides and punishes people in the eyes of other people. It's virtually the Law of Karma, which says that people get paid in this life for sins committed in a previous life. What does that do? Go to India and find out. A caste system develops in which all the hurting people are set aside as gross sinners. Their pain becomes a reason to reject them rather than to care about them.

This was precisely the thing that happened with Job. Everyone began to reject him because they believed he must have committed some terrific sin.

It was the same argument we find in John 9 where the disciples ask Jesus why a blind man was born blind. They say, "Who sinned, this man or his parents, that he should be born blind?" Jesus answers that it had nothing to do with sin, but it was "in order that the works of God might be displayed in him" (John 9:1–3).

In their day the same argument was foisted by the devil on the world. Its effect was to divide the healthy from the unhealthy. The healthy felt superior because they were "good." The unhealthy were rejected and hated because they were so obviously "bad." No good can come from such reasoning. It's one more way Satan uses to pit brother against brother, saint against saint, and sinner against sinner.

It Turns God into an Arbitrary Gift-Dispenser

In such a scenario, God becomes little less than an arbitrary and biased giver of blessings. Where do we find that the good ends and the bad begins? How much good must one do before he's good enough to be blessed in this world? How much bad must he do before he loses that blessing? God is forced into the position of making such judgments for all the world to see.

Furthermore, what happens when bad happens to you and you disagree like Job did? You end up accusing God of being unfair. As a result, this philosophy destroys real faith in God. Lesser people than Job would have cursed God long ago to His face—which is precisely what Satan wants. How many people have rejected Christ and truth because they've secretly believed this lie of Satan?

At a train wreck, a father cried out and cursed God because his son was killed in the wreck. "Where was God when my son was killed?" he challenged. A wise conductor on the same train quietly replied, "I suppose He was in the same place He was when His own Son was placed on the cross."

Ultimately, this principle causes us all to become judges of God because His so-called judgments are so apparent.

It Forces People into a "Works" Mentality

Even worse than these thoughts is the fact that this principle teaches people to trust in their own works, rather than in the work of Christ. If you believe that doing good wins God's blessing, then you'll do good to get the blessing, not out of love for God. Doing good becomes little less than an exercise in selfishness. Real faith is destroyed.

On days when I felt terrifically depressed, even more than usual, I'd often begin scouring the previous day or week, looking for some hidden sin in my life. I became an endless nitpicker, concentrating on what I'd done rather than on what I was doing. My focus was ripped from loving Christ to wondering what I'd done wrong.

God has no desire that we live this way.

When I was in Mexico City, I visited a huge cathedral set on a wide square. All over the square people were walking on their knees. Many would take a step, say a prayer, or go over a bead of their rosary, then take another step. Obviously, they were convinced that doing this won God's attention and favor. But how can anyone think that God is so low He would require such demeaning things of people? It turns God into a wicked tyrant rather than the loving, compassionate person of Jesus.

It Doesn't Promote True Accountability

On the surface, this principle appears to offer a sense of accountability. "If you sin, you'll be paid back for it. So don't sin." But actually there's no real accountability. Too many people escape in this world. Like Paul said, some people's sins "are quite apparent, going before them to judgment; for others, their sins follow along after" (1 Timothy 5:24). We are truly accountable to God only when we realize that we will all one day stand before Him to review all that we've done. He will "repay everyone according to his deeds" (Romans 2:6).

If there was to be true accountability through such a principle, God would be forced to judge people immediately after each good or bad work. Our world would be turned into a tit for tat, "you-did-this, I-do-that" situation. "An eye for an eye and a tooth for a tooth" would be the standard of the day. When people saw that the principle wasn't being done to their satisfaction, they would be tempted to take matters into their own hands.

It Limits the Power and Person of God

Moreover, this principle limits God. It binds Him to a process that is impossible in any practical sense. He is no longer free to operate in human events as He sees fit in His infinite wisdom. Rather, He's compelled to make a judgment in each situation as it happens.

Instead, God has chosen to let all of human history run its course with minimal interference from Him. At the end He will bring about the great judgments which will bring in perfect justice for every creature. With this ahead, He's able to work within human events without distraction.

People Don't Believe It

But the ultimate problem with this theological assumption is that most people simply don't believe it. Evil people disdain it, being sure that they'll escape with the goods without reprisal. Good people note that it doesn't work out in real life at all. Why then do people promote it?

Because it's a simple way of explaining things. We like plain, easy-to-understand principles. We want life to be wrapped up neatly, packaged and squared according to proper specifications. We don't want the interference of too many variables.

Furthermore, it's typical of many theologians to latch onto a principle because it *sounds* good regardless of whether it's true or not. People want everything tied together tightly and neatly so their leaders serve it up to them that way. That's the primary reason so many cults and false religions get started. A tidy explanation of things is offered. Simple minds accept it hook, line, and sinker for the sake of not having to think through the logic or truth of it themselves.

Recently I've been reading some books on the life and death of the people involved in People's Temple with Jim Jones. It's disturbing how many people were willing to submit to a harebrained maniac because they thought certain things he was doing were good. A little decency in the midst of gross immorality held them. One family endured numerous indignities and slams because Jim Jones, they felt, was the first real leader to promote and provide social programs through his church.

The End of Such Arguments

Where did these theological mistakes get these three comforters?

When God had finally spoken, His first judgment was to tell Eliphaz, "My wrath is kindled against you and against your two friends, because you have not spoken of Me what is right as My servant Job has" (Job 42:7). God's wrath was kindled because all three of them claimed to be speaking for God. When one "speaks for" God, he'd better be sure he has his facts and principles right. Otherwise, he may win God's judgment himself.

18

A Brief Explanation of Job 12–14

David J. A. Clines

Something quite new and dramatic has happened in this speech. Standing as it does at the junction between the first and second cycles of speeches it signals a climax in the progress of Job's emotions and lays down a marker for the future development of the plot of the work as a whole.

The dramatic development in this speech is that after all his desire to be put out of his misery as soon as possible (6:8–9), after his acknowledgment of the danger—not to say to the impossibility—of calling God to account (9:3, 14, 16), after his conviction that if he goes to law with God he is bound to be found guilty (9:29), after his demand for an assurance of safe conduct if he is to approach God (9:34–35), here he does the unthinkable and acts as he had not imagined himself acting. Here, at the center of the speech, he unequivocally calls on God to provide the evidence on which God would justify his severity toward him. It matters not which of them is to be plaintiff,

From David J. A. Clines, *Job 1–20,* Word Biblical Commentary (Waco: Word, 1989), 337–39. Used by permission of Word Books.

and which defendant (13:22); what Job seeks is a formal judicial process, in which an obligation is laid upon God to supply a catalogue of Job's supposed crimes (13:23). This is an utterance which, once made, cannot be unsaid; Job is now committed to confrontation with God, whatever the risks.

What outcome to this legal battle does Job expect? He has no illusions, and no hope; of one thing he is confident, that his temerity will issue in his death (13:15). But he has not gone to court to plead for his life or to beg for mercy, but to clear his name. He has no faith in the goodness of God, and not a lot in his justice; but he believes so strongly in the rightness of his own cause that he cannot doubt that in the end, whether before or after his death, he will be vindicated (13:18). He seeks the triumph, certainly not of God, and not even of himself, but of truth.

All this talk of lawsuits and summonses is metaphor, of course. But that does not make it decorative language gilding some plainer truth. The language of the metaphor is the language of feeling; the terminology of plaintiff and defendant, cases, crimes, deposition, affidavit and subpoena signals what it feels like to be involved in dispute with God. Job has a lifetime behind him of godfearingness (1:1), of calling upon God in reverent prayer and being answered (12:4), of harmonious relation with the divine. In a moment, that harmony has been shattered, and he has had to learn a new and more abrasive language to embody the discord in his universe. Now it must be the language of compulsion and division, of contest and defeat. The grimmest irony of all is that the quintessential phraseology for the old harmony, the calling and the answering, turns out to be the technical terminology for the power struggle of the lawsuit ("call, and I will answer," 13:22); what he had known as the language of personal reciprocity has been denatured into a language for isolation and conflict, plaintiff against defendant and defendant against plaintiff.

This is the heart of Job's fourth speech; and by itself this movement in the drama would be rich enough. But there are two further elements enlarging the scope of its significance.

The first concerns the friends. Now that they each have spoken, it is time that Job tell them, and us, what he has made of their words. Hitherto, we have learned from him that he thinks little of their loyalty (6:14, 20), and that he feels disregarded by them (6:26); we have seen him agreeing, on one point at least, with them (9:2). But on the whole he has ignored them; while they have addressed him throughout, he has tended either to soliloquize or to address himself to God. Here, on the contrary, he addresses them directly in 12:2–3 and 13:1–12, and parodies their speeches to him in 12:7–12. His tone is assertive, sarcastic, disputatious. He does not here speak of his feelings about them (as in 6:14, 20), but contrasts himself with them on the intellectual plane. When he says his wisdom is not inferior to theirs (12:2; 13:2), he means that his is superior; he has abandoned the idea of them as friends and he is treating them as conversation partners, colleagues at a theological seminar. It is a token of his greater psychic stability, now that he has made his decision about confronting God, that he speaks of looking to them not for solidarity but for explanation, and can even esteem himself their superior for his greater experience of reality. In the end, he can even become patronizing toward them, proffering them good advice (13:9) and laboring the point that now a legal process is in motion between himself and God their status has changed. No longer can they delude themselves that they speak for heaven against Job; now that they have become nothing but witnesses, partisans for neither party in the dispute, they can testify only to the facts, not to theological theories. But of course they have scant acquaintance with facts, having always believed that wisdom is inherited from one's elders (12:12) rather than fashioned in the crucible of experience; so on pain of having their stupidity exposed, or worse, of falling foul of the deity for unbecoming partisanship, their best course of action is to fall silent (13:5, 13).

The friends are characters in the drama of the book, and it is instructive, not to say entertaining, to see how their role develops—not through any changes internal to themselves, but in step with the forward march of Job's psychological and religious progress. But there is more: they are also Job's alter ego, representations of what Job would be without his calamity. In struggling with them, Job is struggling with the Job of yesteryear; and in affirming his superior intelligence to theirs, Job is committing himself all the more irrevocably to his new religious orientation.

The further weighty element in this speech is to be found in Job's elegy on the human condition in chap. 14. This is not the first time that he has made of his own unhappy state a paradigm for the lot of humanity at large (cf. also 3:20–23; 7:1–2, 17–18), but this is his most extended meditation on the significance of his own experience for what may be said about human life as such. Only in vv. 13–17, in the center of this chapter, does he focus on himself; at beginning and end his thought is for "man born of woman" (14:1). There is nothing new, and nothing unconventional, in his assumption that there can be no life beyond death, that there is more hope for a tree than for a human being (14:7). All the wistful lines about death perhaps being a kind of refuge in which a human could be protected from the divine wrath and from which one could, after an appointed time, arise, into a life of renewed communion with God, a restored intimacy of a calling and answering (14:15), are nothing but an impossible dream, and Job knows it. Human experience goes only to show that, time upon time, "thou destroyest the hope of man" (14:19). What Job, or even the poet, does not acknowledge is that impossible dreams have a surprising habit of coming true; and that even if they never do come true, they can create shape and structure for their dreamers. What this impossible dream will do for Job is impel him into taking action here and now against a wrathful God; would he have been better off if he had believed his dream were possible?

19

THE ARGUMENTS OF JOB'S THREE FRIENDS

David J. A. Clines

What I am offering here is a rhetorical analysis of rhetoric, that is, an application of certain methods of rhetorical criticism in the broadest sense to rhetoric in a narrower sense (declamatory speech designed to persuade). I hope to show that awareness of rhetorical devices can lead to large-scale exegetical gains, and, at the least, can help to preserve the interpreter from major errors.[1]

It would be a very considerable undertaking to argue in detail for the coherence of the speeches of Job's three interlocutors, and the distinctive

1. A preliminary form of this paper was read to the Rhetorical Criticism Section of the Society of Biblical Literature in New York, November, 1979.

From David J. A. Clines, "The Arguments of Job's Three Friends," in *Art and Meaning: Rhetoric in Biblical Literature,* ed. David J. A. Clines, David M. Gunn, and Alan J. Hauser, Journal for the Study of the Old Testament Supplement Series, vol. 19 (Sheffield: JSOT, 1982), 199 214. Used by permission of Sheffield Academic Press.

viewpoints each represents. The concern of this paper is more limited: it is first to treat four rhetorical elements in their speeches that are relevant to the questions of their coherence and of their distinctiveness, and secondly to set out some general arguments for their coherence and their distinctiveness.

Rhetorical Elements

Tonality

The mood, or tone, of each of the speakers in each of their speeches is fundamental to interpretation. Perception of tonality depends partly on the subjective impression of the reader, and certainly cannot be determined in advance of engagement with the whole of the speech, or indeed of the three speeches, of the friends. Clues to tonality are sometimes given rather unmistakably by the exordium and conclusion of a speech; e.g. Eliphaz in ch. 4 begins: "Are we to speak to you a word? You cannot bear it. But neither can we bear to hold back our words," and in ch. 5 he concludes: "Hear, and know for your own good." The tone in this speech thus appears to be deferential, positive, sympathetic.

But exordium and conclusion tones can be misleading: the first speeches of both Bildad and Zophar each end with a similar contrast between the fate of the righteous and that of the wicked, the final verse marking a downbeat note in each case (8:22; 11:20). We might infer from the similarity that the tonality of the two speeches is identical; but in fact it is different, since in Bildad's speech the final contrast proceeds from an unconditional affirmative, "He will yet fill your mouth with laughter" (8:21), whereas in Zophar's speech it proceeds from a hypothetical "If you set your heart aright . . . surely then . . . you will lie down with no one to frighten you" (11:13, 15, 19). Similarly, in the second cycle, all the friends' speeches conclude with a lengthy elaboration of the fate of the wicked (Eliphaz, 15:20–35; Bildad, 18:5–21; Zophar, 20:5–29), but the significance of these depictions varies considerably, as we will see below.

Some further clues in the text to the tonality of the speech—beyond those of exordium and conclusion—must be sought.

Nodal Sentences

In most of the speeches there appear one or two sentences, usually addressed to Job directly, which further define the tonality of the speech as well as pinpointing the content of the speech's argument.

Eliphaz's first speech provides two good examples. In 4:6, "Is not your piety your source of confidence? Does not your blameless life give you hope?" Eliphaz's mood may be felt to be mildly reproachful or wholly encouraging, but certainly not hostile, sarcastic, or dismissive. Unless he says "piety" and "blameless life" with a sneer—which the rest of the speech gives us no reason to suppose—he is essentially affirming Job in speaking without qualification of his "piety" *(yir'āh)* and his "blameless life" *(tōm d^erākim)*. To be sure, the previous verse has—at first hearing—a rather ambiguous tonality: "Now, when it meets with you, you cannot bear it! It strikes at you, and you are dismayed" (v. 5). By itself, it could be heard as a rather aggressive assessment of Job's impatience; but in the shadow of the clear tonality of v. 6, it can only be heard as sympathy, even if expressed with a mild and unhurtful irony.

A second nodal sentence may be found in 5:8: "As for me, I would seek God; it is to God that I would commit my suit." Here Eliphaz puts himself in Job's shoes and suggests what he would do in the same situation. It is not exactly non-directive counselling, but it is certainly non-authoritarian. Eliphaz does not command, threaten, cajole or humiliate Job in any way, but enters into his situation with all the imagination and sympathy he can muster. The facts that he is far from recognising Job's real situation, that patience is for Job the "hard thing" (as Hopkins' sonnet has it,[2] that the author of the book may be, via Eliphaz, mocking the incapacity of theoretical wisdom to handle the realities of human experience[3]) are all beside the point. This remains a crucial sentence for perceiving Eliphaz's mood and message.

Other nodal sentences in the friends' speeches, which cannot be examined in detail here, can be identified in the following: of Bildad: 8:4–6; 18:4; 25:4; of Zophar: 11:4–6; 20:4–5; [27:13–14]; of Eliphaz: 15:4–5; 22:21, 30.

Topoi

All the speeches of the book use stylized descriptions or accounts, which I propose to call *topoi*. E. C. Kingsbury[4] in another context, defined *topoi* as "general rhetorical patterns which may be used as building blocks for literary structures," a somewhat loose definition, but in line with what I have in mind. William J. Urbrock's Harvard dissertation discussed twelve such *topoi* (which he called "themes") in Job.[5] Such *topoi* frequently form the bulk of a speech (as they do in the second cycle of speeches), and account for the discursiveness of the book that many modern readers find tiresome. More significant exegetically is the fact that the function of a *topos* is often far from its obvious significance when considered out of context. A *topos* on a particular subject may serve quite different purposes in different speeches according to the tonality and argument of the speech.

The first speech of Eliphaz again offers us a useful example. In 4:8–9 (or 4:8–11, if the destruction of the lions is a symbol of the destruction of the

2. "Patience, hard thing! the hard thing but to pray,/ But bid for, Patience is" *(Poems and Prose of Gerard Manley Hopkins,* selected by W. H. Gardner [1953], 62).

3. K. Fullerton, "Double Entendre in the First Speech of Eliphaz", *JBL* 49 (1930), 320–74 (340).

4. E. C. Kingsbury, "The Theophany *Topos* and the Mountain of God", *JBL* 86 (1967), 205–210 (205 n. 1).

5. See W. J. Urbrock, "Formula and Theme in the Song-Cycle of Job", *SBL 1972 Proceedings,* vol. 2, 459–87 (487 n. 20).

wicked) we have a brief *topos* on the fate of the wicked. Some commentators, like Dhorme[6] and Weiser,[7] find Eliphaz to be intentionally insulting Job by assuming him to be the cause of his own misfortune. Any reader, indeed, must wonder why, in a speech that has set out to be reassuring, the retribution of the wicked and their destruction by God should find a place. But in the light of the tonality of the speech, and especially of the nodal v. 6, it becomes impossible to view this description as any kind of criticism or warning. On the contrary, precisely because Eliphaz's intention is encouraging, this *topos* depicts a fate that is the opposite of what is in store for Job. Job is among the righteous (v. 6); the innocent and upright are not cut off, that is, die in their prime (v. 7); the wicked, on the other hand, are suddenly brought to an end (vv. 8–9). Precisely because Job is righteous he need have no fear that he is about to die; he can have hope. This interpretation is confirmed by Eliphaz's words of encouragement in 5:18–26, which assures Job that he will not die until he has reached a ripe old age (5:26). In this context, the function of the *topos* is plain; in other cases it must be admitted that its function is not so obvious.

In Eliphaz's second speech (15:1–35) there is a lengthier *topos* on the miserable life and the fearsome fate of the wicked (vv. 17–35). Some have argued that Eliphaz has by now become convinced that Job is an evildoer, and have read this *topos* as Eliphaz's prognostication of the fate in store for Job.[8] It is true that in this speech Eliphaz takes a firmer line with Job: he reproaches him for so letting his tongue run away with him that, with his multitude of windy words, Job has ceased to behave like the wise man he really is (v. 2). And even though this sentence may be more a recognition of the tempestuousness of Job's speech than a reproach of his language in demanding vindication from God and in speaking of God's destructive power (cf. 12:13–25), Job has without question been irreligious ("doing away with the fear of God," v. 4); indeed, Job's mouth, tongue and lips have been leading him into sin ("Your mouth increases your wrongdoing," v. 6).[9] The same point, that Job is not being wise in letting his tongue lead him into sin, is reiterated in the second strophe of the speech (vv. 7–16): Job has not the wisdom of Adam (v. 7), nor that of the prophets (v. 8a), nor even that of his older friends (vv. 9–10). It is through lack of wisdom, Eliphaz is charitable enough to think, that Job is venting his anger (v. 13; cf. NEB) against God.

But as for the relevance of the life and destiny of the wicked, which is the subject of the *topos* that occupies the second half of his speech, although

6. E. Dhorme, *A Commentary on the Book of Job* (ET, 1967), 46.

7. A. Weiser, *Das Buch Hiob* (ATD, ^{4}1963), 48.

8. Thus G. B. Gray, in S. R. Driver and G. B. Gray, *A Critical and Exegetical Commentary on the Book of Job* (ICC, 1921), 132.

9. For the translation, cf. F. I. Andersen, *Job: An Introduction and Commentary* (TOTC, 1976), 176.

Eliphaz insists (as in 4:17–19) that no man can be perfectly righteous and therefore must expect *some* suffering (vv. 14–16), he is clearly maintaining that Job is *not* one of the truly wicked, and so this *topos* concerns what does *not* apply to him. Job has not, like the wicked, "writhed in pain all his days" (v. 20), nor does he "conceive mischief and bring forth evil" (v. 35). He does not belong to "the company of the godless" (v. 34), and if he "bids defiance to the Almighty" (v. 25), that only shows that he is making a serious mistake and forgetting where his loyalty lies. First appearances to the contrary, then, this *topos* does not function as a judgment upon Job's character but as an elaborate sketch of the kind of person Job is *not,* but is in danger of becoming.

In the case of Zophar's second speech (20:1–29), however, a *topos* on the same subject probably has quite a different intention. Zophar's attitude towards Job has been established by the nodal sentences of 11:5–6: Job is a secret sinner from whom God exacts less than his guilt deserves. Zophar's disquisitions on the brevity of the happiness of the wicked (20:4–11), on the "fate-producing deed" (20:12–22), and on the sudden end of the wicked (20:23–29) all apply directly to Job. Far from being an encouragement to Job, this portrayal of the end of the wicked is not even a warning: it is a prediction.

The *topoi* do not therefore offer, of themselves, insight into their function in the argument of Job's friends, but must rather be interpreted from the matter that lies outside them. This is not a very surprising conclusion to reach in the case of such traditional or stock material, but it is remarkable what an important role the *topoi* play in some commentators' analysis of the Joban arguments. Especially if the commentator adopts the principle of synopsis, i.e. compression of the content of each speech to a few lines of prose,[10] the *topoi* come to hold a disproportionate and often misleading place in the interlocutors' argument.

Verb Modality

Another aspect of Hebrew rhetoric that is frequently ignored is the range of modalities covered by the indicative form of the Hebrew verb in the "imperfect."[11] Combined with the range of temporal senses the imperfect has (future, present, past continuous; and perhaps also it is sometimes identical with "preterite" or "point" tense) is the series of modal implications it may convey, such as we would represent in English by the modal auxiliaries "may," "should," "can," "would," and so on. The student of the rhetoric of these speeches cannot assume that the speaker affirms everything he expresses with an "imperfect" verb (and most verbs in these speeches are "imperfects"). Rhetoric thrives on the modulation of possibility, obligation, probability, and

10. This is a particular feature of H. H. Rowley's commentary (*Job* [NCB], 1970); see for example pp. 175f. on Zophar's second speech.

11. Cf. E. König, *Historisch-Comparative Syntax der Hebräischen Sprache* (1897), 70–97.

reality, and trades in hypotheticals and exhortatives. In the poetry of these speeches, most of these nuances are not explicit linguistically, and may only be grasped by the sensitised reader.

Simply to illustrate the point, and to remark on how a rather straightforward example of a modal use of a verb directly affects the argument of a speech, I direct attention to a short passage in Eliphaz's first speech; concerning "those who dwell in houses of clay" (4:19), viz. humankind generally. Of them he says, if we read his speech in the RSV:

> Between morning and evening they are destroyed;
> they perish for ever without any regarding it.
> If their tent-cord is plucked up within them,
> do they not die, and that without wisdom?

Translations and commentaries alike universally assume that Eliphaz is speaking of humankind in general.[12] It seems far more likely, however, that verbs in these sentences are to be read modally. They are not statements of general actuality but of particular possibility. Verse 20 means, not that all human lives are ephermeral, but that humankind is so fragile that a person may be destroyed (*yukkattû*, "pulverized") between a dawn and a dusk. All people do not expire so rapidly, for some suffer lingering deaths. Nor do all die between dawn and dusk, for some—to be prosaic—die between dusk and dawn (cf. a Babylonian text, "he who in the evening was alive is dead in the morning").[13]

Plainly also it is untrue that humans in general perish "without anyone setting it to heart" (if that is how *mibbᵉlî mēśîm* is to be translated); what serves Eliphaz's point about the fragility of human beings as "dwellers in houses of clay" (v. 19) is that they can be of such slight account that they may die without their passing being noticed. Likewise, it can hardly be imagined that Eliphaz maintains that humankind as a whole (himself included!) invariably dies "without wisdom"; rather he argues the insubstantiality of the human frame from the fact that it is possible for a person to live and die without ever gaining the wisdom that he, as one of the wise, regards as essential for a truly human life.

By understanding the verbs of these sentences modally, that is, in this case, as equivalent to "*may* be destroyed . . . *may* perish . . . *may* die," we not only restore the emphasis of Eliphaz to the *fragility* of human existence, rather than its *brevity*, and relieve him of the responsibility of wildly untrue generalizations, but also help to re-create coherence in the speech. For if these verses are taken as general statements about humankind, Eliphaz will have de-

12. See H. H. Rowley, *Job*, 56; G. Fohrer, *Das Buch Hiob* (KAT, 1963), 145; M. H. Pope, *Job* (AB, ^{3}1973), 39.

13. Cited by Dhorme, *Job*, 55.

stroyed, by the time he reaches the mid-point of his speech, the premise from which he began, and on the basis of which alone he can offer consolation to Job; namely that humankind is divided into two camps, the innocent and the wicked (vv. 7–8), that each camp receives its proper reward (v. 8), and that Job unquestionably belongs to the former camp (vv. 3–4, 6). It is always possible, of course, that the speech lacks coherence, but such is an unhappy conclusion to which we may finally be driven only when we have allowed for the possibility of modal interpretations.[14]

The foregoing are elements of rhetoric that can, if we make due allowance for them, influence our analysis of the arguments in the Book of Job.

Coherence and Distinctiveness

My concern here is a more ambitious one. It is to affirm: (A) the coherence of the speeches of Job's three friends; and (B) the distinctive viewpoints of the three friends. For convenience, I shall discriminate in (A) between coherence within a single speech (A_1: micro-coherence) and coherence throughout the whole body of the speeches of each of the friends in turn (A_2: macro-coherence). I shall interpose between my claims for micro- and macro-coherence the evidence for (B), the distinctive viewpoints of the individual speakers.

Micro-coherence (A_1)

It is customary to despair of the possibility of discovering coherence, even on the scale of the single speech, within the Book of Job. G. von Rad, for example, concluded that Eliphaz's first speech (chs. 4–5), "does not in any sense consist of a fairly unified sequence of thought, but is a series of entities of very different kinds, each of which has its own structure of thought and thesis within itself. Eliphaz offers Job at least five different and remarkably slightly connected propositions to ponder."[15]

As against such a position, we may allow that it is not necessary to affirm the logical validity of an argument in order to maintain its coherence. We may, for example, deny that in 4:18–21, part of which we have examined above, a logic operates which is valid by standards either of the author's day or of our own: for, at least in our judgement, it does not follow that men are more untrustworthy than angels just because they "dwell in houses of clay" whereas angels presumably do not. But the *coherence* of these verses is beyond question: they are linked by an *a maiore ad minus* argumentation that is superficially, at least, plausible.

14. For a more extended treatment of this passage, see D. J. A. Clines, "Verb Modality and the Interpretation of Job IV 20–21", *VT* 30 (1980), 354–57.

15. G. von Rad, *Old Testament Theology*, vol. 1 (ET, 1962), 410.

Granted such an understanding of "coherence," especially if the subordinate role of *topoi* and the dominating role of nodal sentences is taken into account, and if allowance is made for the range of verb modality (which may, for example, transform what is apparently an assertion into a statement of possibility), I would claim that coherence within each speech always emerges—except perhaps toward the end of the third cycle of speeches. The arguments of the nine speeches of the friends may thus be briefly stated:

1. In the first cycle, Eliphaz's speech (chs. 4–5) starts from the fundamental position that the innocent are never "cut off." Job is an innocent man and therefore can expect to continue living (4:6). That general point made, Eliphaz can proceed to nuance the concept of "innocence." In fact, he argues, perfect innocence, "purity" or "righteousness" (4:17), is not to be found among men, so even the most innocent, like Job, must expect to suffer deservedly on occasion. Job is suffering on this occasion, so the only practical advice Eliphaz can give to Job is to be patient (commit his case to God, 5:8), since his suffering is bound to be soon over.

2. The first speech of Bildad (ch. 8) is no less coherent. Like all the friends, he believes that suffering is punishment, and that the death of Job's children is proof of that (8:4, "Your children have sinned against him; so he has abandoned them to the power of their own transgression"; the "if" *[ᶜim]* of "if your children have sinned" is not hypothetical, as NEB has rightly recognised). God does not pervert justice (8:3); so if there is suffering, there has been sin. Job himself, however, has not been struck dead, so the possibility is still open that he is innocent of any sin deserving of death. Bildad therefore affirms that if Job is "pure and upright" he will be delivered from his affliction. The comparatively cheerful note on which Bildad concludes (8:21–22) leaves open the question of Job's innocence, and the *topos* of 8:8–19 on the theme "no effect without a cause" (the death of the wicked [vv. 13–19] being a prime example of this truth) serves only to reinforce Bildad's fundamental position: justice is not perverted.

3. In Zophar's speech in the first cycle (ch. 11), the argument is again plain. Starting from the same presupposition as the other friends, that suffering is deserved, he concentrates wholly upon the fact that Job *is* suffering. This can only mean that he is a sinner; and since Job has failed to acknowledge his sinfulness, claiming that he is "clean in God's eyes" (11:4), it follows that Job is a *secret* sinner. In fact, Zophar argues, if the truth were known it would no doubt be apparent that God exacts of Job *less* than his guilt deserves (v. 6c)! The logic of Zophar's argument is on this point rather shaky, but the coherence of his rhetoric is beyond question.[16] Zophar's reference to the wisdom of God (v. 6) leads him into a digressive *topos* on that theme (vv. 7–12), but the thread of his speech is picked up again at v. 13 where he, like

16. Contra N. C. Habel, *The Book of Job* (CBC, 1975), 62.

all the friends, offers direct practical advice to Job: Job must, in a word, repent (v. 14). The lot of the repentant and therefore righteous man is contrasted with that of the wicked in a concluding *topos* (vv. 15–20).

4. In the second cycle, Eliphaz's speech (ch. 15) takes cognizance of Job's responses and asserts that Job is not speaking like a wise man but allowing his tongue to run away with him (15:2–6; v. 5 should probably be translated "your mouth makes you guilty of great wrongdoing, and your tongue chooses guileful words"). Indeed, it is lack of adequate wisdom that is Job's chief fault (vv. 7–16): he has not the wisdom of Adam (v. 7) nor of the friends themselves (vv. 8–9). If we were wise, he would know that no man—nor any angel—is wholly innocent, and that a certain amount of suffering can only be expected (vv. 14–16). Nevertheless, Job is not *wicked*, and the *topos* on the wicked and their fate (vv. 17–35) is a description of precisely what Job is not. He is therefore not destined for ultimate disaster or continued suffering.

5. Bildad's second speech (ch. 18) is almost entirely devoted to a *topos* on the fate of the wicked, and as such is thoroughly coherent. What he means by it as far as Job is concerned cannot be discerned from the speech itself, but must be assessed in the context of all three of his speeches.

6. Zophar's second speech (ch. 20) is even more thoroughly preoccupied with an extended *topos* on the fate of the wicked, developing three themes: the brevity of the rejoicing of the wicked (vv. 4–11), the self-destructive nature of sin (vv. 12–22), and the sudden end of the wicked (vv. 23–29). Its content is not essentially different from the speeches of Eliphaz and Bildad, but, as with theirs, its function must be understood in the context of his other speeches.

7. In the third cycle, Eliphaz (ch. 22) eschews extensive *topos* material and delivers a three-pronged address to Job. In its first movement (vv. 2–11), he asks, "Is not your wickedness great?" (v. 5); it must be, for only guilt explains suffering, and, presumably, only great guilt can explain great suffering. In the second movement (vv. 12–20), since Job admits to great suffering but not to great guilt, it follows that the guilt must be hidden (we note that Eliphaz is being pushed toward Zophar's position). In the third movement (vv. 21–30), Eliphaz's continuing conviction of Job's essential innocence surfaces again, and the most convincing picture of the restoration Job can rightly hope for is painted (we note that Eliphaz retreats from the logic of Job's suffering to the logic of Job's character).

8. Bildad's third speech (ch. 25), as it stands, simply rehearses the by now conventional idea that nothing in the created order, and especially not man, can show any kind of "cleanness" (vv. 4f.). If some disturbance to the text has occurred in the course of transmission, and if 26:5–14 also is rightly to be attached to this third speech of Bildad,[17] the speech continues with a *topos*

17. So Rowley, *Job*, 213f., citing many others of the same opinion.

upon the creatorial wisdom and power of God (the two attributes are frequently virtually equated in Job). God's unsearchable wisdom in company with his irresistible power (cf. 26:14) is the guarantee that "uncleanness" in the world of nature and man will be detected and dealt with by God.

9. Zophar's third speech does not, of course, appear in the present form of the text (and we could therefore immediately forego an attempt to display its coherence). Suppose, however, that it has been erroneously incorporated (not by the final editor, but in the course of transmission) into Job's tenth speech (27:1–28:28) and that it consisted of 27:13–28:28 (so Hoffmann).[18] It should occasion no surprise that a speech from Zophar should dwell upon "the portion of a wicked man with God" (27:13–27), to be followed immediately by a disquisition on the secret wisdom of God (28:1–28), since these two themes have been combined in Zophar's first speech (ch. 11). The argument, not so clearly stated as in ch. 11, will be the same: the fate of the wicked is lodged with God (*ʿim ʾēl,* "with God," 27:13), because God alone is the master of the knowledge required to dispense justice among human beings (28:23–28). Even the profound and intricate knowledge acquired by humankind (28:1–11) gives them no sure hold upon real "wisdom," hid as it is "from the eyes of all living" (28:21). The best wisdom humanity can have is to acknowledge the omniscient Yahweh and keep his commandments (28:28). A less bold reconstruction of Zophar's third speech, that allocates 27:7–23 together with 24:18–24 to it,[19] will have even less difficulty in discerning coherence in the speech; for the preoccupation of the speech will be with the "portion" of the wicked, a *topos* simply prefaced by a few sentences of exordium (27:7–12).

Only a closer analysis can demonstrate the validity of the general argument presented here; but enough has perhaps been said to suggest that in each of the speeches of the three friends a high degree of coherence is to be found.

Distinctive Viewpoints (B)

Students of the Book of Job have frequently attempted to discriminate between the friends on psychological grounds. Thus, Arthur Quiller-Couch, a literary critic of a former era, observed: "I find Eliphaz more of personage than the other two; grander in the volume of the mind, securer in wisdom; as I find Zophar rather noticeably a mean-minded greybeard, and Bildad a man of the stand-no-nonsense kind."[20] A British acquaintance confides that he has always seen Eliphaz as a smooth southerner from the Home Counties, Bildad as a provincial Midlander, and Zophar as a blunt Yorkshireman. Robert Gordis finds Eliphaz "the most dignified and urbane of the Friends . . . the

18. G. Hoffmann, *Hiob* (1891), ad loc.
19. See Rowley, *Job,* 222.
20. A. Quiller-Couch, *The Art of Reading* (Cambridge, 1920), 172–95.

profoundest spirit among them"; Bildad is purely "a traditionalist who contributes little more to the discussion than a statement of accepted virus"; while Zophar, "probably the youngest, possesses the brashness and dogmatism associated with youth."[21] There may be a modicum of truth in some of these distinctions, but what one really wants to see—and what one looks for in vain among the commentaries—is a set of notations of the distinctiveness, logical or theological, in their various argumentations. Only genuinely distinctive argumentation would fully justify the introduction of *three* interlocutors into the body of the book. If they all have the same point to make, the book is indeed long-winded and flabby; but if, as I argue, the friends each take a distinctive position vis-á-vis Job in spite of sharing the most fundamental presuppositions, their presence is not only not gratuitous but positively essential for the exploration of the problem raised by the book.

What I see as their distinctive viewpoints has already become partly visible in outlining the coherence of each of their speeches. But to put it directly, I can do no better than quote some sentences that are somewhat buried away in a corner of Marvin Pope's commentary, in which alone I have found, in embryonic form at least, a presentation of the friends' distinctive viewpoints which jibes with my own.

> Eliphaz appears to concede that Job's piety and conduct have been exemplary. Job, thus, should have confidence and hope that God will deal with him accordingly . . . To concede that Job was innocent would wreck [Bildad's and Zophar's] argument completely. What Bildad says is conditional: if Job were innocent, God would restore him. Zophar is sure that God must have something against Job and could make it known if he cared to speak about it.[22]

I should wish to nuance Pope's presentations a little: Eliphaz does not only *appear to concede* Job's piety to be exemplary; he actually assumes it and argues from it. And Zophar's point is not precisely that God *could* make known, if he cared to, what it is that he has against Job, but that no matter whether or not God divulges what he knows to be Job's sin, he is certainly punishing Job for it (God knows which men are worthless and marks them down for punishment, 11:11).

The distinctiveness of the friends' arguments can be expressed in two further ways: first, Eliphaz argues from the piety of Job in order to offer consolation; Bildad argues from the contrast between the fates of Job and Job's children in order to offer warning; Zophar argues from the suffering of Job in order to denounce Job. Secondly, as becomes clear from the friends' directives to Job, Eliphaz's intention is to encourage Job to patience and hope (5:8; 4:6), Bildad's intention is to urge Job to search his heart before God in

21. R. Gordis, *The Book of God and Man: A Study of Job* (Chicago, 1965), 77.
22. Pope, *Job,* 36.

order to ensure that he is not guilty of crimes such as those for which his children have died (8:5–6); Zophar's intention is to summon Job to repentance for sins that he clearly has already committed (11:6c).

It may be added, parenthetically, that the position of Elihu represents yet another variation on the same fundamental supposition of the causal nexus between sin and suffering: viz., suffering may be discipline, though not in the way the other friends have viewed it; for it may be not the penalty for sin already committed, but a warning, given in advance, to keep a man back from sin (33:19–28).[23] In advancing this view Elihu correctly proclaims himself opposed both to the three friends and to Job (32:6–12; 33:5, 12).

Macro-coherence (A_2)

The coherence of the stance taken by each of the friends throughout his set of three speeches (macro-coherence) has already been to some extent established by the analysis given above of the argument of each individual speech. What we have to remark upon here is that the macro-coherence of each of the three arguments depends upon our recognizing the stance adopted in the first cycle as determinative for the whole of the particular friend's utterances.

From that position, we may go on to allow the content of the second and third cycles of speeches, largely consisting of *topos* material, to be interpreted according to the previously announced intention of the speaker. As for the second cycle, I have noted above how Eliphaz's affirmation of Job's piety in the first cycle (chs. 4–5) requires us to read his description of the fate of the wicked in the second cycle (ch. 15) as a depiction of what Job's fate is certainly *not*. Likewise, Bildad's exhortation to Job in his first cycle speech (ch. 8) to search his heart and take warning from the fate of his children becomes the hermeneutical clue for the reading of his second cycle speech (ch. 18): the fate of the wicked is a *possibility* that confronts Job, but may yet be avoided by him. In similar fashion, the first cycle speech of Zophar (ch. 11), asserting that Job's present suffering proves him to be a sinner (albeit a secret sinner), demands that his second cycle speech (ch. 20) be understood as descriptive of the future he sees in store for Job—assuming, of course, that Zophar's plea for Job's repentance (11:13f.) is ignored.

As for the third cycle of speeches, the same principle applies, that the *topos* material is to be interpreted in the light of the speaker's stance distinctively spelled out in the first cycle. The most striking, and perhaps the only significant, apparent exception to this generalization is the speech of Eliphaz in the third cycle (ch. 22), and for this reason it deserves our special attention. In two respects Eliphaz's argument in this speech is in full accord with his posi-

23. If this reading of Elihu's argument is correct, 33:27, a confession of sin accompanying the sufferer's thanksgiving for deliverance, must refer to sin contemplated (cf. v. 17) but not executed.

tion in his first speech (chs. 4–5): he believes that Job will be delivered "through the cleanness of [his] hands" (22:30), and his advice is to "come to terms with God" (v. 21, NEB) and "be at peace." In another respect, however, he seems to be wholly at variance with his former position: he seems to accuse Job of untold wickedness ("no end to your iniquities," v. 5), mainly in the nature of social injustice: "you have exacted pledges of your brothers for nothing . . . withheld bread from the hungry . . . sent widows away empty (vv. 6–9). These are the most specific, most harsh, and most unjust words spoken against Job in the whole book, and it is strange to find them on the lips of Eliphaz, out of all the friends.

Of course it is possible to maintain that there has been a change in Eliphaz's attitude, and to argue that Eliphaz has lost patience with Job, and in his exasperation has charged Job with crimes that he could not possibly have believed Job had committed when he addressed him in chs. 4–5. Most commentators, indeed, take Eliphaz's accusations at their face value, but there is one indication that Eliphaz's strictures may be read somewhat differently. That is the fact that in all the cases Eliphaz mentions it is the *neglect* of some social duty that Job is charged with. Eliphaz believes, as do all the friends, that Job is suffering for some cause—brief though the suffering may be (4:5); and since the cause cannot be found in any wrong that Job had done, for he seems to have done none, his sin must lie in what he has *failed* to do. To say that Job has stripped the poor of their clothing need not mean that he has actively done any such thing, but rather that he must have failed to offer clothing to some needy person; and so on. (In the same way, the psalmist who reproaches God for having "forsaken" him [Ps. 22:2] does not mean that God has actively departed from him, but that he has failed to come to his help; hence the psalmist's plea is not "return to me," but "hasten to my help," v. 20). Doubtless, since Job is not absolutely perfect (nor omnicompetent), there will be certain members of Job's community untouched by his social concern; in hyperbolic fashion Eliphaz pictures their plight as Job's willful fault. Only in this way can he explain why "snares are round about" Job and why his "light is darkened" (vv. 10–11).

From this perspective the meaning of 22:2–4 becomes plain. When Eliphaz asks, "Is it any pleasure to the Almighty if you make your ways blameless?" (v. 3), he does not disparage righteousness or the fear of God. He is rather saying that it is not for Job's righteousness—which Eliphaz fully recognizes—that God "enters into judgment" with him (v. 4), but for leaving undone those things that ought to have been done (vv. 6–9). They must be sins of omission rather than sins of commission (which admittedly his language describes, prima facie) that are Job's "great wickedness" (v. 5); for Eliphaz has no other way of explaining Job's suffering. It is true that he has moved somewhat beyond the position he had adopted in chs. 4–5, where he first affirmed Job's piety, and then allowed that the righteous are not perfectly so. Now he will specify in what ways he conceives Job to have been open to reproach. But this is only a development of his original position, and no doubt need be cast on the overall coherence of Eliphaz's attitude and argument.

Less taxing is the question of the relation of the third cycle speeches of Bildad (? and Zophar) to their general position outlined in their opening speeches. If we adhere to the Masoretic assignment of ch. 25 alone to Bildad, his insistence upon the "uncleanness" of all created beings harmonises with his original affirmation that since God does not pervert justice (8:3) sin must inevitably be punished. If we extend Bildad's speech by the addition of 26:5–14, we may see in these verses further illustration of the incontrovertible justice of the Almighty. And if Zophar's third speech is to be salvaged for the material of chs. 27 and 28, we find only further illustration of the twin themes of the all-seeing wisdom of God (cf. 11:7–11) and the doom of the wicked foreseen and prepared by that selfsame wisdom (cf. 11:20) which we have observed in Zophar's initial speech.

The intentions of this paper have been to show that the arguments of Job's three friends, though sharing the presupposition of a causal nexus between sin and suffering, are distinct from one another; that every speech exhibits coherence, and that each set of speeches delivered by each friend maintains the same position throughout the course of the dialogue; and that the detection and display both of coherence and distinctiveness are materially assisted by the recognition of certain rhetorical features characteristic of such speeches.

A final implication of the present study is that the author of Job does not portray any development in the position, theology, or argument of Job's friends: their minds are set in familiar patterns. By contrast—though this must be the subject of another paper—Job's mind is confused, flexible, experimental, and his argument constantly in course of development. Even in their style of argumentation, the friends provide a static stylized background against which the tortured but adventurous hero of the book excites our imagination and sympathy.

20

The Certainty of Seeing God: A Brief Exposition of Job 19:23–29

Roy B. Zuck

Just after Job was at his lowest ebb, he rose to his highest peak. Forlorn, wracked by pain, and maligned by both God and people, he then mounted in spirited confidence to a future vindication of his cause. This was a "magnificent burst of faith" (W. B. MacLeod, *The Afflictions of the Righteous*. London: Hodder & Stoughton, n.d., p. 173).

19:23–24. Job expressed his desire for a permanent written record of his **words** of innocence and protest, either **on a scroll** or **engraved in rock** in

From Roy B. Zuck, "Job," in *The Bible Knowledge Commentary (Old Testament)*, ed. Roy B. Zuck and John F. Walvoord (Wheaton, Ill.: Victor, 1985), 741–42. Used by permission of Victor Books.

letters filled with **lead.** Then present and future generations could know of his guilelessness.

19:25. In his jubilation of faith Job affirmed his certainty that God his **Redeemer lives.** Though Job believed God was against him, he knew that only God could vindicate his innocence. Job would die, but God lives on as his Defender, Protector, or Vindicator (*gō'ēl,* "a person who defended or avenged the cause of another, or who provided protection or legal aid for a close relative who could not do so for himself"; cf. Lev. 25:23–25, 47–55; Num. 35:19–27; Prov. 23:10–11; Jer. 50:34). Job knew **that in the end** God would **stand upon the earth** and, like a witness for the defendant at a court trial, would testify that Job was innocent. In that way all would not only read of his uprightness (Job 19:23–24) but also all would hear of it—from God Himself!

19:26. After my skin has been destroyed may be rendered, "After my skin has been flayed" (or "stripped off"), that is, after he had died from the constant peeling away of his skin (another symptom of pemphigus foliaceus; cf. comments on 2:7 and see 30:30) or after worms (cf. 17:14; 24:20) in his grave had eaten away his skin (though "worms," supplied in the KJV, is not in the Heb[rew] text).

After he was dead, Job then would **see God**. He would continue in a conscious existence; he would not be annihilated or sink into soul sleep. But how could he say he would see the Lord **in his flesh** after **he had** just said he would die? Either he meant he would receive a resurrection body (in which case the Heb[rew] preposition *min,* here trans[lated] "in," would be trans[lated] "from the vantage point of"; in 36:25 *min* is used in that sense) or he meant he would see God "apart from" any physical flesh at all (*min* normally means "without"; cf. 11:15b), that is, in his conscious existence after death but before the resurrection. Favoring the first view is the point that whereas *min* normally means "without," it takes on the meaning of "from the vantage point of" when it occurs with the verb "to see" (*ḥāzāh).* Favoring the second view is the fact that since 19:26a speaks of his condition in death, one would expect that verse 26b in Hebrew parallelism would also refer to death rather than to an afterdeath resurrected condition.

19:27. So certain was Job of his seeing God that he repeated this point. The Hebrew word for **see** (*ḥāzāh*) is the same in verses 26 and 27a. Also Job twice emphasized the word **I** (vv. 25, 27)—literally, "I, even I, know," and "I, even I, will see" **Him.** This gazing on God for all eternity will be **with** his **own eyes** (either the eyes of his resurrected body, or figuratively the eyes of his soul). Job would no longer be like a stranger to God, for God would be on his side.

This thought so overwhelmed Job that he exclaimed, **My heart yearns** (lit., "my kidneys," considered the seat of the emotions, "waste away") **within me!** He was emotionally drained by the very thought of meeting God and having Him once and for all vindicate rather than vitiate his cause.

19:28–29. If Job's friends continued to **hound** (the same word is trans[lated] "pursue" in v. 22) **him**—to get him to accept their view that sin had precipitated his suffering, and that the trouble lay within **him**—God would eventually strike them down by **the sword** (perhaps a retort to Eliphaz's word about the sword in 15:22). *Then* they would see that God punished the sin of the wicked. Rather than God punishing *Job* for being wicked, *they* would be the recipients of God's **wrath** for they had repeatedly harassed an innocent victim. Confident that they were wrong about his spiritual state and that he was right, Job was able to look beyond death to his being acquitted by God and fellowshiping with Him.

21

Job 19:25–29

Albert Barnes

25 For I know *that* my Redeemer liveth, and *that* he shall stand at the latter day upon the earth:

25. *For I know that my Redeemer liveth.* There are few passages in the Bible which has excited more attention than this, or in respect to which the opinions of expositors have been more divided. The importance of the passage (ver. 25–27) has contributed much to the anxiety to understand its meaning—since, if it refers to the Messiah, it is one of the most valuable of all the testimonials now remaining of the early faith on that subject. The importance of the passage will justify a somewhat more extended examination of its meaning than it is customary to give in a commentary of a single passage of Scripture; and I shall (1.) give the views entertained of it by the translators of the ancient and some of the modern versions; (2) investigate the meaning of the *words* and *phrases* which occur in it; and (3) state the argu-

From Albert Barnes, "Job" (2 vols.), in *Notes on the Old Testament: Explanatory and Practical,* ed. Robert Frew (1846; reprint, Grand Rapids: Baker, 1963), 1:324–35.

ments, *pro* and *con,* for its supposed reference to the Messiah. The Vulgate renders it, "For I know that my Redeemer—*Redemptor meus*—lives, and that in the last day I shall rise from the earth; and again, I shall be enveloped—*circumdabor*—with my skin, and in my flesh shall I see my God. Whom I myself shall see, and my eyes shall behold, and not another—this, my hope, is laid up in my bosom." The LXX translate it, "For I know that he is Eternal who is about to deliver me—ὁ ἐκλύειν με μέλλων—to raise again upon earth this skin of mine, which draws up these things—τὸ ἀναντλοῦν ταῦτα—[the meaning of which, I believe, no one has ever been able to divine]. For from the Lord these things have happened to me of which I alone am conscious, which my eye has seen, and not another, and which have all been done to me in my bosom." *Thompson's trans. in part.* The Syriac is in the main a simple and correct rendering of the Hebrew. "I know that my Redeemer liveth, and in the consummation he will be revealed upon the earth, and after my skin I shall bless myself in these things, and after my flesh. If my eyes shall see God, I shall see light." The Chaldee accords with our version, except in one phrase. "And afterwards my skin shall be inflated, אתפח מַשׁכ׳—then in my flesh shall I see God." It will be seen that some perplexity was felt by the authors of the ancient versions in regard to the passage. Much more has been felt by expositors. Some notices of the views of the moderns, in regard to particular words and phrases, will be given in the exposition.

I know. I am certain. On that point Job desires to express the utmost confidence. His friends might accuse him of hypocrisy—they might charge him with want of piety, and he might not be able to refute all that they said; but in the position referred to here he would remain fixed, and with this firm confidence he would support his soul. It was this which he wished to have recorded in the eternal rocks, that the record might go down to future times. If after ages should be made acquainted with his name and his sufferings—if they should hear of the charges brought against him and of the accusations of impiety which had been so harshly and unfeelingly urged, he wished that *this* testimony might be recorded, to show that he *had* unwavering confidence in God. He wished this eternal record to be made, to show that he was not a rejecter of truth; that he was not an enemy of God; that he had a firm confidence that God would yet come forth to vindicate him, and would stand up as his friend. It was a testimony worthy of being held in everlasting remembrance, and one which has had, and will have a permanency much greater than he anticipated.

That *my Redeemer.* This important word has been variously translated. Rosenmüller and Schultens render it, *vindicem:* Dr. Good, *Redeemer;* Noyes and Wemyss, *vindicator;* Herder, *avenger,* Luther, Erlöser—*Redeemer;* Chaldee and Syriac, *Redeemer.* The Hebrew word, גֹּאֵל—*goël,* is from גָּאַל—*gáál,* to redeem, to ransom. It is applied to the redemption of a farm sold, by paying back the price, Lev. 25:25; Ruth 4:4, 6; to any thing consecrated to God that is redeemed by paying its value, Lev. 25:13, and to a slave that is ransomed, Lev. 25:48, 49. The word גּאֵל—*goël,* is applied to one who redeems a field, Lev. 25:26; and is often applied to God, who had redeemed his people from bondage, Ex. 6:6; Isa. 43:1. . . . Among the Hebrews, the גּאֵל—*goël* occupied an important place, as a *blood-avenger,* or a vindicator of violated rights. See Num. 35:12, 19, 21, 24, 25, 27; Deut. 19:6–12; Ruth 4:1, 6, 8; Josh. 20:3. The word גּאֵל—*goël,* is rendered *kinsman,* Ruth 4:1, 3, 6, 8; *near kinsman,* Ruth 3:9, 13; *avenger,* Num. 35:12; Josh. 20:3; *Redeemer,* Job 19:25; Ps. 19:14; Isa. 47:4; 63:16; 44:24; 48:17; 54:14; 49:26; 60:16; *kin,* Lev. 25:25, *et al.* Moses *found* the office of the *goël* or avenger, already instituted . . . and he adopted it into his code of laws. It would seem, therefore, not improbable that it prevailed in the adjacent countries in the time of Job, or that there may have been a reference to this office in the place before us. The *goël* is first introduced in the laws of Moses, as having a right to redeem a mortgaged field, Lev. 25:25, 26; and then as having a right, as kinsman, to the restoration of anything which had been iniquitously acquired, Num. 5:8. Then he is often referred to in the writings of Moses as the blood-avenger, or the kinsman of one who was slain, who would have a right to pursue the murderer, and to take vengeance on him, and whose *duty* it would be to do it. This right of a near relative to pursue a murderer, and to take vengeance, seems to have been one that was early conceded every where. It was so understood among the American Indians, and probably prevails in all countries before there are settled laws for the trial and punishment of the guilty. It was a right, however, which was liable to great abuse. Passion would take the place of reason, the innocent would be suspected, and the man who had slain another in self-defence was as likely to be pursued and slain as he who had been guilty of wilful murder. To guard against this, in the unsettled state of jurisprudence, Moses appointed *cities of refuge,* where the man-slayer might flee until he could have a fair opportunity of trial. It was impossible to put an end at once to the office of the *goël.* The kinsman, the near relative, would feel himself called on to pursue the murderer; but the man-slayer might flee into a sacred city, and remain until he had a fair trial; see Num. 25; Deut. 19:6, 7. It was a humane arrangement to appoint cities of refuge, where the man who had slain another might be secure until he had an opportunity of trial—an arrangement which eminently showed the wisdom of Moses. On the rights and duties of the *goël,* the reader may consult Michaelis's Com[mentary] on the laws of Moses, art. 136, 137. His essential office was that of a *vindicator*—one who took up the cause of a friend, whether that friend was murdered, or was oppressed, or was wronged in any way. Usually, perhaps always, this pertained to the nearest male kin, and was instituted for the aid of the defenceless and the wronged. In times long subsequent, a somewhat similar feeling gave rise to the institution of chivalry, and the voluntary defence of the innocent and oppressed. It cannot now be determined whether Job in this passage has reference to the office of the *goël* as it was afterwards understood, or whether it existed in his time. It seems probable that the office would exist at the earliest periods of the world, and that in the rudest stages of society the nearest of kin would feel himself called on to vindicate the wrong done to one of the feebler members of his family. The word properly denotes, therefore, either *vindicator*, or *redeemer;* and so far as the term is concerned, it may refer either to God, as an avenger of the innocent, or to the future Redeemer—the Messiah. The meaning of this *word* would be met, should it be understood as referring to God, coming forth in a public manner to vindicate the cause of Job against all the charges and accusations of his professed friends; or to God, who would appear as his vindicator at the resurrection; or to the future Messiah— the Redeemer of the body and the soul. No *argument* in favour of either of these interpretations can be derived from the use of the *word.*

Liveth. Is alive—חי Sept[uagint] *immortal*—ἀένναός. He *seems* now to have forsaken me as if he were dead, but my faith is unwavering in him as a *living* vindicator. A similar expression occurs in ch. 16:19. "My witness is in heaven, and my record is on high." It is a declaration of entire confidence in God, and will beautifully convey the emotions of the sincere believer in all ages. He may be afflicted with disease, or the loss of property, or be forsaken by his friends, or persecuted by his foes, but if he can look up to heaven and say, "I know that my Redeemer *lives,*" he will have peace.

And that *he shall stand.* He will stand up, as one does who undertakes the cause of another. Jerome has rendered this as though it referred to Job, "And in the last day *I shall rise from the earth*"—*de terra surrecturus sum*—as if it referred to the resurrection of the body. But this is not in accordance with the Hebrew, יָקוּם=—"*he* shall stand." There is clearly no necessary reference in *this* word to the resurrection. The simple meaning is, "he shall appear, or manifest himself, as the vindicator of my cause."

At the latter day. The word "day" here is supplied by the translators. The Hebrew is, וְאַחֲרוֹן—and *after, afterwards, hereafter, at length.* The word *literally* means, hinder, hinder part—opposite to foremost, former. It is applied to the Mediterranean sea, as being behind when the eye of the geographer was supposed to be turned to the East; . . . then it means after, later, applied to a generation or age. Ps. 48:14, to a day—to future times—’ום אחרום, Prov. 31:25; Isa. 30:8. All that this word necessarily expresses here is, that *at some future period* this would occur. It does not determine *when* it would be. The *language* would apply to any future time, and might refer to the coming of the Redeemer, to the resurrection, or to some subsequent period in the life of Job. The meaning is, that however long he was to suffer, however protracted his calamities were, and were likely to be, he had the utmost confidence that God would *at length,* or *at some future time,* come forth to vindicate him. The phrase, "the latter day," has now acquired a kind of technical meaning, by which we naturally refer it to the day of judgment. But there is no evidence that it has any such reference here. . . .

Upon the earth. Heb. על עפר—*upon the dust.* Why the word *dust* is used, instead of ארץ *earth,* is unknown. It may be because the word *dust* is emphatic, as being contrasted with heaven, the residence of the Deity. *Noyes.* What *kind* of an appearance God would assume when he should thus come forth, or how he would manifest himself as the vindicator and Redeemer of Job, he does not intimate, and conjecture would be useless. The *words* do not necessarily imply any *visible* manifestation—though such a manifestation would not be forbidden by the fair construction of the passage. I say, they do not necessarily imply it; see Psalms 44:5, "For the sighing of the needy, now will I arise, (Heb. *stand up*—=אקום), saith the Lord." Ps. 44:26, "Arise (Heb. קומה—*stand up*) for our help." Whether this refers to any *visible* manifestation in behalf of Job is to be determined in other words than by the mere meaning of this word.

> 26 And *though* after my skin *worms* destroy this *body,* yet in my flesh shall I see God:

26. *And* though. Marg. Or, *after I shall awake, though this* body *be destroyed, yet out of my flesh shall I see God.* This verse has given not less perplexity than the preceding. Noyes renders it,

> And though with this skin this body be wasted away,
> Yet in my flesh shall I see God.

Dr. Good renders it,

> And, after the DISEASE hath destroyed my skin,
> That in my flesh I shall see God.

Rosenmüller explains it. "And when after my skin (*seil,* is consumed and destroyed) they consume (*seil,* those corroding, or consuming, *i.e.,* it is corroded, or broken into fragments) *this,* that is, this structure of my bones—my body (which he does not mention, because it was so wasted away that it did not deserve to be called a body)—yet without my flesh—with my whole body consumed, shall I see God." He translates it,

> Et quum post eutem meam hoc fuerit consumptum,
> Tamen absque carne mea videbo Deum.

The Hebrew is literally, "and after my skin." Gesenius translates it, "After they shall have destroyed my skin, this shall happen—that I will see God." Herder renders it,

> Though they tear and devour this my skin,
> Yet in my living body shall I see God.

The fair and obvious meaning, I think, is that which is conveyed by our translation. Disease had attacked his skin. It was covered with ulcers, and was fast consuming; comp[are] ch. 2:8, 7:5. This process of corruption and decay he had reason to expect would go on until all would be consumed. But if it did, he would hold fast his confidence in God. He would believe that he would come forth as his vindicator, and he would still put his trust in him.

Worms. This word is supplied by our translators. There is not a semblance of it in the original. That is, simply, "they destroy;" where the verb is used impersonally, meaning that it would be destroyed. The *agent* by which this would be done is not specified. The word rendered "destroy" (נקפו from נקף), means to cut to strike, to cut, down . . . , and here means *to destroy;* that is, that the work of destruction might go on until the frame should be wholly wasted away. It is not quite certain that the word here would convey the idea that he expected *to die.* It *may* mean that he would become entirely emaciated, and all his flesh be gone. There is nothing, however, in the word to show that he did not expect to die—and perhaps that would be the most obvious and proper interpretation.

This body. The word *body* is also supplied by the translators. The Hebrew is simply זאת—*this.* Perhaps he *pointed* to his body—for there can be no doubt that his body or flesh is intended. Rosenmüller supposes that he did not mention it, because it was so emaciated that it did not deserve to be called a body.

Yet in my flesh. Heb. "From my flesh"—מבשרי. Herder renders this, "In my living body." Rosenmüller, *absque carne mea*—"without my flesh;" and explains it as meaning, "my whole body being consumed, I shall see God." The literal meaning is, "from, or out of, my flesh shall I see God." It does not mean *in* his flesh, which would have been expressed by the preposition ב—but there is the notion that *from* or *out* of his flesh he would see him; that is, clearly, as Rosenmüller has expressed it, tho' my body be consumed, and I *have no flesh,* I shall see him. Disease might carry its fearful ravages through all his frame, until it utterly wasted away, yet he had confidence that he would see his vindicator and Redeemer on the earth. It cannot be *proved* that this refers to the resurrection of that body, and indeed the natural interpretation is against it. It is, rather, that though *without* a body, or though his body should all waste away, he would see God as his vindicator. He would not always be left overwhelmed in this manner with calamities and reproaches. He would be permitted to see God coming forth as his Goël or Avenger, and manifesting himself as his friend. Calmly, therefore, he would bear these reproaches and trials, and see his frame waste away, for it would not always be so—God would yet undertake and vindicate his cause.

Shall I see God. He would be permitted to behold him as *his* friend and avenger. What was the nature of the vision which he anticipated, it is not possible to determine with certainty. If he expected that God would appear in some remarkable manner to judge the world and to vindicate the cause of the oppressed; or that he would come forth in a special manner to vindicate *his* cause; or if he looked to a general resurrection, and to the trial on that day, the *language* would apply to either of these events.

> 27 Whom I shall see for myself, and mine eyes shall behold, and not another; though my reins be consumed within me.

27. *Whom I shall see for myself.* It will not come to be by mere report. I shall not merely hear of the decision of God in my favour, but I shall myself behold him. He will at length come forth, and I shall be permitted to see him, and shall have the delightful assurance that he settles this controversy in my favour, and declares that I am his friend. Job *was* thus permitted to see God (ch. 42:5), and hear his voice in his favour. He spake to him from the whirlwind (ch. 38:1), and pronounced the sentence in his favour which he had desired.

And not another. Marg. *a stranger.* So in the Hebrew. The meaning is, that *his own* eyes would be permitted to see him. He would have the satisfaction of seeing God himself, and of hearing the sentence in his favour. That expectation he deemed worthy of a permanent record, and wished it transmitted to future times, that in his darkest days and severest trials—when God overwhelmed him, and man forsook him, he still firmly maintained his confidence in God, and his belief that he would come forth to vindicate his cause.

Though *my reins.* The margin renders this, "*my reins within me are consumed with earnest desire* for that day." Noyes translates it, "For this my soul panteth within me." Herder,

> I shall see him as my deliverer,
> Mine eyes shall behold him, as mine,
> For whom my heart so long fainted.

So Wemyss, "My reins faint with desire of his arrival." Jerome renders it *(Vulgate), reposita est luce spes mea in sinu meo*—"this, my hope, is laid up in my bosom." The LXX, "All which things have been done—συντετέλεσται—in my bosom," but what they understood by this it is difficult to say. The word rendered *reins* כליה—or in the plural כליות—in which form only it is found, means properly the reins, or the kidneys (Job 16:13), and then comes to denote the inward parts, and then the seat of the desires and affections, *because* in strong emotions the inward parts are affected. *We* speak of the *heart* as the seat of the affections, but with no more propriety than the Hebrews did of the upper viscera in general, or of the reins. In the Scriptures the heart and the reins are united as the seat of the affections. Thus, Jer. 11:20, God "trieth the reins and the heart;" Jer. 17:10; 20:12; Ps. 7:10. I see no reason why the word here may not be used to denote the *viscera* in general, and that the idea may be, that he felt that his disease was invading the seat of life, and his body, in all its parts, was wasting away. Our word *vitals*, perhaps, expresses the idea.

Be consumed. Gesenius renders this, "Pine away." So Noyes, Wemyss, and some others. But the proper meaning of the word is, to consume, to be wasted, to be destroyed. The word כלה *strictly* means to finish, complete, render entire; and thence has the notion of *completion* or *finishing*—whether by making a thing perfect, or by destroying it. It is used with reference to the *eyes* that fail or waste away with weeping, Lam. 2:11, or to the spirit or heart as fainting with grief and sorrow. Ps. 84:3; 143:7; 69:4. It is used often in the sense of *destroying*. Jer. 16:4; Ezra 5:13; Ps. 39:11; Isa. 27:10; 49:4; Gen. 41:30; Jer. 14:12; *et sæpe al.* This, I think, is the meaning here. Job affirms that his whole frame, external and internal, was wasting away, yet he had confidence that he would see God.

Within me. Marg. *in my bosom*. So the Hebrew. The word *bosom* is here used as we use the word *chest*—and is not improperly rendered "within me." In view of this exposition of the words, I would translate the whole passage as follows:

> For I know that my Avenger liveth,
> And that hereafter he shall stand upon the earth;
> And though after my skin this [flesh] shall be destroyed,
> Yet even without my flesh shall I see God:
> Whom I shall see for myself,
> And mine eyes shall behold, am I not another,
> Though my vitals are wasting away within me.

It has already been observed, that very various views have been entertained of this important passage of Scripture. The great question has been, whether it refers to the Messiah, and to the resurrection of the dead, or to an expectation which Job had that God would come forth as his vindicator in some such way as he is declared afterwards to have done. It may be proper, therefore, to give a summary of the arguments by which these opinions would be defended. I have not found many *arguments* stated for the former opinion, though the belief is held by many, but they would be probably such as the following:—

1. Arguments which would be adduced to show that the passage refers to the Messiah and to the future resurrection of the dead. (a.) The *language* which is used is such as would appropriately describe such events. This is undoubted, though more so in our translation than in the original; but the original would appropriately express such an expectation. (b.) The impression which it would make on the mass of readers, and particularly those of plain, sober sense, who had no theory to defend. It is probably a fact, that the great body of the readers of the Bible suppose that it has such a reference. It is usually a very strong presumptive proof of the correctness of an interpretation of Scripture when this can be alleged in its favour, though it is not an infallible

guide. (c.) The probability that some knowledge of the Messiah would prevail in Arabia in the time of Job. This must be admitted, though it cannot be certainly demonstrated; comp. Num. 17:24. The amount of this is, that it could not be regarded as so improbable that any such knowledge would prevail as to demonstrate certainly that this could not be referred to the Messiah. (d.) The probability that there would be found in this book some allusion to the Redeemer—the great hope of the ancient saints, and the burden of the Old Testament. But this is not conclusive or very weighty, for there are several of the books of the Old Testament which contain no distinct allusion to him. (e.) The pertinency of such a view to the case, and its adaptedness to give to Job the kind of consolation which he needed. There can be no doubt of the truth of this; but the question is, not what *would* have imparted consolation, but what knowledge he actually had. There are many of the doctrines of the Christian religion which would have been eminently fitted to give comfort in such circumstances to a man in affliction, which it would be exceedingly unreasonable to expect to find in the Book of Job, and which it is certain were wholly unknown to him and his friends. (f.) The importance which he himself attached to his declaration, and the solemnity of the manner in which he introduced it. His profession of faith on the subject he wished to have engraved in the eternal rocks. He wished it transmitted to future times. He wished a permanent record to be made, that succeeding ages might read it, and see the ground of his confidence and his hope. This, to my mind, is the strongest argument which has occurred in favour of the opinion that the passage refers to the Redeemer and to the resurrection. These are all the considerations which have occurred to me, or which I have found stated, which would go to sustain the position that the passage referred to the resurrection. Some of them have weight; but the prevailing opinion, that the passage has such a reference, will be found to be sustained, probably, more *by the feelings of piety* than by solid argument and sound exegesis. It is favoured, doubtless, by our common version, and there can be no doubt that the translators supposed that it had such a reference.

2. On the other hand, weighty considerations are urged to show that the passage does not refer to the Messiah, and to the resurrection of the dead. They are such as the following:

(a.) The language, fairly interpreted and translated, does not necessarily imply this. It is admitted that our translators had this belief, and without doing intentional or actual violence to the passage, or designing to make a forced translation, they have allowed their feelings to give a complexion to their language which the original does not necessarily convey. Hence, the word "Redeemer," which is now used technically to denote the Messiah, is employed, though the original *may*, and commonly *does*, have a much more general signification; and hence, the phrase "at the latter day," also a technical phrase, occurs, though the original means no more than *afterwards* or *after this*; and hence, they have employed the phrase "in my flesh," though the original means no more than "though my flesh be all wasted away." The following I believe to express fairly the meaning of the Hebrew: "I know that my deliverer, or avenger, lives, and that he will yet appear in some public manner on the earth; and though after the destruction of my skin, the process of corruption shall go on till *all* my flesh shall be destroyed, yet when my flesh is entirely wasted away, I shall see God; I shall have the happiness of seeing him for myself, and beholding him with my own eyes, even though my very vitals shall be consumed. He will come and vindicate me and my cause. I have such confidence in his justice, that I do not doubt that he will yet show himself to be the friend of him who puts his trust in him."

(b.) It is inconsistent with the argument, and the whole scope and connection of the book, to suppose that this refers to the Messiah and to the resurrection of the body after death. The Book of Job is strictly an *argument*—a train of clear, consecutive reasoning. It discusses a great inquiry about the doctrine of divine Providence and the divine dealings with men. The three friends of Job maintained that God deals with men strictly according to their character in this life—that eminent wickedness is attended with eminent suffering; and that when men experience any great calamity, it is proof of eminent wickedness. All this they meant to apply to Job, and all this Job denied. Yet he was perplexed and confounded. He did not know what to do with *the facts* in the case; but still he felt embarrassed. All that he could say was, that God would *yet* come forth and show himself to be the friend of those who loved him and that though they suffered now, yet he had confidence that he would appear for their relief. Now, had they possessed the knowledge of the doctrine of the *resurrection of the dead,* it would have needed the whole debate. It would not only have met all the difficulties of Job, but we should have found him perpetually recurring to it—placing it in every variety of form—appealing to it as relieving his embarrassments, and as demanding an answer from his friends. But, on the supposition that this refers to the resurrection, it is remarkable that the passage here stands alone. Job never adverted to it before, but allowed himself to be greatly embarrassed for the want of just such an argument, and he never refers to it again. He goes on to argue again *as if* he believed no such doctrine. He does not ask his friends to notice this; he expresses no surprise that they should pass by, in entire neglect, an argument which *must have been seen* to be decisive of the controversy. It is equally unaccountable that his friends should not have noticed it. If the doctrine of the resurrection was true, it settled the case. It rendered all their arguments worthless, and would have met the case just as we meet similar cases now. It was incumbent on them to show that there was not evidence of the truth of any such doctrine as the resurrection, and that this could not be urged to meet their arguments. Yet they never allude to so important and unanswerable an argument, and evidently did not suppose that Job referred to any such event. It is equally remarkable that neither Elihu nor God himself, in the close of the book, make any such allusion, or refer to the doctrine of the resurrection at all, as meeting the difficulties of the case. In the argument with which the Almighty is represented as closing the book, the whole thing is resolved into a matter of *sovereignty* and men are required to submit because God is great, and is inscrutable in his ways—not because the dead will be raised, and the inequalities of the present life will be recompensed in a future state. The doctrine of a *resurrection*—a great and glorious doctrine, such as, if once suggested, could not have escaped the profound attention of these sages—would have solved the whole difficulty: and yet, confessedly, it is never alluded to by them—never introduced—never examined—never admitted or rejected—never becomes a matter of inquiry, and is never referred to by God himself as settling the matter—never occurs in the book in any form, unless it be in this. This is wholly unaccountable on the supposition that this refers to the resurrection.

(c.) The interpretation which refers this to the resurrection of the dead, is inconsistent with numerous passages where Job expresses a contrary belief. Of this nature are the following: ch. 7:9. "As the cloud is consumed, and vanisheth away, so he that goeth down to the grave shall come up no more;" 7:21, "I shall sleep in the dust—thou shalt seek me in the morning, but I shall not be;" see ch. 10:21, 22, "I go whence I shall not return—to the land of darkness, and the shadow of death; a land of darkness as darkness itself;" ch. 14: throughout, particularly vs. 7, 9, 11, 12, "For there is hope of a tree, if it be cut down, that it will sprout again, and that the tender branch thereof will not cease. But man dieth, and wasteth away; yea, man giveth up the ghost, and where is he? As the waters fail from the sea, and the flood decayeth and drieth up, so man lieth down and riseth not; till the heavens be no more, they shall not awake, nor be raised out of their sleep." Ch. 16:22, "When a few years are come, then I shall go the way whence I shall not return." These passages all imply that when he should die, he would not appear again on the earth. This is not such language as one would use who believed in the resurrection of the dead. It is true, that in the discourses of Job, various and sometimes apparently contradictory feelings are expressed. He was a severe sufferer; and under strong conflicting emotions he sometimes expressed himself in a manner which he at other times regrets, and gives vent to feelings which, on mature reflection, he confesses to have been wrong. But how is it *possible* to believe that a man, in his circumstances, would ever deny the doctrine of the resurrection if he held it? How could he forget it? How could he throw out a remark that *seemed* to imply a doubt of it? If he had known of this, it would have been a sheet-anchor to his soul in all the storms of adversity—an unanswerable argument to all that his friends advanced—a topic of consolation which he could never have lost sight of, much less denied. He would have clung to that hope as the refuge of his soul, and not for one moment would he have denied it, or expressed a doubt of its truth.

(d.) I may urge as a distinct argument what has before been hinted at, that this is not referred to as a topic of consolation by either of the friends of Job, by Elihu, or by God himself. Had it been a doctrine of those times, his friends would have understood it, and it would have reversed all their theology. Had it been understood by Elihu, he would have understood it, and it would have reversed all their theology. Had it been understood by Elihu, he would have urged it as a reason for resignation in affliction. Had God designed that it should be known in that age, no more favourable opportunity could be conceived for the purpose than at the end of the arguments in this book. What a flood of light would it have thrown on the design of afflictions! How effectually would it have rebuked the arguments of the friends of Job! And how clear is it, therefore, that God did not *intend* that it should then be revealed to man, but meant that it should be reserved for a more advanced state of the world, and particularly that it should be reserved as the grand doctrine of the Christian revelation.

(e.) A fifth consideration is, that on the supposition that it refers to the resurrection, it would be inconsistent with the views which prevailed in the age when Job is supposed to have lived. It is wholly in advance of that age. It makes little difference in regard to this whether we suppose him to have lived in the time of Abraham, Jacob, or Moses, or even at a later period—such a supposition would be equally at variance with the revelations which had then been given. The clear doctrine of the resurrection of the dead, is one of the peculiar doctrines of Christianity—one of the last truths of revelation, and is one of the glorious truths which seem to have been reserved for the Redeemer himself to make known to man. There are, indeed, obscure traces of it in the Old Testament. Occasionally we meet with a hint on the subject that was sufficient to excite the hopes of the ancient saints, and to lead them to suppose that more glorious truths were in reserve to be communicated by the Messiah. But those hints occur at distant intervals; are obscure in their character, and perhaps if all in the Old Testament were collected, they would not be sufficient to convey any very intelligible view of the resurrection of the dead. But on the supposition that the passage before us refers to that doctrine, we have here one of the most clear and full revelations on the subject, laid far back in the early ages of the world, originating in Arabia, and entirely in advance of the prevailing views of the age, and of all that had been communicated by the Spirit of inspiration to the generations then living. It is admitted, indeed, that it was *possible* for the Holy Spirit to communicate that truth in its fulness and completeness to an Arabian sage; but it is not the way in which revelation, in other respects, has been imparted. It has been done *gradually.* Obscure intimations are given at first—they are increased from time to time—the light becomes clearer, till some prophet discloses the whole truth, and the doctrine stands complete before us. Such a course we should expect to find in regard to the doctrine of the resurrection, and such is exactly the course pursued, unless *this* passage teaches what was in fact the highest revelation made by the Messiah.

(f.) All which the words and phrases fairly convey, and all which the argument demands, is fully met by the supposition that it refers to some such event as is recorded in the close of the book. God appeared in a manner corresponding to the meaning of the words here upon the earth. He came as the Vindicator, the Redeemer, the *Goël,* of Job. He vindicated his cause, rebuked his friends, expressed his approbation of the sentiments of Job, and blessed him again with returning prosperity and plenty. The disease of the patriarch may have advanced, as he supposed it would. His flesh may have wasted away, but his confidence in God was not misplaced, and he came forth as his vindicator and friend. It was a noble expression of faith on the part of Job; it showed that he ***had*** confidence in God, and that in the midst of his trials he truly relied on him; and it was a sentiment worthy to be engraved in the eternal rock, and to be transmitted to future times. It was an invaluable lesson to sufferers, showing them that confidence could, and should be placed in God in the severest trials. So far as I can see, all that is fairly implied in the passage, when properly interpreted, is fully met by the events recorded in the close of the book. Such an interpretation meets the exigency of the case, accords with the strain of the argument and with the result, and is the most simple and natural that has been proposed. These considerations are so weighty in my mind that they have conducted me to a conclusion, contrary I confess to what I had ***hoped*** to have reached, that this passage has no reference to the Messiah and the doctrine of the resurrection. We do not ***need*** it—for all the truths respecting the Messiah and the resurrection which we need, are fully revealed elsewhere; and though this is an exquisitely beautiful passage, and piety would love to retain the belief that it refers to the resurrection of the dead, yet ***truth*** is to be preferred to indulgence of the wishes and desires of the heart, however amiable or pious, and the ***desire*** to find certain doctrines in the Bible should yield to what we are constrained to believe the Spirit of inspiration actually taught. I confess that I have never been so pained at any conclusion to which I have come in the interpretation of the Bible, as in the case before us. I would like to have found a distinct prophecy of the Messiah in this ancient and venerable book. I would like to have found the faith of this eminent saint sustained by such a faith in his future advent and incarnation. I would like to have found evidence that this expectation had become incorporated in the piety of the early nations, and was found in Arabia. I would like to have found traces of the early belief of the doctrine of the resurrection of the dead sustaining the souls of the patriarchs then, as it does ours now, in trial. But I cannot. Yet I can regard it as a most beautiful and triumphant expression of confidence in God, and as wholly worthy to be engraved, as Job desired it might be, in the solid rock for ever, that the passing traveller might see and read it; or as worthy of that more permanent record which it has received by being "***printed*** IN A BOOK"—by an art unknown then, and sent down to the end of the world to be read and admired in all generations.

The opinion which has now been expressed, it is not necessary to say, has been held by a large number of the most distinguished critics. Grotius says that the Jews never applied it to the Messiah and the resurrection. The same opinion is held by Grotius himself, by Warburton, Rosenmüller, Le Clere, Patrick, Kennicott, Dalthe, and Jahn. Calvin seems to be doubtful—sometimes giving it an interpretation similar to that suggested above, and then pursuing his remarks as if it referred to the Messiah. Most of the fathers, and a large portion of modern critics, it is to be admitted, suppose that it refers to the Messiah, and to the future resurrection.

> 28 But ye should say, Why persecute we him? seeing the root of the matter is found in me.

28. *But we should say.* Noyes renders this, "Since ye say, 'How may we persecute him, and find grounds of accusation against him?'" Dr. Good,

> Then shall ye say, "How did we persecute him?"
> When the root of the matter is disclosed in me.

The Vulgate, "Why now do ye say, let us persecute him, and find ground of accusation *radicem verbi* against him?" The LXX, "If you also say, What shall we say against him? and what ground of accusation—ρίζαν λόγου—shall we find in him?" Rosenmüller renders it, "When you say, let us persecute him, and see what ground of accusation we find in him, then fear the sword." Most critics concur in such an interpretation as implies that they had sought a ground of accusation against him, and that they would have occasion to fear the divine displeasure on account of it. It seems to me, however, that our translators have given substantially the fair sense of the Hebrew. A slight variation would, perhaps, better express the idea: "For you will yet say, Why did we persecute him? The root of the matter was found in him—and since this will be the case, fear now that justice will overtake you for it, for vengeance will not always slumber when a friend of God is wronged."

Seeing the root of the matter. Marg. *and* what *root of matter is found in me.* The word rendered *matter* דבר means, properly, *word* or *thing*—and may refer to *any* thing. Here it is used in one of the two opposite senses, *piety* or *guilt*—as being *the thing* under consideration. The interpretation to be adopted must depend on the view taken of the other words of the sentence. To me it seems that it denotes piety, and that the idea is, that the root of true piety was in him, or that he was not a hypocrite. The word *root* is so common as to need no explanation. It is used sometimes to denote the *bottom,* or the lowest part of any thing—as e.g. the foot (see chap. 13:27, *margin*), the bottom of the mountains (Job 38:9), or of the sea, Job 38:30, *margin.* Here it means the foundation, support, or source—as the root is of a tree; and the sense, I suppose, is, that he was not a dead trunk, but he was like a tree that had a root, and consequently support and life. Many critics, however, among whom is Gesenius, suppose that it means that the root of the controversy, that is, the ground of strife, was in *him,* or that he was the cause of the whole dispute.

> 29 Be ye afraid of the sword: for wrath *bringeth* the punishments of the sword, that ye may know *there is* a judgment.

29. *Be ye afraid of the sword.* Of the sword of justice, of the wrath of God. In taking such views, and using such language, you ought to dread the vengeance of God, for he will punish the guilty.

For wrath bringeth *the punishments of the sword.* The word *"bringeth"* is supplied by the translators, and as it seems to me improperly. The idea is, that wrath or anger such as they had manifested, was proper for punishment; that such malice as they had shown was a crime that God would not suffer to escape unpunished. They had, therefore, every thing to dread. Literally it is, "for wrath the iniquities of the sword;" that is, wrath is a crime for the sword.

That ye may know that there is a judgment. That there is justice; that God punishes injuries done to the character, and that he will come forth to vindicate his friends. Probably Job anticipated that when God should come forth to vindicate *him,* he would inflict exemplary punishment on *them;* and that this would be not only by words, but by some heavy judgment, such as he had himself experienced. The vindication of the just is commonly attended with the punishment of the unjust; the salvation of the friends of God is connected with the destruction of his foes. Job seems to have anticipated this in the case of himself and his friends; it will certainly occur in the great day when the affairs of this world shall be wound up in the decisions of the final judgment. See Matth. 25.

22

Job's Discourse on God's Wisdom: An Exposition of Job 28

Roy B. Zuck

Many scholars assign [Job 28] to Zophar, Bildad, or even God, or treat it as a poem that was not part of the Book of Job originally. It does seem to be unrelated to what precedes and follows it, and it is in a different mood, but the subject matter—man's inability to discover God's wisdom—is in keeping with Job's words (26:14, as well as 9:10–12; 12:13; 17:10; 23:8–10).[1] This chapter is fittingly Job's, for he had been refuting the three counselors, who had maintained that they knew God's ways. Job now affirmed that it is not possible for man to presume that he can discern the inscrutable mysteries of the majestic God. As Michaelis states so clearly:

1. Andersen's view that chapter 28 is an interlude written by the author of the book (thus serving as a transition from the three rounds of dialogues to the three rounds of monologues by Job, Elihu, and Jehovah) is intriguing, but it (1) does not explain why 29:1 states that "Job again

From Roy B. Zuck, *Job,* Everyman's Bible Commentary (Chicago: Moody, 1978), 122–26. Used by permission of Moody Bible Institute of Chicago.

> But to man this wisdom [by which God made and governs all things] must remain inscrutable. To him God said: Trouble not thyself with inquiring how I govern the world; why I permit the tyrant to be victorious, or innocence and truth to be oppressed: decide not what evil I can or cannot suffer to exist in the world. This is too high for thee: let thy wisdom consist in fearing me, upon whose will all things depend. . . .[2]

Man, in spite of his engineering skills (28:1–11), cannot discover or purchase wisdom (28:12–22); only God knows where true wisdom is to be found (28:23–28). Job spoke of the metals (silver, gold, iron, copper, and precious stones) that are mined by man (28:1–2, 6), and he spoke of the ingenious ways by which the metal sand stones are discovered beneath the surface of the earth (28:3–5, 7–11). Silver was mined in Arabia (2 Chron. 9:14) and Tarshish (Jer. 10:9), gold was imported from Arabia (2 Chron. 9:14) including Ophir (1 Kings 10:11) and Sheba (1 Kings 10:2).

The mining shafts bring light to the dark recesses of mines (28:3), where people have never lived (28:4). Miners, forgotten by people walking above the mine, hang and dangle, apparently while being lowered by ropes into mining holes far below the sight of men on the surface (28:4).[3] From the surface of the earth comes food (from vegetative growth), but from beneath the surface "it is turned up as fire" (28:5). This latter clause may mean that "the overturning that goes on underground produces confused rubble like that caused by fire,"[4] or that the precious stones that are disclosed by the overturning of the earth seem to glow like fire,[5] or that the ore-containing rocks had been produced by volcanic fire[6] or mine blasting. The first of these views seems preferable. The sapphires mentioned next (28:6) are lapis lazuli, the ore of which contains particles that look like gold. The inaccessibility of the mines to animals is then specified: bird of prey with keen insight like the falcon, lions ("proud beasts" probably means lions) with their courage, and serpents[7] with their sly movements are unable to see or touch what man does in mining (28:7–8). The falcon is above the earth, the lion on the earth, and the serpent in it.

Verses 9–11, like verses 3–4, speak of man's mining operations. He breaks

---

took up his discourse," (2) overlooks similarities between chapter 28 and Job's words elsewhere (e.g., 28:24–27 and 26:5–13), (3) does not account for the possibility that Job may have changed from speaking about the wealth of the wicked (chap. 27) to man's ability to unearth much of that wealth (chap. 28), (4) disregards Job's continued frustration with and recognition of his inability to discover God's ways, and (5) assumes an author outside the circle of the five major conversants in the book.

2. J. D. Michaelis, quoted by E. P. Barrows, "Interpretation of the Twenty-Eighth Chapter of Job," *Bibliotheca Sacra* 10 (1853): 271.

3. This is one way of understanding this verse. Numerous other renderings of the obscure Hebrew are revealed by a glance at various versions.

4. Rowley, p. 228.

5. Albert Barnes, *Notes, Critical, Illustrative, and Practical, on the Book of Job*, 2:64.

6. Marvin H. Pope, *Job*, p. 201.

through solid rock, overturns mountains at their base (literally, by the roots), cuts channels (tunnels) in the rocks, and is thus enabled to see valuable metals. In addition, he dams up underground streams so that they do not trickle or seep into the mine and thus hamper his mining operations.

All this activity results in his bringing to light the metals and stones that were hidden in the darkness.

In spite of man's technological abilities to mine precious stones and ores that lie beyond the sight of man, bird, and beast, he cannot find wisdom (28:12). Its value is unknown, its location has not been found in all "the land of the living" (the inhabited earth), in the deep waters beneath the earth, or in the sea. Not only can man not find wisdom, he cannot even purchase it with the precious metals he has found (28:15–19). Job used almost a dozen different words of various metals, including three words that are found only here in the Old Testament ("pure gold," "glass," and "crystal"); the meanings of those three words are therefore difficult to know with precision. Verse 20 is almost identical with verse 12, and verses 21 and 22 are close in thought to verses 13 and 14. As the deep and the sea (28:14) were personified, saying that wisdom is not in them, so Abaddon (a synonym for Sheol; it is used three times by Job in his closing oration; cf. 26:6; 31:12) and Death stated that they have heard rumors about wisdom, the implication being that they do not possess it and know little about it (28:22).

Job concludes the chapter (28:23–28) by answering the questions "Where can wisdom be found?" (28:12) and "Where then does wisdom come from?" (28:20). By being first in the sentence in Hebrew, the word "God" (Elohim) is emphasized (28:23). Only God knows where wisdom is to be found (28:23), for he alone is omniscient (28:24). His looking "to the ends of the earth" and his seeing "everything under the heavens," all in one immediate glance, contrast sharply with man's laborious searching and probing for wisdom without finding it and with the inability of even "birds of the sky," with their vast sweep of vision, to see it (28:7, 21).

Job's appreciation of God's sovereignty over and providential care for His creation is again seen in His establishment of regulations that govern four aspects of nature (28:25–26). Although storms appear to be without order, their elements were determined by His wise, creative genius. The weight (i.e., force) of the wind, the measure (i.e., amount) of water, a limit (literally, decree, law, rule, regulation) for the rain (thus indicating that rain is not haphazard or by chance), and the path followed by the thunderbolt—all were determined by God.

When God, in His creative work, prescribed laws for the wind, waters, rain, and lightning, He explored wisdom, which is treated as a tangible object

7. Sigmund Mowinckel suggests that the mythological griffin (lion-dragon) is suggested here (*Hebrew and Semitic Studies*, ed. D. Winton Thomas and W. D. McHardy [Oxford: Clarendon, 1963], pp. 95–103).

or idea (28:27). (Cf. Prov. 8:27–30, which is strikingly similar.) He saw it, probed it (a possible rendering for the word "declared"), established it, and investigated it. Together these verbs suggest that He perfectly fathomed the nature of wisdom—in stark contrast to man's inability even to *find* it. The verb "established" may point to His setting forth laws regarding the relationship of wisdom to man. The necessity of divine, propositional revelation is indicated next: "to man He said" (28:28). Although man is impotent to discover or purchase wisdom, he can know its very essence, for God has unveiled what otherwise would remain "hidden from the eyes of all living" (28:21). That essence of wisdom is twofold, "the fear of the Lord [Adonai]" and "to depart from evil."

All man's scientific investigations, technological advances, and intellectual achievements—remarkable as they are, whether in Job's day or the present—fail miserably to provide "a full explanation of [God's] government [or to] disclose all that we would wish to know about God."[8] Instead, real wisdom consists in establishing one's life in submissive veneration before God, in revering God in an attitude of confidence that He does all things right (although that rightness may not always be apparent to man). True wisdom also consists in a rejection of evil, in a regulating of one's conduct in paths of piety, and in actions and attitudes that accord with God's standards of holiness and godliness. Fearing God and turning from evil may be summarized as adoration of God and obedience to God. Thus the truly wise man is the one whose life is centered on God, not self, and is regulated by God. Man in right relationship to God, worshiping him, serving him, obeying him—*that* is wisdom and understanding!

This chapter may be seen as Job's rebuke to the shortsighted wisdom of his antagonists,[9] an effort to demonstrate that their limited theological outlook was false. Seen as a disclaimer to their accusations that he was not fearing God and needed to turn from evil, the chapter is unquestionably fitting as the words of Job. Also, it is consistent with God's earlier assessment of Job (1:1, 8; 2:3), thus demonstrating to the reader that the three friends were mistaken in their demand that Job must begin to revere God and repent of sin. Chapter 28 argues that he had been fearing God and hating evil, but that they had not! Seen in this way, the final verse of the chapter becomes "one of the great, climactic moments in the Book."[10]

The closing verse of chapter 28 also serves as an apposite link to chapters 29–31. In chapter 29 Job rehearsed his past virtues—evidences that he feared God; and in chapter 31 he recounted his innocence with regard to numerous sins—evidences that he turned from evil.

8. Barnes, 2:73.

9. Gleason L. Archer, Jr., *A Survey of Old Testament Introduction* (Chicago: Moody, 1964), p. 447.

10. Victor E. Reichert, *Job,* p. 145.

23

Wisdom in the Book of Job

Norman C. Habel

In his study of *The Wisdom of God in the Book of Job,* Peter Zerafa concludes:

> The Book of Job is not so accommodating; it does not give the sages a chance. Not only does it depreciate all human wisdom—this is competently achieved by the human protagonists themselves, who incessantly delapidate *(sic!)* each other's wise perorations—but outrightly denies it both in the theophany (chs. 38ff) and in the hymn to wisdom (ch. 28). Wisdom is out of man's reach, it is not found on earth; man cannot discover it and cannot buy it. In this way the doctrinal edifice of the wisdom schools which sought to encase Yahweh's designs within the scheme of their scholarly speculations is

From Norman C. Habel, "Of Things Beyond Me: Wisdom in the Book of Job," *Currents in Theology and Mission* 10 (1983): 142–54. Used by permission of The Lutheran School of Theology at Chicago.

completely demolished. Only God is wise, and His ways cannot be controlled by man's foolish mind.[1]

How valid are Zerafa's conclusions? I have long been struck by the fact that the author of Job never has any of the human participants actually designating himself as 'wise,' though each in turn lays claim to an authoritative source of knowledge as if he were a sage.[2] This raises the question of precisely how the author of Job uses the term "wisdom" *(ḥokmâ)*. An answer to this question is important if we are to appreciate the charge of God that Job is obfuscating his 'design' *(ʿēṣâ)* without "knowledge" (38:2), a charge to which Job eventually agrees:

> Indeed I spoke without discernment,
> Of things beyond me, which I did not know. (42:3)[3]

Our task in this limited paper will be to explore the theme of wisdom in the Book of Job using the author's poem on wisdom (ch. 28) as our starting point and taking into account the various near synonyms of wisdom employed in the Book.[4]

Wisdom in Job 28

The problem of how to understand and define wisdom in ancient Israel has long exercised the minds of scholars. Some have emphasized its practical dimensions. Thus Zerafa, following the tradition of von Rad considers the basic meaning of wisdom to be 'the art of success.'[5] Others have argued that wisdom is essentially superior intelligence gained through appropriate training and instruction.[6] Still others incorporate various categories of wisdom in their definition. Crenshaw defines wisdom as 'the quest for self-understanding in

1. P. P. Zerafa, *The Wisdom of God in the Book of Job* (Rome: Herder, 1978), p. 184.

2. Though Eliphaz claims an unusual revelatory experience (4:12–16), he, like Bildad (8:8) and Zophar (20:4), cites the tradition of the first fathers (15:18) as the source of his knowledge. Job appeals primarily to his own experience (13:1) and Elihu to his inner spirit (32:8; 33:4).

3. The rendering 'Of things beyond me' is taken from the fine translation by M. Greenberg, J. Greenfield and N. Sarna, *The Book of Job* (Philadelphia: The Jewish Publication Society, 1980). All subsequent translations in the paper are my own.

4. The relevant near synonyms are *bînâ*, 'discernment' (28:12, 20, 28; 28:4, 36; 39:17, 26), *ḥēqer*, 'profound truth' (8:8; 11:7; cf. 5:9; 9:10 and the verb *ḥqr* 28:3, 27), *tûšiyyâ*, 'understanding/know-how' (11:6; 12:16; 26:3; cf. 5:12; 6:13), and *ʿēṣâ*, 'design/counsel' (12:12; 38:2; 42:3; cf. 5:13; 29:21). Zerafa, op. cit., p. 105, also includes *dēaʿ*, 'knowledge,' but the parallels are less explicit.

5. Op. cit., p. 105, G. Von Rad, *Theology of the Old Testament* (London: Oliver and Boyd, 1962), Vol. 1, 418, defines wisdom as 'practical knowledge of the laws of life and the world, based on experience'.

6. R. N. Whybray, *The Intellectual Tradition in the Old Testament* (Berlin: de Gruyter, 1974), 12, speaks of wisdom as basically a 'superior mental ability'.

terms of relationships with things (nature wisdom), people (juridical and practical wisdom), and the Creator (theological wisdom).'[7] Our task here is not to debate the merits of these definitions, but to ascertain the particular way in which wisdom is understood by the author of Job.[8]

Most studies of wisdom begin with human wisdom as a special skill or superior mental ability without any moral or religious reference.[9] Thus skillful women who spin (Exodus 35:25) or experienced sailors who navigate (1 Kings 9:27) may be designated 'wise.' In such studies divine wisdom is usually interpreted as a development from a prior understanding of human wisdom. The author of Job, however, is a theologian and a poet. It seems appropriate, therefore, to take as our starting point the pivotal poem where his position is articulated (ch. 28).[10] I now accept this poem as integral to the Book of Job and view it as a closure for the cycle of speeches between Job and his friends.[11] As a closure this poem may be viewed as the poet's own commentary on the efforts of the preceding participants to probe the hidden side of wisdom and understand the riddle of Job's case.

The governing theme of this poem is the search for wisdom. This search is compared with the quest of mortals for precious gems and metals. In both quests three motifs dominate: the source or "place" of the precious item, the "way" or means of access to it, and the process of discovering it. Human beings may be able to discover the way to, and place of, precious gems in the most obscure regions of the earth, but they cannot find "wisdom." God alone finds her.

The poem culminates in the following finely honed conclusion:

> God understood the way to her (i.e., wisdom)
> And he knew her place,
> For he looked to the ends of the earth
> And saw everything under heaven.
> When making the weight of the wind
> And meting out the waters by measure,
> When making a rule for the rain
> And a way for the thunderstorm,

7. J. L. Crenshaw, "Method in Determining Wisdom Influence upon Historical Literature," *JBL* 88 (1969), 132.

8. J. Lévêque, *Job et son Dieu* (Paris: Gabalda, 1970), vol. 2, ch. 3, classifies all references to the root *ḥkm* under the categories of a) human wisdom, b) divine wisdom at work in creation, c) divine wisdom as revelatory or educational, and d) wisdom as fear of God.

9. For example, R. B. Y. Scott, *The Way of Wisdom* (New York: Macmillan, 1971), pp. 6ff.

10. Zerafa, op. cit., p. 53, also views ch. 28 as the close of the first part of the Book of Job. This hymn, he writes, 'proves that man cannot attain wisdom: only God is wise'.

11. I argue the case for authenticity of this chapter as a closure statement in my forthcoming commentary on Job in the Old Testament Library series (Philadelphia: Westminster Press). Cf., Zerafa, op. cit., p. 53. On closure forms see B. Herrnstein-Smith, *Poetic Closure* (Chicago: University Press, 1968).

Then he saw her and appraised her,
Established her and *probed* her.
(28:23–27)

A close scrutiny of this passage reveals a number of key elements about the nature of wisdom.

1. Wisdom is here not a natural attribute of God, but something acquired or found. Wisdom is explicitly portrayed as a discrete entity with a "place" of her own and a "way" to that place (v. 23). God "looks" to the ends of the earth to locate her (v. 24). Finally he "sees" her, "appraises" her, and "probes" her (v. 27). Thus wisdom is a separate entity which God discovers and scrutinizes closely like the most precious gem of all. Bruce Vawter has shown that in the related text of Prov. 8:22 wisdom is also "acquired" rather than "begotten" or "created."[12]

2. Wisdom is acquired in the process of God creating the domain where she operates. The creative activity of God in this passage is the celestial ordering of the celestial forces of "wind," "rain" and "thunderstorm" (vv. 25–26). These phenomena are presumably illustrations of God's total creative activity. The key expression "when making" which introduces both verses 25 and 26, refers to the process or activity of creating.[13] In that process God discovers wisdom.

3. Hence wisdom is the principle or design which governs the activity to which she relates. The specific ordering activity of God described in this passage involves determining weights and measures (v. 25), establishing "rules" (cf. 38:33), and designing "ways" (cf. 38:24–25) or laws according to which various celestial forces operate (v. 26). In this creative "ordering" of things wisdom is obviously not herself any one of these "laws" or "rules," but is discovered in their establishment. She must therefore be the basic overall design or principle which governs them. She informs all "ordering" and is discovered in the process of ordering.

When God discovers this principle which governs all other laws and principles of the cosmos he "probes" her. The verb "probe" *(ḥqr)* in Job refers to penetrating hidden depths (28:3; cf. 5:27; 29:16; 32:11; Prov. 25:2). The derived noun *ḥēqer* comes to mean something very deep and profound (38:16; cf. 5:9; 19:10), and as such is a near synonym for wisdom (8:8; 11:7). Thus wisdom is apparently the deep and mysterious principle behind all other laws, principles, and designs of the cosmos.

The priority of wisdom as a governing principle in the ordering of creation also implies her primordiality, that is, her absolute priority as the original prin-

12. B. Vawter, "Prov. 8:22: Wisdom and Creation," *JBL* 99 (1980), 205–216, especially pp. 214–215.

13. "When making" renders the infinitive forms *laʿăśōt* (v. 25a) and *baʿăśōtô* (v. 26a). The "when" of the creative process is balanced by the explicit "then" (*ʾāz*) of the discovery (v. 27a). That *ʾāz* may mean the original "then" of the primordial is evident from Prov. 8:22.

ciple of the created order. Vawter's study of the related text of Prov. 8:22 supports this conclusion. According to Vawter, wisdom is identified as "the beginning" of his works. That is, wisdom is the *principium*, the "first principle" or "model" which precedes and informs the creation of the cosmos. In similar vein, I argued elsewhere that "way" in Prov. 8:22 refers to the foundation principle which precedes Yahweh's "work" or creation.[14] It remains to be tested whether the rendering "governing principle(s)" or "underlying design" is basic to the meaning of wisdom in other contexts.

By employing the definite article with *ḥokmâ* in the body of the poem (28:1–27), the author may be stressing that this wisdom is "the" first principle which governs all other principles of the universe.[15] In any case, the meaning of "governing principle" or "design" fits the sense of the poem admirably.

Wisdom in the Dialogue between Job and His Friends

Does this understanding of wisdom illuminate references to wisdom and related terms in the speech cycle between Job and his friends? In his second response to Job Eliphaz asks with ironic tone:

> Were you the first human ever born?
> Were you brought forth before the hills?
> Did you listen in on the *council* of God
> And keep *wisdom* for yourself?
> What do you know that we do not know
> Or discern that we do not?
> (15:7–9)

Once again wisdom is something which precedes the event. The activity involved seems to be the planning of creation in the heavenly council of God.[16] Were Job born before creation he could have participated in that council and acquired wisdom for himself.[17] Thus Job would have first-hand knowledge of the governing principles of the earth and "know" more than his friends.

14. N. Habel, "The Symbolism of Wisdom in Proverbs," *Interpretation* 16 (1972), 154–155.

15. Note R. Gordis, *The Book of Job* (New York: Jewish Theological Seminary of America, 1978), Special Note 23 where he makes a major distinction between 'higher wisdom' and 'lower wisdom', the former being *ḥokmâ* with the definite article. This distinction is hard to maintain since the wisdom of God elsewhere appears without the definite article.

16. For *sôd* as the 'council' where planning and decisions are made see Jer. 23:18, 22.

17. The meaning of wisdom as "first principle" is appropriate whether or not one believes Eliphaz is alluding to a myth about the heavenly first man.

This ironic question of Eliphaz must be seen considered in relation to his subsequent claim to knowledge.

> What *wise men* have announced
> And *the fathers* not hidden
> To whom alone the land was given,
> When no stranger passed among them—(15:18–19)[18]

The fathers here are not the previous generation but those to whom the land or earth was first allocated, presumably by God (Deut. 32:8). This land has not been polluted by strangers. The fathers are therefore those who experienced the land or earth first-hand and discerned the principles of its operation. These fathers are apparently the "wise," that is, those who acquired wisdom at the beginning. For Job to have knowledge superior to that of Eliphaz, he would need to have lived before the wise man from whom Eliphaz claims to have received his knowledge by tradition.

Bildad's claim to knowledge is essentially the same when he urges:

> Ask now of the *first* generation,
> And consider the *profound truth* of the fathers,
> For we are of yesterday and know nothing. (8:8–9a)

Here too the focus is on the "first" generation, that is, the primordial or distant heroic past. What the first generation found is designated *hēqer*, "that which was probed" (*ḥqr*, cf. 28:27). The "probed" or "profound truth" of the fathers recalls the "wisdom" which Yahweh "probed" when ordering the heavens (28:27; cf. 11:7). This "profound truth," therefore, seems to be synonymous with the "wisdom" of the fathers, a wisdom Bildad is claiming as his authority. In making his claim Bildad is following a known practice of appealing to ancient or primordial tradition as the ground for authoritative knowledge.[19] Thus for Bildad true wisdom among human beings is derived from the original fathers who probed the principles of life on earth by first-hand experience at the beginning. Later Zophar appeals to ancient primordial tradition in the same way:

> Do you not know this, that from *time immemorial*
> Since humans were set on the earth . . . (20:2)

In depreciating Job's claims to knowledge,[20] however, Zophar asserts,

18. Whether or not the fathers are synonymous with the wise as in my translation, the focus is on authoritative knowledge being transmitted from the very beginning.

19. N. Habel, "Appeal to Ancient Tradition as a Literary Form," *ZAW* 88 (1976), 253–272.

20. In his preceding speech (chs. 9–10) "knowledge" (the root *yd'*) is a major theme. Note 9:2, 5, 21, 28; 10:2, 7, 13.

If only God would speak
And talk to you himself.
He would expound to you the *secrets of wisdom*
For there are *two sides to understanding.*
(Know that God exacts from you
Less than your guilt deserves.)
Can you find the *profound truth* of Eloah?
Can you find the *limit* of Shaddai?
It is higher than heaven—what can you do?
It is deeper than Sheol—what can you know? (11:5–9)

The "profound truth" of God clearly stands in contrast to the "profound truth" of the fathers (8:8). The profundity of this truth or mystery is emphasized by making it synonymous with the "limit" of Shaddai (cf. 28:3), the inaccessible depths of God's knowledge. This "profound truth" is greater than the extremities of the cosmos. Apparently, therefore, this mystery is equivalent to "wisdom," the underlying design or principle governing the universe. In verse 6 this mystery is explicitly identified as "the secrets of wisdom." "Secrets" *(ta 'ălômôt)* is literally "hidden dimensions." The profundities of God's wisdom are hidden from mortals; "understanding" *(tûšiyyâ)*[21] has two sides—the manifest and the hidden.[22] Wisdom as the underlying principle governing the cosmos is hidden from mortals; what the fathers probed was apparently the manifest side. Thus Zophar concurs in part with the poet of chapter 28 in asserting that wisdom is the hidden first principle, greater than the cosmos itself and inaccessible to human beings.

What of those references to wisdom which do not focus explicitly on the primordial or the profound? How do they relate to the proposed interpretation given above? Eliphaz maintains that mortals are creatures of clay whose ephemeral existence may be terminated at any time without their knowing "wisdom" (4:21). Wisdom is not innate; it is normal for mortals to die without acquiring it. God, adds Eliphaz, foils the "plans" and "design" of the so-called wise (5:12–13). Significantly the "wise" of the world are those who have a "design" or plan by which they operate. Both Job and Elihu contend that wisdom is not with the aged of the community (12:12; 32:7–9). Job argues that God retains wisdom, not the aged (12:12–13).[23] Thus wisdom is conspicuous by its absence among the human participants. "I do not find one wise person among you" concludes Job (17:10; cf. 26:3). At one point Job quips:

21. This noun carries the connotation of "effectiveness" or "success" (cf. 5:12). Perhaps the American expression "know-how" is a suitable rendering.

22. The term *kiplayim* does not mean "manifold" (RSV), but "double, duplex." Cf. M. Pope, *Job* (Garden City, N.Y.: Doubleday, 1965), 84.

23. 12:12 may be taken as a quotation of the friends (Gordis, op. cit., 138, or rendered as an ironic question as in the translation of Greenberg, Greenfield, and Sarna, op. cit).

Truly you are the people
With whom wisdom will die. (12:2)

Job's tone is one of biting sarcasm. Job is not crediting his friends with being wise, but with claiming to be a privileged group who possess wisdom. In reality they are human beings on the same intellectual level as Job (12:3; 13:4). Job closes this speech with a similar sarcastic comment in which he declares that the friends could be counted as "wise" if they kept silent (13:5). The context makes it clear that Job is calling his friends "fools" (cf. Prov. 17:28). Eliphaz, in turn, derides Job for pretending to be wise but instead spouting forth the empty babble of a fool (15:2). These references say little about the essentials of wisdom, but they do underscore its apparent absence. In spite of their claims to knowledge, the protagonists are found berating each other as fools. The claim of the friends that they have inherited the "profound truth" of the first fathers seems discredited. The primal fathers are a spurious source of wisdom if the friends are faithful witnesses to that wisdom.

Wisdom in the Elihu Speeches

Yahweh's design for the natural world included "allocating a portion" of wisdom to each species (39:17). The ostrich is the exception which interprets this rule. She was deprived of her portion of natural wisdom and therefore lacks an instinctive knowledge of the principles of survival and motherhood typical of other creatures (39:13–16). Because the natural world possesses this intuitive understanding of the principles of life, humans can learn from nature (cf. 12:7–8). Or as Elihu says:

(God) who teaches us by the
beasts of the earth
And makes us wise by the birds
of heaven. (35:11)[24]

Elihu seems to argue that human beings possess a natural endowment like innate wisdom of the animal kingdom. That inner wisdom is a gift which is not dependent on age, tradition or length of experience. Thus he asserts:

I said to myself, "Days will testify
And many years teach wisdom."
Surely her spirit is in mortals.[25]

24. This verse is variously rendered. For this translation see Pope, op. cit., 262.

25. I take the pronoun *hî'* as a reference back to 'wisdom.' The text may then be rendered "she is the spirit" or "her spirit." Cf. W. Michel, *The Ugaritic Texts and the Mythological Expressions in the Book of Job* (Ann Arbor: University Microfilms, 1970). Others render "it is the spirit" (RSV). Either way, an intimate like between the indwelling spirit of God and wisdom is evident.

The breath of Shaddai gives them discernment.
But the aged are not wise.
Nor do old men discern justice.
So I say, "Listen to me.
I will speak my mind.[26] Yes, I will." (32:7–10)

Elihu supports the position that wisdom is derived from the breath of Shaddai within. That gift enables him to discern first-hand the underlying factors involved in Job's case. Elihu's alleged understanding of these hidden principles gives him the confidence to claim that he can teach Job "wisdom" (33:33). Elihu's arrogance reaches its zenith when he asserts that his natural endowment makes him "perfect in knowledge" (36:4), an expression he uses later to describe God's level of understanding (37:16). The language of this passionate hothead (32:1–5) convicts him of being a bloated fool (see 32:17–20).[27] The poet thereby leaves the audience with the impression that innate wisdom is a spurious vehicle for interpreting the underlying factors in Job's case. For Elihu makes a fool of himself.

Wisdom in the Yahweh Speeches[28]

We proposed above that wisdom for the author of Job basically means the first principle(s) or underlying design of an activity or order. To possess wisdom is to have probed and understood that principle. The friends claim that the first fathers probed the principles of life and handed down "profound truth" as wisdom. But their claims are not convincing and Job finds them lacking in any understanding of his case. Elihu's claims to an inner wisdom are likewise spurious. Zerafa therefore seems to be correct when he contends that the Book of Job depreciates all human wisdom.[29] The one thing on which all human protagonists agree is that God possesses wisdom. Job, however, maintained that God manipulates wisdom with fickle intent. He controls the governing principles of the cosmos to produce upheavals in nature and disorder in society (12:13–15; cf. 9:4ff.). Job seems to hold that he does not need to return to the primordial to discern the governing principle by which God operates. He knows from personal experience and observation (13:1). Even the animals know God's arbitrary and fickle design (12:7–9).

Yahweh's response to Job's accusations is the challenging question:

26. "Mind" renders the noun *dēaʿ* a word for knowledge found in this form only in Elihu's speeches. Zerafa, op. cit., p. 105, considers it a synonym for wisdom.

27. See N. Habel, "The Role of Elihu in the Design of the Book of Job," in *In the Shelter of Elyon*, ed. W. Boyd Barrick and John R. Spencer, JSOT Supplement Series 13 (Sheffield: JSOT, 1984), pp. 81–98.

28. For a recent exploration into the ambiguous and paradoxical nature of Yahweh's speech see the articles entitled "The Book of Job and Ricoeur's Hermeneutics," in *Semeia*, 19 (1981).

29. Op. cit., p. 184.

> Who is this who clouds ***my design*** with darkness,
> Presenting arguments without knowledge? (38:2)

The charge against Job is not the use of sacrilegious language or the sin of *hubris,* but the obfuscation of Yahweh's design through lack of knowledge. The "design" of Yahweh seems to be a near synonym for the wisdom of the cosmos acquired by God himself in the process of creation (28:23–27). From the details of the speech which follows it is apparent that this underlying design incorporates both the structures and functions of the created world. Wisdom is the first principle which governs that primordial design. Job has obfuscated that design because he lacks the first-hand knowledge of the governing principles at work in the cosmos. In short, he lacks the wisdom which God has acquired. Job would need to have been present at creation to discern the hidden design of the earth:

> Were you there when I laid earth's foundations?
> Tell me, if you have ***discernment.*** (38:4)

"Discernment" is a synonym for "wisdom" in related passages of Job (38:36; 39:17, 26; 28:12, 20, 28). If Job were present at the construction of the earth he would have wisdom, that is, he would know the first principle of its design and be able to answer the repeated challenge questions,[30] including those which ask "Do you know?" (38:18, 21, 33; 39:1–2). The caustic comment "Surely you know, for you were born then!" (38:21a) accentuates the focus on primordial participation as fundamental to an understanding of the blueprints of Yahwehs' cosmic design. The design theme is emphasized especially by the metaphor of earth's creation as the planning and construction of a massive edifice according to divine specifications (38:4–7).

The challenge questions posed by Yahweh expose Job's lack of knowledge about numerous domains in his design for the physical and natural world. If Job possessed wisdom he would understand the underlying structures and functions of Yahweh's design for the cosmos. These structures include fixed limits (38:8–11), designated "places" (38:12, 19), appointed "ways" (38:19–20, 24–25) and "times" (39:1–4), celestial "laws" (38:31–33) and the inbuilt principle of wisdom (38:36; 39:26). The functions of this design include constraint of the wicked (38:12–15), judgment (38:22–23), providence (38:39–41) and celebration (38:7; 39:19–25). Job's lack of knowledge about these features of Yahweh's design exposes his lack of wisdom. Of the numerous challenges addressed to Job the following may be selected for comment:

> Who has the wisdom to count the clouds? (38:37a)

30. On the challenge question form of the speeches of Yahweh see H. Rowold, *The Theology of Creation in the Yahweh Speeches of the Book of Job* (Ann Arbor: University Microfilms, 1977), 57ff.

The image of someone attempting to count clouds whose shapes change constantly as they scud across the sky is rather comical. The question posed, however, is whether anyone, namely Job, has "wisdom," that is, knows a principle or hidden law which will make counting clouds possible. Yahweh alone knows the governing principles of his cosmic design; he alone possesses this wisdom.

Yahweh's response from the whirlwind seems to suggest that if Job lacks wisdom then the same is true of the other human participants. As an answer to the eternal why of innocent suffering Yahweh's response may seem evasive and paradoxical. For it implies that Job's unwarranted affliction is to be understood in the light of a "design" which is hidden.[31] A mortal like Job cannot comprehend that design unless he has wisdom or discernment, that is, first-hand or primordial knowledge of the principle governing this cosmic blueprint.

Does Job Acquire Wisdom?[32]

Does Job finally acquire wisdom through his first-hand experience of suffering? Is his submission to Yahweh (42:2–6) evidence of "fearing the Lord" which is "the beginning of wisdom?" (Prov. 9:10). The closing lines of the wisdom poem cited above read:

> Yet to humans he said,
> Behold to fear the Lord is wisdom,
> To shun evil is discernment. (28:28)

This verse seems to be diametrically opposed to all that preceded in the rest of the poem where wisdom is declared inaccessible to all but God. This verse is therefore deleted by many scholars as a conservative theological postscript designed to redeem the preceding poem.[33] But radical surgery is not required if we ask how this verse fits into the literary design of the poet. The theological approach which developed in Israelite piety maintained that Yahweh imparts wisdom as a special gift (Prov. 2:6) and that the "fear of Yahweh" is the "beginning" or "principle" of wisdom (Prov. 9:10; cf. 1:7; 3:7; 15:33; Ps. 111:10). The relevant passage in Job (28:28) goes a step further and equates the fear of the Lord with wisdom itself. If this equation is true, then Job is

31. It is hard to accept the claim of M. Fox, "Job 38 and God's Rhetoric," *Semeia* 19, op. cit., 60, that the "design" of God is manifest and known. The challenge questions which follow expose Job's ignorance of the underlying principles of that design.

32. J. Kleinig, *The Getting of Wisdom*, Master of Philosophy Dissertation, Cambridge, 1981, contends that in Proverbs the mode of "getting wisdom" differs depending on whether the sage, Dame Wisdom or Yahweh is the source.

33. Zerafa, op. cit., 155, for example, argues that this verse is out of place in a book where human wisdom is "continuously taken to task, parodied and denied."

wise. For the terms used to define wisdom here, namely "fearing God" and "shunning evil," are the very terms employed to characterize Job in the opening lines of the prologue (1:1). The repetition of these terms in 28:28 constitute a major *inclusio* which frames the first half of the Book of Job (chs. 1–28). In terms of the traditional piety reflected in the prologue and the closing verse of this wisdom poem, Job is wise. But this *inclusio*, like the prose legend which frames the Book of Job, serves as a foil and backdrop against which an alternative reality is depicted. In that world the wisdom of piety proves futile; it offers Job no understanding of the reason for his suffering. In the dialogue speeches which fall between these framing references to piety as wisdom, the bankruptcy of that tradition is exposed. Though Eliphaz urged Job to find strength in his past "piety" (4:6; cf. 22:4), Job makes it clear that this "piety" offers him no support (6:14) and neither do any of the traditional answers of the friends who espoused this tradition.

Central to Job's change of attitude is that he no longer sought understanding through past piety or traditional mediated vehicles for knowing God. He sought a first-hand knowledge with God himself present to face Job in court. In fact, Job is no longer interested in finding wisdom, but in finding God (23:3). Because Job seeks personal vindication for his integrity rather than an intellectual solution to the riddle of theodicy, God replaces wisdom in Job's quest. But God, like wisdom, is hidden and impossible to "discern" directly (9:11). Job does not know how to "find" God or penetrate his dwelling place (23:3; cf. 28:12, 20). He cannot "discern" him in the West or "behold" him in the North, because [God], like wisdom, is hidden (23:8–9; cf. 28:21). In spite of his elusive ways and in spite of the "terror" of his presence which intimidate mortals (9:34; 13:21), Job wants to see God face to face to prove his innocence. God's "face" *(pānîm)* or presence is a pivotal theme in several of Job's speeches (especially chs. 13 and 23). Job wants to present his suit before God's "face" (13:35; 23:4), but God hides his "face" (13:24; cf. 23:9, 15, 17).

After Yahweh appears in the whirlwind and confronts Job with a barrage of challenge questions, Job admits:

> Indeed, I spoke without discernment,
> Of things beyond me, which I did not know. (42:3)

In this confession Job reluctantly agrees that he lacks the first-hand knowledge to understand Yahweh's primordial design. In short, he admits he does not possess wisdom. But that was not Job's primary objective. He wanted God to come out of hiding and face him in court. And God does, even if he does not formally acknowledge Job's innocence. Job can therefore declare:

> I have heard of you with my ears,
> But now I *see* you with my eyes. (42:5)

Job has "found" the God he sought to "see" (23:9). Thus Job may lack the wisdom which derives from a primordial knowledge of the principle governing Yahweh's design for the cosmos, but he gains a first-hand knowledge of God through the theophany of the whirlwind. He did not find wisdom, but he found God. That experience makes all other claims to knowledge relative. In the last analysis wisdom, as the principle which governs all other structures and principles of the world, is inaccessible to humans, but to heroic mortals like Job, God himself is not. Job sees God and survives!

24

Job's Asseveration of Innocence

Claus Westermann

The asseveration of innocence *(Unschuldsbeteuerung)* is a fixed form in the psalms of lamentation.[1] Under certain circumstances it can there take the place of the confession of sins. The friends demand of Job such a confession, but Job counters with his asseveration of innocence. This occurs in two acts. In the first, Job faces up to his friends and maintains his innocence. In 6:28–30 this asseveration stands totally within the context of the disputational discourse. Job attempts to convince his friends that he is not the transgressor his friends suspect him of being (despite God's blows against him). This attempt echoes once again in Job's fifth speech, which is to say in

1. Cf. Hermann Gunkel and Joachim Begrich, *Einleitung in die Psalmen* (Göttingen, 1933), p. 253.

From Claus Westermann, *The Structure of the Book of Job: A Form-Critical Analysis*, trans. Charles A. Muenchow (Philadelphia: Fortress, 1981), 97–99. Used by permission of Augsburg Fortress.

the last speech where there is disputational discourse between Job and the friends ("Know then that God has put me in the wrong!" [19:6]). However, none of this is actually asseveration of innocence; it is only a reflection of it. Already in his second speech Job turns to the higher court with an asseveration of innocence. And just as his lament at the beginning is no more than a cry (chap. 3), so here is the affirmation of his innocence no more than a single very short statement voiced to God: "I am blameless" (9:21).[2] But just a little further on this sentence gets transposed into its opposite: "I must indeed be guilty" (9:29).[3] The same thing occurs once again at 10:6, in the same speech. All these clauses from the second speech of Job stand in very close association with the accusation against God. The asseveration of innocence arises out of this other element, initially as the cry of one who has become conscious of his total alienation and despair. By the time of the third speech, however, the situation is different. Here a conclusion gets drawn out of the despairing cry:

> Behold, he will slay me; I have no hope;
> yet will I defend my ways to his face. (13:15; cf. vv. 18, 23)

What it comes down to is that already here, at the end of the first cycle of discourse, the resolve is formed which then gets carried out in chap. 31. In the second cycle of discourse, correspondingly, the asseveration of innocence does not appear as an independent form. The closest thing to it in this cycle is found in 16:17, which shows that Job still stands by his earlier asseveration.[4] The asseveration of innocence reappears in the third cycle of discourse, in Job's answer to the final speech of Eliphaz. Tying in directly and almost word-for-word with 13:5, it occurs in 23:7, 10, 12. In these verses the asseveration of innocence is firmly allied with the wish to stand in the presence of God, where one would be able to present one's case to him (23:2–6). The final speech of Job contains only these two motifs, followed by the accusation against God in 23:13–17. If one ignores for the moment the fragments in chaps. 24–27, then the final speech of Job is followed, after the intervening section comprised of chap. 28, by the large concluding lament in chs. 29–31. Within the fragments, the element of asseveration of innocence occurs only in 27:2–6. These verses have the character of a solemn new point of emphasis, one can even say of an actual introduction. However, the theme here finds no continuation; various fragments following 27:7ff. It has often been noted, on the other hand, how remarkably abruptly the oath of clearance starts out in chap. 31. Houtsma, among others, has suspected that the beginning of chap.

2. The expression *tom 'āni* most likely stems from juristic speech.

3. [Westermann's reading of the text's אנכי ארשע differs slightly from the RSV at this point.—Trans.]

4. On 19:6 see above.

31 is to be found in 27:2–6.[5] This is certainly the case. We can here add two more relevant arguments: (1) In 23:7, 10–12 the asseveration of innocence is conjoined with the accusation against God; the one passes over into the other. The final and definitive appearance of the element of asseveration of innocence in chap. 31 then follows upon the element of accusation. (2) We saw that the asseveration of innocence encompassed two acts: over against the friends—over against God. Now Job, who since the utterance of Eliphaz in chap. 22 had no longer addressed the friends, turns to them one more time right at the end; 27:5 is Job's only rebuttal of the accusation of Eliphaz in chap. 22. From now on, however, with his oath of clearance, Job has nothing more to do with the friends; from here on he deals only with God. All this is not really apparent when one reads 27:2–6 in its present position, but it is readily apparent if these words introduce the concluding speech of Job, namely, his oath of clearance in chap. 31.

It was shown above that the asseveration of innocence, where it occurs in the speeches of Job, corresponds to the asseveration of innocence as found in the psalms of lamentation. Job's oath of clearance in chap. 31 is no more than a development of the same process, which therefore certainly has a cultic background.[6]

Chapter 31 contains only two themes: asseveration of innocence (vv. 1–34, 38–40) and wish (vv. 35–37). The conclusion, vv. 35–37, is certainly a summoning of God in terms of its content; in terms of its form, however, it remains a wish. Here we find a precise correspondence to the beginning of chap. 23, which is the final speech of Job: it begins with the same wish (vv. 2–6), which then passes over into the asseveration of innocence (vv. 7, 10–12). Hence the situation looks like this:

Beginning (chap. 23): The wish to stand before God, together with an asseveration of innocence;

End (chap. 31): An asseveration of innocence, together with the wish to stand before God.

5. Martijn Theodoor Houtsma, *Das Buch Hiob*, Textkritische Studien zum Alten Testament 1 (Leiden, 1925), p. 61.

6. On the religiohistorical background of this "negative confession," cf. Paul Humbert, *Recherches sur les sources égyptiennes de la littérature sapientale d'Israel*, Mémoires de l'Université de Neuchâtel 7 (Neuchâtel, 1929); cf. also Curt Kuhl, "Neuere Literarkritik des Buches Hiob," *Theologische Rundschau*, N. F. 21 (1953): 293.

25

The Legal Metaphor in Job 31

Michael Brennan Dick

Recent studies on the legal pattern in the Book of Job attest to the importance of this metaphor for a full appreciation of the book's theology.[1] However, "legal language" itself does not constitute a distinct literary form,[2] for the juridical sphere encompasses a broad area of human life and does not correspond to a specific situation *(Sitz im Leben)*. Therefore, if

1. Besides the older study of H. Richter, *Studien zu Hiob* (Theologische Arbeiten 11; Berlin: Evangelische Verlagsanstalt, 1959), see the dissertations of S. H. Scholnick, "Lawsuit Drama in the Book of Job" (unpub. Ph.D. Dissertation, Brandies University, 1975); G. Many, "Der Rechtsstreit mit Gott (Rîb) im Hiobbuch" (Diss. Kath.-theol. Fakultät der Ludwig-Maximilian Universität, Munich, 1970); M. B. Dick, "Job 31: A Form-critical Study" (unpub. Ph.D. Dissertation, The Johns Hopkins University, 1977); also see J. J. M. Roberts, "Job's Summons to Yahweh: The Exploitation of a Legal Metaphor," *Restoration Quarterly* 16 (1973) 159-165.

2. See H. W. Hoffman, "Form—Funktion—Intention," *ZAW* 82 (1970) 342.

From Michael Brennan Dick, "The Legal Metaphor in Job 31," *Catholic Biblical Quarterly* 41 (January 1979): 37–50. Used by permission of the *Catholic Biblical Quarterly*.

we are to accurately understand the use and function of this metaphor in Job, we first must establish the legal jurisdiction involved *(jus civile* or *jus gentium*) and then proceed to clarify the exact situation alluded to in the book. The success of recent research on legal language in the prophets highlights the importance of a similar examination in Job. Our knowledge of the prophets has been considerably aided by identifying their use of juridical language as an instance of international *rîb* which arises out of the alleged failure of one party of a treaty to honor its stipulations.[3]

I propose Job 31:35 as the key to the legal metaphor in Job. An examination of biblical and extra-biblical legal documents establishes v 35 as a defendant's official appeal before a third party for a civil hearing at which the judge would compel the plaintiff to formalize his accusations and to present any supporting evidence. As we shall see, this request was ordinarily made only after all attempts at informal arbitration had been exhausted and was often accompanied by a sworn statement of innocence. In Job 31 the oath of innocence[4] has been expanded to embrace the entire chapter.[5]

Job as Defendant

In order to support this thesis, I shall first examine the legal relationship between Job and Eloah. Although many exegetes see Job as the plaintiff and God as the defendant in their *rîb*,[6] the matter is somewht more complicated, as many of the above scholars would concede.[7] We should be quite cautious in sharply delineating the roles of plaintiff and defendant, for ancient documents are often unclear in distinguishing these relationships,[8] and a too rigid imposition of this modern distinction might be anachronistic.[9] Nonetheless it

3. See J. Harvey, *Le Plaidoyer prophétique contre Israël apres la rupture de l'alliance* (Studia travaux de recherche 22; Montreal: Les Editions Bellarmin, 1967).

4. See F. Horst, "Der Eid im Alten Testament" *Gottes Recht: Gesammelte Studien zum Recht im Alten Testament* (Munich: Chr. Kaiser, 1961) 292–314; R. Press, "Das ordal im alten Israel," *ZAW* 10 (1933) 121–140, 227–225. Many of the legal oaths in the OT (e.g. Num. 5:12–28) take place within the trial itself; in Job 31, however, the oath is invoked in order to summon the trial or judicial procedure.

5. For a more detailed study of the oath in Job 31, see the author's dissertation "Job 31: A Form-critical Study", chapter 4.

6. J. J. Stamm, "Die Theodizee in Babylon und Israel," *JEOL* 9 (1944) 104; B. Gemser, "The Rib-or Controversy-Pattern in Hebrew Mentality," VTSup 3 (1955) 135; H. Richter, *Studien zu Hiob,* 71, 73.

7. H. Richter, ibid., 73: "Job knows also . . . that he has been judged by God, that God has a legal case against him." S. H. Scholnick, "Lawsuit Drama," 171 n. 120: "But Job uses the oath [chapter 31] as a defense measure since he feels that God's accusation of offense is implicit in the punishment he has been experiencing."

8. J. G. Lautner, *Die richterliche Entscheidung und die Streibeendigung im altbabylonischen Prozessrechte* (Leipziger rechtwissenschaftliche Studien 3; Leipzig: Theodor Weicher, 1922) 1.

9. H. J. Boecker, *Redeformen des Rechtslebens im alten Testament* (WMANT 14; Neukirchen-Vluyn: Neukirchener Verlag, 1964) 48 n. 1; H. Richter, *Studien zu Hiob,* 20 n. 25.

is germane to establish that in accordance with Ancient Near Eastern principles God appears to initiate the charges and Job seems to be the defendant. Job's request for a writ of particulars implies that he is the victim of a prior juridical action: "How many are my offenses and sins? Tell me my crime and my sin" (13:23).[10] God has afflicted Job with a series of catastrophes because he has apparently been found guilty of sin the nature of which Job does not know. Like Mr. K. in Kafka's *The Trial,* Job remains on the defensive throughout the book, no matter how loudly he asserts his innocence (19:17; 23:11; 27:5–6).

This analysis is corroborated by an examination of Near Eastern hamartiology exemplified in the Akkadian "lament of the individual." Sickness implied guilt even as early as the Third Dynasty of Ur;[11] however, the belief that suffering revealed the sinfulness of the victim was an especially prevalent theologoumenon in Cassite (1400–1200 B.C.) Mesopotamia.[12]

> O my Lord, my wrong-doings are many, great are my sins.
> God in the rage of his heart has confronted me;
> The Goddess has become angry with me and made me ill.[13]

> A terrible disease has weakened my entire body; a terrible illness is afflicting me. For a known and unknown sin—because I was disrespectful, because I sinned, was careless, committed misdeeds—I became fearful and afraid and I brought my life before your great divinity.[14]

10. Cf. J. A. Craig, *Assyrian and Babylonian Religious Texts* (Assyriologische Bibliothek 13; 2 vols.; Leipzig: J. C. Hinrichs, 1895–1897) II 9:3 mi-na-a e-pu-uš-ma še-ir-tam na-šu-ku "What have I done that I bear (this) punishment?" For a similar question asked in a legal context, cf. H. F. Lutz, *Selected Sumerian and Babylonian Texts* (University of Penn. Museum Publications [PBS], 1/2; Philadelphia: University Museum, 1919) no. 73. In this letter from the Cassite era, Ninibašarid has been accused of wrongdoing, but he proclaims his innocence (37–38) by addressing a question to his accuser which is similar to Job's: mi-na-a ḫi-ṭa ah-ti be-li-ia "What offense have I committed against my lord (4; cf. 29)?"

11. W. G. Lambert, *Babylonian Wisdom Literature* (Oxford: Clarendon Press, 1960) 11–12 (abbreviated *BWL*).

12. H. Vorländer, *Mein Gott: Die Verstellungen vom persönlichen Gott im Alten Orient und im Alten Testament* (AOAT 23; Neukirchen-Vluyn: Neukirchener Verlag, 1975) 99.

13. S. Langdon, *Babylonian Penitential Psalms* (Oxford Editions of Cuneiform Texts [OECT], VI; Paris: Librairie Orientaliste Paul Geuthner, 1927) 41:37, 51, 53 for the transliterated text; however, in line 51 I have read: i-lim(sic!) ina uz-zi lib-bi-šu ú-sam!-ḫi-ra-an-ni. The cuneiform text is found in H. C. Rawlinson, *The Cuneiform Inscriptions of Western Asia* (2nd ed.; London: British Museum, 1891) IV 10.

14. E. Ebeling, *Die Akkadische Gebetsserie "Handerhebung"* (Deutsche Akademie der Wissenschaften zu Berlin Institut für Orientforschung 20; Berlin: Akademie-Verlag, 1953) 8:7–12. This explanation for sickness is both geographically and temporally extensive. Such thinking persisted into NT times (John 9:2). Geographically, Mursilis's Plague Prayer (*ANET* 394–396) reveals a similar theology for the Hittite kingdom. In Homer's Iliad, Apollo inflicts a destructive plague on the Achaeans because they committed sacrilege by dishonoring his priest Chryses (*Il.* 1:11–52). For further Greek references, see *TDNT* IV (1967) 1092–1098.

More pointedly there are even Mesopotamian texts which describe in the language of the court man's suffering as a legal judgment of guilt:

> [31] . . . di-nu^{lu}GIG śa DIB-an-ni ana di-ni kàm-sa-ku
> [32] [di-nu di-in EŠ-BAR-]a-a KUD-[us]

> In the (legal) cause of the illness which has seized me, I am lying on my knees for judgment, Judge my cause, give a decision for me.[15]

This causal relationship between sin and illness can be equally documented in the OT:

> Thy indignation has left no part of my body unscarred; there is no health in my whole frame because of my sin. For my iniquities have poured over my head; they are a load heavier than I can bear (Ps 38:3–4).

The theological etiology for human suffering was not restricted to an individual's lamentation, for sin could also explain a national catastrophe (Isa. 1:4–6). The identical theologoumenon could even be expressed conditionally (Exod. 15:26). In short, the ancient Israelite clearly recognized the punishing hand of God at work in human sickness, which was then considered an instance of the doctrine of retribution.[16]

Job's astonishment and indignation in 14:12–17 presuppose the nexus between human suffering and divine judgment. Job's losses and his repeated request for a writ of *habeas corpus* demonstrate that the man from Uz considers himself the victim of a previous, if unaccountable, juridical action. Job is the accused, the defendant. This evaluation is expressly supported by Eliphaz in 22:4:

> Is it for your religiosity that he accuses you? Enters into litigation with you?

Job's lamentable state then is evidence that God has initiated legal action against him.[17]

15. E. Ebeling, *Keilschrifttexte aus Assur religiösen Inhalts* [KAR] (Wissenschaftliche Veröffentlichungen der Deutschen Orient-Gesellschaft 28; Leipzig: J. C. Hinrich, 1919) 184 obv. This text has been reproduced by F. Köcher, *Die babylonisch-assyrische Medizin in Texten und Untersuchungen* (4 vol.; Berlin: de Gruyter, 1971) IV n. 323. My translation is from B. Gemser, "The Rib," VTSup 3 (1955) 127 n. 1; A. Falkenstein and W. von Soden, *Sumerische und akkadische Hymnen und Gebete* (Die Bibliothek der Alten Welt; Zürich: Artemis, 1953) 400: "Shamash is asked [in KAR 184] to revise his earlier judgment which has resulted in the sickness."

16. H. Gunkel, *Einleitung in die Psalmen* (2d ed.; Göttingen: Vandenhoeck und Ruprecht, 1967) 190–191.

17. Job's insistence on his innocence implies that God has misjudged him—a conclusion to which the three friends are sensitive (8:3). Job's defense against Eloah's judgment contains an indictment against God: In virtue of his defense Job becomes a plaintiff! This role exchange can

The Defendant in Ancient Near Eastern Civil Law

To understand the recourse open to a defendant, we should first acquire a familiarity with the pre-trial and trial procedures in Ancient Near Eastern civil law. For this I have found it helpful to begin with Akkadian legal documents, since—with a single exception—we have no contemporary Hebrew law records. I shall next examine two biblical passages (I Sam. 24:10–16, 18 and Gen. 44:3–12) whose importance lies in their being links between the *prima facie* Mesopotamian legal evidence and the literary Job 31. Although the two texts from 1 Samuel and Genesis are not juridical documents *sensu stricto*, they do reveal that the options open to the defendant in the OT are quite similar to those isolated in the cuneiform records.

The Defendant in Mesopotamian Civil Law

When a suit arose *(ragāmu, baqāru)* in Mesopotamia, a trial was usually preceded by attempts at arbitration between the plaintiff and the accused. This preliminary stage at times involved more than verbal disputation, as can be assumed by the terminology involved: the plaintiff was often said "to seize *(ṣabātu)*" or "to bind *(esēru)*" the defendant.[18]

If no private settlement could be achieved by the litigants, they would then be forced to go before the magistrate(s) *(dayyāni kašādu, alāku, sanāqu)*. Such legal recourse could be initiated by either the plaintiff or the defendant, who would be especially inclined to seek a public trial if he had been taken into actual custody *(ṣabātu)* by his accuser (cf. CT VI 8 in n. 18). The committee of judges would study the case *(awātam amāru)*, examine the documents *(kanikū)* presented and interrogate the witnesses *(šibu)* adduced. The procedure could result either in compromise *(magāru)* or judgment *(purussâm parāsu)*. This latter decision was either a demand for evidence in the absence of which the matter was to be considered settled (Lautner's *Beweisurteil*),[19] or a specific adjudication (Lautner's *Leistungsurteil*).[20] Scholars dispute the authority of this judicial decision. J. G. Lautner maintained that the judges functioned merely as arbiters *(Schiedsrichter)* and their

be illustrated by the use of *ḥāmās*, "crime" in the speeches of Job. (On the legal use of *ḥāmās*, see H. J. Boecker, *Redeformen*, 6.) In 16:17 Job declares himself innocent of the charge of *ḥāmās*, this verse presupposes that Job functions as a defendant (cf. Scholnick, "Lawsuit Drama," 11, 14). Job's innocence of *ḥāmās*, implies that the same charge could be leveled against Eloah: "I made a charge 'Lawlessness (*ḥāmās*,)', but I am not answered. I press charges, but there is no litigation (19:7)." (Cf. Scholnick, "Lawsuit Drama," 201, 203, 206.) It should be noted that such a counterchange is implicit in many legal defenses.

18. See T. G. Pinches, *Cuneiform Texts from the Babylonian Tablets in the British Museum* [CT] (London: British Museum, 1898), VI 8:11–14. By the Old Babylonian period, this vocabulary of coercion was largely symbolic, a holdover from an earlier practice. Legal language is frequently conservative. On the use of *ṣabātu* and *esēru*, see Lautner, *Die richterliche Entscheidung*, 12–13.

19. E.g. CT II 9:7–10.

20. E.g. CT II 39:9–12.

judgment *(purussû)* was only a "recommended settlement *(Streitbeendigungsvorschlag)*." Accordingly unless the parties swore to accept this decision and to forego further litigation *(ṭuppu lā ragāmi)*[21] there was no binding legal resolution.[22]

Since I maintain that Job 31 employs the literary fiction of a defendant's formal appeal to a judge for a trial, the transition from private dispute to public judicial hearing warrants further scrutiny. Inability to reach a private settlement in the suit *(rugummû)* could induce either party to request a civil trial.

In the following Old Assyrian text the defendant Pušukēn has petitioned the *Kârum* at Kaniš to appoint a judicial board to settle his dispute with his accuser Aššur-malik:

> Thus says Pušukēn (the defendant) to Aššur-malik (the plaintiff): "For ten days you have constantly [GTN of *ragāmu*) brought charges against me concerning the 5 mines of silver. Come and bring your charges about what I owe you to a court of law."[23]

If the defendant made the appeal, his request was often accompanied by a declaration of innocence. This procedure is especially clear in the following Assyrian legal text:

> To Upri (plaintiff), speak! Thus says Gazru (the judge): "Aššur-bêl-apli (defendant) has petitioned me: 'I am neither a bad debtor nor a criminal, yet he (Upri) has made accusations against me.' To my face you (Upri) stated: 'I have not made an accusation!' What you have accused will not remain unsettled by you. Either give up your accusation against him (Aššur-bêl-apli), or if you do not give up the accusation against him, then come and bring along your witnesses and whatever is necessary for your case. Make your charges during your trial."[24]

The defendant Aššur-bêl-apli petitions the judge Gazru for a hearing in his case with Upri, his accuser. Aššur-bêl-apli's statement of innocence has apparently been successful in bringing about a judicial hearing; Upri is now

21. The *ṭuppu lā ragāmi* is equivalent to the Aramaic *separ mirḥaq;* it is also probably alluded to in Ugaritic RS 1957. 702 Rev. *al ydd mt mrzḥ wyrgm l šmmn* (L. R. Fisher, ed., *The Claremont Ras Shamra Tablets* [*AnOr* 48; Rome: Pontifical Biblical Press, 1971] 37–44). On the *ṭuppu lā ragāmi* see R. A. Veenker, "An Old Babylonian Legal Procedure for Appeal," *HUCA* 45 (1974) 1–15.

22. On the various opinions about the binding force of the judgment rendered, see Veenker, "Babylonian Legal Procedure," 4n. 14.

23. A. T. Clay, *Letters and Transactions from Cappadocia* [BIN] (Babylonian Inscriptions in the Collection of James B. Nies; New Haven: Yale University Press, 1927) IV 107:3–9; G. Eisser and J. Lewy, *Die altassyrischen Rechtsurkunden vom Kültepe* (MVAG 33; Leipzig: J. C. Hinrich, 1930) 248–249.

24. O. Schroeder, *Keilschrifttexte aus Assur verschiedenen Inhalts* [KAV] (WVDOG 35; Leipzig: J. C. Hinrich, 1920) 201.

required to submit witnesses and all relevant documents, if he wishes to prosecute his allegation.

A civil process *(dinu)* could be initiated not only by such statements of innocence as found in KAV 201 but also by written documents and by oaths.

> 11. ù DI-KU$_5$-E-NE Larsam^{ki} im-ḫu-ur-ma
> 12. ka-ni-ik ši-ma-tim ša a-bi-šu
> 13. ú-kal-al-li-im-ma
> He went before the judges of Larsa and presented his father's bill of sale.[25]
> 12. a-na KA tup-pa-a-ti-ši-na
> 13. di-nam ú-ša-ḫi-zu-ši-na-ti-ma
> On account of the content of their documents, they granted them a trial.[26]

At times Mesopotamian records establish that if evidence (such as the declaration in KAV 201:6–7) were to initiate a trial, it must first be certified by an oath. PBS 5:100, a case involving the *inspectio ventris* of Roman law,[27] demonstrates the importance of fortifying appeal evidence with an oath. In this document one set of litigants insists that the testimony of witnesses submitted in this trial appeal be certified by an oath:

> 33. i-na-an-na ši-bu i-na ni-iš DINGIR
> 34. li-bi-ir-ru-šu . . .
> (The defendants said) Now let the witnesses establish it with a divine oath.

Only after requiring the oath of the witnesses (Col. II) did the judges hear this case. This example also illustrates that the party making the appeal could make evidential demands of his opponent when requesting the public hearing.

This pattern was not confined to Mesopotamia and is attested in the Yabneh-Yam legal ostracon (KAV § 200) from the seventh century (ca. 625 B.C.).[28] The anonymous petitioner has apparently been accused by the agent of the commander *(haššār)* of neglecting his periodic corvée labor;[29] the agent Hošiah ben Šobay has impounded the defendant's[30] cloak *(bgd)* as a penalty of surety. This ostracon is a written appeal for an official adjudication

25. V. Scheil, "Notules" *RA* 14 (1917) 95–96.

26. CT 48:8; see Veenker, "Babylonian Legal Procedure," 5–6, 6 n. 23.

27. M. Schorr, "Ein Anwendungsfall der *inspectio ventris* im altbabylonischen Rechte," *WZKM* 29 (1915) 74–96.

28. For a bibliography, J. C. L. Gibson, *Textbook of Syrian Semitic Inscriptions*, vol. 1: *Hebrew and Moabite Inscriptions* (Oxford: Clarendon Press, 1971) 28. There is also extrinsic evidence of the legal nature of this ostracon, for it was found at the city gate, the ancient Near Eastern site of legal proceedings.

29. F. M. Cross, Jr., "Epigraphic Notes on Hebrew Documents of the Eighth-Sixth Centuries B.C.: II. The Murabbaʿat Papyrus and the Letter found near Yabneh-Yam," *BASOR* 165 (1962) 45–46; S. Talmon, "The New Hebrew Letter from the Seventh Century B.C. in Historical Perspective," *BASOR* 176 (1964) 29–38.

30. Since the anonymous author has apparently not been the victim of theft, but rather stands accused of neglecting an obligation, he can rightly be called the defendant.

(12–14). The request of the accused, like its cuneiform counterpart, employs the testimony of witnesses:

> 10. wkl ʾḥy. yʿnw ly
> And all my brothers will testify for me.[31]

Likewise the defendant swears his innocence:

> 11. ʾmn[32] nqty mʾ
> 12. [šm[33]
> In truth I am free from any guilt.

The Defendant in the Old Testament

The legal procedures which we have just investigated in primary legal sources—Mesopotamian and Israelite—are also evidenced in OT literary texts. The two examples which follow both exploit the familiar pattern of the defendant's request for a civil proceeding. These two examples used by H. J. Boecker will enable us to make the transition from *prima facie* legal records to the metaphoric use of this legal device in Job 31.

1. 1 Sam. 24:10–16, 18.[34] In this pericope David is accused of plotting evil against King Saul (v. 10). The persecuted David seeks adjudication of the false allegations against him:

> yišpōṭ YHWH bênî ûbênekā . . . . wehayā YHWH
> lĕdayyān wešāpat bênî ûbênekā weyēreʾ weyārēb
> ʾet-rîbî wēyišpĕtēnî miyyādekā (vv. 13, 16)

> Let Yahweh be the judge between me and you. . . . Let Yahweh be the judge; he will decide between me and you. May he see this and take my part and grant me justice away from your hands.

31. See S. Talmon, "The New Hebrew Letter," *BASOR* 1764 (1964) 34.

32. The reading and understanding of *ʾmn* in line 11 are disputed. W. F. Albright, cited by F. Cross, "Epigraphic notes," 45 n. 49, suggests reading the *nun* as a diplography, thus *ʾm nqty* would be parallel to the reading *wʾm l* (line 12): "If I am innocent . . . if I am not . . ." Although Cross (ibid.) also reads *w ʾmʾ* in line 12, he maintains the written text in line 11 and reads *ʾmn* as "strengthening the petitioner's claim." J. C. L. Gibson (*Textbook,* 30) accepts *ʾmn* but divides the line differently and reads it with the preceding *yʿnw*: "bear witness that it was as I said." S. Talmon (pp. 34–35) compares *ʾmn* with the biblical *ʾomnâ/ʾomnām* rather than with the affirmative *ʾāmēn* (Cross and J. Naveh ["A Hebrew Letter from the Seventh Century B.C.," *IEJ* 10 (1960) 129–139]). Talmon finds a parallel in Josh 7:20 *ʾomnā ʾanokî haṭ aʾtî* "I swear that I have done wrong." On the use of *ʾmn* in oaths, see S. H. Blank, "The Curse, the Blasphemy, the Spell, the Oath," *HUCA* 23/1 (1950/1) 89 n. 53.

33. S. Talmon, "The Hebrew Letter," 35, would restore as follows: *ʾmn nqty mʾ [ltk* "I testify that I had discharged myself of what you had imposed on me." Cf. *ʾlh* in Gen. 24:41.

34. See H. J. Boecker, *Redeformen,* 47–48; J. Begrich, *Studien zu Deuterojesaja* (Theologische Bücherei 20; Munich: Kaiser, 1963) 27.

As motivation for this trial, David proclaims his innocence:

> kî ʾen bĕyādî rā ʿâ wāpešaʿ wēlōʾ-ḥāṭāʾ tî lāk (v. 12b)
> I am responsible for no evil nor offense and I have not rebelled against you.

David further adduces as material evidence the strip which he cut from the king's cloak in the cave (vv. 10–12).

2. Genesis 44:3–12.[35] Judah and his brothers have been accused of theft by the vizier of Egypt, their unrecognized brother Joseph. Although Jacob's sons do not explicitly request a hearing with a formula such as *yišpōṭ bên*, etc., the context makes it evident that they are in fact making an appeal.[36] In similarity with the oath of innocence in Job 31, the brothers express their request using a complete oath:[37]

> ʾăšer yimmāṣēʾ ʾittô mēʿabādekā wāmēt wĕgam-ʾănaḥnû nihyeh laʾdōnî la-ʿă bādîm (v. 9)
>
> If any of your servants is found to have (the goblet), he shall die, and as for the rest of us, we shall become my lord's slaves.

Chapter 31: Job's Trial Appeal

Job has become a defendant faced with Eloah's mysterious accusations. As seen previously, Job's disturbing new relationship with his God is expressed in the legal metaphor.[38] Arbitration seems excluded since Eloah is unreachable and the three friends misrepresent God (13:7–11). Job would prefer to confront Shaddai directly (23:4–5), but the inaccessibility of God precludes an out-of-court settlement.[39] Job is confident that if he could only face Eloah a reconciliation could be effected (13:15–16).

Following the structure described in the previous legal sources, either party could now appeal for the intervention of an arbiter who would preside over a public civil process.

35. See G. von Rad, *Genesis* (ATD 4; Göttingen: Vandenhoeck und Ruprecht, 1953) 343: "This passage (Gen. 44:3–12) has a strongly legal character." See also C. Westermann, *Die Joseph-Erzählung* (Calwer Predigthilfen 5; Stuttgart: 1966) 98; G. Liedke, *Gestalt und Bezeichnung alttestamentlicher Rechtssätze* (WMANT 39; Neukirchen-Vluyn: Neukirchener Verlag, 1971) 47 n. 7.

36. H. J. Boecker, *Redeformen*, 57.

37. In contrast to von Rad (*Genesis*, pp. 343–344), H. J. Boecker (*Redeformen*, p. 52) does not consider v 9 to be an oath.

38. S. H. Scholnick, "Lawsuit Drama," 107.

39. E. Ebeling cites a Middle Assyrian text which documents a similar difficulty in conducting a legal hearing when one of the parties makes himself inaccessible. "Drei gerichtliche Ladung aus Mittelassyrischer Zeit," *AFO* 1933 Max Freiherrn von Oppenheim Festschrift, 36.

Then make a plea and I shall be the respondent; or let me make a charge and you reply to me (13:22).[40]

Job's desire for a trial has been expressed in his wish in 9:33:

lûʾ[41] yēš-bênênû môkîaḥ yāšēt yādō ʿal-šĕnênû

If there were only a judge between us, someone who could lay his hand onš both of us.

The *ôkîaḥ* is the ancient Near Eastern judge *(Schiedsrichter)*. Unlike the modern magistrate who represents the state and functions with its authority, this arbiter could probably only suggest a settlement which possessed no authority unless one party swore the *ṭuppu lā ragāmi*.[42] That the hiphil of *YKḤ* describes this type of judicial arbitration is clear from Gen 31:37 *wĕyôkîḥû bên šĕnênû*, "And let them choose between us." Furthermore, a comparison between 1 Chr. 12:18 and Exod. 5:21 shows the parallelism between *šāpaṭ* and *yôkîaḥ*. The use of the term *môkîaḥ* places this metaphor within the domain of *jus civile*, as is supported by the position of this official *baššaʿar*, "at the gate" in Isa. 29:21 and Amos 5:10.[43]

Although either litigant could request that a judge preside over a trial, Eloah has not taken advantage of his prerogative but has remained silent:

ʾašawwaʿ ʾēlēkā wēlōʾ taʿănēnî ʿāmadtî wattitbōnen bî (30:20)

I cried to you, but you do not respond; I take a stand; but you look at me.[44]

In accordance with ancient civil law, there remained only one recourse for Job so frustrated by his aloof persecutor. Chapters 29–31 signal a new strategy. In these chapters Job recapitulates the internal dialectic of his earlier speeches by completely turning away from his friends to face his real *ʾîš rîb* "opponent," God. C. Westermann assigns these three chapters generally to the genre of the lamentation. Chapter 29 describes Job's former fortune—a feature most common in the "lament of the people"; chapter 30 is a more standard lamentation pattern. However, instead of completing this lamenation with the customary plea for help, the author of Job has altered the pattern so that it culminates in the trial request before a judge *(šōmēaʿ, môkîaḥ, gōʾēl)*.[45]

40. S. H. Scholnick, "Lawsuit Drama," 233.

41. MT *lōʾ* has been read here as *lûʾ* "would that" following the LXX and the Peshitta.

42. See Veenker, "Babylonian Legal Procedure," 4 n. 14.

43. This verb is also used in Isa. 2:4 and in a parallel passage in Micah 4:3, where it refers to Yahweh's judging the nations; however, Yahweh's activity here seems to be derived from the standard divine epithet as found in the Akkadian *dajjān kibrāti* "Universal Judge."

44. Cf. Scholnick, "Lawsuit Drama," 212, who translates *'ăšawwaʿ* "I press charges (against you)." The language in 30:20 is from the genre of the individual lamentation.

45. See G. Many, "Der Rechtsstreit," 230; C. Westermann, *Der Aufbau des Buches Hiob* (*BHT* 23; Tübingen; J. C. B. Mohr, 1956) 73.

The petition for a trial, as we have seen, included a declaration of innocence by the accused. Occasionally this took the form of an oath. However, the extensive exculpatory oath of Job 31 is particularly striking. The oath of clearance was a common juridical procedure in civil cases throughout the Near East from Babylon to Elephantine. Its widespread usage in Israel is implied by the reference in Solomon's temple prayer (1 Kgs. 8:30–32//2 Chr. 6:22–23).[46] In chapter 31 an extended version of this oath has dramatically replaced the shorter more prosaic statement of innocence. This chapter is particularly striking not only for its unparalleled length, but because the complete oath with an expressed self-imprecation is quite rare. S. H. Blank is correct in seeing this type of oath as an emphatic adjunct to Job's formal petition.[47]

At the end of chapter 31, Job makes his official plea:

mî yitten-lî šōmēaᶜ lî / hen-tāwî šadday yaᶜănēnî / wĕsēper kātab ᵓîš rîbî (v. 35)

If only I had someone to give me a hearing! / Here is my mark! Let Shaddai answer me! / Let my opponent write out an indictment.[48]

I interpret the participle *šōmēaᶜ* as the equivalent of the earlier desired *môkîaḥ*, the arbitration-judge.[49] The forensic use of *ŠMᶜ* to designate the activity of a judge is widespread in the Ancient Near East.[50] In cuneiform records *šēmû* can be used, as in Englsih, of "hearing a case":

dēnšu DI.KU, lā išammû[51]

The judges did not hear his case.

46. For a bibliography on the oath, cf. n. 4.

47. S. H. Blank, "An Effective Literary Device in Job XXXI," *JJS* 2 (1951) 105–107.

48. For a complete philological analysis of 31:35, see the author's Dissertation ("Job 31: A Form-critical Study"), 70–73. I have taken *kātab* as the perfect precative (cf. Peshitta *nktwb*); for a bibliography on this usage, see A. Blommerde, *Northwest Semitic Grammar and Job* (*BibOr* 22; Rome: Pontifical Biblical Institute, 1969) 17–18. Some scholars think that *kātab* in v. 35 refers to the Egyptian legal practice where the emphasis was on written charges (cf. Diodorus Siculus 1:75). However, legal ostraca such as that of yabneh-Yam have been found in Palestine. There are also references in Isa. 65:6a, Dan 7:10 and Ps. 149:9 to written court documents. We need not suppose that written indictments such as that requested by Job were peculiarly Egyptian. Cf. Z. W. Falk, "Hebrew Legal Terms," *JSS* 5 (1960) 351; A. Alt, "Eine neue Provinz des Keilschriftrechts" *Die Welt des Orients* (Munich: C. H. Beck, 1959) 1/2 78–92.

49. K. Budde, *Das Buch Hiob* (2d ed.; HKAT; Göttingen: Vandenhoeck und Ruprecht, 1913) 194; G. Many, "Der Rechtsstreit," 80.

50. See Scholnick, "Lawsuit Drama," 192 for a survey of the forensic use of *ŠMᶜ*; see also M. Weinfeld, *Deuteronomy and the Deuteronomic School* (Oxford: Clarendon, 1972) 245–246.

51. C. H. W. Johns, *Assyrian Deeds and Documents* (Cambridge: Cambridge University, 1898) 471 r. 13; M. Schorr, *Urkunden des altbabylonischen Zivil-und Prozessrechts* (Vorderasiatische Bibliothek 5; Leipzig: J. C. Hinrich, 1913) 280: 39 iš-mu-u.

The Ugaritic *šmᶜ rgm* reported in several personnel lists (2011:10, 2084:12, 171:3) are "hearer(s) of a case (cf. Akkadian *ragāmu*)." They are probably legal magistrates.[52] In Egyptian the verb *sḏm* "to hear" is the root of the noun *sḏmyw* "judges."[53]

The important juridical function of the *šōmēaʿ* became involved in the power struggle between King David and his ambitious son. Absalom warned those who had submitted lawsuits for adjudication:

> Your suit is good and just, but there is no one to hear you in the King's name (wĕšōmēaᶜ ʾên-lĕkā mēʾēt hammelek) . . . If only I could be appointed judge *(šōpēt)* in the land! Then everyone who has a lawsuit to be decided might come to me (2 Sam. 15:3–4 NAB translation).

It is clear from this passage that the *šōmēaʿ* was an official appointed by the king to mediate legal disputes.[54]

Job 31:35 seeks the assemblage of the tripartite judicial board necessary for the orderly adjudication of a defendant's complaint: defendant (Job), *ʾîš* (Shaddai) and the judge *(šōmēaʿ)*. Job's mention of his *tāw*[55] is admittedly troublesome, but it is probably semantically related to the defendant's presentation of documentation *(kanîkum, ṭuppum, kunukkum)* in the Mesopotamian appeal for a trial.[56] Job's request that his opponent *(ʾîš rîb)* produce a written account *(wĕsēper kātab)* corresponds to the similar demand in KAV 201:19–22 (cf. n. 24). "come and bring along your witnesses and whatever is necessary for your case." Job expresses his petition in the optative *(mî yitten-lî)*, possibly this hesitancy betrays his awareness of the incongruity of applying a civil law metaphor to his relationship with God. As in the prophetic *rîb*, God here is not only the plaintiff but also *judex in causa sua*.

The foregoing treatment establishes that Job 31 functions as the legal appeal of a defendant for a formal judicial hearing. In this way Job hopes that a judge *(šōmēaʿ)* will compel his accuser to present in writing his as yet unspecified charges. The author has shown characteristic artistic freedom in the use of this legal pattern. The petition itself appears as the final element of a lament

52. C. Gordon, *UT* Glossary §2441.

53. A Gardiner, *Egyptian Grammar* (3d ed.; London: Oxford University, 1964) 593.

54. C. F. Keil, *Die Bücher Samuels* (2d ed.; Bib. Commentar über das AT; Leipzig: Dörffling und Franke, 1875) 323: "*Šōmēaʿ* i.e. that judiciary official whose responsibility it was to receive those with complaints, to investigate their cases and to present them to the king for decision." W. Nowack, *Die Bücher Samuelis* (HKAT; Göttingen: Vandenhoeck und Ruprecht, 1902) 208: "In v. 3 *šmʿ* designates the official installed by the king to conduct inquests. . . . " See also G. Mendenhall, "Ancient Oriental and Biblical Law," *BA* 17 (1954) 45 n. 42; J. J. Finkelstein, "The Middle Assyrian Sulmanu-Texts," *JAOS* 72 (1952) 79.

55. Cf. Ezek 9:4, 6 where the *tāw* also functions as evidence of innocence; in Ezekiel as in Job, the *tāw* is written. For further discussion of the *tāw* in Job 31:35, cf. the author's Dissertation ("Job 31: A Form-critical Study"), 71–72.

56. See V. Scheil, "Notules," *RA* 14 (1917) 95: 12–13.

(chapters 29–30) and replaces the normal plea for help.[57] The expansion of the customary sworn statement/document of innocence usually accompanying appeals of this type has considerable force: in no more emphatic way could Eloah be made to justify himself. The theological implications of Job's appeal are reminiscent of the legal anomaly encountered in the prophetic *rîb.*

The Legal Metaphor in Job and the Prophets: *Ne Quis Judex in Propria Causa*

The Book of Exodus formulates Israel's rapport with Yahweh in the language of the international suzerainty treaty.[58] The prophets adopt the same legal metaphor, for they treat accusations of infidelity in accordance with the format of the international *(jus gentium)* dispute between a suzerain and his vassal.[59]

In the Near Eastern agreement, the deities invoked in the treaty guarantee the contracted relationship between lord and vassal. These gods would adjudicate any disputes. This procedure is evident from the beginning of Yarim-Lim's case against Tašub-Yaḫad:

> Let Shamash investigate my conduct and yours, let him judge (ù li-ša-ḫi-iz).[60]

Of course Israel's staunch monotheism necessitates compromise in the application of this metaphor derived from the *jus gentium,* for Yahweh was not only the suzerain in the treaty *(bĕrît),* but he was simultaneously the guarantor deity. Therefore in any dispute one of the litigants (whether defendant or plaintiff) would likewise turn out to be the ultimate judge.[61]

The Book of Job, as we have seen, also uses the legal metaphor in treating Job's relationship with Eloah; but the juridical language of Job differs from that of the prophets in that it arises from *jus civile* rather than from *jus gentium.* The pattern in Job, however, suffers from the same theological difficulty. Job seems fully aware that his unjust accuser is also his judge. Eloah's awkward dual legal role forms the basis of Job's plea in 10:2 "I will say to God 'Don't condemn me! Let me know your case against me.'" As S. H. Scholnick has correctly observed, in this passage Job requests that God function as an opponent and inform him of the charges rather than function as a judge who declares him guilty.[62] Similar sections such as 9:28 and 10:14–15

57. See H. Gunkel, *Einleitung,* 218–231.

58. See G. E. Mendenhall, "Ancient Oriental and Biblical Law," *BA* 17 (1954) 26–46; D. R. Hillers, *Covenant: The History of a Biblical Idea* (Baltimore: Johns Hopkins, 1969).

59. See J. Harvey, *Le plaidoyer prophétique.*

60. G. Dossin, "Une Lettre de Iarim-Lim, roi d'Alep, a lašub-Iaḫad, roi de Dîr," *Syria* 33 (1956) 66, lines 5–6.

61. Harvey, *Le plaidoyer prophétique,* 23.

62. Scholnick, "Lawsuit Drama," 136.

illustrate Job's dilemma in challenging an opponent who is also the ultimate arbiter. Job's pleas for a neutral party to hear his case[63] are all the more pitiful since Job himself appears to be aware of his legal impasse.

The disconsonant use of the legal idiom in Job 31:35 also serves a theological purpose, for it is the juridical metaphor which most forcefully communicates the thesis of the Book of Job that religious piety is not amenable to the *quid pro quo* principle of divine retribution.[64] From his tragedy Job concludes that Eloah has violated his rights. Since the Satan, Job, Eliphaz, Bildad, and Zophar have all conceived of religion as a relationship protected and stabilized by retributive justice, it is only logical that Job attempt to bring God into court in order to redress his supposed grievances. Ultimately Job can only summon Eloah before this same God, who is thus both judge and plaintiff. This incongruity reduces the legal metaphor to the absurd and thereby reveals the bankruptcy of conceiving the man-God relationship along the lines of legal justice.

63. Job 9:33, 16:19, 19:25, 31:35.
64. See M. Tsevat, "The Meaning of the Book of Job," *HUCA* 37 (1966) 73–106.

26

JOB 31

Edwin M. Good

Job gets a good press for this part of his speech. Gordis calls it "the code of a man of honor" and emphasizes that Job declares his freedom from fourteen sins—twice seven, an important symbolic if not magical number.[1] The implied ethical system indeed seems impressive by our standards, involving not merely external actions but also inner attitudes and principles of ethical thinking. Several recent studies concentrate on the legal implications of the chapter, some referring to the disclaimers that the dead Egyptian king makes in the Book of the Dead in order to gain entrance to his full destiny, others discussing the analogy of Job's oaths to the oath of innocence that an accused person takes in court.[2]

1. Gordis, *Book of Job*, p. 339. I count not fourteen but fifteen curses, and I think that vv. 19–20 have one curse rather than two. The matter can be argued.

2. See, e.g., Dick, "Oath" and "Legal Metaphor"; and Roberts, "Job's Summons." For a different view of this matter, see Holbert, "Rehabilitation."

From Edwin M. Good, *In Turns of Tempest: A Reading of Job* (Stanford: Stanford University Press, 1990), 309–18. Used by permission of the publishers, Stanford University Press.

We have seen before that Job wants a trial to establish his innocence, and the notion of an oath of clearance prior to the judge's appearance and the trial procedure would seem to make very good sense. His rehearsals of his own administration of justice in chap. 29 point in the same direction. Yet we had reason earlier to wonder whether he might have dropped the idea. Especially 27:7–23 suggested that Job had given up all hope of a trial that acknowledged his real character, and 30:20 almost proposed that a trial had already in effect taken place, in an atmosphere that was not conducive to justice.

> I cry out to you, and you don't answer me,
> I stand (silent), and you examine me.

In chap. 9, Job had already written off the trial as a waste of energy:

> If I'm innocent, my own mouth condemns me;
> if I'm perfect, he'll do me fraud. (v. 20)
>
> I'll be condemned—
> why do I struggle with the breeze?
> If I wash myself with snow water,
> purify my palms with lye,
> then you'll plunge me into the muck,
> and my clothes will make me disgusting. (vv. 29–31)

He had changed his mind in the interim:

> How long! I'll take my flesh in my teeth,
> grasp my throat with my hand.
> He's going to kill me; I cannot wait,
> but I must argue my ways to his face. (13:14–15)

He was ready to start the procedure right then, though he asked [God] for some safeguards (vv. 20–21):

> Call, and I will answer,
> or I will speak, and you respond to me. (v. 22)

Later he advised the friends:

> Fear for your lives before the sword,
> for the sword is fury on wrongdoing,
> so that you may know that there is a trial. (19:29)

And in chap. 23 he reached the high point of his conviction that, if the trial could be fair and he could maintain his position, he would be vindicated in it.

I would know the words of his answer,
understand what he says to me.
Would he prosecute me by an attorney?
No, he himself would attend to me.
There a moral person could argue with him,
and I should bring forth my case successfully. (vv. 5–7)

But the redefinitions in chap. 27 seemed, like much of chaps. 29–30, to render the notion of a trial quite impossible. If [God] had become Job's vicious enemy, then by definition the trial would be unjust, and Job could hope only for death (30:23), as he had done much earlier (6:8–10).

Yet now it seems that Job makes the final preparations for the trial, if indeed this series of curses upon himself is an oath of innocence, a response to a charge, implicit or explicit, that inaugurates the legal procedure he wishes. Four kinds of expressions are mixed up together in this chapter: questions, rhetorical and ordinary (e.g., vv. 11–12, 28, 30, 32); an exclamation (v. 35); and curses (e.g., vv. 5, 7–8, 9–10, 13). There are two kinds of curses: (1) eleven (or twelve, depending on how we read vv. 19–20) are the kind of "if (not)" curses without result clauses that we have seen again and again through out the book; (2) unusually, four are "if (not)" curses with result clauses:

If my step has strayed from the way,
my heart has gone after my eyes,
a stain has stuck to my palms,
may I sow and another eat,
and my descendants be uprooted. (vv. 7–8)

If my heart has been fooled over a woman,
and at my neighbor's door I have lain in wait,
may my woman grind for another,
others kneel over her. (vv. 9–10)

If I have shaken my fist at the orphan
because I saw my helpers in the gate,
may my arm fall from my shoulder,
my forearm be broken at the elbow. (vv. 21–22)

If my ground cries against me,
its furrows weep together,
if I have eaten its strength without silver,
made its Baals gasp,
instead of wheat may thorns come up,
instead of barley, stinkweed. (vv. 38–40)

It is structurally interesting that these four curses are spread out through the chapter: the first two are the second and third curses in the chapter, the third is the seventh (or eighth, if vv. 19–20 are two curses), and the last is the fifteenth and last curse. It is also structurally interesting that the curses with result clauses are always preceded by curses without result clauses, though a statement (v. 6) intervenes between the first pair (vv. 7–10) and the preceding curse (v. 5). Other structurally interesting points about the chapter may be shown in this outline:

1. Questions: retribution (vv. 1–4; 8 lines)
2. Curses and statements (vv. 5–12; 17 lines)
   a. Curse without result: fraud (v. 5)
   b. Statement: integrity (v. 6)
   c. Curse with result: impurity (vv. 7–8)
   d. Curse with result: adultery (vv. 9–10)
   e. Statement with ***kī***, "for": crimes (vv. 11–12)
3. Curses, questions, and statement (vv. 13–18; 13 lines)
   a. Curse without result: justice for slaves (v. 13)
   b Questions: [God] and common origin (vv. 14–15)
   c. Curse without result: aloofness (vv. 16–17)
   d. Statement with ***kī:*** care for the poor (v. 18)
4. Curses and statement (vv. 19–23; 10 lines)
   a. Curse without result: clothing for the poor (vv. 19–20)
   b. Curse with result: fairness (vv. 21–22)
   c. Statement with ***kī:*** fear of disaster (v. 23)
5. Curses and statement (vv. 24–28; 10 lines)
   a. Curse without result: wealth (v. 24)
   b. Curse without result: power (v. 25)
   c. Curse without result: idolatry (vv. 26–27)
   d. Statement with ***kī:*** crimes (v. 28)
6. Curses and statements (vv. 29–34; 13 lines)
   a. Curse without result: arrogance (v. 29)
   b. Statement: curse (v. 30)
   c. Curse without result: food (v. 31)
   d. Statement: hospitality (v. 32)
   e. Curse without result: hypocrisy (with ***kî;*** vv. 33–34)
7. Statement and curses (vv. 35–40; 13 lines)
   a. Statement (exclamation): challenge to trial (v. 35)
   b. Curse without result: pride (vv. 36–37)
   c. Curse with result: soil (vv. 38–40)[3]

3. By far the most sensible account of the structure of this chapter is Habel's (*Book of Job*, pp. 427–31). I disagree with him in detail only, but some of the detail forces a quite different perception of structure. For example, in the interest of a most intriguing, symmetrical outer frame (A: covenant and curse, vv. 1–3; B: challenge, vv. 4–6; C: catalog of crimes, vv. 7–34; B1: challenge, vv. 35–37; A1: covenant witness and curse, vv. 38–40), Habel associates v. 4 not with the ques-

The structure is not symmetrical, though sections 3–6 with their chiastic structure of thirteen, ten, ten, and thirteen lines almost are. The occurrence of the particle *kî* ("for, because") with the statements at the ends of sections 2–5 and in the oath that closes section 6 is the most compelling clue to the architecture of the speech for me. Nevertheless, the design is a way by which we may more efficiently see what Job is saying. It allows us to see, for example, how the poem moves from the steps in verse 4 to the walking and hurrying in verse 5, and how the steps in verse 4 are matched by numbering steps in verse 37. The threat of "disaster" in verse 3 is matched by the fear of "disaster" in verse 23. Such linkages between sections (see, e.g., "eyes," vv. 1, 7; "orphan," vv. 17, 21; "fist" [*yad,* "hand"], v. 21, and "hand," vv. 25, 27, "rejoice," vv. 5, 29) show that the speech is not mere words flung into the air or onto the page, but structured, carefully calculated thought.

Not surprisingly, the thought is complex and self-serving. Job is ill-inclined to take his pain in silence, and here he engages in the most forthright defense of his life and value system. He would surely accept Gordis's tag, "the code of a man of honor." From the cultic covenant of verse 1 to the covenant with his agricultural land in verse 38–40,[4] he ranges over the sins he has not committed and the attitudes he has had. I need not list the vices avoided and the virtues cultivated. The curses that Job calls down upon himself "if" he has done such crimes as fraud (v. 5), idolatry (vv. 26–27), adultery (vv. 9–10), overbearing arrogance in the presence of assistants (vv. 21–22), and senseless exploitation of the soil (vv. 38–40) are matched by statements of assurance that [God] knows his integrity (the familiar *tummah,* v. 6), that certain crimes are notoriously actionable (vv. 11, 28), that he has refrained from loose cursing (v. 30), and that he has hospitably opened his doors (v. 32). He wishes disaster on himself not only for overt actions like withholding food from the starving (vv. 16–17) but also for inward attitudes: despising the justice due to the slave (v. 13), depending on wealth and power (vv. 24–25), being pleased ("stirred," *ʿrr,* "emotionally moved") at an enemy's misfortune (v. 29), and concealing himself because of fear of someone else's displeasure (vv. 33–34).

The claims fall for us on appreciative ears. These are sins we take seriously, attitudes we wish inwardly to avoid. Through its whole ethical history, our culture has taught us to avoid precisely these deeds and these thoughts. The principles Job espouses are those we are enjoined to have, those we accept as "right," even if viewed through eyes that a heart has followed into impurity (v. 7). Job depicts himself as the epitome of the ethical man, as he depicted

tions of vv. 1–3 but with vv. 5–6, partly because the word *saʿad* ("step") occurs both in v. 4b and in v. 37a. I do not think that balance is enough to justify the pursuit of so rigid a symmetry as Habel finds. I see structural uses of the particle *kî,* "for, because," that suggest a division of the whole that is almost too close to symmnetry, especially in the light of an often-noticed tendency in Hebrew poetry to skew structures that threaten to become symmetrical.

4. Habel, *Book of Job*, pp. 427–28, 440.

himself in chap. 29 as the epitome of the successful leader. Both inwardly and outwardly, this speech lends credence to the first characterization of the man we saw: *tam w'yašar*, "scrupulously moral" (1:1, 8; 2:3). The narrator said it, [God] said it, Job himself has claimed it in passing before. Now he describes in detail just what it means, both in outward act and inward thought, to be *tam w'yašar*.

The chapter has another side, however. The series of curses is, after all, designed to prepare the ground for Job's trial with [God]. The litigant claims in this remarkable speech attention from his adversary. And he claims it in the strongest possible way. The frequent use of the term "oath of clearance" by scholars may mask that,[5] because scholars are prone, as I have complained before, to take the self-curse as more or less equivalent to a strong denial or affirmation and to deal with these statements as affirmations and denials, not as self-curses. Our culture does not know what to do with curses, because we do not believe in their magical efficacy. No such disability informed ancient Hebrew culture. A curse was not a casual expression, to be trifled with or tossed aside. It was the most powerful way people had of setting in train forces of action and reaction, and no one would take a curse lightly. I have argued that the curse is a way of forcing [God] to respond, requiring his attention, because the curse cannot go unattended.[6] It will work ineluctably through to its end result, and [God] himself is under its sway. Habel calls this series of oaths "a barbed provocation."[7] His only error is that the words are too weak.

The most common form of the curse is "If A (or not A)—" without specifying the result the curser calls down upon himself. That was the form of the Prosecutor's self-curse in 1:11: "If he does not curse you to your face—." The Prosecutor left unspoken the terrible result for himself in that event and we saw no catastrophe, though we see nothing further of the Prosecutor after chap. 2. This kind of curse is present in eleven of the fifteen curses in chap. 31 (vv. 5, 13, 16–17, 19–20, 24, 25, 26–27, 29, 31, 33–34, 36–37). In each case Job implies some disaster for himself.

In four of the curses (vv. 7–8, 9–10, 21–22, and 38–40), Job specifies the disaster. The result in verse 22 exceeds the evil from which Job wishes to clear himself.

> If I have shaken my fist [*yad*, hand] at the orphan
> because I saw my helpers in the gate,
> may my arm fall from my shoulder,
> my forearm be broken at the elbow. (vv. 21–22)

5. See works cited in n. 2; Fohrer, "Righteous Man"; and Janzen, *Job*, pp. 210–13.

6. See my "Job and the Literary Task."

7. Habel, *Book of Job*, p. 431. Janzen's similar but milder metaphor of the "prick of conscience" (*Job*, pp. 210–12) strikes me as even weaker, especially because it seems to find in this chapter nothing more than Job's reflection on himself. Janzen specifically objects to the language of coercion I used in "Job and the Literary Task."

For raising his hand, Job calls down the fracture of his arm. In each case, the result is correlated with the evil. In verses 38–40, the evil is exploitation of the soil, and the result is that the soil will grow inedible produce. But the other two curses with result clauses are very curious. In verses 7–8, the result of Job's hypothetical straying from the "way" or his having an impure stain on his palm is the producer's loss of consumption ("may I sow and another eat"), a penalty presumably upon himself, and the "uprooting" of his descendants, a penalty on those involved only by association. To be sure, the law allows the penalty for a person's crime to fall upon that person's descendants (Exod. 20:5), but Job opposed that idea in 21:19–20.

Even more shocking is 31:9–10, where Job's possible adulterous behavior will issue in the bondage of his "woman," who becomes the slave of "another" (singular) and the sexual toy of "others" (plural). The retribution for his sexual misdeeds, if any, is to fall not upon himself but upon her! For a speech full of high-flown ethical principles, this one falls with a crash to earth. Significantly, I find no commentator who sees in verses 9–10 cause to criticize the ethical honor of the hero. Slaves are promised far better treatment than Job's "woman." Such oppressiveness is quite enough decisively to undercut the consistent picture of "honor" that interpreters see in chap. 31.

Pondering the Prosecutor's self-curses in chaps. 1–2, I found them crucial to the situation of Job's suffering. In fact, they brought that suffering about by putting the Prosecutor at hazard of disaster. Now, having begun the dialogue by cursing his birthday (3:3–10), Job ends it with this catalog of fifteen curses upon himself.[8] One might wonder whether one or two would have been enough to accomplish what Job wished. Perhaps the provocation of fifteen curses is a blunt rather than a barbed instrument. At any rate, Job puts the heat on [God] in a way that matches the heat the Prosecutor applied in the first two chapters.

Not only does Job specifically call out for a trial:

> Oh that I had someone to hear me—
> here is my mark; let Shaddai answer me—
> and the inscription my accuser has written! (31:35)

8. Gordis (*Book of Job*, pp. 542–43) claims not that there are fourteen curses, but that Job affirms freedom from fourteen separate sins. I am as interested in the structure of curse combined with statement and question as I am in the ethical content, and I suspect that the structure of fifteen curses combined with eight statements and two groups of questions (totaling, if I count them correctly, six questions) efficiently masks the fourteen sins for readers. I would also quibble with Gordis over reading vv. 1–2 as having to do with lust (I think that the "virgin" refers to the goddess Anat, hence that the sin is false worship, the same sin as in vv. 26–27) and over combining vv. 24–25 into a single sin, where I read "trusting" in gold (v. 24) and "rejoicing" over power (v. 25) as two different bad attitudes.

The "hearer" is no doubt a "hearing officer" in the legal sense. Job puts his signature, his *taw* (we would say his X), on the claim for a trial, and the very word may echo *tummah*, his "integrity" (v. 6b). The accuser's "inscription" is somewhat confusing,[9] in that the sentence appears to imply that Job does not have the "inscription" and wishes he did have it. Carrying on a hypothetical cross-examination (13:23), he had demanded information about his faults but had no satisfaction of it.[10] Now he proceeds to another self-curse. Translators are at one in rendering 31:36–37 as strong statements, but they have the familiar "If I do not" form:

> If I do not carry it [*sc.*, the inscription] on my shoulder,
> tie it on me like a wreath,
> the number of my steps imprint upon him,
> like a prince approach him—

Job reverts to the same kind of royal language that he used at the end of chap. 29, though he used "leader" *(nagîd)* for his subordinates in 29:10a. But he emphasizes the word here by the nice wordplay in the verb "imprint," *'aggîdenû*. This curse calls attention to his determination to deal with [God] as an equal. An element of comedy is also present. Job, "the disheveled victim arising from his ashes to parade with his 'paper crown,'"[11] is a parody of his arrogant parading to his seat of justice in 29:7–10, flaunting as a badge of honor or a crown of glory both the hypothetical document, which he does not possess, and his own self-assurance. Job will "inform" *('aggîd)* [God] of the count of his steps, which [God] has long been not only tracking (cf. 13:27) but "numbering" (31:4).

The provocation is barbed, to be sure, but it is greater than that. It includes an element of sarcasm as well as of irony, of comic parody as well as of serious argument. And as an overwhelming series of curses upon himself, it puts Job's future (and, as vv. 7–10 show, the futures of others) absolutely on the line.

The remaining factor in this speech, most surprising of all, is perhaps most clearly seen at the very beginning:

> What is Eloah's portion from above,
> Shaddai's inheritance from on high?
> Is it not disaster for the vicious,
> calamity for evildoers?
> Does he not see my ways,
> number all my steps? (vv. 2–4)

9. See Gehman, "*Sēper.*" *Sēper* is often translated "book," which is anachronistic. Perhaps "document" is our closest equivalent.

10. Habel (*Book of Job*, pp. 231,438) reads 13:23 as demanding a "bill of particulars," implying a written indictment.

11. Ibid., p. 439.

Verse 4 denies that Job qualifies for the "inheritance" from Shaddai that verse 3 describes as applying to the "vicious." That "portion" and "inheritance" (*ḥēleq* and *naḥᵃlah*, respectively) are what Job described in 27:13 as the "portion" and "inheritance" from El and Shaddai for the wicked. There Job was redefining terms to mean their opposites, and "vicious" was his reversal word for [God] himself in 27:7. Here, we have two simultaneous possibilities. If "vicious" in 31:3a has the same referent as the word has in 27:7 (it is singular in both places), Job now claims that the logical outcome of [God's] own bequeathing is disaster for [God] himself. There is a catastrophic inconsistency within [God's] single front.

But 31:4 also seems to distinguish Job from the "vicious" and the "evildoers" of verse 3, and that seems consistent with the following series of self-curses, designed to assert the hero's high moral stature. On the other hand, if verse 3 is aimed at the destruction of the deity, the curses sound like a kind of self-immolation by the hero, who takes to flaunting his goodness before an evil and doomed god.

If, however, Job distinguishes himself from the malefactors of verse 3, he has returned to conventional reference. The series of curses demonstrates that he has been the very model of the ethical man, the assiduous follower of all the rules and the attitudes that the ancient Hebrew super-ego inculcated. In that case, Job has dropped back to the full retributionist position, has departed the depth of his despair about receiving a fair trial (chap. 23) and the savage redefinition of terms that in chap. 27 portrayed him as [God's] moral superior. Now he trots out the standard terms of reward and punishment to which he so furiously objected when the friends enunciated them. The other meaning, consistent with chap. 27, is certainly present, but it stays beneath the surface, as an ominous subtext. Retributionism is now the heart on Job's sleeve.

His assurance about the trial rests on his certainty that he *deserves* reinstatement and acquittal, precisely because he is free of all the actions and attitudes from which he so vigorously dissociates himself in this chapter. The man of honor (except for the lapse in vv. 9–10) demands his due, will wear the claim to the contrary as proudly as a prince wears a crown. It is an astounding reversion to a position it seemed Job had definitively left, especially as he first defined the objects of [God's] favor as the wicked in chap. 21, then accounted for [God's] avoidance of a trial for him by his own excellence in chap. 23, began in chap. 24 to show the divine power as arbitrarily whimsical, admitted its tremendous scope in chap. 26, and finally defined it as evil and vicious in chap. 27. Accounting for the sudden reversal here is difficult. Perhaps it is an effect of the nostalgic recollection in chap. 29 of his "autumn days," when everything was nice for him, if not for others. Perhaps Job has been so enraptured by his self-portrait in power and influence, in contrast to his present debility, as to want to recapture not only the circumstances of social authority but also what he recollects were their grounds and ground rules. He got where chap. 29 showed him to be by attention to [God's] rules, and if he wishes to get there again, perhaps he must resume obedience to those rules.

Surely we can understand the wistful longing for those good days. Especially does it show up in the interlocking conclusions of the three parts of this summation speech. Job proudly remembered his royal authority and his function as "a happy person who consoles mourners" (*ᵃbēlîm*, 29:25c). By contrast, his present hapless state is one where

> my lyre has become mourning *['ē bel]*,
> my flute a weeping *[bōkîm]* voice. (30:31)

Now his last self-curse in the interests of reinstatement denies that his actions have caused his "ground" (*ᵃdamah;* cf. *'adam*, 31:33a) to cry out or its furrows to "weep" (*yibbayūn*, 31:38). He has moved from consoling mourners through mourning and weeping to denying weeping.

The narrator has the last word: "Job's words were spent" (*tammū*, v. 40c). They were finished (the verb's surface meaning), completed, used up; they were perfected, in a connotation corresponding to Job's own *tummah,* his integrity, her perfection *(tam)*. But they are none of those. Job will have more to say, twice; he has not arrived at his final stance yet; and he has at least one, perhaps two, important changes yet to make.

A question remains to the reader: what will come next? No matter that we have already read the book and know. To read carefully is to read as if one did not know, to read along the book's own line, watching it unfold, letting it disclose our disguise itself. What now? Surely Job has come to the end of his rope, has said everything he has to say, has spent his entire psychic and intellectual capital. He has made as thorough and effective a challenge to [God] as he could. The Prosecutor's curses upon himself brought an immediate response and activity with Job, and we must expect the same of Job's curses. There *must* be some divine response. Will it be a trial? A rational dialogue? A denunciation? A show of threatening force? A frontal attack? At one time or another in the discussion with the friends, Job has wished for or expected each of these. Informed by the background of the dialogue, the reader must think of some response. That [God] would remain silent is surely impossible. That anything but his direct entry on the scene must come next seems highly unlikely.

27

The Speeches of Elihu

Édouard Dhorme

From ch. 32 a new person appears on the scene. Nothing has prepared us for his intervention. A short prose prologue explains why he has so far remained silent (32:1–5). But since he was not introduced to us in the narrative which opens the book, we were not concerned with his attitude. His genealogy, country, and family are given, whilst for the three friends of Job it was felt to be sufficient to give their country. Elihu is a young man and has listened patiently while old age speaks. But his impetuosity can no longer be restrained, and he will speak so much that neither Job nor his three friends will have an opportunity of saying a word. The speeches of Elihu will be monologues. The formula of introduction repeats the name of his father and country: Elihu, the son of Barachel the Buzite, is to speak.

We are given a long exordium, to explain how Elihu has been waiting for these old men to display their wisdom (32:6–7), and how his expectation has been disappointed, for it is the spirit in man and not the age which renders

From Édouard Dhorme, *A Commentary on the Book of Job*, trans. Harold Knight (1926; reprint, London: Thomas Nelson & Sons, 1967), liv–lvii. Used by permission of Thomas Nelson Publishers.

him wise and intelligent (32:8–13). Elihu will take care not to follow the method of the aged, since it has resulted only in their confusion, and Job has reduced them to silence (32:14–15). Elihu has done his duty by listening; he will now do it by talking (32:16–17). Furthermore, he can no longer remain silent; too many ideas crowd upon his brain (32:18–20). He will have no regard for any one whomsoever (32:21–2).

He begins by directly apostrophising Job, with whom he proposes to enter on a discussion (33:1–5). There is nothing to fear since the argument is between two men, not between a man and God (33:6, 4, 7).

Elihu then sums up the contention of Job: I am innocent and yet God persecutes me (33:8–11)! Such is the position which Job has clung to throughout the debate. Further, Job has complained because God does not answer him (33:12–13). It is this second complaint which will first be dealt with. The former will be the object of ch. 34.

God does speak, and it is for man to hear Him when He does (33:14). Sometimes it is in dreams and apparitions (33:15–16), so that man may be delivered from pride and death (33:17–18); sometimes by pain and illness which are the gates of death (33:19–22). It is an angel who plays the part of intermediary between God and the sufferer, and of intercessor with God on behalf of the sufferer (33:23–4), to save him. The effect of this intervention is healing, return to grace, joy, salvation (33:25–8). The action of God, in these various aspects, has as its aim and effect to save man from death (33:29–30).

After this first theory, Elihu demands the attention of Job and even invites him to speak (33:31–3). But it is now Job who adopts the role of listener in silence. Elihu turns to the friends and proposes to them a serious examination of what Job has said (34:2–4). The first point to be attacked (33:8–11) has as its corollary the injustice of God, since God is persecuting an innocent man (34:5–6). This is an impious and untenable thesis (34:7–8), since it is tantamount to saying that there is no advantage in serving God (34:9).

This is precisely the opposite of the truth. God is supremely righteous. He renders to each according to his works; it is impossible for Him to act unjustly (34:10–12). And, in fact, it is God to whom the world belongs, it is He who must govern it, He who is above kings, noblemen, princes, and the rich; how could He exercise justice if He were not Himself just (34:13–20)?

God is supremely righteous. Besides, He knows all things, nothing escapes Him (34:21, 22, 25). He has no need to make investigations or appointments (34:23–4); He chastises as He pleases those who have become estranged from Him and have oppressed their neighbour (34:26–8). He intervenes in the life of societies as in that of individuals, for His justice is independent of all (34:29–30). The passage which follows, and of which the text is corrupt, seems to confront Job with a case of conscience and to throw on him the onus of a reply, so that his ignorance may be exposed to all (34:31–3). Elihu triumphs (34:34–5). But he wishes to pursue his examination and silence Job, for he cannot suffer that he does not admit his fault and speaks against God (34:36–7).

The concatenation of ideas in ch. 35 is somewhat difficult to grasp, and it will be necessary to make constant reference to the Commentary on each verse. This is how we think it possible to understand the thought of Elihu.

A new grievance against Job is his having claimed that his fault was of no consequence to God (35:2–3; cf. 7:20). Doubtless, replies Elihu, God is too exalted for us to be able to reach Him either in bad fortune or good, by our faults or by our righteousness (35:4–7). But there is man, and it is our brother man who is either profited or harmed by our conduct (35:8).

Job had complained of the excess of violence and of the fact that God paid no attention to the cries of the oppressed (24:12). Elihu takes up this idea, of which he is reminded at this point by his observation that man harms his fellow-man (35:9). If God fails to intervene, it is because the unfortunate utter vain cries without turning directly to God, the Creator and Governor of all things (35:10–13). Still more justifiably will God refrain from replaying if man refers to Him by remarks such as Job has uttered and which have been heard by all (35:14–16).

Once again Elihu calls for attention. He insists on his veracity and his knowledge (36:2–4). This time it is a long dogmatic and historic exposition to which he subjects Job. God is great and righteous, rendering to each man according to his works (36:5–7). He takes an example drawn from the history of Judah. Kings have been placed on the throne by God, but the only result is that they become proud (36:7). They are then punished with captivity and affliction (36:8). God reveals to them their sin (36:9, 10). The guilty man is faced with the alternative either of being converted and thus attaining salvation (36:11), or else of refusing to hearken and that means death without more ado (36:12). Some remain insensible in the face of misfortune; only death can punish them (36:13–14). In brief, misfortune is an instrument in the hands of God to save the guilty (36:15). Job may therefore hope that his misfortunes will result not in his ruin but in his happiness and glory (36:16–17). In that case he should be careful to avoid a further lapse (36:18–21).

And now Elihu abandons his harsh reasonings on the case of Job. He rises to a more exalted plane, and soars on the wings of doxology. He will make the sublimity of God apparent (36:22). God is above all things: man can only sing His praises and contemplate His works (36:23–5). God is not to be measured by time (36:26). He is the author of all meteoric phenomena: rain, storm, snow, showers, cold, ice, lightning, and thunderbolts. These phenomena are described, with more or less detail, but with a somewhat high-flown poetic style, in 36:27–37:13. Elihu draws Job's attention more especially to certain extraordinary facts such as the lightning, the balancing of the clouds, the heat (37:14–18). He interrupts the flow of his eloquence in order to declare that there is no more to be said in the presence of these wonders (37:19–20). But suddenly, as though a storm had occurred during his speech, he stresses the action of the wind which has just swept the clouds away (37:21–2). The conclusion is that God is not within our reach: He is Eloah, Shaddai, the Almighty, by reason of His power and righteousness; He must be feared and reverenced; He has no accounts to render us (37:22–4).

The striking feature of this long monologue of Elihu is that it is conceived with a subtlety to which the three friends of Job had not accustomed us. The latter had confined themselves to the essential point of the thesis: the relation between virtue and happiness, as between sin and misfortune. Elihu tries to discover the meaning of sorrow and trial; he explains the various ways in which the divine justice may manifest itself; he shows how in societies this justice, which is sometimes so little apparent, does in fact operate, and he concludes with an exalted treatise on the action of God in the world of nature. He envisages the case of Job only to a very secondary degree, although quite often he addresses the hero, even by his name. His thesis is the summing up of a whole body of theological teaching the sources of which it will be easy for us to recognise.

28

The Meaning of *Mišpāṭ (Justice)* in the Book of Job

Sylvia Huberman Scholnick

Central to an understanding of the Book of Job is the meaning of divine justice.[1] A look at the author's use of the word for justice, *mišpāṭ,* shows that the definition changes during the course of the work and through these changes he is able to dramatize Job's search for the meaning of justice. The poet presents two dimensions of the word: the juridical and the

1. The most recent discussion of the meaning of divine justice in Job is that of John Briggs Curtis in "On Job's Response to Yahweh," *JBL* 98 (1979) 498–511.

From Sylvia Huberman Scholnick, "The Meaning of *Mišpāṭ* in the Book of Job," *Journal of Biblical Literature* 101 (1982): 521–29. Used by permission of the *Journal of Biblical Literature.*

executive. Job and his friends draw their definitions from the sphere of the court, while God understands it as executive sovereignty, the prerogative of the ruler. Much of the tension of the drama grows out of this difference in understanding of justice.

Job and his friends view his loss of health, family and wealth as punishment from God the Judge for some unspecified offense. Knowing nothing he has done to warrant such a severe sentence, Job demands litigation with God as plaintiff to charge him formally with specific offenses or as defendant to answer the charge of unlawful seizure of Job's property. Justice for Job, then, is the equitable resolution through formal judicial proceedings of his case with God.[2] Yahweh's appearance before the hero and his friends signals his acceptance of the challenge for litigation. But in his testimony, rather than pressing charges or presenting a defense, God focuses on the more fundamental question of the nature of divine justice. Excluding any mention of man's system of justice through litigation, he speaks instead of his own authority over the universe, which he labels *mišpāṭ* in 40:8. His concern for Job is expressed through teaching him that justice goes beyond the human legal system to include a system of divine kingship. The hero's response to God's speech is an acceptance of divine power (42:2) with the resultant retraction of his lawsuit (42:6).

Because of the rich tradition of the ancient Semitic root *špṭ/ṯpṭ*, the poet is able to use *mišpāṭ* in Job in two distinct ways, as jurisprudence and sovereignty. Contained within this single root are two ideas which in the English language are distinct: judging and ruling. Clear examples of the judicial meaning are its usage in Hammurabi's Code 81–90, which speaks of *a-šar ši-ip-ṭi-im,* "the place of sentence," and in the Ugaritic Epics of Aqhat (3 Aqhat 5:8) and Keret (127:33, 34), where the noun and verb are used forensically in the context of the judicial duties of the king who sits at the gate to hear and settle disputes. On the other hand, the administrative meaning of the root is particularly interesting in the Ugaritic equivalent of *mišpāṭ*, *mṯpṭ*, which means "dominion," when used in parallel with *mlkk*, "kingship."

> I yhp. ksa. mlkk
> yṯbr. ht. mṯpṭ
>
> Overturn thy throne of kingship.
> Break thy staff of dominion (49: VI:29).

2. M. B. Dick in "Legal Metaphor in Job 31" (*CBQ* 41 [1979] 37–50) presents the thesis that Job 31:35 is a key to understanding the legal metaphor in the book. Dick sees this verse as an official appeal by Job the defendant for a hearing where God the plaintiff in the civil case would be compelled by a judge to press charges formally and to present evidence. For a full discussion of Job's lawsuit with God, see my *Lawsuit Drama in the Book of Job* (dissertation, Brandeis, 1975).

In the Biblical Hebrew root *špṭ*, these ideas of judging and ruling continue side by side, although the juridical usage gains dominance. The noun *mišpāṭ* in a forensic context is used in a wide range of meanings: place of judgment (as in Isa. 28:6); procedure by which a dispute is settled, namely litigation (as in Deut. 17:8); case (as in Num. 27:5) or claim (as in 2 Sam. 15:4) presented in court; trial or arguing of a case (as in Num. 35:12); and finally, sentence (as in Jer. 49:12). There are several usages which develop from the forensic meaning of *mišpāṭ:* legal procedure (as in Num. 27:11); codification of legal practice (as in Exod. 21:1); and proper conduct, that is, how a person ought to behave so that if challenged in court he would be found innocent (as in Prov. 2:9).

While the majority of occurrences of the root *špṭ* in the Hebrew Bible fall into the forensic category, there are many that refer to governance. The best example of the administrative use of *mišpāṭ* is found in 1 Samuel 8 as evidenced by its use with the verb *mlk*. In answer to the people's request for a king, God instructs Samuel to tell them the prerogatives of such a ruler: "Tell them the jurisdiction of the king *(mišpāṭ hammelek)* who will be ruler over them" (1 Sam. 8:9). In v. 11 the *mišpāṭ hammelek* is defined by what his royal power allows him to do in order to rule his people, including drafting men for an army, taking servants from among the people, and appropriating property.

The author of Job draws on this twofold usage of the root *špṭ/ṯpṭ* when he uses the word *mišpāṭ* to explore the nature of justice. He dramatizes Job's process of education from his preoccupation with justice as forensic to his discovery that in the divine realm it refers to Yahweh's executive authority. This Hebrew word is so important in Job that it is used from the first speech of Bildad (8:3) to the long speech of God (40:8) by every character with the single exception of Zophar. *Mišpāṭ* is used in the juridical category by Eliphaz (22:4) and Elihu (34:12) as "divine judgment" through a system of moral recompense; by Job (9:19, 32; 14:3; 19:7) and Elihu (32:9) as "litigation" in man's court of law; and by Job (13:18; 23:4; 27:2; 31:13) and Elihu (34:4, 5, 6; 35:2) as "case." It is used in the executive category by God (40:8) as a term for divine governance of the world.

Job appeals to God for an understanding of the nature of divine justice: how can a just deity punish an innocent human being? The hero's challenge to God to justify the suffering of the innocent echoes the earlier biblical intercession of Abraham, who asks God about the justice of killing the upright with the guilty when he destroys Sodom and Gomorrah: *hašōpēṭ kāl-'āreṣ lō' ya'ăśeh mišpāṭ* "Shall not the Judge of all the earth deal justly?" (Gen. 18:25). In the Genesis story, God agrees to save the blameless from death, but in the prologue of Job, Yahweh permits Satan to test the depth of the hero's integrity by depriving him first of his property and family, then of his health and physical well-being. The decision is an executive, not a judicial one. Job's insistence in the drama on his innocence is justified. Not only does God praise the exemplary hero in the prologue as "a blameless and upright man who fears God and shuns evil!" (1:8), but acknowledges in the epilogue the truth of his statements (42:8). Job's error is believing that man's fate is entirely the result of God's judicial decisions. The author of the book is trying to expand the understanding of the nature of God to include a realization that He is King of the universe. Yahweh's decisions may reflect His use of sovereign authority, removing the property and family of a subject as he deems necessary for the smooth operation of his realm, something which is clearly within the jurisdiction of a human king, according to 1 Samuel 8. The prologue enables the reader to understand that God is acting as Ruler to test His subject, not as Judge to punish him for wrongdoing.

The three friends, Eliphaz, Bildad and Zophar, express the conventional philosophy that God, acting as supreme Judge, rewards the innocent and punishes the guilty. When they see the tremendous loss Job has suffered, these men immediately assume that the hero has committed a commensurate offense. Eliphaz defines this system of divine retribution in 4:7–8 and Bildad provides the identifying label, *mišpāṭ,* which may be translated simply "justice," *ha'ēl ye'awwēt mišpāṭ wĕ'im-šadday yĕ'awwēt ṣedeq* "Will God pervert justice? / Will the Almighty distort the right?" (8:3). An example of the systems operation is given in the verse immediately following, *'im-bāne(y)kā ḥāṭ'û-lô wayĕšallĕḥēm bĕyad-piš'ām* "If your children sinned against him, / He paid them for their sin" (8:4). So great is their faith in this system of divine justice that these friends feel no obligation to find substantiating evidence of Job's wrongdoing before assuming his guilt. As far as they are concerned, the hero's misfortune is proof enough that he has lost his case before God the Judge. However, when Job insists on his innocence, Eliphaz concocts an undocumented bill of particulars against his tormented friend (22:6–9). The only consolation these three offer is the possibility of a return to God's favor through proper conduct, as for example Bildad advises in 8:5–6.

Job shares the belief that he is being punished by God, yet he knows of nothing he has done to deserve the severe verdict and sentence. In chapter 9, Job expresses his frustration that God has found him guilty without providing the opportunity for testimony. In the system of moral recompense, there is no court of appeal for the accused who believes he is innocent and unjustly punished. A new direction in his thinking is seen in 9:32: *kî-lō'-'îš kāmōnî'e'ĕnennû nābô' yaḥdāw bammišpāṭ,* "He is not a man, like me, whom I could challenge (by saying), 'Let us enter litigation together.'" Job recognizes that unlike settling a dispute with another human being, a conflict with God is not justifiable. *Bô' bĕmišpāṭ* is an idiom which literally means "go to the place of judgment," but here, as in Ps. 143:2, should be translated "enter litigation." In contrast to the occurrence in Psalm 143 where man appears before God the Judge, Job speaks in 9:32 of the impossibility of legal proceedings against Yahweh as an equal adversary, emphasized by the adverb *yaḥdāw*, "together." Job has definitely begun to consider the advisability of adjudication with Yahweh.

It is not surprising that Job should think of litigation when he is in a conflict situation. He is portrayed as a prominent figure in the judicial assembly of his community who takes pride in legal settlement of disputes (15:17; 29:12; 31:21). As his crisis intensifies, Job is desperate to see justice done and turns to the only process he knows to accomplish his goal, a lawsuit. What at first had seemed to him an impossibility now becomes a necessity: entering litigation with God whom he identifies as his opponent in 13:3. *Hinnē-nāʾ ʿarakti mišpāṭ yādaʿtî kî-ʿănî ʾeṣdāq*, "See, now, I have prepared a case. / I know I will be acquitted" (13:18). The idiom *ʿārāk mišpāṭ* which Job uses here and in 23:4 means "prepare a case." That *mišpāṭ* may be translated "case" is clear from its use in Num. 27:5 and its use without a pronoun in 2 Sam. 15:4. While *dbr* and the hiphʿil of *qrb* are more common in the idiom "prepare a case," the author of Job prefers *ʿrk* as does the psalmist in 50:21.[3]

Job takes the unprecedented step of initiating legal proceedings against Yahweh, but the results are not immediately rewarding. God does not appear at once for the adjudication of the case. *Hēn ʾeṣʿaq ḥāmās wĕlōʾ ʾĕʿāneh ʾăšawwaʿ wĕʾên mišpāṭ*, "I make a charge 'Lawlessness,' but I am not answered. / I press charges, but there is no litigation" (19:7). *Mišpāṭ* is found in parallel construction with the niphʿal of *ʿnh* which in a forensic context refers to finding a response from an opponent in court.[4] As in Num. 35:12, *mišpāṭ* here refers to proceedings in court. It is interesting to note that in this verse Job mentions the offense with which he is charging Yahweh: *ḥāmās*, a technical term for wrongdoing in Exod. 23:1 and Deut. 19:6. The use of the word in Prov. 4:17 suggests that *ḥāmās* refers to what is gained by illegal means. Job may well use this term to charge God with unlawful seizure of his property. But even with a formal charge against him, Yahweh fails to respond immediately.

As Elihu answers Job and his friends, his pivotal role in the drama becomes clear. He uses the word *mišpāṭ* as a juridical term in three different ways: like Job as "litigation" (32:9) and "case" (34:4, 5, 6; 35:2), and like the friends as "moral recompense" (34:12). He also prepares the reader for God's use of

3. *ʾrk* is considered by B. Gemser in "The Rib- or Controversy-Pattern in Hebrew Mentality" (in *Wisdom in Israel and in the Ancient Near East* [ed. M. Noth and D. Winton Thomas; VTSup 3; Leiden: Brill, 1955] 123) and Donald A. McKenzie in "Judicial Proceedings at the Town Gate" (*VT* 14 [1964] 102) as meaning "to lay the case before the assembly of judges, as witnesses and adversaries," to use Gemser's words. In Ps. 50:21, *ʾrk* is used without an object with the meaning being forensic: "confront with charges" (NJPS). The verb in Ps. 50:21 is parallel to *ykḥ*.

4. BDB 773, #3. McKenzie (p. 102) cites as the meaning of *ʿnh* in Exod. 20:16 and 23:2 "to bear witness." S. R. Driver and G. B. Gray (*A Critical and Exegetical Commentary on the Book of Job Together With A New Translation* [ICC; New York: Scribner's, 1921] 60) discussing Job 9:16 and E. Dhorme (*A Commentary on the Book of Job* [London: Nelson, 1967] 135) discussing 9:32 and 15:6 recognize that *ʿnh* has a forensic meaning.

the word in 40:8 as an executive rather than a judicial term when he speaks in 37:23 of justice and power as attributes of Yahweh. The three friends had refused to consider Job's lawsuit against God as justiciable, but Elihu eagerly weighs the merits of the case.

kî-'ōzen millîn tibḥan wĕḥēk yit'am le'ĕkōl
mišpāṭ nibḥărāh[5] *lānû nēdʿāh*[6] *bênênû mah-ṭôb*[7]

For the ear tests arguments
As the palate tastes food.
Let us examine a case for ourselves.
Let us know among us what is defensible (34:3–4).

Men must judge the words of a *mišpāṭ,* "a case," in a way that the ear and palate evaluate sensory experience. Elihu encourages those assembled to consider the case before them. He quotes key points in Job's testimony: 27:3 quoted in 34:5, 16:17 in 34:6[8] and either 6:29 or 13:18 in 35:2.

Elihu's response to Job's case is that God cannot be held accountable in a human court of law. He echoes Job's forensic vocabulary, using the idiom *hlk bammišpāṭ* in 34:23 as Job uses the comparable *bw' bammišpāṭ* in 9:32 and 14:13. *kî lō' ʿal-'îš yāśîm 'ôd*[9] *lahălōk 'el-'ēl bammišpāṭ,* "For He sets no man a date to enter into litigation with God" (34:23). For Elihu a calendar and a

5. *bḥr* can be seen to refer to the evaluation of people in Tg. Jer. where in 6:27, 12:3, 17:10 and 20:12 it is given as the equivalent of Hebrew *bḥn*.

6. The verb *yḏʿ* is used with the sense "to judge" here as in 2 Sam. 19:36 where Barzillai says: *ha'ēdaʿbên-tôb lᵉrāʿ,* "Can I judge between right and wrong?" Herbert B. Huffmon has written an informative article or the term *ydʿ* called "Treaty Background of Hebrew *YADAʿ*" (*BASOR* 181 [1966] 31–37) where he points out that "'Know' may be used as a technical term for (legal) recognition in international treaties and related texts." He cites (on p. 37) passages from the Hebrew Bible such as Dan. 11:32 where *ydʿ* means in a legal sense "acknowledge, recognize (authority, claims)." Gemser (p. 124) concludes that this verb has a forensic usage in Jer. 29:23, indicating knowledge of ear- and eye-witnesses.

7. An example of *ṭôb* meaning "defensible" is found in a prose passage, 2 Sam. 15:3, in a phrase "defensible cases." The term *ṭôb* is found in Job 13:9 where it may be translated "defensible," referring to the action of the friends showing bias for God in litigation, an action whose defensibility Job questions.

8. *'akazzēb* in 34:6 is problematical. Many translators follow the G which has *yĕkazzēb,* "he lies," referring to God lying about Job. It is thought that the original text might have been changed from *yĕkazzēb* to *'akazzēb* to avoid making a blasphemous statement. N. H. Tur-Sinai (*The Book of Job, A New Commentary* [rev. ed.; Jerusalem: Kiryath Sepher, 1967] 477) offers an attractive solution, emending the text from *'akazzēb* to *ak zak,* "quite pure," which modifies *mišpāṭi*. This would then be a paraphrase of Job's statement in 16:17: *ûtpillāti zakkāh,* "my petition is legitimate." NJPS chose *'akazzēb* , translating 34:6a: "I declare the judgment against me false."*miš*

9. The emendation of *yaśim 'ôd* to *yaśîm môʿ ed* has been widely accepted by translators, including NJPS, M. H. Pope (*Job, Introduction, Translation, and Notes* [2d ed.; AB; Garden City, N. Y.: Doubleday, 1973]), Dhorme, and A. Guillaume (*Studies in the Book of Job* [ed. John McDonald; ALUOS Sup 2; Leiden: Brill, 1968]), NEB and RSV.

system of cross-examination are extraneous in Job's case since, like the friends, he believes that justice between man and God is accomplished through a divine system of moral retribution, identified and labelled *"mišpāṭ"* in 34:11–12. Elihu does not make the kind of accusations against the hero that the others have made. He is simply trying to teach Job that justice with God is not accomplished through litigation.

Elihu shares with Job and the three friends the conception of God as supreme Judge, describing this role in 36:1–26. It is when he hears Yahweh's voice in chapter 37 that Elihu begins to perceive God in a new way, as Sovereign over the natural world: over rain (36:27–28, 37:8), snow (37:6), cold (37:9), ice (37:10) and lightning (37:11–18).

šadday lō'-měṣā' nuhû śaggî'-kōaḥ
ûmišpāṭ wěrōb[10]*-ṣĕdāqāh lō' yĕ'anneh*

Shaddai—we cannot attain to Him;
He is great in power and judgment.
And abundant in righteousness. He does not torment (37:23)

For the first time in the book the ideas of power *(kōaḥ)* and judgment *(mišpāṭ)* are linked, reminiscent of Isa. 40 (vv. 14, 26) and Ps. 89 (v. 15, *gĕbûrāh* in v. 14) where the emphasis is on God's role as King (Isa. 40:22; Ps. 89:19), Creator and Ruler of the world. Elihu presents justice with power as attributes of Yahweh, who is not simply Judge but Sovereign.[11] But in the very last lines of his speech (37:23–24), he returns to an emphasis on God's role as Judge who evaluates man according to his merit. The characters in the drama continue until God's appearance to understand *mišpāṭ* as juridical: Job, believing in his innocence, insists God has acted unjustly toward him and must submit their conflict to litigation; the others, concluding that the hero is guilty of wrongdoing, affirm the infallibility of the divine system of retribution.

God's appearance helps answer the question about the nature of justice. Matching the hero's request in 13:22, Yahweh in 38:3 and again in 40:7 challenges Job to participate in a lawsuit, validating Job's juridical understanding of *mišpāṭ*. *'Ĕzār-nā' kĕgeber ḥălāṣe(y)kā wĕ'eš'ālkā wĕhôdî'ēnî*, "Gird your loins like a hero; / I will ask and you tell me" (38:3). The verb *gzr*, "to gird," means get ready to face a challenge, either unpleasant as in battle (Ps. 18:40) or pleasant (Ps. 30:12). The forensic force of the idiom in Jer. 1:17

10. *wērōb*, a noun, ought to be vocalized *wĕrab* as an adjective describing a characteristic of God.

11. Thorkild Jacobsen in "Primitive Democracy in Ancient Mesopotamia" (*JNES* 2 [1934] 160) describes the role of the ruler in ancient Mesopotamian city-states: "One individual, the ruler, united in his hands the chief political powers: legislative, judiciary, and executive." God viewed as king has these three powers within his control.

elucidates its meaning in God's speech. Jeremiah girds his loins for a legal battle as God's advocate against Israel. The author of Job draws on the forensic usage of the request to "gird the loins" with the significant difference that Job is challenged to oppose God. The meaning of the idiom has been clarified independently by two scholars, Cyrus Gordon and Tur-Sinai, who cite Nuzi tablet JEN 331 as an example of the belt-wrestling ordeal used for settlement of a court case where there is contradictory testimony.[12] The poet uses the challenge of the belt-wrestling ordeal to signal God's willingness to continue proceedings and his acceptance of Job's position that justice may be accomplished through litigation.

Yahweh, ignoring Job's request for a bill of particulars (13:23), testifies instead about His own dominion over the universe; His creation of the world (38:1–13); His knowledge of its structure (38:16–22); His command over natural forces (38:24–38), animals (39; 40:14–24), and man (40:11–13); and finally, His ability as provider (38:39–41). God presents evidence, through His intimate knowledge of the workings of the world, that He is Ruler. When He uses the word *mišpāṭ* in 40:8, the context makes the meaning clear. *Ha'ap tāpēr mišpāṭî taršî'ēnî lĕma'an tiṣdaq*, "Would you impugn My sovereignty, / Would you condemn Me that you may be right?" (40:8). *Mišpāṭ* refers to the sovereignty over the universe which God elaborately describes in His long speech. The use of this word in 1 Sam. 8:9 helps to illuminate its meaning in Job 40:8: the ruler has authority *(mišpāṭ)* which attaches to his position of power. He may treat his people and their property according to his own interests without their prior consent. For example, the king described by God to Samuel has the right to appropriate his subject's property when he wishes without the transaction being a punishment for an offense or a payment for a debt. When Job hears God use the word *mišpāṭ* in the context of His Divine Sovereignty in the universe, he may then understand that his loss of health, family and wealth need not be a punishment for wrongdoing. God's actions are his prerogative as Ruler and a sign of His total control.

Once God reveals Himself as the Ruler of the world, Job is able to accept His authority, as he acknowledges in 42:2. He learns from Yahweh that divine justice is ruling power, the sovereign having the authority to control the well-being and wealth of his subjects. While God acknowledges that justice for man may be accomplished through litigation and therefore is willing to participate in a suit with Job, the case has been left pending. The hero's final words of response in 42:6, however, signify his retraction of the lawsuit: *'al-kēn 'em'as wĕniḥamtî 'al-'āpār wā'ēper.* The specific meaning of the verbs *m's* and *nḥm* in this verse are difficult to determine since they lack objects. Some translators follow the Septuagint and Vulgate, supplying the object "myself,"

12. Cyrus H. Gordon, *Ugaritic Literature* (Rome: Pontificium Institutum Biblicum, 1949), 134, citing L. Manross and Tur-Sinai, p. 442.

while others prefer "my words."[13] It is quite likely that the author is using a shortened form of *m's mišpāṭ* in 42:6 since the object of this verb in 31:13, part of Job's last major speech, is *mišpāṭ* The idiom is used forensically in the sense of a judge refusing to hear a case. And further, Job uses the comparable idiom, *śwr mišpāṭ,* in 27:2 to accuse God of rejecting his lawsuit. He turns the tables on himself in 42:6, repudiating his own case against Yahweh.

The second verb in 42:6, *nḥm,* has generally been translated "repent,"[14] with the phrase *'al-'āpār wā'ēper* being adverbial. This verb has a forensic usage in prophetic lawsuit literature in the Hebrew Bible as "retract," a translation which warrants consideration in 42:6. Cyrus Gordon suggests that *nḥm* may be used "apparently in the sense of a judge retracting and lightening his decision."[15] An example of this usage is found in Jer. 15:6b where the statement *nil'ētî hinnāḥēm* means "I am weary of (continually) retracting." Gordon supports his conclusion with an example of the pi'el of the verb in Isa. 49:13. The possibility ought to be considered that *nḥm* in the pi'el in Job 42:6 has the forensic sense of a plaintiff's retraction of his case. An acceptable translation of the verse would then be: "Therefore, being but dust and ashes, / I withdraw and retract [my case]" (42:6). This translation helps answer the question of the resolution of Job's lawsuit against God. The answer is that the hero no longer wishes to continue his case when he realizes that there is a dimension of justice outside the sphere of the court which supersedes the purely forensic.

The Book of Job dramatizes God's involvement with the important human question: "What is justice?" Yahweh is responsive to the issue of the suffering of the innocent. When Job challenges him to explore his legal status through litigation, God appears ready to participate in juridical proceedings. But beyond this, and more important, Yahweh shows His concern by communicating a dimension of *mišpāṭ* previously outside of Job's knowledge. Somehow in his preoccupation with juridical matters, the hero ignores a dimension of *mišpāṭ* as ruling power, a meaning which has been an integral part of the Semitic root *špṭ/ṯpṭ* from its earliest use. He and his friends thought of God only as Judge of man's behavior, ignoring the deity's all-encompassing role as King of the universe. Job acknowledges his ignorance in 42:3bc where he says: "Indeed I spoke without understanding / Of things beyond me, which I did not know." The book explores the nature of man's

13. Robert Gordis (*The Book of Job: Commentary, New Translation and Special Studies* [New York: The Jewish Theological Seminary of America, 1978] 491), NEB and RSV choose "myself" as an object while Tur-Sinai, Pope, Driver-Gray and Guillaume prefer "my words." NJPS gives no object.

14. The list of translators who use "repent" for *nḥm* includes Dhorme, Driver-Gray, Gordis, Pope, Tur-Sinai, NEB, RSV and W. B. Stevenson (*The Poem of Job, A Literary Study with a New Translation* [London: Oxford University, 1947]).

15. Cyrus H. Gordon, "Legal Background of Hebrew Thought and Literature," M.A. thesis, University of Pennsylvania, 1928.

knowledge of God and divine justice. What Job learns is that the divinely ordained justice in the world is God's governance. Job speaks at the end of the drama not as an innocent hero who rejects the divine Judge for improperly accusing him of wrongdoing, but as an enlightened and humbled man who accepts an all-powerful King. His acceptance is based on a full understanding that *mišpāṭ* integrates the ideas of human jurisprudence and divine sovereignty.

29

The Theophany of Job

James G. Williams

Interpretations of Job abound, both in modern scholarship and in modern literature.[1] These interpretations show that perspective on the Book of Job and methodology have a strong bearing on the conclusions attained. If it is viewed as basically a philosophical statement on religion then one searches for primary concepts and conceptual alternatives (Tsevat). If Job is viewed as a literary masterpiece, one sets aside philosophical and theological concerns and analyzes the structure and movement of the book (Robertson; Whedbee; also Good to some extent). One could also compare it to other lit-

1. Bibliographical note: The following are sources which have been of special interest and aid to me, and which will be cited in this essay. The later citations of these writings will state only author and pages. G. Fohrer, *Das Buch Hiob,* KAT 16 (Gütersloh, 1963); N. Glatzer, ed., *Dimensions of Job* (New York, 1969); E. Good, *Irony in the OT* (Phila., 1965); R. Gordis, *The*

From James G. Williams, "Deciphering the Unspoken: The Theophany of Job," *Hebrew Union College Annual* 49 (1978): 59–72. Used by permission of the Hebrew Union College.

The place where life gets figured out is important too; you could not have known many things about yourself unless you had come here.

erary works. A modern commentary would exhibit historical and philological concerns (e.g., Fohrer; also Pope, though his is not really a commentary). Ancient commentaries and discussions would view Job in terms of the respective religious frameworks. Christians, for example, have usually viewed Job christologically: they have viewed Christ as the answer to Job or Job is taken as an adumbration of Christ (see selections in Glatzer).

There has been an explosion of interpretations of Job in the modern Western world. Most interpreters, however, will agree on one thing: the theophany or speeches of God in chapters 38–41 of Job provide the key to the book. Some modern critical interpreters have had so much difficulty with this section of Job that the God-speeches (one or both) are not attributed to the original work.[2] It is now probably more common for scholars to understand

---

Book of God and Man: A Study of Job (Chicago, 1965); M. Heidegger, *Aus dier Erfahrung des Denkens*, 2. Auflage (Pfullingen, 1965); C. G. Jung, *Answer to Job*, tr. R. F. C. Hull (Cleveland, 1960); R. S. Kluger, *Satan in the OT* (Evanston, 1967); R. Polzin, "The Framework of the Book of Job," *Interpretation* 28 (1974). pp. 182–200; M. Pope, *Job*, The Anchor Bible, 15 (Garden City, N. Y., 1965); D. Robertson, *The OT and the Literary Critic* (Phila., 1977); M. Tsevat, "The Meaning of the Book of Job," *HUCA* 37 (1966), pp. 73–106; G. von Rad, "Job 38 and Old Egyptian Wisdom," in *The Problem of the Hexateuch and Other Essays* (Edinburgh and London, 1965), pp. 281–91; J. W. Whedbee, "The Comedy of Job," *Semeia* 7 (1977), pp. 1–39; J. G. Williams, "'You Have Not Spoken Truth of Me': Mystery and Irony in Job," *ZAW* 83 (1971), pp. 231–55, and "Comedy, Irony, Intercession: A Few Notes in Response," *Semeia* 7 (1977), pp. 135–45 (when the latter article is cited its date will be given; otherwise the references are to the 1971 article). The essays by Tsevat, and von Rad have been republished in the anthology edited and introduced by J. Crenshaw, *Studies in Ancient Israelite Wisdom* (New York, 1976).

Works that I have found helpful in literary interpretation, but which are not discussed in this paper, are: B. Allemann, "Irony and the Unspoken"—(unpublished?) paper presented at the Fourth Consultation on Hermeneutics, Syracuse University, 1970; E. Auerbach, *Mimesis: Representation of Reality in Western Literature*, tr. W. Trask (Garden City, New York); R. W. Corrigan, ed., *Comedy: Meaning and Form* (Scranton, Pa., 1965); D. Crossan, *The Dark Interval: Towards a Theology of Story* (Niles, Ill., 1975); A.-J. Greimas, *Sémantique Structurale* (Paris, 1966); S. Hopper, "Irony—The Pathos of the Middle," *Cross Currents* 12 (1962), pp. 31–40; V. Jankélévitch, *L'Ironie* (Paris, 1964); W. McCollom, *The Divine Average: A View of Comedy* (Cleveland and London, 1971); D. Robertson, "The Book of Job: A Literary Study," *Soundings* 56 (1973), pp. 446–69 (basically a longer version of chapter 3 in his 1977 book); S. Sandmel, "The Enjoyment of Scripture: An Esthetic Approach," *Judaism* 22 (1973), pp. 455–67; R. F. Scholes, *Structuralism in Literature* (New Haven, 1974); D. O. Via, Jr., *Kerygma and Comedy in the NT* (Phila., 1975).

Here are some modern authors of literary works who draw upon Job as paradigmatic: Robert Frost, *A Masque of Reason;* Thomas Hardy, *Jude the Obscure;* A. MacLeish, *J. B.;* I. A. Richards, *Job's Comforting;* E. Wiesel, *Night*, etc.; Neil Simon, *God's Favorite*. Cf. S. Hopper on Kierkegaard and Kafka in R. Shinn, ed., *Restless Adventure: Essays on Contemporary Expressions of Existentialism* (N.Y., 1968), pp. 110–16. Hopper calls the Job drama "the representative anecdote of existentialism in its Kierkegaardian forms" (p. 110).

2. See the discussion of M. Pope, "Job, Book of," *IDB*, vol. 2, *The OT: An Introduction* (N. Y. and Nashville, 1962), pp. 921 f. Fohrer, pp. 487 ff., reconstructs the "original" speech as 38:1–40:2, 6–14 (although 40:6–7 are "repetitive glosses" from 38:1–3). Tsevat inclines "to the critical opinion that 40:15–41:26 are not authentic" (p. 84, n. 26).

the theophany as integral to the whole book, to try to determine its relation to Job's complaints and accusations (even if the relation is negative), and to comment on the seemingly tenuous connection of the theophany and Job's repentance (38–42:6) to the epilogue.[3]

What I propose here is a literary interpretation of the theophany which will show that the speeches of God are related to the rest of the book in a highly subtle fashion and that their meaning lies in the irony of what is not spoken (what is not directly expressed and what is omitted). This approach will not deal directly with Job as theology, ethics, philosophy, comparative religion, etc. On the other hand, it may be of value to those who use the book for these purposes. Such a literary methodology has two main working principles which must be accepted as valid in their own context: the work in question is assumed to be a coherent whole, and it *can* be studied as literature, however else it has been and is studied.

Some Interpretations of the Theophany

Before moving into the main body of the study, I would like to discuss briefly some recent interpretations of the theophany which I consider important. My own approach has been informed by them. Then I would like to indicate my overall view of the Book of Job before concentrating on the speeches of God.

G. von Rad has identified the form of Job 38 as an ancient form of instruction through the use of rhetorical questions. The life-setting of the form would thus have been the school.[4] Von Rad's use of comparative data and his interpretive conclusions may help one towards a grasp of the *irony* in Yahweh's speeches.

M. Tsevat's conceptual grasp of what is at stake in the Book of Job is impressive. He points out that Job is shattered because his view of the world has not explained his suffering. This view of the world is based on the principle of retributive justice (R). Job wants God (G) to be faithful to the principle of retributive justice. What Job learns, concludes Tsevat, is that he cannot have both R and G. God subject to R is no longer God. Job subject to R would be a man unenlightened. Job therefore "sees" by giving up R for G. He learns that "He who speaks to man in the Book of Job is neither a just nor an unjust god but God."[5]

Be it noted that Tsevat does not think the epilogue plays any role in the

3. Discussed in Williams, pp. 231–37.

4. Fohrer, p. 496, has disputed von Rad's identification of the form. He maintains that it is rather a *Streitrede* (controversy speech). But he concedes that at least three forms have been brought together in Job 38–41, including catechetical questions of the wisdom teacher (Fohrer, p. 497).

5. Tsevat, p. 105.

poet's treatment of Job's dilemma. Robert Polzin deals with the problem of the epilogue in relation to the theophany, and in so doing he both assumes and seeks to show that the total framework of Job is patterned in a structure of sequences. Polzin's analysis is a very technical structural study, so what follows indicates only some highlights of his analysis. He unfolds a fourfold movement in Job: Act of God, Vision, Repentance and Word; each of these movements resolves a previous contradiction and poses a new contradiction until the fourth or final one. Then God's word establishes the experience of God as transcending all human belief, while affirming that belief and justice are divinely willed. For example, when Job avows his vision and repents, he affirms his new visionary experience but seemingly contradicts his previous cry for justice. The epilogue pulls together his cry for justice and his new experience. I have thus found Polzin's essay helpful in seeing Job as a spiritual journey which moves from "equilibrium without insight" to "equilibrium with insight."[6]

David Robertson has advanced the treatment of Job as irony further than anyone else. He demonstrates that Job correctly predicts God's coming in a tempest, and he says this shows that Job correctly anticipates the insensitive, indeed brutal manner of Yahweh's approach and speaking. Robertson also points out that Yahweh's pompous, overbearing way of speaking is reminiscent of the friends. Yahweh does not care at all for justice, as Job charged (12:13ff.), and his pride in Behemoth and Leviathan is an indication that they are manifestations of himself. When Job repents, it is tongue in cheek. When Yahweh condemns the friends and says that they have not told the truth about him as has Job, Yahweh condemns himself! He is the *alazon,* the buffoon who is shown up by his human subject. Job did not win the trial, but he won a moral victory over the cosmic tyrant who doesn't play fair.

Robertson's interpretation is suggestive in its tracing of irony, and it is a pioneering literary critical study. His understanding of irony, however, is rather simplistic, and he does not seem to take seriously the principle of assuming that the literary work is an integral whole. The epilogue, especially vv. 10–17, seems to dangle with no function except to betray Yahweh as the *alazon* and perhaps to end things as a conventional audience would have wanted.[7]

Finally, the essay by J. William Whedbee in *Semeia* 7 has opened up a promising new sphere in interpreting Job. In a compact yet comprehensive discussion he poses the thesis that Job is comedy. He points out that comedy is profoundly a matter of vision rather than funny lines eliciting laughs, its central ingredients being incongruity and a final upswing in the plot to happiness and restoration of the hero who becomes reconciled with his world. Whedbee views the friends as caricatures of the wise counselor, repeating themselves in a windy way while they accuse Job of windiness. Job repudiates

6. Polzin, p. 200.
7. Robertson, pp. 34, 53–54.

them with sarcasm and satire, and turns to God as his true adversary, eventually demanding a cosmic trial at which he would defend himself. Meanwhile, Elihu interrupts and provides a comic interlude. When Yahweh speaks from the whirlwind he does not answer Job directly and unambiguously, and this serves to give Job a profound and comic view of himself: "He sees God and through God's eyes he now sees the world."[8] Then, when Job repents the first time and we expect the show to be over, Yahweh surprises the audience by continuing with a speech parallel to the first. "The stylistic technique of structural parallelism serves to heighten the sense of incongruity in Yahweh's renewed challenge to Job and Job's second capitulation in the act of repentance."[9] Whedbee also calls attention to the playful, festive note in the portrayal of creation.[10] Whedbee has thus made the greatest contribution so far to setting the irony of Job within the larger framework of comedy.

My own concept of the Book of Job is that it is a comedy, though I am less concerned with the name of a genre than with trying to see its literary and religious dimensions in a new way. I accept most of the features of Whedbee's general perspective on Job. One thing he neglects is any discussion of Job as intercessor in the epilogue, whereas I see the *intention* of the book as one of relating how Job experiences a "spiritual journey" and finally becomes intercessor for the friends; this role as intercessor produces an enormous irony.[11] This spiritual journey is made up of four "acts" or "movements":

1. Once upon a time (chapters 1–2). Folk tale setting. Divine doubt and human faith.
2. Once in time (chapters 3–31). Job doubts and suffers. God is silent. Job disputes with friends who represent wisdom of the ancients; Job is torn between accusing God of being an unjust adversary and affirming the necessary goodness and fairness of God.
   —Intrusion of Elihu (chapters 32–37). Comic interlude, although Elihu is a kind of Elijah preparing the way of the Lord.[12]
3. Once out of time (38–42:6). Theophany, Job's vision (to be discussed below).
4. Twice upon a time (42:7–17). Condemnation of friends, restoration of Job who prays for friends. Twofold restoration of possessions and sons; three beautiful daughters—implication that marriage will soon occur.[13]

8. Whedbee, p. 25.
9. Whedbee, p. 28.
10. Whedbee, p. 24.
11. This is developed in Williams (1977), pp. 239–40.
12. See Gordis, p. 116.
13. See Fohrer, pp. 544–45.

The Theophany

In the theophany Job gets what he wants. And there is always a comic element in getting what one wants, whether or not it is finally funny. From a purely literary standpoint Job has "forced the hand" of God by uttering the oath of clearance: from Job's point of view God *must* now come to speak to him. Otherwise, Job is innocent and justified if the curses do not rebound upon him. If, on the other hand, he is struck down, God will have lost his wager with the Satan. So God comes in a whirlwind, speaks, and Job is questioned by way of a panoramic vision of the cosmos.

Yet the speeches of God are strange and elusive. In terms of the verbal level it is simply a fact that Yahweh makes no affirmation about himself that Job had not already expressed in the dispute: God is omnipotent, omniscient, omnipresent, etc. Neither does the Voice directly respond to Job's questions, complaints and laments. Is it true or not that there is no moral order in the universe? That Elohim is terrible, the Almighty a supernatural tyrant who acts capriciously, unwisely, and unjustly? Is it true that the doctrine of retribution is an illusion, that the just man is not rewarded nor the wicked punished?

Yahweh does not address himself to these questions. Why not? There is an incongruity about the different parts of the Book of Job: there is no direct and obvious relation of one part to another. It is as if one could jump into the book or play at almost any point and then understand the play as well as one who heard or read it from the beginning—provided one is given a minimal explanation of the story-line. For example, one could be told, "A righteous man named Job has suffered greatly and complained about his fate and divine justice. Now God is speaking to him." This person would probably be no more and no less puzzled than someone who had followed the major sequences assiduously.

What I hope to demonstrate is that what is *said* but unspoken is what constitutes the meaning of the speeches of God. This said but unspoken also serves to bind the parts (movements or acts) of the Book of Job together. Seeing the said but unspoken requires the recognition of irony in the text as potentially significant.

Everything that follows is interpretive. However, I shall try to move carefully from the more easily demonstrable to the more speculative, i.e., from what is generally accepted as "factual" or tightly related to the factual to that which must be seen in vaguer outlines from afar. This will involve: A. establishing those ways and instances in which the theophany is obviously or visibly related to the rest of the book, as well as to the biblical and ancient Near Eastern context. B. focusing on the form, content and manner of God's speaking. C. eliciting the implications of the unspoken in God's speaking.

The Theophany as Related to Its Context

This study presupposes that its subject, the Book of Job, is a literary whole which is not to be truncated. The logic of the literary study requires a search for signs of the relation of the part to the whole, and vice versa, even if these signs are subtle. In the case of the God-speeches, there are words and images that appear to be related to other parts of the book. Some of these relations cannot be established without question, but they are all of interest.

The most obvious instance of a tie between theophany and the rest of the work is the arrival of Yahweh to speak from a tempest (*sᵉʿarāh*, 38:1). Job had predicted that if Yahweh were to answer him, it would be out of a tempest (9:17). One question here is whether Job's anticipation of the unjust and inhumane treatment he would receive is also correct:[14]

> [he] would bruise me in a tempest,
> and multiply my wounds without cause

Yahweh affirms that he is hunter of prey for the lioness and her young (38:39). In the dispute Job viewed Yahweh as one hunting him as a lion (10:16), and graphically described being tortured by his divine enemy as a lion's victim would be (16:12). Yahweh also describes the horse's strength, beauty, and lust for the blood of battle (39:19–25). The horse's strength is divinely given; he cannot be turned back in his fierceness (*wᵉlo' yašuv mipᵉnĕ ḥerev*, 39:22). This is reminiscent of Job's depiction of God (*mī yᵉšivenu*, 9:12; cf. 9:4).

These three instances afford interesting verbal connections. I think that our certainty concerning the *intended* connection should be high in the case of 38:1/9:17 and then diminish a bit with each of the other two instances. But all three would be fairly strong examples. More tenuous but worthy of note are three others: 40:15; 38:8; and 39:5.

God tells Job that he made Behemoth as well as Job (40:15). This latter clause, *ʾašer ʿaśiti ʿimmak*, is interesting.[15] It indicates that Behemoth and Job, as God's creatures, have something most basic in common. What that is, outside of their creaturehood, is not obvious. At any rate, I would raise the question whether the description of Behemoth is an allusion to Job's consternation in 10:8:

> Your hands shaped me and made me *(wayaʿaśuni)*
> together round about—and you would destroy me?

In 38:8 two things are interesting: the use of the verb *suk* and the image of the sea. The verb appears only here and in Job 3:23. The variant, *śuk*, occurs

14. See Robertson, p. 48.

15. Fohrer, p. 522, holds that this clause is a gloss, but it makes perfect sense. Cf. Pope, pp. 270f. At any rate, one of the working principles of this study entails considering every part of the work as belonging to it. Whether or not such an assumption is "correct" in terms of source and redaction criticism, it is necessary for the new literary criticism, in order to test the results. See Chapter 1 of Robertson.

only in Job 1:10 and Hos. 2:8. If we begin with the prologue we move along an interesting route in the usage of ***suk*** and ***śuk***: the Satan claims that Yahweh has hedged Job about (protected him); Job claims that God has hedged him about (stifled him); God, by a rhetorical question, indicates his power in shutting up the sea (established order). Concerning the sea, Job asked,

> Am I Sea, or Sea-serpent,
> that you place a guard over me? (7:12)

Is Yahweh's rhetorical question an allusion to the image that Job applies to himself?

Yahweh asks Job,

> Who sent the wild ass to freedom?
> The bonds of the wild ass—who loosed them? (39:5)

The first word for "wild ass," *pere'*, is one that Job has used as an analogy to himself: "Does the *pere'* bray when it has no grass (6:5)?" The question is whether Yahweh alludes to that analogy.

Finally, to take another kind of instance, Job's statement of repentance, 42:2–6, seems to contain two near-quotations of Yahweh's speeches (vv. 3 and 4; cf. 38:2 and 40:7). The other possibility is that 42:2–6 is a dialogue with Yahweh speaking in 42:3, 5. If it is not a dialogue, one wonders *how* Job is citing the speeches of God.

If we turn to the relation of the theophany to its biblical and ancient Near Eastern context, the figures of Behemoth and Leviathan immediately call for comment.[16] In his second speech Yahweh boasts first of Behemoth and asserts that he is "the first of El's sovereign acts" (40:19). The mythical hintergrund of this assertion is evidently the battle of the high god with the monster(s) of chaos. Whether the mythologem of the battle for creation now stands as the intention of the text is not clear. Probably there is here an allusion to a primordial victory over Behemoth: "(only) his maker can bring near his sword," i.e., only Yahweh-El can conquer him.

One of the significant aspects of 40:19 involves a comparison with Prov. 8:22ff. In the latter passage we read that Ḥokhmah, Wisdom, was acquired by Yahweh as the first of his sovereign acts. Comparing the texts brings us to this relationship: Behemoth: Ḥokhmah: Chaos: Order. Behemoth, like Leviathan, symbolizes primordial powers of chaos, whereas Ḥokhmah symbolizes primordial potentials for ordering chaos. David Robertson has argued that the significance of this relationship is that according to the views of the respective poets each figure is a symbol of God.[17] Suffice it to note here that

16. The notes of Pope, pp. 247ff., are especially good.
17. Robertson, p. 50.

Yahweh is very proud of Behemoth, and the image of the divine creator is that of a warrior. It is also necessary to keep in mind that, as Yahweh points out, Behemoth and Job are fellow creatures (40:15, supra).

The mythological significance of Leviathan is well known. Appearing as the Lothan of seven heads that Baal destroys in the Ugaritic myths, he is likewise the sea-serpent of many heads that Elohim defeated in the beginning (Ps. 74:12–14). One mythical tradition of the eschaton represents a final battle of Yahweh with Leviathan (Isa. 27:1). This Leviathan is doubtless the mythical origin of the dragon of seven heads in Rev. 17. Leviathan, as well as Behemoth, appears with eschatological significance in Enoch 60:7–9, IV Ezra 6:49–52, and Apoc[ryphal] Baruch 24:4.

From the nostrils of the great Leviathan issues smoke, from his mouth flames shoot out (Job 41:12, 13). this is almost exactly the description of Yahweh in a psalm:

> There arose smoke from his nose
> and fire from his mouth consumed;
> coals flamed forth from him. (Ps. 18:9, II Sam. 22:9)

We are also told that even the gods are seized with fear before Leviathan (41:17). The ancient Israelite tradition implies that none other could strike terror in the gods except Yahweh (Exod. 15:11). The compared texts thus give many indications that Yahweh and Leviathan are much alike. This conclusion is reinforced by 41:2: Yahweh, like Leviathan is unapproachable.

Provisional Conclusions:

1. Yahweh comes as Job said he would, in a tempest (38:1; 9:17). A tempest or whirlwind is an overwhelming natural force, to say the least.
2. Yahweh uses images of himself (38:39) and his creatures (39:22) that Job has used of God (10:16; 9:12).
3. Behemoth and Leviathan have an important place in Yahweh's view of himself.
4. Yahweh may be making allusions to Job in speaking of some of his creatures (38:8/7:12, 3:23, 1:10; 39:5/6:5). An explicit connection between Job and Behemoth is drawn in 40:15.[18]

Form, Content and Manner of God's Speaking

It is probably correct that a number of forms of speech have been brought together in Job 38–41.[19] I follow von Rad, however, in viewing the divine

18. Job's response, 42:2–6, cannot enter into discussion here because it poses a difficult problem of interpretation. See the treatment of this passage in Williams, pp. 232–33.

19. Discussion and references in Williams, pp. 39–41.

speeches as predominantly in the form of *instruction* which stems from the life-setting of the school, where the master drills his pupils by means of ironic testing and teaching.[20] The form of Yahweh's speeches combines a cataloguing of natural phenomena with satirical questioning. Von Rad has pointed out the form of Hori's satirical questions to Amen-em-opet in the Egyptian Onomasticon of Amen-em-opet:

> What is it (Byblos) like?
> Pray, instruct me about Sidon and Sarepta.
> Where is the stream of the Litani?

These are, of course, questions about geography, but the form is much the same as Job 38–41:

> Where were you? . . .
> Tell me. . . .
> Who did thus-and-so?
> What is the way to? . . .

God is instructing Job, and in the course of the didactic discourse Job hears a beautiful and glowing, albeit rather boastful recital of the world outside of man and man's domain. The forces of the cosmos and the wild animals are paraded before Job: the earth, the sea, the morning, the Dog-star, the springs of the deep, the gates of death, the home of light, the dwelling of darkness, the storehouse of the snow, the heat and the rain, the constellations, the clouds, the lightning, the lioness and the raven, the mountain-goats, the wild ass, the wild ox, the ostrich (which is rather stupid), the horse, the hawk, the vulture, the whale, and above all, the Leviathan and the Behemoth. But what does Job know of all these? Their wildness and the incomprehensibility of their origin—in short, their mystery—must strike Job dumb.

But Job had never pretended to have knowledge of the mysteries of life. He simply wanted justice to be done: a fair trial, his divine adversary appearing to state the charges and hear Job's side. But Job's desires and questions receive no direct response. Is there an indirect response?

Robert Gordis has said yes, God does respond to Job's questions in a fashion appropriate to subtle Oriental rhetoric. The God-speeches, says Gordis, point to the order and harmony of the cosmos; this cosmic order described by God implies another order, an "*order and meaning in the moral sphere, though this is often incomprehensible to man.*"[21] I find it difficult to adduce evidence against Gordis's interpretation. It has the virtue of assuming the importance of irony and allusion, and of presupposing that the Book of Job is

20. Von Rad, pp. 288–89.
21. Gordis, p. 133.

a coherent literary work. But it does not satisfy the literary question of how one would really establish the relation of this inferred order and harmony to the rest of the book. And the literary context gives rise to a metaethical question: do Job's questions and his moral view have anything to do with the divine nature? To hold that God implies that there is, after all, a moral order comes across rather as an anodyne to Job, as Tsevat has noted.[22] It is not satisfying within the context that the book marks out.

Is there an indirect "answer to Job"? I say yes. With respect to form, the speeches of Yahweh are ironic: they are in form rhetorical questions that the pupil cannot answer and that the master does not want him to answer. It is a rhetorical form whose purpose is to humble the pupil and send him back to his books or whatever sources of investigation he may have.

Moreover, the speeches are replete with allusions to the rest of Job, as well as to the total religious and cultural heritage of the Jews. We probably have only scratched the surface of such allusions. If it is firmly established that there are such allusions (whether or not given instances are debatable), and if it becomes a reasonable premise that the theophany is ironic in form, then new and exciting lines of study are opened up.

We now have irony and allusions. It is clear that Job's demand for a trial and a verdict of guilt or innocence is ignored. One more observation will constitute the basis of my interpretation of Job 38–41: man is missing from Yahweh's recital of the cosmic panorama. Job is not there, man is not there, Israel is not there. One expects man to appear. As a general rule, the telling of origins not only relates the beginning of the cosmos but explains how and where one becomes continuous with his ancestors.[23] Nothing of that here. Specifically in terms of the biblical context, man is the crown of creation (Gen. 1), even if man is a paradox or surprising phenomenon in the midst of the wonders of the created order (Ps. 8). Even the psalms that sing praise to God's majesty and power in nature attribute to Israel the responsibility of relating and singing the divine greatness (e.g., Pss. 29, 104). But no man, no Job, no Israel in Yahweh's speeches. The man Job is, however, addressed by Yahweh.

The Irony of the Unspoken

What is spoken and what is said are two different things in any human context of communication.[24] Two important aspects of the unspoken (what is not directly verbalized) are allusions which signal certain meanings and omissions which are pregnant with implications for the attentive audience. From the occurrence of allusions I conclude that Yahweh playfully alludes to a "beastliness" that binds God, man and animals together. And from the omis-

22. Tsevat, p. 94.
23. This is dealt with in Williams, pp. 248–49.
24. Heidegger, p. 21: "Nie ist das Gesprochene und in keiner Sprache das Gesagte."

sions I conclude that God sees man neither as a simple given in creation nor as able to justify himself.

The "beastliness" of God, man and animals. God is so proud of his wild animals that it is fair to conclude that they are, indeed, manifestations of the divine. It seems that in viewing the lioness Job also "sees" the one who hunts prey for her (38:39). This is the Hunter who has stalked Job (10:16; cf. 16:12). The strength of the horse is reminiscent of the power of El (39:19; 9:4); neither the horse nor El can be turned back in his fierceness (39:22; 9:12).

And there is Behemoth, that savage, massive *thereness.* The name is actually the Hebrew plural of *b^ehemah,* "wild animal, beast" (thus *theria* in the LXX). He is the "beasts," and Yahweh is proud of him as his "primordial production."[25]

And Leviathan, monster of sparkling eyes, flaming mouth and smoking nostrils (41:11–13). Is this not a face of God? Is Yahweh not like a dragon? (Cf. Ps. 18:9; 2 Sam. 22:9.)

Yahweh reveals himself as beastly. There is something monstrous about the divine reality, and something divine in beasts and monsters. But if Yahweh shows himself in a veiled manner, he also shows Job Job's self. Though Job compares himself to a wild ass whose cry is not without cause, Yahweh points out that he is the one who sets the wild ass free. Perhaps—may we infer?—there is also hope for Job to be free of his troubles, but in any case the wild ass is under the dominion of his creator. Like the surging, deep tumultuous sea, which was enclosed within doors when it bursts forth from the womb, so also—may we read?—Job has to be enclosed and held within bounds for his good and for God's (38:8; 7:12; 3:23; 1:10). In other words, Job has also an instinctive, beastly, monstrous side. Like the sea, like the Behemoth, he has to be overcome.

I have discussed and partly agreed with Jungian interpretations of the theophany, according to which Yahweh discloses his dark, irrational side to Job.[26] Where I would part from such an interpretation is over the issue of Yahweh's self-knowledge: I think that the poet depicts Yahweh as cognizant of his dark and chaotic side, of which he subtly allows Job a glimpse. It is for this reason that I must also disagree with Robertson, who views Yahweh as the *alazon* and Job as the *eiron:* Yahweh is shown up for what he is, though he does not realize it, and even incriminates himself in the return to the prose story (42:7–9).[27] There *is* a tremendous irony in the return to the prose story,[28] but

25. Robertson's rendering, p. 50.

26. The interpretations of Jung and Kluger are noted in Williams, pp. 235–36, 246, 247; critique on pp. 252–54.

27. Robertson, pp. 53–54.

28. Cf. Williams, pp. 231–33.

I think that it is more a matter of Yahweh and Job as *alazon* and *eiron* to each other. Both are dissimulating, both are exposed, both are "shown up."

So—if the world does not always operate according to human ideas of rationality, if its structures and powers are beyond man's grasp, if unpredictable chaos takes over from time to time, then that's the way it is. Job was right. Also wrong, because that animal element, that *anima,* is within him, too.

Man is not simply given in the creation. Why this omission of man is noteworthy is discussed above. Note that I say not *simply* given. Man is there: Job is addressed by Yahweh. However, his beginning in a mythical sense is not presented. He shares a certain *anima* with Yahweh and the animals, but beyond that he is an open question. It is as though he is in the process of being created.

Man can neither justify himself nor be justified. It is a simple fact that Job is neither justified by Yahweh nor condemned. Overwhelmed, perhaps. But not justified or condemned. Justification in the sense of acquittal or declaration of innocence on the basis of conforming to statutes and doctrines, or to a world-view, is simply by-passed in the theophany. Job is liberated from self-justification, and from the belief that man is a preordained, fixed system. Self-justification leads to punishment of self or others; liberation therefrom leads to understanding of self and others. Now one can see the irony of Yahweh's command in Job 40:11–12:

> Unleash your furious anger,
> and regard everyone proud and abase him,
> and look on everyone haughty and bring him low,
> and tread down the wicked in their place.

If Job or anyone were to do this, there wouldn't be any humans left!

If this interpretation of the theophany is fundamentally sound, then it has unlocked the door to the poet's vision of the world. This vision is that of comedy. Comedy's essential features are incongruity and an eventual upswing to the reconciliation of the hero with his world. The inner being of the Job poet's comic vision is the recognition of man's common being with the mysterious structures and vitalities of the world, of the groundlessness of any putative human nature, of the ultimate hopelessness of self-justification. Pretense, defensiveness, and airs of superiority are thus given their due: they are exposed as part of the comedy.

Concluding Reflection

This has been a literary study. One does not have to agree with it. I cannot completely accept the vision of Job as I have set it forth, although I have learned much from trying to understand it. As appealing and full of immense insight as this vision is, I think it is impossible for most of us to live in it and to try to realize it. It is practically amoral, bursting from an older world view as it does, like the young Sea that Yahweh must enclose. In practice we need a concept of human nature. "Selfhood," however understood, has to include some defenses and mechanisms of self-justification, even if they are enfolded in a larger reality of the "self," that I would want to affirm with some poets, mystics and modern religionists.

So it is not a matter of saying that Job is right or wrong, but that Job discloses a profound view of human existence in an uncanny world and does so in a literary style that is superb and perfectly matched to the complexities and ironies of existence itself. The engagement with such a vision, which may question and balance our own cultural drifts and personal predilections, is well worth the effort. And that in itself is enough to claim.

30

Mystery and Faith in Job 38:1–42:16

D. A. Carson

Job and God (Job 38:1–42:6)

Finally God himself speaks, answering Job out of the storm (chaps. 38–41). "Who is this that darkens my counsel with words without knowledge? Brace yourself like a man; I will question you, and you shall answer me" (38:2–3). There follows question after question, each designed to remind Job of the kinds of things he cannot do, and that only God can. "Where were you when I laid the earth's foundation? Tell me, if you understand" (38:4). "Have you ever given orders to the morning, or shown the dawn its place . . . ?" (38:12). "Have you entered the storehouses of the snow or seen the storehouses of the hail, which I reserve for times of trouble, for days of war and battle?" (38:22–23). "Can you bind the beautiful

From D. A. Carson, *How Long, O Lord? Reflections on Suffering and Evil* (Grand Rapids: Baker, 1990), 171–78.

Pleiades? Can you loose the cords of Orion? Can you bring forth the constellations in their seasons or lead out the Bear with its cubs?" (38:31–32). "Do you hunt the prey for the lioness and satisfy the hunger of the lions when they crouch in their dens or lie in wait in a thicket? Who provides food for the raven when its young cry out to God and wander about for lack of food?" (38:39–41). God then goes on to describe some of the more spectacular features of the mountain goat, the wild donkey, the ox, the ostrich, the horse, the hawk, the eagle. "Will the one who contends with the Almighty correct him? Let him who accuses God answer him!" (40:2).

Job had wanted an interview with the Almighty. He had, as it were, sworn an affidavit demanding that the Almighty appear and put his indictment in writing (31:35). But God's defense wasn't quite what Job had in mind. At the first pause, Job answers, "I am unworthy—how can I reply to you? I put my hand over my mouth. I spoke once, but I have no answer—twice, but I will say no more" (40:4–5).

But God hasn't finsihed yet. "Brace yourself like a man; I will question you, and you shall answer me" (40:7). Then come the most blistering questions: "Would you discredit my justice? Would you condemn me to justify yourself? Do you have an arm like God's, and can your voice thunder like his? Then adorn yourself with glory and splendor, and clothe yourself in honor and majesty. Unleash the fury of your wrath, look at every proud man and bring him low, look at every proud man and humble him, crush the wicked where they stand. Bury them all in the dust together; shroud their faces in the grave. Then I myself will admit to you that your own right hand can save you" (40:8–14).

It is important to recognize that God does not here charge Job with sins that have brought on his suffering. He does not respond to the "whys" of Job's suffering, nor does he challenge Job's defense of his own integrity. The reason he calls Job on the carpet is not because of Job's justification of himself, but because of Job's willingness to condemn God in order to justify himself. In other words, God does not here "answer" Job's questions about the problem of evil and suffering, *but he makes it unambiguously clear what answers are not acceptable in God's universe.*

The rest of chapter 40 and all of chapter 41 find God asking more rhetorical questions. Can Job capture and subdue the behemoth (40:15ff.) and the leviathan (41:1ff.)? These two beasts may be the hippopotamus and the crocodile, respectively, but they probably also represent primordial cosmic powers that sometimes break out against God. The argument, then, is that if Job is to charge God with injustice, he must do so from the secure stance of his own superior justice; and if he cannot subdue these beasts, let alone the cosmic forces they represent, he does not enjoy such a stance, and is therefore displaying extraordinary arrogance to call God's justice into question.

Job's response must be quoted in full (42:2–6), along with two or three explanatory asides: "I know that you can do all things," Job tells God, "no plan of yours can be thwarted. You asked, 'Who is this that obscures my counself without knowledge?' [38:2]. Surely I spoke of things I did not understand, things too wonderful for me to know. You said, 'Listen now, and I will speak; I will question you, and you shall answer me' [38:3; 40:7]. My ears had heard of you but now my eyes have seen you [i.e., Job has come to have a far clearer understanding of God than he had before]. Therefore I despise myself and repent in dust and ashes."

What shall we make of this exchange between God and Job?

Many doubtful interpretations have been put forward by various writers. Because God refers to so many natural phenomena, one writer argues that a major purpose of God's speech is to tell Job that the beauty of the world must become for him an anodyne to human suffering, a kind of aesthetic aspirin. When one basks in the world's beauty, one's problems become petty, "because they dissolve within the larger plan" of the harmony of the universe."[1] But to someone suffering intensely, the beauty of the world can just as easily become a brutal contrast that actually intensifies the suffering. Worse, it does not dissolve pain; rather, it is in danger of "dissolving" the sufferer in some kind of pantheistic sense of the fitness of things. This is surely a massive misunderstanding of God's response. Not once does God minimize the reality of Job's suffering.

Others, such as George Bernard Shaw, simply mock God's answer. Job wants an answer as to why he is suffering, and the best that God can do is brag about making snowflakes and crocodiles. A comtemporary author like Elie Wiesel, writing in the aftermath of the Holocaust, holds that Job should have pressed God further. Doubtless Job needed to repent of his attitude, but he still should have pressed God for an answer: Why do the righteous suffer?

Both of these approaches misunderstand the book rather badly. They have this in common: they assume that everything that takes place in God's universe *ought* to be explained to us. They assume that God owes us an explanation, that there cannot possibly be any good reason for God not to tell us everything we want to know immediately. They assume that God Almighty should be more interested in giving us explanations than in being worshiped and trusted.

The burden of God's response to Job is twofold. The first emphasis we have already noted: Job has "darkened God's counsel" by trying to justify himself at the expense of condemning God; and Job is in no position to do that. "God's speeches show Job that his lowly station point was not the appropriate place from which to judge whether cosmic orders were sufficiently askew to justify the declaration 'let there be darkness.'"[2] The second emphasis

1. So Robert Gordis, *The Book of God and Man: A Study of Job* (Chicago: University of Chicago Press, 1965), 133, 304.

2. Stuart Lasine, "Bird's-eye and Worm's-eye Views of Justice in the Book of Job," *Journal for the Study of the Old Testament* 42 (1988): 344.

is implicit: if there are so many things that Job does not understand, why should he so petulantly and persistently demand that he understand his own suffering? *There are some things you will not understand, for you are not God.*

That is why Job's answer is so appropriate. He does not say, "Ah, at last I understand!" but rather, "I repent." He does not repent of sins that have allegedly brought on the suffering; he repents of his arrogance in impugning God's justice, he repents of the attitude whereby he simply demands an answer, as if such were owed him. He repents of not having known God better. "My ears had heard of you but now my eyes have seen you. Therefore . . . I repent" (42:5–6).

To those who do not know God, to those who insist on being God, this outcome will never suffice. Those who do know God come in time to recognize that it is better to know God and to trust God than to claim the rights of God.

Job teaches us that, at least in this world, there will always remain some mysteries to suffering. He also teaches us to exercise faith—not blind, thoughtless submission to an impersonal status quo, but faith in the God who has graciously revealed himself to us.

Job's Happy Ending (Job 42:7–16)

These verses may be divided into two parts. The first, which we have already glanced at, reports God's wrath with Eliphaz and his two friends for not speaking of God what was right, as Job did (42:7–8). They are required to offer sacrifice to God, and Job, whom they have despised and abused, must pray for them, for God will accept his prayers for them (and, by implication, not their own!).

In the second part (vv. 10-17), after Job prays for his friends, the Lord makes him prosperous again. His siblings and acquaintances gather around him and provide gifts, presumably to help him start up again. He sires another family, seven more sons and three more daughters, and gains herds twice the size of what he had before. No women were more beautiful than his daughters, and Job left them an inheritance along with their brothers —further evidence of Job's compassionate and enlightened treatment of those traditionally squeezed to the periphery of life (cf. chap. 31). He lived to a ripe old age, seeing his children and their children to the fourth generation. Eventually he died, "old and full of years"—an epitaph reserved for the choicest or most favored of God's servants (Abraham [Gen. 25:8], Isaac [Gen. 35:29], David [1 Chron. 29:28], and Jehoiada the priest [2 Chron. 24:15]).

If some critics are displeased with God's answer to Job out of the storm, even more are incensed by this "happy ending." The story, they argue, should have ended with Job's repentance. Whether he was restored is irrelevant; in any case it is untrue to the experience of many, who suffer at length without reprieve. To end the story this way makes the doctrine of retribution basically right after all. The conclusion is therefore anticlimactic at best, contradictory at worst.

This is, I think, a shallow reading of the text. Perhaps the following reflections will help unpack the purpose of this conclusion a little:

1. We must beware of our own biases. One of the reasons why many people are dissatisfied with this ending is because in the contemporary literary world ambiguity in moral questions is universally revered, while moral certainty is almost as universally despised. The modern mood enjoys novels and plays where the rights and wrongs get confused, where every decision is a mixture of right and wrong, truth and error, where heroes and antiheroes reverse their roles.

Why this infatuation with ambiguity? It is regarded as more mature. Clear-cut answers are written off as immature. The pluralism of our age delights in moral ambiguity—but only as long as it costs nothing. Devotion to contemporary moral ambiguity is extraordinarily self-centered. It demands freedom from God so that it can do whatever it wants. But when the suffering starts, the same self-centered focus on *my* world and *my* interests, rather ironically, wants God to provide answers of sparkling clarity.

2. Throughout his excruciating suffering, Job has demonstrated that he serves the Lord out of a pure heart. True, he has said some stupid things and has been rebuked; but at no point does he simply curse God and turn his back on him. Even his demand that God present himself before Job and give an answer is the cry of a believer seeking to find out what on earth God is doing. Even while sitting in the ashpit, Job trusts God enough to express extraordinary confidence in him, and for no ulterior motive.

In that sense, God has won his wager with the devil. Job may utter words that darken God's counsel, but he does not lose his integrity or abandon his God. Is it therefore surprising that there should be full reconciliation between God and Job? And if the wager has been won, is there any reason for Job's afflictions to continue?

3. No matter how happy the ending, nothing can remove the suffering itself. The losses Job faced would always be with him. A happy ending is better than a miserable one, but it does not transform the suffering he endured into something less than suffering. A survivor of the Holocaust has not suffered less because he ultimately settles into a comfortable life in Los Angeles.

4. The Book of Job has no interest in praising mystery without restraint. All biblical writers insist that to fear the Lord ultimately leads to abundant life. If this were not so, to fear the Lord would be stupid and masochistic. The book does not disown all forms of retribution; rather, it disowns simplistic, mathematically precise, and instant applications of the doctrine of retribution. It categorically rejects any formula that affirms that the righteous always prosper and the wicked are always destroyed. There may be other reasons for

suffering; rewards (of blessing or of destruction) may be long delayed; knowledge of God is its own reward.

Job still does not have all the answers; he still knows nothing about the wager between God and Satan. He must simply trust God that something far greater was at stake than his own personal happiness. But he has stopped hinting that God is unjust; he has come to know God better; and he enjoys the Lord's favor in rich abundance once again.

5. The blessings that Job experiences at the end are not cast as rewards that he has earned by his faithfulness under suffering. The epilogue simply describes the blessings as the Lord's free gift. The Lord is not nasty or capricious. He may for various reasons withdraw his favor, but his love endures forever.

In that sense, the epilogue is the Old Testament equivalent to the New Testament anticipation of a new heaven and a new earth. God is just, and will be seen to be just. This does *not* smuggle mathematical retribution in through the back door. . . .

6. Although I have repeatedly spoken of God entering into a wager with Satan, or winning his wager with Satan, I have done so to try to capture the scene in the first chapter. But there is a danger in such language: it may sound as if God is capricious. He plays with the lives of his creatures so that he can win a bet.

Clearly that is not true. The challenge to Satan is not a game; nor is the outcome, in God's mind, obscure. Nothing in the book tells us *why* God did this. The solemnity and majesty of God's response to Job not only mask God's purposes in mystery, but presuppose they are serious and deep, not flighty or frivolous.

Nevertheless, the wager with Satan is in certain ways congruent with other biblical themes. God's concern for the salvation of men and women is part of a larger, cosmic struggle between God and Satan, in which the outcome is certain while the struggle is horrible. This is one way of placing the human dimensions of redemption and judgment in a much larger framework than what we usually perceive.

7. We are perhaps better situated now to understand precisely why God says that his servant Job spoke of him "what was right," while the three miserable comforters did not. True, Job is rebuked for darkening the Lord's counsel: he became guilty of an arrogance that dared to demand that God give an account of his actions. But Job has been genuinely groping for the truth, and has not allowed glib answers to deter him. He denies neither God's sovereignty nor (at least in most of his statements!) God's justice. Above all, so far as the wager between God and Satan is concerned, Job passes with flying colors: he never turns his back on God.

Contrast the three friends. Although they are trying to defend God, their reductionistic theology ends up offering Job a temptation: to confess sins that weren't there, in order to try to retrieve his prosperity. If Job had succumbed, it would have meant that Job cared more for prosperity than for his integrity or for the Lord himself; and the Lord would have lost his wager. Their counsel, if followed, would have actually led Job *away* from the Lord; Job would have been reduced to being yet one more person interested in seeking God for merely personal gain.

This is, at the end of the day, the ultimate test of our knowledge of God. Is it robust enough that, when faced with excruciating adversity, it may prompt us to lash out with hard questions, but will never permit us to turn away from God?

But perhaps it is better to put the matter the other way round: the God who put Job through this wringer is also the God of whom it is said that, with respect to his own people, "he will not let [them] be tempted beyond what [they] can bear. But when [they] are tempted, he will also provide a way out so that [they] can stand up under it" (1 Cor. 10:13). God could not trust me with as much suffering as Job endured; I could not take it. But we must not think that there was any doubt in God's mind as to whether he would win his wager with Satan over Job!

When we suffer, there will sometimes be mystery. Will there also be faith?

31

God's Revelation and Job's Repentance

David McKenna

In answer to Job's plea, God speaks, but in his own time and way. Rather than entering the fray as one of the disputants, God comes as God—speaking out of the whirlwind about the mystery of the universe. His first speech challenges Job to understand and to participate in the creation of the natural universe. Acknowledging his impotence and admitting his ignorance, Job submits in silence.

God's second speech begins with the admission that there are margins of sin and suffering that appear to be out of His control. Yet, these are the areas covered by the mystery of His grace in the creation of living things. As proof, He presents the leviathan and the behemoth, two of the most ludicrous—or better yet, comical—creatures of God's creation. Still, God loves them, cares for them, and finds joy in them. A higher level of faith breaks through for

From David McKenna, *Job*, The Communicator's Commentary (Waco: Word, 1986), 280–316. Used by permission of Word Books.

Job. For the first time, he sees the God of grace, who is not only just but loving and caring. Job is reconciled with God and ready for healing.

God—The Mystery of Creation

God does not directly answer any of the issues in the debate. He has no need to defend Himself. He does, however, obliquely address Job's initial question *why* from the perspective of his power at work in the natural universe. Does Job have the power to create and to understand heaven and earth, stars and sea, morning and night, light and darkness, snow and hail, flood and lightning, rain, dew, frost, and clouds? To think that these are the "mere edges" of God's power! Job is overwhelmed.

Without waiting for an answer, God adds the mystery of His living creation—the lion's cub, the mountain goat, the wild ass, the buffalo, the ostrich, the horse, the hawk, and the falcon. They are God's glory and in His care. Confessing that he is impotent and ignorant before the mystery of creation, Job repents with the realization that he cannot judge God or understand the moral order of the universe.

38:1 Then the LORD answered Job out of the whirlwind, and said:
2 "Who is this who darkens counsel
By words without knowledge?
3 Now prepare yourself like a man;
I will question you, and you shall answer Me.
4 "Where were you when I laid the foundations of the earth?
Tell Me, if you have understanding.
5 Who determined its measurements?
Surely you know!
Or who stretched the line upon it?
6 To what were its foundations fastened?
Or who laid its cornerstone,
7 When the morning stars sang together,
And all the sons of God shouted for joy?
8 "Or who shut in the sea with doors,
When it burst forth and issued from the womb;
9 When I made the cloud its garment,
And thick darkness its swaddling band;
10 When I fixed My limit for it,
and set bars and doors;
11 When I said,
'This far you may come, but no farther,
And here your proud waves must stop!'
12 "Have you commanded the morning since your days began,
And caused the dawn to know its place,
13 That it might take hold of the ends of the earth,
And the wicked be shaken out of it?

14 It takes on form like clay under a seal,
And stands out like a garment.
15 From the wicked their light is withheld,
And the upraised arm is broken.
16 "Have you entered the springs of the sea?
Or have you walked in search of the depths?
17 Have the gates of death been revealed to you?
Or have you seen the doors of the shadow of death?
18 Have you comprehended the breadth of the earth?
Tell Me, if you know all this.
19 "Where is the way to the dwelling of light?
And darkness, where is its place,
20 That you may take it to its territory,
That you may know the paths to its home?
21 Do you know it, because you were born then,
Or because the number of your days is great?
22 "Have you entered the treasury of snow,
Or have you seen the treasury of hail,
23 Which I have reserved for the time of trouble,
For the day of battle and war?
24 By what way is light diffused,
Or the east wind scattered over the earth?
25 "Who has divided a channel for the overflowing water,
Or a path for the thunderbolt,
26 To cause it to rain on a land where there is no one,
A wilderness in which there is no man;
27 To satisfy the desolate waste,
And cause to spring forth the growth of tender grass?
28 Has the rain a father?
Or who has begotten the drops of dew?
29 From whose womb comes the ice?
And the frost of heaven, who gives it birth?
30 The waters harden like stone,
And the surface of the deep is frozen.
31 "Can you bind the cluster of the Pleiades,
Or loose the belt of Orion?
32 Can you bring out Mazzaroth in its season?
Or can you guide the Great Bear with its cubs?
33 Do you know the ordinances of the heavens?
Can you set their dominion over the earth?
34 "Can you lift up your voice to the clouds,
That an abundance of water may cover you?
35 Can you send out lightnings, that they may go,
And say to you, 'Here we are!'?
36 Who has put wisdom in the mind?
Or who has given understanding to the heart?
37 Who can number the clouds by wisdom?
Or who can pour out the bottles of heaven,

38 When the dust hardens in clumps,
And the clods cling together?
39 "Can you hunt the prey for the lion,
Or satisfy the appetite of the young lions,
40 When they crouch in their dens,
Or lurk in their lairs to lie in wait?
41 Who provides food for the raven,
When its young ones cry to God,
And wander about for lack of food?
39:1 "Do you know the time when the wild mountain goats bear young?
Or can you mark when the deer gives birth?
2 Can you number the months that they fulfill?
Or do you know the time when they bear young?
3 They bow down,
They bring forth their young,
They deliver their offspring.
4 Their young ones are healthy,
They grow strong with grain;
They depart and do not return to them.
5 "Who set the wild donkey free?
Who loosed the bonds of the onager,
6 Whose home I have made the wilderness,
And the barren land his dwelling?
7 He scorns the tumult of the city;
He does not heed the shouts of the driver.
8 The range of the mountains is his pasture,
And he searches after every green thing.
9 "Will the wild ox be willing to serve you?
Will he bed by your manger?
10 Can you bind the wild ox in the furrow with ropes?
Or will he plow the valleys behind you?
11 Will you trust him because his strength is great?
Or will you leave your labor to him?
12 Will you trust him to bring home your grain,
And gather it to your threshing floor?
13 "The wings of the ostrich wave proudly,
But are her wings and pinions like the kindly stork's?
14 For she leaves her eggs on the ground,
And warms them in the dust;
15 She forgets that a foot may crush them,
Or that a wild beast may break them.
16 She treats her young harshly, as though they were not hers;
Her labor is in vain, without concern,
17 Because God deprived her of wisdom,
And did not endow her with understanding.
18 When she lifts herself on high,
She scorns the horse and its rider.

19 "Have you given the horse strength?
Have you clothed his neck with thunder?
20 Can you frighten him like a locust?
His majestic snorting strikes terror.
21 He paws in the valley, and rejoices in his strength;
He gallops into the clash of arms.
22 He mocks at fear, and is not frightened;
Nor does he turn back from the sword.
23 The quiver rattles against him,
The glittering spear and javelin.
24 He devours the distance with fierceness and rage;
Nor does he come to a halt because the trumpet has sounded.
25 At the blast of the trumpet he says, 'Aha!'
He smells the battle from afar,
The thunder of captains and shouting.
26 "Does the hawk fly by your wisdom,
And spread its wings toward the south?
27 Does the eagle mount up at your command,
And make its nest on high?
28 On the rock it dwells and resides,
On the crag of the rock and the stronghold.
29 From there it spies out the prey;
Its eyes observe from afar.
30 Its young ones suck up blood;
And where the slain are, there it is."

Job 38:1–39:30

Out of the Whirlwind

At last! The Lord comes. All of us who have felt the tedium and the tension, the anguish and the anger, the doggedness and despair of the Jobian drama—we are more than ready for God to speak.

The setting is significant. Elihu has concluded his speeches in one of those treasured moments after a storm when the splendor of a golden calm bathes the soul in glowing hope. Then, like an intruder in the tranquility, an isolated whirlwind spirals into view, sending tumbleweeds end over end in its wake.

Whirlwinds in the desert are not out of place. On the barren stretch of sand between Needles, California, and Hoover Dam, Nevada, the air burns with temperatures above one hundred and twenty degrees in the summertime. But against the visible waves of thermal heat, you can see the dust-filled cones of whirlwinds dipping and dancing over the desert floor. At one and the same time, they are partners with the desert, yet independent of it. God comes to us the same way—in sequence with our surroundings, but also with surprise. A burning bush, a ladder of angels, a still, small voice, a wheel in a wheel, a lofty throne, a solar eclipse, a sheet filled with animals, a trumpet sound—all announce the coming of the Lord. To our chagrin, God seldom, if ever, comes the same way twice. Attempts to fix the way He comes as doctrinally correct or spiritually superior are to put God in a box from which He will inevitably escape. Certainly, God does not come as Job expects. He tried to arraign God's appearance in a somber and orderly courtroom setting. Instead, he gets the sound of fury and the spin of chaos in a whirlwind.

Once again, we must stop to give credit to Elihu's claim that he spoke with the "voice of the Almighty." While the whirlwind out of which God spoke seems to come as an interruption, the actual transition is more like a natural line of progression from one scene to another. *"Then the LORD answered Job out of the whirlwind"* (38:1) suggests that Elihu prepared the way for God, and the voice of God followed in natural sequence with the voice of Elihu.

How much this sequence is like the role of the preacher in the pulpit. The sermon may begin with the sound of a human voice but only in preparation for the voice of God. As we say to our seminarians, "You do not preach until another Voice is heard." Elihu served the Spirit well.

God knows how to get our attention. How often have you heard the story about the soft-spoken Quaker who tamed a recalcitrant mule by hitting him over the head with a two-by-four? When asked to explain the contradiction between his violent act and pacifistic personality, the Quaker explained that before you can train a mule, "Thee must first get his attention." As a boy growing up, I remember just the opposite kind of training. My father never spanked or threatened me. One silent look from his eyes struck fear into my heart, stopped my protest, changed my direction, and modified my behavior. God has that same sensitivity to our individuality. Pompous, wordy, and defiant—Job needs a whirlwind.

So, like a voice out of a windstorm, God confronts Job with a question that arrests, indicts, tries, convicts, and sentences him:

> *Who is this who darkens counsel*
> *By words without knowledge?* (v. 2)

Job has spoken as if his innocence gives him direct access to the mind of God and as if his wisdom earns him an explanation from God. His greatest fault, however, is to presume that his own finite mind can comprehend the infinite mind of God. With such presumption, Job has been staggering along the borderline between limiting God's power and denying His justice. Notably, God does not condemn him for sin. Instead, He chides him for throwing up a barrage of empty words about a subject beyond his knowledge. *"Words without knowledge"* only smog the sky and keep him from seeing through to God's purpose.

The image of ack-ack guns, sending up a skyful of flak to protect the cities of London and Berlin during World War II, comes to mind. As an admission that the aircraft gunners could not turn back the invaders by aiming at the hundreds of planes droning over the cities, the defenders resorted to a strategy of desperation by shooting up a screen of smoke and shrapnel through which the bombers had to fly. Hits came by a gambler's chance rather than a gunner's aim.

God sees Job's words as a similar tactic. Bombarded by suffering beyond his comprehension or control, Job sends a screen of verbal scattershot to defend his ignorance and his impotence. Because his faith is too small to cover the contingency of the innocent suffering, Job projects the blame on God and, in so doing, creates a shadow of darkness over the mind of God through which he cannot see.

Words are a common defense for our insecurity. In an interview with a prospective field representative for a Christian organization, I asked one simple question that triggered a veritable fifteen-minute barrage of words. Only by interrupting could I ask a second question. Another fifteen-minute fusillade followed. The prospect missed all of the cues I gave—shifting in my seat, leaning forward as if to ask another question, raising a hand to make a suggestion, and even pleading *stop* with my eyes. Finally, a colleague inserted his own question. I almost choked with laughter when he asked in a matter-of-fact tone, "How do you rate yourself as a listener?" The candidate blushed red as if to understand and answered, "It is an area I have to work on." Then, believe it or not, with hardly a breath, he went on for another ten minutes until my impatience got the best of me, and I concluded the interview by standing up, shaking his hand, and saying, "Thank you for coming." More unbelievable yet, when he got his letter of rejection, he wrote back to ask, "What did I do wrong?" He failed to see that in representing the organization with friends in the field his verbiage would throw up a dark screen through which the purpose of a spiritual ministry could not be seen.

Was I unfair in not saying to the wordy candidate, "You talk too much?" God does not hesitate to confront Job bluntly about the same problem. He does not "swallow him up" as Job feared. Instead, He comes down to Job's level, meets him where he is, and adopts his tactic of asking questions. The gauntlet falls as God takes the initiative:

> Now prepare yourself like a man;
> I will question you,
> and you shall answer Me. (38:3; 40:7)

Job has challenged God; now it is God's turn to challenge Job. He will test his knowledge and push his wisdom to its outer limits. God will be like the professor who told his class at examination time, "If anyone gets 100 percent on my test, it means that I have not examined the limits of your knowledge." God says the same thing to Job, "I will test the limits of your knowledge." *Creation* is the theme of the test and three specific questions are asked of Job:

Do you know the *sources* from which the universe began? (38:4–21).

Do you understand the *systems* upon which the earth depends? (38:22–38).

Do you appreciate the *specialties* by which the animals are distinguished? (38:39–39:30).

None of the questions purports to answer the ethical issues for which Job demands a response. Evidently, God has something else in mind.

Do You Know the Sources from Which the Universe Began?

With unsurpassed poetic beauty, God opens the examination with a series of questions about his work as the architect and engineer of the universe:

> *Where were you when I laid the foundations of the earth?* (38:4)
> *Or who shut in the sea with doors?* (v. 8)
> *Have you commanded the morning since your days began,*
> *And caused the dawn to know its place?* (v. 12)
> *Have you entered the springs of the sea?* (v. 16)
> *Where is the way to the dwelling of light?* (v. 19)

Time collapses on Job. His beginning does not precede the Creator of the universe. His existence does not give him power to limit the sea, command the dawn, probe the underworld, or discover the source of light. Yet, Job has asked the question *why* about his suffering. It is a legitimate question because it arises from his God-given curiosity. To ask *why* is to inquire about the "first cause" of creation. To know the answer is to be God himself. Therefore, if the question *why* is twisted into Satan's promise that Adam and Eve can be as wise as God, natural curiosity can lead to sin and death.

Robert Oppenheimer, reputed to be the father of the atomic bomb, followed the scientist's curiosity when he said of the bomb, "It was so technologically sweet, it had to be invented." But after he heard about the devastation of Hiroshima when the bomb was dropped, he declared, "The physicists have known sin."

As the "Intermediate Adam," Job's curiosity has taken him into the same temptation. By demanding that God explain his suffering, Job assumes that he can be as wise as God. His first lesson must be that he is a created being with a brief history in time and space. As represented by the origins of the universe, Job will have to accept the tension of being able to ask *why* without the privilege of knowing all the answers. God is asking Job to trust Him.

Do You Understand the Systems upon Which the Earth Depends?

Without a pause, God's questions flow into a recital of the seasons of the earth. Winter's snow and hail fall as a time of trouble, stopping armies in their tracks (vv. 22–23). Spring floods followed by summer's thunderstorms bring rain to a parched land (vv. 26–27). In one case, God uses the snow and hail for the purpose of stopping war. In the other case, He brings rain to the wasteland to grow green grass for no apparent reason all, except for His own good pleasure.

Behind the question *why* is always the question *how.* Sin is more than the desire to be as wise as God; it is also the urge to be as powerful as God. If the cause of suffering, for instance, can be broken down into explainable pieces, it is assumed that solutions can be found to control the problem. This is the path of scientific process that has made miracles so common among us. God is not condemning science by His questions about the systems of the earth which remain a mystery to the human mind and ultimately out of human control. He is saying that the human mind can take the world apart, but it cannot put it back together again.

Fred Smith, one of the most creative of Christian minds in this century, heard a well-known philosopher say, "Whatever man can undo, man can do." Fred answered, "I'd like to break an egg over his head and say, 'Now you *do* what I have *undone.*'" Like the good theology in the nursery rhyme of Humpty-Dumpty's fall, all of the king's horses and all of the king's men cannot put that delicate shell back together again.

The mystery of the control of creation is further illustrated by the answer a panel of economists gave to the moderator's final question on a television program, "What is the greatest influence upon the world economy?" As one, the economists answered, "The weather." After all of our efforts to manage money and stock markets in order to control the economy, the honest confession is that the weather—a factor completely out of human control—will determine bull markets and bear markets, prosperity and depression, deficits and surpluses.

The lesson is that God is in control of what he creates. Job cannot understand *why* God controls His creation as he does any more than Job can comprehend creation itself. To believe in God is to live with mystery. Yet, God assures Job that the seasons do not come and go by whimsy. The movements of the celestial constellations—Pleiades, Orion, Mazzaroth, the Great Bear (vv. 31–33)—are bound, freed, started, and guided at His command to control the seasons of the earth. In between the heavens and the earth, there are the clouds that contain the water, rain, and electricity for lightning—falling and flashing upon his command. Is it possible what God is bringing to Job's mind is the lightning that caused the fire, killing his sheep and his servants in the first round of Job's catastrophes? Is there any connection in the fact that God is speaking out of a whirlwind, the very force of nature that took the lives of his children? If so, God is not saying that He caused their deaths, but He is saying that the lightning was not out of His control.

A fine line of mystery divides creation, control, and causation in human suffering. If God is the Creator of all and the Controller of all, is He not then the Cause of all, including natural catastrophes and the consequence of human suffering? Insurance companies carry this theology of causation through to their policies, which define natural catastrophes—such as earthquakes, tornadoes, floods, and fire caused by lightning—as "acts of God." According to God's word to Job, they are and they are not. He creates all of the elements of nature and controls them through His laws, but this does not mean ipso facto that God causes them to favor some people and to destroy others. He may, of course, intervene in nature to bring about His blessing or His judgment, but this does not mean that every act of nature can be explained as divine intervention.

Once again, we are suspended in a paradox, best defined as "truth held absurdly." With Job, we must believe that God is the Creator of all, the Controller of all, and the Cause of all, but not the one who intervenes in natural law so that every evidence of prosperity or punishment can be interpreted as a cause-and-effect relationship initiated by God. This was the fatal trap into which Eliphaz, Bildad, and Zophar fell. They insisted that human reason could understand everything that happens to human beings by applying the cause-and-effect formula in which God automatically rewards justice and punishes wickedness. No room is left for God's grace or mankind's faith.

Do You Appreciate the Speciality by Which Animals Are Distinguished?

Creation involves three categories, each unique on its own level: ***inanimate creation, animate creation,*** and ***human creation.*** The faultline of evolutionary theory is not just the question of origins, Did life begin by intelligent design or random accident? The theory also presumes a continuous line of upward development through the categories of creation. It is assumed that out of inanimate creation came the animals and out of the animals came human beings. No one doubts that animals are made up of chemical elements or that humans share the nervous, respiratory, and visceral systems with animals. But does this mean that each level of creation is a direct extension of the other? The frustrated search for the "missing link" between animals and human beings illustrates the efforts to prove the theory.

In Genesis, the six days draw the lines of distinction among the three categories of creation. Human creation, especially, is singled out when God declares, "Let Us make man in Our image, according to Our likeness" (1:26).

God's creative act is as special as His words. In the complementary account of creation in the second chapter of Genesis, the commonality and the uniqueness of human beings is clearly stated in the scriptural record: "And the LORD God formed man of the dust of the ground, and breathed into his nostrils the breath of life; and man became a living being [soul]" (2:7).

God teaches Job the lesson of special creation with illustrations from the animal kingdom. A dozen different animals are mentioned: lion, raven, goat, onager, deer, donkey, ox, ostrich, horse, locust, hawk, and eagle. Each has the common characteristic of being a living animal, but each is made fearfully and wonderfully different. Lions and ravens are animals that need help in finding food for their young (38:39–41). Lions tend to wait in ambush for their prey to come, while ravens tend to flit around in search of seeds. In both cases, God cares for them.

For the first time in the theophanies of Job, God's care for His creation is specifically introduced. A sequence is unfolding. God is not only the Creator of all, but He cares about each of His created beings. James Herriot must have been inspired when he entitled his books about the animal kingdom—*All Creatures Great and Small, All Things Wise and Wonderful,* and *All Things Bright and Beautiful.*

Centuries earlier, God preceded him in the Book of Job as He creates verbal pictures of the animals He loves—the ***unpredictability*** of the birthing and development of goats and deer (39:1–4); the ***freedom*** of the foraging donkey and onager (vv. 5–8); the ***stubbornness*** of the working ox (vv. 9–12); the *foolishness* of the speeding ostrich (vv. 13–18); the ***courage*** of the warring horse (vv. 19–25); the ***wisdom*** of the migrating hawk (v. 26); and the ***perspective*** of the high-nesting eagle (vv. 27–30).

Note that each animal in God's menagerie is not only unique in itself, but within each animal are complementary gifts and flaws, graces and faults, charms and handicaps. The ostrich, for instance, is at once the fastest and the most foolish of the animal creation. Deprived of the simple wisdom of maternal instinct, she lays her eggs and abandons them. Motherhood is so fundamental with us that we tend to write off the ostrich as a cruel trick of nature and a waste upon the earth. God doesn't think or act as we do. Even in the ostrich, He notes the compensating value of its ability to survive by sheer speed, outrunning the fastest horse and rider.

God is paying Job the greatest compliment that a teacher can give a student. Instead of giving him answers, God only asks questions. Instead of stating conclusions, God presents only the facts. Induction, not deduction, is God's method of teaching. He might have pronounced His conclusion to Job and then presented the supporting facts as a deductive teacher. If He had done so, Job's fear of being "swallowed up" would have been realized. But God shows how much He cares for His creation by refusing to violate Job's freedom or insult his intelligence. He gives him assorted facts and counts upon him to make the connections, see the meaning, and apply his understanding to the next higher and more complex level of learning. Underneath the process, however, God is at work on faith development. Facts and faith go hand in hand. When we have the facts, we need no faith. But when the facts add to the mystery of the unknown, even greater faith is required.

Job has been suffering in the "no-man's-land" between known facts and his unknown future. By demanding that God answer his question *why,* he has assumed that God owes him the facts to explain his affliction and defend divine justice. Inadvertently, Job has started on the path that leads to humanism, agnosticism, and atheism. Nietzsche, the atheist, said, "He who knows the *why* can bear with any *how!*"

Why is the question for which Satan promised the answer to Eve in the Garden. To her, he said, "You will be like God, knowing good and evil" (Gen. 3:5). As the Intermediate Adam, Job is tempted with the same question. Throughout his contest with his friends and his God, he demands answers to the question *why*. In his own way, he feels that his innocence has earned him the right to be as wise as God, knowing good and evil.

God honors Job's spiritual potential as well as his human intelligence by ignoring the question *why* in His response. To answer the question is to speed the human mind down the dead-end street where Nietzsche ran until he hit the wall of atheism, which in turn spawned the atrocities of the Nazi regime. As evidence of His loving care, when Job asks *why* God answers *who*. Faith is never created out of facts that answer the question *why*. Only out of mysteries beyond human comprehension comes the trust in *who*.

Job—Submitting in Silence

A conundrum begins to clear. "Why," we ask, "does God speak to Job without answering any of his questions?" The answer is that Job is casting a dark shadow between his mind and God's mind with the *why* of ethical questions about his suffering, which the human mind cannot comprehend or understand. We lack the perspective of God's view in *creating* the universe, *controlling* its forces, and *caring* about its creatures. Job needs to learn that the issue is not ethical, the question is not *why*, and the need is not understanding. The issue is spiritual, the question is *who*, and the need is trust.

> 1 Moreover the LORD answered Job, and said:
> 2 "Shall the one who contends with the Almighty correct Him?
> He who rebukes God, let him answer it."
> 3 Then Job answered the LORD and said:
> 4 "Behold, I am vile;
> What shall I answer You?
> I lay my hand over my mouth.
> 5 Once I have spoken, but I will not answer;
> Yes, twice, but I will proceed no further."
>
> Job 40:1–5

Job has two answers that he didn't expect to give. One is the answer to God's question, *"Who am I?"* He now sees the God who is purposeful in His creation, pervasive in His control, and personal in His care. The answers tell us about the gaps in Job's faith. His suffering has raised hidden doubts about God's purpose in creation, His power of control, and His personal interest in His creatures. At one and the same time, the question *why* reflects Job's deepest fears that all human beings know. Do we have doubts about God's purpose in our lives? Ask *why*. Do we have fears that He may not have control in every facet of our lives? Ask *why*. Do we have concerns about His personal interest in us? Ask *why*. These are the hidden and prior questions of trust that must be answered by an "I-Thou" relationship with God, not by a recitation of facts or reasons.

"Who am I?" is God's way of introducing Himself personally to us. For all his righteousness, Job has not met God in the depth and breadth of a relationship that includes the possibility of unexplained suffering.

The second question that God answers for Job is *"Who are you?"* By showing him the uniqueness of the animal creation and the complementary gifts and gaffs of the individual animals, God let Job draw the inference that he is a special creation of God above and beyond the animals, with untold capability for good and evil that escapes the limits of animal instinct and explores the realm of God's image through human intelligence. Yet with all this potential, human wisdom flounders on the shore of an uncharted ocean. At their best and at their highest, the miracles of human intelligence only open new vistas of mystery that prompt the breathless confession, I don't know, as the true expression of human wisdom. Hulme, in his book on Job entitled *Dialogue in Despair*, tells about a scientist who was asked to describe his research in one hundred fifty words. For his answer, the scientist wrote fifty times the three-word sentence, "I don't know."[1]

Job is a good, quick learner. After God puts question after question to him about His creation, His control, and His care, the challenge is repeated:

> *Shall the one who contends with the Almighty correct Him?*
> *He who rebukes God, let him answer it.* (40:2)

Job's rehearsed speech, which he planned to give in the presence of God, sticks in his throat. Like Isaiah who saw the Lord high and lifted up, he can only cry,

> *Behold, I am vile;*
> *What shall I answer You?* (v. 4)

The snowman of self-righteousness melts before God in the confession, "I am unworthy," and in the admission, "I don't know." The impotence of Job's righteousness and the ignorance of his wisdom is exposed. Job is reduced to silence—the last thing he expected to do in the presence of God, but the first thing that he needed to do in order to save himself from another flurry of words with which he would try to defend himself.

. . . Words had become his strategic defense and his offensive weapon. After all, he had reduced Eliphaz, Bildad, and Zophar to silence. Before God,

1. Hulme, *Dialogue in Despair*, p. 142.

however, he is the one who is reduced to confession and silence. With his hand over his mouth, Job no longer relies on his own weapon of words. He is learning to listen to God, but hearing alone is not healing. God has more to say and Job has more to learn.

God—The Mystery of Grace

God is not yet finished. Passing by Job's repentance, God unveils the mystery of His grace. Two exceptions to the beauty and harmony of the created order are noted. One is the margin of evil that appears to be out of God's control—an apparent exception to his omnipotence. The other is the ridiculous animals—the behemoth or hippopotamus and the leviathan or crocodile—who appear to be out of harmony with the rest of creation. For these exceptions, God's grace is sufficient. For the first time, Job sees his suffering from the perspective of God's view. In a leap of faith, he shouts, "I see"—the beauty of God's power, the harmony of His creation, the justice of His ways, and the sufficiency of His grace. Job is more than reconciled to God—he is redeemed.

> 6 Then the LORD answered Job out of the whirlwind, and said:
> 7 "Now prepare yourself like a man;
> I will question you, and you shall answer Me:
> 8 "Would you indeed annul My judgment?
> Would you condemn Me that you may be justified?
> 9 Have you an arm like God?
> Or can you thunder with a voice like His?
> 10 Then adorn yourself with majesty and splendor,
> And array yourself with glory and beauty.
> 11 Disperse the rage of your wrath;
> Look on everyone who is proud, and humble him.
> 12 Look on everyone who is proud, and bring him low;
> Tread down the wicked in their place.
> 13 Hide them in the dust together,
> Bind their faces in hidden darkness.
> 14 Then I will also confess to you
> That your own right hand can save you.
> 15 "Look now at the behemoth, which I made along with you;
> He eats grass like an ox.
> 16 See now, his strength is in his hips,
> And his power is in his stomach muscles.
> 17 He moves his tail like a cedar;
> The sinews of his thighs are tightly knit.
> 18 His bones are like beams of bronze,
> His ribs like bars of iron.
> 19 He is the first of the ways of God;
> Only He who made him can bring near His sword.

20 Surely the mountains yield food for him,
And all the beasts of the field play there.
21 He lies under the lotus trees,
In a covert of reeds and marsh.
22 The lotus trees cover him with their shade;
The willows by the brook surround him.
23 Indeed the river may rage,
Yet he is not disturbed;
He is confident, though the Jordan gushes into his mouth,
24 Though he takes it in his eyes,
Or one pierces his nose with a snare.
41:1 "Can you draw out Leviathan with a hook,
Or snare his tongue with a line which you lower?
2 Can you put a reed through his nose,
Or pierce his jaw with a hook?
3 Will he make many supplications to you?
Will he speak softly to you?
4 Will he make a covenant with you?
Will you take him as a servant forever?
5 Will you play with him as with a bird,
Or will you leash him for your maidens?
6 Will your companions make a banquet of him?
Will they apportion him among the merchants?
7 Can you fill his skin with harpoons,
Or his head with fishing spears?
8 Lay your hand on him;
Remember the battle—
Never do it again!
9 Indeed, any hope of overcoming him is false;
Shall one not be overwhelmed at the sight of him?
10 No one is so fierce that he would dare stir him up.
Who then is able to stand against Me?
11 Who has preceded Me, that I should pay him?
Everything under heaven is Mine.
12 "I will not conceal his limbs,
His mighty power, or his graceful proportions.
13 Who can remove his outer coat?
Who can approach him with a double bridle?
14 Who can open the doors of his face,
With his terrible teeth all around?
15 His rows of scales are his pride,
Shut up tightly as with a seal;
16 One is so near another
That no air can come between them;
17 They are joined one to another,
They stick together and cannot be parted.
18 His sneezings flash forth light,
And his eyes are like the eyelids of the morning.

19 Out of his mouth go burning lights;
Sparks of fire shoot out.
20 Smoke goes out of his nostrils,
As from a boiling pot and burning rushes.
21 His breath kindles coals,
And a flame goes out of his mouth.
22 Strength dwells in his neck,
And sorrow dances before him.
23 The folds of his flesh are joined together;
They are firm on him and cannot be moved.
24 His heart is as hard as stone,
Even as hard as the lower millstone.
25 When he raises himself up, the mighty are afraid;
Because of his crashings they are beside themselves.
26 Though the sword reaches him, it cannot avail;
Nor does spear, dart, or javelin.
27 He regards iron as straw,
And bronze as rotten wood.
28 The arrow cannot make him flee;
Slingstones become like stubble to him.
29 Darts are regarded as straw;
He laughs at the threat of javelins.
30 His undersides are like sharp potsherds;
He spreads pointed marks in the mire.
31 He makes the deep boil like a pot;
He makes the sea like a pot of ointment.
32 He leaves a shining wake behind him;
One would think the deep had white hair.
33 On earth there is nothing like him,
Which is made without fear.
34 He beholds every high thing;
He is king over all the children of pride."

Job 40:6–41:34

"The God of Contingencies"

Submissive and silent, Job awaits God's response. No spoken acceptance of his confession is given or needed. By advancing to His next subject, God assumes that Job has learned his first lesson—he is small before the bigness of God; his knowledge is limited in time and scope; and his words are symbols of his security rather than his wisdom. Like a hungry baby bird reaching upward with its mouth wide open, Job is ready and eager to learn again.

God begins by letting Job know that He has another subject in mind. Out of the whirlwind, God repeats His challenge:

Now prepare yourself like a man;
I will question you,
and you shall answer Me. (40:7)

Still in a confrontational mood, God goes straight to the point with four questions that pick up on Job's earlier demands:

> *Would you indeed annul My judgment?*
> *Would you condemn Me that you may be justified?*
> *Have you an arm like God?*
> *Or can you thunder with a voice like His?* (vv. 8–9)

In paraphrase, God is asking:

> Do you *refute* My wisdom?
> Do you *condemn* My justice?
> Do you *doubt* My power?
> Do you *reject* My voice?

Once again, God sets the agenda for His teaching. The subject is the justice and the power of God. Time after time, Job has raised questions about God's moral government which permitted him to suffer even in his innocence. From his viewpoint, God has to be either unfair in His justice or limited in His power. Job has raised the ethical questions and moral issues upon which faith or fatalism turns. In his opening address, God ignored these issues. His first task was to soften the heart and open Job's mind for learning beyond human wisdom. Sweeping generalizations about the physical universe and special examples from the animal kingdom show Job the mysteries of God's creation, control, and care which he can never fully comprehend. When Job admits his limited wisdom and drops his verbal guard, he is ready to face the tougher questions that God will ask.

Consistent with His character, God continues to honor the personhood and respect the intelligence of Job by asking him questions and letting him draw the conclusions. Job has acknowledged that the wisdom of God's general and special creation is beyond the time or scope of his understanding. God now asks him to understand the apparent *exceptions* in His power and wisdom that perplex and confound the wisest of the wise among human minds.

In management circles, the "critical incident" has been identified as the factor that distinguishes between effective and ineffective executives. Any job has routine matters that almost anyone can handle. Executives earn their money, however, when they must make crucial decisions that determine the destiny of their people and their organization. Such decisions arise out of "critical incidents" for which there is no company policy or standard practice. When Harry Truman said, "If you can't stand the heat, get out of the kitchen," he was referring to the decisions on "critical incidents" that the president of the United States is called to make. Critical incidents in the careers of American presidents include Truman's firing of General Douglas MacArthur, Dwight D. Eisenhower's priority for the space program, John F. Kennedy's blockade of Cuba, Lyndon B. Johnson's bombing of Hanoi,

Richard Nixon's failure to destroy the tapes, Jimmy Carter's attempt to free the Iranian hostages, and Ronald Reagan's risk on the "Star Wars" system.

Suppose, for example, that the president of a corporation is informed that a vice-president is suspected of embezzlement. How does he handle the volatile situation? All of the accumulated experiences of a lifetime are needed to weigh all the evidence, balance responsibilities for the individual and the institution, consider the long-term consequences for all parties, and still make a fair and clean decision. The issue is a "critical incident." The decision makes the difference between an effective and an ineffective executive.

Three exceptions to the moral order of the universe, which God created and controls, are presented to Job as "critical incidents." To begin, God asks Job to change roles and assume that he has in his hands the power of God. Now, as the new executor of the universe, Job must make decisions on three "critical incidents":

> Would you *crush the wicked?* (vv. 8–14)
> Would you *create the useless?* (vv. 15–24)
> Would you *control the hostile?* (41:1–34)

In each case, power is the issue and justice is the principle with which Job must deal.

Would You Crush the Wicked?

Job has complained about the apparent inconsistency of God letting him suffer while the wicked prosper. Indirectly, God admits that this is a problem with which He also struggles. Strict justice, not unlike the king in which Eliphaz, Bildad, and Zophar believed, dictated swift punishment for the wicked and abundant prosperity for the righteous. Certainly, such action is within His power. Why then, does He not crush the wicked to prove that He is just? Job, who has questioned God's justice, is asked what he would do if God's power were in his hands. God imagines that Job would

> *Disperse the rage of your wrath;*
> *Look on everyone who is proud,*
> *and humble him.*
> . . . .
> *Tread down the wicked in their place.*
> *Hide them in the dust together,*
> *Bind their faces in*
> *hidden darkness.* (40:11–13)

If Job would do this, God agrees to bow before him, confess his greatness, and acknowledge his power to save himself (v. 14). In other words, Job would prove to be the omnipotent God of justice, but something would still be missing. He would not be the God of grace who delays his judgment in order to save the wicked. Later on, this attribute of grace will become flesh and blood in the person of Jesus Christ. As an intimation of that time, God is showing Job his grace in a situation where justice rules and when he owes the wicked nothing but punishment. Yet, he does not destroy them as Job might wish because of his genuine love for his creation.

Whenever human beings have the power to play God and use that power to punish the wicked, evil triumphs. The Spanish Inquisition and the Holy Wars are horror stories in human history. Prompted by the motive to punish evil in the name of Christ, they concocted greater evil than the sins they sought to punish. In the Garden of Gethsemane, when the Roman guard came to arrest him, Jesus rebuked Peter for brandishing the sword and cutting off the Roman servant's ear, "Put your sword in its place, for all who take the sword will perish by the sword" (Matt. 26:52).

Job is quick to understand the point. If he exercised swift and certain justice upon the wicked, he too would die because he has acknowledged that he is not without sinful nature. What appears to be God's injustice, then, is in reality the patience of redeeming grace.

Would You Create the Useless?

God illustrates this question with a graphic portrayal of the behemoth, perhaps the animal better known to us as the hippopotamus. At best, the monstrous animal is a riddle of creation. He eats grass like an ox, but is not an ox; he has strength in his hips, his stomach, and his thighs, and yet he is useless for work. He is blessed with a tail like a tree, bones like bronze, and ribs like iron (vv. 17–18).

But for what purpose? The hippopotamus has no place among the birds and beasts of earlier listing because it has no unique function or special quality that sets it apart in the animal kingdom. The hippopotamus is ugly and useless.

Humor is a part of God's grace. The hippopotamus is a ludicrous creature who fouls up a neat and orderly universe in which everything makes sense and everything makes a contribution. Not the hippo. It is a maverick beast known for crashing through the jungle, upsetting the harmony of nature, or sinking up to its bulbous eyeballs in a muddy riverbed. If the hippopotamus has a reason for being, it is to keep us laughing at the ludicrous in ourselves as well as in the universe.

God has another view of the hippopotamus. Is his tongue in his cheek when he tells Job how much he prizes the hippopotamus?

> *I made* [him] *along with you.* (v. 15)
> *He is the first of the ways of God.* (v. 19)

God is not kidding. The big, dumb, ugly, useless animal called the hippopotamus is a special object of God's care. Whether feeding on the mountains, playing in the fields, lying under a lotus tree, or letting the river gush into his eyes, nose, and mouth, the beast is a tranquil picture of playful trust.

Beauty and function are not the conditions of God's grace. Among the contingencies of His creation are ugly and useless creatures or circumstances for which the purpose seems unknown.

Among the frequent cries that surround the suffering of the innocent souls are "What a waste!" and "How senseless!" Very legitimately, Job feels the same way about his suffering. But then, God gives him the opportunity to assume the power and answer the questions, "Would you create the ugly and useless?" and "Would you do away with all creatures or circumstances for which there is no obvious purpose?" Some suffering would disappear if the useless were erased from the earth, but what would be lost? Learning the lesson from the hippopotamus, there would be no need for the humor of God's grace, and because each of us has some of the ugly and the useless in us, there would be no need to trust God.

To judge the value of persons or events on their utilitarian merits is another dangerous doctrine that must be avoided at all costs. One of the first stirrings of moral decadence in a civilization is to devalue or destroy persons who are not deemed useful to the culture. Girl babies who could not contribute to the "macho" image of Rome were tossed out in the street after one look by the father. Eskimo and Indian societies sent their elderly into the wilderness to die when they could no longer fight, work, or move with the tribe. Our society may be on the borderline of such decadence. The premium upon utilitarian values is so high that uselessness may be among the motives behind abortion without cause. A baby who restricts freedom, requires unselfish attention, costs $200,000–$300,000 to raise, and offers nothing useful in return may be an unwanted child.

If this attitude persists as a characteristic of our culture, a major moral crisis may be in the making. People over the age of sixty-five are the fastest-growing segment of our population, and, of that category, people over one hundred years old are the fastest-growing segment of all. To this time, however, we have failed to utilize effectively the skills and experience of the aged. If utility is equated with worth, we will have to find a meaningful function for the elderly or face the dilemma of living wills, negotiated deaths, suicide pacts, and varied forms of euthanasia.

On another level, a society that is dominated by utilitarian values has little appreciation for the creative arts or recreative play. A sculpture or a symphony may have value only in themselves, but they are the "grace notes" that are prized by great societies and devalued by declining civilizations.

Learning from a hippopotamus may seem to be a bizarre way to appreciate what appears to be ugly and useless in the realm of God's creation. But without the hippopotamus, we would lose another example of God's loving grace for an undeserving creature. With Job, we learn to laugh and cry when we realize that there is some of the ugly and the useless in each of us. Never again can we see water gushing up to the bulgy eyes, over the pointy ears, and out of the snubby snout of a hippopotamus resting on a riverbed without seeing a prized creature of God's creation and a precious example of God's grace.

Would You Control the Hostile?

At the other extreme of creation is the leviathan, an amphibious monster of land and sea, which may be the animal we know as the crocodile. In contrast with the playful trust of the useless hippopotamus, the crocodile is a creature of violent hostility. God uses the crocodile to symbolize the forces of evil that exist for one persistent and malicious purpose in the universe—to oppose the will of God. In the most vivid and complete portrait of any of the animals, God details every incorrigible characteristic of the crocodile in a chapter that might be entitled, "Everything You Always Wanted to Know about Crocodiles but Were Afraid to Ask." The horny, hostile monster is described as uncatchable, unfeeling, untrustworthy, unmanageable, unplayful, undesirable, unhospitable, and unethical (41:1–6).

Attempts to capture or control the crocodile are vain. Furthermore, wisdom suggests that it is foolish to aggravate the crocodile because of all the beasts of the earth, he is the most ferocious of all. What is the difference between a crocodile and an alligator? According to an attendant at a zoological park, the crocodile will attack people without provocation while the alligator will strike only as provoked.

It takes God to subdue the crocodile. Where human beings fail, He can control:

> *Who then is able to stand against Me?*
> *Who has preceded Me,*
> *that I should pay him?*
> *Everything under heaven is Mine.* (vv. 10–11)

No doubt remains. All of the forces of evil, no matter how fierce, are not outside of God's command. Why, then, doesn't God wipe evil from the face of the earth? This is the question that is posed to Job. God asks, "If you had the power to subdue evil, would you do it?" Sin would end, suffering would cease, and God's justice would be vindicated. But what would be lost? Once again, the answer is ***human freedom*** and ***divine grace***. Job might have been relieved of suffering, but he could not have been redeemed from sin. In the symbol of the crocodile, God makes a choice. He prefers a loving relationship with his creation more than a perfect world. Thus, he permits evil to exist until he has fulfilled his redemptive purpose. Saints as well as sinners will be victims of evil, but out of suffering, God will work his good purpose.

God has more to say about evil. With descriptive overkill, he introduces Job to the biological details of the crocodile:

limbs that are mighty and graceful (v. 12);
skins that cannot be removed and a ferocity that will not respond to a double bridle (v. 13);
jaws that cannot be opened and teeth that cannot be counted; (v. 14);
scales that are like a coat of armor (v. 15);

sneezings that flash with light and eyelids that lift like the dawn; (v. 18);
breath that resembles fire (v. 19);
strength that centers in the neck (v. 22);
flesh that defies penetration (v. 23); and
a heart that is as hard as stone (v. 24)

All of the human weapons that are arrayed against the crocodile will fail:

sword, spear, dart and javelin bounce off him (vv. 26–27);
iron is as straw and bronze is as rotting wood (v. 27);
arrows do not faze him and slingstones are like stubble against him (v. 28); and
darts are like straw and javelins are a laugh to him (v. 29).

Once the crocodile is aggravated, however, he

slashes the mire with pointed marks (v. 30);
makes the deep boil like a pot and turns the sea into seething ointment (v. 31); and
leaves a shining wake behind him (v. 32).

Nothing on earth is like him—fearless, ferocious, and formidable. Symbolizing Satan, the crocodile *"is king over all the children of pride"* (v. 34). Among God's creatures, he is the epitome of evil.

God has brought Job full cycle to the issue of evil in the universe. He permits evil in order to reveal His grace, but He will not provoke evil by exercising his power. Contrary to the opinion of Rabbi Harold Kushner that God is limited in his power to heal, Job is taught that God in His wisdom will not always act to subdue evil if a greater evil is the result or if his redemptive purpose is sacrificed. Only an administrator of justice can understand the dilemma of making moral decisions in which the choice is for the lesser evil as well as the greater good.

Elton Trueblood, one of my mentors in philosophy and faith, shook me up the first time that I met him. He accepted the invitation to be our commencement speaker at Spring Arbor College when I was president. When we met for breakfast prior to the commencement service, Trueblood said that he had to miss an important Monday morning class to give the commencement address. "I had to choose," he said, "between lesser evils. Would my students missing the class suffer more than the audience not hearing me speak?" At the time, I reacted against this negative outlook because I wanted every decision to be made in the context of the greater good, not the lesser evil. Later, I learned that Trueblood's realism put a perspective on decision-making that I had missed. Our decisions for the greater good can result in the greater evil. To impose Christian values on a sinful society, for instance, may be consistent with the greater good, but, more often than not, the long-term consequence is a greater evil. Furthermore, in practical decision-making as an administrator, another of my mentors in the university presidency, Dr. Charles Odegaard, often said, "Whenever I make an executive decision, I must ask who it is that I will alienate." Through the symbol of the crocodile, God is teaching Job that He does not always act to punish short-term evil because the long-term consequences may be a greater evil.

God has introduced Job to the most profound and perplexing problem of the universe. Without direct references, He has invited him into the inner sanctum of heaven's council, where He accepted the challenge of Satan to test the faith of His servant Job. Evil is the ultimate contingency of the universe which God permits in order to show His grace, and He will not provoke long-term evil for a short-term good. No higher compliment could be given by God to Job than to unveil this truth with the confidence that His servant will understand. A ferocious creature as incorrigible as the crocodile is God's way of explaining the existence of evil as an opportunity for His grace.

The God of the orderly creation and the God of the disorderly contingency has now introduced Himself to Job. He does not answer the plaintiff's question *why,* but He does address the ultimate question *who.* When it comes down to the rub of our fears, we are afraid that some corner of creation is out of God's control. No conundrum is greater than the suffering of the innocent. This is why God addresses Himself to Job's fear rather than answering His questions of fact. Unless we have all of the facts of the omniscient mind—back to the origins, systems, and distinctions of creation—our fears will remain. If, however, we are confident that there is no contingency or creature outside the command of the God who cares, we can bear the pain of suffering and live with mystery. Unencumbered trust is God's goal for His servant Job.

Job—Seeing through Suffering

As quickly as the whirlwind appeared, it vanishes. The voice of God is gone, finishing on a strange note; not a call to faith, but a statement of fact about the crocodile as the symbol of evil in the world,

> On earth there is nothing like him,
> Which is made without fear.
> He beholds every high thing;
> He is king over all the children of pride. (vv. 33–34)

God has revealed the character of Satan—fearing no one of earth, lording it over the high of the earth, and presiding over the pride in human hearts.

Job is left with a decision. Can he affirm his faith in God knowing that Satan is still permitted to work evil in the world? Can he put his trust in God who will not answer his question *why*? Even more personally, can he believe in God who will give him no promise of immunity from the mysterious accidents of nature or from the deliberate actions of Satan whose obsession is to make him curse God and die?

> 1 Then Job answered the LORD and said:
> 2 "I know that You can do everything,
> And that no purpose of Yours can be withheld from You.
> 3 You asked, 'Who is this who hides counsel without knowledge?'
> Therefore I have uttered what I did not understand,
> Things too wonderful for me, which I did not know.
> 4 Listen, please, and let me speak;
> You said, 'I will question you, and you shall answer Me.'
> 5 "I have heard of You by the hearing of the ear,
> But now my eye sees You.
> 6 Therefore I abhor myself,
> And repent in dust and ashes."
>
> Job (42:1–6)

For Job, the question is no longer *why* but *who*. This is a two-sided question that every person must answer, whether suffering in innocence or devasted by sin: *Who am I?* and *Who is God?*

Spiritually, the answer to the first question is a *confession of need;* the answer to the second question is an *affirmation of faith*. Job does not disappoint us.

Who Am I?

When God first spoke to Job out of the whirlwind, he asked the question "Who is this?" (38:2). Now, in a human confession of need, Job repeats the question and answers, "Who am I?" He makes a humble confession of need: I am *weak* (42:2), I am *unwise* and *wordy* (v. 3), and I am *unworthy* (v. 6).

Job needs to confess each of these deficiencies. Although he has not sinned, his pride has taken him perilously close to blasphemy when he demands that God come down to his level of power and understanding. God must have had him in mind when He closed his speech with the warning about Satan, "He is king over all the children of pride" (41:34). Job gets the message. His pride in his own righteousness has taken him within a hair's breadth of Satan's control. Therefore, before he can affirm his faith, he must confess his pride.

My mother used to say, "Confession is good for the soul." Job is not confessing either the overt sins of the rich of which Eliphaz accused him (22:2–11) or the hidden sins of the hypocrite which Bildad tried to uncover (8:11–18). He is confessing his reliance upon the power of his own righteousness and the wisdom of his own knowledge. In part, Job is a victim of his background. Schooled in the oral tradition and mastered by self-discipline, the strength of his background could have been a weakness in his faith.

Tragedy dogs the steps of people who have let religious tradition or self-discipline become their barrier to God. A friend of mine who is dying of cancer still blames his fundamentalist background for keeping him from God. If he is to be healed in spirit, if not in body, he must confess that he has used his background as an excuse for his cynicism. Without his confession, Job would have fallen into the same cynical mire. He had followed every fundamentalist step toward faith—living blamelessly and uprightly, fearing God and shunning evil (1:1). By all human counts, he was righteous and wise. His suffering, then, becomes the pivot upon which he can grow in faith or sink in cynicism. Job chooses to grow. Confessing that he is weak, unwise, wordy, and unworthy, Job progresses to an affirmation of faith that is big enough to include the question, Why do the innocent suffer?

Who Is God?

If a person never goes beyond asking "Who am I?", fatalistic despair is inevitable. After a lifetime of asking "Who am I?", the humanist Walter Kauffman summed up his philosophy of life by saying, "Just do the best you can, and, if possible, face death with a smile."

If Job had stopped with the confession that he was weak, unwise, wordy, and unworthy, the book that bears his name would be lost among other literary tragedies.

In modern literature, the works of Elie Wiesel represent that kind of tragedy. Wiesel, who coined the word *holocaust,* suffers all of the wounds of a child who somehow survived both Auschwitz and Buchenwald. Wiesel said, "So heavy was my anguish that in the spring of 1945 I made a vow: not to speak, not to touch upon the essential for at least ten years. Long enough to unite the language of humanity with the silence of the dead."[2]

Today, his books such as *Night, The Jews of Silence, One Generation After,* and *The Fifth Son* still carry the theme of his first book, when he broke the silence: "A child watches the hanging of another child: 'Where is God? Where is He?' . . . And I heard a voice within me answer: 'Where is He? Here He is—He is hanging here on this gallows.'"[3]

Wiesel cannot separate the murder of the innocent from the martyrdom of faith. Ever so slowly, such as with the birth of his own son, Wiesel is beginning to believe again. He, with Job, balances upon the pivot that can turn to festering cynicism or affirming faith. The pivot is the suffering of the innocent.

Only the redeeming grace of God can bring us through tragedy to an affirming faith that covers every contingency—known and unknown, useful and useless, good and evil. This is not a flippant statement of faith; it is a fact of life. To limit ourselves to the question "Who am I?", whether for ourselves or for humanity, will ultimately lead to the martyrdom of faith. Only by ask-

2. Elie Wiesel, *Time* magazine, March 18, 1985, p. 79.
3. Elie Wiesel, *Night/Dawn, The Accident* (New York: Hill and Wang, 1972), p. 10.

ing the companion question "Who is God?" can faith be resurrected, expanded, and affirmed.

Critical scholars find redundance in Job's first confession of submission and silence and his second confession of weakness, lack of wisdom, wordiness, and unworthiness. They fail to understand the full meaning of the gospel that Jesus proclaims at the announcement of his public ministry, "Repent and believe the Gospel." In his confession, Job *repents;* in his affirmation, Job *believes.* A creed of faith can be written out of the affirmations that Job speaks in response to the question "Who is God?"

> I know that *Your power* can do anything for me, and that *Your purpose* will be accomplished for me (42:2),
> I know that *Your will* is good for me (v. 3),
> I know that *Your presence* is real to me (v. 5), and
> I know that *Your grace* is given to me (v. 6).

Two words are key to understanding Job's affirmation of faith. One is the word *"wonderful"* (v. 3), the other is the word *"sees"* (v. 5).

Eliphaz, Bildad, Zophar, and Elihu expressed the grandest of poetic eloquence in their hymns of praise to the power and majesty of God. None of them, however, used the word *"wonderful"* to exalt his works. At the thought of his presence, they quaked with "fear." Now we know why. *Fear* is the logical response to the justice of God; *wonder* is the experiential response to the grace of God. Mystery, wonder, and grace are inseparable. God expects us to marvel at the mysteries of his creation. More than that, he wants us to enjoy the wonders of his creation with him. But most of all, he wants us to see the wonder of his grace and the mystery of his creation. Adults tend to fear mystery but children find glee in the unknown. So when Job speaks of *"things too wonderful for me,"* he is like a child reveling for a moment in the wonders of God. Elizabeth Akers Allen wished for such a moment when she wrote,

> Backward, turn backward
> O time, in your flight
> Make me a child again
> Just for tonight.[4]

Rachel Carson is best known for her book *Silent Spring,* in which she foresees the pollution of nature by the use of pesticides. A lesser-known book, which I prize, is entitled *A Sense of Wonder.* With her nephew Roger at her side, Miss Carson explores the beach and woods through the eyes of a child. In one of the most beautiful passages in contemporary literature, she writes,

4. Elizabeth Akers Allen, *Saturday Evening Post,* May 1960.

> A child's world is fresh and beautiful, full of wonder and excitement. It is our misfortune that for most of us that clear-eyed vision, that true instinct for what is beautiful and awe-inspiring is dimmed and even lost before we reach adulthood. If I had influence with the good fairy who is supposed to preside over the christening of all children, I should ask that her gift to each child in the world would be a sense of wonder so indestructible that it would last throughout a life, as an unfailing antidote against the boredom and disenchantment of later years, the sterile preoccupation with things that are artificial, the alienation from our source of strength.[5]

If only Rachel Carson had known God. Her sense of wonder led her to the threshold of His presence, but she died before she finished her book or declared her faith. Job, however, crosses the threshold of wonder into the very presence of God. In the wonders of creation, he catches a glimpse of the grace of God. With the writer of the Proverbs, he worships as he wonders:

> There are three things which are too wonderful for me,
> Yes, four which I do not understand:
> The way of an eagle in the air,
> The way of a serpent upon a rock,
> The way of a ship in the midst of the sea,
> And the way of a man with a virgin. (Prov. 30:18–19)

Before this experience, the power of God in creation provoked in Job the fear that is reputed to be the "beginning of wisdom." Now, he advances in faith as a sense of wonder leads him into the presence of Wisdom itself. Like a child who is at home with the wonders of creation, if Job were alive today, he would smile, nod his head, and join in the chorus of George Beverly Shea's well-known song,

> There's the wonder of sunset at evening,
> The wonder of sunrise I see;
> But the wonder of wonders that thrills my soul
> Is the wonder that God loves me.

Seeing is the other word that opens up our understanding of Job's affirmation of faith. Elihu, in his second speech, introduced us to the "inner ear" of human reason,

> For the ear tests words
> As the palate tastes food. (34:3)

5. Rachel Carson, *A Sense of Wonder* (New York: Harper and Row, 1956), pp. 42–43.

Job, exemplar of the Wisdom School, confesses that he has relied upon the same teaching-learning process in his approach to God: *"I have heard You by the hearing of the ear"* (42:5).

The teaching of his elders and the logic of his mind had served as Job's way of knowing God. Out of the same oral tradition as Eliphaz, Bildad, and Zophar, Job had only extended their line of thinking on the straight line of human reason. They had become fixed in the tradition of orthodoxy that equated suffering with sin and prosperity with righteousness. Job had not really refuted their position; he had only extended it by continuing to conceive God within the limits of his own mind. Taking a "me-He" rather than an "I-Thou" approach to God, Job demanded an answer from God on human terms. While protesting his innocence, Job was really demonstrating his arrogance. He spoke only with the authority of what he had heard about God from the oral tradition and what he had thought about God in his own mind.

No wonder that God came to Job out of a whirlwind. A breakthrough is needed before Job's faith can be transformed from hearsay to experience. Job's own testimony is witness to that breakthrough: *"But now my eye sees You"* (v. 5).

Throughout Scripture, the "eye" symbolizes the spiritual perception that comes from a life-changing encounter with God. While no mortal man can actually "see" God and live, it is possible to know his person and his presence so intimately that one can say, *"My eye sees You."*

Malcolm Muggeridge is a severe critic of television, because he says that it makes us *see* as spectators, not as participants. Edmund Blake's verse supports Muggeridge:

> This Life's dim windows of the soul
> Distorts the Heavens from Pole to Pole,
> And leads you to believe a lie,
> When you see with, not through, the eye.[6]

Job's self-confessed wordiness blurred his view of God—His person, His presence, and His purpose. Once he clapped his hand over his mouth and confessed his ignorance, he began to see clearly through to the person, presence, and purpose of God. All of the wonders of creation began to make sense. They are not just accidents of nature, or displays of power, but expressions of a person—God himself. Through the seeing of the eye, Job's world comes together. He has perspective. Usually, we think of perspective as the ability to see the larger scene so that the parts of the picture fit into a meaningful whole. We forget that perspective is gained only by "seeing through" to the center point to which all other parts are related.

6. Malcolm Muggeridge, *Christ and the Media* (Grand Rapids: Wm. B. Eerdmans, 1977), p. 62.

In my office are three original color prints of geometric figures done by Brian Halsey, a Christian artist. Each print is perfect in symmetry. To appreciate them, however, you must "see through" to the center point from which all of the patterns and figures emerge. To help lead your eye to the point of perspective, the artist uses variations of the same color to focus the brightest light at the center from which all lines diverge in relationship to the center point and to each other. It is no surprise to learn that Halsey entitled the series "Creation." God is the point of perspective, and his creation is in perfect unity with him. After "seeing through" to the perspective of the prints and appreciating the perfection of every line, it is easy to understand how God stepped back to view his own creative work and said, "It is good."

Job "sees through" to God. No longer does he rely upon tradition or hearsay about God; he knows God for himself. No longer does he have to depend upon human reason to define the nature of God; he has been in the presence of God. No longer does he have to tremble in fear before the power of God; he has seen the grace of God. No longer does he have to demand an explanation for every mystery; he has put his trust in God. Through the perception of the soul, Job sees the answer to the question, Who is God? *He is the God of grace.* With the Bishop of Cambrai, Job can now say, "Smite or heal / Depress or build me up / I adore Thy purposes without knowing them." Better yet, he can add experience to insight and speak again the grand affirmation of his faith, "Though He slay me, yet will I trust Him" (13:15).

He can sing his hope with new meaning,

> I know that my Redeemer lives,
> And He shall stand at last on the earth;
> And after my skin is destroyed,
>   this I know,
> That in my flesh I shall see God. (19:25–26)

Job can now bear his suffering through his seeing,

> He knows the way that I take;
> When He has tested me,
> I shall come forth as gold. (23:10)

Knowing the answer to the question *who,* Job no longer needs to ask the question *why.*

Why then does Job conclude his response to God by bowing and repenting once again? The answer is that one who "sees through" to the great grace of God bows humbly and repents sincerely. By bowing, grace lifts him; by repenting, grace liberates him. So, like the phoenix bird rising out of the dust and ashes with the colors of the sun, God will lift Job to his feet and set him free—reconciled, restored, and ready to serve others with new-found grace. Job has "seen through" to God.

32

The Design of Yahweh's Speeches

Norman C. Habel

The speeches of Yahweh are majestic poems, rich in lyric artistry, literary ambiguity, and theological profundity. In these poems language, form, and theme are integrated into a structural unity (cf. Kubina, *Die Gottesreden im Buche Hiob*). The intent of the poet in these speeches is revealed in the design for this final poetic segment of the book. The balanced components of that design are evident in the following outline:

Any interpretation of Yahweh's speeches must take into account both their framework and core. The opening narrative report (38:1) introduces

From Norman C. Habel, *The Book of Job, A Commentary*, Old Testament Library (Philadelphia: Westminster, 1985), 526–35. Used by permission of Westminster/John Knox Press.

A Introductory formula with report of theophany event	38:1	A1 Introductory formula with report of theophany event	40:6
B Thematic challenge	38:2–3	B1 Thematic challenge	40:7–14
i Theme A Who is this who clouds my *design* . . . ?		i Theme B Would you impugn my *justice?*	
ii Summons Gird your loins		ii Summons Gird your loins	
C Elaboration of theme		C1 Elaboration of theme	
i in the physical world	38:4–38	i with Behemoth	40:15–24
ii in the animal kingdom	38:39–39:30	ii with Leviathan	40:25–41:26 [41:1–34E]
D Challenge to Legal Adversary	40:1–2		
E Answer of Job	40:3–5	E1 Answer of Job	42:1–6

three key literary features: *(a)* ironic fulfillment, *(b)* thematic shock, and *(c)* structural integration. God's personal appearance is what Job both desired and feared. In an earlier speech he cried:

> If I summoned him to court and he answered,
> I do not believe he would hear my voice.
> He would crush me with a whirlwind *(ś^{e}‘ārā)*
> And increase my wounds without cause. (9:16–17)

Ironically Yahweh does appear in a whirlwind and he overwhelms Job with a battery of challenges (cf. Robertson, *The Old Testament and the Literary Critic*, 48–50). Job had feared that if God appeared in court, his "terror" would so intimidate Job that he would be prevented from having a fair trial (9:34; 13:21). Yet Job's great passion was to confront God face to face (see on 13:15, 20, 24), and his final challenge to God is a summons for God to present his case in writing and in person (31:35–37). For Job to expect God to appear in person, however, was absurdly presumptuous. According to Israelite tradition, no mortal could see God and live. Or as Elihu says:

> It is not for a mortal to set a time
> To come before El in litigation.
> (34:23)

Elihu expressed the force of this tradition clearly when he proclaimed the transcendence of God (ch. 35) and announced that his just governance was discernible in the established course of events. Direct private revelation for a reprobate individual was unthinkable. Then comes the shock ending. Yahweh appears to Job as he did to heroic figures like Noah and Abraham. The God of the heroic past is not an otiose high god who has retired into oblivion. God's earlier silence, the wager of the prologue which has never been disclosed to Job, and the traditional theology of Elihu, which provides a legitimate answer for Job, prepares the audience for the appropriate silence of God. To our surprise God does appear and does speak. But he confounds Job with questions, not with his "terror." By having God appear as Yahweh, rather than Shaddai or El, the author integrates God's speeches with the other narrative elements of the book where the name of Yahweh is used. The God who appeared to Israel in later theophanies is the deity who appears to Job, even though Job remains ignorant of his name. Thus, when the Creator God El moves from behind the scenes of his creation to establish a direct personal relationship with Job we are confronted with a veiled allusion to Yahweh, the covenant God. Job's heroic faith has provoked the *deus absconditus* into becoming the *deus revelatus,* even before Sinai.

The second feature of the design for these speeches is the key thematic challenge. The opening challenge in 38:2–3 is balanced by a second major challenge in 40:7–14, with 40:2 standing at a pivotal point between the two balanced speeches of Yahweh. The overt challenge dimension of these opening gambits is clear from the imperative "Gird your loins as a hero" (38:3; 40:7). Job, the hero, had challenged God to appear in court with his case in writing. Yahweh appears, but instead of specifying charges, he presents his case from a whirlwind and challenges Job to reveal his wisdom. These challenging questions are tantamount to Yahweh's defense against the accusation and claims of Job, a defense which sends Job reeling.

Two explicit themes in Yahweh's defense are identified in these opening challenges: his "design" (*'ēṣā,* 38:2) and his just governance (*mišpāṭ*) of the world (40:8). The "design" of Yahweh is a broad term for the mysterious and paradoxical way in which the world is ordered and operates. That "design" includes the primal, past and present creative acts of Yahweh. It is forcing the text to demand, as Kubina does (pp. 122–123), that "design" *('ēṣā)* refers necessarily to "history" rather than "creation." "Just governance," the second major theme, was a subject of major concern for Job and his friends (see on 40:8). Job is challenged to match God's containment of evil in his governance of earth (40:9–14).

The challenge at the pivot point between the two speeches of Yahweh (40:2) is also significant since it specifies the formal relationship between Yahweh and Job in this context. Yahweh explicitly addresses Job as "the one with a suit against Shaddai," and "the one arraigning/accusing Eloah" (40:2). Thus the juridical background still obtains; Yahweh does not dismiss Job's demand for litigation. Rather, having presented a defense of his own in the form of challenging questions, he now summons Job to "answer" *('ny)* as

Job had promised he would do if God arraigned him (13:22). Job's efforts to make God the accuser and specify his charges against Job are completely bypassed. Yahweh's defense operates from the assumption that Job is innocent but ignorant. Thus the formal relationship between Yahweh and Job in this context is not primarily that of Creator/creature, teacher/pupil, or Lord/worshiper, but of adversary/accuser. God as the "adversary at law" (31:35) assumes the offensive in his defense against Job's accusations. Rather than indulging Job's obsession with his own integrity, he forces Job to come to terms with God's integrity as the Creator of a complex world. In his answers (40:2–5; 42:1–6) Job relinquishes his stance as plaintiff, admits his ignorance, and declares his willingness to drop his suit. Job's answers are therefore equivalent to a legal retraction which sets aside his demand for formal vindication as the injured party.

This leads us to the substantive core of Yahweh's speeches and the question of their basic form. Westermann argues that the structure of the book of Job is like an expanded lament and that the speeches of Yahweh fall at the point when the "salvation oracle" *(Heilsorakel)* would normally be spoken by the priest to the individual crying for deliverance (*Structure*, 106). Job's cry is for litigation, however, not deliverance. H. Richter proposes a *Naturweisheit* genre incorporated within a disputation speech (*ZAW* 70, 1958, 1–20). G. von Rad argues for the influence of Egyptian onomastica such as the Onomasticon of Amenemope, which lists 610 objects as a "compendium concerning all that Ptah created, the heavens and their appurtenances, the earth and all that is in it" (*The Problem of the Hexateuch and Other Essays*, 281). The order of the listing in Job and Egyptian onomastica indicates a traditional order according to which certain phenomena were cataloged in wisdom circles (cf. Ps. 148; Sirach 43; and Song of the Three Young Men).

More recently Kubina (pp. 131–142) and Rowold *(Theology of Creation)* have drawn attention to parallels between the form and function of the Yahweh speeches in Job and Yahweh's trial speeches in Second Isaiah, where similar challenge questions are posed. According to Rowold the typical challenge question consists of a pronominal subject (e.g., I, you, who), a verb describing Yahweh's lordship in action (e.g., create, measure, command), and an object describing the extent of that lordship (e.g., earth, sea, stars). These verses do not solicit information, but challenge the party to whom they are directed. The answer to these questions is intended to focus on God as the only possible power who could perform the action described in the question. The answer to the question, "Who hemmed in the Sea behind doors?" is not "Who knows?" or "I did not," but "You alone did." According to Westermann, "In the trial speeches of Second Isaiah (Isa. 41:1–5, 21–29; 43:8–15; 44:6ff.; 45:20–25) Yahweh and the gods of the nations confront each other in a legal process, the purpose of which is to decide who is truly god" (*Isaiah 40–66*, p. 15). The answer to the challenge question "Who measured the waters?" (Isa. 40:12) or "Who created these?" (Isa. 40:26) is

"Yahweh alone. No other deity was involved." These challenge questions are thus designed to expose the inefficacy and impotence of all rival deities. In the Yahweh speeches, the opposing parties are Yahweh and the hero Job, who is challenged to gird his loins as a rival. Job is expressly designated "the one with a suit against Shaddai" (40:2). Yahweh's speech is therefore a defence against his rival and accuser. This lawsuit is not a covenant court trial *(rîb)* in which Yahweh prosecutes his people for breach of covenant (cf. Micah 6:1–8; Jer. 2:4–13). In the trial speeches of Yahweh in Job and Second Isaiah, Yahweh is under attack from a rival; his defense is to pose challenging questions which remove the ground from under his rival's feet. Thus the closing court speeches in Job consist of three basic components: *(a)* the formal summons in which the challenge is issued and the theme of the challenge specified (38:2–3; 40:7–14), *(b)* the defense proper governed by a series of challenge questions (38:4ff.; 40:15ff.), and *(c)* the rival's retraction (40:3–5; 42:1–6; cf. Kubina, 131ff.).

The announced theme of Yahweh's first defense speech (38:2) is his "design" of the cosmos. That theme is developed by a seriatim treatment of major phenomena of the universe. With each treatment both structural and functional features of this cosmic design are considered. As a defense the speech also makes repeated allusions, innuendos, and ironic hints at earlier claims and accusations of Job. These aspects of Yahweh's first speech are summarized in the following table.

Plan of Yahweh's First Speech

38:4–39:30

Domain in Cosmic Design	Key Features of Design	Related Claim of Job
A *The Inanimate Physical World*		
1 The Earth 38:4–7	Earth is constructed according to Yahweh's design The heavens celebrated the earth's construction	God overthrows the structures of earth (9:5–7)
2 The Sea 38:8–11	The chaos waters of Sea are *hedged* in by *limits* These limits protect the earth	God *hedges* in the way of mortals (3:23) and muzzles Job as if he were *Sea* (7:12)
3 The Dawn 38:12–15	Dawn has her assigned *locus* Her advent exposes and limits the *wicked*	God smiles on the design of the *wicked* and hands over the earth to them (9:22–24; 10:3; cf., 12:5–6; 21:7ff.)

4 The Netherworld 38:16–18	Yahweh's design includes the underworld at its nethermost extremity The gates of Death control Sheol	Sheol is a realm free from the cruel hand of God (3:16–19) and a potential refuge from his anger (14:13–14)
5 Light and Darkness 38:19–21	Both light and darkness have any allotted *way* These regulate night and day in the calendar	Job sought to remove the day and night of his origins from the calendar of destiny (3:3–10; cf. 12:22–25)
6 Weather Forces 38:22–30	Each element in the weather pattern has its assigned *locus* and *way* At set *times* these elements have appointed roles for judgment or blessing	God's *design* is to manipulate the weather to destructive ends (12:13–14)
7 Constellations 38:31–33	The constellations are governed by celestial *laws* These laws control the *order* of things on earth	God employs his eternal wisdom to create chaos on earth (12:13–25)
8 The Thunderstorm 38:34–38	An inbuilt *wisdom* operates the cloud canopy of heaven Rain from this cloud cover brings new life to the dusty earth	(Note vs. 22–30; cf. 22:13)
B *The Animal and Bird Kingdoms*		
9 The Lion and the Raven 38:39–41	In his providence Yahweh *hunts* for wild creatures when they *cry*	God *hunts* Job like a *lion* (10:16–17; 16:9) and does not heed his *cry* (19:7)
10 The Ibex and the Hind 39:1–4	Yahweh establishes *times* in the life cycle of animals for their benefit	God fixes the brief life span of mortals to oppress them (7:1–3, 17–21)
11 The Wild Ass 39:5–8	Yahweh *frees* creatures and gives them a place on the earth	The place of freedom is Sheol, far from God's oppressive voice (3:17–19)
12 The Wild Ox 39:9–12	Yahweh imbues the wild ox with a will that cannot be tamed or *trusted* by humans	God cannot be *trusted* to answer Job's cry (9:16)
13 The Ostrich 39:13–18	Some creatures were given no *portion* of wisdom in the design of things	God is arbitrary in the way he allocates *portions* of fate (31:2)
14 The Horse 39:19–25	The horse is a reminder of Yahweh's *terror* and theophanic splendor	Only if God restrained his *terror* would a fair trial with him be possible (9:34; 13:21)
15 The Hawk and the Eagle 39:26–30	The hawk soars by Yahweh's *discernment*; the *eye* of the eagle detects food	The *eye* of God spies on mortals (7:8, 20)

The governing motifs developed in the elaboration of Yahweh's design for the universe can be divided into three major categories: the structural, the functional, and the celebrative. The structural motifs emphasize the wise order and depth of this design, the functional motifs focus on the containment of evil and providential care, while the celebrative motifs reach beyond structure and function to the festive and incongruous dimensions of this design.

The eternal order of Yahweh's cosmic design is characterized by primordial *measurement* (38:5), established *limits* (38:10), assigned *places* (38:12, 19; 39:6), designated *ways* (38:19–20, 24–25), fixed *times* (38:23; 39:1–2), and celestial *laws* (38:33). Yahweh's design for the cosmos is a meticulously controlled network of structures and processes. The depth of that design is marked by its inclusion of the world's extremities. The construction of earth lies in the distant primordial before the era when mortals pondered such mysteries (38:4, 21). The invisible recesses of the Deep and the gates of Death are encompassed in this design (38:16–17). The faintest star in the galaxy belongs to a celestial order (38:31–33). The mystery of these unseen realms is complemented by the mystery of wisdom implanted in the canopy of heaven (38:26; cf. vv. 12, 19, 33) and in the creatures of the wild (39:26–27). All such creatures, with the exception of the ostrich, have a *portion* of this wisdom (38:26–27).

These structural elements are balanced by functional or teleological aspects which are indicated in the purpose clauses of the speech and the ironic allusions to Job's earlier arguments. The structures of the cosmos control the waters of chaos (38:8–11), expose and contain the wicked (38:13–15), and enable judgment in times of war (38:23). The cycles and seasons of this order govern the flow of divine blessings: light and darkness (38:19–20), rain and grasses (38:24–27, 38), prey and provender (38:39–41), birth and maturation (39:1–4), and pasture and protection (39:8, 26–30). Keel (*Jahwes Entgegnung an Ijob,* 61ff.) argues that five animal pairs in Yahweh's speech are not selected at random, but reflect associations with realms of opposition (enemies, demons, etc.) against human society which are kept under control by Yahweh as the "Lord of the Animals." He supports his argument with strong iconographic evidence from the ancient Near East. The alien forces in the structure of society are also in Yahweh's design and under his control.

Beyond the structure and function of the cosmic design appear certain elements which seem to exist for celebrative rather than pragmatic reasons. They point to the aesthetic, the playful and comic in Yahweh's design. The construction of earth is marked by singing stars (38:7); Yahweh swaddles a baby monster called Sea (38:8–9); dawn and lightning are personified as messengers (38:12, 35); Yahweh does the hunting for lions (38:39); the ostrich persists as a ludicrous anomaly (39:13–17); the liberated ass, the exalted ostrich, and the prancing horse all enjoy laughing (39:7, 18, 22), and a magnificent animal with a neck robed in thunder cries "aha" when he smells the thunder of war (39:19–25). Both the majestic and the absurd seem to celebrate this design; and Yahweh seems to rejoice in his paradoxical creations (cf. Ps. 104:31).

Does Yahweh's poetic defense of his cosmic design answer the questions and claims of Job? Scholars such as Robertson (pp. 48–50) argue that God fails utterly in his attempt to prove his own innocence and answer Job's accusations. God comes off as a blind force, a blustery orator, and a charlatan deity. But does this judgment reflect the poet's intention or a facile identification with the perspective of the hero? The preceding table indicates some of the points at which ironic allusions and indirect answers to Job's charges and complaints are made. Yahweh's answer, however, does not follow the style of Elihu who cites lines from Job's speeches and attempts to refute them directly. Nor does Yahweh challenge Job's protestation of innocence, his accusation that the innocent suffer unjustly, his claim to have been afflicted unjustly, or his complaint against the hardships of mortal existence. He avoids the problem of innocent suffering in general and Job's case in particular. Yet he recognizes that Job is the one demanding litigation to vindicate his integrity (40:2). Thus Yahweh avoids the simplistic replies of the friends who adhered to a mechanical application of the law of reward and retribution. Instead Yahweh challenges Job to change his orientation and view his case in the light of the total cosmic design of his Creator. In that design the structural, functional, and celebrative dimensions express the paradox of reality. In the elucidation of that paradox, literary artistry and theological motif are happily integrated.

In his world of paradoxes, Yahweh continues to operate with the opposites of life and death, chaos and order, freedom and control, wisdom and folly, evil and blessing. What he challenges Job to do, he himself has done or continues to do. The incongruous and the bizarre are as much a characteristic of his style as the majestic and the beautiful. The King of heaven is found playing nursemaid to a baby chaos monster (38:8–11). The forces of chaos are not annihilated, but reduced to manageable monsters (40:15ff.) and kept within bounds like an infant (38:10–11). The power and domain of death is balanced by the annual cycle of birth and life (38:16–17; 39:1–4). The Lord of life goes hunting for lions and kills lesser life to satisfy the lions' lust for blood (38:39–41). As a wise designer Yahweh established a universe with laws which govern the location and movement of natural phenomena (38:19–20, 24–25, 33); yet he has the freedom to direct dawn, hail, and lightning when he wills (38:12, 22–23, 34–35). In his enigmatic arrangement of creatures he liberates the wild ass (39:5–8) and creates a wild ox untamable (39:9–12). Yet he makes the horse a thunderous beast who thrills to human wars (39:19–25). The peaceful providence experienced by the hinds in the moutains (39:1–4) is matched by the awesome terror of the horse charging into battle (39:19–25). Natural wisdom is implanted in numerous creatures and operations of the universe (38:36; 39:26–27). The ostrich is the comic anomaly which interprets that rule. She has no wisdom but she laughs at the awesome horse; she has no discernment but her young find food just as the eagle's do; she cannot soar like the hawk but her stubby wings rejoice (39:13–18).

In a world where paradox and incongruity are integral to its design, there is no simplistic answer to the problem of innocent suffering. The baby eagle survives because another young creature dies. God does not eliminate the forces of chaos, the role of Death, or the presence of the wicked. They operate within the eternal constraints of his design. Light is balanced by darkness. Each night the wicked function, but with each dawn they are exposed and contained (38:12–15). No mechanical law of reward and retribution operates in this design. The "wasted wasteland" is as much God's concern as the rain that breaks the drought (38:26–27, 37–38). For there is a celebrative aspect to the world which puts all structural and functional features into perspective. In his design there is a measure of the comic with the controlled, the bizarre with the beautiful, the serendipitous with the serious. Yahweh challenges Job to show the discernment necessary to keep this paradoxical world in balance. From these parallels in the natural world Job is left to draw the necessary conclusion relevant to his personal world. Job's complaint that the innocent suffer unjustly is never refuted. It stands side by side with the answers of Yahweh as part of the paradox of that design. Yahweh's theophanic appearance honors Job; his speech challenges Job; his enigmatic design throws Job back into a bewildering world of wonder. In that world Job reluctantly forgoes his demand for litigation.

33

POETRY IN THE COURTROOM: JOB 38–41

Sylvia Huberman Scholnick

Anguished by the devastating loss of his children, health and wealth, the righteous hero of the Book of Job calls God to account for his abusive action. When the Almighty makes his dramatic entrance from the whirlwind in chs. 38–41, he dazzles the man from Uz with a vision of the cosmos from the divine perspective. He reveals intimate details about the nature and structure of the universe he created and rules. But God never directly mentions the profound suffering of the hero which occasioned the call for his appearance. In fact, he seems to dismiss Job's powerful speeches with one brief question:

From Sylvia Huberman Scholnick, "Poetry in the Courtroom: Job 38–41," in *Directions in Hebrew Poetry,* ed. Elaine Follis (Sheffield: JSOT, 1987), 185–204. Used by permission of Sheffield Academic Press.

mî zeh maḥšîk ʿēṣâ
bᵉmillîn bᵉlî-daʿat

Who is this that darkens my plan
By words without knowledge? (38:2)

Instead of explaining this condemnation, the Almighty proceeds to enlighten Job with an elaborate description of his *ʿēṣâ,* his plan or design for the universe,[1] previously beyond human comprehension.

The answer God gives to Job raises a difficult critical problem in the book. What is the underlying artistic structure which unifies God's words with Job's? In what way is the creation poetry in Job 38–41 an adequate response to the hero's complaints about the unjust treatment he, an innocent man, is receiving from his divine opponent? The problem of the artistic integrity of the Book of Job has most recently been raised by Robert Alter in 'The Voice from the Whirlwind.' He makes progress toward its solution by analyzing the 'essential role *poetry* plays in the imaginative realization of revelation' and by exploring 'how its language and imagery flow directly out of the poetic argument that has preceded.'[2] While Alter sees a continuity in language and imagery between the speeches of Job and his friends and that of God, he identifies what appears to be a troublesome discontinuity in the poetic drama:

> God chooses for His response to Job the arena of creation, not the court of justice, the latter being the most insistent recurrent metaphor in Job's argument after Chapter 3. And it is, moreover, a creation that barely reflects the presence of man, a creation where human concepts of justice have no purchase.[3]

For Alter, then, there is a discontinuity between the issues of human justice which Job raises in the courtroom and the response that God provides in what appears to be the far-removed arena of creation.[4]

1. *ʿēṣâ* is used in the creation poetry of Isa. 40:13 to speak of God's design for the universe. It is used to refer to the divine plan for mankind in Isa. 5:19; 46:10; Jer. 32:19; 49:20; 50:45; Mic. 4:12; Ps. 33:11; 73:24; 106:13; 107:11; Prov. 19:21.

2. Robert Alter, 'The Voice from the Whirlwind', *Commentary* (January, 1984), p. 34. Alter focuses on the beginning of what he calls 'the poetic argument' in the Book of Job, Job's death-wish which he introduces in ch. 3. He contrasts the hero's self-involvement, his turning inward, with God's expansiveness, his 'panoramic vision' (p. 35), in chs. 38–41.

3. Alter p. 39.

4. While Alter does say that 'the poet works with an exquisite sense of the descriptive needs at hand and of the structural continuities of the poem and the book' (p. 41), his statements about the relationship between Job's speeches and those of God show his concern that there appears to be a degree of structural discontinuity. For example, he says: 'Obviously there can be no direct answer to Job's question as to why, having been a decent and God-fearing man, he should have lost all his sons and daughters, his wealth, and his health . . . Job surely does not have the sort of answer he expected, but he has a strong answer of another kind' (p. 41).

As many scholars have recognized, the poet chooses the court of justice as the setting for the dialogue between Job and his friends.[5] He dramatizes the hero's search for an acceptable definition of the meaning of divine justice by structuring the work around a lawsuit which the man from Uz initiates against God.[6] The case is comprised of several interwoven complaints. But when God speaks from the whirlwind, the setting of the drama appears to shift to what Alter calls the 'arena of creation.' Apparently ignoring the accusations made by his human legal opponent, God describes his creation and administration of the universe. The creation poetry in chs. 38–41 evokes the rich ancient Near Eastern tradition of the divine warrior who has sufficient power to bring the forces of chaos under control and to order the cosmos. As is typical of poetry with a creation motif, God's speeches are concerned with the affirmation of his credentials as King.[7]

There is, however, no discontinuity of setting in the drama. The entire poetic Dialogue is staged in the human court of justice where God addresses the juridical issues raised by the man from Uz. The traditional conventions of creation poetry have been adapted so that the Almighty's speeches can function as testimony in the suit initiated against him by his human opponent. Paradoxically, by entering the court of law, God has the opportunity to lead Job beyond the narrow confines of this legal order to a plane which allows the hero to see justice from the divine perspective. By accepting accountability in man's forensic forum for what Job charges is injustice in his role as Judge of mankind, God enlightens the hero about his design for the cosmos where human juridical categories cease to be central and where man must assume accountability for his proper role in the Lord's kingdom. Creation poetry, then, has a unifying artistic function within the drama: as testimony it continues the lawsuit, while at the same time as revelation it facilitates its resolution.

There can be no doubt that chs. 38–41 were intended by the poet to be understood as the testimony of the divine defendant in the lawsuit brought by the plaintiff from Uz. This is confirmed in 38:3 and 40:7 by his use of the metaphor of belt-wrestling to express the Almighty's challenge to continue juridical proceedings in his presence:

5. These scholars include B. Gemser, 'The *Rib*- or Controversy-Pattern in Hebrew Mentality', *Wisdom in Israel and in the Ancient Near East* (ed. M. Noth and D. Winton Thomas; VTSup, 3; Leiden: Brill, 1955), p. 135; James Limbug, 'The Lawsuit of God in the Eighth Century Prophets', ThD thesis, Union Theological Seminary (Virginia), 1969; M.H. Pope, *Job, Introduction, Translation and Notes* (2d ed; AB; Garden City, N. Y.: Doubleday, 1973), p. lxxi; Heinz Richter, *Studien zu Hiob, Der Aufbau des Hiobbuches, dargestellt an den Gattungen des RechtslebenI* (Theologische Arbeiten, 11; Berlin: Evangelische Verlagsanstalt, 1959); and Claus Westermann, *Der Aufbau des Buches Hiob* (Beiträge zur historischen Theologie, 23; Tübingen: J. C. B. Mohr [Paul Siebeck], 1956).

6. This subject is explored in my earlier article, 'The Meaning of *Mišpāṭ* in the Book of Job', *JBL* 104 (1982), pp. 521–29.

7. Dennis J. McCarthy, S. J., '"Creation" Motifs in Ancient Hebrew Poetry', *Creation in the Old Testament* (ed. Bernhard W. Anderson; Philadelphia: Fortress Press, 1984) p. 83.

**zor-nā kᵉgeber ḥălāṣêkā wᵉešʾālkā wᵉhôdîʿēnî*

Gird your loins like a hero;
I will ask and you inform me. (38:3; 40:7)[8]

Still another indication that God acknowledges his active participation in a *rîb*, a lawsuit, is found in 40:2 when he asks his human co-litigant:

hărōb ʿim-šadday yissôr
môkîaḥ ʾĕlôah yaʿănennâ.

May one who reproves contend against Shaddai?
May one arraigning testify against him? (40:2)

Although the Hebrew of this verse is difficult, as the NJPS notes, there is no question that the poet continues to use the root *rîb* in God's answer, as he has in the speeches of Job (10:2; 13:6; 19; 23:6 and 31:35) and Elihu (33:13), to refer to the hero's lawsuit against his divine opponent.[9] Here the infinitive of *rîb* is used, as Tur-Sinai points out, as a substitute for the finite verb.[10] The language and imagery of jurisprudence, used in the previous section of the book, is carried over into the vocabulary of the Lord, as evidenced in 38:3, 40:2 and 7, and demonstrate God's eagerness to accept the challenge of his human opponent to engage in litigation.

There are several accusations comprising Job's case against God, which the divine litigant will need to answer in his testimony. He gives the most serious consideration perhaps to Job's charge that he has committed what in human terms would be considered a justiciable offense. In 19:7 the plaintiff charges that God has committed *ḥāmās*, 'offense,' which is a juridical term in the Hebrew Bible for the broad category of unlawful conduct.[11] Job complains in

8. Evidence for a juridical interpretation of the belt-wrestling metaphor is reviewed in my article, 'The Meaning of *Mišpāṭ* in the Book of Job', p. 527.

9. In Job 29:16 and 31:13, Job uses the root *rîb* to speak of former litigation in which he was involved. All other occurrences of the root in the book refer to the lawsuit the hero initiates against God. The root in 13:8 refers to the friends' participation in the suit on behalf of God. James Limburg (p. 67) argues that *rîbôt* in 13:6 refers to the hero's arguments in a second suit against his friends. But his request for their silence in 13:13 argues against this interpretation because, were the companions litigants in a suit, they would be required to testify, as Job says about this responsibility of a defendant in 13:22. As the hero makes clear with the idiom *rîb lĕ*, 'to testify in behalf of', in 13:8, a meaning known from its use in Judg. 6:31, he considers the friends as witnesses for God.

10. N. H. Tur-Sinai, *The Book of Job: A New Commentary* (rev. ed, Jerusalem: Kiryath Sepher, 1967) p. 554.

11. *ḥāmās* is a technical term for 'wrongdoing' or 'offense', as verified by its use in the Hebrew law in Exod. 23:1 and Deut. 19:16 where, in construct with ʿ*ēd*, meaning 'offending witness', it refers to one who testifies falsely in a case-at-law. Giving false testimony is a justifiable offense, according to Deut. 19.

9:12 that God has robbed him *(yaḥtōp),* but the specific wrongdoing on which he is basing his case is to be found in 10:3a: *hăṭôb'*[12] *lᵉkā kîta'ăšōq,* 'Is it defensible for you to commit a wrongful taking?' It is not possible to identify in Anglo-American law an exact equivalent to the ancient Hebrew and Aramaic offense *'šq,* the closest being 'conversion,' which *Black's Law Dictionary* defines as: 'an unauthorized assumption and exercise of the right of ownership over goods or personal property belonging to another, to the alteration of their condition or the exclusion of the owner's rights. Any unauthorized act which deprives an owner of his property permanently or for an indefinite time. Unauthorized and wrongful exercise of dominion and control over another's personal property, to the exclusion of or inconsistent with rights of ownership.'[13] 'Wrongful deprivation' is its general intent or meaning, as can be documented from Hebrew and Aramaic law.[14] The Prologue of the book, important within the whole artistic work for introducing the facts of the case,[15] clearly states that God has taken from the hero his health (2:7), family (1:19), and wealth (1:10, 14–15) 'without cause *(ḥinnām)*' (2:3), not as punishment for wrongdoing, but simply as a test of his loyalty (1:8–11; 2:3–6). In the poetic Dialogue Job's case is one of wrongful seizure against God for the losses he has sustained: he was once a vigorous and prosperous man (29:2–17) who was highly regarded in his community (29:7–9, 21–25); now his property is gone (as in 3:24); and he holds God responsible for the abusive treatment, a point to which he gives special emphasis (as in 6:4; 9:12; 10:8, 16, 17; 12:9; 16:9–14; 19:8–12, 21; 30:18–23). Central to his case is his claim to innocence of wrongdoing that would justify the Lord's action, a claim which he reiterates throughout his speeches, from ch. 9 through ch. 27 (9:15, 20, 21; 10:7; 16:17; 23:7, 10–12; 27:5–6). For example, in 23:10–12, he attests to his righteousness:

kî-yāda' derek 'immādî
bᵉḥānanni kazzāhāb 'ēṣē'.

12. In this verse *ṭôb* may have the force of 'defensible', as its meaning in 2 Sam. 15:3, 'defensible cases (*aᵉbārekā ṭibîm)*', would indicate.

13. *Black's Law Dictionary* (5th ed, 1979), p. 300.

14. Although most translators of the term into English choose the non-technical 'oppress', the NJPS correctly recognizes its juridical force with 'defraud'. But 'defraud' in English civil law refers to deprivation of a right, usually property, through false representation, and therefore does not accurately convey the meaning of the Hebrew. The technical forensic intent of the root *'šq* in Hebrew and Aramaic law is documented in 'A Case of Wrongful Deprivation: Job's Lawsuit Against God', a paper I delivered at the 1983 AAR/SBL/CTS Southeast Region Annual Meeting.

15. Moshe Greenberg, 'Reflections on Job's Theology', *The Book of Job: A New Translation According to the Traditional Hebrew Text* (Philadelphia: The Jewish Publication Society of America, 1980), pp. xvii–xviii. There has been disagreement among scholars as to whether the Prologue and Epilogue may have been written by an earlier of later author than the one who wrote the poetic Dialogue. Regardless of the process of writing and editing that may have occurred, the book must finally be treated as a whole in the form in which it appears in the Hebrew Bible. In that sense, it is possible to speak of the author of Job.

ba'ăšurô 'āḥazâ raglî
darkô šāmartî wᵉlō'-'āṭ.
miṣwat śᵉpātāyw wᵉlō' 'āmîš
mēḥūqqî ṣāpantî 'imrê-pîw.

But he knows the way I take;
Would he assay me, I should emerge pure as gold.
I have followed in his tracks,
Kept his way without swerving,
I have not deviated from what his lips commanded;
I have treasured his words more than my daily bread. (23:10–12)

He charges that the divine defendant did not have the necessary or sufficient justification to seize his property, and therefore, the action constitutes *ʿšq*, unlawful appropriation.

A second important accusation against him that the Lord will address in the answer he files is an extension of the first: God is unjust in his role as Judge. Job and his friends share the assumption that God acts as Judge of human behavior. While his friends testify that the hero must have committed some offense that would justify the punishment he is receiving from God (8:4; 22:5–9), the plaintiff, holding firmly to his innocence, accuses the divine magistrate of injustice. He presents evidence from his own case (9:20c) as well as his observations on the widespread prosperity of the wicked (21:7–34; 24:1–25) to prove that the system of divine retribution is corrupt. His painful and shocking experience at the hands of the divine Judge leads the innocent man from Uz to complain before his peers:

'aḥḥat-hî'[16] *ʿal-kēn 'āmartî tām wᵉrāšā hû' mᵉkalleh*

It is all one; therefore I say, 'He destroys the blameless and the guilty' (9:22)

Job hopes to resolve the issue of the miscarriage of divine justice through the human system of justice—litigation.

God appears before the tribunal to answer the charges Job brings against him. The author adroitly uses poetry about creation to provide the defendant with the opportunity to clear himself. He responds directly to the first charge,

16. The words *'aḥḥat-hî'*, which may be translated 'It is all one', could be interpreted to mean that it doesn't matter whether one lives or dies, as S. R. Driver and G. B. Gray (*A Critical and Exegetical Commentary on The Book of Job Together with a New Translation* [Edinburgh: T. & T. Clark, 1921], p. 92) suggest, or that God treats guilty and innocent alike, a more common interpretation preferred, for example, by E. Dhorme (*A Commentary on the Book of Job* [transl. Harold Knight; New York: Thomas Nelson, 1967], p. 139); Robert Gordis (*The Book of Job: Commentary, New Translation and Special Studies* [New York: The Jewish Theological Society of America, 1978], p. 108; Pope (p. 71); and Tur-Sinai (p. 167).

that of wrongful appropriation, by asserting his rightful title to the universe he created and rules. God testifies in 41:3: *taḥat kol-haššāmayim lî-hû'*, 'Everything under the heavens is mine.' In addition to this clear assertion of his own right of ownership, God dismisses through a series of cross-examining interrogatories any possible prior claim to title that Job might make:

'êpoh hāyîtā b^eyosdî-'āreṣ
haggēd 'im-yāda'tā bînâ.
mî- śām m^emaddêhā kî tēdā'
'ô mî-nāṭâ 'ālêhā qāw.

Where were you when I laid the earth's foundations?
Speak if you have understanding.
Do you know who fixed its dimensions,
Or who measured it with a line? (38:4–5)

The creator has original title. If Job cannot establish his participation in the work of creation, he would have no grounds for any claim to the property he has charged was unlawfully seized. God continues to present his defense when he closely questions the plaintiff about his knowledge of the creative process:

'al-mâ 'ădānêhā hoābā'û
'ô mî-yārâ 'eben pinnātāh.
b^eron-yaḥād kôk^ebê bōqer
wayyārî'û kol-b^enê 'ĕlōhîm.

Onto what were its bases sunk?
Who set its cornerstone
When the morning stars sang together
And all the divine beings shouted for joy? (38:6–7)

The creator would know the specifications for laying the foundation of the universe, as well as the nature of the celebration that accompanied it. If Job is claiming title to any property in this world, he would have to prove to the court that he has information about the construction details:

'ê-zeh hadderek yikon-'ôr
w^eḥošēk 'ê-zeh m^eqômô.
kî tiqqāḥēnnû 'el-gĕbûlô
w^ekā tābîn n^etîbôt bêtô.

Which path leads to where light dwells,
And where is the place of darkness,
That you may take it to its domain
And know the way to its home? (38:19–20)

This cross-examination is intended to dramatize before the court that a human being cannot assume . . . ownership over any part of the universe. If Job is unable to respond effectively to these interrogatories, he would in effect confirm God's defense against the charge of unlawful appropriation—that everything under the heavens does indeed belong to the divine Creator.

Continued cross-examination by the divine litigant is directed at establishing the defense that he has never transferred the original title he holds to the universe he created. If Job, then, is claiming the right of ownership over any property he charges God has seized, he ought to be able to demonstrate that he has assumed or even is capable of assuming the responsibilities of ownership. The Almighty asks a series of questions intended to reveal the plaintiff's inability to exercise the most fundamental care for any land:

hăyādaʿtā ḥuqqôt šamāyim
ʾim-tāśîm miśṭārô bāʾāres.
hătārîm lāʿāb qôlekā
w^{e}*šipʿat-mayim t*^{e}*kassekkā.*

Do you know the laws of heaven
Or impose its authority on earth?
Can you send up an order to the clouds
For an abundance of water to cover you? (38:33–34)

Job is challenged to explain how he can charge God with appropriation of property clearly dependent upon the Lord for its continued survival.

Poetry about creation is appropriate for refuting Job's charge against God of wrongful deprivation. Traditionally, the concepts of creation and title are linked in Biblical Hebrew poetry. The founder of the universe automatically assumes title. A good example of the connection between these ideas is found in Psalm 24:

la-yhwh hāʾāreṣ ûm^{e}*lôʾah*
  tēbēl w^{e}*yôš*^{e}*bê bāh*
kî-hûʾ ʿal-yammîm y^{e}*sā-dāh*
  w^{e}*ʿal-n*^{e}*hārôt y*^{e}*kōnĕnehā*

The earth is the Lord's and all that it holds,
  the world and its inhabitants.
For he founded it upon the ocean,
  set it on the nether-streams. (Ps. 24:1–2)[17]

17. Other psalms in which there is a link between the ideas of creation and title include Pss. 89:12 and 95:3–5.

Creation poetry makes clear that the Lord has never transferred title to any part of the universe he formed.

If creation poetry in Hebrew Scripture has traditionally affirmed that the Lord who established the world has title to it, how then was the biblical audience to understand the gifts that God promises to give in return for obedience? Moses, for example, assures the Israelites that, in return for obedience, they will be given the land promised to their forefathers (Deut. 6:10–12) and prosperity (Deut. 28:11). It would be easy to misconstrue the meaning of the verb *ntn* in these promises. Its intended meaning is not the transfer of title to property, but a grant for its use. Moses makes this clear to Israel in Deut. 10:14:

> *hēn la-yhwh ʾĕlōhêkā hāššāmayim ûš*^{e}*mê haššamāyim hāʾāreṣ w*^{e}*kol-ʾăšĕr-bāh*
>
> Mark, the heavens to their utmost reaches belong to the Lord your God, the earth and all that is on it!

Lev. 25:23–24 confirms this understanding:

> *w*^{e}*hāʾāreṣ lōʾ timmākēr liṣmitut kî-lî hāʾāreṣ kî-gērîm w*^{e}*tôšābîm ʾattem ʿimmādî*
>
> But the land must not be sold beyond reclaim, for the land is mine; you are but strangers resident with me.

An additional example of God's clarification of the issue of title is found in Exod. 19:5–6:

> *w*^{e}*ʿattâ ʾim-šāmôaʿ tišm*^{e}*û b*^{e}*qôlî ûš*^{e}*martem ʾet-b*^{e}*rîtî wihyîtem lî s*^{e}*gullâmikkol-hāʿammîm kî-lî kol-hāʾāreṣ*
>
> Now, then, if you will obey me faithfully and keep my covenant, you shall be my treasured possession among all the peoples. Indeed, all the earth is mine, but you shall be to me a kingdom of priests and a holy nation.

The author of the Book of Job firmly builds God's defense against the plaintiff's misconceived accusation on the foundation of accepted biblical tradition.[18] The Lord never authorized the hero's assumption of the right of ownership over any of his property, but has simply given a grant for its use. There can have been no wrongful deprivation committed by the Almighty against the man from Uz.

18. Job in the Prologue responds to his loss with the pious statement: 'The Lord has given (*nātan*), and the Lord has taken away (*lāqāḥ*); blessed be the name of the Lord' (1:21). The poetic Dialogue explores the hero's process of coming to terms with the meaning of divine giving and taking.

The second accusation which God answers simultaneously in his testimony is that of injustice in his role as Judge of the earth because of his indiscriminate punishment of the innocent Job. He does this first by describing his primary role in the universe as that of King rather than Judge, so that the hero can realize that the treatment he is receiving from God is not the result of a juridical decision but an administrative one. And second, God answers the complaint that he acted unjustly by defining for Job the true nature of divine justice as sovereignty. The redefinition frees the hero to see the divine action as the prerogative of the Ruler.

To establish that his primary role is that of King rather than Judge, God describes in intimate detail his dominion over the universe: His creation of the world (38:4–11); his knowledge of its structure (38:16–22); his command over natural forces (38:24–30) and animals (39:1–30); and his ability as provider (38:39–41). God's administrative activity extends to all details of operating his realm. With a rapid series of interrogatories, he challenges the ability of his opponent as a human being to provide the necessary governance. Does the man from Uz need to concern himself as the ruler does with the details of the life of the planet: the cycle of night and day (38:12, 19–20), the formation of the constellations (38:31–33), the wind and rain (38:24–28), and the welfare of the wild life (38:39–40)?

hămibbînāt^{e}kā ya'ăber-nēṣ
yiprōś k^{e}nāpāw l^{e}têmān.
'im-'al-pîkā yagbiah nāšer
w^{e}kî yārîm qinnô.

Is it by your wisdom that the hawk grows pinions,
Spreads his wings to the south?
Does the eagle soar at your command,
Building his nest high,
Dwelling in the rock,
Lodging upon the fastness of a jutting rock? (39:26–27; cf. 38:39–41)

Although the poet mentions briefly in 38:12–13 and 40:11–13 the Lord's responsibilities as divine judge of human beings, the emphasis of the speech is clearly on his duties as sovereign over a kingdom dependent on him for its continued existence:

mî yākîn lā'ōrēb ṣêdô
kî-y^{e}lādāw 'el-'ēl y^{e}šawwē'û
yit^{e}'û liblî-'ōkel.

Who provides food for the raven,
When his young cry out to God
And wander about without food? (38:41)

It is interesting to note that the poet uses the verb *šw'* 'cry out,' in this verse to show the dependency of the young ravens on God. This use of the verb echoes its earlier use in 19:7 where it signifies Job's legal action against the divine Judge for injustice in the punishment he is receiving:

hēn 'eṣ'aq ḥāmās wᵉlō' 'ē'āneh
'ăšawwa' wᵉ'ēn mišpāṭ

Behold, I cry out 'Offense!' but I am not answered;
I call out, but there is no litigation (19:7).

There is irony in the poet's use of this verb in verses which contrast the wild birds' intuitive appeal to God as the very source of their continued life with Job's myopic appeal to the human court of law for justice with the divine Judge.

In the course of his testimony that he is primarily King not Judge in the world, God indirectly answers Job's charge of injustice by defining the nature of divine justice. When he uses the word *mišpāṭ* in 40:8 the context leaves no doubt that he is speaking not simply about his system of retribution but about his governance.

ha'ap tāpēr mišpāṭî
taršî'ēnî lᵉma'an tiṣdāq.

Would you impugn my sovereignty,
Would you condemn me that you may be right? (40:8)

As I discussed in an earlier article, 'The Meaning of *Mišpāṭ* in the Book of Job,' the ancient Semitic root *špṭ/ṯpṭ* has two meanings—that of judging and that of ruling.[19] While Job and his friends have drawn their definitions from the sphere of the court, when God uses the term *mišpāṭ,* he draws his definition also from the alternate meaning of the root: ruling. This usage is verified in 1 Sam. 8:9 where God describes to Samuel the authority *(mišpāṭ)* of the king. By using *mišpāṭ* in this context in 40:8 God teaches Job that he need not understand his profound loss as the result of the Lord's judgment for wrongdoing, but of his exercising his divine prerogative to administer a complex kingdom. This conforms with the characterization in the Prologue of God's action toward Job—testing of his subject's loyalty (1:8–11; 2:3–6).

Most commonly poetry with a creation motif is used in the Hebrew Bible to praise God as King or to petition his intervention.[20] But the author of the

19. Scholnick, p. 522.

20. Poetry with a creation motif is used to praise God, as in Isa. 40:12; 51:9–10; Am. 4:13; Pss. 8; 24:1–2; 33:6–7, 9; 89:10–13; 95:4–5; 96:5; 100; 119:73, 90; 147:4, 8–9, 16–18; and to petition his intervention, as in Pss. 65:6–8; 74:13–17; and 90:1–2.

Book of Job adapts the poetry for use in the arena of the courtroom, and therefore, several distinct characteristics emerge. First, it is spoken by God in chs. 38–41 in the first person, rather than in the usual second or third person, because he is a litigant testifying in the hero's lawsuit.[21] His opening challenge emphasizes this characteristic: *wᵉʾešʾālᵉkā wᵉhôdîʿēnî*, 'I will ask and you inform me' (38:3b). Second, it is uniquely framed in an often rapid-fire series of interrogatories which God uses to cross-examine his co-litigant. For example:

hᵃtittēn lassûs gᵉbûrâ
hᵃtalbîš ṣawwāʾrô raʿmâ.
hᵉtarʿîšennû kāʾarbeh
hôd naḥrôʾēmâ.

Do you give the horse his strength?
Do you clothe his neck with a mane?
Do you make him quiver like locusts,
His majestic snorting (spreading) terror? (39:19–20)

The force of these queries is to discredit Job's accusation that his divine opponent unlawfully appropriated his property, and their effect is to establish God's power over the universe he created and his prerogative to administer it as he wills. How can the man from Uz accuse God of injustice when in fact he knows little about the very meaning of divine justice or the nature of God's responsibilities in the world?

The only possible equivalent biblical use in a juridical context of what might be considered a creation motif may be found in Psalm 50.[22] But here, rather than cross-examining the human plaintiff in a lawsuit brought against him, God is the initiator of litigation for breach of covenant. He testifies in the first person that his people are fulfilling only the ritual laws for sacrifice while neglecting the rest of the covenant (Ps. 50:8, 16–21). What the Almighty requests is that Israel:

zᵉbaḥ lēʾlōhîm tôdâ
wᵉšallēm lᵉelyôn nᵉdārêkā

21. Praise about God in the third person is found in Isa. 40:12; 51:9–10; Pss. 24; 33; 95:1–5; 96; 100; 147 and in the second person in Pss. 8; 65; 74; 89; 90; 119. It is a general characteristic that poetry with a creation motif is in the second or third person. In these verses, God speaks in the first person, as he does in Job, about his creation.

22. Although Ps. 50 does not mention God's founding of the universe, it might broadly be classified as creation poetry because of its description of his kingship, if we accept Loren Fisher's definition of the genre in 'Creation at Ugarit and in the Old Testament' (*VT* 15 [1965], pp. 313–24). He writes: 'Those who say "no creation at Ugarit" must have a very narrow definition of creation. Certainly they do not consider "re-creation" or the ordering of chaos as creation . . . I hope to show . . . that conflict, kingship, ordering of chaos, and temple building are all related to an overarching theme that I would call "creation"' (pp. 315–16).

Offer to God praise as your sacrifice,
fulfill your vows to the Most High. (Ps. 50:14)

But the interesting element of this juridical psalm is God's explanation of why sacrifice is an insufficient fulfillment of the covenant.

lōʾ-ʾeqqaḥ mibbêtᵉkā pār
mimmiklᵉʾōtêkā ʿattûdîm.
kî-lî kol-ḥayᵉtô-yāʿar
bᵉhēmōt bᵉharᵉrê-ʾālep.
yādaʿtî kol-ʿôp hārîm
wᵉziz śāday ʿimmādî.
ʾim-ʾerʿab lōʾ-ʾōmar lāk
kî-lî tēbēl ûmᵉlōʾāh.

I claim no bull from your estate,
  no he-goats from your pens.
For mine is every animal of the forest,
  the beasts on a thousand mountains.[23]
I know every bird of the mountains
  the creatures of the field are subject to me.
Were I hungry, I would not tell you,
  for mine is the world and all it holds. (50:9–12)

The Lord makes clear to his people that the sacrificial animal may not be considered their gift to him, since he already has title to it. The praise that motivates or accompanies the physical offering constitutes for God the gift. Although the legal issues are different in Psalm 50 and in the Book of Job, the former being the legitimacy of a gift from man to God while the latter concerns the appropriation by God of what Job contends was a divine gift,[24] the answer filed by God in the two lawsuits is the same. Human beings simply cannot claim title to any part of the universe in which they reside. The meaning of the elaborate descriptions in Job 38–41 of the birds and animals living in God's realm is elucidated by Psalm 50. Curiously, in Ps. 50:11, God supports his claim to title with the assertion *(yādaʿtî)* that he has knowledge of the creature living in his kingdom. This kind of knowledge evidently is considered necessary and sufficient evidence of title.

While creation poetry is used in Job 38–41 as testimony which allows God to enter the courtroom, accept accountability to man, and see the world from Job's perspective, it also works paradoxically to open divine vistas for the man from Uz beyond the limited confines of the human legal forum. God's open-

23. As the NJPS points out, the Hebrew of this verse is uncertain.

24. In the Book of Job, the hero is presented in the Prologue as considering his property and family as gifts of God (1:21) which he takes back and, in the poetic dialogue, he speaks of his life as a divine gift (10:12).

ing challenge to Job in 38:2 (*mî zeh maḥšᵉîk ʿēṣâ / bᵉmilîn bᵉlî-dāʿat,* 'Who is this that darkens my plan, / by words without knowledge?') criticizes the hero for his earlier speeches which obscured the divine design for the universe.

It is important to understand how Job may have darkened God's plan in order to appreciate the impact of his resulting enlightenment after hearing the Lord's speech. The hero's testimony obscured God's design, not simply because he wished for the blackness of extinction (ch. 3) after God had granted life, although that is, as Robert Alter suggests, an important purpose of the poet's imagery of darkness.[25] The hero darkens God's plan by having tunnel-vision in viewing divine justice in human juridical terms. The shadowed world that Job describes is a perverse one in which the wicked are free to operate in the dim night without punishment while he, an innocent man, is assumed by his peers to have the taint of sinfulness because of his loss at God's hands. The poet uses the imagery of darkness on this level to describe the world of the wicked who are 'rebels against the light *(bᵉmōrĕdê-ʾôr)*' (24:13a), using the cover of night to commit the crimes of adultery and theft. Job complains that his world, once lighted with God's lamp (29:3), has been destroyed by darkness (23:17):

wᵉhiṣṣigani limšōl ʿammîm
wᵉtōpet lᵉpānîm ʾehyeh.
watēkah mikkaʿaś ʿênî
wiṣuray kaṣṣēl kullām.

He made me a byword among the people;
I have become like Tophet of old.
My eyes fail from vexation;
All shapes seem to me like shadows. (17:6–7)

The blackness Job is experiencing is interpreted by Eliphaz as proof of his wickedness. This friend charges:

ʾalmānôt šillaḥtā rêqām
ûzᵉrōʿôt yᵉtōmîm yᵉdukkāʾ.
ʿal-kēn sᵉbîbôtêkā paḥîm
wibahelᵉkā paḥad pitʾōm:
ʾô-ḥōšek lōʾ-tirʾeh
wᵉšipʿat-mayim tᵉkassekkā.

You have sent away widows empty-handed;
The strength of the fatherless is broken.
Therefore snares are all around you,
And sudden terrors frighten you,

25. Alter, pp. 35–36.

Or darkness, so you cannot see;
A flood of waters covers you. (22:9–11)

Job sees that the only hope for light is litigation that will clarify his legal status. Because God does not answer immediately his accusations (30:20), the man from Uz says:

kî ṭôb qiwwîtî wayyābō' rā'
wa' ăyaḥălâ le'ôr wayyābō' 'ōpel.

I looked forward to good fortune, but evil came;
I hoped for light, but darkness came. (30:26)

When God does testify before the court, the illumination that Job hoped for comes. The Lord's testimony does, as we have seen, enlighten Job about the reason for his action. But the clarification extends far beyond receiving specific answers to his juridical complaints. Creation poetry allows God to elucidate for Job his *'ēṣâ,* his design for the universe. He extends the hero's vision beyond the human realm, best exemplified in the legal forum where scrutiny and evaluation of man's behavior is of ultimate concern. Previously Job characterized God as a 'watcher of man *(nōṣēr hā'adām)*' (7:20) who is preoccupied with human judgment:

mâ-'enôs kî tegaddelennû
wekî tāšît 'ēlāyw libbekā

What is man, that you make much of him,
That you fix your attention upon him? (7:17)

God is portrayed in the creation poetry of chs. 38–41 as Watcher over the cosmos, his attention fixed on the forces of nature, the land, and animals. By questioning Job, the Almighty wishes to teach him how little awareness he has had of the complexity of the world in which man lives and how myopic his previous vision of the Lord's relationship to the cosmos has been. For example, Job thought of darkness on one level as the extinction of human life which he wishes for and on another, as the black world of the sinner into which he was thrust by God's abusive action. But the Almighty shows him how little he really understands about darkness when he asks:

'ê-zeh hadderek yiškon-'ôr
wehōšek 'ê-zeh meqômô.
kî tiqqāḥennû 'el-gebûlô
wekî tābîn netîbôt bêtô.

Which path leads to where light dwells,
And where is the place of darkness,

That you may take it to its domain
And know the way to its home? (38:19–20)

The Lord is talking in these verses about events of creation beyond Job's previous understanding. Darkness has a reality of its own, not simply in relationship to human beings. Job's horizon is being extended.

God describes for Job in chs. 38–39 his broad, all-encompassing vista of the cosmos—earth (38:4–6), sea (38:8–11), the gates of death (38:17), snow (38:22), hail (38:22), wind (38:24), rain (38:25–28), grass (38:27), dew (38:28), ice (38:29–30), the constellations (38:31–32), clouds (38:34), lightning (38:35), the lion (38:39–40), ravens (38:41), mountain goats (39:1), the wild ass (39:5–8), the wild ox (39:9–12), the ostrich (39:13–18), the horse (39:19–25), and the hawk (37:26–30). Job is given a perspective once available only to the Creator.

While the poetic vision of the natural world in chs. 38–39 is broad and general, it is detailed and particular in chs. 40–41 in which God describes Behemoth and Leviathan.[26] The extensive cataloguing of the characteristics of these two creatures is the poet's way of demonstrating their deep significance to the Creator who says:

hinnēh-na'bᵉhēmôt 'ăšer-'āśîtî 'immāk
ḥāṣîr kabbāqār yō'kēl.
hinnēh-nā'kōḥô bᵉmotnāyw
wᵉ'ōnô bišrîrê biṭnô . . .
hû' rēšit darᵉkê-'ēl
hā'ōśô yaggēš ḥarbô.

Take now behemoth, whom I made as I did you;
He eats grass, like the cattle.
His strength is in his loins,
His might in the muscles of his belly . . .
He is the first of God's works;
Only his maker can draw a sword against him. (40:15–16, 19)

26. In the context of God's speeches in chs. 38–41, Behemoth and Leviathan are treated as natural creatures described in a landscape which includes other real animals: the ibis and cock (38:36), the lion (38:39–40), the raven (38:41), the mountain goat (39:1–4), the wild ass (39:5–8), the wild ox (39:9–12), the ostrich (39:13–18), the horse (39:19–25), the hawk (39:26–30). Robert Gordis in Special Note 37 (pp. 569–72), after reviewing the two interpretations that these animals have historically been given—as mythical and as real creatures—presents a strong case for viewing these two beasts as real animals described by God as part of the natural world in which Job lives. After giving five reasons why it makes sense contextually to understand Behemoth and Leviathan as real rather than mythical beasts, Gordis concludes by saying: 'We are, therefore, convinced that only a description of actual flesh-and-blood monsters, unbeautiful in man's eyes, but a source of delight to God, is relevant to the poet's purpose. Hence, *Behemoth* is to be identified as the hippopotamus and *Leviathan* as the crocodile' (p. 571).

The Lord provides information not readily accessible to human beings of Leviathan when he tells about his back (41:7), his scales (41:8–9), his sneezings (41:10), his eyes (41:10), his mouth (41:11), his nostrils (41:12), his breath (41:13), his neck (41:14), his flesh (41:15), his breast (41:16), and his underparts (41:22). The poetry communicates a divine caring that cannot be exceeded by the Lord's love for human beings:

hăyarbeh ʾēlêkā taḥănûnîm
ʾim-yᵉdabbēr ʾēlêkā rakkôt.
hăyikrōt bĕrît ʿimmāk
tiqqāḥennû lᵉʿebed ʿôlām.

Will he plead with you at length?
Will he speak in soft words to you?
Will he make a covenant with you
To be taken as your lifelong servant? (40:27–28)

God's relationship with Leviathan, as with man, is structured and defined by a *bᵉrît*. The Almighty provides the hero with an opportunity to see his place in the universe in relationship to these enormous and fascinating beasts. He says about Leviathan in his closing words:

ʾên-ʿalʿāpār mošlô
heʿāśû liblî-ḥāt.
ʾēt-kol-gābōah yirʾeh
hûʾ melek ʿal-kol-bᵉnê-šaḥaṣ.

There is not on earth his like,
Made as he is without fear.
He sees all that is haughty;
He is king over all proud beasts. (41:25–26)

The creation poetry in God's speeches, which works successfully as testimony in the courtroom, paradoxically opens for Job a transcendent perspective of the cosmos created and governed by God.

Job's initial response to the panoramic vision of God's *ʿeṣâ* is silence. God's questions remain unanswered. When he does speak briefly in 40:4 before lapsing again into speechlessness, he expresses a new realization of his own insignificance in so vast a design for creation.

hēn qallōtî mâ ʾăšîbekkā
yādî śamtî lᵉmô-pî.

See, I am of small worth; what can I answer you?
I clap my hand to my mouth. (40:4)

Job's final response in 42:6 shows his understanding that the creation poetry of God's speeches has worked on two levels: as testimony in his lawsuit, and as revelation of the divine plan for the universe:

ʿal-kēn ʾemʾas wᵉniḥamtî
ʿal-ʿapār wāʾēper.

Therefore, I withdraw and retract (my case),
being but dust and ashes. (42:6)

As I discussed in 'The Meaning of *Mišpaṭ* in the Book of Job,'[27] the final stich of this verse communicates the plaintiff's perception that until that moment the lawsuit has been in progress. Job ends the case with a formal retraction.

The hero's final concession works in a second way. He acknowledges with the phrase *ʿal-ʿāpār wāʾēper* that God's speech has helped him put his life in a cosmic perspective. The exact intent of this short phrase is difficult to determine precisely, the NJPS translating it adverbially as 'being but dust and ashes,' while most translations prefer 'in/on/upon dust and ashes.'[28] A case may be made for each of these interpretations. It may be intended to communicate, as the NJPS translators might argue, Job's new realization that he is simply one part of a complex cosmos, made of dust and ashes, the very stuff God used to create the universe. While he once complained against the Almighty for fashioning him of clay only to turn him back into dust (10:9), he now shows an acceptance of his humble composition, just as Abraham does when he acknowledges his being dust and ashes while boldly challenging the justice of God's destroying Sodom and Gomorrah (Gen. 18:27). Some translators prefer the English '(sitting) in/on/upon dust and ashes' for the Hebrew *ʿal-ʿāpār wāʾēper.* If this is the intended meaning, Job, having just heard the description of Leviathan who cannot be dominated by any creature on earth (*ʿal-ʿāpār,* 41:25), would be symbolically expressing an acceptance of his modest place in the animal kingdom by sitting on earth and ashes.[29] The poet may have left this phrase intentionally ambiguous to evoke both meanings, a play on words that would be difficult to reflect in an English translation. In the very act of sitting upon dust and ashes, Job symbolically affirms that he is made of the same elements, dust and ashes, which God used in creating the earth.

Regardless of the precise English translation of *ʿal-ʿāpār wāʾēper,* the author's intent in 42:6 is clear. The verse communicates Job's awareness of

27. Scholnick, pp. 528–29.

28. *ʿal-ʿāpār wāʾēper* is rendered 'in/on/upon dust and ashes' in the majority of modern translations of the Book of Job into English, most recently in Gordis, p. 491.

29. Edouard Dhorme, translating *ʿal-ʿāpār wāʾēper* as 'on dust and ashes', suggests that 'This self-humiliation springs from an act of repentance' (p. 647).

the complexity of God's answer. To its juridical dimension, the plaintiff answers by retracting his case, recognizing the force of the divine litigant's defense. To its cosmic dimension, the man from Uz, by confirming the elemental nature of his being, acknowledges his humble place in the divine *ʿēṣâ*.

The Almighty's speech from the whirlwind has had a profound impact on Job in his search for the meaning of divine justice. God, accepting accountability in man's court of law for the force of his action, has acknowledged the importance of the human system of jurisprudence within his universal order. But the creation poetry enlightens the man from Uz about a system of justice far more complex and awesome than the one he had known in the legal forum. Job accepts God's revelation that divine justice is the Lord's sovereignty over his universe.

34

Job: Repentant or Rebellious?

B. Lynne Newell

Although differing in their views about a number of issues with regard to the Book of Job, in general, scholars have agreed that Job's replies to Yahweh in 40:4–5 and 42:2–6 indicate that Job repented,[1] or at least relented and changed his attitude. Even scholars such as K. Fullerton, C. G. Jung, and D. A. Robertson, who reject the possibility that Job could have repented, nevertheless agree that 42:2–6 in particular indicates that he did. K. Fullerton maintains that 42:2–6 is absolutely opposed to the content

1. Of what Job repented is debated. Most scholars favor the view that he repented of his words and/or attitude towards God during the dialogue with his friends.

From B. Lynne Newell, "Job: Repentant or Rebellious?" *Westminster Theological Journal* 46 (1984): 298–316. Used by permission of Westminster Theological Seminary.

of the dialogues and could not have been written by the author of that section, hence he rejects the whole of 40:6–42:17 as a gloss.[2] C. G. Jung and D. A. Robertson see Job's replies as hypocritical. C. G. Jung says that most probably Job prostrated himself before God as if he were a defeated antagonist, realizing that God was a being who could not be judged morally.[3] D. A. Robertson says it is only a "tongue-in-cheek" confession, made to calm God's whirlwinds.[4]

A few scholars do not believe that Job is expressing remorse or regret in any sense in his final reply. For example, M. Tsevat says that Job only acknowledges in 42:2–6 that he now knows, from the content of God's speeches, that justice is not an integral part of the universe and that one cannot, and should not, expect anything for one's behavior. Freed from that misconception, Job is then prepared to live a truly pious and moral life with no such false hopes or claims.[5] Dale Patrick translates 42:6, "Therefore I repudiate and repent of dust and ashes," and interprets vv. 2–6 as Job declaring that, because of the wonder of God's ways, he will change his speech from lament and accusation of God to praise and rejoicing.[6] Although not seeing Job as repentant in the usual sense, these views nevertheless agree that Job changed his attitude, speech, and behavior, and that he worshipped God.

In 1979 J. B. Curtis presented a radically different translation and interpretation of Job's responses.[7] He argued that Job did not repent, but totally and unequivocally rejected Yahweh. This represents a complete reversal of the traditional interpretation. He paraphrases 40:4 as follows:

> Although I dealt with matters that to you are trivial when I spoke earlier, I will now with contemptuous revulsion cease speaking altogether.

He sees Job here sarcastically expressing his hostility by saying it is useless to try and talk to a god who is so concerned with great things that he is not even aware of the existence of such small problems as the suffering of the innocent. He views 42:3a and 4 as Job "daring to hurl back in God's teeth his own words," and "sarcastically attacking the god who thinks that his might answers all questions."[8] J. B. Curtis adds that 42:4–5 indicate that God had wanted to question Job, and he did, but about irrelevancies. The experi-

2. K. Fullerton, "The Original Conclusion to the Book of Job," *ZAW* 42 (1924) 116–36, esp. pp. 125–28.
3. C. G. Jung, *Answer to Job* (New York: Pastoral Psychology Book Club, 1955) 31.
4. David A. Robertson, "The Book of Job: A Literary Study," *Soundings* 56 (1973) 466.
5. M. Tsevat, "The Meaning of the Book of Job," *HUCA* 37 (1966) 73–106, esp. pp. 92, 104.
6. Dale Patrick, "Job's Address of God", *ZAW* 91 (1979) 268–82, esp. p. 281.
7. John B. Curtis, "On Job's Response to Yahweh," *JBL* 98 (1979) 497–511.
8. Ibid., 509.

ence of seeing God had confirmed the reports Job had heard about God and had proved his injustice. So, according to J. B. Curtis's translation of 42:6, Job, "totally disenchanted with this god," said:

> Therefore I feel loathing contempt and revulsion
> (toward you, O God);
> and I am sorry for frail man.

Job thus totally and finally rejects this unjust, unfeeling, and irrelevant deity.[9]

The variety of opinions about Job's response to Yahweh and especially the radically different translation and interpretation by J. B. Curtis demand that we reexamine and reevaluate this portion of the text of Job. That is the purpose of this article.

To understand the meaning of Job's responses, we need to consider them within their context. So, before focusing on the Hebrew text of Job's replies, we shall first consider relevant factors from the literary context of the Book of Job (ancient Near Eastern parallel literature), and then the immediate context (the meaning and intent of the Yahweh speeches to which Job responded).[10]

Ancient Near Eastern Literary Parallels

The date of composition of the Book of Job is much debated, nevertheless its setting is generally considered to be in the second millennium B.C. Archaeology has provided from that era several other wisdom texts that consider the issue of human suffering. These texts are commonly referred to by scholars as the "innocent sufferer" texts and are often considered to be a subgenre within the wisdom literature.

Although these "innocent sufferer" texts originated in Mesopotamia, they, as with other Mesopotamian literature, were probably known throughout the Near Eastern area. The findings of archaeology have demonstrated that economic and cultural exchange took place. In the field of literature, a fragment of the Mesopotamian Gilgamesh Epic from about the thirteenth century B.C. has been found at Megiddo in Palestine.[11] Mesopotamian wisdom texts have also been found at Ugarit. Among them is one J. Nougayrol has called "Juste Souffrant" because it presents an innocent man struggling with the problem of his experience of suffering. The suggested date for this text is ca. 1300 B.C.[12] Similarities of literary format, poetic style, and certain theological con-

9. Ibid., 510.

10. A fuller discussion of these factors and related issues can be seen in my Th.M. thesis, "Job, Repentant or Rebellious?" (Westminster Theological Seminary, 1983).

11. John Gray, "The Book of Job in the Context of Near Eastern Literature," *ZAW* 82 (1970) 251–69, esp. p. 262. A. Goetze and S. Levy, "A Fragment of the Gilgamesh Epic from Megiddo," *Atiqot* 2 (1959) 121–28.

cepts (e.g., divine retribution according to man's behavior) as well as of theme, indicate that these texts may constitute part of the literary context of the Book of Job. So, we shall examine these texts to see what attitudes they present as acceptable in a sufferer. If these documents do not allow for attitudes of revulsion and rejection of the deity as their conclusion, then it is less likely that Job responded thus to Yahweh.[13] That would lessen the likelihood that J. B. Curtis's interpretation is correct. Conversely, if repentance and submission are found consistently in the sufferers, more likely Job's attitude would be similar and the historical conventional interpretation correct.

The oldest extant text which deals theologically with the problem of human suffering is from Sumer. Its title is "Man and His God"[14] and it is often referred to as "The Sumerian Job." The "hero" is a righteous man who nevertheless is stricken with severe sickness and bitter suffering. He describes his suffering, then laments over it. He concludes with three pleas for deliverance alternating with two confessions of sin. The first is just a general confession of his sinfulness as a human being, but the second is a confession of the sins his god made known to him. His lament and repentance are accepted by the god who then restores his health and prosperity. The Sumerian "Letter to Enki" shows this same pattern—the need for confession of sin and repentance so that the god would end the man's sufferings and restore his happiness.[15]

Three Babylonian texts, AO 4462, "Ludlul bĕl nĕmeqi" ("I will praise the Lord of Wisdom," often called "The Babylonian Job") and "The Babylonian Theodicy," resemble the Book of Job thematically.[16] The attitude considered to be correct for a sufferer is clear from these texts. He should examine himself to see if he had committed any errors, and if he had he should repent of them. Whether or not his own sin was the cause of his suffering, he should accept the suffering and not complain, rebel, or blaspheme his god. He should continue to serve his god faithfully and seek his god's compassion. The Akkadian "Righteous Sufferer" text found at Ugarit demonstrates the same concept of the correct attitude in a sufferer.

12. J. Nougayrol, *Ugaritica* 5 (1968) 265–73. Gray, "Job in the Context of Near Eastern Literature," 262.

13. See Chapter Two, "The Validity, Procedure and Benefit of a Comparative Approach to Akkadian Autobiography," in Tremper Longman III, "Fictional Akkadian Royal Autobiography: A Generic and Comparative Approach" (Ph.D. dissertation, Yale University, 1983).

14. S. N. Kramer, "Man and His God: A Sumerian Variation on the 'Job' Motif," in *Wisdom in Israel and in the Ancient Near East* (ed. M. Noth and D. W. Thomas; Leiden: E. J. Brill, 1955) 170–82; *ANET,* 589–91.

15. William W. Hallo, "Individual Prayer in Sumerian: The Continuity of a Tradition," *JAOS* 88 (1968) 82–88; Thorkild Jacobsen, *The Treasures of Darkness: A History of Mesopotamian Religion* (New Haven & London: Yale University Press, 1976) 153–54.

16. J. Nougayrol, "Une version ancienne du 'Juste souffrant,'" *RB* 59 (1952) 239–50; *ANET* 434–37, 596–600, 438–40, 601–4; W. G. Lambert, *Babylonian Wisdom Literature* (Oxford: Clarendon Press, 1960) 21–62, 63–91.

If we accept the consensus of scholarly opinion which holds that the Book of Job is also one of the "innocent sufferer" texts, then we expect to find this same attitude from Job. After the theophany, Job's wrong attitude would change, and he would praise and worship God once more. He would no longer complain, nor would he rebel against God and reject him. Conversely, he would repent of any sin God showed him. This, I maintain, is what did occur.

The general interest in "the fear of the Lord" found in wisdom literature introduces another factor relevant to Job's response to Yahweh. At the beginning of the Book of Job, Job was a man who feared the Lord and shunned evil. The book's genre as wisdom literature requires that Job repent and return to fearing the Lord when at the end of his suffering Yahweh charged him with wrongdoing. He would not rebel.

Immediate Context

Understanding and interpreting Job's responses in the light of their immediate context involves taking account of the specific content and purpose of Yahweh's speeches to which he was responding. To understand the purpose, and hence the meaning, of the Yahweh speeches, we must see them, too, in context. They are addressing specific statements, questions, and attitudes of Job in the preceding dialogues. Actually, Job's speeches in the dialogues exhibit a mixture of features, e.g., questioning, agony, faith, hopelessness, perplexity, and confidence. He argues with his friends, defending himself against their accusations and maintaining his righteousness. He addresses God, and speaks about him, as he wrestles to reconcile his theology and past experience of God with his present experience of suffering and the wickedness he sees about him. Job believed God was the sovereign Lord, and he recognized no second causes.[17] So, as he wrestled to reconcile this with his loss and suffering, he concluded that God had changed from being his friend (29:2–4) who cared for him to his enemy who persecuted and maltreated him (10:8–12; 13:24–27; 30:21).

Throughout the dialogue, as he wrestled to reconcile his theology with his experience and to refute the accusations of his friends, Job accused God of a number of things. He said God oppressed him while he smiled on the schemes of the wicked (10:3), attacked him in anger and shattered him (16:9, 12), wronged him and counted him an enemy (19:6–11), denied him justice (27:1) and maltreated him ruthlessly (30:19–21).

Although he may not have been conscious of the full implications of what he was saying, Job was actually passing judgment upon God by thus accusing him. Job also passed judgment on God for not fulfilling his duties as a ruler

17. 1:21; 2:10. He knew the Sabeans and Chaldeans had robbed him (1:15, 17) but he did not mention them. Cf. 9:24, "If it is not he, then who is it?"

when he allowed the widow, the orphan, the poor, and the needy to be oppressed by the wicked and did not intervene on their behalf (24:1–12). In thus judging God, Job was in fact exalting himself above God and implying that he would be a better ruler.

However, we need to remember that these things were said within the context of Job's wrestling to reconcile his beliefs about God with the reality he was experiencing and witnessing. Alongside the above statements we find others that reveal Job's continued faith in God and in his righteousness and justice (e.g., 12:13; 13:15, 14:15–17; 17:3; 19:25; 23:6, 7, 10–12). In all that he said, Job does that appear to be spurning God, but rather Job is seeking God and his answers.

In Yahweh's speeches[18] every pericope except one begins with a question. That one, the behemoth pericope, closes with a question. The use of questions is a very effective teaching method. They involve the "learner" by calling forth from him a personal response. So, Yahweh's use of them may indiate that his speeches were not designed to be merely a display of his power and authority, but also for a relationship purpose. They were designed to teach Job about God and about himself, and to draw forth a response.

In his speeches Yahweh brought three accusations against Job, all of them relating to Job's words and attitudes in the dialogue with his friends. In his first speech Yahweh charged Job with using words without knowledge (38:2), contending with God, and accusing him of wrongdoing. Job had done all of this, thus, as it were, putting himself on at least equal footing with God. Yahweh dealt with Job's sin here by asking him a series of questions centered around his work of creating and sustaining the universe and some of the animals that inhabit it. Yahweh asked Job repeatedly what his part was in this work, both past and present, and whether he had the knowledge, power, and authority to perform it. Each question was so framed that Job could only answer that he did not possess those qualities, only God did.

As well as thus emphasizing that he is infinite in wisdom, power, and authority, God also spoke to Job of his care of and concern for his creation, both animate and inanimate. He sends rain on the dry land, provides food for lions and ravens, and cares for other animals. All of creation is shown to be in the control and care of God. At that point, Yahweh challenged Job with "Let him who accuses God answer him" (40:2), and Job makes his first response (40:3–5).

18. Some scholars reject the ostrich pericope (39:13–18) and the behemoth and leviathan sections (40:15–41:34) as later additions. However, I do not find the reasons they give convincing. See my thesis, "Job, Repentant or Rebellious?" chap. 6. See also E. Dhorme, *A Commentary on the Book of Job* (London: Nelson, 1967) xcii–xcv; Robert Gordis, *The Book of God and Man: A Study of Job* (Chicago: University of Chicago Press, 1965) 122–23, and *The Book of Job* (Moreshet Series 2; New York: The Jewish Theological Seminary of America, 1978) 557–59, 566–68; Francis I. Anderson, *Job: an Introduction and Commentary* (Tyndale OT Commentaries; Downers Grove: InterVarsity Press, 1976) 49, 53.

In his second speech Yahweh focuses on his third charge against Job: "Would you discredit my justice? Would you condemn me to justify yourself?" (40:7). Job was guilty of this too, so that, though he may have been unconscious of the implication, it was as if he were a rival god.

So, Yahweh challenges Job to take over the administration of justice on earth in his stead, if he can (40:9–14). It is clear he cannot. Yahweh then confronts Job with behemoth and leviathan, creatures and/or chaos forces before whom Job as man was helpless and over whom he had no control. Once again Yahweh revealed Job's weakness and inadequacy and at the same time showed his, Yahweh's, power, authority, and control, not only over the natural creation but also over chaos forces and evil.

Yahweh stated explicitly that no man had a claim against him that he must pay (41:11). Yet God had come to Job and spoken to him, to teach, rebuke, correct, and enlighten him. All of this, from God's own initiative, was not because of some "claim" but of grace. To this God, Job responded.

Job's Responses

Now we shall consider the text of Job's responses in 40:4–5 and 42:2–6 to establish a translation and an interpretation of them. We shall, of course, establish word-meanings that are in line with the meanings of those words in other parts of the Old Testament, and interpret Job's replies in the context described above.

As we examine that text of Job's responses, we find that the LXX and the Qumran targum of Job (11QtgJob) differ from the MT in some verses. However, the nature of the LXX translation of Job causes most careful scholars to agree that great caution is needed in the use of it for textual criticism.[19] Certainly with regard to the text of Job's responses the weight of evidence is not in favor of the variant translations found in the LXX.

11QtgJob is, on the whole, a sober, literal translation, supportive of the MT.[20] However, some divergences from the MT are found in Job's response in 42:1–6. The most significant of these is the replacing of 42:3 by 40:5. We cannot consider this as proof, though, that originally Job made only one

19. Dhorme, *Job,* cxcvi–ccvi; Henry S. Gehman, "The Theological Approach of the Greek Translator of Job 1–15," *JBL* 68 (1949) 231–40; Donald H. Gard, *The Exegetical Method of the Greek Translator of the Book of Job* (JBL Monograph Series 8; Philadelphia: SBL, 1952); Donald H. Gard, "The Concept of Job's Character According to the Greek Translator of the Hebrew Text," *JBL* 72 (1953) 182–86; Gillis Gerleman, "Studies in the Septuagint, I: The Book of Job" (Lunds Universitets Arsskrift, n.s. 1/43/2; Lund: Gleerup, 1947); Harry M. Orlinsky, review of *The Exegetical Method of the Greek Translator of the Book of Job,* by Donald H. Gard, in *JBL* 73 (1954) 251–52.

20. Joseph A. Fitzmyer, *A Wandering Aramean: Collected Aramaic Essays* (Missoula: Scholars Press, 1979) 161–81. G. W. Parsons, "A Biblical Theology of Job 38:1–42:6" (Th.D. dissertation, Dallas Theological Seminary, 1980) 313–15.

response to Yahweh. Although in the targum 40:4–5 is illegible, in 40:6 Yahweh answers Job, thus indicating clearly that Job must have spoken in at least v. 5.[21] Also, Job's expressed intention in 40:5 to say no more seems to better fit the interpretation that his first response ends there rather than continuing for a number of verses more.

For the translation of 42:6, 11QtgJob has "Therefore I am poured out and boiled up (or dissolved), and I am become dust and ashes," a translation differing from both the LXX and the MT. The translator has taken different roots for both of the verbs—*mss* instead of *m's,* and *hmm* (Nifal) instead of *nḥm.*[22] Whereas divergences from the MT are not common in this targum, the accumulation of divergences in these verses witnesses to the difficulty the translator was having here. His obvious difficulty and his choice of roots that would not yield the words in the MT without some emendation decrease the value of his translation for determining the meaning of the MT in these verses.

Job's First Response, 40:4–5

hēn qallōti māh 'ăšibekā yādi śamti lēmô pî
'aḥat dibbartî wēlō' 'e'ĕneh ûśtayim wēlō' 'ôsip

The translation I suggest for these verses is:

Indeed, I am worthless (of no account). What (How) shall I answer
you? I put my hand to (over) my mouth.
I have spoken once, but I shall not reply (again);
even twice, but I shall not add more (I shall not continue).

Scholars agree that the relevant basic meaning of the root *qll* is "to be light, to be small, to be of little account."[23] Tsevat draws our attention to the fact that the root *qll* is anonymous to *kbd.*[24] Used of a person, the noun *kābôd* can mean "weightiness, splendor, distinction, honor."[25] Job had spoken of his *kābôd* in 29:20 (also 19:9). In 31:37 Job had said he would approach God like a "prince," and a prince would be a man of *kābôd.* But after Yahweh's first speech, which brought Job to realize his finitude and his

21. J. P. M. van der Ploeg, O. P., and A. S. van der Woude, *Le Targum de Job de la Grotto XI de Qumran* (Leiden: E. J. Brill, 1971). M. Sokoloff, *The Targum to Job from Qumran Cave XI* (Ramat-Gan: Bar-Ilan University, 1974).

22. Sokoloff, "Targum to Job," 100, 101, 167.

23. BDB, 886. W. L. Holladay, *A Concise Hebrew and Aramaic Lexicon of the Old Testament* (Grand Rapids: Eerdmans, 1978) 319.

24. Tsevat, "The Meaning of the Book of Job," 91. See also V. Kubina, *Die Gottesreden im Buche Hiob* (Freiburg: Herder, 1979) 78.

25. Holladay, *Lexicon,* 151.

lack of knowledge, power, and authority, Job responded that he was the opposite of ***kābôd,*** i.e., he was without intrinsic honor and worth.[26] The LXX has ***outhen ōn,*** "(I) being nothing," which is the same basic idea.

Two scholars give different translations for ***hēn qallōtî.*** E. Dhorme translates, "If I have been thoughtless," although he too states that the basic meaning is "to be light." He chooses that translation to suit the interpretation he gives for the meaning of Job's responses, i.e., he has spoken out of ignorance.[27] His translation does not really convey the meaning of the Hebrew word.

Curtis translates verse 4a as "Although I was too light in what I answered you." He considers that "this is bitter sarcasm, slashing out against a god who is irrelevant."[28] His argument for translating ***hěn*** as "although" cannot be sustained.[29] Also, the Hebrew here does not require the translation he gives. He states that verse 4a should be rendered in this way so that it is in keeping with the meaning he proposes for 42:6. He then suggests as a paraphrase for verse 4a, "although I dealt with matters that to you are trivial when I spoke earlier."[30] This paraphrase moves further toward subjective interpretation.

The expression "to put the hand to the mouth" is found six times in the Old Testament. There is some variation in the Hebrew expressing this phrase, but the variations are not significant. In Judges 18:19 the expression follows immediately after a command to be quiet, and is really a repetition of that command. It appears to add emphasis. The writer of Prov. 30:32 says "hand to mouth"—a verb is not used. Again it is a command, apparently emphatic, to be silent.

In Job 21:5, having asked his friends to listen carefully to his words, Job then says, "look at me and be astonished, and put your hand over your mouth." Here too the expression indicates that they should be silent, probably because of feeling astonishment and horror. When describing the respect paid to him in his presuffering days, Job says that "the chief men refrained from speaking and covered their mouths with their hands" (29:9). Again the expression means that they were silent but this time because of a feeling of deep respect. Mic. 7:16 describes how, as a result of seeing the Lord's wonders, nations will be ashamed, lose their power, "lay their hands on their mouths and their ears will become deaf," and then (v. 17) they go on to fear the Lord. Once more this expression indicates that the nations become silent, apparently because of feelings of shame and awe, and possibly as a sign of submission.

26. Kubina, *Die Gottesreden im Buche Hiob,* 78.

27. Dhorme, *Job,* lix, 615, 646–47.

28. Curtis, "Job's Response," 507.

29. See the Appendix on "The Particle ***hēn***" in my Th.M. thesis, "Job, Repentant or Rebellious?"

30. Curtis, "Job's Response," 507.

Two ancient reliefs contain scenes which portray the placing of the hand to or upon the mouth as a sign of respect and in one of them possibly amazement. One of those reliefs shows a man being carried skyward on a lion-headed eagle. To our left of that eagle is a man with his hand up towards his mouth. This gesture could be because of amazement or because of respect.[31] In the other relief, King Darius is seated on his throne with Crown Prince Xerxes, attendants and guards standing behind him. In front of King Darius is a Median dignitary who is bowing slightly from the waist and with a hand upon his mouth.[32] Clearly this posture shows respect and homage.

In summary, the five biblical uses examined above all indicate that a person putting the hand to the mouth signifies silence. With the usages in Judges. 18:19 and Proverbs 30:32, no emotional involvement is evident, though they may be considered emphatic. In the other three usages, the person is silent because of a feeling of astonishment, shame or awe, or as an indication of deep respect or even submission. The association of this gesture with respect and homage, and possibly with amazement, is confirmed by the reliefs described above.

So, as we consider Job's use of that expression in 40:4, we expect it to mean that Job is saying he will be silent. This certainly fits the immediate context as Job emphasizes in v. 5 that he is not going to speak. Also the question "what (how) shall I answer you?" indicates that Job is not going to speak. Job uses this expression in responding to Yahweh's first speech. It follows Job's acknowledgement that he is "worthless, of little account." So, to say that with this gesture Job was conveying his feeling of unworthiness, shame, awe, reverence, and even submission to Yahweh, accords well with both the context and other usages of the gesture.

Curtis gives a different interpretation of this expression. He agrees that its basic meaning is "to become silent" but says this meaning is usually "overlaid with strongly emotional overtones." Although he mentions the feelings of awe, profound respect, and remorse as the emotions seen in other biblical uses of the expression, yet apparently he feels free to suggest any feeling as long as it is a strong emotion. He says that the emotion Job feels here would be that of "profound revulsion." So, he paraphrases v. 4b as "I will now with contemptuous revulsion cease speaking altogether."[33] By interpreting the gesture in this way, Curtis has introduced an emotion which is the opposite of feelings associated with the expression in all other places extant. To do thus is to contravene sound exegetical procedure.

Scholars agree about the basic meaning of 40:5, although they differ about the interpretation of it as part of Job's response. Some scholars would emend *ʿeʾĕneh* to *ʿešneh*, which means "I shall repeat it." However this emendation is

31. *ANEP*, #695, pp. 222, 333.
32. *ANEP*, #463, pp. 159, 303.
33. Curtis, "Job's Response," 507.

unnecessary. The idea of repetition is frequently left unexpressed in Hebrew. For example, in both Ps. 51:20 and Isa. 9:9 *bnh* only is used to mean "build again." In the same way, *ʿeʾĕneh* in the MT can mean "respond again."[34]

The use of ascending numeration, such as "once . . . twice . . . " in verse 5, is common in biblical and Semitic poetry. It is particularly a feature of wisdom literature. It may simply mean "several" as it does here. (See, e.g., Amos 1:3, 6, 9, 11, 13; Eccles. 11:2.)[35]

How do we interpret this first response of Job's? First, Yahweh's speech to which Job was responding was designed to teach him his lack of knowledge, power, and authority—i.e., his finitude—and at the same time remind Job of God's omniscience, omnipotence, and benevolence. This purpose was accomplished and Job responded, "indeed, I am worthless [of no account]." As Job was confronted by his Creator, he recognized once more, and in fuller measure (as seen from his second response), his "creatureliness."

Secondly, Yahweh accused Job of speaking "words without knowledge" and of "accusing God." Job responded to this accusation by what he said in vv. 4b and 5. I would suggest that by putting his hand over his mouth he was acknowledging the truth of God's accusation and expressing shame for this. In v. 5, also, Job was acknowledging that he had indeed spoken as God charged, but he would not do so again. Job repeatedly expressed the desire to come before God so that God should present his charges against him, and Job was sure he would be able to answer those charges. Then God would declare him not guilty. Now God has confronted Job, he has presented charges (though not those Job expected), and Job has no answer. He is guilty of these charges, and he thus acknowledges it.

Job's Second Response, 42:2–6

Most scholars now recognize that vv. 3a and 4 are virtual quotations of Yahweh's challenges to Job in 38:2–3 and 40:7.[36] However, some regard them as misplaced variants.[37] I concur that they are Job's words quoting God's challenges in order to respond to them.

In the Kethib of the first word in 42:2, we find a defective spelling of the first person singular form of the verb. The yod is missing from the end of the word. The Qere gives the full spelling. The text itself clearly requires the verb to be in the first person and not the third. Also, both the LXX and 11QtgJob translate it "I know." The same type of defective spelling is found in other

34. Gordis, *Job*, 466.

35. Ibid., 58.

36. Robert Gordis, "Virtual Quotations in Job, Sumer and Qumran," *VT* 31 (1981): 413; Anderson, *Job*, 291–92.

37. Dhorme, *Job*, 645–46; H. H. Rowley, *The Book of Job* (The New Century Bible Commentary; Grand Rapids: Eerdmans, 1980) 265; Marvin H. Pope, *Job: a New Translation with Introduction and Commentary* (AB 15; 3d ed. Garden City, N.Y.: Doubleday, 1973), 348.

verses (e.g., Ps. 16:2; 140:13; Ezek. 16:59). So, we do not hesitate to accept the Qere form.

The translation of 42:2–5 presents no problem. Verse 6, however, contains three problems which we shall examine in some detail. I suggest the following translation for 42:2–5.

> I know that you can do all things, and that no purpose[38] of yours can be thwarted.
> "Who is this obscuring counsel without knowledge?"
> Indeed I have spoken, but I did not understand, of things too wonderful for me (which) I did not know.
> "Listen, now, and I will speak; I will question you, and you answer/inform me!"
> (By hearsay) my ears had heard of you, and now my eyes have seen you.

These verses indicate that Job now reaffirms his belief in God's omnipotence and sovereignty. In Yahweh's second speech, Job was confronted with situations he could not handle. God, however, could handle them. As a result of both speeches Job acknowledges that, as Yahweh said, he has spoken from ignorance and lack of understanding. God revealed to Job something of his ways and purposes in creation, in the functioning of the natural elements that he controlled, and in his care of the animals. Job had not understood these—they were too wonderful and difficult for him. As a result of Yahweh's second speech Job realized that he did not understand God's mercy in judgment. He had not comprehended the exaltedness and might of God the Creator. And he did not understand God's restraint of chaos powers. He confesses here that he had indeed spoken from ignorance and lack of understanding.

God came and spoke directly to Job. God began each of his speeches, "I will question you, and you answer me!" God did question Job. Job summarizes his answer in vv. 5 and 6. Formerly, Job knew of God only by hearsay. Yet he believed in God and lived for him, fearing, worshipping, and trusting him. Now Job has had a personal, direct encounter with God. God has revealed himself to Job. What Job's physical eyes saw we do not know—that was not important. Undoubtedly the storm from which God spoke gave some physical impression of God's presence. But Job's increased knowledge of God from what God said to him and the awareness of the immediacy of the divine presence as God spoke were such that Job said "now my eyes have seen you." Verse 6 begins with "therefore" and hence is a result of Job's "seeing God":

> *ʿal kēn ʾemʾas wĕniḥamti ʿal ʿāpār wāʾēper:*

38. *Mĕzimmāh* is used for God's purpose in Jer. 23:20; 30:24 and 51:11.

Before I propose a translation for this verse, it is necessary to investigate the usage and probable meaning of the verbs *m's* and *nḥm,* the object of *m's,* and the significance of the phrase associated with "dust and ashes."

(1) *m's.* In Holladay's *Lexicon* (180) the meaning is given as "refuse, reject." In BDB (549) the meanings "refuse, reject" are given and also the meaning "despise." An exmaination of seventy-three usages of this word in the Old Testament shows that in the vast majority of cases its meaning is "reject." In twelve verses the meaning "despise" is preferable.[39] In a number of places an element of both meanings seemed to be involved, though one or the other is prominent. In the verses where it means "reject" the "rejection" is due to a variety of causes.

Curtis mentions fourteen verses in which he says *m's* is used with great emotional depth.[40] He says nothing about the other fifty-nine verses. On the basis of the few verses he mentions, and the emotion he sees in them, he concludes that *m's* "has a fundamental meaning like 'to feel loathing contempt and revulsion.'"[41] However, his argument cannot be sustained. In a number of the verses he mentions the word simply means "reject" (e.g., Ps. 15:4; 36:5; 118:2; Isa. 7:15–16; 33:15). Other connotations he mentions are only his subjective speculation, e.g., that in Judges 9:38 and Jeremiah 4:30 "*m's* connotes malicious hatred with intent to kill."[42] In any case, one cannot take an emotion that may accompany an action and substitute it for the action itself. They are not synonymous. Many other usages of *m's* are not related to an emotion at all. See, e.g., Isa. 7:15–16; 33:15; Jer. 31:37; Ezek. 5:6; 20:13, 16, 24.

Although it is clear that *m's* means "to reject" and/or "to despise" there is still a problem in Job 42:6 because the object of the verb is not specified. In four verses in the Old Testament the Qal of this verb does not have its object expressed. All of these verses are in Job—7:16; 34:33; 36:5, and 42:6.

A comparison of Job 9:21 with 7:16 confirms that in 7:16 Job is despising and rejecting his life of suffering which he described in the preceding verses, so that he wants no more of them. This meaning is also clarified by the statement that follows *m's,* "not forever would I live."

In 34:33 also, the context makes it clear that the object of *m's* is what has just been described in the preceding verses, i.e., to repent. So, Elihu is saying of Job "when you refuse/reject to repent." Similarly with 36:5, the context

39. Judg. 9:38; Job 9:21; 19:18; Ps. 53:6(5); 106:24; Prov. 3:11; 15:32; Isa. 33:8; Ezek. 21:15(10), 18(13); Amos 5:21; and possibly Jer. 4:30. The meaning of *m's* in Job 7:16, 36:5 and 42:6 is discussed later in this chapter.

40. Jer. 14:19; Lev. 26:43–44; Lam. 3:45; Judg. 9:38; Jer. 4:30; Job 30:1; Ps. 15:4; 118:22; Isa. 7:15–16; 33:15; Ps. 36:5; 89:39. See Curtis, "Job's Response," 503.

41. Curtis, "Job's Response," 503.

42. Ibid., 503.

indicates what the object of *m's* should be, but this time from the verses that follow it, not those that precede it.

(2) *nḥm*. Before we can understand what the object of *m's* in 42:6 may be, we need to consider the meaning of the verb *nḥm* in this verse. It is in the Nifal. Holladay's *Lexicon* (p. 234) gives as its meanings, "to regret, have a change of heart, relent, turn from a former attitude, and hence repent; to allow oneself to be sorry; to comfort or console oneself." The meanings given in BDB (pp. 636–37) are similar.

The Nifal form of *nḥm* is used forty-eight times in the Old Testament. God is the subject of thirty-four of those occurrences;[34] man is the subject of the other fourteen. Sixteen of the verses in which God is the subject speak of his relenting, and a change of action or situation takes place as a result. Thirteen other verses speak of God's feeling grief, sorrow, regret, pity, or compassion, and again there is action to change the situation.

Eight of the verses in which man is the subject are concerning his being comforted after bereavement and are not relevant to our concern. In Judg. 21:6 and 15 *nḥm* indicates sorrow ("grieved for") over a situation such that the sorrow instigated action to change the situation. Exodus 13:17 indicates as its meaning, regret that produced a change of mind which was followed by a change of plans. The context of both Jeremiah 8:6 and 31:19 indicate probable sorrow or regret because of doing wickedness or straying from the Lord, accompanied by the change needed to remedy the situation, i.e., turning from wickedness or returning to the Lord. Hence in both of these verses *nḥm* is translated "repent."

So, in Job 42:6 we would expect *nḥm* to have a similar meaning. This means that Job would feel sorrow or regret over something and that he would either turn from the cause or make necessary changes.

From the above investigation of the usage of *nḥm* we see that it is the quality of feeling, be it compassion, grief, or regret, that is either accompanied by change-generating action, or which instigates it. It does not necessarily mean "repent." However, it may do so. Whenever *nḥm* is caused by sin or by turning or straying from the Lord, it means "repent." The connotation of *šûb* is more particularly that of "returning" to the Lord, without any necessary designation of emotion. On the other hand, *nḥm* meaning "repentance" implies sorrow and regret because of the sin together with the action of leaving sin and resulted in turning to the Lord.

J. B. Curtis denies that *nḥm* ever means "repent," maintaining rather that it means "to be sorry." On the basis of Genesis 18:27 and Job 30:19, where Job says he has become like dust and ashes (but note; because he says God

43. Gen. 6:6–7; Exod. 32:12, 14; Judg. 2:18; 1 Sam. 15:11, 29(2), 35; 2 Sam. 24:16; 1 Chr. 21:15; Ps. 90:13; 106:45; 110:4; Isa. 1:24; 57:6; Jer. 4:28; 15:6; 18:8, 10; 20:16; 26:3, 13, 19; 42:10; Ezek. 24:14; Joel 2:13, 14; Amos 7:3, 6; Jonah 3:9, 10; 4:2; Zech. 8:14.

has thrown him to the ground!), he says that the expression "dust and ashes" has the idiomatic meaning "man in his utter frailty before the divine."[44] So, he translates Job 42:6 as follows:

> Therefore I feel loathing contempt and revulsion
> [toward you, O God];
> and I am sorry for frail man.[45]

Once again his conclusions are based on too little evidence and reveal a strong subjective bias. An example of this is his statement that "there can be little doubt that the unexpressed object of the loathing is God," with only brief and speculative suggestions as support for his statement.[46] His translations cannot be sustained, therefore his argument that Job did not repent collapses.

Dust and ashes, separately or together, were often associated with mourning or with humbling oneself in the Old Testament. When Job's friends came, they wept, tore their robes, and sprinkled dust on their heads (2:12). Joshua and the elders of Israel tore their clothes and put dust on their heads as they humbled themselves before the Lord (Josh. 7:6; see also Lam. 2:10). After Job was afflicted he sat among the ashes (2:8). The wearing of sackcloth and ashes when mourning and humbling oneself is mentioned in 2 Samuel 13:19; Esther 4:1, 3; Psalm 102:9 (10); Isaiah 58:5; 61:3; Jeremiah 6:26; Daniel 9:3; and Jonah 3:6. The use of both dust and ashes together is mentioned in Ezekiel 27:30. So, strong support exists for seeing this connotation in Job 42:6 also and for translating *ʾal ʿāpār wāʾēper* literally, "upon [or with] dust and ashes."

So, I would translate Job 42:6 as follows:

> Therefore I will have nothing more to do with (i.e., despise and reject) the sins of which you charged me which I committed by my speaking without understanding, and I repent upon dust and ashes.

From the examination of the text of Job's responses that I have presented, I believe it is clear that Job did respond to Yahweh's speeches as Yahweh desired. Job recognized that he had sinned, and he repented of that sin. This sin was not committed prior to his suffering—it was not the cause of his suffering. Rather, his sin was in the words he spoke, accusing and condemning God, though in measure unconsciously, as he justified himself. He also sinned in thus exalting himself as a "rival god."

Job's responses also reveal that he came to a deeper, more intimate knowledge of God and relationship with him. He reaffirmed his confidence in the

44. Curtis, "Job's Response," 500–501.
45. Ibid., 505.
46. Ibid., 504. See also n. 25.

supreme power and sovereignty of God. He accepted the fact that he could not understand God's works and his ways.

Job's relationship with God was renewed by his repentance, and enriched and strengthed by God's self-revelation to him. Now, not only did Job know that God is sovereign, but also he knew, intimately, the God who is sovereign. In that knowledge and that relationship is the resolution of life's problems.[47]

47. I wish to thank Dr. R. B. Dillard, Dr. T. Longman III, and Dr. M. Silva for their helpful suggestions, which have served to improve this paper.

Select Bibliography

Books

Andersen, Francis I. *Job: An Introduction and Commentary.* Tyndale Old Testament Commentaries. Downers Grove, Ill.: InterVarsity, 1976.

Archer, Gleason L., Jr. *The Book of Job: God's Answer to the Problem of Undeserved Suffering.* Grand Rapids: Baker, 1982.

Baker, Wesley C. *More Than a Man Can Take: A Study of Job.* Philadelphia: Westminster, 1966.

Barnes, Albert. *Notes, Critical, Illustrative, and Practical on the Book of Job.* 2 vols. New York: Leavitt, Trow & Co., 1846.

Bergant, Dianne. *Job, Ecclesiastes.* Collegeville, Minn.: Liturgical, 1982.

Cox, Samuel. *Commentary on the Book of Job.* London: C. Kegan Paul, 1880.

Davidson, A. B. *The Book of Job.* Cambridge Bible for Schools and Colleges. Cambridge: At the University Press, 1903.

Delitzsch, Franz. *Biblical Commentary on the Book of Job.* Translated by Francis Bolton. 2 vols. Grand Rapids: Eerdmans, 1949.

Dhorme, Édouard. *A Commentary on the Book of Job.* Translated by Harold Knight. London: Thomas Nelson & Sons, 1967.

Driver, S. R., and G. B. Gray. *A Critical and Exegetical Commentary on the Book of Job.* International Critical Commentary. Edinburgh: T. & T. Clark, 1908.

Ellison, H. L. *A Study of Job: From Tragedy to Triumph.* Grand Rapids: Eerdmans, 1958.

Fohrer, Georg. *Das Buch Hiob.* Kommentar zum Alten Testament. Gütersloh: G. Mohn, 1963.

Garland, D. David. *Job: A Study Guide.* Grand Rapids: Zondervan, 1971.

Gibson, Edgar C. S. *The Book of Job.* 1899. Reprint. Minneapolis: Klock & Klock, 1978.

Gibson, J. C. L. *Job.* Daily Bible Study. Philadelphia: Westminster, 1985.

Good, Edwin M. *In Turns of Tempest: A Reading of Job.* Stanford: Stanford University Press, 1990.

Gordis, Robert. *The Book of God and Man: A Study of Job.* Chicago: University of Chicago Press, 1966.

———. *The Book of Job: Commentary, New Translation, and Special Studies.* New York: Jewish Theological Seminary of America, 1978.

Green, William H. *The Argument of the Book of Job Unfolded.* New York: Hurst & Co., 1873.

Guillaume, A. *Studies in the Book of Job.* Edited by John McDonald. Leiden: E. J. Brill, 1968.

Habel, Norman C. *The Book of Job.* Cambridge Bible Commentary on the New English Bible. London: Cambridge University Press, 1975.

———. *The Book of Job: A Commentary.* Old Testament Library. Philadelphia: Westminster, 1985.

Hartley, John E. *The Book of Job.* The New International Commentary on the Old Testament. Grand Rapids: Eerdmans, 1988.

Janzen, J. Gerald. *Job.* Interpretation. Atlanta: John Knox, 1985.

Job, John. *Job Speaks to Us Today.* Atlanta: John Knox, 1980.

Johnson, L. D. *Out of the Whirlwind: The Major Message of the Book of Job.* Nashville: Broadman, 1971.

Jones, Edgar. *The Triumph of Job.* London: SCM, 1966.

Kidner, Derek. *The Wisdom of Proverbs, Job, and Ecclesiastes.* Downers Grove, Ill.: InterVarsity, 1985.

Littleton, Mark R. *When God Seems Far Away.* Wheaton, Ill.: Harold Shaw, 1987.

McKenna, David. *Job.* Communicator's Commentary. Waco: Word, 1986.

Polzin, Robert, and David Robertson, eds. *Semeia 7: Studies in the Book of Job.* Missoula, Mont.: Scholars Press, 1977.

Pope, Marvin H. *Job.* Anchor Bible. Garden City, N. Y.: Doubleday, 1973.

Reichert, Victor E. *Job.* London: Soncino, 1946.

Rowley, H. H. *Job.* Century Bible. New York: Thomas Nelson, 1970. Rev. ed. Grand Rapids: Eerdmans, 1980.

Shaper, Robert N. *Why Me God?* Glendale, Calif.: Regal, 1974.

Simundson, Daniel J. *The Message of Job: A Theological Commentary.* Minneapolis: Augsburg, 1986.

Stedman, Ray C. *Expository Studies in Job: Behind Suffering.* Waco: Word, 1981.

Terrien, Samuel. *Job: Poet of Existence.* Indianapolis: Bobbs-Merrill, 1957.

Thomas, David. *Book of Job: Expository and Homiletical Commentary.* Reprint. Grand Rapids: Kregel, 1982.

Tur-Sinai, N. H. *The Book of Job: A New Commentary.* Rev. ed. Jerusalem: Kiryath Sepher, 1967.

Westermann, Claus. *The Structure of the Book of Job: A Form-Critical Analysis.* Translated by Charles A. Muenchow. Philadelphia: Fortress, 1981.

Zuck, Roy B. *Job.* Everyman's Bible Commentary. Chicago: Moody, 1978.

Articles and Essays

Albertz, Rainer. "The Sage and Pious Wisdom in the Book of Job: The Friends' Perspective." In *The Sage in Israel and the Ancient Near East,* edited by John G. Gammie and Leo G. Perdue. Winona Lake, Ind.: Eisenbrauns, 1990.

Alter, Robert. "Truth and Poetry in the Book of Job." In *The Art of Biblical Poetry.* New York: Basic, 1985.

Beeby, H. D. "Elihu—Job's Mediator?" *Southeast Asia Journal of Theology* 7 (October 1965): 33–55.

Clines, D. J. A. "Job 5, 1–8: A New Exegesis." *Biblica* 62 (1981): 185–94.

Curtis, John B. "On Job's Response to Yahweh." *Journal of Biblical Literature* 98 (1979): 497–511.

Dahood, Mitchell J. "Chiasmus in Job: a Text-Critical and Philogical Criterion." In *A Light to My Path,* edited by Howard N. Bream, Ralph D. Heim, and Carey A. Moore. Philadelphia: Temple University Press, 1974.

Danin, Avinoam. "Do You Know When the Ibexes Give Birth?" *Biblical Archaeology Review* 50 (1979): 50–51.

Denk, Dan. "The Impatience of Job." *His,* May 1983, 22, 24, 26.

Dick, Michael Brennan. "The Legal Metaphor in Job 31." *Catholic Biblical Quarterly* 41 (1979): 37–50.

———. "Job 31, the Oath of Innocence, and the Sage." *Zeitschrift für die Alttestamentliche Wissenchaft* 95 (1983): 31–53.

Feinberg, Charles L. "The Book of Job." *Bibliotheca Sacra* 91 (1934): 78–86.

———. "The Poetic Structure of the Book of Job and the Ugaritic Literature." *Bibliotheca Sacra* 103 (1946): 283–92.

Fohrer, Georg. "The Righteous Man in Job 31." In *Essays in Old Testament Ethics,* edited by James L. Crenshaw and John T. Willis. New York: KTAV, 1974.

Freedman, Donald N. "The Structure of Job 3." *Biblica* 49 (1968): 503–8.

Good, Edwin M. "Job: The Irony of Reconciliation." In *Irony in the Old Testament.* Philadelphia: Westminster, 1965.

Gordon, Cyrus W. "Leviathan: Symbol of Evie." In *Biblical Motifs: Origins and Transformations,* edited by Alexander Altmann. Cambridge: Harvard University Press, 1966.

Guillaume, A. "The Arabic Background of the Book of Job." In *Promise and Fulfillment,* edited by F. F. Bruce. Edinburgh: T. & T. Clark, 1963.

Habel, Norman C. "Naked I Came . . . : Humanness in the Book of Job." In *Die Botschaft und Die Boten,* edited by Jorg Jeremias and Lothar Perlitt. Neukirchen-Vluyn: Neukirchener Verlag, 1981.

———. "'Only the Jackal Is My Friend.'" *Interpretation* 31 (1977): 227–36.

———. "Of Things Beyond Me: Wisdom in the Book of Job." *Currents in Theology and Mission* 10 (1983): 142–54.

———. "The Role of Elihu in the Design of the Book of Job." In *In the Shelter of Elyon,* edited by W. Boyd Barrick and John R. Spencer. Sheffield: JSOT, 1984.

Harris, R. Laird. "The Book of Job and Its Doctrine of God." *Grace Journal* 13 (Fall 1972): 3–33.

Hartley, John E. "Job." In *The International Standard Bible Encyclopedia,* edited by Geoffrey W. Bromiley, 4 vols. Grand Rapids: Eerdmans, 1979–1988. 2:1064–76.

Hengstenberg, E. W. "Interpreting the Book of Job." In *Classical Evangelical Essays in Old Testament Interpretation,* edited by Walter C. Kaiser, Jr. Grand Rapids: Baker, 1972.

Monsey, Rudolph E. "Exegetical Paper on Job 19:23–27." *Wisconsin Lutheran Quarterly* 67 (July 1970): 153–206.

Howe, George F. "Job and the Ostrich: A Case Study in Biblical Authority." *Journal of the American Scientific Affiliation* 15 (December 1963): 107–10.

Janzen, J. Gerald. "Another Look at God's Watch over Job (7:12)." *Journal of Biblical Literature* 108 (1989): 109–14.

Laurin, Robert. "The Theological Structure of Job." *Zeitschrift für die Alttestamentliche Wissenchaft* 86 (1974): 86–89.

Louis, Kenneth R. R. Gros. "The Book of Job." In *Literary Interpretations of Biblical Narratives,* edited by Kenneth R. R. Gros Louis et al. Nashville: Abingdon, 1974.

Michel, Walter L. "Job's Real Friend: Elihu." *Criterion* (Spring 1982): 29–32.

Newell, B. Lynne. "Job: Repentant or Rebellious?" *Westminster Theological Journal* 46 (1984): 298–316.

Parsons, Gregory W. "The Structure and Purpose of the Book of Job." *Bibliotheca Sacra* 138 (1981): 139–57.

———. "Literary Features of the Book of Job." *Bibliotheca Sacra* 138 (1981): 213–29.

Patrick, O. "Job's Address of God." *Zeitschrift für die Alttestamentliche Wissenschaft* 91 (1979): 268–82.

Rowley, H. H. "The Book of Job and Its Meaning." *Bulletin of the John Rylands Library* 41 (1958): 167–207.

Ryken, Leland. "Drama." In *Words of Delight: A Literary Introduction to the Bible,* 341–52. Grand Rapids: Baker, 1987.

Sarna, Nahum M. "Epic Substratum in the Prose of Job." *Journal of Biblical Literature* 76 (1957): 13–25.

Scholnick, Sylvia Huberman. "The Meaning of *Mišpāṭ* in the Book of Job." *Journal of Biblical Literature* 101 (1982): 521–29.

———. "Poetry in the Courtroom: Job 38–41." In *Directions in Biblical Hebrew Poetry,* edited by Elaine Follis. Sheffield: JSOT, 1987.

Smick, Elmer B. "Another Look at the Mythological Elements in the Book of Job." *Westminster Theological Journal* 40 (1978): 213–28.

———. "Architectonics, Structural Poems, and Rhetorical Devices in the Book of Job." In *A Tribute to Gleason Archer,* edited by Walter C. Kaiser, Jr., and Ronald F. Youngblood. Chicago: Moody, 1986.

———. "Job." In *The Expositor's Bible Commentary,* edited by Frank E. Gaebelein, 12 vols. Grand Rapids: Zondervan, 1979–. 4:843–1060.

———. "Mythology and the Book of Job." *Journal of the Evangelical Theological Society* 13 (1970): 101–8.

Terrien, Samuel. "Job as a Sage." In *The Sage in Israel and the Ancient Near East,* edited by John G. Gammie and Leo G. Perdue. Winona Lake, Ind.: Eisenbrauns, 1990.

Tsevat, Matitiahu. "The Meaning of the Book of Job." *Hebrew Union College Annual* 37 (1966): 73–106.

Webster, Edwin C. "Strophic Patterns in Job 3–28." *Journal for the Study of the Old Testament* (1983): 33–60.

———. "Strophic Patterns in Job 29–42." *Journal for the Study of the Old Testament* (1984): 95–109.

Westermann, Claus. "The Two Faces of Job." In *Job and the Silence of God,* edited by Christian Duquoc and Casiano Floristan. New York: Seabury, 1983.

Whedbee, J. William. "The Comedy of Job." *Semeia* 7 (1977): 1–39.

Williams, James G. "'You Have Not Spoken Truth of Me': Mystery and Irony in Job." *Zeitschrift für die Alttestamentliche Wissenschaft* 83 (1971): 231–55.

Zuck, Roy B. "Job." In *The Bible Knowledge Commentary,* edited by John F. Walvoord and Roy B. Zuck. 2 vols. Wheaton, Ill.: Victor, 1983, 1985. 1:715–77.

General Index

Scripture Index

Extrabiblical Literature